SECRETS

OF

HEAVEN

SECRETS

OF

HEAVEN

The Portable New Century Edition

EMANUEL SWEDENBORG

Volume 2

Translated from the Latin by Lisa Hyatt Cooper

SWEDENBORG FOUNDATION

West Chester, Pennsylvania

Second printing with minor corrections, 2018

Originally published in Latin as *Arcana Coelestia,* London, 1749–1756. The volume contents of this and the original Latin edition, along with ISBNs of the annotated version, are as follows:

Volume number in this edition	Text treated	Volume number in the Latin first edition	Section numbers	ISBN (of hardcover except where noted)
1	Genesis 1–8	1	§§1–946	978-0-87785-486-9 978-0-87785-504-0 (pb)
2	Genesis 9–15	1	§§947–1885	978-0-87785-487-6
3	Genesis 16–21	2 (in 6 fascicles)	§§1886–2759	978-0-87785-488-3
4	Genesis 22–26	3	§§2760–3485	978-0-87785-489-0
5	Genesis 27–30	3	§§3486–4055	978-0-87785-490-6
6	Genesis 31–35	4	§§4056–4634	978-0-87785-491-3
7	Genesis 36–40	4	§§4635–5190	978-0-87785-492-0
8	Genesis 41–44	5	§§5191–5866	978-0-87785-493-7
9	Genesis 45–50	5	§§5867–6626	978-0-87785-494-4
10	Exodus 1–8	6	§§6627–7487	978-0-87785-495-1
11	Exodus 9–15	6	§§7488–8386	978-0-87785-496-8
12	Exodus 16–21	7	§§8387–9111	978-0-87785-497-5
13	Exodus 22–24	7	§§9112–9442	978-0-87785-498-2
14	Exodus 25–29	8	§§9443–10166	978-0-87785-499-9
15	Exodus 30–40	8	§§10167–10837	978-0-87785-500-2

ISBN (Portable)   Volume 2: 978-0-87785-411-1
ISBN (e-book of Portable Edition) Volume 2: 978-0-87785-607-8
(The ISBN in the Library of Congress data shown below is that of volume 1.)

Library of Congress Cataloging-in-Publication Data

Swedenborg, Emanuel, 1688–1772.
  [Arcana coelestia. English]
  Secrets of heaven / Emanuel Swedenborg ; translated from the Latin by Lisa Hyatt Cooper. — Portable New Century ed.
    p. cm.
  Includes bibliographical references and indexes.
  ISBN 978-0-87785-408-1 (alk. paper)
  1. New Jerusalem Church—Doctrines. 2. Bible. O.T. Genesis—Commentaries—Early works to 1800. 3. Bible. O.T. Exodus—Commentaries—Early works to 1800. I. Title.
  BX8712.A8 2010
  230'.94—dc22
                                                                    2009054171

Senior copy editor, Alicia L. Dole
Text designed by Joanna V. Hill
Typesetting by Alicia L. Dole
Ornaments from the first Latin edition, 1749
Cover design by Karen Connor

For information about the New Century Edition of the Works of Emanuel Swedenborg, contact the Swedenborg Foundation, 320 North Church Street, West Chester, PA 19380 U.S.A. Telephone: (610) 430-3222 • Web: www.swedenborg.com • E-mail: info@swedenborg.com

Secrets
of
Heaven

Genesis 9

The Hells (Continued):
A Different Set Than Those Already Mentioned

THERE are some dishonest people who think they can get anything they want by trickery and schemes, and whose success at this kind of fraud during bodily life has confirmed them in their belief. They see themselves as living in a kind of vat called Hell's Cask, off to the left. The vat has a lid, and outside it on a pyramid-shaped stand is a globe that they believe to be the universe, which they watch and control, or so it seems to them. **947**

The ones who preyed on the innocent stay there for centuries. I was told that some have remained there for twenty centuries now.

When they are released, their hallucinations cause them to imagine that the universe is a globe, which they walk around and trample underfoot, believing themselves gods of the universe.

I have seen them several times and talked with them about their fantasy, but since they thought the same way in the world, they cannot be weaned from it.

I have also perceived on occasion how subtly, how craftily they can twist another's thinking, instantly redirect that person's thoughts, and substitute other ideas. They are so sly about it that it was hard to tell they were the ones doing it—and the way they do it is quite incredible. As this is their nature, they are barred from all contact with people on earth, for they inject quantities of venom so secretly and stealthily that no one can tell they have done it.

There is another vat off to the left too, as it seems to them, and in it are some who during physical life thought they had done well when they had done wrong and vice versa. So they put evil in place of goodness. They stay there for a time, and all the while they are being deprived of their rationality. Once stripped of reason, they go into a kind of sleep, and they are not held responsible for anything they then do. They still seem to themselves to be awake, however. **948**

3

When rationality returns to them, they regain consciousness and are like other spirits.

949 Out in front on the left is a room that holds no light, only pure darkness, which as a result is called the black room. The occupants are people who envied others their belongings and could not stop thinking about them. They stole without remorse whenever they could do so under a plausible pretext. Some there had been fairly prominent when they lived in the world and had honored duplicity as a mark of prudence. In the room they conspire with each other—as they had done while living in their bodies—about ways to deceive and defraud others. The darkness of the place delights them.

I was shown an image of the swindlers living there, in which I saw as clear as day what they eventually come to be like: their faces look worse than a dead person's, as gray as that of a corpse, with horrible pockmarks, as they pass their time in a torment of anxiety.

950 There was a troop of spirits surging out on one side of Gehenna, rising high up in front. From their aura I could tell that they held the Lord in contempt and despised all worship of God. (At the first approach of spirits, one can sense their character just from their aura.) Their speech rose and fell. One of them made scandalous charges against the Lord and was immediately tossed down to one side of Gehenna.

From in front they moved back over my head, intent on finding kindred souls they could band together with in order to dominate others. They were slowed down along the way, though, and told that they should give up their plan because it would turn out badly for them. So they came to a halt. I then had a look at them. Their faces were black, and around their heads each wore a white headband, meaning that they saw the worship of God—and the Lord's Word too—as something black, useful only for binding the fetters of conscience on the great mass of people.

Their residence is near Gehenna, and nonpoisonous flying snakes live there, which is why it is called a snakes' nest. But since they are not charlatans, their hell is not very oppressive.

People like this ascribe everything to themselves and their own shrewdness and boast that they fear nothing, but they were shown that a mere hiss can drive them to terrified flight. Hearing one once, they assumed in their fright that all hell was rising up to carry them off, and from being heroes they suddenly became like women.

People who considered themselves saintly during bodily life are in an **951** underground region in front of the left foot. There it sometimes seems to them that they have shining faces—an effect that stems from their picture of sainthood. The outcome for them, however, is that they remain there in the grip of a strong urge to climb to heaven, which they think is up high. Their desire swells and is gradually transformed into anxiety, which increases beyond all measure, until at last they acknowledge that they are not saints.

When released from there, they are allowed to smell their own stench, which is disgusting.

One individual felt he had lived a holy life in the world, his purpose **952** being to win public admiration for his piety and in this way earn heaven. He said he had led a devout life and made time for prayer, believing that it was enough for us each to take care of ourselves and our own welfare. He added that he was a sinner and wanted to suffer, even to the point of being trampled underfoot by others (which he called Christian patience), and that he wanted to be the humblest person there was, in order to be the greatest in heaven. Questioned as to whether he had done or wished to do anyone any good—to perform works of charity, in other words— he declared that he had no idea what these were, that he had simply lived a holy life. Because this man's goal was to be better than others, whom he consequently deemed his inferiors, and most of all because he viewed himself as a saint, he appeared at first in a shining white human form that was visible down to the pelvis. Then he turned a dusky shade of blue and finally black. Since he wished to domineer over other people and held them in contempt, he ended up blacker than others.

Concerning those who want to be greatest in heaven, see above at §§450, 452.

I was led through certain settlements of the first heaven, from which **953** I had the opportunity to see a vast, distant sea, heaving with massive waves and stretching to an unseen shore. The people who fantasize such things and see a body of water like this are afraid they will drown. I heard that they are the ones who aimed for worldly eminence, not caring whether they achieved it by fair means or foul as long as they could win glory for themselves.

In the next life, the fantasies that people have had during physical life **954** alter, although the new fantasies still correspond to the old ones. Some people, for instance, were ruthless and violent on earth. Their violence and lack of mercy turns into unbelievable cruelty, and whenever they happen upon an acquaintance, they seem to themselves to kill the person. They also torture the person in various ways that bring them great satisfaction—so great that these are their supreme pleasures.

People who had been bloodthirsty take delight in abusing spirits to the point of drawing blood; they suppose that the spirits are mortal, not knowing any better. When they see blood (such is their fantasy that they seem to see blood), they are in ecstasy.

Greed spurs a proliferation of fantasies in which spirits seem to be overrun by rats and other vermin, depending on the variety of greed.

Those who enjoyed pleasures that were purely sensual and who regarded these as the ultimate goal, the highest good, and their "heaven," linger with utmost delight in latrines, sensing intense pleasure there. Some spend their time in puddles of foul-smelling urine, some in muck, and so on.

955 There are also various other ways of punishing the evil severely in the next world, and they incur these penalties when they return to their vile obsessions. The punishment inflicts shame, terror, and revulsion for their evil on them, until eventually they abstain.

The penalties come in different forms. In general they entail being humiliated, ripped in pieces, placed under shrouds, and so on.

956 Some people are tenaciously vindictive and consider themselves more important than anyone else, judging all others worthless compared to themselves. Their punishment is to be humiliated, and this is what it is like: Their bodies and faces are disfigured, so that there is hardly anything human-looking left of them. Their faces end up looking like big rounds of flatbread; their arms, like rags. With these stretched out, they spin around, high in the air, always rising toward heaven, and someone shouts out a description of their character for all to hear. Eventually they are struck to the depths with shame. So they are driven to beg humbly for mercy, and the words are dictated to them. Afterward they are taken to a pool of muck near the foul Jerusalem and are rolled and dipped in it until they look as though they have turned into mud. They go through this process several times, until they lose all desire for vengeance and superiority.

In the pool of muck are malicious women from the area of the bladder.

957 There are individuals who acquired for themselves in bodily life the habit of talking one way and thinking another. These people, especially the ones who pined after others' wealth under cover of friendship, wander around and ask to stay with people wherever they go, claiming to be impoverished. Once they are admitted, an inborn craving leads them to covet everything they see.

When their true nature is discovered, they are fined and banished and sometimes racked most painfully—in different ways, depending on the nature of the facade they adopted in order to delude. In some cases the whole body is ripped apart; in others it is the lower legs, or the lower torso, the upper torso, the head, or just the part around the mouth. They are jostled back and forth in indescribable ways. Their body parts are violently smashed together and torn off in the process, so that they imagine they have been shredded into tiny pieces. Resistance is also induced in them so as to increase the pain.

Such are the ways—with a great deal of variety—in which people are punished by racking. The punishments are repeated at intervals enough times to instill in them a terror and horror for false, deceptive speech. Each repetition takes away a little more of their desire.

Those doing the shredding said they enjoy inflicting punishment so much that not in all eternity would they want to leave off.

There are gangs of roving spirits of whom other spirits are intensely **958** afraid. They attach themselves to the lower part of the back and cause pain by a rapid, audible, back-and-forth motion that no one is able to block. It is a pressing, squeezing motion, which they channel upward into the point of a conical shape. Any who are sent inside the cone, especially those near the tip, are wretchedly ripped apart at every joint.

It is the imposters who are sent in there and punished in this way.

One night I awoke from sleep and heard around me spirits who had **959** wanted to ambush me while I lay asleep. Soon drifting off, I had a nightmare but then woke up again, and suddenly, to my surprise, found some scourging spirits at hand. They inflicted bitter punishment on the spirits who had plotted against me in my sleep, by giving them a kind of body—a visible one—and physical sensation and then torturing them by violently knocking their limbs back and forth. They also enhanced the pain by inducing resistance. The scourgers fully intended to kill the spirits, if they could, so they used extreme violence.

Most of them were sirens, who are described in §831. The punishment lasted a long time and spread out around me to include many other gangs. What amazed me was that all of the spirits who had ambushed me were tracked down, even though they wanted to hide.

Because they were sirens, they tried many tricks for escaping punishment, although they failed at the attempt. First they wanted to slip away to a more hidden plane of existence. Then each wanted to pretend to be someone else. Then they tried to divert the punishment to others by projecting their thoughts. Then they created the illusion that they were babies, whom the castigators were punishing, then good spirits, then angels. They attempted many other ruses too, but all in vain.

Although I was surprised to see how severely they were disciplined, I perceived that this kind of behavior is intolerable because of our need to sleep in safety, since if we could not sleep safely, the human race would die out. That was why the penalty simply had to be so harsh.

I sensed that the same events also occur in the vicinity of other people whom spirits endeavor to attack by stealth in their sleep, although the people themselves are unaware of it. If they are unable to talk with spirits and be present with them by way of an inner perception, they cannot hear, still less see, any such thing, despite the fact that similar occurrences are taking place around them.

The Lord guards us with utmost care when we sleep.

960   There are certain deceptive spirits who secretly committed fraud while they were living in the body. Some of them had been fiendishly clever at projecting an angelic image of themselves in order to dupe people. In the next life they learn how to disappear into a less substantial mode of existence and escape the gaze of others, so they consider themselves safe from all retribution. Like others, however, not only do they suffer different kinds of punishment by the rack (depending on the nature and malevolence of their fraud), they are also glued to each other. When this happens, the more they long to free themselves, or split apart, the more tightly they are bound together. This punishment entails fairly intense pain, as it comes in response to their rather well concealed deceits.

961   There are people who in casual conversation make trivial and derisive comments using phrases from Sacred Scripture—some out of habit and some out of contempt. They believe they are being sophisticated, with their jokes and ridicule. But thoughts and words of this kind cling to the base, unclean notions of such an individual and inflict much damage in the other life, because they come back to the individual with profane ideas attached. Such people too undergo racking punishments, until finally they give up the practice.

Genesis Chapter 13

Genesis Chapter 14

Genesis Chapter 15

Contents

Volume 2

Conventions Used in This Work

MOST of the following conventions apply generally to the translations in the New Century Edition Portable series. For introductory material on the content and history of *Secrets of Heaven,* and for annotations on the subject matter, including obscure or problematic content, and extensive indexes, the reader is referred to the Deluxe New Century Edition volumes.

Volume designation *Secrets of Heaven* was originally published in eight volumes; in this edition all but the second original volume have been divided into two. Thus Swedenborg's eight volumes now fill fifteen volumes, of which this is the second. It corresponds to approximately the second half of Swedenborg's volume 1.

Section numbers Following a practice common in his time, Swedenborg divided his published theological works into sections numbered in sequence from beginning to end. His original section numbers have been preserved in this edition; they appear in boxes in the outside margins. Traditionally, these sections have been referred to as "numbers" and designated by the abbreviation "n." In this edition, however, the more common section symbol (§) is used to designate the section numbers, and the sections are referred to as such.

Subsection numbers Because many sections throughout Swedenborg's works are too long for precise cross-referencing, Swedenborgian scholar John Faulkner Potts (1838–1923) further divided them into subsections; these have since become standard, though minor variations occur from one edition to another. These subsections are indicated by bracketed numbers that appear in the text itself: [2], [3], and so on. Because the beginning of the first *subsection* always coincides with the beginning of the *section* proper, it is not labeled in the text.

Citations of Swedenborg's text As is common in Swedenborgian studies, text citations of Swedenborg's works refer not to page numbers but to section numbers, which unlike page numbers are uniform in most editions. In citations the section symbol (§) is generally omitted after the title of a work by Swedenborg. Thus "*Secrets of Heaven* 29" refers to section 29

(§29) of Swedenborg's *Secrets of Heaven,* not to page 29 of any edition. Subsection numbers are given after a colon; a reference such as "29:2" indicates subsection 2 of section 29. The reference "29:1" would indicate the first subsection of section 29, though that subsection is not in fact labeled in the text. Where section numbers stand alone without titles, their function is indicated by the prefixed section symbol; for example, "§29:2".

Citations of the Bible Biblical citations in this edition follow the accepted standard: a semicolon is used between book references and between chapter references, and a comma between verse references. Therefore "Matthew 5:11, 12; 6:1; 10:41, 42; Luke 6:23, 35" would refer to Matthew chapter 5, verses 11 and 12; Matthew chapter 6, verse 1; Matthew chapter 10, verses 41 and 42; and Luke chapter 6, verses 23 and 35. Swedenborg often incorporated the numbers of verses not actually represented in his text when listing verse numbers for a passage he quoted; these apparently constitute a kind of "see also" reference to other material he felt was relevant. This edition includes these extra verses and also follows Swedenborg where he cites contiguous verses individually (for example, John 14:8, 9, 10, 11), rather than as a range (John 14:8–11). Occasionally this edition supplies a full, conventional Bible reference where Swedenborg omits one after a quotation.

Quotations in Swedenborg's works Some features of the original Latin text of *Secrets of Heaven* have been modernized in this edition. For example, Swedenborg's first edition generally relies on context or italics rather than on quotation marks to indicate passages taken from the Bible or from other works. The manner in which these conventions are used in the original suggests that Swedenborg did not feel it necessary to belabor the distinction between direct quotation and paraphrase; neither did he mark his omissions from or changes to material he quoted, a practice in which this edition generally follows him. One exception consists of those instances in which Swedenborg did not include a complete sentence at the beginning or end of a Bible quotation. The omission in such cases has been marked in this edition with added points of ellipsis.

Italicized terms Any words in indented scriptural extracts that are here set in italics reflect a similar emphasis in the first edition.

Special use of vertical rule The opening passages of the chapters treating Genesis 1–15, as well as the ends of all chapters, contain material that derives in some way from Swedenborg's experiences in the spiritual world. Swedenborg specified that the text of these passages be set in continuous italics to distinguish it from exegetical and other material. For this edition, the heavy use of italic text was felt to be antithetical to modern tastes, as well as difficult to read, and so such passages are instead marked by a vertical rule in the inside margin.

Changes to and insertions in the text This translation is based on the first Latin edition, published by Swedenborg himself (1749–1756); it also reflects emendations in the third Latin edition, edited by P. H. Johnson, John E. Elliott, and others, and published by the Swedenborg Society (1949–1973). It incorporates the silent correction of minor errors, not only in the text proper but in Bible verse references. The text has also been changed without notice where the verse numbering of the Latin Bible cited by Swedenborg differs from that of modern English Bibles. Throughout the translation, references or cross-references that were implied but not stated have been inserted in brackets; for example, [John 3:27]. Occasionally such brackets represent an insertion of material that was not present in the first edition, but no annotation concerning these insertions is supplied in this Portable edition. By contrast, references that occur in parentheses reflect references that appear in the first edition; for example, (1 Samuel 30:16), (see §42 above). Words not occurring in the first Latin edition, but necessary for the understanding of the text, also appear in square brackets; this device has been used sparingly, however, even at the risk of some inconsistency in its application.

Biblical titles Swedenborg refers to the Hebrew Scriptures as the Old Testament and to the Greek Scriptures as the New Testament; his terminology has been adopted in this edition. As was the custom in his day, he refers to the Pentateuch (Genesis, Exodus, Leviticus, Numbers, and Deuteronomy) as the books of Moses, or simply as "Moses"; for example, in §1001:4 he writes "Moses says," and then cites a passage from Leviticus. Similarly, in sentences or phrases introducing quotations he sometimes refers to the Psalms as "David," to Lamentations as "Jeremiah," and to both the Gospel of John and the Book of Revelation as simply "John." References given in parentheses after these and other Bible quotations specify their sources in accordance with the conventions set out above. Conventional references supplied in parentheses after such quotations specify their sources more precisely.

Problematic content Occasionally Swedenborg makes statements that, although mild by the standards of eighteenth-century theological discourse, now read as harsh, dismissive, or insensitive. The most problematic are assertions about or criticisms of various religious traditions and their adherents—including Judaism, ancient or contemporary; Roman Catholicism; Islam; and the Protestantism in which Swedenborg himself grew up. These statements are far outweighed in size and importance by other passages in Swedenborg's works earnestly maintaining the value of every individual and of all religions. This wider context is discussed in the introductions and annotations of the Deluxe Edition mentioned above. In the present format, however, problematic statements must be retained without comment. The other option—to omit them—would obscure some aspects of Swedenborg's presentation and in any case compromise its historicity.

There is also a punishment in which spirits' thoughts are torn apart, **962** so that their inner thinking clashes with their outer thinking. This is accompanied by deep pain.

One of the more common penalties involves throwing a shroud **963** over a spirit. In it, spirits gain the impression, from delusions they have brought on themselves, that they are under a shroud stretching far out around them. It is like a blanket of fog that thickens as they fantasize about it. Ablaze with the desire to break loose, they run back and forth under it at varying speeds until they grow exhausted. The experience usually lasts an hour, more or less, and entails pain of different kinds, depending on the intensity of their eagerness to free themselves.

The shroud is the lot of those who see the truth but still do not want to admit to it, because they love themselves, and who take constant offense that the truth should be what it is.

Some of the people under the shroud feel such anxiety and terror that they lose hope of ever gaining their freedom, as one who escaped once told me.

There is another kind of shroud, too—a piece of cloth, it seems, that **964** is wound around people, so that they appear to themselves to be bound hand, foot, and body, while a desperate desire to unwrap themselves is inspired in them. Since it is wrapped just once around them, they figure it must be easy to undo; but when they start unwinding, the cloth grows longer and longer and the unwinding continues endlessly, until they reach the point of despair.

These are the facts concerning the hells and different forms of pun- **965** ishment. The tortures of hell are not pangs of conscience, as some suppose, because the inhabitants of hell have no conscience and therefore cannot feel the torment of one. People who *have* had a conscience are among the happy.

It needs to be noted that we never undergo punishment or torment **966** in the next life on account of evil we have inherited, only on account of evil that we ourselves have actually committed.

When the evil are being punished, angels are always present, temper- **967** ing the punishment and easing the anguish of the wretched. They cannot eliminate the pain, though, because everything in the other world is balanced in such a way that evil punishes itself. Unless wickedness was removed from wicked people by punishment, they would have to be kept in some hell forever. Otherwise they would infest communities of good people and inflict violence on the system of order established by the Lord, which ensures the welfare of the universe.

968 Some people have taken with them from the world the idea that we must not talk to devils but avoid them. But I have taught them that talking to a devil is not the least bit dangerous for people whom the Lord protects, even if the whole of hell were to besiege them within and without. This I was able to recognize from such long and miraculous experience that in the end I had no fear. I was not even afraid of talking with the worst members of hell's crew—an experience granted to me for the sake of learning what they were like.

To those who have wondered at my conversations with devils I have been allowed to add this: Not only does it do me no harm, but devils in the other life were once people. They are the ones who led lives of hatred, revenge, and adultery when they lived in the world. Some of them were even more highly respected than other people at the time. In fact I counted some of them as acquaintances of mine during their physical life. All that "the Devil" means is a mob of such people in hell.

While we are living in the body, we have with us at least two spirits from hell, in addition to two angels from heaven. In bad people, the spirits from hell are in charge, but in good people they are subdued and forced to be useful.

So it is a mistake to believe that any devil has existed from the beginning of creation other than those who once were people of this type.

When the people listening to me hear these things, they are dumbfounded and confess that they had held a completely different opinion of the Devil and the Devil's crew.

969 The spiritual realm is the gathering place for the souls of all people from the beginning of creation, of which almost a million a week come from our planet. They all have their own bent of mind and their own personality, different from that of others. Everybody's ideas are all communicated to others, and yet all things as a whole and in particular must continually be brought into order.

A realm of this size, of course, contains countless phenomena that people on earth have never even imagined. Hardly any of them have formed more than a single vague idea of hell, any more than they have of heaven. As a result, these facts cannot help striking them as strange and astounding. This is chiefly due to the belief that spirits have no sensation, when in reality they have much keener sensation than we do. (Evil spirits also use skills unknown in the world to make others feel sensations

almost exactly like those of the body, although bodily sensations are
actually much more blunted.)

What follows at the end of the present chapter [§§1106–1113] has to
do with spiritual devastation.

970

Genesis 9

1. And God blessed Noah and his sons and said to them, "Reproduce
and multiply and fill the earth.

2. And may fear of you and terror of you be on every beast of the
earth and on every bird of the sky. As for everything that the ground
causes to creep out, and as for all the fish of the sea—into your hands let
them be given.

3. Every creeping thing that is alive will serve you for food. I have
given it all to you as I gave you the green plants.

4. Only flesh in its soul [you must not eat], its blood you must not eat.

5. And assuredly the blood of your souls I will seek; at the hand of
every wild animal I will seek it, and at the hand of a human—at the hand
of a man, [the victim's] brother—I will seek that person's soul.

6. Those shedding the blood of a person in a person will have their
own blood shed, because [blood] has made humankind into God's image.

7. And you, reproduce and multiply; pour out into the earth and
multiply on it."

*   *   *   *

8. And God said to Noah and to his sons with him, saying,

9. "And I—yes, I—am setting up my pact with you and with your
seed after you,

10. and with every living soul that is with you: bird, beast, and every
wild animal of the earth with you, from among all those coming out of
the ark, including every wild animal of the earth.

11. And I am setting up my pact with you; and no more will all flesh
be cut off by the waters of a flood, and no more will there be a flood to
destroy the earth."

12. And God said, "This is the sign of the pact that I make between me and you and every living soul that is with you, to everlasting generations:

13. My bow I have put in the cloud, and it will serve as a sign of the pact between me and the earth.

14. And it will happen in my clouding the earth over with cloud that a bow will be seen in the cloud,

15. and I will remember my pact, which is between me and you and every living soul within all flesh. And no more will there be water as a flood to destroy all flesh.

16. And there will be a bow in the cloud; and I will see it, to remember the eternal pact between God and every living soul within all flesh that is on the earth."

17. And God said to Noah, "This is the sign of the pact that I am setting up between me and all flesh that is on the earth."

*   *   *   *

18. And the sons of Noah coming out of the ark were Shem and Ham and Japheth; and Ham was the father of Canaan.

19. These three were Noah's sons; and from them the whole earth scattered out.

20. And Noah started as a man of the soil and planted a vineyard.

21. And he drank some wine and became drunk and was uncovered in the middle of his tent.

22. And Ham, father of Canaan, saw his father's nakedness and pointed it out to his two brothers outside.

23. And Shem and Japheth took a garment, and both of them put it on their shoulder and went backward and covered their father's nakedness; and their faces were backward, and they did not see their father's nakedness.

24. And Noah woke up from his wine and realized what his younger son had done to him.

25. And he said, "A curse on Canaan! A slave of slaves he will be to his brothers."

26. And he said, "A blessing on Jehovah, God of Shem! And Canaan will be slave to him."

27. May God broaden Japheth! And he will live in Shem's tents, and Canaan will be slave to him."

28. And Noah lived after the flood for three hundred fifty years.
29. And all Noah's days were nine hundred fifty years; and he died.

Summary

NEXT to be treated of is the condition of a person reborn—first the mastery exerted by the inner self and the obedience of the outer self. **971**

To be specific, everything belonging to the outer self submits to the inner and must serve it (verses 1–3). But we ought to be very careful not to merge the good impulses and true ideas of faith with our appetites; we should not use the good impulses and true ideas of the inner self to support bad impulses and wrong ideas. To do so inevitably condemns us to death and brings punishment on us (verses 4, 5) and in the process destroys our spiritual self, or God's image in us (verse 6). If these missteps are not taken, all turns out well (verse 7). **972**

Then the text describes the situation of people who lived after the Flood. The Lord formed them in a way that enabled him to be present with them through neighborly love. As a consequence they would no longer be annihilated as the final generation of the earliest church had been (verses 8, 9, 10, 11). **973**

Next, the condition of people living after the Flood who can accept charitable feelings is portrayed by the bow in the cloud, which those people resemble (verses 12, 13, 14, 15, 16, 17). The bow refers to people in the church, or in other words, the regenerate individual (verses 12, 13). It refers to all people in general (verses 14, 15) and to one who can be reborn in particular (verse 16). So the bow has to do not only with people inside the church but also with people outside it (verse 17). **974**

The final subject, in general, is the ancient church. Shem means inner worship in that church; Japheth, outer worship corresponding to inner worship; Ham, faith detached from charity; and Canaan, outer worship detached from inner (verses 19–end). Because the ancient church wanted to explore religious truth in a self-directed way, through the use of rational argumentation, it fell into error and perversions for the first time (verses 19, 20, 21). On the basis of such misconceptions, people who engage in outer worship detached from inner worship sneer at what faith truly teaches (verse 22). But people who worship inwardly, and those whose outward worship results from inward worship, put a good **975** interpretation on such things and excuse them (verse 23). Those whose external worship is detached from internal are the lowest of the low (verses 24, 25), and yet they are capable of serving the church in lowly ways (verses 26, 27).

976   The closing verses use the years of Noah's age to depict the duration and condition of the first ancient church (verses 28, 29).

Inner Meaning

977   BECAUSE the subject under discussion here is people who have been reborn, a brief statement needs to be made explaining what they are like compared to unregenerate people. From this comparison the character of the one kind and of the other can be recognized.

Regenerate people have a conscience for what is good and true; conscience moves them to do good, and conscience moves them to think truly. The good they do is the good associated with charity, and the truth they think is the truth embraced by faith. People who are not regenerate do not have a conscience. If they do, it is not a conscience that requires them to do what is good out of kindness, or to think what is true because they believe it, but to do so out of some form of love for themselves or the material world. They have either a false conscience or a distorted one.

Regenerate people feel joy when they do what conscience bids, and distress when forced to act or think against conscience. With the unregenerate, on the other hand, this is not so. Most do not know what conscience is, much less what obeying conscience or violating it is. They only know how to live by principles that advance their own interests, which gives them joy. Going against these principles creates distress for them.

[2] Regenerate people have a new will and a new intellect. The new will and intellect are their conscience, or rather exist in their conscience, through which the Lord puts neighborly kindness and religious truth to work. People who have not been reborn do not have a will but appetite instead, and are therefore attracted to every kind of evil. They do not have true intellect but shallow logic, and therefore sink into every kind of falsity.

Regenerate people have heavenly and spiritual life, but unregenerate people have only bodily and worldly life. Any ability the unregenerate have to think about and understand what is good and true derives from the Lord's life force. This force comes by way of the remnant [of truth and goodness] described earlier [§§561, 661:2], which gives them the capacity to reflect.

[3] In regenerate people, the inner self is in charge and the outer self obeys. In people who have not been reborn, the outer self is in charge, while the inner self retires and seems to disappear.

Regenerate people recognize what the inner self is and what the outer self is, or at least they *can* recognize it if they ponder. People who are not regenerate have no idea at all what the inner and outer self are. They cannot tell even if they think about it, because they have no idea what the goodness and truth of a faith based on kindness is.

All this evidence shows what the regenerate person is like and what the unregenerate one is like—that they are as different as summer and winter, or light and darkness. So the regenerate person is a living individual, while the unregenerate one is a dead individual.

Few if any today know what the inner self and the outer self are. They consider the two selves to be one and the same, primarily because they believe they do good and think truth on their own. That is one of the effects of a sense of autonomy. The inner self, though, is as distinct from the outer as heaven is from earth.

978

When they contemplate the subject, neither those who are well educated nor those who are untaught conceive of the inner person as anything but the faculty of thought, since this is internal. They consider the outer person to be the body with its sensory abilities and pleasures, since these are external. But the thinking that they consider part of the inner self is not in fact part of it. The inner self contains nothing but good impulses and true concepts, which are the Lord's; and the intermediate self contains conscience implanted by the Lord. Yet bad people—even the worst of them—have the ability to think, and people devoid of conscience do too. This leads to the conclusion that a person's faculty of thought belongs to the outer rather than the inner self.

To see that the body with its sensory abilities and pleasures is not the outer person, consider the fact that spirits, who have no such body as they had while living in the world, are still just as much in possession of an outer self.

[2] No one can ever see what the inner person and the outer person are without knowing that each of us has: a heavenly and spiritual plane (corresponding to the heaven of angels); a rational plane (corresponding

to the heaven of angelic spirits); and a relatively deep sensory plane (corresponding to the heaven of spirits).

There are three heavens, all of them present inside us, and the distinctions among them are very clear. That is why people with a conscience first find themselves in the heaven of spirits after death, then are raised by the Lord into the heaven of angelic spirits, and finally come into the heaven of angels. This could never happen unless we had the same number of heavens inside us, so that we could relate to those heavens and to conditions in each.

These things have made it clear to me what constitutes the inner self and what the outer. Heavenly and spiritual qualities form the inner self, rational thinking forms the intermediate self, and sense impressions (not direct physical sensation but something derived from it) form the outer self. These are present not only in people on earth but in spirits too.

[3] To address the scholars among my readers, the three planes interrelate in the way goal, means, and result do. People recognize that no result can ever exist without means and no means without a goal. Result, means, and goal are as clearly distinguished from one another as the outer, inner, and inmost levels.

Strictly speaking, our sensory being (the part of us that thinks on the basis of sense impressions) is the outer person. Strictly speaking again, our heavenly and spiritual being is the inner self. Our rational being is halfway in between, and through it, or through our rational capacity, the inner self communicates with the outer.

I realize that few will grasp these concepts, for the reason that we live on the surface and base our thinking on superficial things. That is why some people identify with animals and believe that when their own body dies they will die altogether.

After we die, however, we first start to live. Good people in the other world then begin by living a life full of sensory experience in the world of spirits—that is, in the heaven of spirits. Later they live a life of deeper sense experience in the heaven of angelic spirits, and finally they live a life marked by the deepest kind of sensation in the heaven of angels. This last kind of life—angelic life—is the life of the inner self, but almost nothing can be said about it that people will be able to understand.

[4] Only regenerate people can see that angelic life is the life of the inner self, and only if they reflect on goodness and truth, and on conflict

[between the inner and outer selves]. After all, the life of the inner self is the Lord's life in us, because it is through the inner self that the Lord puts charitable goodness and religious truth to work in our outer self.

Anything from the inner self that rises to awareness in our thoughts and feelings is a general impression containing countless elements that come from the inner self. These elements are imperceptible to us until we arrive in the angels' heaven. For a description of their general effect and its nature, see the lesson of experience in §545.

But what has been said here about the inner self is not necessary for salvation, since it exceeds many people's grasp. Simply let them be aware that there is an inner and an outer self, and acknowledge and believe that everything good and true comes from the Lord.

These remarks on the state of a person reborn and on the way the inner self influences the outer self appear at the outset because this chapter is talking about regenerate people, the mastery that the inner self exerts over the outer, and the obedience of the outer self.

979

Genesis 9:1. And God blessed Noah and his sons and said to them, "Reproduce and multiply and fill the earth."

980

God blessed symbolizes the Lord's presence and favor. *Noah and his sons* symbolize the ancient church. *Reproducing* symbolizes the good effects of charity; *multiplying* symbolizes the true ideas of faith, which now increased. *Filling the earth* means [that they increased] in the outer self.

God blessed symbolizes the Lord's presence and favor, as can be seen from the symbolism of blessing.

981

In the Word, on its surface, *blessing* people means enriching them with every earthly, personal benefit. This is how the Word is interpreted by all who restrict themselves to its surface meaning—Jews of the past and present, for instance, and Christians as well, today especially. So they have identified and continue to identify divine blessings with wealth, an abundance of every resource, and glory for themselves.

In a deeper sense, though, blessing people means enriching them with every kind of spiritual and heavenly goodness. As the Lord is the only one who grants this kind of blessing, or is even capable of granting it, the act of blessing symbolizes the Lord's presence and favor. The Lord's presence and favor carry such a blessing with them.

[2] The word *presence* is used because only in charity is the Lord present, and the subject here is a regenerate spiritual person, who acts out of charity. The Lord is present in each of us, but the further we distance

ourselves from neighborly love, the more the Lord's presence is absent, so to speak—which is to say, the more remote the Lord is.

The word *favor* is used rather than *mercy* because of something I believe is unknown today: people of heavenly character speak not of favor, [or grace,] but of mercy, while those of spiritual character speak not of mercy but of grace. The reason for the difference is this: Heavenly people acknowledge that the human race is sheer filth, that in itself it is made of excrement and is hellish. On this account they beg the Lord for mercy, since mercy is the fitting word for people who feel this way. [3] Spiritual people, on the other hand, might know intellectually that the human race is such, but they do not accept it internally, because they hold fast to their sense of self-sufficiency and love it. As a consequence, they have a hard time saying the word *mercy* but an easy time saying *grace*. This results from the type of humility in each of the two.

The more we love ourselves and consider ourselves capable of doing good on our own in order to earn salvation, the less able we are to plead for the Lord's mercy. The reason some are able to ask the Lord's grace, [or favor,] is that it has become a customary way of speaking. When the request is merely formal, grace contains little of the Lord, but is full of oneself. You can examine this in yourself, when you call on the Lord's grace.

982 The symbolism of *Noah and his sons* as the ancient church has already been stated and illustrated [§§531, 764–765, 768, 773, 788, 915] and can be seen in what follows [§§1025:3, 1062–1063].

983 The symbolism of *reproducing* as the good effects of charity and of *multiplying* as the true ideas of faith, which now increased, can be seen from the symbolism of both terms in the Word. Everywhere in the Word, reproducing (that is, bearing fruit) is used in connection with charity, and multiplying in connection with faith. See earlier statements about their symbolism in §§43 and 55. For even stronger confirmation of that symbolism, let me cite the following passages. In Jeremiah:

> Come back, rebellious children. I will give you shepherds after my own heart, and they will pasture you with *knowledge* and *understanding*. And it will come about that you will *multiply* and *reproduce* on the *earth*. (Jeremiah 3:14, 15, 16)

The multiplying clearly stands for growth in knowledge and understanding, that is, in faith, and reproducing stands for growth in the good effects of charity. The passage is talking about the planting of a church, and faith (multiplication) comes first in this process. [2] In the same author:

> I will gather the remnant of my flock out of all the lands to which I dispersed them, and I will bring them back to their folds, and they will *reproduce* and *multiply.* (Jeremiah 23:3)

This is about a church that has been planted, saying that it will reproduce or be fruitful in regard to the good effects of charity and multiply in regard to the true ideas of faith. In Moses:

> What is more, I will look on you and make you *reproduce* and make you *multiply.* And I will set up my compact with you. (Leviticus 26:9)

The inner meaning here has to do with a heavenly type of church, so that the good inspired by love and kindness is said to *reproduce,* while the good impulses and true concepts of faith are said to *multiply.* In Zechariah:

> I will redeem them, and they will *multiply* as they used to *multiply.* (Zechariah 10:8)

The use of *multiply* in this verse to describe religious truth is evident from the fact that they were to be redeemed. [3] In Jeremiah:

> The city will be rebuilt on its own [ruin] mound, and praise will come out of them, as will the sound of people frolicking, and I will make them *multiply,* and they will not dwindle; and [Jacob's] offspring will be as they once were. (Jeremiah 30:18, 19, 20)

This passage is about positive responses to truth and about religious truth. Praise and the sound of people frolicking indicate positive responses to truth. Multiplication indicates an increase in the amount of religious truth. Here too the offspring, or sons, stand for truth.

The fact that *filling the earth* means [that the good effects of charity and the true ideas of faith increased] in the outer self is established by the symbolism of the *earth* as the outer self, which several earlier sections discuss [§§16, 27, 82, 909, 913].

The case with the good impulses of charity and the true ideas of faith in a regenerate person is that they are implanted in the person's conscience. Since they are implanted through faith—that is, through "hearing the Word"—they first lodge in the person's memory, which is part of the outer self. When the person has been reborn, and the inner self is active, fruitfulness and multiplication follow the same pattern; the good impulses of charity make themselves evident in the feelings belonging to the person's outer self, and the true ideas of faith do so in the memory. In both places, they increase and multiply.

Anyone who has regenerated can see what this multiplication is like. Regenerate people are always gaining new confirmation from the Word, from their rational side, and from facts they have learned. All three of these give them greater and greater assurance. This kind of multiplication is one of the effects of neighborly love, an effect the Lord alone produces, working through that love.

985 Genesis 9:2. *"And may fear of you and terror of you be on every beast of the earth and on every bird of the sky. As for everything that the ground causes to creep out, and as for all the fish of the sea—into your hands let them be given."*

Fear of you and terror of you symbolizes mastery exerted by the inner self; *fear* has to do with evil and *terror* with falsity. *On every beast of the earth* means over cravings in the lower mind. *On every bird of the sky* means over falsities produced by skewed logic. *As for everything that the ground causes to creep out* symbolizes a passion for what is good. *As for all the fish of the sea* symbolizes facts. *Into your hands let them be given* symbolizes what properly belongs to the inner self as it exists in the outer self.

986 The symbolism of *fear of you and terror of you* as mastery exerted by the inner self—*fear* having to do with evil and *terror* with falsity—can be seen from the circumstances of a regenerate person. Before we have regenerated, our circumstances are ones in which the cravings and falsities of the outer self remain in perpetual control, and this causes a struggle. When we have regenerated, the inner self takes control over the outer, or in other words, over its cravings and falsities. When the inner self is in charge, we respond to evil with fear and to falsity with terror, because both violate conscience, and acting against conscience horrifies us.

[2] The inner self, though, is not afraid of evil or frightened of falsity; only the outer self is. So the present verse says that "fear of you and terror of you" will be on "every beast of the earth and every bird of the sky," that is, on all the cravings symbolized by a beast and on the falsities symbolized by a bird of the sky.

The fear and the terror seem to be ours, but here is the actual situation: As mentioned before, we each have with us at least two angels connecting us to heaven and two evil spirits connecting us to hell [§697]. When the angels are in charge, as they are in a person reborn, the evil spirits that are present do not dare to make the slightest assault on goodness or truth, because they are then in chains. When they do try to do anything bad or say anything false—or rather try to goad us into doing so—a hellish fear and terror immediately fall on them. Their fear and terror is what we feel when we face anything that violates conscience. In consequence, as soon as we do or say anything that offends conscience, we undergo inner struggle and suffer pangs of conscience, or in other words, experience a kind of torment that feels like hell.

[3] The reason *fear* is used for evil and *terror* for falsity is that the spirits we have with us are not as fearful of doing wrong as they are of telling lies. It is through the true concepts of faith that people find rebirth and gain conscience, so spirits are not allowed to stir up falsities.

Each of these spirits is mere evil, so that they live in evil; their whole nature and consequently their every effort is evil. And since they live in evil, and the vital energy that is their very own consists in evil, the wrong they do is overlooked if they are being useful in some way. Spreading falsity, however, is not permitted. The reason for this prohibition is to enable them to learn what is true and so improve as much as they can, in order to serve some menial use. I will have more to say on this later, though, the Lord's divine mercy permitting [§§5846–5865, 5976–5993].

The situation is similar in regenerate people, because their conscience is formed out of the truth taught by faith. As a result, their conscience focuses on correctness, and to them the evil that one commits is actually falsity, because it violates religious truth. (It was different for the people of the earliest church, who had perception. They perceived the evil that one commits as evil, and the falsity that one believes in as falsity.)

The fact that *on every beast of the earth* means over cravings in the lower mind is established by the symbolism of a *beast* in the Word. There beasts symbolize passions, or cravings. Beasts that are tame, useful, and clean symbolize passions for something good. Beasts that are savage, useless, and unclean symbolize passions for evil, or cravings. For more on this, see §§45, 46, 142, 143, 246, 776.

Because they symbolize cravings here, they are called beasts of the earth, not beasts of the field.

In respect to the mastery exercised by regenerate people over their cravings, everyone needs to realize the tremendous error and totally unregenerate nature of people who imagine that they can subdue evil by their

987

own efforts. Human beings are nothing but evil. We are a mass of evils. Our whole will is unmitigated evil. That is why Genesis 8:21 said, "What human hearts fabricate is evil from their youth."

Personal experience has shown me that people and spirits—and even angels, viewed in themselves (that is, their whole selfhood)—are the most worthless excrement. It has also shown me that when left to themselves, all they meditate is hatred, vengefulness, cruelty, and the foulest adulteries. These are their own impulses; these are their will.

[2] Anyone can see the same thing simply by musing on this, that at birth we are the basest living creatures among all the wild animals and beasts. After growing up and coming into our own, we would plunge into atrocities of every kind if various restraints did not stop us—external legal restraints, and restraints we place on ourselves in seeking to grow as influential and rich as possible. We would not stop until we had overpowered every person in the universe and raked up everyone's wealth. We would spare none but those who submitted to us as lowly slaves. That is what each of us is like, although we do not perceive it when we have no opportunity or power to achieve it, and when we are under restraint, as mentioned. If opportunity and ability presented themselves and the restraints were loosened, we would run just as wild as we could.

Animals are not at all the same. They are born into a kind of preordained system of nature. The savage predators among them do hurt other animals, but only to protect themselves; and when they eat other animals, they are satisfying their hunger. Once satisfied, they inflict no more harm. Humans are completely different.

These things demonstrate what human selfhood and human will are like.

[3] Since we are such a horrible, massive heap of wickedness and dung, we obviously have no ability whatever to conquer evil on our own. It is absolutely self-contradictory to say that evil can control evil, and not only that it can control evil but that it can control hell. Each of us communicates with hell by means of evil spirits, and it is this contact that arouses the evil in us.

From this anyone can see or (if sane) come to the conclusion that only the Lord can control the evil and the hell we harbor within.

In order to subdue the evil in us—or in other words, to subdue hell, which spends every second trying to attack and destroy us forever—the Lord regenerates us and gives us the gift of a new will, which is conscience. Through it, the Lord alone achieves every positive result.

Faith teaches that we are nothing but evil and that everything good is from the Lord, so we must not only learn it but also acknowledge and believe it. If we do not acknowledge and believe it in this life, it will be vividly demonstrated to us in the other life.

The fact that *on every bird of the sky* means over falsities produced by skewed logic can be seen from the symbolism of a *bird*.   **988**

In the Word, birds symbolize matters of understanding. Those that are tame, useful, and pretty symbolize true ideas in the intellect, but those that are savage, useless, and ugly symbolize misconceptions in the intellect, or falsities produced by the misuse of reason.

See §§40, 776, 870 for evidence that birds symbolize matters of understanding. The same evidence can lead to the conclusion that they symbolize shady logic and the false ideas it produces. For the removal of all doubt on this score, the following passages (in addition to the statements in §866 about ravens) will serve as proof. In Jeremiah:

> I will exact punishment of four kinds on them: with the sword, to kill; and with dogs, to drag; and with the *bird of the sky* and the *beast of the earth,* to devour and destroy. (Jeremiah 15:3)

In Ezekiel:

> On its wreckage will live every *bird of the sky,* and among its branches will stand every wild animal of the field. (Ezekiel 31:13)

In Daniel:

> Then at last upon the abominable *bird*—ruin. (Daniel 9:27)

In John:

> Babylon is a prison for every unclean and loathsome *bird.* (Revelation 18:2)

The prophets frequently say that a corpse would be given as food to the *bird of the sky* and *beast of the earth* (Jeremiah 7:33; 19:7; 34:20; Ezekiel 29:5; 39:4; Psalms 79:2; Isaiah 18:6). The meaning was that people would be destroyed by false notions (the birds of the sky) and evil impulses, or cravings (the beasts of the earth).

In regard to mastery over falsities, it is like mastery over evil; that is to say, we have not the least ability to overcome false thinking on our own.   **989**

The discussion here is about the mastery regenerate people exercise over their corrupt desires (the beast of the earth) and their falsities (the bird of the sky). In view of this, it needs to be known that we have no right at all to say we have regenerated until we acknowledge and believe that charity is the most important part of our faith and until we feel love for our fellow humans and show mercy to them. Love for others forms the regenerate person's new will. Love for others—and not faith devoid of love—is the means by which the Lord does good in the world and puts the resulting truth to work.

Some people do acts of kindness purely out of obedience, because the Lord commanded it, even though they are not regenerate. If they avoid the attitude that good deeds make us righteous, they regenerate in the other life.

990   *As for everything that the ground causes to creep out* symbolizes a passion for what is good, as suggested both by remarks above and by the symbolism of the ground from which those animals are produced or creep out. Remarks above [§§986–989] suggest this symbolism because the subject there is evil and falsity, which the reborn person gains control over. The subject here, then, is the passion for good that is given into such a person's hands. As for the symbolism of the ground from which those animals are produced or creep out, the ground in a general sense means the people of the church and any quality that exists in it. So in the present verse it means whatever the Lord produces in the outer self by way of the inner. The actual ground is in the outer self—in the feelings and the memory of the outer self.

Since we seem to produce good results ourselves, it says, "Everything that the ground causes to creep out." This is an appearance, however. It is the Lord working through our inner self who does so since, to repeat, nothing good or true exists except from the Lord.

991   *As for all the fish of the sea* symbolizes facts, as the symbolism of a fish indicates.

Fish in the Word symbolize facts that rise out of sensory information. There are three kinds of fact: facts truly understood, facts seen rationally, and facts coming from the senses. All three kinds are sown in the memory, or rather in different types of memory, and in a regenerate person it is from the memory by way of the inner self that the Lord calls on them. The last type—facts gleaned from sensory evidence—comes to our awareness or notice while we are physically alive, because we base our thinking on it. The other two, which are deeper, do not do so until we have put off our bodies and entered the other world.

For the symbolism of fish, or the creeping things that the waters produce, as facts, see §40 above. For the symbolism of a large sea creature, or whale, as general categories of fact, see §42.

The symbolism can be further established by the following passages in the Word. In Zephaniah:

> I will make human and animal die out, I will make the *bird in the heavens* and the *fish in the sea* die out. (Zephaniah 1:3)

The bird in the heavens stands for rational concepts, the fish in the sea for rational concepts on a lower plane, that is, for human thought that develops out of facts supplied by the senses. [2] In Habakkuk:

> You will make humankind like the *fish of the sea,* like a *creeping thing,* which has no ruler. (Habakkuk 1:14)

Making humankind like the fish of the sea stands for making us entirely sense-oriented. In Hosea:

> The earth will mourn, and everything living in it will lose strength, including the wild animal of the field and the *bird of the heavens;* and the *fish of the sea* will also disappear. (Hosea 4:3)

The fish of the sea stand for facts yielded by sensory evidence. In David:

> All things you have put under his feet: the animals of the fields, the *flying thing in the heavens,* and the *fish in the sea*—that which travels the thoroughfares of the seas. (Psalms 8:6, 7, 8)

This is about the Lord's power to rule in us. The fish in the sea stand for facts. Seas symbolize facts—knowledge—gathered together, as may be seen earlier, in §28. In Isaiah:

> The *fishers* will lament, and all who cast a hook into the river will mourn, and those spreading a net on the face of the water will languish. (Isaiah 19:8, 9)

The fishers stand for those who rely exclusively on the testimony of the senses, from which they hatch false ideas. The passage has to do with Egypt, or factual knowledge.

Into your hands let them be given symbolizes what properly belongs to the inner self as it exists in the outer self—as the things already said show. It can also be seen from the symbolism of a *hand,* dealt with above in §878. The text says "Into your hands let them be given" because that is how it appears.

993　　Genesis 9:3. *"Every creeping thing that is alive will serve you for food. I have given it all to you as I gave you the green plants."*

Every creeping thing that is alive symbolizes any lower pleasure that contains some goodness, which is the living aspect. *Will serve you for food* symbolizes the joy that people would have in these pleasures. *Green plants* symbolize the humblest kinds of pleasure. *All of it given to you* means enjoying it because it is useful.

994　　*Every creeping thing that is alive* symbolizes any lower pleasure that contains some goodness, which is the living aspect. This can be seen from the symbolism of a *creeping thing,* discussed previously [§§44, 594, 674, 746, 800, 807, 909–911].

Anyone can see that the creeping things mean all clean animals and birds, because it says that they were supplied as food. Strictly speaking, creeping things are those that were the most contemptible of all (listed in Leviticus 11:23, 29, 30) and unclean. In a wider sense, though—the sense used here—they are animals supplied as food. They are being called creeping things because creeping things symbolize lower pleasures. In the Word, clean animals symbolize our more tender emotional responses, as noted [§§45, 46, 142, 143, 246, 776, 987]; but since we are not aware of those responses except as revealed in our lower pleasures (so much so that we actually refer to them as pleasures), they are called creeping things here.

[2] There are two kinds of lower pleasures: those that involve the will and those that involve the intellect. These are the general types of pleasure: pleasure in owning property and having other wealth; the pleasure of rank and high office in government; pleasure connected with love in marriage and with love for babies and children; pleasure in friendship and social contact; the pleasure of reading, writing, learning, and growing in wisdom. And there are many others.

There are also pleasures of the senses. For instance there is auditory pleasure, which in general is pleasure in the sweetness of song and music; visual pleasure, which in general is pleasure in many different kinds of beauty; olfactory pleasure, which is pleasure in sweet scents; gustatory pleasure, which is pleasure in the wonderful flavor and useful qualities of food and drink; and tactile pleasure, which is pleasure in a variety of agreeable sensations.

These general kinds of gratification are felt in the body and so are called bodily pleasures, but the body never experiences any kind of pleasure unless the pleasure springs from some deeper emotion that also sustains it. And no deeper emotion ever exists unless it comes from one still deeper that holds within it a use and purpose.

[3] These layers of emotion that go deeper and deeper, all the way to our inmost reaches, are not something we sense while we are living in the body. Most people hardly even realize that they exist, let alone that the lower pleasures stem from them. In reality, though, nothing can emerge on the surface if it does not come from progressively deeper sources. Sensual gratification is only an outward effect. As long as we live in the body we cannot see what lies within, unless we reflect on it.

Deeper elements first reveal themselves in the next life, and they do so sequentially as the Lord lifts us up toward heaven. Inner emotions, with their satisfactions, reveal themselves in the world of spirits. Emotions yet deeper, with their delights, appear in the heaven of angelic spirits. And emotions yet deeper again, with their blessings, reveal themselves in the heaven of angels. (There are, indeed, three heavens, each deeper, more perfect, and more blessed than the last, as may be seen in §§459 and 684.)

These things unfold in order this way and disclose themselves to our awareness in the other world. But while we live in the body, since our whole focus and concentration is on bodily concerns, deeper elements are essentially put to sleep, being overwhelmed by those concerns. Still, the thoughtful individual can see that our pleasures all reflect the layered depths of our emotional responses and derive their whole existence and character from them.

[4] The progressively deeper layers of emotion are called creeping things because we experience them as pleasures that lie on the surface, in our body. But this is only a physical manifestation, the effect of inner processes, as anyone can see merely from the power of sight and the pleasures that accompany it. Unless there is an inner power of sight, the eye cannot possibly see. The vision of the eye arises from inner vision, for which reason we can still see just as well after the body's death as when we were alive in the body, and much better. We simply do not see what is worldly and material but rather what belongs to the other life. People who had been blind in physical life see as clearly in the next life as those who had been veritable Lynceuses. For the same reason, when we are asleep we see as well in our dreams as when we are awake. By means of inner sight, I have been allowed to see the objects of the next life more clearly than I can see the objects of the world.

These considerations establish the fact that outer sight arises from inner sight, and this from sight still deeper, and so on. Likewise with each of the other senses, and with all the lower pleasures.

[5] Other places in the Word as well call the lower pleasures creeping things, and those places also differentiate between clean and unclean ones—that is, between pleasures enjoyed in a living or heavenly way and pleasures enjoyed in a dead or hellish way. In Hosea, for example:

> I will strike a pact with them on that day—with the wild animal of the field, and with the bird in the heavens and the *creeping thing* of the ground. (Hosea 2:18)

This passage demonstrates that the wild animal of the field, the bird in the heavens, and creeping things symbolize the kinds of things in us that I have already mentioned, since it is talking about a new church. In David:

> Let the heavens and the earth, the seas and every *creeping* thing in them praise Jehovah. (Psalms 69:34)

The seas and the creeping things in them cannot praise Jehovah, only the living, human attributes they symbolize. That is to say, he can be praised only from the living quality of those attributes. In the same author:

> Praise Jehovah, you wild animal and each of you beasts, you *creeping thing* and bird on the wing. (Psalms 148:[7,] 10)

The same is true here.

The fact that these passages use creeping things to mean positive emotions from which gratifications stem can also be seen from the consideration that creeping things were unclean to the people of that time. This will become evident from the following quotations. [6] In the same author:

> Jehovah, the earth is full of your possessions. This sea is large, and wide in its extent. In it is the *creeping thing,* and there is no counting them. They all look to you to *give* them their *food* in its season. You give to them; they gather. You open your hand; they receive abundant good. (Psalms 104:24, 25, 27, 28)

In the inner meaning, the seas symbolize spiritual entities, while the creeping things symbolize everything that receives its life from them.

Giving them food in its season and receiving abundant good depict the enjoyment [of pleasure]. In Ezekiel:

> And it will happen that every *living* soul that *crawls* in any place where the rivers go will *survive;* and the fish will be very numerous, because that water goes there and is cured, and everything will *live,* wherever the river goes. (Ezekiel 47:9)

This is about water flowing from a new Jerusalem. Water stands for spiritual traits from a heavenly origin. The living soul that crawls stands for positive desires and the gratifications they give rise to, both those that are personal and those that are sensory. The fact that these receive life from the water—from spiritual traits of heavenly origin—is obvious.

[7] Tainted pleasures, which trace their origin to self-absorption and so to the sordid cravings of self-absorption, are also called creeping things, as can be seen in Ezekiel:

> And I went in and looked, and here, every shape of *creeping thing* and animal (an abhorrence) and all the idols of the house of Israel—a painting on the wall all around. (Ezekiel 8:10)

The shape of a creeping thing symbolizes foul pleasures, within which lie corrupt desires, within which again lie hatred, vengeance, cruelty, and adultery. Such urges are creeping things, or the thrill of a lower pleasure springing from love for ourselves and for worldly advantages, which is to say, from self-absorption. These are the idols of the self-absorbed, because these are the things they consider agreeable, love, view as gods, and therefore venerate. Because these creeping things symbolized such vile attributes, the representative church deemed them so unclean that it was not permissible even to touch them, and anyone who did so much as touch them was unclean, as shown by Leviticus 5:2; 11:31, 32, 33; 22:5, 6.

The symbolism of *will serve you for food* as the joy that people would have in this pleasure can be seen from the fact that each of our pleasures not only touches us but also nourishes us the way food does.

A pleasure that is not enjoyable is not pleasure but some lifeless thing. Joy is what makes it pleasurable in name and in fact. But the nature of the joy involved determines the quality of the pleasure. In themselves, personal and sensory rewards are only material things, lifeless and dead. From delight, however, which emerges from progressively deeper sources

995

inside us, they receive life. Plainly, then, the quality of the life we have in our deeper dimensions determines the nature of the enjoyment in our pleasures, because enjoyment has life in it. Delight that contains something good from the Lord is the only thing that is alive, because in that case it flows from the genuine life within goodness. That is why the verse says, "Every creeping thing that is *alive* will serve you for food," that is, for enjoyment.

[2] Some believe that no one who wants to be happy in the other world should ever live among personal or sensual pleasures but should renounce them all. They assert that these are bodily and worldly distractions that hinder us from living a spiritual and heavenly life. But people who think this way and willingly subject themselves to misery while living in the world are misinformed as to the true situation.

No one is ever forbidden to enjoy personal and sensory pleasures, which are these: pleasure in owning property and having other wealth; the pleasure of rank and high office in government; pleasure connected with love in marriage and with love for babies and children; pleasure in friendship and social contact; auditory pleasure, or pleasure in the sweetness of song and music; visual pleasure, or pleasure in the many kinds of beauty that exist, such as elegant clothes, fine mansions with all their furnishings, beautiful gardens, and similar objects whose symmetry makes them delightful; olfactory pleasure, or pleasure in sweet scents; gustatory pleasure, or pleasure in the wonderful flavor and useful qualities of food and drink; and tactile pleasures.

These are, after all, our most outward emotional responses—physical responses—rising out of inward responses, as noted. [3] Inward responses, which are alive, all derive their appeal from goodness and truth, and goodness and truth derive theirs from charity and faith and beyond that from the Lord, so that they derive it from life itself. As a result, emotional responses and the lower pleasures that come from them are alive. And since true pleasure springs from this source, it is never denied to anyone. In fact when it springs from there, the thrill it offers outstrips by far any thrill that does not originate there. The other kind of delight is dirty by comparison.

Take for example the sensual pleasures connected with love in marriage. When those pleasures rise out of true marriage love, they surpass immeasurably any pleasure that does not. So superior are they that people who have true marriage love are virtually in the blissful elation of heaven, since it comes down to them from heaven. The people who belonged to the earliest church testify to this. The delight an adulterer feels in adultery was so loathsome to them that merely thinking about it made their hair stand on end. From this we can draw conclusions about the nature of any pleasure that does not flow from the true fountain of life: the Lord.

[4] Again, the pleasures mentioned above are never denied to us. So far are they from being denied to us that they do not even begin to feel good until we obtain them from their true origin. Further corroboration for this fact is the consideration that many people who enjoyed power, importance, and wealth during their earthly lives and abundant gratifications of all kinds, both personal and sensory, are among the blessed and happy in heaven. Deeper joys and a deeper happiness are now alive in them, because these feelings originated in the good impulses of neighborly love and in the true ideas constituting faith in the Lord. Because the joy and happiness originated in charity and in faith in the Lord, such people viewed all their lower pleasures in terms of usefulness, since usefulness was their goal. The usefulness itself was intensely exhilarating to them and was what made their lower pleasures enjoyable. See the lesson of experience in §945.

The symbolism of a *plant* as the humblest kinds of pleasure is established by the statements above.

996

Those kinds of pleasure are called green plants because they are nothing more than worldly and physical kinds—superficial kinds. As I said, the pleasure we feel in our bodies, or on the surface of existence, traces its source back to increasingly deeper levels of enjoyment. The pleasures felt on the surface, or in one's body, are relatively inferior. All agreeable sensation is such that the shallower it grows, the poorer it is, while the deeper it grows, the more blissful it is. So to repeat, as the external layers are unwrapped or peeled off, the elation grows sweeter and more blissful. This is sufficiently apparent from the fact that our enjoyment of the lower pleasures during our physical lives is quite paltry compared to the sensations we enjoy afterward, when we enter the world of spirits. It is so inferior, in fact, that good spirits absolutely spurn the creature comforts of the body and would refuse to return to them even if given all the pleasure in the whole world.

[2] The pleasure these spirits enjoy in turn loses its luster when the Lord lifts them into the heaven of angelic spirits, because they then shed those deeper delights and don ones still deeper. The exhilaration that angelic spirits felt in their heaven likewise pales when the Lord raises

them into the angelic or third heaven. In this heaven, where inner qualities are alive and mutual love reigns supreme, the happiness is indescribable. (For more on inner pleasure or happiness, see the account from experience in §545.)

This shows the meaning of *I have given it all to you as I gave you the green plants.*

Since creeping things symbolize both personal pleasures and the pleasures of the senses, and these are being described as green plants, the original language has an expression that means both "plants" and "greenery." "Plants" refers to earthly pleasures stemming from matters of will, or from heavenly kinds of feelings, while "greenery" refers to those stemming from matters of understanding, or from spiritual feelings.

[3] The symbolism of green plants or grass as something lowly can be seen in the Word, as for instance in Isaiah:

> The waters of Nimrim will be wastelands, because the grain has dried out, the grass has been consumed, there is no *greenery*. (Isaiah 15:6)

In the same author:

> Their residents, their hand shortened, have felt panic and shame. They have become field grass and grain *plants,* hay on the roofs. (Isaiah 37:27)

Grain plants stand for what is humblest. In Moses:

> The land that you enter, to possess it, is not like the land of Egypt, which you came out from, where you would sow your seed and irrigate it by foot like a *vegetable garden.* (Deuteronomy 11:10)

The vegetable garden stands for something humble. In David:

> The evil are suddenly cut down like grain and are consumed like *green plants.* (Psalms 37:2)

The grain and the green plants stand for what is humblest.

997   *All of it given to you* means enjoying it because it is useful, which is the same as receiving it as food, since anything given as food is given for a useful purpose.

As far as usefulness is concerned, the case is this: People who have charity inside, that is, love for their neighbor (which is the source of any living kind of appeal in the lower pleasures) look at the enjoyment of pleasure solely in terms of its usefulness.

Charity, after all, is nothing without the work of charity. Charity consists in doing—in being useful, in other words. If we love our neighbor as ourselves, we do not feel any delight in charity unless we are being active or useful. As a consequence, the life of charity is a life of usefulness. This is the life found throughout heaven, because the Lord's kingdom, since it is a realm of mutual love, is a realm of useful activity. Accordingly, all the gratification that charity offers acquires its appeal from usefulness. The more marked the usefulness, the greater the appeal. That is why the essential nature and quality of an angel's occupation determines the kind of happiness the Lord gives him or her.

[2] The situation is the same with all lower pleasures; the more marked their usefulness, the greater their appeal. Take for a single example the pleasure that married love entails. Because this pleasure provides the breeding ground for human society and through it for the Lord's realm in the heavens, and because this is the most important function there is, it holds within it such ecstasy that it is, as they say, heavenly bliss.

Circumstances are similar for all other kinds of gratification, with variations due to the importance of the service they perform. Those services are so richly varied that it would be hard to break them down into their major and minor categories. They all look toward the Lord's kingdom, that is, to the Lord, some more closely and directly and others more distantly and indirectly.

This again leads to the conclusion that all kinds of lower pleasures are granted to us, but only for the sake of their use, and that as a result, because of the use they perform, each in its own way is brimming and alive with heaven's happiness.

Genesis 9:4. *"Only flesh in its soul [you must not eat], its blood you must not eat."*   **998**

Flesh symbolizes human volition. A *soul* symbolizes new life. *Blood* symbolizes neighborly love. *Not eating* symbolizes not mingling. So *not eating flesh in its soul, [not eating] blood,* is not mingling profane things with holy.

The symbolism of *flesh* as human volition is established by the symbolism of *flesh* in its proper sense, having to do with our depraved self. [In the Word,] flesh symbolizes all people in general and those in particular who are oriented toward their bodies. (See the earlier demonstration of this in §574.) Since flesh symbolizes all people and particularly body-oriented ones, it also symbolizes selfhood and consequently volition.   **999**

Our volition or will is nothing but evil. This being so, when the term *flesh* refers to people, it symbolizes every craving or all greed. Our will consists wholly of cravings, as shown several times already [§§105, 568, 594, 634, 801:1, 977:2]. Since this is what flesh symbolizes, the same thing was represented by the flesh that the people craved in the wilderness, described by Moses in these words:

> The rabble that was in their midst had a *strong craving*. So they wept again and said, "Who will feed us *flesh?*" (Numbers 11:4)

Clearly flesh is being called a craving, since it says, "They had a strong craving. Who will feed us flesh?" The words that follow these also illustrate the meaning:

> The *flesh* was still between their teeth, before it was shredded, and Jehovah's anger blazed out against the people, and Jehovah struck a very strong blow among the people. And he called the name of that place *the Graves of Greed,* because there they buried the people who had had a *greedy craving.* (Numbers 11:33, 34)

[2] Anyone can see that such a blow [or plague] would never have been brought on the people just because they craved flesh; it was not their longing for meat that was to blame. Such a longing is only natural, when people used to eating meat are deprived of it for a long time, as was then true for the people in the wilderness. The real reason—a spiritual one—ran deeper: the people were such that they felt utter disgust for what the manna symbolized and represented (as verse 6 of that chapter [Numbers 11] also shows), and they longed only for the kind of things that flesh symbolized and represented. Those things are the self-centered impulses of the will, the stirrings of greed, which in themselves resemble dung and are inherently profane. It was because that church was a representative one (as a consequence of such representations) that a plague of these proportions was inflicted on the people. The events that took place among them, you see, were represented in a spiritual way in heaven, where manna represented what is heavenly and the flesh the people craved represented a sordid urge of the will. The result, because they were the kind of people described, was punishment.

These and other places in the Word demonstrate that flesh symbolizes the will—in this case, human will. Review the discussion concerning the beast of the earth at verse 2 of this chapter [§987] to see how unclean that will is.

1000   The symbolism of *soul* as life is established by the symbolism of the soul in many passages of the Word. In the Word, soul in general symbolizes all

life, both inward life (or that of the inner self) and outward life (or that
of the outer self). Since it symbolizes all life, it also symbolizes the specific kind of life possessed by the people to whom it is attributed. Here
it is used in connection with the life that a regenerate person has, which
is separate from the person's will. As noted earlier, the new life that a
spiritual person who has been reborn receives from the Lord is completely separate from human will or human autonomy [§§730:1; 731;
848; 933:2, 3]. That is to say, it is completely separate from the person's
own life, which is not life (although that is what it is called) but death,
because it is the life of hell. So in the present verse, the flesh in its soul
that they were not to eat means flesh together with its soul. That is,
they were not to mingle this new life, which is the Lord's, with the evil,
unsavory life that is a human being's. In other words, they were not to
mingle the new life with human will, or human selfhood.

There is a great deal of evidence for the symbolism of *blood* as neigh-   **1001**
borly love. As a result, blood symbolizes a new will that the spiritual person who has been reborn receives from the Lord. This new will is the
same thing as neighborly love, because the new will is formed of that
love. Charity—love—is the vital essence itself of the will, or the life of
the will. The only possible reason for saying we will something is that we
favor or love it. We might say we think something, but that is not the
same as willing it, unless the will lies behind the thought.

This new will, which is neighborly love, is the blood. The new will is
not ours but is the Lord's in us. And since it is the Lord's, it must never
be mixed together with the promptings of our own will, which again are
quite foul. That is why the representative church had this proscription
against eating flesh in its soul, that is, in its blood, meaning that people
were not to mix the two together.

[2] Because blood symbolized charity, it symbolized what was holy;
and because flesh symbolized human will, it symbolized what was profane.
Since the two, being opposites, are separate, people were forbidden to eat
blood. The reason was that the eating of flesh together with blood in those
days presented to heaven a picture of profanation, or the intermingling of
something sacred and something profane. Such a picture could not help
striking the angels of the time with horror. In those days, everything that
was happening among members of the church was being turned into a
corresponding spiritual representation among the angels, in accord with
its inner-sense symbolism.

Since meanings always depend on the individual they apply to, so
does the symbolism of blood. In relation to a regenerate spiritual person,

blood symbolizes charity, or love for one's neighbor. In relation to a
regenerate person of heavenly character, it symbolizes love for the Lord.
In relation to the Lord, however, it symbolizes his core human essence
and therefore Love itself, that is, his mercy toward the human race. Since
blood, then, symbolizes love and anything connected with love, in general it symbolizes heavenly traits, which are the Lord's alone. So in relation to humans, it symbolizes heavenly qualities that we receive from the
Lord. The heavenly qualities that a regenerate spiritual person receives
from the Lord are heavenly-spiritual ones (discussed elsewhere, by the
Lord's divine mercy).

[3] This fact—that blood symbolizes heavenly qualities and that
in the highest sense it symbolized the Lord's core human essence and
so love itself, or his mercy toward the human race—can be seen from
the holiness that the representative Jewish religion was commanded to
accord blood. On that account it was called the blood of the covenant
and was spattered on the people. Along with the anointing oil, it was also
spattered on Aaron and his sons. And the blood of every burnt offering
and sacrifice was spattered on and around the altar. On these subjects,
see Exodus 12:7, 13, 22, 23; 24:6, 8; Leviticus 1:5, 11, 15; 4:6, 7, 17, 18, 25,
30, 34; 5:9; 16:14, 15, 18, 19; Numbers 18:17; Deuteronomy 12:27.

[4] The reason the eating of blood was so strictly forbidden was that
blood was considered this holy and human will is this profane, and the
practice represented the profanation of something holy. Moses says, for
instance:

It is an eternal statute throughout your generations, everywhere you
live: you shall *not eat* any *fat* or any *blood*. (Leviticus 3:17)

Fat stands for heavenly life, and blood (in this verse) for heavenly-
spiritual life.

(A heavenly-spiritual entity is something spiritual that develops out of
something heavenly. For example, love for the Lord was the heavenly trait
belonging to people in the earliest church, because it was planted in their
will. Their heavenly-spiritual possession was the faith that grew out of it,
as described in §§30–38, 337, 393, 398. With spiritual people, on the other
hand, a heavenly attribute is not possible, since love for others is planted in
their intellectual side; they can have only a heavenly-spiritual dimension.)

In the same author:

Any from the house of Israel or from among the immigrants residing
in your midst who may have *eaten any blood*—I will set my face against

the souls *eating blood,* and I will cut them off from the midst of their people, because the *soul of the flesh* is *in the blood.* And I have given it to you [for use] on the altar, to make atonement over your souls, because the *blood* itself must atone for the soul. The soul of all *flesh* is its *blood;* everyone *eating* it will be cut off. (Leviticus 17:10, 11, 14)

This says explicitly that the soul of flesh is in the blood and that the soul of flesh *is* the blood—the heavenly aspect, the sacred element, the Lord's possession. [5] In the same author:

Set yourself firmly against *eating blood,* because the *blood* itself is the soul, and you shall not *eat* the soul with the flesh. (Deuteronomy 12:23, 24, 25)

These verses again show that blood is being called the soul, that is, heavenly life, or a heavenly quality, as represented by the burnt offerings and sacrifices of that religion. The prohibition in Exodus 23:18 and 34:25 against offering the *blood* of a sacrifice on top of yeast bread also represented a ban on mingling any heavenly aspect, which belongs to the Lord—and only what belongs to him is heavenly and sacred—with any distinctly human aspect, which is profane. Anything containing yeast symbolized what was corrupt and tainted.

[6] The reason blood is called soul and symbolizes the holiness of charity, and the reason it represented the holiness of love in the Jewish religion, is that it constitutes the life of the body. Since blood constitutes the life of the body, it is the body's outermost soul, so that we can call it the physical soul, or the vehicle of our physical life. And since external objects represented inner attributes in the representative churches, blood represented the soul, or heavenly life.

The symbolism of *not eating* as not mingling now follows.

Regarded in itself, eating meat is a profane custom, since people of the very earliest times never ate the flesh of any animal or bird but only grains (particularly wheat bread), fruit, vegetables, different kinds of milk, and milk products (such as butter). Butchering living creatures and eating the flesh was heinous, in their eyes, and characteristic of wild beasts. It was only on account of the menial labor and the functions the animals performed for them that they captured any. This can be seen from Genesis 1:29, 30.

But when time passed and people turned as savage as wild animals and in fact more savage, for the first time they started to butcher animals and eat the meat. In view of the fact that people were like this, the practice was also tolerated, as it still is today. To the extent that people follow it in good conscience, it is permissible, because everything we consider true and consequently allowable forms our conscience. For this reason, no one these days is ever condemned for eating meat.

1003 This now shows that *not eating flesh in its soul, [not eating] blood* means not mingling profane things with holy. Eating blood with flesh never mingles profane things with holy, as the Lord also taught explicitly in Matthew:

> It is not what goes into the mouth that renders a person unclean but what comes out of the mouth; this renders a person unclean, since the things that come out of the mouth come out of the heart. (Matthew 15:11, 17, 18, 19, 20)

Still, it was forbidden in the Jewish religion because, again, eating blood with the flesh at that time presented heaven with an image of profanation. Everything that took place in that religion turned into a corresponding representation in heaven. Blood turned into something sacred and heavenly. Flesh (aside from sacrifices) turned into something profane, because it symbolized cravings, as shown [§999:1]. And the actual eating of both turned into a mixing together of holiness and profanation. That is why it was so strictly banned.

After the Lord's Coming, though, when outward rituals were abolished, so that representative forms died out, such practices no longer turned into corresponding representations in heaven. When people develop depth and learn about inner dimensions, superficial things lose all value for them. They realize what is truly holy, namely, charity and the faith growing out of it, which provide them with a perspective on their outer dimension, or the amount of charity and faith in the Lord they have outwardly. As a result, ever since the Lord's Coming, heaven views us not in terms of outer but inner attributes. If angels do look at any of us on the basis of external considerations, it is due to a simplicity in us, and to an innocence and kindness within the simplicity. These come from the Lord and reside within our outward traits, or our outward worship, although we are unaware of it.

1004 Genesis 9:5. *"And assuredly the blood of your souls I will seek; at the hand of every wild animal I will seek it, and at the hand of a human—at the hand of a man, [the victim's] brother—I will seek that person's soul."*

Seeking the blood of your souls means that the violence inflicted on charity will inevitably punish itself, *your blood* meaning violence, and *souls* meaning those who inflict the violence. *At the hand of every wild animal* means by everything inside a violent person. *At the hand of a human* means by everything in that person's will. *At the hand of a man, one's brother,* means by everything in the person's intellect. To *seek a person's soul* means to avenge profanation.

Seeking the blood of your souls means that the violence inflicted on charity will inevitably punish itself, the *blood* meaning violence, and *souls* meaning that which inflicts the violence. This can be seen from statements above and below; from the symbolism of blood in the negative sense; and from the symbolism of a soul in the negative sense.

From statements above: The last verse dealt with the eating of blood, which symbolizes profanation, as was shown.

From statements below: The next verse deals with the shedding of blood. The present verse, then, is about the condition and punishment of those who combine sacred things with profane.

From the symbolism of blood in the negative sense: In a positive sense blood symbolizes heavenly traits and, in respect to a regenerate spiritual person, charity (which is spiritual people's heavenly side); but in its negative sense blood symbolizes the violence inflicted on charity. Accordingly it symbolizes the opposite of charity and therefore all hatred, all vengefulness, all cruelty, and especially profanation, as the passages from the Word quoted in §§374 and 376 indicate.

From the symbolism of a soul in the negative sense: In the Word, a soul generally symbolizes life and so all living people. Our character, though, determines what kind of life we live, so a soul also symbolizes the person who inflicts violence. Many passages in the Word are capable of demonstrating this, but for the moment take just this one from Moses:

> Whoever may have eaten blood, I will set my face against the *souls* eating blood, and I will cut *them* off from the midst of their people, because the *soul* of the flesh is in the blood. And I have given it [for use] on the altar, to make atonement over your *souls,* because the blood itself must atone for the *soul.* (Leviticus 17:10, 11, 14)

This passage uses *soul* to mean life in three senses. Many other passages also [demonstrate these senses].

What follows [§§1011–1012] will show that the violence inflicted on charity inevitably punishes itself.

The fact that *at the hand of every wild animal* means by everything inside a violent person can be seen from the symbolism of a wild animal.

1005

1006

In the Word, a wild animal symbolizes something living, as §908 showed; but in the opposite sense it symbolizes something that resembles a wild animal and so anything bestial inside us, as was also shown earlier [§908]. Consequently it means a person whose life is bestial, which is to say a violent individual, or one who inflicts violence on charity. That is the person who resembles a wild animal.

It is love and charity that make us human; it is hatred, vengefulness, and cruelty that make us wild animals.

1007 *At the hand of a human* means by everything in that person's will, and *at the hand of a man, one's brother,* means by everything in the person's intellect. This is established by the symbolism of *a human,* because the essential nature and life of human beings is their will, although the character of the will determines what kind of people they are. It is also established by the symbolism of *a man, one's brother.* Our intellectual side is called a man and brother, as shown above in §367. Whether it is a true intellect, a sham one, or a misguided one, it is still called a man and brother, because the intellect is called a man (§§158, 265) and the brother of the will (§367).

The reason the terms *a human* and *a man, a brother,* are used here to refer to a polluted will and polluted intellect is that the current passage is talking about profanation. Heaven cannot bear to hear profanation mentioned or see it represented without rejecting it vigorously and immediately. That is why such mild words appear here and why the meaning of the words in this verse is fairly ambiguous: so that heaven need not even see that this is the burden of the passage.

1008 To *seek a person's soul* means to avenge profanation, as can be seen from the things said in the last verse and in the present verse, since the topic is the eating of blood, which symbolizes profanation.

Few people know what profanation is, let alone what the punishment for it is in the other world.

There are many kinds of profanation. People who flatly deny the tenets of the faith (such as nations outside the church that lack access to basic religious knowledge) do not commit profanation. The people who commit profanation are those who know religious truth—especially those who acknowledge, profess, and preach it, and convince others it is true—and yet live a life of hatred, revenge, cruelty, larceny, and adultery. They also justify such behavior by numerous passages that they scrape together out of the Word, perverting them and immersing them in that same vile behavior. They are the ones committing profanation. These actions more than any others bring death on a person.

Evidence that such a practice incurs death can be seen in the fact that profane and holy matters remain completely separate in the other life—profane ones in hell and holy ones in heaven. When the kind of people just described enter the next life, sacred elements cling to profane ones in every single thought they think, the same as during physical life. Now, however, in the new setting, those people cannot present even a single holy idea without exposing something profane attached to it, just as clear as day. That is how it is in the next world when one person perceives another's thoughts. Profanation displays itself in every single thing such a person thinks, then, and since profanation fills heaven with horror, the profaner is inevitably thrust down into hell.

[2] Hardly anyone knows how our mental processes work. People think an idea is a simple thing, but each individual idea contains innumerable details linked together in many different ways, so that it is almost an image and thus a portrait of the person, which others perceive and observe in its entirety in the next life. To offer just a few examples:

When the idea of any place occurs to us—whether it is a whole region or a town or a building—then at the same time the thought and mental image of everything we have ever done there emerges, and spirits and angels see it all. Or if the thought of an individual we hated comes up, then at the same time an idea of every thought we harbored, every word we spoke, and every action we took against that person comes out.

The case is the same with our thoughts on all abstract issues. When our thoughts on a given subject come out, each and every idea that we conceived and that left its mark on us lies open to view. When our thinking on marriage comes up, for instance, then if we had been adulterers, all the filth and smut of adultery (even adultery we had merely imagined) comes out too. So do all the arguments we used for justifying adultery, whether they were based on the evidence of our senses, on a line of reasoning, or on the Word. So too do all the ways we adulterated and perverted the truth in the Word.

[3] Besides this, the idea of one thing bleeds into the idea of another and stains it, as if a scant drop of black dye released in water darkened the whole pool.

As a result, spirits are recognized by their thoughts, and amazing to say, every single idea they have is an image or model of them. When this image or model is presented to view, it is so ugly that looking at it would make you shudder.

This shows what the condition of those who profane holy things is like and what their image is like in the next life.

Those, however, who have believed implicitly in what the Word says can never be said to have profaned holy things even if they have believed what is not true, because the Word speaks according to appearances. (On this last subject, see §589.)

1009   Genesis 9:6. *"Those shedding the blood of a person in a person will have their own blood shed, because [blood] has made humankind into God's image."*

Shedding the blood of a person in a person means obliterating charity; *within a person* means as it exists with us. *Will have their own blood shed* symbolizes their damnation. *Because [blood] has made humankind into God's image* symbolizes charity, which is God's image.

1010   *Shedding the blood of a person in a person* means obliterating charity, and *in a person* means as it exists with us, which the following shows: *Blood* (discussed earlier [§§1001, 1003, 1005]) symbolizes the holiness of charity. And it says, "the blood of a *person in a person*," meaning our inner life, which is not in us but exists with us. The Lord's life is charity, which is not in people (since people are unclean and profane) but exists with them.

The fact that shedding blood is inflicting violence on charity can be seen from various passages in the Word, and from those quoted above in §§374 and 376, showing that the violence inflicted on charity is called blood.

[2] The literal meaning of bloodshed is murder, but the inner meaning is hatred for our neighbor, as the Lord teaches in Matthew:

> You have heard that among the people of old it was said, "You shall not *kill;* whoever kills will be subject to judgment." I say to you, though, that any who *are angry* at their brother or sister without cause will be subject to judgment. (Matthew 5:21, 22)

In this passage, being angry symbolizes a departure from neighborly love; see the discussion above at §357. Consequently it means hatred. Anyone who feels hatred not only lacks charity but also inflicts violence on it, or in other words, sheds blood. Hatred carries murder itself within it, as is clear from this, that those who hate another cherish no greater wish than to kill that person and if external restraints did not interfere would commit the murder. So the murder of a fellow human and the shedding of that person's blood is hatred; and since this is what hatred is, it lurks in every thought we nurture against that person.

The same is true with profanation. Anyone who profanes the Word not only hates truth but also blots it out, or kills it, as I said [§1008]. This can be seen clearly in the next life from those who had committed profanation. No matter how upright, wise, and devout they had appeared outwardly while living in their bodies, in the other world they nurse a deadly hatred for the Lord and for any kind of loving goodness or religious truth. After all, these things combat their deep-seated hatred, their thievery, and their adulteries, which they had veiled in sanctimony and misrepresented to their own advantage.

[3] In addition to the passages quoted earlier, in §374, the following passage from Moses shows that profanation is equated with blood:

> Anyone from the house of Israel who slaughters an ox or lamb or goat in the camp or who slaughters one outside the camp and does not bring it to the doorway of the meeting tent to offer it as an offering to Jehovah in front of Jehovah's dwelling place, *blood[guilt]* will be imputed to that man; he has *shed blood.* And that man will be cut off from the midst of his people. (Leviticus 17:3, 4)

Consecrating something anywhere but on the altar next to the tent represented profanation. Sacrifice was a holy act, but if performed inside or outside the camp, it was profane.

The fact that *will have their own blood shed* symbolizes their damnation is established by the things said.

From the literal meaning comes the idea that one who sheds blood, or a murderer, should be sentenced to death. In the inner meaning, though, we find that the verse condemns to death—that is, hell—those who hate their neighbor. In Matthew the Lord teaches the same thing:

> Any who say, "Idiot!" to their brother or sister will be subject to fiery Gehenna. (Matthew 5:22)

This is because when charity has been eliminated, we are left to ourselves and our own devices. No longer does the Lord rule us through the inner restraints of conscience but through external restraints that the law lays on us and that we subject ourselves to in our drive for power and riches. When the latter chains are loosened, as does happen in the other life, we plunge into the cruelest and most obscene behavior and so into our own damnation.

1011

"Those who shed blood will have their own blood shed" is a retaliatory law that was very familiar to ancient people. It was the standard they used in judging evildoing and crime, as is clear from many passages in the Word. This legal principle derives its origin from the universal law that we must do to our neighbor only what we would want others to do to us (Matthew 7:12). It also results from the pattern that everything in the next life follows, in which evil actually punishes itself, as does falsity, so that evil and falsity carry their own punishment. Since this is the pattern—that evil punishes itself or, what is the same, incurs a penalty mirroring itself—from it ancient people also drew their law of retaliation. The current verse symbolizes the same thing by saying, "Those who shed blood will have their own blood shed"—that is, they will plunge into damnation.

1012   In a literal sense, *those who shed the blood of a person in a person will have their own blood shed* is about shedding another person's blood. In an inner sense, however, it is not about anything belonging to others but about the charity in oneself. That is why the text goes on to speak of "the blood of a person in a person." When the literal sense mentions two things, sometimes the inner sense means just one. The inner self is the "person in a person," so all those who extinguish charity (which belongs to the inner self, or rather *is* the inner self) will have their own blood shed. That is, they will condemn themselves.

1013   The fact that *because [blood] has made humankind into God's image* symbolizes charity, which is God's image, follows logically. The last section discussed the charity symbolized by blood. The fact that it was not to be snuffed out is symbolized by the fact that people were not to shed blood. Now the verse proceeds to say that *it has made humankind into God's image,* which indicates that charity is God's image.

Hardly anyone today knows what God's image is. People say God's image was thoroughly destroyed in the first human, whom they call Adam. They also say that Adam had previously had God's image within him, which they describe as a certain perfection unknown to themselves. Perfection is what it was, too, because Adam or Humankind means the earliest church, which was a heavenly individual, with perception of a type that no later church possessed. So that church was the Lord's likeness as well. (The Lord's likeness symbolizes love for him.)

[2] After this church gradually died out, the Lord created a new one that was not a heavenly church but a spiritual one. This church was not the Lord's likeness but his image. (An image symbolizes spiritual love,

that is, love for one's neighbor, or charity, as also shown earlier, in §§50, 51.) Spiritual love—charity—made this church an image of the Lord, as indicated by the present verse. The reality that charity is itself the Lord's image can be seen from the fact that it says, "because it has *made* humankind into God's image," which is to say that charity itself *made* people so.

The fact that charity is God's image is very clear from the essential nature itself of love, or charity. Only love and kindness can create a likeness or an image of anyone. The essential nature of love and kindness is to form something like a single entity out of two things. When we love another as ourselves—and more than ourselves—we see the other in ourselves and ourselves in the other. Anyone can recognize this simply by observing love, or people who love one another. The will of one is the will of the other; they seem to be deeply bound together; only their bodies are distinct from each other.

[3] Love for the Lord makes us one with him, or makes us his likeness. Charity—love for our neighbor—does too, but it makes us his image. An image is not a likeness of something but is *in* the likeness of that thing.

This oneness rising out of love is something the Lord himself describes in John:

> I pray that they may all be *one;* as you, Father, are in me, and I in you, that *they* too may be *one in us.* I have given them the glory that you have given me, so that they can be *one* as we are *one*—*I in them* and you in me. (John 17:21, 22, 23)

This oneness is the mystical union that some people contemplate—a union achieved only through love. In the same author:

> I live and you will live; on that day you will know that I am in my Father and *you are in me* and *I am in you.* Whoever has my commandments and does them, that is the person who loves me. If any *love me,* they will keep my word, and my Father will love them, and we will come to them and *make a home in them.* (John 14:19, 20, 21, 23)

These things show that love is what binds together, and that the Lord has a home in those who love him and who love their neighbor (since loving our neighbor is loving the Lord).

[4] This union that makes us likenesses and images is not as clear to see in the human race as it is in heaven, where mutual love makes all angels into something like a single being. Each community, consisting of many people, forms an individual person, so to speak. And all the

communities taken together—the whole of heaven, in other words—
form an individual person who is also called the universal human (see
§§457 and 550). Heaven as a whole is the Lord's likeness, because he is
their all-in-all. Each community is also a likeness. So is each angel. Heavenly angels are likenesses; spiritual angels are images. Heaven consists of
as many likenesses of the Lord as there are angels, and this comes from
mutual love alone—from their loving each other more than themselves
(see §§548 and 549).

The reality is that for a whole (all of heaven) to be a likeness, the
parts (individual angels) have to be likenesses, or images that are *in* the
[Lord's] likeness. If a whole does not consist of parts that resemble it, it
is not a united whole.

With these principles in mind, we can easily see what makes us
God's likeness and image: love for the Lord and love for our neighbor.
As a result we can see that love, or charity, which comes from the Lord
alone, makes every regenerate spiritual person an image of the Lord. People motivated by a sense of charity received from the Lord, furthermore,
display a perfection, or wholeness. (Later sections, by the Lord's divine
mercy, will discuss this perfection [§§5113:2, 3; 5658:2].)

1014 Genesis 9:7. *"And you, reproduce and multiply; pour out into the earth
and multiply on it."*

Reproduce and multiply here as above [§§983–984] symbolizes increasing goodness and truth in our intermediate self; *reproducing* has to do
with goodness and *multiplying* with truth. *Pour out into the earth and
multiply on it* symbolizes increasing goodness and truth in our outer self,
which is the *earth; pouring out* has to do with goodness and *multiplying*
with truth.

1015 The fact that *reproduce and multiply* symbolizes increasing goodness
and truth in our intermediate self, and that *reproducing* has to do with
goodness, and *multiplying* with truth, can be seen from explanations
above at verse 1 of this chapter [§983], which uses the same words.

Evidence that the increase takes place in the intermediate self is
provided by the next clause, which repeats the word *multiply*. Redun-
dancy would make the second instance pointless if it did not have its
own meaning—a meaning different from that of the first. From this and
other statements made along the way it stands to reason that the reproducing and multiplying have to do with goodness and truth in our intermediate self.

The term "intermediate self" is used because the heavenly and spiritual traits in us, which belong to the Lord alone, supply us with an internal self, as shown earlier. Our rational processes, on the other hand, supply us with an intermediate self, or one midway between internal and external. And our responses to goodness, and the facts in our memory, create an external self for us.

[2] Section 978 in the remarks introducing this chapter shows that we have these levels, but the reason we are unaware of it while living in our bodies is that we are absorbed by bodily interests. As a consequence we do not even recognize the existence of deeper elements, let alone the fact that they are arranged into these distinct layers. If we are willing to reflect on it, though, we can see it clearly enough by drawing our thoughts up out of our body and thinking in our spirit, so to speak.

The reason that *reproducing* and *multiplying* have to do with the intermediate self—the rational self—is that we do not feel the operation of the internal self except in a very general way, at that intermediate level. A single general impression or even a comprehensive general impression is created in our intermediate self by a boundless number of individual components. Just how far beyond counting they are, what they are like, and how they create a dim, general impression can be seen from the demonstration offered earlier at §545.

The fact that *pour out into the earth and multiply on it* symbolizes increasing goodness and truth in our outer self, which is the *earth,* and that *pouring out* has to do with goodness, and *multiplying* with truth, can be seen from the remarks just above. It can also be seen from the symbolism of the *earth* as the outer self. For these meanings, see the statements and illustrations at verse 1 of the present chapter, in §983.

1016

[2] The reason the text speaks of pouring out into the earth and *consequently* multiplying on it is this: In the outer self of a regenerate person, nothing multiplies—nothing good or true increases—if charity does not have an effect on it. Charity is like springtime or summertime warmth, which makes grain, grasses, and trees grow. Without charity, or spiritual warmth, nothing grows. That is why the current verse says "pour out into the earth" first. This clause has to do with goodness, which is a matter of charity and which causes goodness and truth to multiply.

Anyone can grasp what the situation is here: nothing inside us grows or multiplies without some kind of affection [or desire]. The pleasure afforded by affection makes things not only put down root but also grow.

Everything proceeds in accord with affection's influence. [3] What we love we willingly seize, hold on to, and keep. Anything that supports our desires we likewise seize, hold on to, and keep. If something fails to support our desires, we have no interest in it; we discount and in fact reject it.

The kind of affection we have, however, determines how things multiply in us. When we have been reborn, our affection for goodness and truth develops out of an impulse for charity granted by the Lord. So any argument supporting a charitable affection is something we seize, hold on to, and protect, and we use it to strengthen the goodness and truth inside us. This is what "pour out into the earth and multiply" means.

1017   Let the following example serve to illustrate the idea that the kind of affection we have determines how things multiply in us.

Some people adopt the principle that faith alone saves them, even if they have never done a charitable deed—that is, even if they possess no charity—and in this way they detach faith from charity. It is not only because they took up such a principle in childhood that they think like this. It is also because they imagine that if we were to claim charitable acts, or neighborly love, to be the essential ingredient of faith and for this reason lived devoutly, we could not help viewing good deeds as earning us credit. (This is untrue, though.) Accordingly, they reject charity and consider acts of charity worthless. They restrict themselves exclusively to the concept of faith, which is nothing without its essential ingredient—charity.

When they corroborate this principle in themselves, it is never from a desire for goodness but from a desire for pleasure; they like being able to follow freely a life devoted to their appetites. The ones who use many arguments to defend the principle do so not because they love truth but for the sake of their own glory. They want to appear more important, scholarly, and profound than others and so to be elevated to the ranks of the influential and rich. So it is the pleasure afforded by their predilection that drives them. This pleasure makes them multiply supportive arguments, because, to repeat, the kind of affection we have determines how things multiply in us.

[2] In general, when the premise is wrong, only falsity can result from it, because everything conforms with the premise. As a matter of fact—and I learned about this through experience, as will be reported elsewhere, with the Lord's divine mercy—those who confirm themselves in principles of this kind concerning faith alone, and who have no

charity, lack any interest in the many things the Lord so often said about love and charity. They seem not even to see those statements. Examples are Matthew 3:8, 9; 5:7, 43–48; 6:12, 15; 7:1–20; 9:13; 12:33; 13:8, 23; 18:21, 22, 23–end; 19:19; 22:35–40; 24:12, 13; 21:34, 40, 41, 43; Mark 4:18, 19, 20; 11:13, 14, 20; 12:28–34; Luke 3:8, 9; 6:27–38, 43–end; 7:47; 8:8, 14, 15; 10:25–28; 12:58, 59; 13:6–9; John 3:19, 21; 5:42; 13:34, 35; 14:14, 15, 20, 21, 23; 15:1–8, 9–19; 21:15, 16, 17.

The reason this verse repeats the *reproduce and multiply* of the first **1018** verse in the present chapter is that the words form a closure. In addition, [it makes the point] that all will turn out well for people and will reproduce and multiply if they do not take the missteps symbolized by the eating and the shedding of blood—in other words, if they do not obliterate charity through hatred and profanation.

Genesis 9:8. *And God said to Noah and to his sons with him, saying, . . .* **1019**

God said to Noah and to his sons with him, saying, symbolizes the truth of the themes that follow, concerning the spiritual church meant by Noah and his sons with him.

This symbolism can be seen by considering the nature of the text **1020** from Genesis 1 through the mention of Eber in Genesis 11. Everything assembled into the story there has a different meaning than appears in the letter, and the narrative details are pure fiction. This was the custom of the earliest people. When they were testifying to the truth of a matter, they would say "Jehovah said" (although here it is expressed as "God said," since the text is talking about a spiritual religion). They said the same thing when anything was to come true or had come true.

The symbolism of *Noah and his sons with him* as the ancient church **1021** has already been demonstrated and will also be evident later in the chapter [§§531, 764–765, 768, 773, 788, 915, 1025:3, 1062–1063], so there is no need to spend time corroborating it here.

Genesis 9:9, 10. *"And I—yes, I—am setting up my pact with you and* **1022** *with your seed after you, and with every living soul that is with you: bird, beast, and every wild animal of the earth with you, from among all those coming out of the ark, including every wild animal of the earth."*

And I—yes, I—am setting up my pact symbolizes the presence of the Lord in charity. *With you* symbolizes a spiritual person who has been reborn. *And with your seed after you* symbolizes those who are created anew. *With every living soul that is with you* symbolizes everything in general that has been reborn in us. A *bird* symbolizes our intellectual abilities in particular. A *beast* symbolizes what belongs to our new will in particular. *Every wild animal of the earth* symbolizes our lower capacities of intellect and will, coming from those higher ones. *With you* here again means with a spiritual person who has been reborn. *From among all those coming out of the ark* symbolizes people in the church. *Including every wild animal of the earth* symbolizes people outside the church.

1023   The symbolism of *And I—yes, I—am setting up my pact* as the presence of the Lord in charity can be seen from the symbolism of a *pact,* given in §§[665,] 666. That section showed that a pact symbolizes rebirth, and more especially the Lord's close connection with a regenerate person through love. It also showed that the heavenly marriage is the most genuine compact, and in consequence that the heavenly marriage inside everyone who has regenerated is such a covenant too.

The nature of this marriage—this covenant—has also been shown before [§§155, 162, 252]. [2] For the people of the earliest church, the heavenly marriage existed within the sensation that they had their own power of will. For the people of the ancient church, however, the heavenly marriage developed within the sensation that their power of understanding was their own. When the human race's willpower had become thoroughly corrupt, you see, the Lord split our intellectual sense of self off from that corrupted voluntary sense of self in a miraculous way. Within our intellectual selfhood he formed a new will, which is conscience, and into conscience he injected charity, and into charity innocence. In this way he joined himself to us or, to put it another way, entered into a compact with us.

[3] To the extent that our self-will can be detached from this sense of intellectual autonomy, the Lord can be present with us, or bind himself to us, or enter into a pact with us.

Times of trial and other similar means of regeneration suppress our self-will to the point where it seems to disappear and almost die out. To the extent that this happens, the Lord can work through the conscience implanted in charity within our intellectual selfhood. This, then, is what is being called a pact in the present verse.

1024   The symbolism of *with you* as a spiritual person who has been reborn is established by a plethora of earlier statements to the effect that Noah and his sons symbolize a spiritual church that took the place of the earliest, heavenly church [§§597–598, 605, 726, 765, 788:1, 851]. Since they symbolize a church, they symbolize every member of that church and so a spiritual person who has been reborn.

The symbolism of *with your seed after you* as those who are created **1025** anew can be seen from the symbolism of *seed* and from subsequent verses.

From the symbolism of seed: Seed on a literal level means descendants, but in an inner sense it means faith. And since no faith exists except where there is charity (as stated many times before [§§32, 34, 345, 379, 585, 590, 628, 859, 863, 880, 896:2]) charity is what seed really means in an inner sense.

From subsequent verses: The text is obviously speaking not only of people inside the church but also of people outside it and so of the entire human race. Wherever charity exists—even in the nations farthest removed from the church—seed exists, because heavenly seed is charity. After all, none of us can do good on our own; all goodness is from the Lord. The good that people of non-Christian nations do comes from him too. (These nations will be discussed below [§§1032–1033, 2589–2605, 2861, 3263:2], with the Lord's divine mercy.)

Section 255 above showed that God's seed is faith. *Faith* there and elsewhere means the charity that gives rise to faith, since no faith that really is faith can exist except the faith that comes of charity.

[2] This is also true in other places in the Word that mention seed. Where Abraham's, Isaac's, or Jacob's seed is spoken of, for instance, it symbolizes love, or charity. Abraham represented heavenly love, and Isaac, spiritual love, both of them belonging to the inner self. Jacob represented the same things but in the outer self. The symbolism holds true not only in the prophetic books but also in the narratives, or histories.

Heaven does not notice the Word's story line, only the things that the narrative details symbolize. The Word was written not just for us but also for angels. When we read the Word, taking it solely at face value, the angels grasp not the literal but the inner meaning. The mental images we form when reading the Word, tied as they are to matter, to the world, and to our bodies, turn into spirit- and heaven-oriented ideas among the angels. When we read about Abraham, Isaac, and Jacob, for example, angels never think about Abraham, Isaac, and Jacob but about the attributes they represent and therefore symbolize.

[3] The case is similar with Noah, Shem, Ham, and Japheth. Of these individuals the angels are unaware; all that comes to their minds is the ancient church. With angels who are on a deeper level, it is not even that church but its faith that comes to mind, and also the state of the affairs being discussed, as seen in context.

Likewise when the Word mentions seed. Here, for instance, in speaking of Noah [and his sons], it says that a pact would be set up with them and with their seed after them. Angels do not picture those people's posterity—since there was no Noah, this being merely a name for the ancient church—but take *seed* to mean love for others, which was the essential component of faith in that church. Again, where the narratives of Abraham, Isaac, and Jacob mention their seed, angels never take it to mean their personal descendants. They take it as speaking of everyone throughout the world whether inside or outside the church in whom heavenly seed (or charity) lodges. Angels at the deeper levels, in fact, perceive the actual love that is heavenly seed, without any reference to people.

[4] The following places indicate that seed symbolizes love, as well as everyone who possesses love. In a passage speaking of Abram:

> Jehovah said, "To your *seed* I will give this land." (Genesis 12:7)

Again:

> All the land that you see, to you I will give it, and to your *seed,* forever. And I will make your *seed* like the dust of the earth. (Genesis 13:15, 16)

People who focus on the literal meaning have no idea that *seed* does not mean Abram's descendants or that *the land* does not mean the land of Canaan, especially because that land was indeed given to his descendants. People who focus on the inner meaning, though, as the whole of heaven does, see nothing else in *Abram's seed* than love, or in *the land of Canaan* than the Lord's kingdom in heaven and on earth. All they see in the gift of the land to those descendants is a representative meaning, which will be treated of elsewhere [§§1445–1448, 1606–1610], by the Lord's divine mercy. Again, in another place that speaks of Abram:

> Jehovah led him outside and said, "Look up, now, toward the sky and count the stars, if you can count them"; and he said to him, "So will your *seed* be." (Genesis 15:5)

Here too, since Abram represented love, or the kind of faith that saves us, in the inner sense his seed means no other descendants than everyone in the whole world who is under love's influence. [5] Likewise:

> I will *set up* my *pact* between me and you and your *seed* after you, and I will give you and your *seed* after you the land of your travels—all the land

of Canaan—as an eternal possession; and I will become their God. This
is *my pact* that you shall keep, between me and you and your *seed* after
you: that every male be circumcised to you. (Genesis 17:7, 8, 10)

Once more, setting up a pact symbolizes the Lord's close connection,
through love, with people throughout the world, and that love was represented by Abram. This shows what Abram's seed symbolizes: everyone in
the whole world who is governed by love. The pact consisted in circumcision (the subject of the passage), which heaven never takes as circumcision
of flesh but as circumcision of the heart—and this is the circumcision of
people governed by love. Circumcision was a practice that represented
rebirth through love, as Moses clearly explains:

> Jehovah God will *circumcise* your heart and the heart of your seed, [to
> cause you] to *love Jehovah your God* with all your heart and all your
> soul, so that you will *live*. (Deuteronomy 30:6)

These words show what the inner meaning of circumcision is. Wherever
circumcision is mentioned, it simply means love and charity and consequently life.

[6] The symbolism of Abraham's seed as everyone throughout the
world who has love is also demonstrated by the Lord's words to Abraham
and to Isaac. To Abraham (after he had shown his willingness to sacrifice
Isaac, as commanded):

> I will surely bless you and surely multiply your *seed* like the stars of the
> heavens and like the sand that is on the seashore, and your *seed* will
> inherit the gate of your foes, and in your seed all the *nations* of the
> earth will be blessed. (Genesis 22:17, 18)

In these verses it is obvious that seed means everyone everywhere who
has love.

[7] Just as Abraham represented heavenly love, as noted, Isaac represented spiritual love. Isaac's seed, then, symbolizes nothing else than
every person in whom spiritual love (charity) is found. These words
describe such a person:

> Reside as an immigrant in this land and I will be with you and bless
> you; because to you and your *seed* I will give all these lands. And I will
> confirm the oath that I swore to Abraham your father and will multi-
> ply your *seed* like the stars of the heavens. And I will give your *seed* all

these lands, and in your seed *all the nations of the earth* will be blessed.
(Genesis 26:3, 4, 24)

It is evident that *all the nations* means those who live in charity. Heavenly
love, represented by Abraham, is like the father of spiritual love, represented by Isaac, because spiritual things are born of heavenly ones, as
already shown [§§775:2, 880:2].

[8] Jacob represented outward traits of the church springing from
inner qualities. So he represented every trait of the outer self originating
in love and charity. As a consequence, his seed symbolizes everyone in
the whole world whose outward worship contains inward reverence and
whose deeds of charity contain neighborly love from the Lord. This seed
was mentioned to Jacob after he dreamed of the ladder:

I am Jehovah, God of Abraham your father and God of Isaac. The land
on which you are lying, to you will I give it and to your *seed,* and your
seed will be like the dust of the earth. And in you *all the clans of the
ground* will be blessed, and in your *seed.* (Genesis 28:13, 14; 32:12; 48:4)

[9] In addition to the passages in the Word that §255 above cites, the
following indicate that seed has no other symbolism. In Isaiah:

You are Israel, my servant; Jacob, whom I have chosen; the *seed* of
Abraham, my friend. (Isaiah 41:8)

This verse is talking about our regeneration, and it distinguishes Israel
and Jacob, as so many other places do. Israel symbolizes the inner spiritual church, and Jacob, the outer part of that church. Both are called the
seed of Abraham, that is, of the heavenly church, because heavenly, spiritual, and earthly elements come one after the other. In Jeremiah:

I had planted you as a superior grapevine through and through, the
seed of truth. How could you turn into the degenerate [stems] of a foreign grapevine before my eyes? (Jeremiah 2:21)

This is about the spiritual church, which is the superior grapevine and
whose charity—or faith rising out of charity—is called the seed of truth.
[10] In the same author:

As the army of the heavens cannot be counted and the sand of the sea
cannot be measured, so will I multiply the *seed* of *David,* my servant,
and the Levites waiting on me. (Jeremiah 33:22)

Clearly the seed stands for heavenly seed, because David symbolizes the Lord. Everyone recognizes that David's seed was not the uncountable army of the heavens or the immeasurable sand of the sea. In the same author:

> "Look! The days are coming," says Jehovah, "when I will raise up for David a just offshoot, and he will reign as monarch. He will act with understanding and exercise judgment and justice in the land. In his days Judah will be saved and Israel will live securely. And this is his name that they will call him: Jehovah our justice. So look! The days are coming," says Jehovah, "when they will no longer say, 'As Jehovah lives, who summoned up the children of Israel from the land of Egypt,' but 'As Jehovah lives, who summoned up and who withdrew the *seed of the house of Israel* from the land of the north.'" (Jeremiah 23:5, 6, 7, 8)

In this passage, very different things are meant than those that appear in the letter. David does not mean David nor Judah Judah nor Israel Israel, but David means the Lord, Judah means a heavenly quality, and Israel means a spiritual one. Accordingly, the seed of Israel means those who have charity, or the faith that rises out of charity. [11] In David:

> You who fear Jehovah, praise him. All you *seed of Jacob,* give him glory. Be afraid of him, all you *seed of Israel.* (Psalms 22:23, 24)

Here too the seed of Israel means no other kind of seed than the spiritual church. In Isaiah:

> Its stump will be *holy seed.* (Isaiah 6:13)

This stands for remaining traces [of goodness and truth], which are holy because they are the Lord's. In the same author:

> From Jacob I will bring forth *seed,* and from Judah, one to own my mountains; and the ones I have chosen will own it, and my servants will live there. (Isaiah 65:9)

This is about the heavenly church, both outer and inner. In the same author:

> They will not *bear children* for turmoil. They are the *seed* of those blessed by Jehovah, as are their children with them. (Isaiah 65:23)

This is about the new heavens and the new earth, that is, the Lord's kingdom. The people in it, born or rather reborn of love, are called the seed of those blessed by Jehovah.

1026   *With every living soul that is with you* symbolizes everything in general that has been reborn in us. This can be seen from statements above and below [§§1022, 1036, 1040] and from the symbolism of *living*. Everything that receives life from the Lord is called living; everything in regenerate people that lives from that life is called a living soul. The extent to which we receive life when we are regenerate determines the extent to which individual elements inside us—both our reasoned ideas and our feelings—have life. This living force in the individual aspects of all we think and say is evident to angels, although it is not very evident to human beings.

1027   The fact that a *bird* symbolizes our intellectual abilities in particular can be seen from several previous remarks and explanations, like those in §§40 and 776.

1028   The fact that a *beast* symbolizes what belongs to our new will in particular can likewise be seen from previous remarks and explanations about beasts and their symbolism, as in §§45, 46, 142, 143, 246, 776.

1029   The fact that *every wild animal of the earth* symbolizes our lower capacities of intellect and will, coming from those higher ones, again is established by earlier demonstrations concerning the symbolism of a wild animal [§§45, 46, 246, 908].

Each of us has deep capacities and shallow capacities. The deeper ones are rational thoughts (symbolized by the bird) and feelings (symbolized by the beast). The shallower ones are learned facts and sensual pleasures (symbolized by the wild animals of the earth).

The bird, beast, and wild animal do not literally mean a bird, beast, or wild animal but a living quality in a person who has been reborn. Anyone can see this or figure it out by considering that God cannot enter into a pact with brute animals, even though it says, "I am setting up a pact with every living soul that is with you: bird, beast, and wild animal of the earth with you." He can enter into a pact only with human beings, whose deeper and shallower capacities are portrayed by those creatures.

1030   The symbolism of *from among all those coming out of the ark* as people in the church and of *including every wild animal of the earth* as a person outside the church can be deduced from the line of reasoning in the inner meaning. Everything that came out of the ark has already been named, in the words *every living soul, including bird, beast, and wild animal of the earth*. Now it is repeated: *from all those coming out of the ark, including every wild animal of the earth*. So the wild animal of the earth is mentioned a second time, which it would not be if it did not have another meaning here. The next verse, moreover, continues with the words *and I*

am setting up my pact with you, which was also said before. This indicates
that *those coming out of the ark* symbolizes regenerate individuals, or people in the church, while *the wild animal of the earth* symbolizes everyone
in the entire world outside the church.

[2] In Scripture, when the word for "wild animal" does not mean living things, the wild animal of the earth symbolizes things that are rather
base and that partake more or less of a wild animal's nature. The nuances
involved depend on the topic that is being dealt with. Where the subject
is the attributes inside us, a wild animal of the earth symbolizes the lower
capacities of our outer self and our body, as it did in the immediately preceding part of this verse. So it symbolizes rather base things. Where the
subject is a whole group of people, which is called a composite person,
a wild animal of the earth symbolizes those who are not in the church,
because these people are relatively lowly. And so on, depending on the
subject at hand. In Hosea, for example:

> I will strike a *pact* with them on that day—with the *wild animal* of
> the field, and with the bird in the heavens and the creeping animal of
> the earth. (Hosea 2:18)

In Isaiah:

> The *wild animal* of the field will honor me because I have put water in
> the desert. (Isaiah 43:20)

In Ezekiel:

> In its branches nested every bird of the heavens, and under its branches
> bred every *wild animal* of the field, and in its shade lived *all the great
> nations.* (Ezekiel 31:6)

Genesis 9:11. *"And I am setting up my pact with you; and no more will*   **1031**
*all flesh be cut off by the waters of a flood, and no more will there be a flood
to destroy the earth."*

And I am setting up my pact with you symbolizes the Lord's presence
in every person who has charity; it refers both to *those coming out of the
ark* and to *every wild animal of the earth,* that is, to people inside the
church and to people outside the church. *And no more will all flesh be cut
off by the waters of a flood* means that they will not be obliterated, as the
descendants of the earliest church were. *And no more will there be a flood
to destroy the earth* means that the same kind of deadly, suffocating delusion will not come into being.

1032　　*And I am setting up my pact with you* symbolizes the Lord's presence in every person who has charity; it refers both to *those coming out of the ark* and to *every wild animal of the earth,* that is, to people inside the church and to people outside the church. This can be seen from the remarks just above.

The Lord also enters into a pact with people outside the church, called "Gentiles"—that is, he binds himself to them through charity. This is the situation: People who belong to the church suppose that none of those outside the church, called Gentiles, can be saved, because they lack any knowledge of the faith and are therefore totally ignorant of the Lord. Church members say that without the faith and without any knowledge of the Lord there is no salvation. So they consign everyone outside the church to damnation. In fact many of these church members are the kind of people who subscribe to a doctrine (even a heretical one) that teaches them to consider anyone outside it—anyone whose opinion differs from theirs—incapable of salvation. The reality, however, is entirely different.

[2] The Lord has mercy on the whole human race. He wants to save everyone in the entire world and to draw all people to himself. The Lord's mercy is infinite; it does not allow itself to be restricted to the few within the church but reaches out to everyone on the face of the earth. When people are born outside the church and as a result into ignorance about the faith, it is not their fault; besides which, failure to believe in the Lord because of a lack of knowledge about him never condemns anyone.

What right-thinking person would ever assert that most of the human race will suffer eternal death because they were not born in Europe, whose population is relatively small? What right-thinking person would say that the Lord allowed such an immense number of people to be born in order to die an eternal death? This would be contrary to the divine nature and to mercy. What is more, people outside the church, called Gentiles, live a much more ethical life than those inside the church and embrace teachings of the genuine faith much more easily.

[3] Souls in the other world illustrate this even more clearly. The so-called Christian world yields up the worst of all—people who nurse a murderous hatred for their fellow humans and for the Lord and who are more adulterous than any others in the whole earth. Not so with souls from the other parts of the planet. A large number of those who had worshiped idols are disposed to abhor hatred and adultery and to fear Christians, since Christians are hateful and adulterous and want to hurt everyone else.

Non-Christians, in fact, are such that when angels teach them the truth of the faith and tell them that the Lord governs the universe, they easily pick it up, easily absorb the faith, and as a consequence reject their idols. So non-Christians who have lived a moral life marked by charity for one another and by innocence are reborn in the other life. While they live in the world, the Lord is present with them in their charity and innocence, because not a whit of charity or innocence exists that does not come from the Lord.

The Lord also gives them the gift of a conscience for what is right and good, according to their religious tradition, and into this conscience he instills innocence and neighborly love. When innocence and neighborly love reside in their conscience, they allow themselves to absorb easily the truth of genuine faith that grows out of goodness. The Lord himself said the same thing in Luke:

> Someone said to Jesus, "Lord, are there few who are saved?" He told them, "You will see Abraham, Isaac, and Jacob and all the prophets in God's kingdom but will see yourselves thrown out of doors. On the other hand, from the east and west and from the north and from the south will come those reclining [at table] in God's kingdom. And indeed there are people in the last place who will be first, and there are people in first place who will be last." (Luke 13:23, 28, 29, 30)

Abraham, Isaac, and Jacob mean everyone motivated by love, as shown above [§1025:2].

Non-Christians also receive the gift of a conscience for what is right and good, according to their religious tradition, as noted. This is how it stands:

1033

The general kinds of conscience are true conscience, spurious conscience, and false conscience.

A true conscience is one that the Lord forms out of genuine religious truth. When we have been gifted with this conscience, we are afraid to go against the truth that the faith teaches, because to do so is to violate conscience. No one can receive this kind of conscience but those who are imbued with the truths of the faith. For this reason not many in Christendom do, since everyone sets up her or his own theology as religious truth. Still, those who are reborn receive a conscience, and charity along with it, since charity is the foundation of conscience.

[2] A spurious conscience is one formed in non-Christians out of the tradition they were born into and brought up in. For them, acting

contrary to this is acting contrary to conscience. When their conscience is founded on charity and mercy, and on obedience, they are the kind of people who can and do receive true conscience in the other life, since there is nothing they love better or more fervently than the truth that the faith teaches.

[3] A false conscience is one formed not from internal but from external considerations, that is, not from charity but from selfishness and materialism. People with this kind of conscience see themselves as violating conscience when they offend their neighbor and also imagine that they feel an inward torment then. But the reason for their qualms is that in their mind's eye they see their offense as endangering their own life, position, reputation, wealth, or income, and as doing harm to themselves. Some acquire a certain softness of heart by heredity, some by effort; but it is false conscience.

1034   *No more will all flesh be cut off by the waters of a flood* means that they will not be obliterated, as the final generation of the earliest church was. This can be seen from the things said earlier about the pre-Flood people who died off—the people "cut off by the waters of a flood" [§§310–311, 591–595, 792–813]. In §310 above, the nature of the situation was explained: The final generation to inherit the earliest church was such that when their volitional side had been perverted, their intellectual side was too. Their intellectual side could not be detached from their volitional side, allowing a new will to be formed in it, so tightly did the two parts of their mind cling together.

Because the Lord foresaw that this would happen, he provided for the ability of our intellectual side to detach from our voluntary side and in this way be renewed. Accordingly, since he provided that people like that pre-Flood race would never come into existence again, the current verse says that no more would any flesh be cut down by the waters of a flood.

1035   *And no more will there be a flood to destroy the earth.* The fact that this means that the same kind of deadly, suffocating delusion will not come into being again can be seen from the symbolism of a flood in relation to the pre-Flood people who died off, discussed earlier [§§310, 560, 563, 660, 705, 790, 794]. It can be seen from their appalling delusions as well, described in §§310, 563, 570, 581, 586a. It can also be seen from statements about the next church, called Noah [§705], and in addition from remarks below on the rainbow [§1051].

Genesis 9:12, 13. *And God said, "This is the sign of the pact that I make* **1036** *between me and you and every living soul that is with you, to everlasting generations: My bow I have put in the cloud, and it will serve as a sign of the pact between me and the earth."*

And Jehovah said means so it was. *This is the sign of the pact* means an indication of the presence of the Lord in neighborly love. *That I make between me and you* symbolizes the Lord's close connection with us through neighborly love. *And every living soul that is with you* symbolizes (as it did before [§1026]) everything in us that has been reborn. *To everlasting generations* means all who are created anew, without end. *A bow I have put in the cloud* symbolizes the circumstances of a spiritual person who has been reborn, which resemble a rainbow. A *cloud* symbolizes the dim light in which a spiritual person lives, as compared to a heavenly person. *And it will serve as a sign of the pact between me and the earth* again means an indication of the presence of the Lord in charity; the *earth* here is human selfhood.

All these details have to do with a regenerate spiritual person, or the spiritual church.

The fact that *and God said* means that it was so has already been **1037** stated and demonstrated [§§630, 708, 926, 1020], because *to say* and *God* (or in other words, *Jehovah*) *says* means that a thing is so.

The earliest people constructed stories out of their religious affairs, so when they wanted to affirm that a thing was so, they said "God said" or "Jehovah said," and for them this was a standard way of asserting a thing and vouching for it.

The meaning of *this is the sign of the pact* as an indication of the pres- **1038** ence of the Lord in neighborly love is established by the symbolism of a *pact* and of a *sign of a pact.* The symbolism of a pact as the presence of the Lord in neighborly love was illustrated above at Genesis 6:18 and earlier in the present chapter, at verse 9 [§§665–666, 1023].

The fact that a pact is the presence of the Lord in love and charity is evident from the nature of a pact. Every covenant exists to tie people together; that is, the goal is for people to live in mutual friendship, or in a state of love. This is why marriage too is called a compact or covenant.

The Lord cannot unite with us except in love and charity, because the Lord is love itself and mercy; he wants to save us all and draw us to heaven—that is, to himself—with a powerful force. So we can all see and conclude that no one could ever be united to the Lord except through that which is the Lord, or in other words, without doing as he does, or making common cause with him. To do this is to love the Lord in return and to love our neighbor as ourselves. This is the only means of union. This is the most essential element of a compact. When union does grow out of it, then the Lord, of course, is present.

It is true that the Lord is actually present with every individual, but he is closer to or farther from us to the exact extent that we approach love or distance ourselves from it.

[2] Since a pact is the Lord's close connection with us through love or, to put it another way, is the presence of the Lord with us in love and charity, the Word calls the pact itself a pact of peace. This is because peace symbolizes the Lord's kingdom, and the Lord's kingdom consists of mutual love, which is the only thing that affords peace. In Isaiah, for instance:

> "The mountains will withdraw and the hills recede, but my *mercy* will not withdraw from you, and my *pact of peace* will not recede," Jehovah has said, who shows you *compassion*. (Isaiah 54:10)

Mercy, which is a matter of love, is being called a pact of peace. In Ezekiel:

> I will raise up over them a single shepherd (and he will pasture them): my servant David. He will pasture them, and he will serve them as shepherd, and I will cut a *pact of peace* with them. (Ezekiel 34:23, 25)

David obviously means the Lord, whose presence with a regenerate person is depicted in the words *he will pasture them.* [3] In the same author:

> My servant David will be monarch over them, and there will be a single shepherd for them all. And *I will strike a pact of peace with them;* it will be *an eternal pact* with them. And I will place them and make them multiply and put my sanctuary in their midst forever. And I will become their God, and they will become my people. (Ezekiel 37:24, 26, 27)

Again David means the Lord. The sanctuary in their midst means love. The statement that he would become their God and that they would become his people means the Lord's presence and unity with us in love, that presence and unity being called a pact of peace and an eternal pact. In Malachi:

> "You will know that I have sent you this commandment: that *my compact* should be with Levi," Jehovah Sabaoth has said. "*My compact* with

him was one of *life and peace;* and I gave them to him along with fear, and he will fear me." (Malachi 2:4, 5)

In the highest sense, Levi is the Lord, and as a result he is any person who has love and charity. So the compact of life and peace with Levi involves love and charity. [4] In Moses, where he is speaking of Phinehas:

Here, now, I am giving him *my pact of peace,* and for him and for his seed after him it will be a *pact of eternal priesthood.* (Numbers 25:12, 13)

Phinehas does not mean Phinehas but the priesthood that he represented, which symbolizes love in all its aspects, just as the whole priesthood of that religion did. Everyone realizes that Phinehas's priesthood was not eternal. In the same author:

Jehovah your God, he is God, a faithful God, keeping his *pact* and his *mercy with those who love him* and keep his commandments, to the thousandth generation. (Deuteronomy 7:9, 12)

The pact is quite explicitly the presence of the Lord with us in love, since the passage says it is with those who love him and keep his commandments.

[5] Since a pact is the Lord's close connection with us through love, it follows that it is also a connection through all the by-products of love, which consist of religious truth and are called commandments. All the commandments—and in fact the Law and the Prophets—are based on one solitary law, that we should love the Lord above all and our neighbor as ourselves. The Lord's words in Matthew 22:35–40 and Mark 12:28–34 make this clear. So the tablets on which the Ten Commandments were written are called the tablets of the covenant [Deuteronomy 9:9, 11, 15; Hebrews 9:4].

Since a pact or a close bond is achieved through the laws of love, or the commandments, such a bond was also achieved through societal laws that the Lord laid down for the Jewish religion, which are called testimonies. It was achieved through the Lord's requirements for religious ritual—called statutes—as well. All these rules are described as part of the pact, because they look to love and kindness as their goal. As we read of King Josiah:

The king stood by the pillar and *struck a pact* before Jehovah, to walk after Jehovah and to keep his *commandments* and his *testimonies* and his *statutes,* with all his heart and with all his soul, to secure the *words of the pact.* (2 Kings 23:3)

[6] These considerations now indicate what a pact is and show that it is an inward thing, since internal ties—never external ties separately from internal ones—are what bind us to the Lord. External practices are only tokens or representations of what lies inside. Our actions, for example, are tokens representing our thoughts and intentions, while the charitable deeds we do are tokens representing the love we cherish for our neighbor in heart and mind. In the same way, all the rituals of the Jewish religion foreshadowed and represented the Lord, and as a result they provided an image and representation of love and charity and all the effects of both. So it is our inner attributes that make the pact and the union possible; outward attributes are merely *signs of the pact,* and this is also what they are called.

The fact that inner attributes make the pact and the union possible is plain to see. In Jeremiah, for example:

> "Look! The days are coming," says Jehovah, "when I will *strike* a *new pact* with the house of Israel and with the house of Judah unlike the *pact* that I struck with their ancestors, because they nullified *my pact.* But this is the *pact* that I will strike with the house of Israel after these days: I will put *my law in the midst of them, and upon their heart I will write it."* (Jeremiah 31:31, 32, 33)

This is about a new church. It says openly that the actual covenant itself depends on inner qualities and in fact on those present in a conscience that has written on it the law, which has entirely to do with love, as noted.

[7] External observances, again, are not the pact, unless deeper impulses are attached to them and consequently work together with them toward one and the same end, by being united to them. Externals are signs of the pact, rather, their purpose being to bring the Lord to mind as tokens representing him. Evidence for these things is the fact that the Sabbath and circumcision are called signs of the pact. The Sabbath is so designated in Moses:

> The children of Israel shall keep the *Sabbath,* to perform the *Sabbath* throughout their generations as an *eternal pact.* Between me and the children of Israel this is a *sign* forever. (Exodus 31:16, 17)

Circumcision receives the designation in the same author:

> This is my *pact,* which you will keep, between me and you and your seed after you: that every male be *circumcised* to you. And you will

circumcise the flesh of your foreskin, and it will serve as a *sign of the pact* between me and you. (Genesis 17:10, 11)

Blood, for the same reason, is also called the blood of the covenant in Exodus 24:7, 8.

[8] The main reason external rituals are called signs of the pact is that they serve to bring to mind inner attributes—that is, the entities they symbolize. None of the rituals of the Jewish religion had any other purpose. As a result, the aids they had to remind them of deeper realities were also called signs. An example is their practice of binding the first great commandment on their hand and in a box on their brow, as described in Moses:

> You shall love Jehovah your God with all your heart and with all your soul and with all your powers. And you shall bind these words as a *sign* on your hand, and they shall be as brow pieces between your eyes. (Deuteronomy 6:5, 8; 11:13, 18)

The hand symbolizes the will because it symbolizes strength, since strength belongs to the will. The brow pieces between the eyes symbolize the intellect. So the sign symbolizes remembering the first great commandment (which is the law in condensed form) in order to keep it constantly in the will and constantly in the thought. In other words, the goal is the presence of the Lord and of love in all our willing and all our thinking. This is how the Lord, and mutual love received from him, are present with angels. With the Lord's divine mercy, the nature of this continual presence will be discussed later [§§1276–1277, 6849, 7926:2, 9682].

Likewise here, where it says, "This is the sign of the pact that I make between me and you: My bow I have put in the cloud, and it will serve as a sign of the pact between me and the earth." No other sign is meant here than one indicating the presence of the Lord in neighborly love, and consequently it symbolizes recollection on our part.

How this sign—the bow in the cloud—served as an indication and reminder, though, will be told below [§1042], with the Lord's divine mercy.

That I make between me and you symbolizes the Lord's close connection with us through neighborly love. This can be seen from the remarks just above on pacts and the sign of a pact. A pact means the presence of the Lord in charity; *between me and you* means the close connection it creates; *making* it means bringing it about.

1039

1040   The symbolism of *and every living soul that is with you* as everything in us that has been reborn can be seen from the symbolism of a living soul, discussed above at verse 10 [§1026].

In the Word, a *soul* symbolizes all life, both our inner life and our outer life, as I have said [§§1000, 1005]. It symbolizes the life in animals as well, for the reason that animals symbolize human traits. Strictly speaking, however, a living soul means something that receives life from the Lord, or in other words, something that has been regenerated, since only something regenerate is alive. And because a soul symbolizes both our inner and our outer life, a living soul symbolizes the whole range of attributes that have been reborn in us.

We have inside us properties of will and properties of intellect, which are quite distinct from each other. Every single effect of those properties is alive in a person who is alive.

[2] This is the situation: Whatever we ourselves are like, that is what everything in us is like. Life itself as a general force is present in every single element in us, because out of individual elements—specifics, so to speak—rises a general whole. Otherwise no general whole could possibly exist, since a thing is called general because it is made up of specifics. The quality of our life in general, then, determines the quality of our life in particular and even in the most specific details of all. This includes the details both of our efforts and intentions (our will) and of our thinking. As a result, not the least scintilla of an idea can possibly exist that does not contain the same type of vital force.

Those who are arrogant, for example, display arrogance in each and every thrust of their will and in each and every conception of their thought. Those who are greedy display greed in the same way; those who nurse hatred for their neighbor, likewise. Again, those who are stupid display stupidity in all the particulars of their will and in all the particulars of their thought, while those who are insane display insanity.

As this is what people are like, just a single item of our thought allows others in the next life to recognize our character.

[3] When we are regenerate, every single thing in us is regenerate, or in other words, has life. Indeed it has life just to the extent that our self-will, which is unclean and dead, has been able to be separated from the new will and intellect that the Lord gives us. So since the present verse is speaking of people who have been reborn, the living soul symbolizes everything in them that has been reborn—to put it generally, the contents of their intellect and will, on both deeper and shallower planes. Verse 10 above uses the words *bird* and *beast* and the words *wild animal*

of the earth to stand for these things, since it says, "I am setting up my pact with every *living soul:* bird, beast, and wild animal of the earth."

To everlasting generations means all who are created anew, without end, as can be seen from the symbolism of *everlasting generations. Generations* are offspring that result from earlier events—their "parents." *Everlasting* means what has no end. The subject here is things that have been regenerated, so everlasting generations mean people who are constantly being reborn out of those things, that is, who are being created anew. (The inner meaning depends entirely on the topics under discussion.)

1041

A bow I have put in the cloud symbolizes the circumstances of a spiritual person who has been reborn, which resemble a rainbow.

1042

It might be hard to believe that a *bow in the cloud*—a rainbow—is taken as a sign of a pact in the Word, when a rainbow is nothing but the effect that results when rays of sunlight are modified as they pass through raindrops. Unlike other signs of the pact in the church (discussed just above [§1038]), it is nothing more than a physical phenomenon.

No one can recognize that a bow in the cloud represents regeneration—and symbolizes the circumstances of a spiritual person who has regenerated—except a person who has been permitted to see and learn how matters stand.

In the other world, when spiritual angels (all of whom were once regenerate people of the spiritual church) are so presented to view, a kind of rainbow appears around their head. The rainbows that appear, though, are simply an expression of the angels' state. This allows their nature to be recognized in heaven and in the world of spirits.

The reason this iridescent display appears is that those angels' earthly-type attributes, corresponding to spiritual ones, present this image. It is a modification of spiritual light from the Lord as received in their earthly characteristics. These angels are the ones said to be reborn of water and the spirit [John 3:5]; heavenly angels, though, are reborn of fire [Matthew 3:11; Luke 3:16].

[2] In the world of nature, this is how it works: For color to exist, there has to be dark and light, or black and white. When sunlight falls on the dark and light (or black and white), variations in the balance of the two modify the rays in such a way as to create color. Some colors partake more or less of dark and black, some more or less of light, or white. That is what produces different colors.

The situation in the realm of spirit is comparable. There, a dark color is intellectual conceit, or wrong thinking, while black is self-will, or evil, which absorbs and blots out rays of light. But a light color and white are the true and good things we imagine we do on our own, which reflect rays of light and bounce them back. The rays of light that fall on those colors and seemingly change them come from the Lord in his manifestation as a sun composed of wisdom and understanding. That is exactly what spiritual light rays are and exactly where they come from.

Earthly objects correspond to spiritual entities, and this is why something like a bow in a cloud appears (when the sight is presented in the other life) around a spiritual person who has been reborn. The bow is a representation of spiritual attributes within that person's earthly capacities.

People who are regenerate and spiritual have the sense that their power of understanding is their own, and into this intellectual selfhood the Lord instills innocence, kindness, and mercy. The way they receive these gifts determines how their rainbow looks, when displayed, and the more their self-will has been moved out of the way, conquered, and reduced to obedience, the more beautiful it is.

[3] When prophets were experiencing visions of God, they too saw a bow like that in the cloud. In Ezekiel, for instance:

> Above the expanse that was over the head of the guardian beings was a seeming appearance of sapphire stone, like a throne, and what looked like the appearance of a person on it, high above. And I saw the seeming form of an ember, gleaming with the appearance of fire, within the form, all around, from the appearance of his hips and above. And from the appearance of his hips and below I saw the seeming appearance of fire, which had a brilliance all around. Like the appearance of a *bow when it is in a cloud on a rainy day,* so was the appearance of brilliance all around. This was the appearance of the likeness of Jehovah's glory. (Ezekiel 1:26, 27, 28)

Anyone can see that it was the Lord who was seen in this way, and that he was then representing heaven, because he *is* heaven; in other words, he is the all-in-all of heaven. He is the person described in these verses; the throne is heaven; the ember gleaming with the appearance of fire from his hips and above is the heavenly quality of love; the brilliance of the fire all around from his hips and below, like a bow in a cloud, is a heavenly-spiritual quality. So the heavenly heaven, or the heaven of heavenly angels, was represented by the pelvic area and what was above it, while the spiritual heaven, or the heaven of spiritual angels, was represented by the pelvic area and what was below it. In the universal human, the lower extremities from the pelvis down through the feet to the soles symbolize earthly elements.

This also shows that our earthly traits appear in the form of a bow in the cloud when spiritual light from the Lord illuminates them in this way.

A rainbow also appeared to John, as described in Revelation 4:2, 3; 10:1.

The symbolism of a *cloud* as the dim light in which a spiritual person **1043** lives, as compared to a heavenly person, is established by the remarks immediately above on the rainbow. A rainbow with all its colors, after all, never occurs except in a cloud. To repeat, the darkness through which the sunbeams shine is itself what turns colorful. The type of darkness that the shaft of light touches, then, determines the color.

So it is for a spiritual person. The darkness in such people—which is being called a cloud—is falsity, which is the same thing as their intellectual selfhood. When the Lord infuses this selfhood with innocence, charity, and mercy, the cloud is no longer seen as something false but as the outward appearance of truth, together with truth that *is* true, which comes from the Lord. This is what creates the effect of a colorful arc. It is a kind of spiritual transformation that is completely impossible to describe. If it is not pictured in terms of color and the generation of color, I do not know whether it can be explained in a comprehensible way.

[2] What this cloud is like in a person reborn can be gleaned from an individual's condition before regeneration. We are regenerated by what we suppose to be religious truth. (We each imagine our own theology to be the truth.) This supplies us with conscience. So for us, after we have acquired conscience, violating the strictures stamped on our minds as religious truth is violating our conscience. This is true of every regenerate person, because the Lord regenerates large numbers of people of every creed. When we have regenerated, we do not receive any direct revelation (except the ideas instilled in us through the Word and preaching from the Word). But since we do receive love for our fellow humans, the Lord works through that love to affect our cloud. Light then floods out of it, as happens when the sun strikes a cloud, making it brighter and variegating its color. The same process also creates something like a bow in the cloud. So the thinner the cloud is—that is, the more religious truth it has mixed in—the lovelier the bow is. The thicker the cloud is, though—or the less religious truth it has—the less attractive the bow is. Innocence adds a great deal of beauty; it lends a vivid glow to the colors, so to speak.

[3] All apparent truths are clouds, and they engross our attention when we focus on the Word's literal meaning, since the Word speaks in appearances. But when we maintain a simple trust in the Word (even if we cling to the appearances) and cultivate a feeling of charity, the cloud is relatively thin. For those inside the church, the Lord forms a conscience within this cloud.

All instances of ignorance about truth are also clouds. We live in these clouds when we do not know what the truth of the genuine faith is, when we more generally do not know what the Word is, and especially when we have never heard about the Lord. For those outside the church, the Lord forms a conscience within this cloud. Ignorance, you see, is itself capable of holding innocence and therefore charity within it.

All falsities, too, are clouds, but these clouds are the shadowy darkness inside either those who have a false conscience (as discussed earlier [§1033]) or those who have no conscience.

These are the general qualities of cloud. As for their quantity, we have such large, thick clouds inside that if we were aware of it, we would be astounded to think that any rays of light from the Lord could ever shine through, or that anyone could be reborn. Those who believe they have the smallest cover of cloud sometimes have a huge amount, while those who believe they have a huge amount have less.

[4] Spiritual people have these kinds of clouds around them, but heavenly people have smaller ones, because they have love for the Lord implanted in the will-related part of their mind. As a result, they also do not have the conscience that a spiritual person has. Instead, the Lord gives them the ability to perceive goodness, together with the truth growing out of what is good. When people's capacity of will is such that it can receive the radiance of a heavenly flame, their capacity for understanding glows with its light, and love enables them to recognize and perceive everything true in the realm of faith. Their power of will is then like a miniature sun shining into their intellectual side. This is what the people of the earliest church were like.

Sometimes our willpower is radically depraved and hellish, though, so that a new will (which is conscience) is formed in our intellectual part. This is what happened with the people of the ancient church, and it occurs with every regenerate individual who is part of the spiritual church. When it does, there is dense cloud, because the person has to learn what is true and good and cannot intuit it. Under these circumstances, falsity flows in endlessly from the person's black, will-related part, or rather through it from hell. This is the dark shadow of a cloud. That is why the intellectual side of a spiritual person can never be enlightened the way it is in a heavenly person. Consequently, the cloud in this verse symbolizes the dim light in which a spiritual person lives, compared to a heavenly one.

And it will serve as a sign of the pact between me and the earth means an indication of the Lord's presence in charity, and the *earth* here means human selfhood, as statements above show [§§1036, 1038]. The symbolism of the earth as human selfhood can be seen from the inner meaning, too, and also from the sequence of thoughts. Earlier the text said, "This is the sign of the pact between me and you and every living soul that is with you," which symbolizes whatever has been reborn. Here, however, the phrasing changes: "It will serve as a sign of the pact between me and the earth." The change—and the repetition of *the sign of the pact* as well—shows that the present verse has another meaning. It shows, in fact, that the earth is that which has not been reborn and cannot be reborn, and this is human self-will.

[2] So far as their intellectual side goes, regenerate people are the Lord's, but so far as their voluntary side goes, they are their own. These two sides in a spiritual person are opposed to each other, but although a person's voluntary part is opposed, its presence is still unavoidable. All the darkness in spiritual people's intellectual part, all the thickening of their cloud, comes from the will side. The darkness constantly streams in from their will side, and the more it does, the more the cloud in their intellectual part thickens. On the other hand, the more the darkness withdraws, the more the cloud thins. That is the reason the earth in this case symbolizes human selfhood. (It was shown earlier that the earth symbolizes our bodily concerns and much else besides [§§16, 17, 28, 29, 82, 566, 620, 662, 800, 895].)

[3] The situation resembles that of two people who were once bound together in a pact of friendship, as will and intellect were among the people of the earliest church. When the friendship breaks down and enmity arises—as it did when humanity completely perverted its power of will— and a new pact is entered into, the hostile party then takes center stage, as if it were the party with which the pact had been struck. The pact is not with this side of our mind, however (since it is diametrically opposed and contrary), but with what streams from it, as noted earlier [§1023]— with intellectual selfhood, that is. The sign or indication of the pact is this: the larger the Lord's presence in our intellectual selfhood, the more remote our self-will.

The case is just like that of heaven and hell. A regenerate person's intellectual half is heaven because of the charity in which the Lord is present. But such a person's will side is hell. The more present the Lord is in heaven, the more hell moves away. When we depend on ourselves, we are in hell. When we depend on the Lord, we are in heaven and are always being lifted up from hell into heaven. The higher we rise, the greater the distance between us and our hell.

The sign or indication that the Lord is present, then, is the withdrawal of our own will. Times of trial and many other means of regeneration work to distance it.

1045 This discussion has dealt with the spiritual person (or the spiritual church) who has been reborn. The discussion that follows focuses on all people in general and then on those who can be reborn in particular.

1046 Genesis 9:14, 15. *"And it will happen in my clouding the earth over with cloud that a bow will be seen in the cloud. And I will remember my pact, which is between me and you and every living soul within all flesh, and no more will there be water as a flood to destroy all flesh."*

And it will happen in my clouding the earth over with cloud means when our self-will blocks any view of a loving faith. *That a bow will be seen in the cloud* means when we are nevertheless the kind of people who can be reborn. *And I will remember my pact, which is between me and you,* symbolizes the Lord's mercy, specifically toward people who have been and people who can be reborn. *And every living soul within all flesh* symbolizes the entire human race. *And no more will there be water as a flood to destroy all flesh* means that our intellectual faculty will no longer be able to absorb delusions so terrible that it will be destroyed, as the descendants of the earliest church were.

These things have to do with all people in general.

1047 The fact that *and it will happen in my clouding the earth over with cloud* means when our self-will blocks any view of a loving faith can be seen from statements directly above concerning the *earth,* or human self-will. Human self-will, it was noted, is such that it pours a continuous stream of darkness (falsity) into our intellectual side, which is the *clouding over.* That is where all falsity comes from.

The fact of the matter is fairly evident from this: All selfishness and materialism—which are matters of human will—are simply forms of hatred, because the more we love ourselves the more we hate our neighbor. Since love for ourselves and love of worldly gain are therefore opposed to heavenly love, they necessarily pour out a constant stream of impulses that go against mutual love. These impulses, as they exist on the intellectual side, are all falsities. From them comes all our darkness and shadow. Falsity clouds truth, exactly as a dark cloud obscures sunlight. And since falsity and truth cannot coexist—just as darkness and light cannot—obviously the one recedes as the other approaches. This happens in cycles, and that is why it says here, "in clouding the earth with cloud," which speaks of times when self-will blocks any view of a loving faith, or of truth and the good it leads to, let alone of goodness and the truth it leads to.

That a bow will be seen in the cloud means when we are nevertheless the kind of people who can be reborn. This is established by the symbolism of a *bow in the cloud,* which, again, is a sign and indication of rebirth [§1042].

1048

To speak further of a bow in the cloud: The character of a person, or of a soul after death, is recognized immediately. The Lord has known it from eternity, and he knows what it will be to eternity. Angels instantly perceive what we are like the moment we first approach them. There is a kind of aura that emanates from our disposition, so to speak, or from the individual traits in us. This aura, amazingly enough, is such that another can tell from it what our beliefs are and what kind of love we have for others. The aura is what becomes visible in the form of a rainbow, when the Lord so pleases. This aura will be discussed again later, the Lord in his divine mercy willing [§§1383–1400, 1504–1520].

This shows what the time when a bow is seen in the cloud means: when we are the kind of people who can be reborn.

The symbolism of *and I will remember my pact, which is between me and you,* as the Lord's mercy, specifically toward people who have been and people who can be reborn, also follows from all this, since remembering, for the Lord, is having mercy. The Lord cannot be said to *remember,* because he knows absolutely everything from eternity. Having mercy, though, is something he can be said to do, because he realizes what we humans are like. He knows that our self-centeredness reflects hell and is our actual hell, because our self-will keeps us in touch with hell. Self-will is such, on its own and by hell's inspiration, that its strongest, keenest wish is to throw itself headlong into hell; and it is not content with this but wants to drag everyone else in the universe along with it. Because this is the kind of devils we are on our own, and the Lord knows it, remembering the pact is consequently the same as showing mercy, using divine means to regenerate us, and drawing us to heaven with a powerful force, so far as our nature allows him to.

1049

1050   The symbolism of *and every living soul within all flesh* as the entire human race can be seen from the symbolism of the living soul within all flesh.

Each of us is called a *living soul* from a living quality in us. Not one of us can live—still less live as a human being—if we do not have something living inside us. In other words, we need to have a measure of innocence, charity, and mercy, or at least something that resembles or approximates it. This measure of innocence, charity, and mercy is something we receive from the Lord in childhood and adolescence, as can be seen from the state of children and the state of adolescents. What we receive at those ages is preserved in us. What is preserved in us is what the Word calls a remnant, or survivors, and it is the Lord's alone in us. These preserved traces are what makes it possible for us to be human when we arrive at adulthood. For more on the remnant, or remaining traces, see §§468, 530, 560, 561, 562, 563, 576.

[2] The fact that the states of innocence, charity, and mercy that we experienced in early childhood and in the years when we were growing up make it possible for us to be human is plainly evident from this: We are not born into any life skills, the way brute animals are, but must learn each and every one of them, and what we learn is then turned into habit and second nature by our practicing it. Unless we learn how, we cannot even walk, or talk, or do anything else. When we practice these activities, they become almost instinctive to us. The case is the same with a state of innocence, charity, and mercy—virtues that we likewise absorb from early childhood on; if those states were not present inside us, we would be much lower than animals. But they are not acquired by education. We receive them as gifts from the Lord, who preserves them in us. These states, along with religious truth, are what are called a remnant, and are the Lord's alone. To the extent that we suffocate them during adulthood, we become dead.

When we are being reborn, these states are the starting points of the process, and we are led into them, because the Lord works through the remnant, as noted before [§§635, 711, 737:1, 857, 977:2].

[3] This remnant in each individual is what is being called the *living soul within all flesh*.

The symbolism of *all flesh* as every individual and so the entire human race can be seen from the symbolism of flesh throughout the Word. (See the illustrations offered at §574.) In Matthew, for example:

> If those days were not shortened, no *flesh* would be rescued. (Matthew 24:22; Mark 13:20)

In John:

> Jesus said, "Father, give glory to your Son, just as you have given him authority over *all flesh.*" (John 17:1, 2)

In Isaiah:

> The glory of Jehovah will be revealed, and *all flesh* will see it. (Isaiah 40:5)

In the same author:

> *All flesh* will recognize that I, Jehovah, am your Savior. (Isaiah 49:26)

No more will there be water as a flood to destroy all flesh means that our intellectual faculty will no longer be able to absorb delusions so terrible that it will be destroyed, as the final descendants of the earliest church were. This can be seen from the many things stated and illustrated already concerning the *flood water* [§§705, 790, 794] and concerning the people predating the Flood who died out [§§310–311, 591–595, 792–813]. (To repeat, they utterly destroyed their power of will and made it hellish, and not only their power of will but their power of understanding too, so that they could not be reborn; in other words, a new will could not be formed in their intellectual part.)

1051

Genesis 9:16. *"There will be a bow in the cloud; and I will see it, to remember the eternal pact between God and every living soul within all flesh that is on the earth."*

1052

And there will be a bow in the cloud symbolizes the stage at which they are. *And I will see it* means it is a stage in which they can be reborn. *To remember the eternal pact* means it is such that the Lord can be present with them in charity. *Between God and every living soul within all flesh that is on the earth* means each individual with whom this is possible.

These things have to do specifically with people who are capable of regenerating.

The symbolism of *and there will be a bow in the cloud* as the stage at which they are, is established by explanations and demonstrations above concerning the *bow in the cloud.* It was noted that people or souls in the next world are recognized by angels from their aura; that when the Lord pleases, an aura also presents itself as a display of rainbow colors; and that variation in these colors depends on an individual's stage of development in regard to faith in the Lord, and so in regard to the good impulses and true ideas of faith [§§1042:1–1043:2, 1048].

1053

In the other life, colors appear whose glow and brilliance makes them far more beautiful than the colors visible to earthly eyes. Each color represents some heavenly, spiritual trait. The colors issue from the light that exists in heaven and from the variegation of spiritual light, as noted above [§1042]. [2] Angels, you see, live in such abundant light that the light of the world, by comparison, is useless. Heaven's light, in which angels live, is to worldly light as noonday sunlight is to candlelight, which fades to nothing when the sun rises.

In heaven there is a heavenly type of light and a spiritual type. Heavenly light, if I may speak in relative terms, is like sunlight, while spiritual light is like moonlight, but with all possible gradations, depending on conditions in the angel who receives the light. The same is true of colors, since they are a product of that light.

In the heaven of angels whose character is heavenly, the Lord himself is the sun, while in the heaven of spiritual angels, he is the moon.

One who has no concept of the life a soul lives after death will find these facts unbelievable, but they are still positively true.

1054 *I will see it* means it is a stage in which they can be reborn, as indicated by the fact that *seeing* someone, when the Lord is said to do so, is being aware of what the person is like. The Lord, after all, has known everyone from eternity past and has no need to "see" what we are like. When we are such that we can regenerate, the Lord is said to see a person, and to lift his face on a person as well.

When we are not able to regenerate, however, the Lord is not said to see or to lift his face but to avert his eyes or face—although it is not the Lord who turns away but we ourselves who do. This is why verse 14 above, which treats of the whole human race (including many who cannot regenerate), does not say "when I see the bow in the cloud" but "when the bow is seen in the cloud."

This matter of the Lord's seeing is similar to his remembering, which in a deeper sense means having mercy, as stated in §§840, 1049. See the earlier explanation [of divine sight] in §626.

1055 The fact that *to remember the eternal pact* means it is such that the Lord can be present with them in charity can be seen from what was said and shown above concerning the symbolism of a *pact*. I noted that there is no eternal compact aside from love for the Lord and love for one's neighbor [§§665–666, 1025:5, 1038]. This pact is eternal, because it stretches from eternity to eternity. The whole of heaven rests on love as its foundation. In fact the whole of creation does, because nothing animate or inanimate in the physical world that involves any kind of union or affiliation can possibly exist without tracing its origin to love. This is because everything in the physical world springs from something spiritual, and everything spiritual, from something heavenly, as mentioned earlier [§§775:2; 880:2–3; 911; 1025:7, 9]. So each and every object has love (or something resembling love) implanted in it. Only humankind lacks love. In us love is replaced by its opposite, since we have destroyed the proper pattern of nature in ourselves. But when we are capable of being reborn, or being restored once more to the proper pattern, and welcoming mutual love, there is a pact. That is to say, charity (the subject here) then creates a bond.

Between God and every living soul within all flesh that is on the earth **1056** means inside each individual with whom this is possible. This meaning is evident from previous statements that people who can be reborn are being discussed. That is why the living soul within all flesh symbolizes those people alone.

Genesis 9:17. *And God said to Noah, "This is the sign of the pact that I* **1057** *am setting up between me and all flesh that is on the earth."*

God said to Noah means the church would know the following. *This is the sign of the pact that I am setting up between me and all flesh that is on the earth* means that not only would people in the church have an indication that the Lord was present in charity but people outside the church would too.

God said to Noah means that the church would know the follow- **1058** ing. This is borne out by the sequence of ideas, which are visible only in the inner meaning, where they connect in this way: The first subject is people inside the church who are regenerate and spiritual. The second is everyone throughout the world. The third is everyone who is capable of regenerating. The present verse rounds out the series by saying that the church would know the following. (It was shown earlier that *Noah* is a church [§§529–531, 597–598, 768, 788:1, 915]; here he is the spiritual church as a whole, since his name is the only one mentioned.) What the church would know now follows.

This is the sign of the pact that I am setting up between me and all flesh **1059** *that is on the earth* means that not only would people in the church have an indication that the Lord was present in charity but people outside the church would too. This meaning is visible from the symbolism of *all flesh* as every individual and consequently as the whole human race. The fact that it is the whole human race, both the portion inside the church and the portion outside it, can be seen not only from the mention of all flesh but also from the fact that the earlier phrase *the living soul within all flesh* is not repeated. The addition of the words *that is on the earth* makes it even clearer.

[2] The Lord is just as much present in charity among those who are outside the church, called Gentiles, as among those who are inside the church. (See what was said above in §§932, 1032.) In fact he is more closely present, because they have less cloud in their intellectual part than so-called Christians usually do. Non-Christians are ignorant of the Word and do not know who the Lord is, so they do not know the truth that the faith teaches. As a result they themselves cannot oppose the Lord or that truth, and therefore their clouds do not oppose the Lord or that truth. Clouds of this kind can be dispelled easily when such people are enlightened.

[3] Christians, though, are capable of having clouds that do block the Lord and the truth of the faith, and these clouds are dark enough to produce gloom. When hatred replaces neighborly love, pitch blackness results. The effect is intensified in those who profane the truth of the faith, which non-Christians cannot do, since they live in ignorance of that truth. None of us can profane a thing whose nature and existence we are unaware of.

This is why more non-Christians than Christians are saved, as the Lord also said in Luke 13:23, 28, 29, 30. In addition, he said that all their little children belong to the Lord's kingdom, in Matthew 18:10, 14; 19:14; Luke 18:16.

1060 Genesis 9:18. *And the sons of Noah coming out of the ark were Shem and Ham and Japheth; and Ham was the father of Canaan.*

The sons of Noah coming out of the ark were symbolizes those who made up the ancient church; *those coming out of the ark* symbolizes the regenerate. *Shem* symbolizes the inner church. *Ham* symbolizes the church corrupted. *Japheth* symbolizes the outer church. *Ham was the father of Canaan* means that the corrupted church gave rise to an outward show of worship without inward content, this worship being symbolized by Canaan.

1061 *And the sons of Noah coming out of the ark were* symbolizes those who made up the ancient church, and *those coming out of the ark* are the regenerate. This can be seen from all that follows, which will clarify how the matter stands.

1062 The symbolism of *Shem* as the inner church, *Ham* as the church corrupted, and *Japheth* as the outer church can also be seen from what follows, since their natures will be described.

The situation that exists in every religion existed in the ancient church too: there were people who had depth, there were degraded people who had depth, and there were shallow people.

People with depth are those who consider charity the most important element of faith. People who have depth but are degraded are those who consider faith without charity the most important aspect of belief. Shallow people are those who do not often think about the inner self but still perform deeds of charity and reverently celebrate the church's rites.

Aside from these three types of people, there are none who can be called part of a spiritual church. And since they were all part of the church, they are said to have *come out of the ark.*

Those in the ancient church who had depth—who considered love for others the principal concern of faith, in other words—were called Shem. Those in the ancient church who had depth but were degraded— who considered faith's chief concern to be faith devoid of charity—were referred to as Ham. Those in the ancient church who were shallow and thought little about the inner self but still did the work of charity and reverently celebrated the church's rites were given the name of Japheth.

What each kind was like is dealt with below [§§1075–1103].

Ham was the father of Canaan, means that the corrupted church gave rise to an outward show of worship without inward content, such worship being symbolized by Canaan. This too will be seen from what follows, the contents of the current verse being a preface to the next verses.

1063

Ham's symbolism as the church corrupted, that is, as those who consider the main element of religion to be faith detached from charity, can be seen in David:

> He struck every *firstborn* in Egypt, *the beginning of their strength* in the tents of *Ham.* (Psalms 78:51)

The firstborn of Egypt represented faith devoid of charity. (For the idea that faith is called the church's firstborn, see earlier at §§352, 367. That is why faith is called the beginning of strength, as it is here in David; see Genesis 49:3, where it is used of Reuben, who as Jacob's firstborn represented faith and is called the beginning of strength.) The tents of Ham are worship based on that faith. (For the symbolism of tents as worship, see prior remarks in §414.) Egypt is consequently called the land of Ham in Psalms 105:23, 27; 106:22.

[2] People like this—referred to as Ham in the ancient church—lived a life devoted to all kinds of cravings, babbling only that their faith could save them no matter how they lived. In ancient eyes they accordingly looked black, from the searing heat of their passions, which is why they were called Ham.

The reason the verse describes Ham as the father of Canaan is that such individuals do not care how one lives as long as one attends religious functions. They do still want some kind of worship. Outward worship is the only kind they have; inward worship, which has exclusively to do with charity, they reject. That is why Ham is called the father of Canaan.

1064   Genesis 9:19. *These three were Noah's sons; and from them the whole earth scattered out.*

These three were Noah's sons symbolizes these three types of doctrinal approach, which all religious movements in general adopt. *And from them the whole earth scattered out* means that these gave rise to all subsequent doctrinal systems, both those based on truth and those based on falsity.

1065   The symbolism of *these three were Noah's sons* as these three types of doctrinal approach, which all religious movements in general adopt, was mentioned just above [§1062].

There are, in fact, many kinds of doctrinal approach that are less universal, but there are no more than three comprehensive types. People who do not acknowledge charity or faith or external worship do not belong to any religion, so at present, where the church is the topic, they are not discussed.

1066   *From them the whole earth scattered out* means that these gave rise to all subsequent doctrinal systems, both those based on truth and those based on falsity, as the symbolism of the earth shows.

The earth, or land, is understood in various ways in the Word. In the most general sense it is taken to refer to the place—the territory—where the church is or was. Examples are the land of Canaan, the land of Judah, the land of Israel. So it is used generally for everyone in the church, since the land is named after the people living there, as is also common in everyday speech. Long ago, then, whenever people spoke of the whole earth, they had in mind not the whole globe but only the land where the church existed and consequently the church itself. The following passages from the Word will illustrate this. In Isaiah:

> Jehovah is emptying the *earth.* The *earth* will be emptied bare. The *earth* will mourn, will be confused. And the *land* will be defiled beneath its inhabitants; on this account a curse will devour the *land.* Therefore

the inhabitants of the *land* will be destroyed by fire, and the humanity left behind will be a pittance. The floodgates in the heights opened and *the earth's foundations* shook. The *earth* was shattered utterly. The *earth* split wide open. The *earth* quaked, tottering. The *earth* staggers helplessly like a drunkard and sways back and forth like a shack; and its transgression will weigh on it, and it will fall and not rise again. (Isaiah 24:1, 3, 4, 5, 6, 18, 19, 20, 21)

The earth, or land, stands for the people in it, specifically the people of the church—and so the church itself—and for those aspects of the church that have been purged. While being purged they are said to be emptied, to shake, stagger like a drunkard, sway, fall, and not rise. [2] In the following verse from Malachi, the land symbolizes humankind and consequently the church, which is composed of humankind:

All nations will proclaim you fortunate, because *you will be a land of pleasure.* (Malachi 3:12)

The earth stands for the church in Isaiah:

Do you not understand the foundations of the *earth?* (Isaiah 40:21)

The earth's foundations stand for the church's foundations. In the same author:

Look—I am creating new heavens and a new *earth!* (Isaiah 65:17; 66:22; Revelation 21:1)

New heavens and a new earth stand for the Lord's kingdom and the church. In Zechariah:

Jehovah is stretching out the heavens and *founding the earth* and forming the human spirit in the middle of it. (Zechariah 12:1)

The earth stands for the church here, as it also does above:

In the beginning, God created heaven and *earth.* (Genesis 1:1)

The heavens and the *earth* were completed. (Genesis 2:1)

These are the births of heaven and *earth.* (Genesis 2:4)

In each of these instances, the earth stands for the church, which was created, formed, and made. In Joel:

Before him the *earth* shook, the heavens trembled; the sun and moon turned black. (Joel 2:10)

The earth stands for the church and for everyone in the church. When the church is being purged, heaven and earth are said to shake, while the sun and moon—love and faith—are said to grow black. [3] In Jeremiah:

> I looked at the *earth* when, indeed, there was void and emptiness; and to the heavens, and these had no light. (Jeremiah 4:23)

The earth clearly stands for a person who has not a bit of religion inside. In the same author:

> *The whole earth* will be stripped bare, yet I will not make a full end. Because of this the *earth* will mourn and the heavens will be draped in black. (Jeremiah 4:27, 28)

Again it stands for the church, whose external aspects are the earth and whose internal aspects are the heavens, which are described as draped in black and as having no light when there is no longer a wise appreciation of goodness or an intelligent understanding of truth. Under those circumstances, the earth is also void and empty, and the same is true of any person in the church who would otherwise *be* a church. There are other places as well in which *the whole earth* means the church and only the church. In Daniel:

> The fourth creature will be a fourth kingdom on the *earth,* which will differ from all the kingdoms and consume the *whole earth* and trample it and crush it. (Daniel 7:23)

The whole earth stands for the church and the people in it. The Word, after all, does not talk about the power exercised by sovereigns, as secular literature does, but about sacred topics and about the conditions in the church symbolized by the earth's monarchies. [4] In Jeremiah:

> A huge storm will be stirred up from the *edges of the earth,* and the people stabbed by Jehovah will on that day reach *from the ends of the earth to the ends of the earth.* (Jeremiah 25:32, 33)

"From the ends of the earth to the ends of the earth" stands for the church and for everyone in the church. In Isaiah:

> The *whole earth* is at rest and quiet; they raised a glad shout. (Isaiah 14:7)

The whole earth stands for the church. In Ezekiel:

> As the *whole earth* rejoices, . . . (Ezekiel 35:14)

Here too the whole earth stands for the church. In Isaiah:

> I swore that the waters of Noah would no longer pass over the *earth*. (Isaiah 54:9)

The earth stands for the church, since the church is the subject in this passage.

[5] Because the earth or land in the Word symbolizes the church, it also symbolizes what is not the church. (Every word like this has contrary or opposite meanings.) This is true of the different lands the surrounding nations lived in, or to put it generally, all lands outside that of Canaan.

For this reason, the earth is also taken as standing for the people, and for a person outside the church, and so for the outer self, with its will, its desire for autonomy, and so on. Rarely does the Word use it to mean the entire globe, unless it is symbolizing the situation of the whole human race in regard to religion or nonreligion.

Moreover, since the earth is what contains the ground (which is also the church) and the ground is what contains a field, the term holds many different nuances and accordingly symbolizes many different things. Just what the term symbolizes is to be gleaned from the subject under discussion, the subject to which the term applies, because this is the reality that underlies the term.

From all this it can now be seen that in this verse the *whole earth,* which *scattered out* from Noah's sons, symbolizes not the whole inhabited world, or the whole human race, but all the doctrinal systems of the various religions—both the systems based on truth and the ones based on falsity.

Genesis 9:20. *And Noah started as a man of the soil and planted a vineyard.*   **1067**

Noah started as a man of the soil symbolizes those in general who are equipped with the doctrinal precepts of faith. *And planted a vineyard* symbolizes the church that results; the *vineyard* is a spiritual church.

The fact that *Noah started as a man of the soil* symbolizes those in general who are equipped with the doctrinal precepts of faith is established   **1068** by the symbolism of the *soil,* or ground, discussed earlier in §§268, 566. The soil is the people in the church or, to put it another way, the church itself, since if a church is to exist, each individual has to *be* a church.

The church is called the soil because it receives the seeds of faith, or in other words, the true concepts and good urges of faith.

The difference between the soil and the earth (which also symbolizes the church, as shown) resembles that between faith and charity. Just as charity is what contains faith, the earth is what contains the soil. So when there is a general discussion of religion, it is referred to as the earth, and when there is a specific discussion of it, it is referred to as soil, which is the term used here. A general category is a composite of the items belonging to it.

The doctrinal teachings that the people of the ancient church possessed came from ideas revealed to and perceived by the earliest church, as noted before [§§519:1, 521, 609, 920:4]. These had been preserved, and the people of the ancient church believed in them, the same way we today believe in the Word. Those articles of doctrine were their Word. So Noah's starting as a man of the soil symbolizes those who are equipped with the doctrinal precepts of faith.

1069   The fact that the words *he planted a vineyard* symbolize the church that results, and that the *vineyard* is a spiritual church, can be seen from the symbolism of a vineyard.

The Word frequently describes religions as gardens, and as trees in a garden too. It also directly calls them gardens and trees because of the fruit they produce, which symbolizes the effects of love, or of charity. (This is why we are said to be recognized by our fruit [Matthew 7:16; Luke 6:44].)

Comparisons of religious movements with gardens, trees, and fruit originate in the representations of heaven. In heaven, gardens that are indescribably beautiful sometimes appear in response to different auras of belief. That is why the heavenly church was portrayed [in Genesis] as a paradisal garden containing trees of every variety. The trees in the garden symbolized the perceptions of that church, while the fruits symbolized every kind of loving goodness.

The ancient church, on the other hand, because it was focused on spirit, is depicted by a vineyard, on account of its fruit—grapes—which represent and symbolize charitable endeavors. This is quite clear from many passages in the Word. [2] In Isaiah, for example:

> I will sing my beloved a song of my beloved, to his *vineyard.* My beloved had a *vineyard* on a horn of the offspring of oil; and he fenced it in and circled it with stones and *planted* it with a *choice grapevine* and built a tower in the middle of it and also hollowed out a wine-press in it. And he waited for it to produce *grapes,* and it produced wild grapes. And now, resident of Jerusalem and man of Judah, judge, please, between me and my *vineyard.* Jehovah Sabaoth's *vineyard* is the house of Israel. (Isaiah 5:1, 2, 3, 7)

The vineyard symbolizes the ancient church (and so a spiritual church), and it says explicitly that the vineyard is the house of Israel, because Israel in the Word symbolizes a spiritual church, while Judah symbolizes a heavenly church. In Jeremiah:

> I will build you again, and you will be rebuilt, virgin of Israel; you will decorate your tambourines again and go out into the dance of the merry. You will *plant vineyards* again on the mountains of Samaria. (Jeremiah 31:4, 5)

The vineyard in this passage stands for a spiritual church. The subject is Israel, which, again, symbolizes a spiritual church. [3] In Ezekiel:

> When I gather the house of Israel from the peoples, they will live on the land in security and build houses and *plant vineyards*. (Ezekiel 28:25, 26)

The vineyard stands for a spiritual church, or Israel. Planting vineyards stands for being supplied with the true ideas and good impulses of faith. In Amos:

> I struck you with blight and mildew; your numerous gardens and your *vineyards* and your fig trees and your olive groves the caterpillar will devour. So will I do to you, Israel. (Amos 4:9, 12)

Gardens stand for different aspects of religion. Vineyards stand for spiritual aspects of religion, fig trees for earthly aspects, and olive groves for heavenly aspects; so they stand for different aspects of a spiritual religion, or of Israel. In the same author:

> I will bring my people Israel back from captivity, and they will rebuild the ruined cities and settle down, and *plant vineyards* and drink wine from them, and make gardens and eat produce from them. (Amos 9:14)

Planting vineyards stands for the planting of a spiritual church, so a vineyard itself stands for the spiritual church, or in other words, Israel.

[4] Since a vineyard symbolizes a spiritual church, a grapevine does too, a grapevine being part of a vineyard. The relationship is like that between a church and a person in the church; so the two of them are the same thing. In Jeremiah:

> Is Israel a slave? Is he a houseboy? Why has he become plunder? I had *planted you as a choice grapevine* through and through, the seed of

truth, and how could you turn into the rebellious stems of a foreign grapevine before my eyes? (Jeremiah 2:14, 21)

The grapevine stands for a spiritual church, or Israel. In Ezekiel:

> Raise a lament over the chieftains of Israel. Your mother was like a *grapevine* that resembled you, *planted* next to the water, fruitful, and leafy because of the many waters. (Ezekiel 19:1, 10)

The grapevine stands for the ancient spiritual church—which is the mother—and consequently for Israel, which is why it also says "that resembled you." In Hosea:

> Israel is an empty *grapevine;* they make the fruit resemble themselves. (Hosea 10:1)

The grapevine stands for a spiritual church (Israel)—in this case, when in ruins. In the same author:

> Return to Jehovah your God, Israel. I will be like dew to Israel. Those living in its shade will return. They will bring the grain to life and blossom like a *grapevine;* its memory will be like the wine of Lebanon. (Hosea 14:1, 5, 7)

The grapevine stands for a spiritual church, or Israel. In Moses:

> . . . until Shiloh comes, tying his young animal to the *grapevine* and his jenny's foal to the *choice vine.* (Genesis 49:10, 11)

This is a prophecy of the Lord. The grapevine and choice grapevine stand for spiritual religions.

[5] The Lord's parables of workers in vineyards, in Matthew 20:1–17; Mark 12:1–13; Luke 20:9–17; and Matthew 21:33–44, likewise symbolize spiritual religions.

In a spiritual religion the main focus is charity, in which the Lord is present, by means of which he binds himself to humanity, and through which he alone accomplishes everything good. Because of this, and because a grapevine symbolizes a spiritual religion, the Lord compares himself to a grapevine and describes the people of the church (or the spiritual church itself) by these words in John:

> I am the true *grapevine,* and my Father is the *vinedresser;* every stem on me *not bearing fruit* he removes. But every one *bearing fruit* he will prune so that it will *bear more fruit. Remain in me; I will also remain in*

you. Just as a stem cannot bear fruit on its own, if it does not remain on the vine, so you cannot either, if you do not remain in me. I am the grapevine; you are the stems. Those who remain in me and in whom I remain bear much fruit; because without me you cannot do anything. This is my commandment: that you love one another as I have loved you. (John 15:1, 2, 3, 4, 5, 12)

This clarifies what a spiritual religion is.

Genesis 9:21. *And he drank some wine and became drunk and was uncovered in the middle of his tent.*

1070

And he drank wine means that they wanted to explore religious questions. *And became drunk* means that they consequently fell into error. *And was uncovered in the middle of his tent* symbolizes the resulting perversions; the *middle of the tent* is that which is the primary concern of one's faith.

The fact that *he drank wine* means that they wanted to explore religious questions can be seen from the symbolism of *wine.* A vineyard or grapevine, as shown, is a spiritual religion, or the people of a spiritual church. Grapes, and clusters and bunches of grapes, are its fruit, and they symbolize charity and the effects of charity. Wine, though, symbolizes the faith that grows out of charity, and everything that goes to make up faith. So a grape is the heavenly side of that church, while wine is the spiritual side. The former—the heavenly part—belongs to the will, as noted so often before, while the latter—the spiritual part—belongs to the intellect.

1071

The fact that *he drank some wine* means that they wanted to explore religious questions, and do so by the use of false reasoning, can be seen from the circumstance that *he became drunk,* which is to say that they fell into error.

The people of this church did not have the perception that the people of the earliest church had. They needed instead to learn what was good and true by studying religious teachings that had been gathered from the perceptions of the earliest church and saved up—teachings that were their Word. Like the Word, these religious teachings in many areas were such that they could not be believed in the absence of perception, because spiritual and heavenly matters rise infinitely beyond human comprehension. That was the reason for their use of skewed reasoning. But people who refuse to believe a thing unless they grasp it [with the senses] are completely incapable of believing, as has been demonstrated many times already; see §§128, 129, 130, 195, 196, 215, 232, 233.

[2] The symbolism in the Word of *grapes* as charity and all it entails, and that of *wine* as the resulting faith and all it entails, can be seen from the following passages. In Isaiah:

> My beloved had a *vineyard,* on a horn of the offspring of oil; he waited for it to produce *grapes,* and it produced wild grapes. (Isaiah 5:1, 2, 4)

The grapes stand for charity and its fruits. In Jeremiah:

> "I will utterly destroy them," says Jehovah. "There are no *grapes* on the *grapevine* and no figs on the fig tree." (Jeremiah 8:13)

The grapevine stands for a spiritual religion and the grapes for charity. In Hosea:

> Israel was like *grapes* in the wilderness when I discovered him. Your ancestors were like first fruit on a young fig tree when I saw them. (Hosea 9:10)

Israel stands for the ancient church, a grape for the fact that its people possessed the gift of charity. The meaning is just the opposite when Israel refers to Jacob's children. In Micah:

> There is no *cluster of grapes* to eat; an early [fig] is what my soul has desired. The godly person has perished off the earth, and an upright person does not exist among humankind. (Micah 7:1, 2)

The cluster of grapes stands for charity, or a godly quality, while the early fruit stands for faith, or what is upright. [3] In Isaiah:

> This is what Jehovah has said: "Just as *new wine* is found in the *cluster,* and they say, 'Do not spoil it, because there is a blessing in it' . . ." (Isaiah 65:8)

The cluster stands for charity, the new wine for the good effects of charity and the truth that they lead to. In Moses:

> He washed his clothing in *wine* and his robe in the blood of *grapes.* (Genesis 49:11)

This prophesies of the Lord. The wine stands for a spiritual element that comes from a heavenly one, and the blood of grapes, for that which plays a heavenly role in spiritual religions. So the grapes stand for charity itself and the wine for faith itself. In John:

> The angel said, "Send in the sharp sickle and harvest the earth's *clusters,* because its *grapes* have ripened." (Revelation 14:18)

This is about the final days, when there is no faith—that is, no charity. After all, there is no faith other than the faith that belongs to charity; in its essence, faith *is* charity. So when the statement is made that there is no longer any faith (as is true in the final days), it means that there is no charity.

[4] Just as grapes symbolize charity, wine symbolizes the faith that develops out of charity, since wine comes from grapes. In addition to the passages speaking of vineyards and grapevines cited here and earlier, the following quotations will demonstrate this fact. In Isaiah:

> Gladness and exultation have been taken away from Carmel, and in the vineyards there is no singing, no jubilation. No treader treads *the wine in the winepresses.* I have put an end to the hedad. (Isaiah 16:10)

This stands for the fact that the spiritual church (Carmel) has been devastated. "No one to tread the wine in the winepresses" stands for the fact that there is no longer anyone with faith. In the same author:

> The inhabitants of the land will be destroyed by fire, and the humanity left behind will be a pittance. The *new wine* will mourn; the *grapevine* will droop; they will not *drink wine* with a song. The *strong drink* will be bitter for those drinking it. A shouting over the *wine* in the streets! (Isaiah 24:6, 7, 9, 11)

These verses deal with a spiritual church that has been devastated. The wine stands for religious truth held cheap. In Jeremiah:

> To their mothers they will say, "Where is the grain and the *wine?*" when they swoon as if stabbed, in the city's streets. (Lamentations 2:12)

"Where are the grain and the wine?" means "Where are love and faith?" City streets symbolize truths here, as they do elsewhere in the Word. Lying stabbed in the streets means that they do not know what truth to believe in. [5] In Amos:

> I will bring my people Israel back from captivity and they will rebuild the ruined cities and settle down and plant *vineyards* and *drink wine* from them. (Amos 9:14)

This is about a spiritual religion, or Israel, which is said to plant vineyards and drink wine when it is the kind of religion whose faith is inspired by charity. In Zephaniah:

> They will build houses but not live in them, and plant *vineyards* but not *drink wine* from them. (Zephaniah 1:13; Amos 5:11)

This stands for the opposite situation, in which a spiritual religion has been devastated. In Zechariah:

> They will be like mighty Ephraim, and their heart will rejoice as if with *wine,* and their children will see and rejoice. (Zechariah 10:7)

This is about the house of Judah, which would be as described because of the goodness and truth that characterize faith. In John:

> . . . that they should not hurt the oil or the *wine.* (Revelation 6:6)

This stands for not hurting anything heavenly or spiritual, which is to say, any attributes of love and faith.

[6] Since wine symbolizes faith in the Lord, in the sacrifices of the Jewish religion faith was also represented by a *libation of wine,* as described in Numbers 15:2–15; 28:11–15, 18–end; 29:7–end; Leviticus 23:12, 13; Exodus 29:40. As a result, these words appear in Hosea:

> Threshing floor and *winepress* will not feed them, and the *new wine* will prove false in that [land]. They will not live in Jehovah's land, and Ephraim will return to Egypt, and in Assyria they will eat what is unclean. They will not *pour a libation of wine* to Jehovah; [their libations] will not be pleasing to him. (Hosea 9:2, 3, 4)

In this case the discussion concerns Israel, or a spiritual religion, and those in it who pervert and defile the sanctity and truth of faith through their desire to investigate such things by the use of secular knowledge and sophistry. Egypt is factual knowledge, Assyria is sophistry, and Ephraim is those who engage in it.

1072   The meaning of *he became drunk* as the fact that they consequently fell into error can be seen from the meaning of a *drunkard* in the Word. The people called drunkards are those who believe only in what they can grasp [with their senses] and who therefore make investigations into the mysteries of faith. Because they conduct their inquiry by consulting the senses or the academic disciplines or philosophy, the process inevitably leads them into error, human nature being what it is. Our thinking is purely earthbound, body-centered, and matter-based, because it is formed out of earthly, bodily, and materialistic notions, which cling tenaciously to it. Those notions form the foundation and resting place of the concepts that make up our thinking, so to think and reason about the Lord on the basis of such concepts is to lead ourselves into error and perversion. It is as impossible for us to construct a faith for ourselves out of these things as it is for a camel to go through the eye of a needle. The resulting error and insanity is what the Word calls drunkenness.

As a matter of fact, souls (spirits) in the next life who reason shallowly about religious truth, and against it, come to resemble drunkards and act drunk too. I will have more to say on this later, by the Lord's divine mercy.

[2] It is easy to tell whether or not a spirit has adopted the faith that comes of neighborly love. Those who have adopted it do not debate religious truth but affirm it and also corroborate it by the evidence of the senses, of organized knowledge, and of rational analysis, so far as they can. As soon as any obscurity interferes, they reject whatever they cannot perceive and refuse to let it bring them into doubt. What they are capable of grasping, they assert, is extremely limited, so that it would be insane to view something as untrue simply because they do not comprehend it. These are the people under the influence of charity.

The case is just the opposite with those who do not adopt a faith that results from charity. They lack interest in anything besides arguing whether a thing is true and knowing exactly how matters stand. Unless they can see what the facts of a case are, they say, they cannot believe it to be so. This in itself instantly gives away their lack of belief; it indicates that they not only doubt everything but even deny it at heart. When they do learn how matters stand, they stubbornly raise all kinds of objections, never resting, even if they have to go on arguing forever. And when they stick fast in this way, they heap error on top of error. These people, or their ilk, are those the Word describes as drunk on wine or strong drink, [3] as in Isaiah:

> These *err* through *wine* and *go astray* through *strong drink*. Priest and prophet *err through strong drink. They are swallowed up by wine; they err from strong drink;* they err in their vision; all the tables are full of coughed-up vomit. Just whom will he teach knowledge, and whom will he cause to understand the message? Those weaned off milk? Those pulled from the breast? (Isaiah 28:7, 8, 9)

That such people are meant here is self-evident. In the same author:

> How can you say to Pharaoh, "I am the offspring of sages, the offspring of the monarchs of old"? Where are your sages now? And have them

tell, please. Jehovah has mixed a spirit of perversities in [Egypt's] midst
and made Egypt go astray in all its work, just as *drunkards go astray* in
their own vomit. (Isaiah 19:11, 12, 14)

Drunkards stand for those who want to explore spiritual and heavenly
phenomena by means of facts. Egypt symbolizes factual knowledge,
which is why it calls itself the offspring of sages. In Jeremiah:

Drink and *get drunk*, and vomit, and fall, and do not rise. (Jeremiah 25:27)

The drunkenness stands for falsities. [4] In David:

They reel and quaver like a *drunkard*, and all their wisdom is swal-
lowed up. (Psalms 107:27)

In Isaiah:

Come, let me take *wine* and let us *get drunk on strong drink*, and tomor-
row as on this day there will be great abundance. (Isaiah 56:12)

This is said of concepts that oppose religious truth. In Jeremiah:

Every bottle will be filled with *wine*, all of Jerusalem's residents with
drunkenness. (Jeremiah 13:12, 13)

The wine stands for faith, the drunkenness for error. In Joel:

Wake up, *drunkards*, and cry and howl over the *new wine*, all you *wine
drinkers*, because it has been cut off from your mouth. For a nation is
coming up over my land; it turns my *grapevine* into a desolation. (Joel
1:5, 6, 7)

This is about the church when its religious truth has been devastated.
In John:

Babylon has given some of the *wine* of whoredom's anger to all the
nations to drink; those inhabiting the land became *drunk* on the *wine*
of whoredom. (Revelation 14:8, 10; 16:19; 17:2; 18:3; 19:15)

The wine of whoredom stands for religious truth that has been adulterated, which is described as causing drunkenness. Likewise in Jeremiah:

Babylon was a *goblet* of gold in Jehovah's hand, *intoxicating* the whole
earth. Of *her wine* the nations *drank*, therefore the nations go mad.
(Jeremiah 51:7)

[5] Since drunkenness symbolized insanity concerning religious truth, it also became a representative condition, one forbidden to Aaron in these words:

> Aaron and his sons must not drink *wine* or *intoxicating drink* when they are about to enter the tent, or they will die—in order to distinguish between what is holy and what is profane, between what is unclean and what is clean. (Leviticus 10:8, 9, 10)

In addition, people who believe nothing but what they grasp through sense experience or factual knowledge are described as "heroic at drinking" in Isaiah:

> Doom to those who are wise in their own eyes and discerning in their own sight! Doom to those *heroic at drinking wine* and to men valiant at *mixing strong drink.* (Isaiah 5:21, 22)

They are called wise in their own eyes and discerning in their own sight because those who argue against religious truth consider themselves wiser than others.

[6] But people who care nothing about the Word or the truth that makes up faith and who are consequently unwilling to learn anything about faith (in this way denying its chief tenets) are described as drunk without wine in Isaiah:

> *They are drunk, and not on wine; they stagger, and not from strong drink,* because Jehovah has poured out a spirit of slumber on you and has sealed your eyes. (Isaiah 29:9, 10)

What comes before and after this in Isaiah establishes the fact that these people's character is the one just described. Drunkards of this type imagine themselves more awake than others, but they are in a deep sleep.

At its inception, the ancient church—especially the people in it who came from the stock of the earliest church—had the nature depicted in this verse, as indicated earlier, in the statements of §788.

The symbolism of *he was uncovered in the middle of his tent* as the resulting perversions can be seen from the symbolism of *being uncovered,* or naked. The person who is portrayed as uncovered and denuded by drunkenness on wine is one who has no religious truth, and even more so one in whom that truth is perverted.

1073

The actual truth that composes faith is compared to clothes, in that it provides a covering for the good that comes of charity, or for charity itself. Charity is the body itself, and truth, as a result, is the clothing. Or, to say exactly the same thing, charity is the soul itself, while religious truth is like the body that clothes the soul. The Word calls religious truths clothes or a covering, which is why verse 23 below says that Shem and Japheth took a *garment* and covered their father's nakedness.

The relationship of spiritual entities to heavenly ones is like that of the body to the soul it clothes, or like that of garments to the body they clothe. In heaven, spiritual things are also represented by clothes. Since the present verse says that [Noah] lay uncovered, the meaning is that people deprived themselves of the truth that faith espouses through their desire to explore this truth through empirical data and therefore shallow logic.

Lying naked from being drunk on wine symbolizes the same things [elsewhere] in the Word, as in Jeremiah:

> Rejoice and be glad, daughter of Edom, living in the land of Uz. The goblet will also pass over you. You will *become drunk* and *go naked*. (Lamentations 4:21)

And in Habakkuk:

> Doom to those who cause their companion to *drink*, . . . and also *intoxicating* them in order to *look on their naked parts*. (Habakkuk 2:15)

1074   The fact that the *middle of the tent* is the primary concern of one's faith can be seen from the symbolism of the *middle* and of a *tent*. In the Word, the middle symbolizes the deepest core, while a tent symbolizes neighborly love, or worship based on that love. Love for others is the core, that is, the primary concern, of faith and worship, which makes it the middle of the tent.

The symbolism of the middle as the deepest core has been demonstrated above [§§200, 225]. For the fact that a tent is the holiness of love, or charity, see above in §414.

1075   Genesis 9:22. *And Ham, father of Canaan, saw his father's nakedness and pointed it out to his two brothers outside.*

Ham and *Canaan* have the same symbolism here as before; *Ham* symbolizes the church corrupted, while *Canaan* symbolizes an outward show of worship without inward content. *He saw his father's nakedness* means that they observed the errors and perversions mentioned above. *And pointed it out to his two brothers outside* means that they sneered at those things. The two are called *his brothers* because these people claimed to have faith.

The symbolism of *Ham* as the church corrupted can be seen from the things said about him previously [§§1062–1063]. A religion is called corrupted when it acknowledges the Word and engages in a kind of worship resembling that of a true religion but still detaches faith from charity and so from its essential quality and its life. In consequence, faith becomes a dead thing, and in consequence, the religion is inevitably corrupted.

1076

What the people of such a religion turn into can be seen from the fact that they cannot possibly have any conscience. No conscience exists that actually is conscience except one that grows out of charity. Charity—or rather the Lord working through charity—is what creates conscience. What else is conscience but refusing to wrong anyone in any way, that is, doing right by everyone in every way? So conscience is a matter of charity and never a matter of faith detached from charity. If the people mentioned do have any conscience, it is a distorted one (concerning which, see above [§§977:1, 1033]). And since they lack conscience, they plunge into every sort of wickedness, so far as external restraints fall away.

[2] As a matter of fact, they do not even know what charity is, only that it is a word with some meaning or other. And because they lack charity, they also do not know what faith is. When asked, they can only answer that it is a form of thought, some saying that it is trust, others that it is religious knowledge, few that it is a life according to that knowledge, and hardly any that it is a life of charity, or mutual love. If you tell them this and give them a chance to think about it, their only response is that all love begins with oneself and that those who fail to take care of themselves and their own are worse than heathens [1 Timothy 5:8]. Accordingly they pursue their own interest and worldly advantages exclusively. The result is that they live a life of self-absorption. (The nature of human selfhood has already been described several times before). These are the people referred to as Ham.

Since the people called Ham and Canaan here—that is, the people who detach faith from charity and therefore consider external acts alone to be worship—cannot see what conscience is or where it comes from, a few words must be said on the subject.

1077

Conscience is formed through religious truth, because the things we hear, acknowledge, and believe are what create conscience in us. From then on, to violate those convictions is, for us, to violate conscience, as anyone can see clearly enough. That is why we can never acquire a true conscience unless the things we hear, acknowledge, and believe are the true tenets of faith. It is by means of religious truth—when the Lord stirs our sense of charity—that we are regenerated. So it is through religious truth that we receive conscience, and conscience is our actual new self.

This demonstrates that the true ideas embraced by faith are means to this end, namely, of living by the lessons that faith teaches, and the chief lesson is to love the Lord above all and to love our neighbor as ourselves. If we do not live by those lessons, what is faith but a meaningless curiosity and a hollow word, or something disconnected from heavenly life? Nothing detached from that life can ever provide salvation.

[2] To believe that we can be saved no matter how we live, as long as we possess faith, is to say that we are saved even if we lack any charity, and even if we lack all conscience. It is to claim that even if we spend our lives hating people, taking revenge, looting, committing adultery—in short, violating charity and conscience in every way—still, as long as we possess faith, even a faith adopted in the final hour of death, we can be saved.

Ponder this, then: If you abide by a principle as false as that, just what kind of religious truth is it that forms your conscience? Is it not falsity? Any trace of conscience that you imagine you have consists only of superficial restraints—fear of the law and fear for your rank, your money, and the prestige these things bring you. Such inhibitions create in you what you call a conscience, preventing you from hurting your fellow creatures and prompting you to do good to them. But because this is not conscience, since it is not love for others, people like you plunge eagerly into the worst possible crimes and obscenities when those external restraints loosen or dissolve.

But your situation [after death] is radically different if you said that faith alone saves and yet lived a life of charity anyway, because in that case your faith contained charity, bestowed by the Lord.

1078   The symbolism of *father of Canaan* as an outward show of worship without inward content has been mentioned before [§1063]. Faith detached from charity can produce no other kind of worship, because the inner self consists in charity, never in faith without charity. So people devoid of neighborly love are completely incapable of any other type of worship than an outward show without inward content. Since it is faith detached from neighborly love that produces this sort of worship, Ham is called Canaan's father, and the following verses speak not of Ham but of Canaan.

The fact that *he saw his father's nakedness* means that they observed **1079** errors and perversions is established by the symbolism of *nakedness* as that which is evil and perverted, discussed just above, as well as earlier, in §§213, 214.

People who adopt faith separated from charity are depicted here by Ham and the notice he took of his father's nakedness, that is, of his father's errors and perversions. Those are the only things that people like this can see in another individual. But it is different for people who have the faith that comes of charity. They take notice of good qualities. Whatever evil or falsity they may see, they excuse it, and if they can, they work to correct it in the offender, as the present passage says Shem and Japheth did.

[2] Where neighborly love is absent, self-love is present, along with hatred for anyone who does not cater to oneself. That is why people who lack neighborly love see nothing in their neighbor besides that neighbor's evil. If they see anything good in the person, they either dismiss it or put a bad interpretation on it.

People governed by charity act in an entirely different way.

These differences form the distinction between the two types of people, particularly when they enter the other life. Those who lack all kindness radiate hatred from every pore. They want to examine and in fact judge everyone and crave nothing more than to find evil, constantly bent as they are on condemning, punishing, and torturing others.

Those who are guided by kindness, on the other hand, hardly even notice evil in another but pay attention instead to everything good and true in the person. When they do find anything bad or false, they put a good interpretation on it. This is a characteristic of all angels—one they acquire from the Lord, who bends everything bad toward good.

The fact that *he pointed it out to his two brothers* means that they **1080** sneered at [others' errors and perversions] now follows logically, since people devoid of charity always feel contempt for others. In other words, they always mock others and broadcast the faults of others whenever they find an opportunity. If they do so discreetly, it is only superficial restraints that impede them—fear of the law, fear for their life, and fear of losing rank, money, and the prestige that accompanies such things. As a result, they nourish these impulses deep down while putting on an outward show of friendship.

In doing so, they acquire two auras, which are clearly perceived in the other world. One—the inner one—is full of hatred; the other—the outer one—mimics goodness. Because these auras are at complete odds with one another, they cannot help clashing, and the consequence is that when such people are stripped of their external aura and can no longer pretend, they hurl themselves into every unspeakable wickedness. When the external aura is not removed, hatred lurks in every word they utter, and is perceived, and this leads to punishment and agony for them.

1081 The two are called *his brothers* because these people claimed to have faith, as can be seen from proofs in §367 showing that charity is faith's brother.

1082 Genesis 9:23. *And Shem and Japheth took a garment, and both of them put it on their shoulder and went backward and covered their father's nakedness; and their faces were backward, and they did not see their father's nakedness.*

Shem, as noted, symbolizes the inner church; *Japheth,* the corresponding outer church. *They took a garment* means that they put a good interpretation on the situation. *And both of them put it on their shoulder* means that they did so with all their might. *And went backward* means that they paid no attention to errors and perversions. *And covered their father's nakedness* means that in doing so they excused those wrongs. *And their faces were backward, and they did not see their father's nakedness* means that this is the proper thing to do, and that we should not concentrate on such wrongs, which are blunders and downfalls resulting from misguided thinking.

1083 The symbolism of *Shem* as the inner church and of *Japheth* as the corresponding outer church has already been mentioned [§§975, 1062].

Where a church exists, there has to be an inner dimension and an outer dimension, since a human being, who *is* a church, has an inner self and an outer self. Until a person becomes a church, that is, until a person has regenerated, he or she lives on the surface. While regenerating, we are led away from superficial considerations (or rather by means of them) to deeper ones, as explained and illustrated already. Afterward, when we have been reborn, external elements form a perimeter around all the contents of the inner self. So in every religion, there has to be an inner church and an outer church.

[2] Take the ancient church, for instance, and the Christian church today. The inner aspects of the ancient church were all the things that go to make up charity and the faith that grows out of it—all humility, all veneration of the Lord resulting from charity, all good feelings toward one's neighbor, and other qualities like these. The external aspects of that

church were sacrifices, libations, and other customs, all of which were reminders of the Lord because of what they represented, and all of which focused on him. There were inner attributes, then, inside the outward practices, and they created a single church.

The inner aspects of the Christian church were exactly like those of the ancient church, although different outward practices took over; sacrifices and so on were replaced by symbolic acts that likewise drew attention to the Lord. So inward and outward elements again formed a single entity. [3] The ancient church and the Christian church differed not at all in their deeper values, only in their outward rituals. Worshiping the Lord in charity can never differ, no matter how much the outward expression varies.

Moreover, since a religion cannot exist unless it has an inner and an outer dimension, as stated, the inner dimension without the outer one—without some external counterpart on which to rest—would be vague and ill defined. People (most of them, anyway) are such that they do not know what the inner self is or what belongs to it. So unless there were external worship, they would not have the least idea what holiness is. [4] As long as such people possess neighborly love and a conscience based on that love, they have inside themselves, within their outward worship, a deeper form of worship. This is because the Lord is at work within them, in their charity and in their conscience, and lends all their worship a deeper quality.

Things are otherwise for those who have no love for others and therefore no conscience. They are able to engage in a show of worship, but it is disconnected from any inward content, just as their faith is disconnected from charity. This kind of worship is called Canaan, and this kind of faith is called Ham; and since a disconnected faith generates this kind of worship, Ham is called Canaan's father.

The fact that *they took a garment* means that they put a good interpretation on the situation follows from earlier comments. Taking a garment and covering someone's nakedness has to symbolize this when an uncovered condition and nakedness symbolize error and perversions. **1084**

The fact that *they put it on their shoulder* means that they did so—that is, put a good interpretation on the situation and excused it—with all their might can be seen from the symbolism of the *shoulder* as all a person's might. In the Word, a hand symbolizes power (demonstrated before [§878]) and an arm symbolizes even greater power, but a shoulder symbolizes all **1085** power. This symbolism can also be seen in the following places in the Word. In Ezekiel:

> With side and *shoulder* you push, and with your horns you strike all the ailing sheep until you scatter them outside. (Ezekiel 34:21)

[To push] with side and shoulder stands for doing so with all one's soul and all one's might, while striking with the horns stands for doing so with all one's strength. [2] In the same author:

> . . . so that all the inhabitants of Egypt will recognize that I am Jehovah, because these have been a staff of reed to the house of Israel. When they seize you by the palm, you will be shattered to pieces and split every *shoulder* of theirs. (Ezekiel 29:6, 7)

This describes people who want to use facts to investigate spiritual truth. The staff of reed stands for the power to do so; seizing by the palm stands for being confident; and splitting every shoulder stands for being stripped of all power, so that they know nothing. [3] In Zephaniah:

> . . . so that they may all call on the name of Jehovah, so that they may serve him with a *single shoulder*. (Zephaniah 3:9)

This stands for doing so with one soul and consequently with united power. In Zechariah:

> They refused to heed and turned a defiant *shoulder*. (Zechariah 7:11)

This stands for the fact that they resisted with all their might. In Isaiah:

> They hire a metalsmith, who makes gold and silver into a god. They worship; they also bow down; they bear it on their *shoulder;* they carry it about. (Isaiah 46:6, 7)

This stands for the fact that they worship the idol with all their might—which is to carry it on their shoulder. [4] In the same author:

> A child has been born for us, a son has been given to us, and sovereignty will be on his *shoulder;* and his name will be called Miraculous, Counselor, God, Hero, Eternal Father, Prince of Peace. (Isaiah 9:6)

This speaks of the Lord, and here specifically of his power and authority, which is why it says, "on his shoulder." In the same author:

> I will put the key of David's house on his *shoulder,* and he will open, and there will be no one closing; and he will close, and there will be no one opening. (Isaiah 22:22)

This verse likewise treats of the Lord. Putting the key of David's house on his shoulder stands for his power and authority.

The fact that *they went backward* means that they paid no attention to errors and perversions can be seen from the meaning of *going backward* as averting one's gaze and not seeing. This meaning is also corroborated below, where it says that they did not see their father's nakedness. In the inner meaning, not seeing something is not paying attention to it.

The fact that *they covered their father's nakedness* means that in doing so they excused those wrongs can again be seen from context. It is also established by the symbolism of nakedness as perversions.

Their faces were backward, and they did not see their father's nakedness, means that this is the proper thing to do, and that we should not concentrate on such wrongs, which are blunders and downfalls resulting from misguided thinking. This can be seen from the repetition involved, since these words are almost exactly the same as those directly above. Taken together, they also bring the matter to an end, because in this parental church—or in a person in this church—misdeeds sprang not from depravity but from naiveté. This is indicated in the very next verse, which says that Noah woke up from his wine, or in other words, learned better.

[2] To delve more deeply into the subject: People lacking in charity think nothing but evil and speak nothing but evil of their neighbor. If they have anything good to say, it is only for their own benefit, or else it is an attempt to ingratiate themselves with the person, under the guise of friendship. But people who love their neighbor think nothing but good and speak nothing but good of others. They do so not for their own sake or to curry favor with another but because it is what results when the Lord stirs their sense of charity.

The former are like the evil spirits and the latter like the angels we have with us. Evil spirits always arouse bad impulses and false ideas in us, and they condemn us. Angels, though, arouse only good impulses and true ideas, and whatever is evil or false they excuse. All of this shows that individuals lacking in charity are under the control of evil spirits, who keep us in touch with hell, while individuals endowed with charity are under the control of angels, who keep us in touch with heaven.

Genesis 9:24. *And Noah woke up from his wine and realized what his younger son had done to him.*

Noah woke up from his wine means when they had learned better. *And realized what his younger son had done to him* means that external worship cut off from internal worship is by nature contemptuous.

1090   The fact that *Noah woke up from his wine* means when they had learned better is evident from the meaning of waking up after drunkenness. Since in verse 21 [§1072] being drunk symbolized falling into error, waking up simply means awakening from error.

1091   *What his younger son had done to him* means that external worship cut off from internal worship is by nature contemptuous. In the literal meaning—the narrative—*his younger son* seems to mean Ham, but the next verse indicates that it means Canaan, because it says, "A curse on Canaan!" And the subsequent verses (26 and 27) say that Canaan will be a slave. For the reason why Ham goes unmentioned, see what is said at the next verse [§1093:3].

The only thing left to explain here is the reason for an arrangement that lists Shem first, Ham second, Japheth third, and Canaan fourth. Charity (Shem) is the first step of religion, faith (Ham) is the second, worship growing out of charity (Japheth) is the third, and an outward show of worship devoid of faith and charity (Canaan) is the fourth.

Charity is the brother of faith, and so too the worship that grows out of charity; but a show of worship without any base in charity is a slave of slaves.

1092   Genesis 9:25. *And he said, "A curse on Canaan! A slave of slaves he will be to his brothers."*

A curse on Canaan means that outward worship detached from inner worship turns its back on the Lord. *A slave of slaves he will be to his brothers* symbolizes the lowliest function in the church.

1093   The fact that *a curse on Canaan* means that outward worship detached from inner worship turns its back on the Lord is established by the symbolism of Canaan and by the symbolism of being cursed. *Canaan* is outward worship detached from inner, as can be seen from what was said about Canaan earlier [§§1063, 1077, 1083:4] and also from his being described as cursed. Again, it can be seen from what follows, where he is called a slave of slaves, and where he is called a slave to both Shem and Japheth. This can only mean something detached from genuine religion, as worship consisting only of external forms is.

The meaning is established by the symbolism of *being cursed* in that being cursed actually means turning one's back. The Lord never curses anyone; he does not even get angry. It is we instead who curse ourselves by turning our backs on the Lord. (For a discussion of this, see what was said and shown above at §§223, 245, 592.) The Lord is as far from cursing or being angry at anyone as heaven is from earth. He is all-knowing and all-powerful and rules the universe in wisdom, so he is infinitely above all weakness. How can anyone believe that he would indulge in anger against such wretched dust as we human beings are, who hardly even know what we are doing and on our own can do nothing but evil? For this reason, the Lord never feels anger but only pity.

[2] Even though Ham was the one who saw his father's nakedness and pointed it out to his brothers, it was not he who was cursed but his son Canaan. This alone indicates that the verse involves a hidden meaning. Canaan was not Ham's only child or even his firstborn but his fourth, as Genesis 10:6 below makes clear, where Ham's children are listed as Cush, Mizraim, Put, and Canaan. What is more, the divine law was that offspring would not bear their parents' sin, as Ezekiel shows:

> The soul that has sinned, that soul shall die. *A child shall not carry the wickedness of the parent,* nor shall a parent carry the wickedness of the child. (Ezekiel 18:20; Deuteronomy 24:16; 2 Kings 14:6)

Yet another indication is the fact that this sin—seeing his father's nakedness and pointing it out to his brothers—was so mild that it never could have been grounds for cursing his entire posterity. These considerations clarify the fact that the verse contains a hidden meaning.

[3] The reason that not Ham but Canaan is mentioned here is that Ham symbolizes faith detached from neighborly love in a spiritual religion. Such faith cannot be cursed, because in a spiritual religion, faith has a holy quality, since it contains truth. Although it is not faith as long as there is no charity, still, since religious knowledge enables us to regenerate, it can be linked with charity. So in some measure it is a "brother," or at least can become a brother. That is why Canaan was cursed and not Ham.

In addition, most of the inhabitants of the land of Canaan were such that they completely identified worship with outward acts—the Jews there just as much as the non-Jews. These are the secrets hidden in the text; and had it not been for them, Canaan would never have been substituted for Ham.

The fact that outward worship separated from inward turns its back and so brings a curse on itself is sufficiently apparent from the focus of people whose worship is external. They look toward worldly, bodily, and earthly values—downward, that is—and immerse their character and their life in such things. People like this are described just below.

1094   The symbolism of *a slave of slaves he will be to his brothers* as the lowliest function in the church can be seen from the nature of outward worship separated from inner.

External worship viewed in itself, without anything internal to sanctify it, is nothing, as anyone can see. What is outward devotion without the heart's devotion but a gesture? What is prayer on the lips without any thought behind it but blather? And what is a given deed without the intent behind it but a kind of nonentity? So every exterior by itself is a lifeless thing; only the interior can give it life.

[2] Many observations in the other life have made it clear to me what outer worship without inner worship is like. People who are witches and sorceresses there attended church and took the sacraments as often as anyone else while still alive in the world. So did cheats (who attended even more faithfully than others). The same is true for those who liked preying on others and for misers. Yet they are hellish and cherish an intense hatred for the Lord and their neighbor. The inner worship within their outward worship had consisted in the effort to be seen by the world, or to obtain their worldly, earthly, and bodily desires, or to deceive people by devout appearances. Either that or it was the result of entrenched habit.

Such individuals are eager to adore any god or idol that caters to them and their corrupt desires. This is especially obvious from the Jews [of the Old Testament], who viewed worship exclusively as a matter of superficial appearance and as a consequence often fell into idolatry. Worship of this kind is inherent, unmitigated idolatry, since outward forms are what the devotees worship.

[3] Non-Jews in the land of Canaan too, who worshiped baals and other gods, had almost the same forms of worship. They had not only temples and altars but sacrifices as well, so that the outer form of their worship differed very little from that of the Jews. The only difference was that they named Baal, Ashtoreth, or some other deity as their god, while the Jews named Jehovah as theirs, just as they do today. They thought that the mere use of Jehovah's name would make them the holy, chosen people. The reality, however, is that it brought them into greater damnation than others, since they were then capable of profaning something holy, which non-Jews were not. Such is the nature of the worship called Canaan, who is said to be a slave of slaves.

To learn how it is that a *slave of slaves* is the lowliest function in the church, see the treatment of the next verse.

Genesis 9:26. *And he said, "A blessing on Jehovah, God of Shem! And*   **1095**
Canaan will be slave to him."

A blessing on Shem's Jehovah means that everything good comes to
those who worship the Lord from deep inside; *Shem* is the inner church.
And Canaan will be slave to him means that the type of individual who
identifies worship exclusively with the outward show of it is among those
who are able to serve people of the church in lowly ways.

The fact that *a blessing on Shem's Jehovah* means that everything good   **1096**
comes to those who worship the Lord from deep inside can be seen from
the symbolism of being *blessed*.

A blessing involves every heavenly and spiritual kind of benefit, and
every earthly kind as well. These are what a blessing symbolizes in an
inner sense. In a shallower sense, it symbolizes every temporal, personal,
and worldly kind of benefit; but if these are to be true blessings, they
have to stem from an inner blessing. Only an inner blessing really is a
blessing, because it is eternal and carries with it a full range of happiness.
An inner blessing is the essential reality of any blessing, because what else
genuinely exists besides what is eternal? Everything else that exists ceases
to exist.

"A blessing on Jehovah!" was a common phrase among the ancients,
and by it they meant that all blessings—everything good, in other
words—came from him. It was also a standard way to thank the Lord for
his benefits in past and present. The phrase occurs in David, for instance,
in Psalms 28:6; 31:21; 41:13; 66:20; 68:19, 35; 72:18, 19; 89:52; 119:12; 124:6;
135:21; 144:1; and in other authors.

[2] The exact wording in this verse is "A blessing on *Jehovah God*"
because it has to do with *Shem,* or the inner church. This church is called
an inner one because of its charity. Charity holds within it the presence
of the Lord, who is accordingly called Jehovah God here. It is not so in
the outer church. In this church the Lord admittedly is present, but not
the same way as he is with the people of the inner church. Those who
belong to the outer church, you see, still believe that they do the good
deeds of charity under their own power, and as a result, the Lord is called
"God" when they are the people being spoken of. The next verse, for
example, which talks about Japheth, says "May God broaden Japheth!"

The fact that everything good comes to those who worship the Lord
from deep inside can also be inferred from the pattern of things. This is
the pattern: the Lord is the source of all heavenly traits, heavenly traits
are the source of all spiritual traits, and spiritual traits are the source of all

earthly traits. This pattern governs the emergence of all things, and it sets the pattern by which those things flow into us.

[3] The heavenly element is love for the Lord and for our neighbor. Where love does not exist, the link is broken and the Lord is not present, since he enters into us only through what is heavenly—that is, through love. When there is no heavenly element, no spiritual element is possible either, because everything spiritual comes from the Lord by way of something heavenly. The spiritual element is faith, so faith is impossible unless it comes from the Lord by way of charity, or love. The same is true of the earthly element.

Everything good flows in according to the same pattern, from which it follows that those who receive it are those who worship the Lord from deep inside, or in other words, from charity. It also follows that people who do not worship him in charity do not receive anything good but the kind of things that merely imitate goodness and are essentially evil. An example is the thrill of hatred and adultery, which, viewed in itself, is no more than a delight in excrement; and this is what it turns into in the other life.

1097 *Canaan will be slave to him* means that the type of individual who identifies worship exclusively with the outward show of it is among those who are able to serve people of the church in lowly ways. This can best be seen from the things that people in the Jewish church represented.

In the Jewish church, Judah and Israel represented the inner church. Judah represented a heavenly church; Israel, a spiritual one; Jacob, the outer church. But people who identified worship exclusively with the outward show of it were represented by non-Jews, whom they called foreigners. These were their *slaves,* who performed menial tasks in that church. In Isaiah, for example:

> *Strangers* will stand and pasture your flock, and the children of a *foreigner* will be your farmers and your vinedressers. And you will be called Jehovah's priests, attendants of our God; it will be said to you, "The wealth of the *gentile nations* you will eat, and their glory you will glory in." (Isaiah 61:5, 6)

Heavenly kinds of people are called Jehovah's priests; spiritual ones, God's attendants. Those who see worship as consisting only in outward appearances are called children of a foreigner, destined to serve in the fields and vineyards. [2] In the same author:

> The *children of a foreigner* will rebuild the walls, and their monarchs will *tend* to you. (Isaiah 60:10)

This verse too mentions their labor as slaves. In Joshua, concerning the Gibeonites:

> "A *curse* on you! And the *slave* will not be cut off from you, or those chopping wood and drawing water for the House of my God." Joshua on that day made them choppers of wood and drawers of water for the assembly—particularly for Jehovah's altar. (Joshua 9:23, 27)

A pact was made with the Gibeonites, though. What kind of people they therefore represented may be seen elsewhere [§§3058, 4431, 6860], but they were among those who would act as servants in the church.

A law was laid down for foreigners, stating that if they accepted peace and opened their gates they would serve as *tribute in the form of slave labor* (Deuteronomy 20:11; 1 Kings 9:21, 22).

Each and every thing written about the Jewish church in the Word represented the Lord's kingdom—a kingdom that by its very nature requires everyone, of whatever identity or character, to do something useful. Nothing but usefulness is regarded by the Lord in his kingdom. Even people in hell have to be useful, but the uses they fill are very lowly. Some of the people doing menial work in the other world are individuals whose worship had been completely external, disconnected as it was from any inner content.

[3] Furthermore, representative meanings in the Jewish church were such that they imply nothing about the person filling a role but only about the phenomenon that the person represented. Jews, for instance, were anything but heavenly people, and yet that is the kind of people they represented. By the same token, Israel was anything but a spiritual person, and yet that is what he represented; and the same for Jacob and all the others—including the monarchs and priests, who nonetheless represented the Lord's royal power and holiness. The point is illustrated even more clearly by the fact that inanimate objects also filled a representative role. These included Aaron's vestments, the altar itself, the tables holding the loaves, the lamps, and the bread and wine, not to mention adult cattle, young cattle, he-goats, sheep, she-goats, lambs, pigeons, and turtledoves.

The children of Judah and Israel merely represented the internal and external worship that takes place in the Lord's church, while more than any other people they considered worship to consist only in outward acts. Consequently they more than any others are the ones who can be called Canaan, in view of his symbolism here.

1098   Anyone who wants to know what Shem and Japheth are—that is, who the people of the inner and outer church are—and by extension what Canaan is, can see from the following.

People in the inner church attribute every good deed they do and every true thought they think to the Lord, but people in the outer church do not know they should do this, although they still do good deeds.

People in the inner church assign crucial importance to charity-based worship of the Lord and in fact to inner worship; outward worship they consider less important. People in the outer church assign crucial importance to outward worship, not knowing what inner worship is, although they do engage in it. So people of the inner church believe they are violating conscience if they do not worship the Lord from within, while people of the outer church believe they are violating conscience if they do not reverently observe the external rituals.

The conscience of a person in the inner church is well supplied, because such a person knows much about the Word's inner meaning. The conscience of a person in the outer church, on the other hand, is less well supplied, since such a person knows little about the Word's inner meaning.

The former (a person in the inner church) is the one called Shem, while the latter (a person in the outer church) is the one called Japheth. But an individual who considers worship exclusively a matter of outward acts, who possesses no charity and therefore no conscience, is called Canaan.

1099   Genesis 9:27. *"May God broaden Japheth! And he will live in Shem's tents. And Canaan will be slave to him."*

Japheth symbolizes the corresponding outer church, as he did above. *May God broaden Japheth!* symbolizes its enlightenment. *And he will live in Shem's tents* means so that the inner dimensions of worship exist within the outward forms. *And Canaan will be slave to him* here as before means that those who identify worship solely with external forms can serve in lowly ways.

1100   I have already said that *Japheth* symbolizes the corresponding outer church [§§1062, 1083]. What is meant by "the outer church" has also been stated; to be specific, it is outward worship, and consequently it is those who do not know what the inner self is, or what belongs to the inner self, but who still live in charity. The Lord is equally present with these people, because he operates through charity, wherever it exists.

The situation resembles that of little children, who have no idea what charity is, still less what faith is, despite which the Lord's presence is much stronger with them than with adults, especially when the children

live a life of shared kindness. It is the same with simple-thinking people
who have innocence, charity, and mercy.

Knowing a lot makes no difference if we do not live by what we
know, since the only point in knowing anything is to be shaped by it—
specifically, into good people. When we have become good, we gain
far more than people who know countless facts without being good,
because what they seek to obtain from their vast knowledge, we already
possess. It is quite different, though, with a person whose knowledge of
truth and goodness is deep and broad, who at the same time has charity
and conscience, and who is part of the inner church, or in other words,
is Shem.

People who know little but possess a conscience become enlightened
in the next life—so enlightened that they turn into angels; and then their
wisdom and understanding is beyond words. These are the people symbolized by Japheth.

May God broaden Japheth! symbolizes that church's enlightenment.
In a literal sense *broadening* means enlarging the borders, but in an inner
sense it means being enlightened. Being enlightened is like having the
borders of one's wisdom and understanding enlarged, as in Isaiah:

1101

> *Broaden* the place of your *tent,* and let the tent curtains of your dwell-
> ings stretch out. (Isaiah 54:2)

This stands for being enlightened in spiritual matters.

People in the outer church are broadened when they learn about the
true ideas and good impulses of faith, and since they are under the influence of charity, they grow more and more convinced of what they learn.
The more they learn, the more it scatters the clouds obscuring their intellectual side, which houses their charity and conscience.

He will live in Shem's tents means so that the inner dimensions of
worship exist within the outward forms. This meaning is established by
all the things said about Shem so far: Shem is the inner church, or inward
worship, and outward worship is only some lifeless, dirty thing without
inward worship to give it life and sanctify it.

1102

The fact that *tents* simply mean holy love and the worship that grows
out of it can be seen from the symbolism of tents, given earlier, at §414.
The ancients habitually used the phrases *travel with tents* and *reside in
tents,* which in an inner sense symbolized sacred worship, because the
earliest people both moved around and settled down in tents, conducting
their sacred worship in them. On an inner level, as a result, migrating
and setting up residence also symbolized living.

[2] In addition to the passages quoted earlier, in §414, let the following serve to confirm that tents symbolize sacred worship. In David:

> God deserted his dwelling place at Shiloh, the *tent* where he *lived* among humankind. (Psalms 78:60)

The tent has the same symbolism as a temple, and God is said to live in it when he is present with humankind in love. The ancients accordingly called an individual who lived a life of sacred worship a tent, and later a temple. In Isaiah:

> Broaden the place of your *tent,* and let the tent curtains of your dwellings stretch out. (Isaiah 54:2)

This stands for enlightenment regarding the elements of true worship. In Jeremiah:

> The whole earth was devastated. In an instant were my *tents* devastated; in a moment, my tent curtains. (Jeremiah 4:20)

Obviously it is not tents but holy worship that is meant here. In Zechariah:

> Jerusalem will still *dwell* in its place—in Jerusalem. Jehovah will save the *tents* of Judah. (Zechariah 12:6, 7)

The tents of Judah stand for worshiping the Lord in the holiness of love.

[3] These passages illustrate what it is to live in Shem's tents: to have inward worship within one's outer worship.

But since the human being called Japheth (the person who is in the outer church) does not really know what the inner dimension is, it must be spelled out briefly. Sometimes we might sense or perceive inside ourselves that we are thinking rightly about the Lord, and that we are thinking rightly about our neighbors and wanting to render them assistance without looking for any financial reward or prestige for ourselves. Sometimes we might also feel sympathy for those who are suffering calamity and even greater sympathy for those who are misled about religious doctrine. At these times we can be sure that we are living in Shem's tents, or in other words, that we have inside us a deeper dimension through which the Lord can work.

1103   The meaning of *Canaan will be slave to him* as the fact that those who identify worship solely with external forms can perform lowly duties is established by the things said about Canaan as a slave above, in the last verses—25 and 26 [§§1094, 1097].

To be sure, people like this are not slaves in the Lord's church on earth. Many of them occupy top positions, higher than anyone else. Nothing that they do has its basis in charity or conscience, although they observe the external requirements of religion very strictly and even condemn those who do not. But there is a consequence to the fact that they have no neighborly love or conscience and consider the outward show, devoid of inner content, to be the whole of worship. The consequence is that they are slaves in the Lord's kingdom (the other life), unfortunates that they are. The tasks they perform are menial and too numerous to discuss in detail. (I will have more to say on them later, however, by the Lord's divine mercy.)

[2] Everyone, no matter who, has to do useful work in the next life. We are born for no purpose but to be useful to the community we live in and to our neighbor as long as we are alive in the world, and to serve at the Lord's good pleasure in the other world.

The situation resembles that in the human body. Every part of our anatomy has to serve a function, including elements that in themselves are worthless—fluids that exist to be excreted, for instance, as the many types of saliva do, and the different types of bile, and others. Not only do they have to work on the food, they also have to extract waste products and clean out the intestines. Another parallel is the manure and dung used on fields and in vineyards. And so on.

Genesis 9:28, 29. *And Noah lived after the flood for three hundred fifty* **1104**
years. And all Noah's days were nine hundred fifty years; and he died.

This symbolizes the length of time the first ancient church lasted and conditions in that church as well.

This symbolism is sufficiently clear from earlier remarks about num- **1105**
bers and years, which may be seen at §§482, 487, 488, 493, 575, 647, 648.

Spiritual Devastation

THERE are many people who in their naiveté and ignorance soaked **1106**
up falsities about religion while they were in the world, developed a certain brand of conscience harmonizing with the principles of their faith, and, unlike some others, did not live a life of hatred, revenge, and

adultery. In the next world, they cannot be admitted into heavenly society as long as their ideas remain false, because if they were, they would contaminate it. So they are kept in an underground region for some time in order to slough off their false assumptions there. The period of their stay in that place is longer or shorter, depending on the nature of their false thinking and the kind of life it led them to adopt, and depending also on the degree to which they have cemented such principles in their minds. Some people suffer rather harshly there, some not so harshly.

This is what is called devastation, and mention of it comes up quite often in the Word.

When their period of devastation has ended, they are lifted into heaven, where as novices they receive instruction in religious truth. The angels who welcome them are their teachers.

1107 Some are very willing to be devastated, or purged, and so rid themselves of the false premises they have dragged with them from the world. (No one can ever shed false assumptions in the next life except over time and through means that the Lord provides.) While they stay in the underground realm, the Lord maintains in them a hope for deliverance. He also keeps them thinking about the goal, which is to change for the better and become ready to accept heaven's happiness.

1108 Some remain in a state midway between wakefulness and sleep, thinking little, except from time to time when they seem to waken and remember the things they had thought and done during bodily life. Then they fall back into a state midway between waking and sleeping. This is the way they are purged.

They are under the left foot, out in front a little.

1109 People who had fully confirmed themselves in misguided principles are reduced to total ignorance, and then they feel so dark and confused that when they merely think about the ideas they had confirmed themselves in, they suffer deep-seated pain.

When their time has finished, though, they are created anew, in a manner of speaking, and they absorb the truth that faith embraces.

1110 Some people had claimed that good deeds would make them virtuous and earn them credit, and in this way they assigned to themselves—not to the Lord and his virtue and merit—the ability to achieve salvation. They had hardened this idea in themselves by the way they thought and the way they lived. In the other life, their misguided assumptions turn into hallucinations, in which they seem to themselves to be cutting wood; this is exactly how it appears to them. I have talked with them;

and if asked while at their work whether they are tired, they answer that they have not yet done enough work to earn heaven.

While they are cutting wood, it appears as though something of the Lord lies under the logs, so that the wood is the merit. The more of the Lord there is in the pieces of wood, the longer they remain wood-cutters, but when it begins to vanish, the period of devastation is drawing to its close.

Finally they arrive at a point where they can be allowed into good communities, but for a long time they continue to go back and forth between a true idea and a false one. Because they have lived a devout life, they are objects of particular care to the Lord, and he repeatedly sends them angels.

These are the ones who were represented in the Jewish religion by the woodcutters in Joshua 9:23, 27.

Some people had lived a life of civic and moral good but had convinced themselves they would earn heaven by their deeds, believing it sufficient to acknowledge the one God as the creator of the universe. In the other life, their false assumptions turn into hallucinations in which they seem to themselves to be mowing grass, and they are called grass cutters. They are cold and do the mowing in an effort to warm up. Sometimes they wander around asking the people they meet, "Would you lend me some warmth?" Imparting warmth is something that spirits are indeed capable of, but the kind these people receive does nothing for them, because it is superficial, when what they crave is inner heat. So they go back to their mowing and warm themselves by their work. I felt their chill.

They are constantly hopeful of being taken up into heaven. Sometimes they seek advice on how to make it there under their own power.

Since they did do good deeds, they are among those who undergo devastation, and when their term is completed, they are finally accepted into good communities, where they receive instruction.

People who had immersed themselves in the good effects and true ideas of faith, on the other hand, and who had in this way acquired conscience and a life of charity, are raised into heaven by the Lord immediately after death.

There are girls who had been led into promiscuity and consequently persuaded that there is nothing wrong with such behavior but whose character had been upright in all other respects. Because they have not yet reached an age at which they can understand or evaluate this way of life, they are given a personal tutor—a fairly strict one—who reprimands them whenever they fantasize about committing such indecencies. This tutor they fear intensely. That is how they are purged.

But full-grown women who were prostitutes and recruited other women do not undergo devastation. They are in hell.

Genesis 10

The Earliest Church, Called "Humankind," or Adam

ANGELS and spirits, or in other words, human beings after death, **1114** can meet anyone they want—anyone they had known in the world or heard of—when the Lord grants it. They can see such people in person and talk with them, and what is amazing, the person desired appears instantly, face to face. So it is possible to converse not only with friends (and friends usually find each other) but also with other people one had admired and revered.

The Lord in his divine mercy has given me the opportunity to talk not only to people I knew when they were alive in the body but also with leading figures in the Word; likewise with people from the earliest church—the one called Humankind, or Adam—and with some adherents of later churches too. The purpose was to show me that the personal names in the early chapters of Genesis only mean different religions and to teach me what people in the churches of that era were like.

The things I learned about the earliest churches, then, are the following.

People who had been part of the earliest church, which was called **1115** Humankind, or Adam—heavenly people—are high up overhead, where they live together in sublime happiness. They said that others rarely approach them, except for the occasional visitor from elsewhere, or as they put it, from the universe.

Their position so high above the head, they added, was not due to inflated pride; on the contrary, the goal was to allow them to govern the people there.

I was shown the houses of the people who belonged to the second **1116** and third generations of this earliest church, and they are magnificent. They are very long, and each displays various beautiful shades of deep red and of blue.

Angels have houses that are simply glorious—so glorious that words could never describe them. I have seen these houses many times. They appear so vividly before the sight of their inhabitants that nothing could strike the eyes more vividly; but the reason why the visual experience is so intense will be explained later [§§1619–1633], in the Lord's divine mercy.

They live in an aura of pearly light (so to speak) and sometimes in one of diamondlike radiance. In the next life, countless different varieties of atmosphere exist, and they are incredible. People are seriously mistaken if they do not consider such things possible there, and infinitely more of them than anyone ever has been or ever will be able to picture. It is true that these things exist as representations, as did some of the sights the prophets saw, but they are so vivid that they are completely real to the inhabitants of the next world and make the objects of this world seem unreal by comparison.

1117 They live in the greatest possible light. The light of the world can hardly be compared to the light in which they live. That light was shown to me in the form of a flame that more or less streamed down in front of my eyes, and the people who had come from the earliest church told me that they had the same kind of light, only brighter.

1118 By means of a kind of inspiration I cannot describe, I was shown how they had talked when they were alive in the world. Their speech was not articulated, as the verbal speech we use today is, but silent, produced not by external but by internal breathing. I also had the opportunity to sense what their internal breathing was like. It moved from the navel to the heart and then out through the lips without a sound. It did not enter another person's ear from outside and vibrate on the part called the ear drum but traced a path through the mouth and in fact through a passageway there that we now call the Eustachian tube.

I was shown that this kind of speech enabled them to express the thoughts of their heart and the ideas in their minds much more fully than articulated sounds or audible words ever could. Audible sounds too travel on the breath (external breath, though), because no word contains any element that can be conveyed without the use of breath. But the process was much more perfect with them, because it relied on internal breathing. Since internal breathing takes place on a deeper plane, it is more perfect and better adapted to the actual ideas in our heads.

In addition, they used subtle motions of the lips and corresponding facial changes. Since they were a heavenly kind of people, everything they thought shone out from their face and eyes, which altered to suit the thought. They were completely incapable of any facial expression that did not agree with their thinking. They considered pretense a heinous crime and deceit even worse.

I had a practical demonstration of the way the internal breathing of the earliest people entered silently into a type of external breathing they had and so into soundless speech. Listeners heard this speech in their inner self.

1119

They said this kind of respiration varied in them, depending on the state of their love for the Lord and faith in him. They told the reason, too, which was that since they were communicating with heaven, they were necessarily breathing in rhythm with the angels who kept them company. Angels do have respiration, and any inner breathing keeps pace with it. They undergo similar changes in their breathing, because when anything arises to oppose love for the Lord or faith in him, they have difficulty breathing, but when they enjoy the good cheer of love and faith, their breathing is free and full. Everyone on earth experiences something similar, but it occurs in connection with our bodily and worldly passions and our convictions. When anything opposes these, we choke, but when anything caters to them, we breathe freely and fully. These facts, however, relate to external breathing.

I will have more to say on the respiration of the angels later [§§3883–3895], though, with the Lord's divine mercy.

I was also shown that the inner breathing of the people in the earliest church, which had flowed from the navel toward the deeper areas of the chest, had altered as time passed—that is, had altered in their descendants. It had withdrawn more toward the back and the belly, or more toward the surface and downward, until finally in the last generation of that church (the generation right before the Flood), hardly any internal breathing remained. In the end, when the breathing inside the chest disappeared, they spontaneously suffocated.

1120

In some people, though, external breathing then took hold, as did articulated sounds, or verbal speech.

As I was shown, these are the ways people living before the Flood breathed, depending on the state of their love and faith. In the end, when there was no longer love or faith but only a convinced belief in falsity, internal breathing stopped, as did direct communication with angels and perceptive knowledge.

The progeny of the earliest church have taught me about the level of perception they had enjoyed. They had possessed the ability to perceive

1121

any proposition of faith, almost to the same degree as angels, with whom they communicated. One reason was that their inner self—their spirit— was united to heaven by means of internal breathing. Another was that love for the Lord and love for one's neighbor carry this communication with them, because these two kinds of love unite people on earth with angels through the essential core of their life, which consists in such love. They said they had the law written in them because they loved the Lord and their neighbor, since everything the laws require consequently agreed with their perception and everything the laws prohibit conflicted with their perception.

They had no doubt that all human laws resembled divine laws in being founded on love for the Lord and charity for one's neighbor and in looking to love and charity as their basis.

Of course since they had a foundation from the Lord inside themselves, they knew everything that was built on it.

They believe too that all those alive in the world today who love the Lord and their neighbor also have the law written in them and are welcomed as citizens anywhere on earth, just as any such people are welcomed in the other life.

1122   I learned further that people in the earliest church had the most pleasant dreams, and visions as well, and that the meanings of the dreams and visions were suggested to them at the same time. This led to their use of paradise and other images as metaphors.

The objects of their outer senses, which belonged to the earth and the world, accordingly meant nothing to them. They felt no pleasure in those things but only in what they symbolized and represented. As a result, when they saw earthly objects, they did not think at all about them but only about the qualities they symbolized and represented. Such qualities inspired them with great pleasure, because these were the kinds of things that existed in heaven and revealed the Lord to them.

1123   I talked to the third generation of the earliest church, and they said that in their day on earth they looked forward to the arrival of the Lord, who was to save the human race. It was common, they said, for them to speak of the fact that the woman's seed would trample the snake's head [Genesis 3:15].

They went on to say that from that time on, the greatest exhilaration of their lives had been to have children, with the result that their highest pleasure was loving their spouse in order to produce offspring. They called this their most enjoyable delight and their most delightful joy. The

perception of this thrill and pleasure, they added, came from the idea
flowing out of heaven that the Lord would be born.

Some of their descendants living before the Flood—not those who
were destroyed in it but others of somewhat better character—were present with me, and at first they exerted a fairly gentle influence that was
not very noticeable. But I was able to perceive that deep down they were
bad, and deep down they worked against love. An aura with the stench
of dead flesh wafted from them, making the spirits around me run away.
They thought they were so subtle that no one would be able to tell what
they were thinking.

§1124

I carried on a conversation with them about the Lord, asking whether
like their forbears they had awaited his Coming. They had represented
the Lord to themselves, they said, as an old and godly individual with a
white beard and because of him became devout and grew beards themselves. That is the origin of the religious scruple about beards that sprang
up among their descendants. Even now they were able to worship him
devoutly, they added, although they did so according to their own lights;
but just then an angel approached whose coming they could not bear.

I was also allowed to talk with some who had belonged to the church
called Enosh, mentioned in Genesis 4:26. They flowed into me gently
and spoke modestly, saying that they live in charity among themselves
and do their social duty by any others who visit them. It was plain,
though, that they extended their charity only to friends.

§1125

They live peaceably, never troubling anyone, as the good citizens
they are.

I saw a narrow room, and through an open door there came into view
a tall man dressed in white—a very intense white. I wondered who he
was. They said that a man in white symbolized those who were referred
to as Noah, or in other words, those who were the very first people in the
ancient church—the church that followed the Flood. Those people were
represented this way, they said, because their numbers were small.

§1126

I had the privilege of talking to people from the ancient church (the
church following the Flood) who had been referred to as Shem. They
flowed in gently through the area of my head into my chest area, heading
for my heart but not reaching it.

§1127

The way spirits flow in indicates what they are like.

I saw someone wreathed in a kind of cloud, on whose face were quite
a few wandering stars, which symbolize falsities. It was said that this was
what the descendants of the ancient church were like when it started to

§1128

die out, especially among those who established a cult involving the use of sacrifices and images.

1129 More on the pre-Flood people who were wiped out follows at the end of the chapter [§§1265–1272].

Genesis 10

1. And these are the births of Noah's sons: Shem, Ham, and Japheth; and sons were born to them after the flood.

2. The sons of Japheth: Gomer, and Magog, and Madai, and Javan, and Tubal, and Meshech, and Tiras.

3. And the sons of Gomer: Ashkenaz, and Riphath, and Togarmah.

4. And the sons of Javan: Elishah and Tarshish, Kittim and Dodanim.

5. From these the islands of the nations dispersed in their lands, each by its tongue, by their clans, in their nations.

6. And the sons of Ham: Cush, and Mizraim, and Put, and Canaan.

7. And the sons of Cush: Seba, and Havilah, and Sabtah, and Raamah, and Sabteca. And the sons of Raamah: Sheba and Dedan.

8. And Cush fathered Nimrod; he began to be mighty on the earth.

9. He was mighty in hunting before the face of Jehovah. For this reason there was a saying: "Like Nimrod, mighty in hunting before the face of Jehovah."

10. And the beginning of his kingdom was Babel, and Erech, and Accad, and Calneh, in the land of Shinar.

11. From that same land, Asshur went out and built Nineveh, and the city Rehoboth, and Calah,

12. and Resen, between Nineveh and Calah (this is the great city).

13. And Mizraim fathered the Ludim, and Anamim, and Lehabim, and Naphtuhim,

14. and Pathrusim, and Casluhim (from whom the Pelishtim came), and Caphtorim.

15. And Canaan fathered Sidon, his firstborn, and Heth,

16. and the Jebusite, and Amorite, and Girgashite,

17. and Hivite, and Arkite, and Sinite,

18. and Arvadite, and Zemarite, and Hamathite. And after that, the clans of the Canaanites scattered.

19. And the border of the Canaanites reached from Sidon as you come to Gerar, as far as Gaza, as you come to Sodom and Gomorrah and Admah and Zeboiim, as far as Lasha.

20. These are Ham's sons by their clans, by their tongues, in their lands, in their nations.

21. And Shem too had offspring. He was the father of all the sons of Eber; he was the older brother of Japheth.

22. The sons of Shem: Elam, and Asshur, and Arpachshad, and Lud, and Aram.

23. And the sons of Aram: Uz, and Hul, and Gether, and Mash.

24. And Arpachshad fathered Shelah, and Shelah fathered Eber.

25. And to Eber were born two sons. The name of one was Peleg (because in his days the land was divided), and the name of his brother was Joktan.

26. And Joktan fathered Almodad, and Sheleph, and Hazarmaveth, and Jerah,

27. and Hadoram, and Uzal, and Diklah,

28. and Obal, and Abimael, and Sheba,

29. and Ophir, and Havilah, and Jobab; all these are the sons of Joktan.

30. And their living space reached from Mesha as you come to Sephar, the mountain of the east.

31. These are Shem's sons, by their clans, by their tongues, in their lands, by their nations.

32. These are the clans of Noah's sons, by their births, in their nations, and from them the nations scattered in the land after the flood.

Summary

THIS whole chapter deals with the ancient church and the propagation of it (verse 1).

1130

Those who engaged in outward worship that corresponded to inner worship are the sons of Japheth (verse 2). Those who engaged in a form of it that was further removed from inner worship are the sons of Gomer and Javan (verses 3, 4). Those whose worship was even further removed are the islands of the nations (verse 5).

1131

Those who revered knowledge, facts, and ritual and separated them from any deeper properties are the sons of Ham (verse 6). The ones who

1132

revered the knowledge of spiritual things are the sons of Cush, while the ones who revered the knowledge of heavenly things are the sons of Raamah (verse 7).

1133 The next subject is those who engage in outward worship that holds evil and falsity within it. Nimrod is that kind of worship (verses 8, 9). The evil in that kind of worship (verse 10). The falsity in it (verses 11, 12).

1134 Those who take facts, apply logic to them, and in this way invent new forms of worship for themselves (verses 13, 14). Those who turn religious knowledge into a mere system of fact (verse 14).

1135 External without internal worship (which is Canaan), and what developed out of it (verses 15, 16, 17, 18). How far it extended (verses 19, 20).

1136 Inward worship (which is Shem) and the fact that it extended to the second ancient church too (verse 21). Inward worship and what developed out of it. Because those developments stem from neighborly love, they have to do with wisdom, understanding, secular learning, and religious knowledge, which the various nations symbolize (verses 22, 23, 24).

1137 A certain religion that came into existence in Syria and that was established by Eber, which should be called the second ancient church. Its internal worship is Peleg; its external worship, Joktan (verse 25). Its rituals, which are the nations named (verses 26, 27, 28, 29). How far this religion extended (verse 30).

1138 There were different kinds of worship in the ancient church, and they suited the character of each nation (verses 31, 32).

Inner Meaning

1139 IT was said earlier that the Word has four different writing modes: (1) the mode of the earliest church, which resembled the manner of writing in Genesis from its first chapter up to the present one, (2) the narrative mode, which is seen in the rest of Moses and in all the other narrative books, (3) the prophetic mode, and (4) a mode midway between the prophetic kind and people's usual way of speaking. For more on this, see §66.

1140 The mode of the earliest church continues through this chapter and the next up to the mention of Eber, but it is halfway between a made-up story and true history. Noah and his offspring—Shem, Ham, Japheth, and

Canaan—did not and do not mean anything but the ancient church in respect to its worship, in the abstract. Specifically, Shem means inner worship; Japheth, outward worship that corresponds to it; Ham, inner worship corrupted; and Canaan, outward worship detached from inner. These particular people never existed. Instead, different kinds of worship were given their names, because all the different forms of worship, or all the specific differences among them, could be reduced to these basic kinds.

Noah, then, simply meant the ancient church in general, embracing all types of worship, as their progenitor.

Still, aside from those of Eber and his descendants, the names in the current chapter mean individual nations, and all of them were nations forming a part of the ancient church. That church was scattered far and wide in the lands surrounding Canaan.

All the people referred to here as Japheth's sons were such that they engaged in outward worship corresponding to inner worship. In other words, they lived in simple innocence, friendship, and mutual kindness, unaware of any doctrinal affairs beyond their outward ritual. **1141**

The people referred to as Ham's sons were those who engaged in inward worship that had been corrupted.

The people called Canaan's sons were those who engaged in external worship detached from internal.

The people termed Shem's sons were people of depth who worshiped the Lord and loved their neighbor, and their church closely resembled the genuine version of our Christian church.

The present chapter does not specify what these people were like, since it merely lists them by name, but the prophets' writings clarify it, where the names of these nations come up, as they often do. In each of those passages, the names have no other meaning [than that mentioned here], although it sometimes applies in a positive sense and sometimes in a negative. **1142**

Despite the fact that these were the actual names of the nations that made up the ancient church, they mean something on an inner level—specifically, the types of worship themselves. **1143**

The inhabitants of heaven have no idea what the names, the lands, the nations, and so on are. No concept of such things exists there, only a concept of the entities they symbolize.

The inner meaning gives the Lord's Word life. That meaning is like a soul whose body is the superficial sense. The case resembles that with human beings; when our body dies—when we join the angels—our soul comes alive, and when our soul lives, we no longer know anything of bodily affairs. By the same token, we no longer know what the literal meaning of the Word is, only what its soul is.

[2] The people of the earliest church were like this, and if they were alive today and read the Word, they would not become bogged down in the literal meaning. It would be as if they did not see the letter but only the inner meaning apart from the letter. In fact it would be as if the letter did not exist. So they would fasten on to the life or soul of the Word.

This is the situation throughout the Word, including the historical parts, which report exactly what happened but contain not even one little word that does not enfold hidden meanings on an inner plane. These meanings are never seen by readers who train their attention on the historical context.

Likewise in the current chapter; in the literal sense or the narrative, the names mean the peoples that made up the ancient church, but in the inner sense they mean the doctrinal concepts of those peoples.

1144 Genesis 10:1. *And these are the births of Noah's sons: Shem, Ham, and Japheth; and sons were born to them after the flood.*

These are births of Noah's sons symbolizes the doctrinal matters and types of worship that developed in the ancient church, which in general is Noah. *Shem, Ham, and Japheth,* have the same symbolism as before; *Shem* symbolizes true inner worship, *Ham* symbolizes inner worship corrupted, and *Japheth* symbolizes outer worship corresponding to inner. *And sons were born to them* symbolizes the doctrinal matters that developed out of their worship. *After the flood* means from the time when this new religion came into existence.

1145 The symbolism of *these are the births of Noah's sons* as the doctrinal matters and types of worship that developed in the ancient church, which in general is Noah, can be seen from the symbolism of births, discussed above [§§89, 469–474, 610].

The superficial or literal meaning of *births,* of course, is the generating of one person from another, but on an inner level everything focuses on heavenly and spiritual elements, or the properties of charity and faith. So the births here have to do with aspects of religion and consequently with doctrinal affairs. This will be easier to see from what follows.

1146 *Shem, Ham, and Japheth* have the same symbolism as before; *Shem* symbolizes true inner worship, *Ham* symbolizes inner worship corrupted, and *Japheth* symbolizes outer worship corresponding to inner. This can be seen from earlier statements about them [§§1062–1063, 1065, 1075–1103]. Those statements not only show that Shem, Ham, and Japheth symbolize these types of worship but also explain what true inner worship (Shem) means, what corrupted inner worship (Ham) means, and what outer worship corresponding to inner (Japheth) means. There is no need, then, to dwell further on the symbolism.

The symbolism of *and sons were born to them* as the doctrinal matters that developed out of their worship can be seen from the symbolism of *sons* on an inner level as religious truth, and as religious falsity too, and accordingly as doctrinal matters. "Doctrinal matters" refers to both true ideas and false ones, since the doctrinal approaches of the churches reflect both kinds of ideas. **1147**

For this symbolism of sons, see above at §§264, 489, 491, 533.

The meaning of *after the flood* as from the time when this new religion came into existence is again established by remarks made in previous chapters, since the *flood* depicts the end of the earliest church, and the beginning of the ancient church as well. **1148**

Please keep in mind that the name of the church that preceded the Flood is the earliest church, while that of the church following it is the ancient church.

Genesis 10:2. *The sons of Japheth: Gomer, and Magog, and Madai, and Javan, and Tubal, and Meshech, and Tiras.* **1149**

The *sons of Japheth* symbolize those who engaged in outward worship corresponding to inward. *Gomer, Magog, Madai, Javan, Tubal, Meshech, and Tiras* were individual nations who practiced this kind of worship; and in an inner sense they symbolize individual systems of doctrine, each different from the others, which were the same as the rituals that they reverently observed.

The symbolism of the *sons of Japheth* as those who engaged in outward worship corresponding to inward has been mentioned already [§§1062, 1083, 1096, 1098, 1099–1102]. **1150**

Outward worship is described as corresponding to inward when it contains the essential ingredient, which is heartfelt reverence for the Lord. Such reverence is not possible in the least except where charity, or love for one's neighbor, exists. Charity, or love for our neighbor, contains the Lord's presence. With it, we can adore the Lord from the heart. When we have charity, our reverence comes from the Lord, since the Lord gives us all the ability to revere him and all the vital essence of our veneration. It follows, then, that the kind of charity we have determines the quality of our adoration, that is, the quality of our worship. All worship is veneration, because it has to have reverence for the Lord within it in order to be worshipful.

[2] Japheth's sons, or the nations and peoples called Japheth's sons, lived together in mutual kindness, friendship, politeness, and simple innocence, so the Lord was also present in their worship. When the Lord infuses outward worship, internal worship is present in external; in other words, external worship then answers to internal.

Most non-Christian nations were once like this, and even today there exist some that view worship as a matter of external acts, unaware of any internal facet or, if they *are* aware, without any thought about it. If they acknowledge the Lord and love their fellow humans, the Lord is within their worship and they are Japheth's children. If they deny the Lord, however, and love only themselves, if they do not care about others or, worse, hate them, their worship is shallow and detached from inner worship. Then they are Canaan's children, or Canaanites.

1151   *Gomer, Magog, Madai, Javan, Tubal, Meshech, and Tiras* were individual nations who practiced this kind of worship; and in an inner sense they symbolize individual systems of doctrine, which were the same as the rituals that they devoutly observed. This is clear from the Word, where the names of these nations recur quite often. In each place, they symbolize outward worship—in one place, outward worship corresponding to inward; in another, outward worship opposed to inward. The reason it sometimes symbolizes worship opposed is that all religions, wherever they exist, have changed with the passage of time and have even become the opposite of what they were.

As noted, other passages from the Word can demonstrate that the nations listed here simply symbolized outward worship and consequently the doctrinal elements of those nations, which were their rituals. The prophets are especially full of such proofs. [2] This is what Ezekiel says about *Magog, Meshech, Tubal,* and *Gomer:*

> Child of humankind, turn your face toward Gog, the land of Magog, the chief, the head of *Meshech* and *Tubal,* and prophesy over it, and you are to say, "This is what the Lord Jehovih has said: 'Here, now, I am against you, *Gog,* you chief, you head of *Meshech* and *Tubal.* And I will bring you back and put hooks into your jaws and lead you and your whole army out—horses and riders, all dressed perfectly, a large assembly, with shield and buckler, all of them grasping swords. And with them will be Persia, Cush, and Put; with them will be *Gomer* and all its wings; *Beth-togarmah*—the flanks of the north—and all its wings. In the aftertime of years, you will come over a land that has returned from the sword, that has been gathered from many peoples,

on Israel's mountains, which have become a wasteland.'" (Ezekiel 38:2, 3, 4, 5, 6, 8)

This whole chapter speaks of the church, which has become perverted and in the end has relegated all worship to external acts, or ritual, blotting out charity, which is symbolized by Israel's mountains. In this passage, Gog and the land of Magog—the chief and the head of Meshech and Tubal—is an outward show of worship.

Anyone can see that Gog and Magog are not the focus. The Lord's Word deals not with worldly subjects but with divine matters.

[3] In the same author:

> Prophesy over *Gog,* and you are to say, "This is what the Lord Jehovih has said: 'Here, now, I am against you, *Gog,* you chief, you head of *Meshech* and *Tubal,* and I will bring you back and destroy a sixth of you. I will bring you up from the flanks of the north and lead you onto Israel's mountains. On Israel's mountains you will fall—you and all your wings and the peoples who are with you.'" (Ezekiel 39:1, 2, 4)

This whole chapter likewise talks about outward worship that has been separated from inward and turned into idolatry, which is what Gog, Meshech, and Tubal symbolize here. The same tribes also mean the doctrinal concepts that people who worship in this way seize on and then confirm by use of the Word's literal meaning. In this way they falsify truth and destroy inner worship. After all, as I said above, the same nations have a symbolism opposite to their positive meaning. [4] In John:

> When the thousand years have ended, Satan will be released from his prison and go out to mislead the nations that are at the four corners of the earth—*Gog* and *Magog*—in order to gather them for battle. They went up over the plain of the earth and surrounded the camp of the godly, the well-loved city. (Revelation 20:7, 8, 9)

Gog and Magog symbolize similar things here. Outward worship cut off from inward—cut off, that is, from love for the Lord and love for others—is just idolatry, which surrounds the camp of the godly and the well-loved city.

[5] This is what Ezekiel says about Meshech and Tubal:

> There are *Meshech* and *Tubal* and its entire horde, its graves all around it, all its people uncircumcised, stabbed by the sword, because they put terror of themselves in the land of the living. (Ezekiel 32:26)

This refers to Egypt, or facts, which people want to use in exploring spiritual issues. Meshech and Tubal stand for ritual as a doctrinal matter. It is described as uncircumcised when it is devoid of love, and this is why it is "stabbed by the sword" and why there is "terror in the land of the living."

[6] *Javan* is spoken of in Joel:

> The children of Judah and the children of Jerusalem you have sold to the children of the *Javanites,* to move them far away from their own border. (Joel 3:6)

The children of Judah stand for heavenly aspects of faith and the children of Jerusalem for its spiritual aspects, so they stand for inner qualities. The children of the Javanites stand for an outward show of worship detached from any inner participation. This kind of worship is distant from inward worship, which is why the passage says that they moved the children of Judah and Jerusalem far away from their own border.

[7] In Isaiah, Javan and Tubal stand for worship in its genuine external form:

> [The time] to gather all nations and tongues is coming, and they will come and see my glory. And I will put a mark on them and send some of them—escapees—to the nations *Tarshish,* Put and Lud (drawing the bow), *Tubal* and *Javan* (the distant islands), which have not heard of my fame and have not seen my glory. And they will tell of my glory among the nations. (Isaiah 66:18, 19)

This is about the Lord's kingdom and his Coming. Tubal and Javan stand for those who engage in external worship that corresponds to internal, who need to be taught about internal qualities.

1152 Genesis 10:3, 4. *And the sons of Gomer: Ashkenaz, and Riphath, and Togarmah. And the sons of Javan: Elishah and Tarshish, Kittim and Dodanim.*

The *sons of Gomer* also symbolize people who engaged in outward worship, but in a form of it that developed out of the kind adopted by the nation of Gomer. *Ashkenaz, Riphath, and Togarmah* were individual nations where this form of worship existed, and they also symbolize individual doctrinal systems that consisted in rituals derived from the outward worship adopted by Gomer. The *sons of Javan* symbolize yet another group: those who had an outward form of worship that developed out of the worship adopted by the nation of Javan. *Elishah, Tarshish, Kittim, and Dodanim* were individual nations where this form of worship existed, and they also symbolize individual doctrinal systems that consisted in rituals derived from the outward worship adopted by Javan.

The *sons of Gomer* also symbolize people who engaged in outward worship, but in a form of it that developed out of the kind adopted by the nation of Gomer. This follows from several previous statements and explanations regarding the symbolism of sons and from the fact that Gomer is one of the nations that engaged in external worship corresponding to internal.

1153

The previous verse names seven nations that practiced this kind of worship; the present verse names seven more, which are called sons of Gomer and Javan. The precise difference between one nation and another cannot be described, because only their names appear here. The prophets, though, where they deal specifically with this or that type of worship in the church, can clarify the differences.

Speaking generally, all differences in outward worship (and in inward worship too) mirror the reverence for the Lord offered in worship; and reverence depends on love for him and love for one's neighbor. The Lord is present in love and so in worship. Accordingly, differences in worship among the nations mentioned reflected the same factors.

[2] To make it still clearer how worship differs, and how it differed among the various nations in the ancient church, the following needs to be known: All genuine worship consists in reverence for the Lord, reverence for the Lord consists in humility, and humility consists in admitting the truth about ourselves. That truth is that there is nothing living and nothing good inside ourselves, that everything inside us is dead and even cadaverous. It also consists in acknowledging that the Lord is the source of everything living and everything good. The more we acknowledge this with our hearts rather than our lips, the more humble we will be. The humbler we are, the more reverence we will have (or in other words, the more truly we will worship), the more love and charity we will feel, and the happier we will be. Each consequence contains the next, and they are tied so tightly together that they cannot be separated. This indicates what the identity and quality of differences in worship are.

[3] The people named here as Gomer's and Javan's sons also engaged in outward worship corresponding to inward (although it was somewhat further removed [from inward worship] than among the people mentioned in the last verse). So the people referred to in the current verse are called sons too. As the generations—or the stages of development—descend in

order, they move from deeper to shallower. The more people depend on their senses, the more superficial they become and consequently the more remote from genuine worship of the Lord. The more our worship partakes of the world, the body, and the earth, the less it partakes of the spirit, and the more distant it is [from true worship].

The people in this verse were called Gomer's and Javan's sons because they focused more on the senses, and for this reason they identified worship with the outward show of it even more strongly than their "parents" or "cousins" did. So they constitute another category here.

1154   *Ashkenaz, Riphath, and Togarmah* were individual nations where this form of worship existed, and they also symbolize individual doctrinal systems that consisted in rituals derived from the outward worship adopted by Gomer. This can be seen in the prophets, where the same nations are mentioned again. In each instance, as usual, they symbolize doctrinal systems or rituals in one of two senses—sometimes in a positive sense and sometimes in a negative.

Ashkenaz is mentioned in Jeremiah:

> Raise a banner in the land! Blow a horn among the nations! Consecrate the nations against [Babylon]! Cause the kingdoms of Ararat, Minni, and Ashkenaz to hear [the call] against it! (Jeremiah 51:27)

This is about the destruction of Babylon, and Ashkenaz stands for its idolatrous worship, that is, for the outward form separated from inward content, which destroyed Babylon. More narrowly, Ashkenaz stands for false doctrines. So it is being used in its negative sense.

Togarmah is mentioned in Ezekiel:

> *Javan, Tubal,* and *Meshech* were your dealers in human souls; and vessels of bronze they sold as your merchandise. Horses and riders and mules from *Beth-togarmah* they sold in exchange for your provisions. (Ezekiel 27:13, 14)

This is about Tyre, which represented those who possessed the knowledge of heavenly and spiritual things. Javan, Tubal, and Meshech once again are different kinds of ritual that had a representative or correspondential meaning, while Beth-togarmah stands for something similar. The outward ritual of the former relates to heavenly matters, but that of the latter (Beth-togarmah) relates to spiritual matters, as shown by the symbolism of the commodities in which they dealt. Here their meaning is a positive one. In the same author:

> There is *Gomer* and all its wings; *Beth-togarmah*—the flanks of the
> north—with all its wings too. (Ezekiel 38:6)

These stand for doctrines that have been perverted, which is what the
flanks of the north are as well. Here the sense is negative.

The *sons of Javan* symbolize yet another group: those who had an
outward form of worship that developed out of the worship adopted by
the nation of Javan. This too can be seen in the prophets [Isaiah 66:19;
Ezekiel 27:13, 19], where the names appear in a certain order, along with
the actual inner phenomena, and in each series they mean those phenomena and nothing else.

1155

The reason only Gomer's and Javan's sons are mentioned, and not
the sons of the others in verse 2 (which lists seven), is that the children of the one belong to the spiritual category and the children of the
other to the heavenly. Gomer's sons belong to the spiritual category, as
is established by the passages from the prophets cited just above. But the
fact that Javan's sons belong to the heavenly category will become clear
in what follows.

What distinguishes the spiritual class from the heavenly is that the
former has to do with the truth that faith embraces while the latter has
to do with the good that faith embraces (which is a matter of charity).
Although these distinctions are completely unknown in the world, they
are very well known in heaven—not only the general ones but the specific ones as well. Not the least difference exists that is not categorized
with minute precision. The world knows only that various types of worship exist and that they differ from each other—and merely in superficial
ways, at that. Heaven, on the other hand, sees the real distinctions (of
which there are too many to count) openly and vividly; and it sees them
as they are on the deeper planes.

Elishah, Tarshish, Kittim, and Dodanim were individual nations where
this form of worship existed, and they symbolize individual doctrinal
systems that consisted in rituals derived from the outward worship adopted
by Javan. The following passages from the prophets demonstrate this.

1156

Elishah comes up in Ezekiel:

> Fine linen with embroidery from Egypt was what you spread out to
> serve you as a banner. Blue-violet and red-violet fabric from the islands
> of *Elishah* was your covering. (Ezekiel 27:7)

This describes Tyre, which symbolizes people who own heavenly and
spiritual riches, or knowledge. Embroidery from Egypt stands for facts

and so for ritual that represents spiritual traits. Blue-violet and red-violet fabric from the islands of Elishah stands for ritual that corresponds to inward worship and so for ritual that represents heavenly traits. Elishah appears in its positive meaning here.

Of *Tarshish,* Isaiah says:

> I will send some of them—escapees—to the nations *Tarshish,* Put and Lud (drawing the bow), *Tubal* and *Javan* (the distant islands). (Isaiah 66:19)

[2] In the same author:

> Howl, you ships of *Tarshish,* because Tyre has been wiped out, so that there is not a house to enter. This has been revealed to them from the land of *Kittim.* (Isaiah 23:1, 14)

There is more on Tarshish in Isaiah 60:9; Jeremiah 10:9; Ezekiel 27:12; and Psalms 48:7; and in these places it stands for ritual, or in other words, doctrinal affairs.

Kittim is mentioned in Jeremiah:

> Go over into the islands of *Kittim* and see, and into Arabia and pay close attention: has anything like this ever happened? (Jeremiah 2:10)

And in Isaiah:

> He said, "You must no longer continue to gloat, oppressed virgin daughter of Sidon. Get up, go over to *Kittim;* even there you will have no rest." (Isaiah 23:12)

Kittim stands for ritual. In Ezekiel:

> Of oaks from Bashan they made your oars; your planking they made of ivory—the daughter of steps from the islands of *Kittim.* (Ezekiel 27:6)

This is about Tyre. Ship planking from the islands of Kittim stands for outward acts of worship—and so for ritual—belonging to the heavenly category. In Moses:

> Ships [are coming] from the shore of *Kittim,* and they will harry Assyria, and they will harry Eber. (Numbers 24:24)

Here too Kittim stands for outward worship and so for ritual.

Such things go to show that on a deeper level all these names symbolize inner phenomena, arranged in their proper order.

Genesis 10:5. *From these the islands of the nations dispersed in their lands, each by its tongue, by their clans, in their nations.*   **1157**

From these the islands of the nations dispersed in their lands means that the worship of many other nations sprang from them. The *islands* are particular regions—and so particular types of worship—that were even further removed; the *lands* are general ones. *Each by its tongue, by their clans, in their nations,* means each according to its mentality: *by its tongue* is each according to its way of thinking, *by their clans* is according to its sense of ethics, and *in their nations* is in respect to both traits more broadly.

From these the islands of the nations dispersed in their lands means that   **1158**
the worship of many other nations sprang from them. The *islands* are particular regions—and so particular types of worship—that were even further removed; the *lands* are general ones. This can be seen from the symbolism of islands in the Word.

Up to this point, the discussion has centered on people who engaged in outer worship that corresponded to inner. Japheth's seven sons symbolized those who came closer to true inner worship. The seven sons that Gomer and Javan had between them symbolized those who stood further from true inner worship. The islands of the nations symbolize those still further off. Strictly speaking, they symbolize people who lived together in mutual kindness yet in ignorance, not knowing anything about the Lord, the church's religious precepts, or inner worship, although they did have a kind of outward worship that they performed with devotion. The Word calls people like this *islands,* so at a deeper level, islands symbolize worship that is more distant [from inner worship].

[2] People alive to the Word in its inner sense (angels, for instance) do not know what islands are because they no longer have a mental image of them. In place of islands they perceive worship that is further removed, like the worship that nations outside the church practice.

In a similar way, they also take islands to mean qualities in the genuine church that are somewhat more remote from charity—qualities like loyalty and politeness. Loyalty is not charity, politeness still less so; both are several steps below charity. The more they partake of charity, though, the more authentic they are.

[3] The following passages in the Word demonstrate that islands symbolize these things. In Isaiah:

> Be silent for me, you *islands,* and let the peoples renew their strength; let them come near. The *islands* saw and were afraid; the *ends of the earth* shuddered; they approached and came. (Isaiah 41:1, 5)

The islands stand for nations outside the church that were honest and that practiced the outward forms of their worship with devotion. The farthest boundaries of the church are called the ends of the earth. In the same author:

> He will not go dark, and will not shatter anything, till he establishes judgment on the earth; and for his law the *islands* wait. Sing Jehovah a new song, his praise from the *end of the earth,* you that go down to the sea and you that fill it, you *islands* and you who inhabit them. They will give glory to Jehovah, and his praise they will tell in the *islands.* (Isaiah 42:4, 10, 12)

Here too islands stand for nations outside the church that have lived in ignorance, simple innocence, and honesty. [4] In the same author:

> Pay attention to me, you *islands,* and listen carefully, you people *from far away.* (Isaiah 49:1)

Once again they stand for those nations that are further removed from worship of the Lord and from knowledge of the true faith and who are therefore described as being "from far away." In the same author:

> In me the *islands* will put their hope, and for my arm they will wait. (Isaiah 51:5)

The islands here stand for the same people. Because these are people who live uprightly, it says, "In me they will put their hope, and for my arm they will wait." In Jeremiah:

> Listen to the Word of Jehovah, you nations, and tell it in the *islands far away.* (Jeremiah 31:10)

They stand for the same people. In Zephaniah:

> Jehovah is fearsome over them, since he will starve all the gods of the earth to death. And all the *islands of the nations* will bow down to him, each individual from her or his own place. (Zephaniah 2:11)

The islands of the nations stand for nations somewhat cut off from any knowledge of the true faith. [5] In David:

> Jehovah is reigning. Let the earth rejoice; let the many *islands* be glad! Cloud and darkness are all around him. (Psalms 97:1, 2)

They stand for the same people. The ignorance of these people is expressed in a representative way by the cloud and darkness; but since they have a simple innocence and honesty, it says that the cloud and darkness are all around Jehovah.

Because islands symbolize what is relatively distant [from true worship], Tarshish, Pul, Lud, Tubal, and Javan—which symbolize outward forms of worship—are also called islands (Isaiah 66:19). So is Kittim (Jeremiah 2:10 and Ezekiel 27:6).

When islands are contrasted with the earth or with mountains, they also symbolize religious truth, and this is because they are set in the sea. In consequence, they mean doctrinal matters—that is, ritual.

Each by its tongue, by their clans, in their nations, means each according to its mentality. *By its tongue* is each according to its way of thinking, *by their clans* is according to its sense of ethics, and *in their nations* is in respect to both traits more broadly. This can be seen from the symbolism of tongue, clans, and nations in the Word, as explained below, by the Lord's divine mercy.

On the inner level, a *tongue* symbolizes a way of thinking, so it symbolizes assumptions and opinions. The reason for the symbolism is that the correlation between our tongue and our intellectual side—that is, our thoughts—is the same as that between an effect and its cause. And not only does a person's thinking flow into the movements of the speaking tongue in this way but heaven does too. The evidence of experience concerning these things will be given elsewhere, the Lord in his divine mercy willing [§§1638, 3741:2, 4044, 4791, 4801].

[2] The inner-level symbolism of *clans* as a sense of ethics, and also as charity and love, is due to the fact that all the bonds of mutual love in heaven resemble blood relationships and family ties and so resemble clans. (For more on this see §685.) In the Word, then, things that have to do with love or charity are depicted as households and clans, although there is no need to spend time proving it here. (For this symbolism of households, see §710.)

[3] The symbolism of *the nations* as both traits more broadly can be seen from the symbolism of a nation or nations in the Word. In a good

sense, they symbolize the contents of the will and the intellect when these faculties have been renewed. As a result they symbolize the good effects of love and the true ideas of faith. In the opposite sense, though, they symbolize evil and falsity, as do households, clans, and tongues. These things can be corroborated by many passages in the Word.

The reason for this symbolism is that the earliest church was divided into households, clans, and nations. A household comprised a married couple together with their children and their male and female servants; a clan comprised a number of households that were not too far apart; while nations comprised several clans. So *the nations* meant all clans taken together, or collectively. The situation in heaven is similar, but all relationships there are determined by people's love for the Lord and faith in him (see §685).

[4] This, then, is why on an inner level the nations symbolize something broader that incorporates attributes of both will and intellect—or aspects of both love and faith, to put it another way—in relation to the clans and households that compose them. (For more on this, see what was said earlier, at §§470, 471, 483.)

These things show that the nations symbolize both traits more broadly and that *each by its tongue, by their clans,* and *in their nations* means the mentality of every person, clan, and nation that inherited its worship from the ancient church.

1160   Genesis 10:6. *And the sons of Ham: Cush, and Mizraim, and Put, and Canaan.*

Ham, here as earlier, symbolizes faith detached from charity. The *sons of Ham* symbolize characteristics of a detached faith. *Cush, Mizraim, Put,* and *Canaan* were individual nations, and on an inner level they symbolize the concepts, facts, and varieties of worship connected with a faith detached from charity.

1161   The symbolism of *Ham* as faith detached from charity can be seen from what was said and shown about Ham in the last chapter [§§1062–1063, 1076–1078].

1162   The symbolism of the *sons of Ham* as characteristics of a detached faith follows logically. In order to see what Ham is, and therefore what Ham's sons are, it is necessary to know what faith isolated from charity is. Faith isolated from charity is no faith at all, and where there is no faith there is no worship, inward or outward. If any kind of worship does exist, it is corrupt worship, so Ham also symbolizes inner worship that has been corrupted.

People who use the term *faith* for a bare knowledge of heavenly and spiritual facts unconnected with neighborly love have the wrong idea. Sometimes the most knowledgeable people are the worst ones, after all. For example, they might be people who live lives of unremitting hatred and revenge, or of adultery—hellish individuals, who turn into devils when bodily life ends. This proves that knowledge is not faith. On the contrary, faith is an acknowledgment of the tenets of faith, and acknowledgment is never external but internal; it is a work the Lord alone accomplishes in us through charity. And acknowledgment is never a matter of lip service but of life; the way we live reveals the quality of our acknowledgment.

[2] "Child of Ham" is a term that applies to all who are well educated in religious concepts but lack charity. No matter whether we have learned the deeper knowledge and sheer mysteries buried in the Word; whether we have learned all the details of its literal sense; whether we have learned other types of truth—whatever name they go under—that give us a new perspective on our knowledge of the Word; or whether we are familiar with all points of ritual belonging to external forms of worship; if we do not have charity, we are children of Ham. The fact that those called the children of Ham are like this can be seen from the nations discussed next.

Cush, Mizraim, Put, and *Canaan* were individual nations, and on an inner level they symbolize the concepts, facts, and varieties of ritual connected with a faith detached from charity. This can be seen in the Word, where these nations are mentioned frequently, since such is their symbolism there. To be specific: Cush (that is, Ethiopia) symbolizes the deeper knowledge in the Word that we use to confirm false premises. Mizraim (that is, Egypt) symbolizes the various kinds of secular knowledge or facts we attempt to use in examining the secrets of faith and justifying the false principles that result. Put (that is, Libya) symbolizes knowledge gleaned from the Word's literal meaning that—yet again—we use for confirming false premises. Canaan (or Canaanites) symbolizes ritual, or outward forms of worship separated from inward. All these practices, when they are detached from charity, are called the children of Ham.

The same nations also stand simply for religious and secular knowledge. Cush symbolizes the deeper knowledge in the Word, Egypt symbolizes secular knowledge, and Put symbolizes knowledge gleaned from the Word's literal meaning. That is why they are taken in both senses, bad and good, as the passages below demonstrate.

1163

1164   The symbolism of *Cush* (that is, Ethiopia) as the deeper knowledge in the Word that we use to confirm false assumptions, can be seen in Jeremiah:

> *Egypt* rises like a river, and like rivers its waters churn. And it has said, "I will go up; I will blanket the land; I will destroy the city and those living in it." Go up, horses, and run mad, chariots, and let your mighty men march out, *Cush* and *Put,* as you grasp your shield. (Jeremiah 46:8, 9)

In this passage Egypt stands for those who believe nothing unless they can comprehend it in terms of the facts they know. This insistence renders everything doubtful, negative, and false, which is what going up, covering the land, and destroying the city is. Cush, here, stands for broader, deeper kinds of knowledge in the Word that we use for shoring up the false principles we have adopted. Put stands for knowledge from the literal level of the Word that accords with appearances presented to us by our senses. [2] In Ezekiel:

> A sword will come into *Egypt,* and there will be agony in *Cush,* when the victim of stabbing falls in *Egypt,* and they seize its mob, and its foundations are destroyed—*Cush* and *Put,* and Lud, and all the Ereb and Chub. And the children of the land of the covenant with them will fall by the sword. (Ezekiel 30:4, 5, 6)

No one would ever know what this meant without the inner meaning; and if the names were not symbolic, it would make hardly any sense at all. Egypt, though, symbolizes facts here—facts that we want to use as a means of entry into religious mysteries. Cush and Put are called Egypt's foundations because they stand for knowledge gained from the Word. [3] In the same author:

> On that day, messengers will go out from before me in ships, to terrify confident *Cush.* And there will be agony upon them as in *Egypt's* day. (Ezekiel 30:9)

Cush stands for knowledge from the Word that we use in proof of falsities we have dreamed up out of various facts. In the same author:

> I will turn the land of *Egypt* into wastelands, a ruinous wasteland, from the tower to Syene even as far as the border of *Cush.* (Ezekiel 29:10)

Egypt stands for factual knowledge in this verse; Cush stands for knowledge of the deeper import of the Word, which is the border to which factual knowledge extends. [4] In Isaiah:

> The monarch of Assyria will lead *Egypt's* captives and *Cush's* captives, young and old, naked and barefoot and with uncovered buttock— the nakedness of Egypt. And they will panic and be embarrassed on account of *Cush,* their hope, and of *Egypt,* their glory. (Isaiah 20:4, 5)

In this passage, Cush stands for knowledge from the Word used to support the falsities that factual knowledge has prompted us to adopt. Assyria is shallow reasoning, which leads us captive. In Nahum:

> *Cush* was its strength, as was *Egypt,* and there was no end to them. *Put* and the *Libyans* were of help to you. (Nahum 3:9)

The subject here is the church when it has been devastated, and once again Egypt stands for secular knowledge, while Cush stands for religious knowledge.

[5] Cush and Egypt can stand simply for religious and secular knowledge—truth, that is, which is useful to people whose faith comes from charity. In other words, Cush and Egypt sometimes have a good meaning. In Isaiah:

> Jehovah has said: "The labor of *Egypt,* and the wares of *Cush* and of *Seba's inhabitants*—sizeable men—will pass over to you and will belong to you. They will walk after you in fetters. They will pass over, and to you they will bow down. To you they will pray: 'Only among you does God exist, and there is no other god besides.'" (Isaiah 45:14)

The labor of Egypt stands for learning; the wares of Cush and of Seba's inhabitants, for the knowledge of spiritual things; [both of] which serve those who acknowledge the Lord. These are the people who possess all learning and knowledge. [6] In Daniel:

> The monarch of the north will rule over the hidden treasures of gold and silver, and over all the desirable things of *Egypt,* and of the *Libyans* [Put], and of the *Cushites,* in your footsteps. (Daniel 11:43)

Put and Cush stand for knowledge from the Word, while Egypt stands for secular learning. In Zephaniah:

> From the ford of *Cush's* rivers come my worshipers. (Zephaniah 3:10)

This stands for people who lack access to religious knowledge and so for non-Christians. In David:

> Nobles will come from *Egypt; Cush* will quickly thrust its hands out to God. (Psalms 68:31)

Egypt stands for learning and Cush for religious knowledge. [7] In the same author:

> I will remember Rahab and Babylon as being among those who know me—yes, Philistia, and Tyre, along with *Cush.* This last was born there [in the city of God]. (Psalms 87:4)

Cush stands for knowledge from the Word, which is why it is said to have been born in the city of God.

It is because Cush symbolizes knowledge buried deep in the Word and an intelligent understanding based on this knowledge that the second river issuing from the Garden of Eden circled the whole land of Cush. For more on this, see §117 above.

1165 In the Word, *Mizraim* (Egypt) symbolizes the various kinds of secular knowledge or facts we attempt to use in examining the secrets of faith and justifying the false principles that result. In addition it simply symbolizes secular knowledge, which is useful. These meanings are visible not only from the passages already quoted but also from many others, which would fill whole pages if they were all to be quoted. See Isaiah 19:1–end; 30:1, 2, 3; 31:1, 2, 3; Jeremiah 2:18, 36; 42:14–end; 46:1–end; Ezekiel 16:26; 23:3; 29:1–end; 30:1–end; Hosea 7:11; 9:3, 6; 11:1, 5, 11; Micah 7:12; Zechariah 10:10, 11; Psalms 80:8 and following verses.

1166 *Put* (that is, Libya) in the Word symbolizes knowledge gleaned from the literal meaning that—yet again—is used for confirming false premises; and in addition it stands simply for the knowledge itself. This can be seen from the passages cited earlier in reference to Cush, which likewise symbolizes knowledge, but knowledge at a deeper level. The Word mentions Put in conjunction with Cush; look at the section concerning Cush [§1164] to see the places, as quoted from Jeremiah 46:9; Ezekiel 30:4, 5, 6; Nahum 3:9; Daniel 11:43.

1167 *Canaan* (or a Canaanite) in the Word symbolizes ritual or outward forms of worship separated from inward, as many passages illustrate, especially in the narrative books. Because Canaanites practiced this kind of worship at the period when the children of Jacob invaded their land, their obliteration was permitted; but in the Word's inner meaning, Canaanites mean everyone who practices outward worship separated from inward. Since Jews and Israelites engaged in this kind of worship more than anyone else, Canaan refers specifically to them in the prophetic parts of the Word, as the two following passages alone show. In David:

> They have shed innocent blood—the blood of their sons and daughters, whom they sacrificed to the idols of *Canaan*—and the land has been profaned with blood. And they have been polluted by their works and have prostituted themselves in their deeds. (Psalms 106:38, 39)

[2] In a deeper sense, shedding the blood of their sons and daughters means that they blotted out all religious truth and all the good effects of neighborly love. Sacrificing their sons and daughters to the idols of Canaan symbolizes profaning the attributes of faith and charity through outward worship detached from inward, which is the same as idolatry. In this way they polluted themselves with their works and prostituted themselves in their deeds. In Ezekiel:

> This is what the Lord Jehovih has said to Jerusalem: "Your trading and your birth origins belong to the land of *Canaan*. Your father is an Amorite and your mother a Hittite." (Ezekiel 16:3)

This says explicitly that they came from the Canaanite land.

For the symbolism of Canaan as external worship detached from internal, see what appears above in §§1078, 1094.

Genesis 10:7. *And the sons of Cush: Seba, and Havilah, and Sabtah, and Raamah, and Sabteca. And the sons of Raamah: Sheba and Dedan.*

1168

The *sons of Cush* symbolize people who did not have inward worship but did have religious knowledge, the possession of which they considered to be religion. *Seba, Havilah, Sabtah, Raamah,* and *Sabteca,* are individual nations among whom that knowledge was extant, while at a deeper level they symbolize the knowledge itself. The *sons of Raamah* also symbolize people who did not have inward worship but did have religious knowledge, the possession of which they considered to be religion. *Sheba* and *Dedan* are individual nations among whom that knowledge was extant, while at a deeper level they symbolize the knowledge itself. The difference is that the sons of Cush symbolize a knowledge of spiritual qualities while the sons of Raamah symbolize a knowledge of heavenly qualities.

The *sons of Cush* symbolize people who did not have inward worship but did have religious knowledge, the possession of which they considered to be religion. This is established by the symbolism of *Cush,* whose

1169

sons they were, as a knowledge of spiritual realities on a deep level, as shown earlier [§§117, 1163–1164]. It can also be seen in the Word, in the places that mention those nations.

1170 The fact that *Seba, Havilah, Sabtah, Raamah,* and *Sabteca,* are individual nations among whom that knowledge was extant, and that at a deeper level they symbolize the knowledge itself, is established by the passages from the Word quoted below.

1171 The *sons of Raamah* also symbolize people who did not have inward worship but did have religious knowledge, the possession of which they considered to be religion; *Sheba* and *Dedan* are individual nations among whom that knowledge was extant, and at a deeper level they symbolize the knowledge itself. This can be seen from the following places in the prophets, beginning with quotations from them about *Seba, Sheba,* and *Raamah.* In David:

> The monarchs of Tarshish and of the islands will bring a gift, and the monarchs of *Sheba* and *Seba* will deliver their tribute, and all monarchs will bow down to him. (Psalms 72:10, 11)

This is about the Lord, his kingdom, and a heavenly type of church. The gift and tribute in this passage symbolize worship, as anyone can see, but no one can tell just who the worshipers are and what their worship is like without knowing what Tarshish and the islands mean, and what Sheba and Seba mean. Tarshish and the islands mean outward forms of worship that correspond to inner worship, as already demonstrated [§§1156:2, 1158]. As a result, Sheba and Seba mean inward forms of worship. Sheba, in particular, means heavenly aspects of worship, while Seba means spiritual aspects of it. [2] In Isaiah:

> I have given Egypt in atonement for you, *Cush* and *Seba* in place of you. (Isaiah 43:3)

Cush and Seba stand for spiritual aspects of faith. In the same author:

> The labor of *Egypt,* and the wares of *Cush* and of *Seba's inhabitants*— sizeable men—will pass over to you. (Isaiah 45:14)

The labor of Egypt stands for secular knowledge; the wares of Cush and of Seba's inhabitants, for a knowledge of spiritual entities. These serve a use to people who believe in the Lord. [3] In the same author:

> A troop of camels will blanket you, the dromedaries of Midian and Ephah; they will all come from *Sheba.* Gold and frankincense they will

carry, and Jehovah's praises they will proclaim. Every flock of *Arabia* will be gathered to you. (Isaiah 60:6, 7)

In this passage, Sheba means heavenly qualities and the spiritual qualities that grow out of them. These are the gold and frankincense and are explained as being Jehovah's praises, or in other words, internal worship. [4] In Ezekiel:

> The dealers of *Sheba* and *Raamah* were your dealers, in the finest of every perfume, and in every precious stone; and gold they traded for your provisions. (Ezekiel 27:22, 23)

This is about Tyre. What Sheba and Raamah symbolize can be seen from the merchandise, which is listed as perfume, precious stones, and gold. On an inner level, perfume is charity, precious stones are the faith that charity yields, and gold is love for the Lord, all of which are the heavenly qualities that Sheba symbolizes. Strictly speaking, the knowledge of these qualities is Sheba, and that is why the passage describes them as different kinds of trade, which people are trained in when they are coming into the church. Without knowledge, no one can become part of the church. [5] Something similar was represented by the queen of *Sheba*, who came to Solomon bringing perfumes, gold, and precious stones (1 Kings 10:1, 2, 3). The same is true for the sages from the East who came to Jesus at his birth, who fell down and worshiped him, and who opened their treasure chests and offered him gifts: gold, frankincense, and myrrh (Matthew 2:1, 11). These gifts symbolize heavenly, spiritual, and earthly types of goodness. In Jeremiah:

> Why should frankincense come to me from *Sheba,* or the best calamus from a far-off land? Your burnt offerings give no satisfaction. (Jeremiah 6:20)

Here too Sheba obviously symbolizes knowledge and acts of reverence, which are the frankincense and calamus; but in this case it is knowledge and reverence devoid of charity that Sheba symbolizes, and these are not pleasing.

Dedan symbolizes knowledge of the lower-level heavenly attributes that are present in ritual, as the following passages from the Word show. In Ezekiel:

> The children of *Dedan* were your dealers; many islands were your traders at hand. Horns of ivory and items of ebony they have brought as your tribute. (Ezekiel 27:15)

In an inner sense, horns of ivory and items of ebony are anything that is outwardly good about worship, or about ritual. In the same author:

> *Dedan* was your dealer in clothes for the chariot that allow free movement. Arabia and all the chiefs of Kedar . . . (Ezekiel 27:20, 21)

Clothes for the chariot that allow free movement are likewise something outwardly good, or what is good about ritual. In Jeremiah:

> Their wisdom has become rank; run away! *Dedan's* inhabitants turned their backs; they took themselves down into the depths to live. (Jeremiah 49:7, 8)

Dedan stands for ritual that holds within it no inward worship of the Lord, that is, no heartfelt veneration of him—this being the proper meaning of Dedan. The passage describes people whose ritual is like this as turning their backs and taking themselves down into the depths to live.

These passages now demonstrate that the children of Cush symbolize a knowledge of spiritual qualities, and the children of Raamah, a knowledge of heavenly qualities.

1173   Genesis 10:8, 9. *And Cush fathered Nimrod; he began to be mighty on the earth. He was mighty in hunting before the face of Jehovah. For this reason there was a saying: "Like Nimrod, mighty in hunting before the face of Jehovah."*

Cush here as before symbolizes the knowledge of spiritual and heavenly attributes on a fairly deep level. *Nimrod* symbolizes those who made internal worship external, and so he symbolizes this kind of external worship. *Cush fathered Nimrod* means that people who possessed a knowledge of deeper things founded this kind of worship. *He was mighty on the earth* means that this kind of religion grew rife in the church; the *earth* is the church, as before. *He was mighty in hunting before the face of Jehovah* means that this religion persuaded many people. *For this reason there was a saying: "Like Nimrod, mighty in hunting before the face of Jehovah,"* means that since so many people were swayed, this became a stock phrase; a further meaning is that this kind of religion ensnares people's minds very easily.

1174   The symbolism of *Cush* as the knowledge of spiritual and heavenly attributes on a fairly deep level can be seen from previous remarks and explanations concerning Cush [§§117, 1163–1164, 1169].

1175   *Nimrod* symbolizes those who made internal worship external, and so he symbolizes this kind of external worship, as can be seen from what follows. Here at the outset it needs to be said what making internal worship external means.

It has already been stated and shown that inward worship—worship that rises out of love and charity—is real worship, and that outward worship without this inward dimension is no worship at all. Making internal worship external is making the show of worship more important than its inward content, which is turning true worship upside down. For instance, it is saying that there is no such thing as inner devotion without outer devotion, when the truth is that there is no such thing as outer devotion without inner.

This aptly describes the religion of those who divide faith from charity. Such people rank matters of belief above matters of neighborly love, or matters of religious knowledge above matters of life. In so doing, they rank matters of form above those of essence. Outward devotion is simply the external form of inward devotion, since inward devotion is its truly essential ingredient, and to create worship from a form that lacks its essence is to make internal worship external. An example is the belief of some that people who live where there is no church, no preaching, no sacraments, and no priesthood cannot be saved or practice any kind of worship, when in fact they can worship the Lord with inner devotion.

[2] The conclusion does not follow, however, that outward worship should be abandoned. To see the issue more clearly, take as an example the tendency to identify the most critical factors in worship as attending church, taking the sacraments, listening to sermons, praying, observing the holy days, obeying any other external, ceremonial requirements, and persuading ourselves that, in terms of religion, this is enough. All such activities are merely the outward forms of worship. Yet those who consider love and charity the most essential ingredients in worship do the same things. They attend church, take the sacraments, listen to sermons, pray, observe the holy days, obey other requirements, and do all this with dedication and care; but they do not consider such deeds the essence of worship.

There is something holy and living about the outward devotion of the latter people, because inward worship lies within it. There is nothing holy or living in the worship of the group described first, though. That which is really essential is what lends holiness and life to things that are matters of form and ceremony. Faith detached from charity is incapable of lending holiness or life to worship, because it lacks essence and life. This kind of worship is called Nimrod. It is born out of the knowledge that Cush stands for, which in turn is born out of the faith detached from charity that Ham stands for. From Ham, that is, from a detached faith, through the knowledge that belongs to such a faith, no other kind of worship can ever be born.

These are the things that Nimrod symbolizes.

1176 *Cush fathered Nimrod* means that people who possessed a knowledge of deeper things founded this kind of worship, as can be seen from what has just been said. The knowledge of deeper things consists of ideas that they call doctrines and distinguish from matters of ritual. Their main doctrine, for instance, is the notion that faith alone saves us. They do not realize that love for the Lord and love for our neighbor is real faith. They also fail to see that the knowledge they call faith exists only to lead us to receive love—love for the Lord and love for our neighbor—from the Lord. They do not know that this is the faith that saves us.

People who call bare knowledge faith are those who father and found the kind of worship described above. They are discussed earlier [§1162:1].

1177 *He was mighty on the earth* means that this kind of religion grew rife in the church, as can be seen from what comes next. The fact that the *earth* is the church has been demonstrated before, in §§620, 636, 662, and elsewhere.

1178 The meaning of *he was mighty in hunting before the face of Jehovah* as the fact that he persuaded many people can be seen from the fact that faith divided from charity has this ability, and from the symbolism of hunting in the Word.

Faith separated from neighborly love is such that people are easily talked into it. The majority of humankind has no idea what internal phenomena are, only what outer ones are. Most people live lives of physical sensation, animal pleasures, and cravings and focus on themselves and the material world. As a result they are easily ensnared by this religion.

As for the symbolism of *hunting,* its general meaning in the Word is persuading people. Its specific meaning is captivating their minds and in this way persuading them, by appealing to their physical senses, sensual pleasures, and cravings, and by arbitrarily interpreting doctrine to agree with the viewpoint of both listener and speaker, for the selfish purpose of obtaining high rank and great wealth. [2] This symbolism can be seen in Ezekiel:

> Doom to those who sew padding together [to go] over all the joints of my arms and who make mantles [to go] over heads of every height, to *hunt* souls. You *hunt* the souls that belong to my people; and the souls that are yours you keep alive. And you profaned me among my people for handfuls of barleycorns and for crumbs of bread, to kill souls that

must not die and to keep souls alive that must not live, lying about yourselves to my people, who were listening to the lie. Look now, regarding your padding, with which you are *hunting* souls, there, to [make them] fly away: I will rip it off your arms and release the souls that you are *hunting,* souls [that you are hunting] to [make them] fly away. And I will rip up your mantles and rescue my people from your hand, and they will no longer be in your hand for *hunting.* (Ezekiel 13:18, 19, 20, 21)

This explains what hunting is: it is deceiving a person with persuasive arguments and with religious concepts that we pervert, interpreting them to advance our own interests and to harmonize with the other person's mindset. [3] In Micah:

The merciful person has perished off the earth, and there is no upright person among humankind; they all lie in wait for blood. Each man *hunts* his brother with a net, while they do evil with their hands in place of doing good. Chieftains are conducting inquiries and passing judgment for the sake of a bribe, and the great are uttering the perversity of their soul; and they twist it. (Micah 7:2, 3)

This passage also explains what hunting is: it is conniving for selfish purposes, or in other words, saying that falsity is truth, and speaking perversity, and twisting things, all for the sake of persuading others. In David:

A man with a tongue must not become established on the earth. A man of violence *hunts* evil to the point of [the earth's] ruination. (Psalms 140:11)

This is about godless people who, for the purpose of deceiving others, persuade them with false arguments, think wrongly, and speak smoothly. The tongue stands for dishonesty.

For this reason there was a saying: "Like Nimrod, mighty in hunting   1179
before the face of Jehovah," means that since so many people were swayed, this became a stock phrase; a further meaning is that this kind of religion ensnares people's minds very easily. This can be seen from the preceding remarks and from the literal meaning itself. Furthermore, since people in ancient times gave personal names to things, they assigned this name to that type of worship. To be specific, they said that *Nimrod* (that type of worship) was *mighty in hunting* (good at ensnaring people's minds). They added *before the face of Jehovah* because people whose worship was like this called a detached faith by the name Jehovah, or "the man Jehovah," as indicated by the remarks of §340 above concerning Cain.

Cain too symbolizes faith detached from charity. [2] But the difference between Cain and Ham is that Cain was part of the heavenly church, which had perception, while Ham was part of the spiritual church, which had no perception. So the earlier group was more culpable than the later.

In ancient times, people of this character were called mighty ones, as in Isaiah:

> All the glory of Kedar will be consumed, and what is left of the number of bows among the *mighty* sons of Kedar will decrease. (Isaiah 21:16, 17)

And in Hosea:

> You have plowed godlessness; wickedness you have reaped. You have eaten the fruit of your lying because you trusted your own way [and] the large number of your *mighty ones*. (Hosea 10:13)

There are other places too. They called themselves men and mighty ones on account of faith, because in the original [Hebrew] language there is a term simultaneously expressing the idea of a mighty one and a man, and in the Word, this term has to do with faith. It is faith in both senses that the term applies to.

1180 Genesis 10:10. *And the beginning of his kingdom was Babel, and Erech, and Accad, and Calneh, in the land of Shinar.*

The beginning of his kingdom was means that this is the way that kind of worship began. *Babel, Erech, Accad, Calneh, in the land of Shinar* means that those were the places it was located; the same nations also symbolize the worship itself, whose outward forms appear holy but whose inner depths are profane.

1181 The fact that *the beginning of his kingdom* means that this is the way that kind of worship began can be seen from the symbolism of Babel in the land of Shinar, discussed in what follows.

1182 *Babel, Erech, Accad, Calneh, in the land of Shinar,* means that those were the places it was located; the same nations also symbolize the worship itself, whose outward forms appear holy but whose inner depths are profane. This can be seen from the symbolism of Babel and of the land of Shinar. The Word has many things to say about Babel, [or Babylon,] and in each instance it symbolizes this kind of worship—that is to say, worship in which the outward forms appear holy but the inward content is profane. Since the next chapter speaks of Babel, however, the proof that it symbolizes these things will appear there. So too will a demonstration of the fact that such worship was not so profane at first as it became later.

Outward worship depends completely on the depths within it for its nature. The more blameless the qualities within it are, the more innocent the outward practice of worship is. But the more disgusting the inner qualities are, the more profane the outward practice is. To put it briefly, the more materialism and self-love there are in a person worshiping outwardly, the less a living, sacred quality lies within the worship. The more hatred for others there is within the self-love and materialism, the more profanity lies within the worship. If malevolence exists within the hatred, the profanation is even greater. And if deceit exists within the malevolence, the profanation is greater still. All these attributes are the inner depths of external worship that Babel symbolizes, as described in the next chapter [§§1317, 1326:1].

It is not as easy to understand the specific symbolism of *Erech, Accad,* **1183** *Calneh, in the land of Shinar,* since the Word does not mention them anywhere else (aside from a reference to Calneh in Amos 6:2), but they are different varieties of this worship.

As for the *land of Shinar,* where these types of worship existed, though, its symbolism in the Word as external devotion that is profane at its core can be seen from its symbolism in verse 2 of the next chapter, Genesis 11. It can also be seen in Zechariah 5:11 and still more clearly in Daniel, where these words appear:

> Into the hand of Nebuchadnezzar, king of Babylon, the Lord gave Jehoiakim, king of Judah, and a portion of the vessels of the House of God. And he carried them into the *land of Shinar,* into the house of his god, and he brought the vessels into the treasure house of his god. (Daniel 1:2)

The meaning of these words is that holy things were profaned. The vessels of the House of God are the holy things. The house of the god of Babylon's king in the land of Shinar is the profane places where the holy things were brought. Although the details are historically true, they still harbor these secret meanings, as all the historical details of the Word do. The symbolism of Shinar is demonstrated further in the profanation of the same vessels, as told about in Daniel 5:3, 4, 5. If the vessels had not represented holy attributes, these events would never have happened.

Genesis 10:11, 12. *From that same land, Asshur went out and built* **1184** *Nineveh, and the city Rehoboth, and Calah, and Resen, between Nineveh and Calah (this is the great city).*

From that same land, Asshur went out, means that those who practiced this shallow kind of worship started to reason falsely about the deeper qualities of devotion; *Asshur* is skewed reasoning. *And built Nineveh, and the city Rehoboth, and Calah,* means that in this way they created doctrines for themselves about faith; *Nineveh* symbolizes the false elements of the doctrines; *Rehoboth* and *Calah* symbolize the same things from a different source. *Resen, between Nineveh and Calah,* means that they also created doctrines for themselves about how to live. *Resen* symbolizes the false elements of doctrine that resulted; *Nineveh* is falsity that rises out of faulty reasoning; *Calah* is falsity that stems from our cravings; and *between Nineveh and Calah* means falsity from both of these. *This is the great city* symbolizes doctrinal positions and the fact that they proliferated.

1185   *From that same land, Asshur went out,* means that those who practiced this shallow kind of worship started to reason falsely about the deeper qualities of devotion. This is indicated by Asshur's symbolism in the Word as true reason and skewed reasoning, to be discussed just below.

Two meanings can be discerned here. One is that Asshur went out from that land; the other is that Nimrod went out from that land into Asshur, or Assyria. It is put this way because both ideas are meant—both that faulty reasoning about spiritual and heavenly matters sprang from this culture (which is Asshur's setting out from the land of Shinar) and that this kind of culture engages in faulty reasoning concerning spiritual and heavenly matters (which is Nimrod's setting out from the land into Asshur, or Assyria).

1186   The fact that *Asshur* is skewed reasoning can be seen from the symbolism of Asshur, or Assyria, in the Word, where it is always taken to mean matters of reason, in both senses—both rational thinking and rationalizations. (Reason and rational thinking, strictly speaking, mean valid mental processes, while rationalizing and rationalizations mean dishonest ones.) Because Asshur symbolizes both reason and rationalization, it is usually connected with Egypt, which symbolizes secular knowledge, since reason and rationalization are based on such knowledge.

Asshur's symbolism as rationalization can be seen in Isaiah:

> Doom to *Asshur,* the rod of my anger! He thinks what is not right, and his heart contemplates what is not right. He has said, "In the strength of my hand have I done this, and in my wisdom, because I have understanding." (Isaiah 10:5, 7, 13)

Asshur stands for rationalization, which is why it is said of him that he thinks and contemplates what is not right and claims that he does so through his wisdom, because he has understanding. [2] In Ezekiel:

> Two women, the daughters of one mother, whored in *Egypt*. In their youthful years they whored. One whored and doted on her lovers— the neighboring *Asshur* [Assyrians], dressed in blue-violet; leaders and rulers; desirable young men, all of them; riders riding horses. To her came the *sons of Babylon,* and they defiled her through their whorings. (Ezekiel 23:2, 3, 5, 6, 17)

Egypt in this passage stands for secular facts, Asshur for rationalization, and the sons of Babylon for false ideas that develop out of corrupt desires. [3] In the same author:

> Jerusalem, you whored with the *sons of Egypt;* you whored with the *sons of Assyria.* You multiplied your whoredom in the land of Canaan all the way to Chaldea. (Ezekiel 16:26, 28, 29)

Egypt again stands for secular facts and Assyria for rationalization. To engage in twisted reasoning about spiritual and heavenly concerns on the basis of facts is called whoredom, both here and elsewhere in the Word. Anyone can see that it does not refer to whoredom with Egyptians and Assyrians. [4] In Jeremiah:

> Israel, why should you go to *Egypt* to drink the waters of the Sihor, and why should you go to *Assyria* to drink the waters of the river [Euphrates]? (Jeremiah 2:18, 36)

Once again Egypt stands for facts and Assyria for flawed reasoning. In the same author:

> A strayed sheep is Israel; lions drove him off. First to eat him was the king of *Assyria,* and this later one, the king of *Babylon,* took his bones. (Jeremiah 50:17, 18)

Assyria stands for flawed reasoning on spiritual subjects. [5] In Micah:

> This will be peace, when *Assyria* comes into our land and when he tramples our palaces. And we will set up over him seven shepherds and eight chiefs of the people, and they will graze on the *land of Assyria* with a sword and on the *land of Nimrod* in its gates. And one will deliver [us] from *Assyria,* when he comes into our land and when he tramples our border. (Micah 5:5, 6)

This is about Israel (the spiritual church), which it says that Assyria (sophistic reasoning) would not invade. The land of Nimrod stands for the kind of worship that Nimrod symbolizes, which contains evil and falsity at a deep level.

[6] Assyria's other symbolism in the Word—as true reason in a member of the church, which allows the person to see truth and goodness clearly—appears in Hosea:

> They will quake like a bird from *Egypt* and like a dove from the land of *Assyria.* (Hosea 11:11)

In this passage, Egypt stands for factual learning and Assyria for reason in a person who is part of the church. A bird is factual knowledge that we really understand, while a pigeon, or dove, is goodness on a rational plane, as shown earlier [§§40, 745, 776–777, 870, 891]. [7] In Isaiah:

> On that day there will be a path from *Egypt* to *Assyria,* and *Assyria* will come into *Egypt* and *Egypt* into *Assyria,* and the *Egyptians* will serve *Assyria.* On that day Israel will be third to *Egypt* and *Assyria,* a blessing in the middle of the earth, whom Jehovah Sabaoth will bless, saying, "A blessing on my people *Egypt* and on the work of my hands, *Assyria,* and on my inheritance, Israel!" (Isaiah 19:23, 24, 25)

The subject here is the spiritual church, which is Israel. Rationality in this church is Assyria, and the secular knowledge in it is Egypt. These three make up the intellectual abilities of people in the spiritual church, and they come in that order.

Assyria, or Asshur, symbolizes either true or false rationality in other places where it comes up too, as for instance in Isaiah 20:1–end; 23:13; 27:13; 30:31; 31:8; 36; 37; 52:4; Ezekiel 27:23, 24; 31:3–end; Micah 7:12; Zephaniah 2:13; Zechariah 10:11; Psalms 83:8. It stands for rationalization in Hosea 5:13; 7:11; 10:6; 11:5; 12:1; 14:3; and likewise in Zechariah 10:10, concerning Ephraim, which symbolizes a property of the intellect—in this case, an intellect that has been perverted.

1187   The meaning of *he built Nineveh, and the city Rehoboth, and Calah,* as the fact that in this way they created doctrines for themselves about faith can be seen from the symbolism of Nineveh, Rehoboth, and Calah, to be detailed directly below. It can also be seen from the symbolism of a *city* in the Word as a true doctrinal concept, or else as a heretical one—a symbolism laid out earlier, in §402.

The symbolism of *Nineveh* as the false elements of the doctrines and **1188**
of *Rehoboth* and *Calah* as the same things from a different source can be
seen from the symbolism of Nineveh in the Word, which will be discussed just below.

Falsities of this kind come from three sources:

1. Illusions of the senses, the darkness of an unenlightened intellect,
   and ignorance. (Falsity from this source is Nineveh.)
2. The same causes, but with some corrupt desire dominating, such as
   an eagerness to innovate or to be superior to others. (Falsity from
   this source is Rehoboth.)
3. The will, and so our cravings; specifically, the refusal to recognize the
   truth of any idea that does not cater to our cravings. (Falsity from
   this source is Calah.)

All of these kinds of falsity come into existence through Assyria, or sophistic reasoning about the true ideas and good effects of faith.

[2] The symbolism of *Nineveh* as falsity rising out of sensory illusions,
darkness in an unenlightened intellect, and ignorance can be seen in the
Book of Jonah. Jonah was sent to Nineveh to pardon the city's people
for being of this type. The symbolism can also be seen in the individual
statements about Nineveh in Jonah. These ideas will be dealt with elsewhere, by the Lord's divine mercy. The narrative there is historical, but
it is still prophetic too, harboring and representing as it does the same
kinds of hidden meanings as all the other historical parts of the Word.

[3] The same is true in Isaiah 37:37, 38 as well, where it talks about
Assyria's king, saying that he stayed in *Nineveh* and while prostrating
himself in the house of Nisroch, his god, was struck by his sons with a
sword. Although these particulars are historical, they are still prophetic,
harboring and representing as they do the same kinds of hidden meanings. Nineveh here symbolizes an outward show of worship that has
false notions at its core; and because this kind of worship is idolatrous,
the king was struck by his sons with a sword. Sons are false notions,
as already shown [§1147], and a sword is the punishment that falsity
carries with it (which is its meaning everywhere in the Word). [4] In
Zephaniah, too:

Jehovah will stretch his hand out over the north and destroy *Assyria,*
and he will turn *Nineveh* into a desolation, into drought like the desert.

And flocks will lie down in its midst, every wild animal of that nation; the spoonbill and the harrier will also spend the night among its pomegranates. A voice will sing in the window. Devastation is at the threshold, because he has stripped its cedar bare. (Zephaniah 2:13, 14)

This describes Nineveh (in a writing mode typical of the prophets) and also the falsity symbolized by Nineveh. Because this falsity is worshiped, it is called the north, the wild animal of the nation, and a spoonbill and harrier among the pomegranates. The idea is also expressed in the statement that a voice sings in the window and the cedar—truth in the intellect—is stripped bare. All these expressions are symbolic of this kind of falsity.

1189 The symbolism of *Calah* as falsity rising out of our cravings cannot be demonstrated by verses from the prophets, yet it *can* be shown from the histories in the Word. The second book of Kings 17:6 and 18:11 says that the king of *Assyria* carried the descendants of Israel off into *Assyria* and settled them in *Calah,* and in Habor on the river Gozan, and in the cities of Media. The historical details here involve no other meaning. All the histories of the Word are symbolic and representative, as noted [§§64, 66:2, 117:2, 755:4–5, 855, 1025:2, 1140, 1143, 1183]. So Israel here is the spiritual church corrupted, Assyria is rationalization, and Calah is falsity rising out of our cravings.

1190 *Resen, between Nineveh and Calah,* means that they also created doctrines for themselves about how to live, and *Resen* symbolizes the false doctrines that resulted. This is established by the evidence given directly above concerning Nineveh and Calah. It is also established by the logical progression: The last verse [§1188] spoke of falsity in doctrine; the present one, of falsity in a person's life. The writing mode of the Word, especially in the prophets, requires that matters of the will be addressed whenever matters of intellect are. The last verse talked about something intellectual—falsity in doctrine—but the present one talks about the falsity we live by, which is what Resen symbolizes. Since the Word does not mention Resen anywhere else, the meaning cannot really be proved, except by two pieces of evidence. One is the fact that Resen was built between Nineveh and Calah, or in other words, between the falsity that comes of faulty reasoning and the falsity that comes of our cravings—a combination producing falsity that we actually live by. The other is the fact that it is called the great city because it rises out of falsity in both the intellect and the will.

The symbolism of *this is the great city* as doctrinal positions and the fact that they proliferated can be seen from the symbolism of a *city* as a true doctrinal viewpoint, or else as a false one. This symbolism was demonstrated in §402. The reason it is called a great city is that all falsity in doctrine and in worship that develops out of doctrine turns into falsity that people actually live by.

1191

Verse 10 just above dealt with evil in worship, as symbolized by Babel, Erech, Accad, and Calneh in the land of Shinar. The two current verses treat of falsity in worship, as symbolized by Nineveh, Rehoboth, Calah, and Resen. Falsity is a product of assumptions that grow out of flawed reasoning; evil is a product of cravings that come from materialism and selfishness.

1192

Genesis 10:13, 14. *And Mizraim fathered the Ludim, and Anamim, and Lehabim, and Naphtuhim, and Pathrusim, and Casluhim (from whom the Pelishtim came), and Caphtorim.*

1193

Mizraim fathered the Ludim, Anamim, Lehabim, and Naphtuhim, and the Caphtorim, symbolizes these individual nations, which in turn symbolize individual types of ritual. *Mizraim* means secular learning; *the Ludim, Anamim, Lehabim, and Naphtuhim,* mean respective types of ritual, which are merely secular. *The Pathrusim and Casluhim* mean nations by these names, and they symbolize doctrinal positions regarding ritual, which come from the same origin and are themselves merely secular. *From whom the Pelishtim came* means the nation that grew out of this tradition, which in turn symbolizes a knowledge of the concepts involved in faith and charity. The fact that they *came from* [the Casluhim] means that with them, religious knowledge exists in the form of facts.

Mizraim fathered the Ludim, Anamim, Lehabim, and Naphtuhim, and the Caphtorim, symbolizes these individual nations, which in turn symbolize individual types of ritual, as was established by evidence above at verse 6 of the present chapter concerning Mizraim, that is, Egypt [§§1163, 1165]. The information there shows that Egypt symbolizes learning, or factual knowledge. Those he is depicted as fathering can be nothing else—nothing but different kinds of ritual, and in fact different kinds of ritual used in an outward show of worship. Deep in its heart—in its inner meaning—the Lord's Word never concerns itself with any other issues than ones that have to do with the Lord's kingdom and so with the church. Here, then, the offspring born of factual information by shallow reasoning are just different kinds of ritual.

1194

1195   The fact that *Mizraim* (Egypt) means secular learning was demonstrated at verse 6 of this chapter. The fact that *the Ludim, Anamim, Lehabim, and Naphtuhim,* mean the respective types of ritual, which are merely secular, can be seen from the remarks directly above.

Ritual that is merely secular is attributed to people who use shallow logic to investigate spiritual and heavenly topics and manufacture a style of worship for themselves out of this. Because the ritual involved in this type of worship develops out of logic and fact, it is called secular. It has nothing spiritual or heavenly inside it, because it comes from human selfhood. This was the source of Egyptian idols and of the magical arts. Since this was the origin of those people's ritual, they completely rejected the rites of the ancient church. In fact they felt disgust and loathing for those rites, as indicated in Genesis 43:32; 46:34; Exodus 8:26. Because these are the things symbolized, those people are said to have been fathered by Mizraim, or Egypt—that is, by secular knowledge. And because they had many different kinds of knowledge, the ritual that sprang from it also came to be of many different types. The general varieties are symbolized by the respective nations.

The fact that *the Ludim,* or Lydians, have such a meaning can be seen in Jeremiah:

> Egypt rises like a river, and like rivers its waters churn. And it has said, "I will go up; I will blanket the land; I will destroy the city and those living in it." Go up, horses; run mad, chariots; and let your mighty men march out, Cush and Put, as you grasp your shield, and *Lydians* as you grasp—as you bend—your bow. (Jeremiah 46:8, 9)

The rivers of Egypt are different categories of information—false information. Going up and covering the land is using factual information as a means of entry into religious questions, or matters of faith. Destroying the city is destroying true ideas. Cush and Put are religious knowledge. Lydians (the subject here) are rituals that have emerged out of factual knowledge. Grasping and bending a bow is indulging in shallow logic.

1196   *The Pathrusim and Casluhim* mean nations by these names, and they symbolize doctrinal positions regarding ritual, which come from the same origin and are themselves purely secular. This is evident from the statements just made and from the position of these nations in the sequence. For passages about the people of Pathros, see Isaiah 11:11, 12; Ezekiel 29:13, 14, 15; 30:13, 14; Jeremiah 44:1, 15.

The fact that *from whom the Pelishtim came* means the nation that grew out of this tradition, which in turn symbolizes the knowledge of concepts involved in faith and charity, can be seen in the Word, where the name comes up many times. The ancient church used the label of *Philistine* for all those who talked and talked about faith and about the idea that salvation is found in faith and yet completely failed to live a life of faith. For this reason, Philistines more than any others were also described as uncircumcised, meaning that they lacked charity. (For passages that refer to them as uncircumcised, see 1 Samuel 14:6; 17:26, 36; 31:4; 2 Samuel 1:20; and other places.)

These people by nature could not help turning religious knowledge into a matter of memorization. The knowledge of spiritual and heavenly realities and even the mysteries of faith become nothing more than objects of memory when the people who are adept at them have no love for others.

Memorized details are dead objects to us unless we live according to them as a matter of conscience. When we do, then as soon as something becomes part of our memory it also becomes part of our life. That is when it first becomes something in us that remains useful to us and our salvation after physical life ends. Neither secular nor religious knowledge means anything to us in the other life—even if we have learned all the secrets that have ever been revealed—unless it permeates our life.

[2] In the prophetic parts of the Word, Philistines always symbolize this kind of people, as they do in the narrative parts too. One example is Abraham's stay in the Philistines' land and the fact that he struck a pact with Abimelech, king of the Philistines (Genesis 20:1–end; 21:22–end; 26:1–33). Since the Philistines symbolized the concepts of faith and Abraham represented the heavenly aspects of faith, he stayed in their land and entered into a pact with them. Isaac, who represented the spiritual aspects of faith, did something similar. But Jacob did not, because he represented the surface aspects of the church.

[3] Philistines in general symbolize the knowledge of religious concepts and in particular those who place faith and salvation in knowledge alone, which they turn into memorized information. This can be seen in Isaiah:

> Do not rejoice through and through, *Philistia,* that the rod striking you has been broken, because from the root of a snake a cockatrice will come out, and its fruit will be a flying fire snake. (Isaiah 14:29)

The root of a snake stands for facts, and a cockatrice, for evil rising out of falsity based on those facts. The fruit that is a flying fire snake means the deeds of those people; and the deeds are referred to as a flying fire snake because they result from cravings. [4] In Joel:

> What are you to me, Tyre and Sidon and all you borders of *Philistia?* Are you repaying me with retribution? I will very speedily bring your retribution back onto your own head, because my silver and my gold you have stolen, and my good, desirable things you have taken into your temples, and the children of Judah and the children of Jerusalem you have sold to the children of the Javanites, in order to make them go far away from their own border. (Joel 3:4, 5, 6)

The meaning of the Philistines and of the whole of Philistia (all its borders) is plain. The silver and gold mentioned mean spiritual and heavenly qualities of faith. Good, desirable things mean knowledge of those qualities. The taking of these items into the Philistines' temples means that they had that knowledge and preached it. But they sold the children of Judah and the children of Jerusalem, which means that they had no love and no faith. Judah in the Word is the heavenly side of faith, while Jerusalem is the spiritual side of it that develops out of the heavenly side, and these were removed far from their own borders. There are other passages in the prophets too, such as Jeremiah 25:20; 47:1–end; Ezekiel 16:27, 57; 25:15, 16; Amos 1:8; Obadiah verse 19; Zephaniah 2:5; Psalms 87:3, 4.

For passages about the people of *Caphtor,* see Deuteronomy 2:23; Jeremiah 47:4; Amos 9:7.

1198 The fact that they *came from* [the Casluhim] means that with them, religious knowledge exists in the form of facts, as the statements just made indicate. They are not said to have been *fathered* by the offspring of Egypt but to have *come from* them, because they do not do as those described above do; they are not the kind of people to invent new doctrines for themselves by reasoning fallaciously about spiritual and heavenly subjects on the basis of earthly knowledge. Instead they learn religious concepts from some other source, and the reasons they have for learning and memorizing the information are no different than their reasons for learning about other subjects. None of the information matters to them—aside from the fact that they know it—unless they can see it as a way to rise to high position and to other advantages. The study of religious concepts is so unlike any discipline in one of the earthly arts or sciences that the two share hardly any common ground. This is why [the Philistines] are said not to have been born to [the Casluhim] but to have come from them.

Because this is what Philistines are like, they too inevitably pervert religious knowledge by sophistic reasoning about it and in the process create false doctrines for themselves. They too, then, are among those who are almost incapable of being reborn and receiving any urge to love their neighbor. Their hearts are uncircumcised, and besides, false assumptions (and consequently the life of their intellect) get in the way and prevent their rebirth.

Genesis 10:15. *And Canaan fathered Sidon, his firstborn, and Heth.* **1199**
Canaan here as before symbolizes outward worship that has no inner content. *Sidon* symbolizes a superficial knowledge of spiritual attributes. Because this is the first knowledge acquired in the kind of outward worship being discussed here, Sidon is called Canaan's *firstborn*. *Heth* symbolizes a superficial knowledge of heavenly attributes.

The symbolism of *Canaan* as outward worship that has no inner **1200** content has been demonstrated in earlier discussions of Canaan [§§1063, 1094, 1103, 1167]. The outward display of worship that is called Canaan is the kind that Jews practiced before the Lord's Coming and after it as well. They had an external form of devotion that they observed very strictly, without realizing what its inner dimension was. In fact they imagined their bodies alone were alive. They had absolutely no idea what the soul was, what faith was, what the Lord was, what spiritual or heavenly life was, or what life after death was. As a result, many of them in the Lord's time denied the resurrection, as Matthew 22:23–34; Mark 12:18–28; and Luke 20:27–41 show. [2] When we are such that we do not believe we live on after death, we also fail to believe that any inner dimension exists, whether spiritual or heavenly.

People who spend their lives on mere self-gratification—especially those mired in sordid greed—are like this too, because they devote their lives exclusively to their person and to worldly advantages. Nonetheless, they engage in worship, one group attending synagogue, another going to church; and they observe traditional rites, some of them doing so very strictly. But since they do not believe in life after death, their worship cannot help being shallow, without any inner content, like a nutshell without the meat, or like a tree without fruit and even without leaves.

This is what the outward devotions symbolized by Canaan are like.

All the other types of inward worship discussed above were types of worship that did contain inner levels.

1201   The symbolism of *Sidon* as a superficial knowledge of spiritual attributes can be seen from the fact that he is called Canaan's firstborn, since what is firstborn in every church is, in an inner sense, faith (§§352, 367). Here, though, where there is no faith, since inner qualities are lacking, it is nothing more than a superficial knowledge of spiritual attributes, which takes the place of faith. So it is the kind of knowledge that Jews had: not only a knowledge of the ritual involved in external worship but a knowledge of other kinds of things that had to do with their worship as well, doctrinal precepts being one example.

The fact that Sidon symbolizes these things can also be seen from the consideration that Tyre and Sidon were the farthest boundaries of Philistia. They even bordered on the sea. So Tyre symbolized deeper knowledge and Sidon symbolized shallower knowledge—a deeper or shallower knowledge even of spiritual concepts—as the Word also demonstrates. In Jeremiah:

> . . . over the day that is coming, to devastate all the *Philistines,* to cut down in *Tyre* and *Sidon* every survivor who helps; because Jehovah is devastating the Philistines, the remnant of the island of Caphtor. (Jeremiah 47:4)

The Philistines stand for a knowledge of the religious concepts involved in faith and charity. Tyre stands for rather deep concepts and Sidon for concepts of spiritual entities. [2] In Joel:

> What are you to me, *Tyre* and *Sidon* and all you *borders of Philistia?* Because my silver and gold you have stolen, and my good, desirable things you have taken into your temples. (Joel 3:4, 5)

Clearly in this passage Tyre and Sidon stand for knowledge and are called the borders of Philistia, since the silver and gold and the good, desirable things are points of knowledge. In Ezekiel:

> [There you find] chiefs of the north, all of them, and every *Sidonian,* who have all gone down with the stabbed into the pit; . . . when Pharaoh with all his horde is made to lie in the middle of the uncircumcised along with those stabbed by the sword. (Ezekiel 32:30, 32)

The Sidonians stand for superficial knowledge, which in the absence of any deeper content is just a collection of facts, and that is why the

Sidonians are mentioned at the same time as Pharaoh, meaning Egypt, which symbolizes facts. In Zechariah:

> Hamath too will border on it, [as will] *Tyre* and *Sidon,* since it was very wise. (Zechariah 9:2)

This is about Damascus. Tyre and Sidon stand for knowledge. [3] In Ezekiel:

> The inhabitants of *Sidon* and Arvad were your rowers; your sages, *Tyre,* were within you; they were your captains. (Ezekiel 27:8)

Tyre stands for rather deep knowledge, so its sages are called captains; and Sidon stands for rather superficial knowledge, so its people are called rowers, since this is the relation of deeper knowledge to shallower. In Isaiah:

> The inhabitants of the island, the trader of *Sidon* crossing the sea, are silent; they have filled you up. But the seed of Sihor, the harvest of the river, its produce, came on many waters, and it was the merchandise of the nations. Blush, *Sidon,* since the sea, the stronghold of the sea spoke, saying, "I was not in labor and did not give birth and did not bring up young men, raise young women." (Isaiah 23:2, 3, 4, 5)

Sidon stands for shallower knowledge that has nothing deeper inside it. Because it has nothing inside, it is called the seed of Sihor, the harvest of the river, its produce, the merchandise of the nations, and also the sea, the stronghold of the sea, and something that does not labor or give birth. The literal meaning of these details could never be grasped, but on an inner level their meaning is quite obvious, as it is with all other passages in the prophets.

Because Sidon symbolizes superficial knowledge, it is also called the periphery of Israel (the spiritual church) in Ezekiel 28:24, 26, since superficial knowledge acts as a surrounding border.

It was explained in the last section that Sidon is called Canaan's *first-born* because this knowledge is the first acquired in the kind of outward worship devoid of inner content being discussed here.   `1202`

The fact that *Heth* symbolizes a superficial knowledge of heavenly attributes follows logically. The prophets customarily link spiritual and heavenly ideas; where they speak of spiritual properties, they also speak of heavenly ones. The one set comes from the other, so a certain perfection is missing unless they are joined. A further purpose is to bring an   `1203` image of the heavenly marriage into each and every part of the Word. These considerations (not to mention other illustrative passages in the Word) show that Sidon symbolizes a shallow knowledge of spiritual qualities while Heth symbolizes a shallow knowledge of heavenly ones. They symbolize this knowledge in both senses—both with and without deeper knowledge. In addition they stand simply for superficial knowledge.

Spiritual entities, as noted many times before, are aspects of faith, and heavenly entities are aspects of love. Again, spiritual traits belong to the intellect, heavenly ones to the will.

[2] The symbolism of Heth as shallow knowledge devoid of deeper knowledge can be seen in Ezekiel:

> This is what the Lord Jehovih has said to Jerusalem: "Your trading and your birth origins belong to the land of *Canaan*. Your father is an Amorite and your mother a *Hittite*. You are the daughter of your mother, who showed disgust for her man and her children; and the sister of your sisters, who showed disgust for their husbands and their children. Your mother is a *Hittite* and your father an Amorite." (Ezekiel 16:3, 45)

In this passage, outward worship without inward is Canaan. Showing disgust for their husbands and children is spurning things that are good and true, which is why their mother is called a Hittite.

Heth in the Word is also taken to stand for a relatively superficial knowledge of heavenly attributes in a good sense. Almost all the names of lands, cities, nations, and individuals do have a good sense, for the reason given earlier [§1151:1]. This symbolism of Heth will be dealt with later [§§2913, 2933, 2986:1, 6461], by the Lord's divine mercy.

Spiritual concepts are those that relate to faith and so to doctrine, but heavenly concepts relate to love and so to life.

1204   Genesis 10:16, 17, 18. . . . *and the Jebusite, and Amorite, and Girgashite, and Hivite, and Arkite, and Sinite, and Arvadite, and Zemarite, and Hamathite. And after that, the clans of the Canaanites scattered.*

The Jebusite, Amorite, Girgashite, Hivite, Arkite, Sinite, Arvadite, Zemarite, and Hamathite were individual nations that also symbolize individual idolatries of different sorts. *And after that, the clans of the Canaanites scattered,* means that all other types of idolatrous worship come from them.

1205   *The Jebusite, Amorite, Girgashite, Hivite, Arkite, Sinite, Arvadite, Zemarite, Hamathite* were individual nations that also symbolize individual idolatries of different sorts. The fact that those nations symbolize idolatries is evident from many places in the Word, because they were inhabitants of the land of Canaan, who were rejected on account of their idolatries, and of whom a portion was eradicated. But in the Word's inner sense, they do not symbolize the nations but the idolatries themselves. In general they symbolize idolatry wherever it exists; the specific reference is to idolatry among the Jews [of that time].

There are people who view worship as consisting solely in outward acts, who flatly refuse to hear about inward elements and reject the very idea when they are taught about it. Such people are strongly drawn to all these types of idolatry, as is strikingly clear from the [Old Testament] Jews. Only in internal worship is there a bond that can hold us back from idolatry. When it breaks, there is nothing left to stop us.

Idolatry, however, comes not only in shallow forms but in deeper forms as well. Superficial types of idolatry attract those practicing an outward worship devoid of inner devotion. The deeper forms of idolatry attract those practicing an outward worship in which the inner depths are foul. Both kinds are equally symbolized by these nations. Inward idolatries are simply so many falsities and impure desires that we love and adulate, which means that they stand in the place of the gods and idols that existed among non-Jewish nations. But explaining exactly which falsities and cravings are adulated [by the various people] symbolized by these nations—the Jebusite, Amorite, Girgashite, Hivite, Arkite, Sinite, Arvadite, Zemarite, and Hamathite—would take too long here. By the Lord's divine mercy, it will be told in the individual places where their names come up.

The meaning of *after that the clans of the Canaanites scattered,* as the fact that all other types of idolatrous worship come from them is evident without explanation.   **1206**

Genesis 10:19. *And the border of the Canaanites reached from Sidon as you come to Gerar, as far as Gaza, as you come to Sodom and Gomorrah and Admah and Zeboiim, as far as Lasha.*   **1207**

Here as earlier, *Sidon* symbolizes superficial knowledge. *Gerar* symbolizes information revealed about faith. *Gaza* symbolizes information revealed about charity. *The border of the Canaanites reached from Sidon as you come to Gerar, as far as Gaza,* symbolizes knowledge extending to include the truth and goodness in people who worship outwardly but not inwardly. *As you come to Sodom, Gomorrah, Admah, Zeboiim, as far as Lasha,* symbolizes the falsity and evil in which that knowledge ends.

The symbolism of *Sidon* as superficial knowledge is established by the illustrations offered above at verse 15 [§1201].   **1208**

1209 The symbolism of *Gerar* as information revealed about faith, and so generally as faith itself, can be seen from passages that mention Gerar, such as Genesis 20:1 and 26:1, 17. Later sections will deal with this symbolism of Gerar, the Lord in his divine mercy willing [§§2504, 3365, 3417].

1210 The symbolism of *Gaza* as information revealed about charity is established by two things. One is that where the Word speaks of spiritual traits it also speaks of heavenly traits in connection with them. In other words, when it talks about matters of faith it also talks about matters of charity. The other is from the Word as well, in places that mention Gaza.

What is more, knowledge extends to include faith, reaching as far as charity, which is its most distant boundary.

1211 *The border of the Canaanites reached from Sidon as you come to Gerar, as far as Gaza,* symbolizes knowledge extending [to include the truth and goodness] in people who worship outwardly but not inwardly. This can be seen from the symbolism of Gerar and Gaza. The boundaries of all knowledge having to do with worship (whether it is shallow worship or deep) reach that far, because all worship comes from faith and charity. Any worship that does not come from them is not worship but idolatry.

Since the subject here is Canaan, that is, outward worship and the things that develop out of it, it is the boundaries and extent not of worship but of knowledge that are meant here.

1212 The fact that *as you come to Sodom, Gomorrah, Admah, Zeboiim, as far as Lasha,* symbolizes the falsity and evil in which that knowledge ends can be seen from the symbolism of those nations in the narrative and prophetic parts of the Word.

Falsity comes from two general sources. One is the cravings that constitute selfishness and materialism; the other is the religious and secular concepts yielded by flimsy reasoning. Falsity from these sources that tries to gain the upper hand over truth is symbolized by Sodom, Gomorrah, Admah, and Zeboiim.

Anyone can see that falsity and the evil stemming from it are the ultimate bounds of outward worship that has nothing inside. This kind of worship contains only what is dead. Wherever the people who practice it turn, they fall into falsity. They have no inner voice to guide them in the path of truth or keep them on it. They have only an external drive that carries them off wherever craving and delusion lead.

The narrative and prophetic books of the Word mention Sodom, Gomorrah, Admah, and Zeboiim, so the specific symbolism of each will be told in the appropriate places, with the Lord's divine mercy.

Genesis 10:20. *These are Ham's sons by their clans, by their tongues, in their lands, in their nations.* **1213**

Ham's sons symbolize the doctrinal views and the varieties of worship that developed out of corrupt inward worship, which is Ham. *By their clans, by their tongues, in their lands, in their nations,* means according to the mentality of each, specifically and generally. *By their clans* means according to their standards of behavior; *by their tongues* means according to their way of thinking; *in their lands* means in respect generally to their way of thinking; *in their nations* means in respect generally to their behavioral standards.

Ham's sons symbolize the doctrinal views and the varieties of worship that developed out of corrupt inward worship, which is Ham. This can be seen from the symbolism of *sons* as doctrinal views and from the symbolism of *Ham* as corrupt inward worship—a symbolism discussed previously. **1214**

The meaning of *by their clans, by their tongues, in their lands, in their nations,* as according to the mentality of each, specifically and generally, was explained above at verse 5 [§1159], where the same words occur, although in a different order. That verse said of Japheth's sons that "from them the islands of the nations dispersed in their lands, each by its tongue, by their clans, in their nations," which symbolized different types of outward worship that had deeper worship within. In that passage, then, the images having to do with doctrine came first, but here those having to do with behavior, or with life, come first. **1215**

By their clans means according to their standards of behavior; *by their tongues* means according to their way of thinking; *in their lands* means in respect generally to their way of thinking; and *in their nations* means in respect generally to their behavioral standards. This is established by the symbolism of each—clan, tongue, land, and nation—in the Word. For those meanings, see what was said above at verse 5. **1216**

Genesis 10:21. *And Shem too had offspring. He was the father of all the sons of Eber; he was the older brother of Japheth.* **1217**

At this point *Shem* symbolizes the ancient church in general. *Shem had offspring* means that from the ancient church sprang a new one. *Eber* symbolizes the new church, which should be called the second ancient church. *He was the father of all the sons of Eber* means that this second ancient church and everything that belonged to it came from the first ancient church, its father. *He was the older brother of Japheth* means that its worship remained on the surface.

1218   The symbolism here of *Shem* as the ancient church in general can be seen from the fact that the person discussed in this verse is Eber, on whom the text now focuses. The symbolism can also be seen from the consideration that this verse describes Shem as Japheth's older brother.

1219   The meaning of *Shem had offspring* as the fact that from the ancient church sprang a new one can be seen from the contents of the present verse, in that it treats of Eber, meaning this new ancient church, which will be described below.

1220   The symbolism of *Eber* as the new church, which should be called the second ancient church, can be seen from what follows, where Eber is discussed in detail. Eber is mentioned here because from him came the new church. Later sections, with the Lord's divine mercy, will tell how the case was with Eber and with this second church.

1221   *He was the father of all the sons of Eber* means that this second ancient church and everything that belonged to it came from the first ancient church, its father. This too will become evident below, where Eber and this church are discussed. The current chapter speaks of Eber in verses 24–30, and the following chapter does so from verse 11 to the end.

1222   The meaning of *he was the older brother of Japheth* as the fact that its worship remained on the surface is established by the symbolism of Japheth as the outer church, dealt with in the last chapter, at verse 18 and later verses, and earlier in the present chapter, at verses 1–5 [§§1062, 1083, 1091, 1098, 1100, 1144–1159]. Here the specific meaning of the fact that Shem was Japheth's older brother is that the inner church and the outer church are brothers, since this is precisely the relation inward devotion bears to the outward worship that holds it. The two are kin, because charity is the main concern of each. The inner church is the older brother, though, since it comes first and is deeper.

The idea of Japheth's older brother here also involves the fact that the second ancient church (called Eber) was like a brother to the first ancient church. In an inner sense, Japheth just means outward worship filled with inward worship, in every church. So he also symbolizes the worship of this new ancient church, which remained mostly on the surface. (The Word's inner meaning is such that we ignore the narrative details of the literal sense when focusing on universal themes abstracted from that sense, because the two meanings concern themselves with entirely different matters.) So in an inner sense, Japheth's older brother symbolizes the way the new ancient church worshiped: a superficial way. If it did not mean this, there would be no need for the verse to mention that he was the older brother of Japheth.

Genesis 10:22. *The sons of Shem: Elam, and Asshur, and Arpachshad, and Lud, and Aram.* **1223**

Shem here as before symbolizes the inner church. The *sons of Shem* symbolize attributes that are forms of wisdom. *Elam, Asshur, Arpachshad, Lud, and Aram* were individual nations, which symbolize attributes that are forms of wisdom. *Elam* symbolizes faith that grows out of love for others; *Asshur* symbolizes the powers of reason that result; *Arpachshad* symbolizes the secular learning that results from this; *Lud* symbolizes knowledge of truth; and *Aram* symbolizes knowledge of goodness.

This shows what these names mean on an inner level. They mean that **1224** the ancient church (the one that had depth) was endowed with wisdom, understanding, secular learning, and knowledge of truth and goodness. Those are the contents in the inner sense, even though they are only names, which reveal nothing on the literal plane but the fact that each was an originator or ancestor of a nation. The literal meaning reveals nothing doctrinal, still less anything spiritual or heavenly. The case is similar in the prophets, which sometimes contain series of names—symbolizing the deeper realities of the inner sense—that progress in the most beautiful order.

The symbolism of *Shem* as the inner church was stated and illus- **1225** trated in the last chapter, at verse 18 and later verses [§§1062, 1083, 1091, 1096:2, 1098, 1102:1, 3].

The *sons of Shem* symbolize attributes that are forms of wisdom. The **1226** fact that Shem is the inner church, whose offspring are nothing else than forms of wisdom, is not the only indication of this symbolism. *Wisdom* is the term for everything that charity fathers, because whatever charity fathers comes by way of charity from the Lord, who is the source of all wisdom, since he is wisdom itself. This is the origin of true understanding, which is the origin of true learning, which is the origin of true knowledge. All three are the offspring of charity, or in other words, children of the Lord by way of charity. Because they are children of the Lord by way of charity, each is described as a form of wisdom. This is because each of them contains wisdom, from which they draw their life. In fact not one of them—not understanding or secular learning or religious knowledge—has any life except that drawn from wisdom, which belongs to charity, which is the Lord's.

The fact that *Elam, Asshur, Arpachshad, Lud, and Aram* were individ- **1227** ual nations is evident from the places they are mentioned in the narrative and prophetic parts of the Word. Their symbolism as attributes that are forms of wisdom can be seen from the remarks just above and by ones that follow too.

The inner church existed among these nations; the outer church existed among others referred to as Japheth's children; the inner church once it was corrupted, among those called Ham's children; and the outer church corrupted, among those called Canaan's children. (Whether one says inward and outward worship or inner and outer church, it is exactly the same.)

1228   The symbolism of *Elam* as faith that grows out of love for others can be seen from the essential nature of the inner church. The inner church is where love for others is the primary basis of thought and action. The first child born of that love is nothing less than faith, since faith comes from that love and not from anywhere else. Elam's symbolism as the faith that comes of charity—that is, the faith that truly forms the inner church—can also be seen in Jeremiah:

> The word of Jehovah came to Jeremiah concerning *Elam:* "Here, now, I am breaking the bow of *Elam,* the beginning of its power, and I will bring to *Elam* four winds from the four ends of the heavens and will scatter the people among all these winds. And there will not be a nation to which some of the exiles of *Elam* will not come. And I will unnerve *Elam* before its enemies and before those seeking its soul, and I will bring evil on them—the blazing of my anger—and I will send the sword after them until I devour them. And I will put my throne in *Elam* and eliminate the monarch and the chieftains from there, and it will happen in the end of days that I will bring *Elam* back from captivity." (Jeremiah 49:34–39)

[2] This passage speaks of faith, under the figure of Elam. What is the same, it speaks of the inner church when this has become perverted and corrupt, and then immediately of the same church when it has been restored. Similar things are said of Judah, Israel, and Jacob many times in the Word, and they symbolize churches too. Judah symbolizes the heavenly church, Israel symbolizes the spiritual church, and Jacob symbolizes the outer church. Their condition when they had been perverted is treated in much the same way in the Word, which says that they would scatter and then that the scattered would be reclaimed from their enemies and brought back from captivity, meaning that a new church would be created. So of Elam, or the inner church when it had become perverted and corrupt, it says here that it would be scattered and then that it would be brought back. Afterward it says that Jehovah would put his throne in Elam—in other words, in the inner church, or in the inner depths of the church, which consist in nothing less than the faith that rises out of neighborly love. [3] In Isaiah:

The burden of the wilderness beside the sea: From the wilderness it comes, and from a fearsome land. A harsh vision was shown to me: the betrayer is betraying and the ravager is ravaging. Go up, *Elam!* Lay a siege, *Madai!* All its groaning I have ended. (Isaiah 21:1, 2)

This is about Babylon's destruction of the church. Elam is the inner church; Madai is the outer church, or outward worship containing inward. The fact that Madai is this kind of church or this kind of worship can be seen above at verse 2 of the current chapter [§§1150–1151:1], where Madai is named as Japheth's son.

The symbolism of *Asshur* as the power of reason can be seen from evidence given above at verse 11 of this chapter [§§1185–1186]. **1229**

The symbolism of *Arpachshad* as secular learning cannot really be established from the Word, but it follows logically from the series of meanings coming before and after it. **1230**

The symbolism of *Lud* as knowledge of truth can be seen by considering that a knowledge of truth comes in this way—from the Lord through charity and so through faith by means of reason and learning. The symbolism can also be seen in Ezekiel: **1231**

> Persia and *Lud* and Put were in your army; they were your men of war. Shield and helmet they hung on you; they themselves gave you your adornment. (Ezekiel 27:10)

Tyre is the subject here. Lud and Put stand for points of knowledge, which are described as being in the army and as being men of war, because they serve to defend truth, with the aid of reason; and this service is also the hanging of shield and helmet. For the symbolism of Put as superficial knowledge of the Word, see above at verse 6 of this chapter [§§1163–1164, 1166].

The symbolism of *Aram,* or Syria, as knowledge of what is good follows logically. It also follows from what the Word says. In Ezekiel: **1232**

> *Aram* was your dealer for the abundance of your works in chrysoprase, red-violet fabric, and embroidery, and fine linen, and ramoth, and carnelian; they traded for your market goods. (Ezekiel 27:16)

This is about Tyre, or in other words, about acquiring knowledge. The works, chrysoprase, red-violet fabric, embroidery, fine linen, ramoth, and carnelian mean nothing else than a knowledge of goodness. In Hosea:

> Jacob fled into the field of *Aram* and worked as a servant in exchange for a wife, and for a wife he guarded [sheep]. And through a prophet Jehovah

brought Israel up out of Egypt, and through a prophet [Israel] was kept
safe. Ephraim provoked [Jehovah] to bitter anger. (Hosea 12:12, 13, 14)

Jacob stands for the outer church here, and Israel stands for the inner,
spiritual church. Aram stands for a knowledge of goodness. Egypt stands
for secular learning that corrupts. Ephraim stands for intelligence that
has been corrupted. What they symbolize within the series could never
be deduced from the literal meaning, only from the inner sense, in which
names symbolize various phenomena in the church, as noted [§§64, 144–
145, 339, 468:1, 1143, 1224]. In Isaiah:

> Here now, Damascus has been rejected as a city and become a heap of
> ruin. The stronghold will disappear from Ephraim and the sovereignty
> from *Damascus,* and the remainder of *Aram* will be like the glory of the
> children of Israel. (Isaiah 17:1, 3)

The remainder of Aram stands for a knowledge of goodness, which is
called Israel's glory. Aram (or Syria) in the opposite sense also stands for
a knowledge of goodness that has been perverted, in Isaiah 7:4, 5, 6; 9:12;
Deuteronomy 26:5. (In the Word it is common for a word to be used in
both senses.)

1233   Genesis 10:23. *And the sons of Aram: Uz, and Hul, and Gether, and Mash.*
Aram here as before symbolizes a knowledge of what is good. The
sons of Aram are further knowledge derived from it and the effects of that
knowledge. *Uz, Hul, Gether, and Mash,* each symbolize a different type
of this knowledge.

1234   The symbolism of *Aram* as a knowledge of goodness was demonstrated directly above.

The symbolism of the *sons of Aram* as further knowledge derived
from it and the effects of that knowledge follows logically. The knowledge derived from a knowledge of goodness is earthly truth. The effects
of that knowledge are actions taken in accord with it. These symbolisms
cannot easily be demonstrated from the Word because the names are not
among those that come up frequently. The only reference is to Uz, in
Jeremiah 25:20 and Lamentations 4:21.

From this it now follows that *Uz, Hul, Gether, and Mash,* each symbolize a different type of this knowledge and of action taken in accord
with it.

1235   Genesis 10:24. *And Arpachshad fathered Shelah, and Shelah fathered Eber.*
Arpachshad was a nation by that name, and it symbolizes secular
learning. *Shelah* was likewise a nation by that name, and it symbolizes

the effect that results from that learning. *Eber* too means a nation, one whose ancestor was Eber, an individual called by that name. He symbolizes the second ancient church, which separated from the first.

The fact that *Arpachshad* was a nation by that name and that it symbolizes secular learning is indicated by remarks about him just above at verse 22 [§§1223–1224, 1226–1227, 1230].

1236

Shelah was likewise a nation, and it symbolizes the effect that results from that learning, as follows from the fact that it says that *Arpachshad fathered Shelah.*

1237

In regard to the fact that *Eber* too means a nation—one whose ancestor was Eber, an individual called by that name—the case is this: The names mentioned so far were nations among whom the ancient church was present. All of them were called children of Shem, Ham, Japheth, or Canaan because Shem, Ham, Japheth, and Canaan symbolized dissimilar cultures in the church. Noah, Shem, Ham, Japheth, and Canaan themselves never existed. But the ancient church in particular (like every religion in general) by its very nature had genuine depths, corrupt depths, genuine externals, and corrupt externals. That is why these names came into being: so that all the different general types could be categorized under the headings represented by these individuals and their offspring.

1238

At their outset, the nations named here also practiced the kind of worship [symbolized by each]. That is why they are called the children of one of Noah's sons, and it is why the names of these nations in the Word symbolize the different cultures themselves.

[2] This first ancient church—the one that Noah and his sons symbolize—did not exist among only a few people but spread out through many countries. One indication is the number of nations mentioned: Assyria, Mesopotamia, Syria, Ethiopia, Arabia, Libya, Egypt, Philistia as far as Tyre and Sidon, and the whole land of Canaan on both the far and the near sides of the Jordan.

Afterward, though, a certain shallow kind of worship took hold in Syria, and it eventually spread far and wide through many lands (especially in Canaan). It was at variance with the worship of the ancient church, and since its existence constituted the start of something like a church distinct and separate from the ancient church, a seemingly new church now arose, which can therefore be called the second ancient church. The founder was Eber, so the religion was named after him.

At that period people were all divided into households, clans, and nations, as already noted [§§470–471, 483:2, 1159:3]. Each nation acknowledged one father, for whom it was named, as the Word demonstrates throughout. So the nation that acknowledged Eber as its father was called the Hebrew nation.

1239   The symbolism of Eber as the second ancient church, which separated from the first, can be seen from the statements just above.

1240   Genesis 10:25. *And to Eber were born two sons. The name of one was Peleg (because in his days the land was divided), and the name of his brother was Joktan.*

Eber was the founder of the second ancient church, and he symbolizes that church. He had *two sons,* who symbolize two kinds of worship—inward and outward. His two sons were called Peleg and Joktan, and *Peleg* symbolizes the inward devotions of that church, while Joktan symbolizes its outward devotions. *Because in his days the land was divided* means that the church was then subverted; the *land* here as before symbolizes the church. *The name of his brother was Joktan* symbolizes the outward devotions of that church.

1241   Concerning *Eber* as the founder of the second ancient church, and his symbolism as that church, this is the situation: The first ancient church, as noted [§1238:2], spread far and wide throughout the world, especially in the Near East. Over time it deteriorated, as all religions everywhere do, and subverters in various places adulterated both its outward and its inward worship. Their main offense was to take all the symbolic and representative lore that the ancient church had received from the mouth of the earliest church—every bit of which focused on the Lord and his kingdom—and make it idolatrous. Some nations even turned it into magic. To prevent the entire church from perishing, the Lord allowed symbolic and representative worship to be restored in some places, and this was done by Eber, whose worship consisted chiefly in external things. The externals of the religion were high places, groves, pillars, and anointings, not to mention priesthoods and the traditions governing them, along with many other rules, which were called statutes.

The deeper aspects of the religion were doctrinal precepts dating back to the time before the Flood, received principally from the people referred to as Enoch. These people gathered together the perceptive knowledge of the earliest church and out of it constructed doctrinal precepts that formed their Word.

The internals and the externals just described formed the worship of this religion. The style of worship was founded by Eber but later enlarged and also changed. In particular, its worshipers started to consider sacrifices more important than other types of ritual. Sacrifice was unknown in the true ancient church. It existed exclusively with certain idolatrous descendants of Ham and Canaan and was tolerated among them to prevent them from sacrificing their own sons and daughters.

These descriptions illustrate the nature of this second ancient church, founded by Eber and maintained among his descendants, who were called the Hebrew nation.

Eber's *two sons* symbolize two kinds of worship, inward and outward, and the two sons were called Peleg and Joktan. *Peleg* symbolizes the inward devotions of that church, while *Joktan* symbolizes its outward devotions. The main evidence for this is as follows. In an inner sense Eber and the nation he founded symbolize this second ancient church. Every church has an inner and an outer dimension, since a church lacking an inner plane is not a church and cannot be called a church but a form of idolatry. It is evident, then, since different aspects of the church are what the sons portray, that one of them symbolizes the church's inner dimension and the other the outer. The same thing happens in many other places throughout the Word. Adah and Zillah, Lamech's wives (see §409), provide one earlier example. Leah and Rachel provide another, and Jacob and Israel (who will be discussed later), another. There are yet others too.

The present chapter deals with Joktan's descendants; the next, with Peleg's.

From this it can now be seen that *because in his days the land was divided* means that the church was then subverted. The *land,* after all, actually means the church, as §§662, 1066 above clearly demonstrated.

The fact that *the name of his brother was Joktan* symbolizes the outward devotions of that church was shown just above. For the fact that outward worship is called a brother, see above at verse 21 of this chapter [§1222], which speaks of Shem as Japheth's older brother. That is why the present verse adds that it was the *brother's* name.

Genesis 10:26, 27, 28, 29. *And Joktan fathered Almodad, and Sheleph, and Hazarmaveth, and Jerah, and Hadoram, and Uzal, and Diklah, and Obal, and Abimael, and Sheba, and Ophir, and Havilah, and Jobab; all these are the sons of Joktan.*

These were individual nations formed from the clans of Eber, and they symbolize individual types of ritual.

The fact that these were individual nations formed from the clans of Eber can be seen from conditions at that period. In earliest times, as previously noted [§1238:2], people lived as nations divided into clans and as

1242

1243

1244

1245

1246

clans divided into households, and each nation acknowledged one father, for whom it was named. When the children of one father multiplied, they likewise formed households, clans, and nations; and so on.

These people, the offspring of Joktan, lived a similar way, as can be seen from the children of Jacob. When they eventually multiplied, they formed tribes, each of which claimed one of Jacob's sons as the father for whom it was named. Yet all of them taken together came from Jacob and were called Jacob. By the same token, all these nations came from Eber and were called Hebrews.

1247 The fact that they symbolize individual types of ritual can be seen from the consideration that names in the Word never have any meaning but a symbolic one. The Word in its inner sense concentrates exclusively on the Lord, on his kingdom in heaven and earth, and consequently on the church and its attributes. The same is true of these names.

Furthermore, since Eber's son Joktan symbolizes the outward devotions of this new church, as I said before, his own children cannot symbolize anything else than features of external worship, which are different kinds of ritual. In fact each must symbolize its own kind. Exactly what those types of ritual were, however, it is impossible to say. They depend for their character on the worship itself, and before the variety of worship is known well, nothing can be said about its rituals, and knowing about them would not be useful to anyone. Besides, the names never recur in the Word, except for those of Sheba, Ophir, and Havilah. And these are not offshoots of Joktan's stock, because the Sheba and Havilah that the Word talks about came from those who are called children of Ham, as verse 7 of the current chapter shows. The same is true of Ophir.

1248 Genesis 10:30. *And their living space reached from Mesha as you come to Sephar, the mountain of the east.*

These words symbolize how far their worship extended: from religious truth to charitable good. *Mesha* symbolizes truth; *Sephar* symbolizes what is good; *the mountain of the east* symbolizes charity.

1249 These words symbolize how far their worship extended: from religious truth to charitable good. *Mesha* symbolizes truth; *Sephar* symbolizes what is good. But these meanings cannot be illustrated from the Word, because the prophets make no mention of Mesha or Sephar. Still, it can be seen from the fact that the verse forms a conclusion for the words leading up to it. In particular, it can be seen from the fact that the mountain of the east is the final image, to which everything before it looks, and in the Word an eastern mountain symbolizes charity from the Lord, as the following section establishes. It can also be seen from the fact that everything about the church looks to charity as its final goal. The logical conclusion, then, is that Mesha symbolizes truth, or the starting point, while Sephar symbolizes goodness and therefore charity (the mountain of the east), or the end point.

The symbolism of *the mountain of the east* as charity, specifically the quality of charity received from the Lord, can be seen from the following symbolism in the Word: A mountain symbolizes love for the Lord and charity toward our neighbor (as shown above at §795). The east symbolizes the Lord and heavenly qualities received from him, which are qualities of love and charity (again, see above, §101). The symbolism can also be seen in the following passages. In Ezekiel:

1250

> The guardian beings lifted their wings. The glory of Jehovah went up from the middle of the city and stood on the *mountain* that was on the *east* of the city. (Ezekiel 11:22, 23)

The sole meaning of the mountain that was on the east is the heavenly quality that belongs to love and charity—these being the Lord's, because it says that the glory of Jehovah stood there. [2] In the same author:

> He led me to the gate, a gate that looks out on the path to the *east,* and there! The glory of Israel's God came by way of the *east.* (Ezekiel 43:1, 2)

The east has a similar meaning here. In the same author:

> And he brought me back by way of the gate of the outer sanctuary looking to the *east,* and it was shut. And Jehovah said to me, "This gate shall be shut; it shall not be opened; and not a man shall go in through it. But Jehovah, God of Israel, will go in through it." (Ezekiel 44:1, 2)

Again the east stands for a heavenly quality, which is the quality of love, which is the Lord's alone. In the same author:

> When the chief makes a voluntary offering, a burnt offering, or peace offerings, it is a voluntary offering to Jehovah. And he shall open to [Jehovah] the gate looking toward the *east* and make his burnt offering and his peace offerings as he does on the Sabbath day. (Ezekiel 46:12)

Here too the east stands for a heavenly quality, which is the quality of love for the Lord. [3] In the same author:

> And he brought me back to the doorway of the House, and look! Water going out from under the doorsill of the House toward the *east;* because the House faces *east.* (Ezekiel 47:1, 8)

This is about a new Jerusalem. The east stands for the Lord and so for the heavenly quality of love. The water means spiritual qualities.

The mountain of the east in the present verse has a similar meaning. In addition, people who lived in Syria were called the children of the east, and they will be discussed later [§§3249, 3762], with the Lord's divine mercy.

1251   Genesis 10:31. *These are Shem's sons, by their clans, by their tongues, in their lands, by their nations.*

These are Shem's sons symbolizes cultures that developed out of the inward worship that is Shem. *By their clans, by their tongues, in their lands, in their nations* mean in harmony with the character of each, specifically and generally. *By their clans* is in accord with their different forms of charity. *By their tongues* is in accord with their different beliefs. *In their lands* is in relation to the effects of faith generally. *In their nations* is in relation to the effects of charity generally.

1252   There is no need for further confirmation that these are the things they symbolize, since the words are the same as those above in verse 20 (see the remarks there [§§1213–1216]). Symbolism (here, for instance, the symbolism of families, tongues, lands, and nations) relates to the subjects being described. Verse 20 dealt with Ham, or in other words, with inner devotion that had been corrupted. The current verse, however, deals with Shem, or true inner devotion. At verse 20, then, the clans and nations had to do with the behavioral standards belonging to a church that had depth but had been corrupted, while the tongues and lands had to do with its way of thinking. But here, the clans and nations have to do with the charity belonging to a church with true depth and the tongues and lands have to do with its faith.

For a discussion of the symbolism of nations and families, see below in the present chapter [§§1254, 1256, 1259–1261].

1253   Genesis 10:32. *These are the clans of Noah's sons, by their births, in their nations.*

These are the clans of Noah's sons, symbolize the specific ways in which the ancient church worshiped. *By their births* means insofar as they were able to reform. *In their nations* symbolizes the general ways that church worshiped.

1254   The symbolism of *these are the clans of Noah's sons,* as the specific ways in which the ancient church worshiped can be seen from the symbolism of a clan, and of a clan of sons, as ways to worship and in fact as specific types of worship.

The nations named in the earlier parts of this chapter only symbolized various ways in which the ancient church worshiped, so the clans that composed the nations cannot have any other meaning. The inner sense cannot be referring to any other clans than those of spiritual and heavenly traits.

The fact that *by their births* means insofar as they were able to reform can be seen from the symbolism of birth as reformation. When we are being reborn or regenerated by the Lord, each and every new thing that we receive is a birth. So in this case, since the ancient church is under discussion, the births mean insofar as its people were able to reform. **1255**

With regard to reformation of the nations, they did not all have the same kind of worship or the same teachings, because they did not all have the same disposition or the same upbringing and education from childhood on. The Lord never breaks the principles we first adopt as children but bends them. Any principles we possess that we have always invested with holiness, any that do not inherently oppose God's plan or the order of the physical world but are inconsequential, those principles the Lord leaves alone and allows to remain in us. This was true of many principles that the second ancient church adopted, which will be discussed below [§§1337, 1343], by the Lord's divine mercy.

The symbolism of *in their nations* as the general ways that church worshiped can be seen from statements above and below concerning nations. **1256**

And from them the nations scattered in the land after the flood. **1257**

From them the nations scattered in the land means that this was the origin of all the varieties of worship in the church, with both their good and their bad aspects, which are symbolized by *the nations;* the *land* is the church. *After the flood* means from the start of the ancient church.

From them the nations scattered in the land means that this was the origin of all the varieties of worship in the church, with both their good and their bad aspects, and these are symbolized by *the nations,* as can be seen from the symbolism of nations. **1258**

As noted before [§§470, 1159:3], a nation means many clans taken together. A large number of clans acknowledging a single father made up one nation in the earliest church and in the ancient church. Yet in an inner sense nations symbolize different kinds of worship in the church, specifically its good and its bad aspects, and this is why: When angels look at clans and nations, they form no picture of a nation but only of the worship that the nation practices. They regard all people in terms of

their true nature or quality, and the nature or quality in us from which
heaven views us is charity and faith.

You can see this clearly by looking carefully at the way you view
any individual, clan, or nation. Chances are that you evaluate others in
terms of what is most important to you personally at the time, and the
first thing that springs to mind is your assessment of their character [in
that regard], which determines your private reflections on them. This
is still more true of the Lord and from him of the angels. They cannot consider any individual, clan, or race except in terms of its charity and faith. So on an inner level, what nations mean is worship in
the church, and specifically its quality—that is, the good embraced
by charity and the truth espoused by the faith that comes of charity.
When the word *nations* occurs in the Word, angels never linger over
the idea of a nation, as the literal meaning of the narrative would have
them do, but over the idea of the goodness and truth in the nation
mentioned.

1259   To continue with the concept that nations symbolize the good and
bad in a way of worshiping: As already noted [§§470–471, 483:2, 1159:3,
1238:2, 1246], humankind in the earliest times lived divided into nations,
clans, and households. The purpose behind this was for the church on
earth to represent the Lord's kingdom, where all the inhabitants are
marked off into separate communities and the communities into larger
communities and these again into still larger ones. It is differences in love
and faith, both general and specific, that determine those divisions. (For
more on this, see §§684, 685.) So the inhabitants are likewise divided
into something like households, clans, and nations.

As a result, different kinds of goodness associated with love and so
with faith are symbolized by households, clans, and nations in the Word,
which carefully distinguishes between nations and peoples. A nation
symbolizes goodness or evil, but a people symbolizes truth or falsity. This
is consistently true, without exception, as the following passages illustrate. [2] In Isaiah, for instance:

> It will happen on that day that Jesse's root will be what is standing as a
> banner of the *peoples;* it will be what the *nations* seek, and its resting
> place will be glorious. On that day, the Lord will apply his hand another,
> second time to secure the remnant of his *people* who were left behind by
> Assyria and by Egypt and by Pathros and by Cush and by Elam and by
> Shinar and by Hamath and by the islands of the sea. And he will lift up

a banner for the *nations* and gather the exiles of Israel, and the scattered elements of Judah he will assemble. (Isaiah 11:10, 11, 12)

The peoples stand for the church's true ideas, while the nations stand for its good qualities, and the two are obviously distinct. The theme is the Lord's kingdom, the church, and (to speak universally) every individual who has been reborn. The names symbolize the same things as before [§§1163–1165, 1183, 1185–1186, 1196, 1205, 1228]. Israel symbolizes the church's spiritual attributes; Judah, its heavenly attributes. In the same author:

> This *people,* walking in shadow, have seen great light. You have multiplied the *nation;* you have enlarged the gladness in it. (Isaiah 9:2, 3)

The people in this passage stand for truth, so they are said to walk in shadow and to see light. The nation stands for goodness. [3] In the same author:

> What answer will the messengers of the *nation* receive? That Jehovah has founded Zion, and the wretched of his *people* will trust in it. (Isaiah 14:32)

The nation again stands for goodness and the people for truth. In the same author:

> Jehovah Sabaoth will swallow up on this mountain the enveloping layers enveloping all the *peoples,* and the mantle veiling all the *nations.* (Isaiah 25:7)

This is about a new church—a church among gentile, or non-Jewish, nations. The people stand for its true ideas, and the nations, for its good qualities. In the same author:

> Open the gates, so that an upright *nation* keeping faith may walk in. (Isaiah 26:2)

The nation explicitly stands for goodness. In the same author:

> All the *nations* will assemble together, and the *peoples* will gather. (Isaiah 43:9)

This too is about a church among non-Jewish nations. The nations stand for its good qualities and the people for its true ideas, and because the two are distinctly different from each other, both are addressed. Otherwise it would be pointlessly repetitive. In the same author:

> The Lord Jehovih has said, "Look, now, I will lift my hand to the *nations,* and for the *peoples* I will raise my signal. And they will bring

your sons in their embrace, and your daughters they will carry here on
their shoulder." (Isaiah 49:22)

This is about the Lord's kingdom. The nations again stand for goodness
and the peoples for truth. [4] In the same author:

To the right and left will you burst out, and your seed will inherit the
nations, and deserted cities they will inhabit. (Isaiah 54:3)

The subject is the Lord's kingdom and the church called the church of the
Gentiles. The nations stand for charitable goodness, or (what is the same)
for individuals who display charitable goodness, as can be seen from the
fact that the "seed" (faith) will inherit them. The cities stand for truth. In
the same author:

Look, now, I have made him a witness to the *peoples,* a chieftain and law-
giver for the *peoples.* Look, now, you will call a *nation* you do not recognize, and a *nation* that has not known you will run to you. (Isaiah 55:4, 5)

The subject here is the Lord's kingdom. The peoples stand for truth, the
nations for goodness. In the church, those who are endowed with the good
impulses of neighborly love are the nations, while those who are endowed
with religious truth are the peoples. Goodness and truth are predicated of
the individuals in whom they exist. In the same author:

The *nations* will walk toward your light, and monarchs toward the
radiance of your dawn. Then you will see and flow toward them, and
your heart will be struck with awe and expand, because the abundance
of the sea will be steered toward you; the armies of the *nations* will
come to you. (Isaiah 60:3, 5)

This passage is about the Lord's kingdom and the church of the Gentiles.
In it, the nations stand for goodness, and the monarchs, who are monarchs of the peoples, stand for truth. [5] In Zephaniah:

The remnant of my *people* will plunder them, and those remaining of
my *nation* will inherit them. (Zephaniah 2:9)

In Zechariah:

Many *peoples* and numerous *nations* will come to seek Jehovah of the
Legions in Jerusalem. (Zechariah 8:22)

Jerusalem stands for the Lord's kingdom and for the church. The peoples
stand for those who possess religious truth, and the nations for those

who exhibit the good impulses of neighborly love, which is why they are mentioned separately. In David:

> You will free me from the quarrels of the *people;* you will put me at the head of the *nations.* A *people* I have not known will serve me. (Psalms 18:43)

Again the people stand for those who have true concepts, and nations for those who have goodness. Since these entities go to make up an individual in the church, both are mentioned. In the same author:

> The *peoples* will acclaim you, God. The *peoples* will acclaim you—all of them; the *nations* will rejoice and exult, because you will judge the *peoples* with uprightness, and the *nations* you will lead into the land. (Psalms 67:3, 4)

The peoples obviously stand for those who have religious truth, and the nations for those who possess charitable goodness. [6] In Moses:

> Remember the days of old; understand the years of generation after generation. Ask your father and he will point out to you; your elders and they will tell you: when the Highest One gave an inheritance to the *nations* and divided the children of humankind, he set the boundaries of the *peoples* by the number of the children of Israel. (Deuteronomy 32:7, 8)

The theme here is the earliest church and the ancient churches, which are the days of old and the years of generation after generation. In those churches, the members who exhibited charitable goodness were called nations, to whom an inheritance was given. The children of humankind and then the peoples were members possessing religious truth that grew out of charity.

Because nations symbolize the church's good qualities and peoples symbolize its true ideas, when Esau and Jacob were still in the womb it was said that:

> Two *nations* are in your womb, and two *peoples* will divide from your belly. (Genesis 25:23)

This evidence now establishes what the term *church of the Gentiles* (or of the nations) really means; the earliest church was the real church of the Gentiles, and after it, the ancient church was.

[7] Because those who have charity are called nations, while those who possess faith are called peoples, the Lord's role as priest is assigned

to the nations (since it involves heavenly attributes, which are different kinds of goodness), while his role as monarch is assigned to the peoples (since it involves spiritual entities, which are true concepts). This was represented in the Jewish religion, whose adherents formed a nation during the time before they had monarchs but became a people after they acquired monarchs.

1260 Since nations symbolized good qualities or good people in the earliest church and in the ancient church, in the opposite sense they also symbolize bad qualities or bad people. By the same token, since peoples symbolized truth, in the opposite sense they also symbolize falsity. A perverted religion turns goodness into evil and truth into falsity. That is why the symbolism of nations and peoples is a negative one many times in the Word, as for instance in Isaiah 13:4; 14:6; 18:2, 7; 30:28; 34:1, 2; Ezekiel 20:32; and many other places.

1261 As nations symbolized good qualities, clans did too, since each nation consisted of a number of clans. The same is true for households, because each clan was made up of many households. (For more about a house or household, see §710.) Yet although clans symbolize goodness when mentioned in connection with nations, they symbolize truth when mentioned in connection with peoples. In David, for example:

> Before you all the *clans of the nations* will bow down, because the kingdom is Jehovah's, and he is ruling over the *nations*. (Psalms 22:27, 28)

And in the same author:

> Give Jehovah—you *clans of the peoples*—give Jehovah glory and strength. (Psalms 96:7)

In the present and preceding verses of this chapter, clans refer to goodness, because they were the clans of the nations.

1262 This evidence now shows that here too the *land* symbolizes the church. When a particular land is mentioned, nothing else comes to mind than the nation or people belonging to that land, and since a nation or people comes to mind, what comes to mind is its character. So the land truly does mean the church, as shown earlier, at §§662, 1066.

1263 The fact that *after the flood* means from the start of the ancient church can be seen by considering that the Flood was the end of the earliest church and the beginning of the ancient, as shown earlier, at §§705, 739, 790.

These remarks now indicate that although the present chapter is composed simply of the names of nations and clans, the contents still include all the different ways in which worship embodied charitable good and religious truth in the ancient church. The chapter describes such differences as they existed not only in the ancient church in general but in each individual church as well. In fact it holds more information than anyone could ever believe. That is the nature of the Lord's Word. **1264**

The Pre-Flood People Who Died Out

SOME distance above my head was a crowd of people who were influ-encing my thoughts and holding them captive, so to speak, so that I was very much in the dark. They pressed down on me fairly heavily. The spirits around me were likewise being held more or less captive by them, so that they could hardly think anything that did not pour in from those others. The situation was severe enough to arouse the spirits' anger. Someone said that these were people who had lived before the Flood, although they were not the ones called Nephilim who had died out, because the Nephilim did not have such forceful persuasive powers. **1265**

The pre-Flood people who were annihilated are in a certain hell under the heel of the left foot. A kind of foggy crag that materializes out of their monstrous hallucinations and delusions covers them, separating them from the other hells and putting distance between them and the world of spirits. **1266**

They are constantly trying to rise up out of there, but they can accomplish nothing more than the attempt. Their nature is such that if they reached the world of spirits, their dreadful hallucinations and the toxic fumes and poisons of their delusions would deprive all the spirits they came across (except the good ones) of the ability to think. Had the Lord not freed the world of spirits from that unspeakable mob by coming in the flesh, the human race would have been destroyed. This is because no spirit could have been present with people on earth, and we cannot survive for even a moment if there are no spirits and angels with us.

The ones that obstinately continue trying to emerge from that hell meet with cruel treatment at the hands of their companions, since they **1267** nurse a murderous hatred for all, even their associates. Their highest pleasure consists in holding each other enslaved and virtually butchering their captives.

The ones who persist even more stubbornly in their effort are sent still farther down under the misty crag. An insane rage to annihilate everyone, ingrained in them, is what goads them on; it is what makes them struggle to break free.

When they come across others, they wrap them in a piece of cloth, lead them away captive, and throw them into what they take to be a sea. Or they abuse them in some other way.

1268 I was taken toward that misty rock under safeguard. (Being led to people like these does not mean moving from place to place but staying in one place while communities of spirits and angels in between effect the change. Still, it feels like a descent.) As I drew near the crag, I came across a spot where the temperature dropped, and this chill invaded the lower part of my back. From that spot I talked with the inhabitants about their delusions, asking what beliefs concerning the Lord they had held in bodily life. They answered that they had thought about God a lot but persuaded themselves that no god could exist and that human beings were gods instead. So they considered themselves gods, they said, and their dreams confirmed them in the belief.

Something will be said below about the fantasies they have that express opposition to the Lord [§1270:3].

1269 To teach me still more about their character, the Lord allowed some of them to come up into the world of spirits. But before this happened, a handsome young man dressed in white appeared, and then in an open door appeared another young man wearing green. Soon two female servants in white headgear also appeared. What these things symbolized was not revealed to me.

1270 Before long, a group of beings issued out of that hell, but the Lord, using spirits and angels to intervene, arranged it so that nothing could hurt me. They came forward out of that depth and seemed to themselves to struggle onward—and so upward—through what appeared to be caves in a cliff. At last they could be seen above on the left, so that from there, at a distance, they would be able to exert an influence on me.

I was told that they were allowed to affect the right half of my head but not the left, and through the right half of my head the left side of my chest, but never the left part of my head. Had they done so, it would have been the end of me, because they would then have flowed in with their self-deceptions, which are horrendous and deadly. Since they were to act on the right part of my head and from there the left part of my chest, they would use various intense desires as their means. This is how the case with spiritual influence stands.

[2] Their delusions are strong enough to snuff out everything true or good, preventing the people they affect from perceiving anything and consequently from thinking anything. So the spirits were also removed.

When they started to work their influence, I fell asleep. Then, while I slept, they worked on me with their cravings. Their influence was so forceful that I would never have been able to resist them while awake. Asleep, I sensed their pressure, but I cannot describe it, except to say that I later recalled how they tried their worst to murder me with a suffocating vapor that was like a vicious incubus. Then I woke up and noticed that they were near me, but when they became aware that I was awake, they escaped to a place up above and acted on me from there.

[3] While they were there, it seemed to me as if they were being wound up in a cloth, of the kind mentioned in §964. I thought it was the pre-Flood people who were being wrapped up, but it was others, and they themselves were doing the wrapping. They accomplish this through hallucinations, but the spirits they are victimizing in fantasy this way have no idea that it is not actually happening. It appeared as though they took the spirits they were binding up and rolled them down the steep face of a rock, but the victims were released and freed. (These were spirits who were unwilling to run away, so the Lord protected them. Otherwise they would have suffocated. They would have come back to life, but only after suffering excruciating pain.)

Next they retreated down the slope of rock. I heard a drilling sound coming from there, as if many huge drills were at work, and I perceived that their fantasies of terrible cruelty against the Lord were the source of the sound. Later they were forced down through the shadowy caves under the foggy crag into their hell.

When they were in the world of spirits, the composition of the atmosphere there changed.

Afterward, there were some deceitful spirits that wanted [the pre-Flood people] to escape and suggested to them the idea of saying that they were completely insignificant, so that they would be allowed to climb out. I then heard the sound of upheaval in that hell, like the sound of a large, rowdy mass. It was the sound of their agitated desire to struggle free. So once more some of them were permitted to rise up, and they

1271

appeared in the same place as the earlier ones. Assisted by the deceitful fiends, they tried to pour their lethal persuasions into me from there, but it was no use, because the Lord was protecting me. Still, I could tell that their persuasive powers were capable of smothering a person.

They thought they could do anything and take life from anyone. But since they considered themselves all-powerful, it was a mere baby that sent them back down. The infant's presence made them stagger so violently that they cried out over the anguish they were in. Their distress was so severe that they resorted to pleading.

The deceivers were punished too. First they were almost smothered by [the pre-Flood people]. Later they were cemented together so that they would stop doing the kind of things they had done. In the end, though, they were set free.

1272   After these things, I was shown how the women among them dressed. On their head they had a long, rounded, black hat with a peak in front. Their faces were small. The men, on the other hand, were shaggy with hair.

I was shown also how proud they were to have large numbers of children. Wherever they ventured, they took their children with them, letting the children walk in front in a curved line. But they were told that animals—even the worst ones—all love their offspring, and that this provides no proof of virtue in them. They could have loved their children not out of conceit or pride, it was said, but out of a desire to increase world population for the sake of the common good, and more especially to swell the number of people in heaven. So they could have made the Lord's kingdom their goal, and then they would have exhibited a genuine love for children.

Genesis 11

Location in the Universal Human; in Addition, Place and Distance in the Other Life

SOULS recently arrived from the world eventually leave the company **1273** of spiritual angels to mix with spirits and finally reach the community they inhabited while alive in their bodies. When the time comes for this, angels take them around to a number of residential areas, which are separate communities (though interconnected). In some places the newcomers are welcomed; in others they are sent on. This continues for some time until they reach the community they resided in while they lived in their bodies, and there they stay. From that moment, their lives start afresh.

When people are insincere, hypocritical, or dishonest, and can deceptively adopt an angelic-seeming personality, good spirits sometimes accept them, but before long they are banished. Then they wander around without angels to escort them, begging to be taken in but meeting with rejection and sometimes punishment. In the end they are relegated to the company of hellish spirits.

[2] People who are released from spiritual devastation to the companionship of angels also change communities, and when they pass from one to another, they are sent on their way politely and with kindness. The process repeats itself until they finally arrive in a community of angels that harmonizes with their disposition for charity, devoutness, honesty, or genuine courtesy.

I was also escorted in the same way through various neighborhoods, where the residents talked with me, so that I could learn what the experience was like. Meanwhile, I was given the opportunity to reflect on these changes of place and to realize that they were only apparent moves—that my state alone changed, while my body stayed put.

Among the marvels of the next life are the following: **1274**

1. Communities of spirits and angels seem to occupy different positions, even though locations and distances in the other world are simply differences in state.

2. Location and distance relate to the human body in such a way that people on our right appear to the right no matter which way we turn our body. The same holds true for those on our left and in other directions too.

3. No spirit or angel is too far away to be seen, and yet no more of them come into sight than the Lord allows.

4. The spirits we are thinking about—people we knew in some way during bodily life, for instance—show up instantly, when the Lord allows it. They are so close that they stand at our ear, in arm's reach, or at a little distance. Although they may have been several thousand miles away, or even up among the stars, it is no obstacle, because the distance of a place does not matter at all in the other life.

5. Angels have no concept of time.

These wonders occur the world of spirits, and they occur in a still more perfect way in heaven. Imagine, then, how the Lord sees it! After all, not a single one of us can help being directly present to him, right under his gaze and providence.

These things seem unbelievable and yet are true.

1275 I was once in a community marked by calm, or rather by a calm condition *approaching* peace, in a way, but not fully reaching it.

I talked there about the state of little children and about location, saying that variations in place and distance are merely appearances and that they depend on each individual's state and changes in state.

While I was being taken there, the spirits around me seemed to be withdrawn and to appear below me, although I was still able to hear them speaking.

1276 In regard to spirits' position in the world of spirits and angels' position in heaven: Angels are on the Lord's right, evil spirits on his left. In front of him live people of a middling sort, at his back live the malicious. Overhead are the vain and ambitious, underfoot are hells that provide a counterpart to them. So all individuals have their own position relative to the Lord, in every quarter, at every height, on the horizontal plane and the vertical and at every angle in between. Everyone's place remains fixed, never changing to eternity.

[2] The heavens in the other world make up what is essentially a single human being, which is therefore called the universal human, and everything in us corresponds to [something in] that human. The correspondence will be discussed later, with the Lord's divine mercy.

As a result, everything positions itself in a similar way around every angel and within every person on earth to whom the Lord opens heaven. The Lord's presence carries this consequence with it. It would not be so if the Lord were not omnipresent in heaven.

The case is similar with people on earth in regard to their souls, which are always tied to some community of spirits and angels. We on earth have a position in the Lord's kingdom too, and it likewise depends on the character of our life and on our state. It makes not the slightest difference whether some of us are far apart on the planet, even if the distance is many thousands of miles; we can still be together in the same community. If we exercise kindness in our lives, we are in an angelic community. If we fill our lives with hatred and similar qualities, we are in a hellish community.

1277

Similarly, it does not matter in the least if a large number of us live together in one place on earth; all of us are still individuals when it comes to the character of our lives and our state of mind, and each of us can be in a different spiritual community.

When people who are several hundred or several thousand miles apart appear before the inner senses, they can be so close (depending on their spiritual location) that they sometimes touch. As a result, if several people were to have their inner eyes opened on earth, they could congregate and talk together, even if one were in India and another in Europe. This has even been demonstrated to me. So each and every person on earth is immediately present to the Lord, directly under his eyes and his loving care.

For a discussion of position, place, distance, and time in the other life, see the continuation at the end of this chapter [§§1376–1382].

1278

Genesis 11

1. And the whole earth had one language and the same words.

2. And it happened when they set out from the east that they found a valley in the land of Shinar and settled there.

3. And they said, a man to his companion, "Come, let us make bricks and bake them until baked." And they had brick in place of stone, and tar they had in place of mortar.

4. And they said, "Come, let us build ourselves a city and a tower with its head in the sky. And let us make ourselves a name, to keep from being scattered over the face of the whole earth."

5. And Jehovah went down to see the city and tower that the children of humankind were building.

6. And Jehovah said, "Look: the people are one and they all have one language, and this is what they are starting to do; and now nothing would be prohibited to them that they thought to do.

7. Come, let us go down and muddle their language there, so that a man will be unable to understand the language of his companion."

8. And Jehovah scattered them from there over the face of the whole earth; and they stopped building the city.

9. For this reason he called its name Babel, because there Jehovah muddled the language of the whole earth. And from there Jehovah scattered them over the face of the whole earth.

10. These are the births of Shem: Shem was a son of one hundred years, and he fathered Arpachshad, two years after the flood.

11. And after Shem fathered Arpachshad he lived five hundred years; and he fathered sons and daughters.

12. And Arpachshad lived thirty-five years and fathered Shelah.

13. And after Arpachshad fathered Shelah he lived four hundred three years; and he fathered sons and daughters.

14. And Shelah lived thirty years and fathered Eber.

15. And after Shelah fathered Eber he lived four hundred three years; and he fathered sons and daughters.

16. And Eber lived thirty-four years and fathered Peleg.

17. And after Eber fathered Peleg he lived four hundred thirty years; and he fathered sons and daughters.

18. And Peleg lived thirty years and fathered Reu.

19. And after Peleg fathered Reu he lived two hundred nine years; and he fathered sons and daughters.

20. And Reu lived thirty-two years and fathered Serug.

21. And after Reu fathered Serug he lived two hundred seven years; and he fathered sons and daughters.

22. And Serug lived thirty years and fathered Nahor.

23. And after Serug fathered Nahor he lived two hundred years; and he fathered sons and daughters.

24. And Nahor lived twenty-nine years and fathered Terah.

25. And after Nahor fathered Terah he lived one hundred nineteen years; and he fathered sons and daughters.

26. And Terah lived seventy years and fathered Abram, Nahor, and Haran.

27. And these are the births of Terah: Terah fathered Abram, Nahor, and Haran. And Haran fathered Lot.

28. And Haran died in the presence of Terah, his father, in the land of his birth, in Ur of the Chaldeans.

29. And Abram and Nahor took themselves wives; the name of Abram's wife was Sarai, and the name of Nahor's wife was Milcah daughter of Haran (the father of Milcah and the father of Iscah).

30. And Sarai was infertile; she had no offspring.

31. And Terah took Abram his son and Lot son of Haran (son of his son) and Sarai his daughter-in-law (wife of his son Abram), and they went out with them from Ur of the Chaldeans to go into the land of Canaan. And they came all the way to Haran and stayed there.

32. And the days of Terah were two hundred five years; and Terah died in Haran.

Summary

VERSES 1–9 treat of the first ancient church, which followed the Flood.   **1279**

Its first phase, in which everyone had the same doctrine (verse 1).   **1280**
Its second, in which the church began to degenerate (verse 2). Its third, in which the falsities engendered by self-interest started to predominate (verse 3). Its fourth, in which people started to exert control through their divine worship (verse 4). As a result, conditions changed in the church (verses 5, 6) in such a way that no one possessed religious goodness (verses 7, 8, 9).

Verses 10–26 deal with the second ancient church, named for Eber.   **1281**
They also discuss what developed out of that church and what conditions were like in it, since it ended in idolatry.

Verses 27–32 speak about the origins of the third ancient church, which   **1282**
was transformed from an idolatrous religion into a representative one.

Inner Meaning

1283 THE present topic is the ancient church in general and the fact that its inward worship was falsified and adulterated as time passed. Its outward worship accordingly suffered the same fate, because outward worship mirrors inward. The falsification and adulteration of inward worship is portrayed as Babel here.

Up to this point the narrative (aside from what it says about Eber) is fiction rather than history, as the story about the Babylonian tower shows. Consider the idea that people set about to build a tower with its head in the sky, for instance; that their language was muddled so that they would be unable to understand one another's language; and that Jehovah is the one who caused the confusion. Another piece of evidence is the claim that Babel grew out of this incident, when verse 10 of the last chapter says that Nimrod built it. This too shows that Babel does not mean a city but some phenomenon; here it means worship that is profane within despite an outward appearance of sanctity.

1284 Genesis 11:1. *And the whole earth had one language and the same words. The whole earth had one language* means that a single broad view of doctrine existed everywhere. A *language* is doctrine; the *earth* is the church. *And the same words* means that a single detailed view of doctrine existed.

1285 The meaning of *the whole earth had one language* as the fact that a single broad view of doctrine existed everywhere can be seen from the symbolism of a language [or lip] in the Word (to be discussed just below).

This verse, in just a few words, describes what conditions had been like in the ancient church, in that it had held a single overall view of doctrine. The next verse portrays the commencement of falsification and adulteration, and the following verses up to verse 9 tell how the church became thoroughly corrupt, so that it no longer had any internal worship. Directly afterward, the text takes up the second ancient church, started by Eber, and eventually it turns to the third ancient church, which was the beginning of the Jewish religion. (Three churches came in a row after the Flood.)

[2] The first ancient church had one language and the same words—that is, a doctrinal view that was united in both its general and its particular

tenets—despite its broad spread throughout the globe. It displayed this unity even though its forms of worship, both deep and shallow, differed everywhere, as the last chapter showed. (Each nation mentioned there symbolized a different doctrinal position and a different style of ritual.) As far as that church and its unity is concerned, the situation is this:

Heaven contains a countless number of communities, each of them different but still united, because the Lord leads them all as one. (For more on this, see §§457, 551, 684, 685, 690.) It resembles a human being, in whom all the elements without exception are regulated as a single whole, by a single soul, despite the vast number of organs and of component parts to the organs, viscera, and limbs, each component acting in a different way from the next. Or it is like the human body, in which all the activities of force and motion, though unlike, are still regulated by a single motion of the heart and a single motion of the lungs, and in which they still form a unified whole.

The reason they are able to act as one in this way is that heaven has a single stream of influence, which each individual receives according to his or her own character. (The stream of influence consists of the emotional effect that the Lord in all his mercy and vital energy has on us.) Even though there is a single stream [received in different ways], all things obey and yield to it as a united whole. This is the result of the love that heaven's inhabitants share.

[3] Such was the case with the first ancient church. There were as many general categories of inner and outer worship in it as there were nations, as many subcategories as clans in the nations, and as many specific types as there were people in the church. Yet they all had one language and the same words, which is to say that they all had one doctrinal view in general and particular.

A doctrinal view is united when everyone loves each other, or displays charity. Mutual love and charity bring such people together into one despite the variety among them, because it draws unity out of variety. When everyone practices charity, or loves each other, then no matter how many people there are—even if they number in the hundreds of millions—they share a single goal: the common good, the Lord's kingdom, and the Lord himself. Variety in doctrine and worship are, again, like the variety of senses and organs in the human body, which contribute to the perfection of the whole. When doctrine or worship varies, then the Lord, working by means of charity, affects and acts on each of us in a way uniquely suited to our personality. In this way he fits each and every one of us into the order of things, on earth just as in heaven. Then, as the Lord himself teaches [Matthew 6:10], his will is done on earth as it is in heaven.

1286   The fact that a *language,* [a *lip,* or *speech*] is doctrine can be seen from the following passages in the Word. In Isaiah:

> The seraphs shouted, "Holy, holy, holy is Jehovah Sabaoth!" The prophet said, "Alas for me! I have been cut off—since I am a man unclean of *lips* and am living in the middle of a people unclean of *lips*—because my eyes have seen the king, Jehovah Sabaoth." And one of the seraphs flew to me, touched my mouth, and said, "Look, now, this one has touched you on your *lips,* and your wickedness is subsiding, and your sin is being atoned for." (Isaiah 6:3, 5, 6, 7)

The lips stand for our inner capacities and so for inward worship, which gives rise to reverence, a fact represented here in the prophet. As anyone can see, the touching of his lips, and the consequent subsiding of his wickedness and atonement for his sin, was a representation of deeper attributes. These attributes—which are facets of charity and of the doctrine of charity—are symbolized by the lips. [2] In the same author:

> Jehovah will strike the earth with the rod of his *mouth,* and with the spirit of his *lips* he will kill the ungodly person. (Isaiah 11:4)

The inner sense contains the idea not that Jehovah will strike anyone with the rod of his mouth or kill an ungodly person with the spirit of his lips but that the ungodly do this to themselves. The spirit of the lips is doctrine, and with ungodly people the doctrine is false. In the same author:

> [I am] the one who creates the produce of the *lips:* peace; peace to one who is far off and to one who is near. And I heal that person. (Isaiah 57:19)

The produce of the lips stands for doctrine. [3] In Ezekiel:

> Child of humankind, come; go to the house of Israel, and you are to speak my *words* to them. Not to a people *deep of speech* and heavy of *tongue* are you sent [but] to the house of Israel; not to numerous peoples *deep of speech* and heavy of *tongue,* whose *words* you would not hear. If I sent you to these, would they not listen to you? And the house of Israel does not want to listen to you, because they do not want to listen to me. For the whole house of Israel has an obstinate forehead, and they are hard of heart. (Ezekiel 3:4, 5, 6, 7)

The people deep of speech stand for the surrounding nations, which had charity, even though their doctrine was wrong. As a result, they are described as listening. Those who have no charity, though, are said to have an obstinate forehead and hard heart. [4] In Zephaniah:

> I will turn toward a people of transparent *speech,* so that they may all call on the name of Jehovah, to serve him with a single shoulder. (Zephaniah 3:9)

The transparent speech plainly stands for doctrine. In Malachi:

> The law of truth was in his mouth, and perversion was not found on his *lips.* For the priest's *lips* will protect knowledge, and people will seek the law from his mouth, since he is the angel of Jehovah Sabaoth. (Malachi 2:6, 7)

This describes Levi, who represents the Lord. The lips stand for doctrine based on charity. In David:

> . . . who say, "By our tongue we will prevail; our *lips* will stand by us." (Psalms 12:4)

The lips stand for falsity. In the same author:

> My soul will be filled, as with grease and fat, and my mouth will give praise with *lips* of song. (Psalms 63:5)

In Isaiah:

> On that day there will be five cities in the land of Egypt speaking the *language* of Canaan and swearing to Jehovah Sabaoth. (Isaiah 19:18)

A language stands for doctrine.

The symbolism of the *earth* as the church has been demonstrated before, at §§662, 1066. **1287**

The fact that *the same words* means that a single detailed view of **1288**
doctrine existed can be seen from what was said above. A language, [a lip, or speech] symbolizes doctrine in general, as shown, but words symbolize doctrine in particular, that is, particular doctrinal teachings. As noted [§1285:2], the specifics do not matter as long as they focus on a united goal, which is to love the Lord above all and to love our neighbor as ourselves, since the specific teachings then fit with these general principles.

[2] A *word* symbolizes the whole body of doctrine concerning neighborly love and the faith that grows out of it, while *words* in the plural symbolize different aspects of the doctrine. This can be seen in David:

> I will acclaim you in uprightness of heart, while I learn the judgments of your justice. Your statutes I will keep. With what will a youth purify his course, to keep it, in accord with your *word?* With my whole heart I have sought you; please do not make me stray from your commandments. In my heart have I hidden your *word,* to prevent my sinning against you. A blessing on you, Jehovah; teach me your statutes. With my *lips* I have recounted all the judgments of your mouth. In the path of your testimonies I have rejoiced. On your requirements I meditate, and I gaze on your paths. In your statutes I take pleasure. I do not forget your *word.* (Psalms 119:7–16)

A word stands for the broad outlines of doctrine. The commandments, judgments, testimonies, requirements, statutes, path, and lips there are distinguished from each other, as is evident, and they are all different types of "word," or doctrinal teaching. Everywhere else in the Word, too, they symbolize distinctly different entities. [3] In the same author:

> A love song: My heart ponders a good *word.* My tongue is the pen of a rapid scribe. More beautiful are you than the children of humankind. Grace is poured out on your *lips.* Ride on the *word* of truth and gentle justice; your right hand will teach you marvelous things. (Psalms 45: heading, 1, 2, 4)

Riding on the word of truth and gentle justice is teaching a doctrine of truth and goodness. As in other places in the Word, a word, mouth, lip, and tongue symbolize different things here. They all have to do with teachings concerning charity, because the psalm is called a song of "loves." Those teachings are portrayed as having more beauty than the children of humankind, and grace on the lips, and a right hand that teaches marvelous things. [4] In Isaiah:

> Jehovah has sent *word* against Jacob, and it has fallen on Israel. (Isaiah 9:8)

The word stands for teachings having to do with inward and outward worship; Jacob here stands for outward worship and Israel for inward. In Matthew:

> Jesus said, "Humankind does not live on bread alone but on every *word* that has come out of God's mouth." (Matthew 4:4)

In the same author:

> When anyone hears the *word concerning the kingdom* and pays no attention, the evil one comes and snatches away what was sown in the person's heart. (Matthew 13:19)

(Verses 20, 21, 22, 23 there also mention "the word.") In the same author:

> Heaven and earth will pass away, but my *words* will not pass away. (Matthew 24:35)

The word in these passages stands for the doctrine concerning the Lord, while words in the plural stand for various parts of that doctrine.

[5] Since words stand for all the precepts of a doctrine, the Ten Commandments are called words in Moses:

> Jehovah wrote on the tablets the *words* of the covenant—the ten *words*. (Exodus 34:28)

In the same author:

> He declared his covenant to you, which he commanded you to do: the ten *words*. And he wrote them on two stone tablets. (Deuteronomy 4:13; 10:4)

In the same author:

> Be careful, and guard your soul intently to keep from forgetting the *words* [things] that your eyes have seen. (Deuteronomy 4:9)

There are other passages as well.

Genesis 11:2. *And it happened when they set out from the east that they found a valley in the land of Shinar and settled there.*   **1289**

When they set out from the east means when they backed away from charity; the *east* is a sense of charity, received from the Lord. *They found a valley in the land of Shinar* means that their worship grew more unclean and profane. *And settled there* symbolizes the way they lived.

The meaning of *when they set out from the east* as a time when they backed away from charity is established by the symbolism of setting out and by that of the east in the Word. It is apparent that *setting out* here means backing away, because it has to do with charity, which is the east that they traveled away from.   **1290**

The fact that the *east* is a sense of charity, received from the Lord, can be seen from previous demonstrations in §§101 and 1250.   **1291**

1292   The meaning of *they found a valley in the land of Shinar* as the fact that their worship grew more unclean and profane can be seen from the symbolism of a *valley* and the symbolism of the *land of Shinar*.

As for a *valley:* In the Word, mountains symbolize love, or charity, because these are the aspects of worship that reach the highest above or (to say the same thing another way) the deepest within. This was shown earlier, at §795. A valley consequently symbolizes what lies at the foot of the mountains—that is, something in worship that is on a lower level or (to put it another way) more on the surface.

The *land of Shinar,* though, symbolizes outward worship that has a profane quality, as shown above at §1183. So "they found a valley in the land of Shinar" here means that their worship grew more unclean and profane.

[2] The first verse spoke of the church, saying that it had one language and the same words, or a single broad and a single detailed view of doctrine. The present verse, however, describes how the church went downhill by "setting out from the east," that is, by starting to draw back from neighborly love. The further the church or its members depart from charity, the further its worship departs from holiness and the closer that worship approaches to being unclean and profane.

The reason their discovery of a valley in the land of Shinar symbolizes the lapse of the church and of its worship into profanation is that a valley is a low spot between mountains, which, again, symbolize the holy qualities of love or of charity that are present in worship. This can be seen from the meaning of a valley in the Word, which expresses the concept through several different words in the original language. Those words, when used in this sense, symbolize varying degrees of profanation in worship. [3] Isaiah provides evidence that valleys have such a symbolism:

> The burden of the *Valley of Vision:* . . . for it is a day of upheaval and trampling and chaos to the Lord Jehovih Sabaoth in the *Valley* of Vision. (Isaiah 22:1, 5)

The Valley of Vision stands for delusions and twisted reasoning that introduce falsity and at last profanation into worship. In Jeremiah:

> How can you say, "I am not defiled; I have not walked after the baals"? Look at your path in the *valley!* (Jeremiah 2:23)

The valley stands for unclean worship. In the same author:

> They built the high places of Topheth that are in the *Valley* of the Children of Hinnom. So watch! The days are coming, and it will no

longer be called Topheth or the *Valley* of the Children of Hinnom but the *Valley* of Murder. (Jeremiah 7:31, 32; 19:6)

The Valley of Hinnom stands for hell, and also for the profanation of what is true and good. [4] In Ezekiel:

> This is what the Lord Jehovih has said to the mountains and hills, the gullies and *valleys:* "Watch! I myself am bringing a sword on you, and I will destroy your high places." (Ezekiel 6:3)

In the same author:

> I will give Gog a place there for a grave in Israel: the *valley* of those going by toward the east of the sea. And they will call it the *Valley* of Gog's Horde. (Ezekiel 39:11, 15)

This is about superficial worship; the valley stands for such worship.

When worship has not yet become quite so profane, though, it is portrayed by use of the same word for valley as in the current verse. An example in Isaiah:

> I will open rivers on the slopes, and in the middle of *valleys* I will set springs; [I will make] the desert into a pool of water, and dry land into outlets of water. (Isaiah 41:18)

People who live in ignorance (without access to knowledge about faith and charity) but still in charity are the focus here, and the valley in this verse stands for them. The valley in Ezekiel 37:1 has a similar meaning.

The symbolism of *and they settled there* as the way they consequently lived can be seen from the symbolism of *settling,* in the Word, as living. The word *settle,* or reside, occurs many times in both the prophetic and narrative books of the Word, and on an inner level it usually symbolizes living one's life. The reason for the symbolism is that the earliest people lived in tents and carried out their holiest devotions there. So tents in the Word also symbolize the holiness of worship, as shown in §414. And since tents symbolized the holiness in worship, settling or residing (in its good sense) also symbolizes life, or the way one lives.

1293

Because the earliest people took their tents with them when they set out on a journey, *setting out* in the Word's inner sense also symbolizes the customs and pattern of a life.

Genesis 11:3. *And they said, a man to his companion, "Come, let us make bricks and bake them until baked." And they had brick in place of stone, and tar they had in place of mortar.*

1294

And a man said to his companion means that it began. *Come, let us make bricks,* symbolizes the falsities that they would invent for themselves. *And bake them until baked* symbolizes evil rising out of self-love. *And they had brick in place of stone* means that they had falsity instead of truth. *And tar they had in place of mortar* means that they had the evil they craved, instead of goodness.

1295　　The meaning of *a man said to his companion* as the fact that it began, or that these things started, follows from the context.

This verse deals with the third phase of the church, when falsity, and specifically greed-driven falsity, started to predominate.

Falsity has two origins; one is ignorance of the truth, the other is corrupt desire. Falsity that springs from ignorance of the truth is not as harmful as falsity that rises out of corrupt desires. We fall into the errors of ignorance when we are taught that way from childhood onward, or when business matters of various kinds distract us from inquiring into the truth, or when we lack the ability to discriminate between truth and falsity. This kind of misinformation does not do much damage, as long as we avoid entrenching ourselves in it with multiple arguments and convincing ourselves—under the goading of some selfish desire—to lend it our support. To do this is to thicken the cloud of ignorance and make it so dark that we cannot see the truth.

[2] But falsity is greed-driven when it starts with corrupt desires, or in other words, with self-love and materialism. We might take up a certain tenet of doctrine, for instance, and avow it publicly in order to seize hold of the popular mind and become a leader. We might interpret or distort that doctrine to our own advantage, arguing from factual evidence and at the same time quoting from the letter of the Word to confirm our views. Worship stemming from such behavior is profane, no matter how pious it seems on the outside, because on the inside it is not worship of the Lord but of ourselves. Furthermore, we fail to acknowledge anything that really is true, except to the extent that we can explain it to our own advantage. This kind of worship is what Babel symbolizes.

The case is different, however, with those who have been born and brought up to this kind of worship, who do not know that the thinking is wrong, and who live a life of love for others. Their ignorance holds innocence inside it, and their worship contains the goodness born of charity. It is not so much the worship itself as the quality of the person worshiping that determines whether it should be described as profane.

1296　　The symbolism of *come, let us make bricks,* as the falsities that they would invent for themselves can be seen from the symbolism of *brick.* In the Word, stone symbolizes truth. So brick, as a human product, symbolizes falsity, since it is artificial, manufactured stone. This symbolism of brick can also be seen from the following passages. In Isaiah:

> I have spread my hands out all day to a defiant people walking on a path that is not good, in pursuit of their own thoughts, sacrificing in gardens and offering incense on *bricks.* (Isaiah 65:2, 3)

To offer incense on bricks is to base one's worship on fictions and falsity, which is why the people are said to be pursuing their own thoughts. In the same author:

> . . . on account of haughtiness and pride of heart in Ephraim and in the resident of Samaria, who say, "*Bricks* have fallen, and we will build with carved stone." (Isaiah 9:9, 10)

Ephraim stands for a discerning person who has sunk into corrupt ways, who calls truth falsity or turns truth into falsity, falsity being the bricks. Carved stone stands for a fabrication. In Nahum:

> Draw water for the siege for yourselves; shore up your strongholds; go into the clay and tread mortar; repair the *brick kiln.* There fire will consume you and the sword will cut you off. (Nahum 3:14, 15)

The treading of mortar stands for falsity; repairing the brick kiln, for worship based on falsity. Fire is the penalty exacted by corrupt desire; a sword, the penalty incurred by false thinking. In Ezekiel:

> Take yourself a *brick* and put it in front of you, and carve the city of Jerusalem on it. (Ezekiel 4:1)

Then comes a command to lay siege to it. This prophetic act involves the idea that worship has been falsified.

The symbolism of brick as falsity stands out even more clearly from the symbolism of stone as truth, to be dealt with just below.

The fact that *and bake them until baked* symbolizes evil rising out **1297** of self-love can be seen from the symbolism of baking and being baked and of fire, sulfur, and tar in the Word. These images are used to portray desire, especially the desires that go with self-love. In Isaiah, for example:

> Our house of holiness and our prize jewel, where our ancestors praised you, has become a *fiery conflagration,* and all our pleasant things have become a ruin. (Isaiah 64:11)

In the same author:

> Conceive garbage; give birth to chaff. Your *fiery* wind will consume you.
> Thus the peoples will be *burned* into lime. Thorn prunings will *kindle*
> *with fire.* (Isaiah 33:11, 12)

There are many other places besides. Burning and fire relate to desire
because they resemble it.

1298   The fact that *they had brick in place of stone* means that they had
falsity instead of truth is established by the symbolism of *brick* (given
just above) as falsity. It is also established by the symbolism of *stone* in a
broad sense as truth (given earlier, in §643).

The reason *stones* symbolized truth was that the earliest people used
stones to mark borders and that they raised stones up as testimony that a
thing was so, or true. This can be seen from the stone that Jacob set as a
pillar in Genesis 28:22 and 35:14; from the pillar of stones between Laban
and Jacob in Genesis 31:46, 47, 52; and from the altar that the children
of Reuben, Gad, and Manasseh built beside the Jordan as testimony in
Joshua 22:10, 28, 34. So in the Word stones symbolize truth. This symbolism is so consistent that not only the altar stones but also the precious
stones on the shoulders of Aaron's ephod and on the breastplate of judgment symbolize the holy truth that comes of love.

[2] In regard to the altar: When sacrificial worship on altars began,
an altar symbolized worship that represented the Lord in a general way.
The actual stones, though, symbolized the sacred truths of that worship.
This was the reason for requiring an altar to be built of whole stones
rather than carved ones and for forbidding any iron implement to be
wielded on them (Deuteronomy 27:5, 6, 7; Joshua 8:31). Carved stones,
and stones on which an iron tool had been wielded, symbolized elements
of worship that were human-made and therefore nongenuine—that is,
the products of human selfhood, the fabrications of people's thoughts
and of their hearts. To invent such elements was to profane worship, as
Exodus 20:25 explicitly says. It was for the same reason that no piece of
iron was wielded on the stones of the Temple (1 Kings 6:7).

[3] The fact that the precious stones on the shoulders of Aaron's
ephod and on the breastplate of judgment likewise symbolized sacred
truth was shown earlier, in §114. It can also be seen in Isaiah:

> Here, now, I will lay your *stones* on garnet and found [you] on sap-
> phires, and I will use carnelian for your suns [windows], and make your
> gates of gem *stones,* and your whole border of desirable *stones.* And all

your children will be taught by Jehovah, and great will be the peace of your children. (Isaiah 54:11, 12, 13)

The stones named here stand for sacred truth, which is why it says, "all your children will be taught by Jehovah." So in John it also says that the foundations of the city wall in Jerusalem the Holy were "adorned with every *precious stone,*" which it then lists (Revelation 21:19, 20). Jerusalem the Holy stands for the Lord's kingdom in the heavens and on earth, and its foundations are sacred truths. The tablets of stone on which the commandments of the law (the ten "words") were written likewise symbolize holy truths, which is why they were made of stone, or had a stone base, as described in Exodus 24:12; 31:18; 34:1; Deuteronomy 5:22; 10:1. The Commandments themselves are absolutely core religious truths, after all.

[4] In ancient times, then, stones symbolized truth, and later, when worship on pillars and altars and in the Temple began, the pillars, altars, and Temple symbolized sacred truth. That is why the Lord too is called a stone. In Moses:

Mighty Jacob, from whom comes the Shepherd, the *Stone of Israel.* (Genesis 49:24)

In Isaiah:

The Lord Jehovih has said, "I am laying as a foundation in Zion a *stone,* a well-tested *stone,* a corner[stone], a precious one, for a firm foundation." (Isaiah 28:16)

In David:

A *stone* that the builders spurned has become the head of the corner. (Psalms 118:22)

Something similar is meant by the *stone* cut out of rock that crushed Nebuchadnezzar's statue, in Daniel 2:34, 35, 45.

[5] The symbolism of stones as truth can also be seen in Isaiah:

By this Jacob's wickedness will be atoned for, and this will be the whole fruit [of atonement]: that they will remove their sin when they have made all the *altar stones* like scattered *stones* of chalk. (Isaiah 27:9)

The altar stones stand for truths expressed in worship that have been done away with. In the same author:

Level a way for the people! Pave a path; pave it! *De-stone it of its stones!* (Isaiah 62:10)

The pathway and stone stand for truth. In Jeremiah:

> I am against you, destroying mountain. I will roll you down from the rocks and make you a mountain *aflame,* and they will not take a *corner-stone* or a foundation *stone* from you. (Jeremiah 51:25, 26)

This is about Babylon. The mountain aflame is self-love. The statement that no stone would be taken from there is the fact that no truth would come from there.

1299　　The fact that *tar they had in place of mortar* means that they had the evil they craved, instead of goodness, can be seen from the symbolism of *tar* and the symbolism of *mortar,* or clay, in the Word.

Since the theme here is the building of the Babylonian tower, building materials are used to express the message. Tar is sulfurous and flammable, and in the Word sulfur and fire symbolize cravings, especially those that come of self-love. So tar here symbolizes the evil they craved, as well as the resulting falsity, which is also an evil. These went into the construction of the tower described in the next verses. It can be seen in Isaiah that this is the symbolism:

> A day of vengeance for Jehovah! [Zion's] watercourses will turn into *pitch,* and its dirt into *sulfur,* and its land will become *burning pitch.* (Isaiah 34:8, 9)

The pitch and sulfur stand for the falsity and evil associated with our cravings. There are other instances elsewhere.

1300　　The symbolism of mortar, or clay, as the goodness that forms the substance of the mind (in other words, that forms people in the church) is also evident in the Word. In Isaiah, for instance:

> Now Jehovah, you are our Father; we are *clay,* and you are our potter, and we are all the work of your hand. (Isaiah 64:8, 9)

Clay stands for the individual in the church who is actually being formed, and so for the charitable goodness that does all the work of shaping or forming us—that is, reforming and regenerating us. In Jeremiah:

> Like *clay* in a potter's hand—that is how you are in my hand, house of Israel. (Jeremiah 18:6)

The meaning is similar. Whether the text speaks of building with clay or of forming from clay, it is the same thing.

Anyone can see that this, now, is what is being symbolized. The clues 1301
are provided both by the symbolism of all the individual elements of
the verse and by the nature of the details mentioned, such as the type of
stones and the type of mortar they were using. Such details would never
be worthy of mention in the Lord's Word if they did not enfold such
hidden meanings as these.

Genesis 11:4. *And they said, "Come, let us build ourselves a city and a* 1302
tower with its head in the sky; and let us make ourselves a name, to keep from
being scattered over the face of the whole earth."

And they said means that it happened. *Let us build ourselves a city and*
a tower means that they made up their own doctrine and worship; a *city*
is doctrine, and a *tower* is self-worship. *With its head in the sky* means
with the eventual purpose of controlling what goes on in heaven. *And let*
us make ourselves a name means so as to gain from this a reputation for
power. *To keep from being scattered over the face of the whole earth* means
that otherwise they would not be acknowledged.

The fact that *and they said* means that it happened follows logically 1303
from context. (In this it resembles the earlier statement "they said, a man
to his companion," which meant that it began.) The passage is using the
tower to describe what Babel [Babylon] is like.

The fact that *let us build ourselves a city and a tower* means that they 1304
made up their own doctrine and worship can be seen from the symbolism of a *city* and from that of a *tower,* given directly below.

The nature of religion is such that when charitable love for our neighbor disappears and love for ourselves replaces it, we disregard what faith
teaches, except so far as we can turn it to the purposes of self-worship.
We also despise everything holy in worship unless it benefits ourselves
and so unless it forms a part of self-worship.

All self-love entails this consequence, because when we love ourselves
more than others, we hate everyone who does not serve us and refuse to
favor such people unless they become our slaves. Not only that, so far as
any restraints on us are loosened, we run wild, even to the point of lifting
ourselves up above God. Personal experience has shown me that self-love
acts like this when it runs loose. These are the things symbolized by the
city and the tower.

Self-love—and every desire that rises out of it—is the vilest, most
profane thing that exists, and it is the epitome of hell. From this everyone can draw her or his own conclusion about what worship is like when
it harbors such a quality inside it.

1305   The symbolism of a *city* as doctrine, or as a doctrinal view, whether genuine or heretical, was shown earlier, at §402.

1306   The fact that a *tower* is self-worship can be seen from the symbolism of a tower. Self-worship exists when we set ourselves up above others, so much so that we seek to be worshiped. As a result, self-love—which is conceit and pride—is called height, loftiness, and elevation, and it is depicted by anything that is high up, as in Isaiah:

> The eyes of human pride will lower, and the loftiness of men will sink, and Jehovah alone will be exalted on that day. For the day of Jehovah Sabaoth will come over all the proud and lofty and over all the haughty (and they will be brought down) and over all the cedars of Lebanon, tall and lifted up, and over all the oaks of Bashan, and over all the lofty mountains, and over all the tall hills, and over every high *tower,* and over every fortified wall. (Isaiah 2:11–18)

The theme here is self-love, which is portrayed by cedars, oaks, mountains, hills, and a tower, which are tall and lofty. [2] In the same author:

> There will be brooks, channels of water, on the day of great slaughter, when *towers* fall. (Isaiah 30:25)

Again it stands for self-love and for mixing conceit with worship. In the same author:

> Look: the land of the Chaldeans! This people was not. Assyria founded [the land] among tsiyim. They will erect their *spy towers;* [the Chaldeans] will raise up their palaces; [Assyria] will make it a ruin. (Isaiah 23:13)

This is about Tyre and its destruction. The spy towers—for which a different [Hebrew] word is being used—stand for the illusions that come from there. In Ezekiel:

> I will bring many nations up against Tyre, and they will destroy Tyre's walls and demolish its *towers,* and I will remove its dirt from it and make it as dry as a rock. (Ezekiel 26:3, 4)

The meaning is similar.

[3] The reason self-love within worship (that is, self-worship) is called a tower is that a city symbolizes doctrine, as shown earlier (§402), and towers patrolled by guards once formed the defenses of a city. Towers also dotted the borders and were accordingly called watchtowers (2 Kings 9:17; 17:9; 18:8) and spy towers (Isaiah 23:13). In addition, when the Lord's church is compared to a vineyard, different facets of worship and

of its preservation are compared to a winepress and to a tower in the vineyard, as can be seen in Isaiah 5:1, 2; Matthew 21:33; Mark 12:1.

The fact that *with its head in the sky* means with the eventual purpose of controlling what goes on in heaven now follows from the above. Having its head in the sky is having the arrogance to reach all the way to heaven, as descriptions of Babel [Babylon] throughout the Word also demonstrate, and as earlier remarks in §257 about lifting one's head indicate.

1307

Self-love is the least harmonious with heavenly life of all possible loves. It is the source of all evil—not only of hatred but of vengefulness, cruelty, and adultery as well. It is even more discordant when it enters into worship and profanes it. Hell consequently consists of people who love themselves, and the higher they wish to raise their heads into heaven, the lower they actually go and the fiercer are the punishments into which they plunge themselves.

And let us make ourselves a name means so as to gain from this a reputation for power, as the symbolism of making a name for themselves shows.

1308

They recognize, after all, that everyone wants to practice some kind of worship. This is a common trait, even among non-Christians. Everyone who contemplates the universe (and especially its order) acknowledges a supreme being, of course, and since we seek our own best welfare, we venerate that being. Besides, there is something inside that tells us to do so, because such a dictate flows in from the Lord by way of the angels present with each one of us. Anyone who does not sense that influence is under the domination of spirits in hell and fails to acknowledge God.

Since people who build Babylonian towers realize this, they make a name for themselves through doctrine and piety. Otherwise they would be unable to win the adulation of others. This is symbolized by the very next clause, that otherwise they would be "scattered over the face of the whole earth," or in other words, would not be acknowledged. From this it also follows that the higher into heaven such people can raise their heads, the more of a name they make for themselves.

Their domination is strongest with those who have a modicum of conscience, since they lead these people anywhere at will; but they have a plethora of external restraints for controlling those who lack conscience.

The fact that *to keep from being scattered over the face of the whole earth* means that otherwise they would not be acknowledged now follows logically from the above. Being scattered over the face of the whole earth is dropping out of sight and so failing to be received and acknowledged.

1309

Genesis 11:5. *And Jehovah went down to see the city and tower that the children of humankind were building.*

1310

Jehovah went down symbolizes a judgment on them. *To see the city and tower* means on their perversion of doctrine and profanation of worship. *That the children of humankind were building* symbolizes things they invented for themselves.

1311 The symbolism of *and Jehovah went down* as a judgment on them is established by remarks above and below and by the symbolism of coming down, when it is Jehovah who does so. With respect to remarks above: earlier sections [§§1302–1309] discuss the building of the city and Tower of Babel. With respect to remarks below: later sections [§§1319–1328] discuss the muddling of their language and the scattering of the people. With respect to the symbolism of coming down, when it is Jehovah who does so: Jehovah is said to come down when there is a judgment.

Jehovah (the Lord) is present everywhere and knows everything from eternity, so he cannot be said to come down to see. Only the letter of the story speaks in these terms, and in doing so it adapts to the human way of seeing things. The true, inner sense does not. That sense presents things not as they appear to be but as they are in themselves. So in the current instance, the inner sense presents "coming down to see" as a judgment.

[2] It is called a judgment when evil reaches its peak. The Word expresses this as a time when things in general culminate or when wickedness does. The situation is that every evil has limits it is allowed to reach. When it goes beyond these limits, it brings evil on itself as a punishment. This is true at a specific and at a general level. The evil it brings on itself as punishment is what is then called a judgment.

At first it seems as though the Lord does not see or notice that anything bad is happening, because when we go unpunished for the evil we do, we think the Lord does not care. The moment we pay a penalty is when we first believe the Lord sees, and we even imagine he inflicts the punishment. It is because of these appearances, then, that the text says Jehovah went down to see.

[3] Jehovah is depicted as descending because he is described as the Highest, or as being on the highest heights, and this too accords with appearances, because he is not on the highest heights but at the deepest inner depths. That is why "highest" and "inmost" mean the same thing in the Word. The actual judging or punishment of evil reveals itself at a lower level or at the lowest, which is why Jehovah is said to come down, as he also is in David:

Jehovah, bend your heavens and *come down* and let me speak with you.
Touch the mountains and they will smoke; hurl lightning and *scatter*
them. (Psalms 144:5, 6)

Here too Jehovah's coming down stands for the punishment of evil, or a
judgment on evil. In Isaiah:

Jehovah Sabaoth will *come down* to do battle on Zion's mountain and
on its hill. (Isaiah 31:4)

In the same author:

You will *come down;* before you, mountains will disintegrate. (Isaiah 64:3)

The descent here is likewise for the purpose of punishment—or judgment—
on evil. In Micah:

Jehovah was leaving his place, and he *came down* and trampled on the
lofty places of the earth, and the mountains melted under him. (Micah
1:3, 4)

To see the city and tower means on their perversion of doctrine and   **1312**
profanation of worship, as is established by the symbolism of a city and a
tower, discussed above [§§1305, 1306].

The symbolism of *that the children of humankind were building* as   **1313**
things they invented for themselves can be seen without explanation.

The *children of humankind* here are the daughters and sons of the
church. People who are not part of the church and do not have knowledge of the faith cannot invent such things. They cannot profane what is
holy, as was already explained in §§301, 302, 303, 593.

Genesis 11:6. *And Jehovah said, "Look: the people are one and they all*   **1314**
have one language, and this is what they are starting to do; and now nothing
would be prohibited to them that they thought to do."

Jehovah said means that it was so. *Look: the people are one and they all*
have one language, means that religious truth and doctrine were the same
for everyone. *And this is what they are starting to do* means that now they
are starting to alter. *And now nothing would be prohibited to them that*
they thought to do means unless their status now changes.

Jehovah said means that it was so, as can be seen from the previously   **1315**
demonstrated fact that this passage is not genuine history but made-up
history [§§482, 1020, 1283]. So when it says, "Jehovah said," the sole thing

it means is that it was so, which is what it meant in many earlier passages [§§630, 708, 926, 1020, 1037].

1316　　*Look: the people are one and they all have one language,* means that religious truth and doctrine were the same for everyone. This can be seen from the symbolism of a *people* as religious truth and from the symbolism of a *language* as doctrine.

The symbolism of a people as religious truth, that is, as those who have religious truth, was illustrated before, at §1259. The symbolism of a language as religious doctrine was illustrated above at verse 1 [§1286]. The people and their language are said to be one when everyone adopts the common good of society, the common good of the church, and the kingdom of the Lord as a goal. Under those circumstances, the Lord—who brings about the unity of all—is present in the goal.

When we adopt our own welfare as the goal, however, the Lord cannot be present in any way. Our very self-absorption pushes him away. Under these circumstances we deflect and divert to ourselves the common good of society, the common good of the church, and even the Lord's kingdom, treating them as if they exist for our own sake. In this way we take what is the Lord's away from him and replace it with ourselves.

When this attitude takes over in us, a reflection of it lurks in each of our thoughts and even in the smallest facets of our thoughts. That is how it is with a person's dominant trait. [2] The fact is not as obvious during bodily life as it is in the other life, where our dominant characteristic reveals itself through a kind of aura that everyone around us perceives. Our aura is like this because it emanates from everything inside us. If we focus on ourselves at every point, our aura usurps and (as people there say) absorbs everything advantageous to us, including all the pleasure of the spirits around us. It destroys all freedom in them. Inevitably, then, people like this are ostracized.

But when the people are one and they have one language, that is, when the common good of all is what people focus on, then no one ever usurps another's happiness or destroys another's freedom but promotes and increases it as much as possible. That is why heavenly communities seem to form a unit, and this is the effect of mutual love alone, which comes from the Lord. The same is true in the church.

1317　　The sequence of events shows that *this is what they start to do* means that now they were starting to alter.

Starting to do symbolizes their thinking, or their intention, and so their goal, as can be seen from the next clause, "and now nothing would be prohibited to them that they thought to do." The reason a goal is symbolized at an inner level is that the Lord regards nothing in us but our goal. No matter what thoughts we have thought or deeds we have done in all their countless permutations, as long as our purpose is good, these things are all good. When our purpose is bad, on the other hand, those things are all bad. Our final goal is what prevails in every single thing we think or do.

The angels with us are the Lord's, and therefore what they govern inside us are our purposes. When they govern these, they also govern our thoughts and deeds, because all our thoughts and deeds are included in our purposes.

Whatever we aim at is our actual life. The aim brings everything we think and do to life, since (again) it embraces everything we think or do. So the nature of our goal determines what our life is like. A goal, or purpose, is nothing but love, because the only thing we can adopt as a purpose is something we love. Even those who think one way and act another still have something they love as their goal. Within the pretense or deceit itself lies the goal, which is self-love or materialism, and this is the joy of their life. Accordingly, as anyone can see, the nature of our life reflects the nature of our love.

These, then, are the things symbolized by *starting to do*.

The fact that *and now nothing would be prohibited to them that they thought to do* means unless their status now changes can be seen from what follows. The Word's inner meaning is such that it constantly focuses on what follows and on the ending, even when this focus is not evident in the literal meaning.

1318

With people like those described above, nothing is prohibited that they think to do, unless their circumstances change. What follows will show that their circumstances did indeed change.

The thought of doing something is the same as an intention, or in other words, a purpose. No human purpose can ever be prevented— changed, in other words—unless conditions change in the person, because our final goal constitutes our actual life, as I said. When conditions change in us, our goal also changes, and with the goal, our thinking. What change in status occurred for the people of this church will be told below, by the Lord's divine mercy.

1319   Genesis 11:7. *"Come, let us go down and muddle their language there, so that a man will be unable to understand the language of his companion."*

Come, let us go down, means that a judgment therefore occurs. *And muddle their language there* means that no one knows any doctrinal truth. *So that a man will be unable to understand the language of his companion* means that they all clash.

1320   The meaning of *come, let us go down,* as the fact that a judgment therefore occurs is established by remarks above at verse 5 about the symbolism of going down [§1311]. The reason it says "*let us* go down" and "*let us* muddle their language" in the plural is that a judgment is being executed and spirits—evil spirits—are the agents.

1321   The meaning of *let us muddle their language* as the fact that no one knows any doctrinal truth can be seen from the symbolism of a *language,* [a *lip,* or *speech*] as doctrine (discussed above at verse 1 [§1286]). This leads to the conclusion that muddling the language is bringing confusion to the things doctrine teaches—that is, to doctrinal truth.

At an inner level, *muddling* something symbolizes not only darkening it but also obliterating it and scattering it to the winds, so that there is no longer anything true about it.

When self-worship replaces worship of the Lord, all truth is perverted. Not only is it perverted, it is also abolished, and in the end falsity is acknowledged as truth, and evil as goodness. All the light of truth comes from the Lord, and every bit of darkness from humankind. When human beings take over the Lord's role in worship, the light of truth becomes darkness. Then people see light as darkness and darkness as light. [2] The same holds true for their existence after death: a life of falsity is like light to them, but a life of truth is like darkness. The light in this false way of life turns into pure darkness, though, when they go near heaven.

During the time they live in the world, admittedly, they can speak the truth. In fact they can do so with eloquence and seeming zeal. And since they never stop mirroring everything back onto themselves, they also see themselves as believing what they say. But their real aim is worship of themselves, and the effect this aim has on their thinking is to keep them from acknowledging the truth, except so far as they can find a self-serving angle to it. When people who carry truth on their tongue are like this, the truth clearly is not true for them. This fact is obvious in the other world, where such people not only fail to acknowledge the truth they proclaimed during bodily life but even hate and attack it. The less they lose of their arrogance and self-adulation, the more they lash out at truth.

So that a man will be unable to understand the language of his companion means that they all clash, or oppose each other, as is clear from the words themselves. *Being unable to understand the language of a companion* is not acknowledging what another is saying. In an inner sense, it means not acknowledging what another teaches, or in other words, not acknowledging another's doctrine, since a *language,* [a *lip,* or *speech*] is doctrine, as shown above at verse 1. They do acknowledge it with their mouth but not with their heart, and harmony of the mouth is nothing in the face of discord at heart.

1322

The situation here resembles that of evil spirits in the next life. Like good spirits, they divide into separate communities, but what keeps them joined together are the ties formed by their having similar hallucinations and cravings. They act as one, then, in attacking what is true and good, and so they have something in common, something that binds them together. As soon as this common bond dissolves, however, each spirit assaults the next, and their pleasure then consists in torturing their companions one and all.

The case is the same with this type of doctrine and culture in the world. Adherents adopt a single doctrinal perspective and style of ritual compatibly enough, but the bond they share is self-worship. So far as they are able to participate in this common activity, they acknowledge [one another's points of view]; but so far as they cannot participate, nor hope to participate, they break apart. The reason, given just above, is that none of them knows any truth. Each takes falsity as truth and evil as goodness. This, now, is what it is for a man to be unable to understand the language of his companion.

Genesis 11:8. *And Jehovah scattered them from there over the face of the whole earth; and they stopped building the city.*

1323

Jehovah scattered them over the face of the whole earth here as before means that they were not acknowledged. *And they stopped building the city* means that doctrine of this kind was not accepted.

The meaning of *Jehovah scattered them over the face of the whole earth* as the fact that they were not acknowledged can be seen from statements above at verse 4 [§§1308–1309], where the same words occur.

1324

[2] The meaning of *they stopped building the city* as the fact that doctrine of this kind was not accepted can be seen from the symbolism of a city as doctrine—demonstrated earlier, in §402—and from

remarks above at verses 4 and 5 about the building of the city and tower [§§1302–1313].

These remarks show that such a doctrine (or such worship), holding self-love (self-worship) deep inside it, was not allowed in this ancient church, for the reason given in the next verse [§1327].

1325   Genesis 11:9. *For this reason he called its name Babel, because there Jehovah muddled the language of the whole earth; and from there Jehovah scattered them over the face of the whole earth.*

For this reason he called its name Babel symbolizes this type of worship. *Because Jehovah muddled the language of the whole earth* symbolizes conditions in this ancient church, in that inward worship started to die out; the *earth* is the church. *And from there Jehovah scattered them over the face of the whole earth* means that inward worship became nonexistent.

1326   The symbolism of *for this reason he called its name Babel* as this type of worship—specifically, the type symbolized by Babel—is evident from what has been said so far. It is worship that has self-love deep inside it and consequently everything that is unclean and profane. Self-love is nothing but the conviction that we answer to ourselves alone, and the filth and profanity of human selfhood can be seen from the explanation presented earlier, in §§210, 215.

From *philautia*—from self-love, that is, or a sense of autonomy—flows every kind of evil, such as hatred, vengefulness, cruelty, adultery, deceit, hypocrisy, and godlessness. So when our worship harbors self-love, or the desire to be our own ruler, it harbors evils like these, but with differences in amount and kind, depending on the amount and kind of influence self-love has. This is where all profanation in worship comes from.

The fact of the matter is that the more self-love or a misplaced sense of independence worms its way into our worship, the more internal worship recedes, or becomes nonexistent. Inward devotion consists in an affection for what is good and an acknowledgment of truth, but the more egoism or self-dependence advances or enters, the more an affection for goodness and the acknowledgment of truth withdraw or leave. Holiness can never coexist with profanation, just as heaven cannot coexist with hell. The one needs to separate from the other; that is what conditions in the Lord's kingdom, and the way it is organized, require. This is the reason why inward worship does not exist in those whose worship is called "Babel." Instead they worship something dead and even cadaverous that lies within. It is evident, then, what outward worship is like when something like this lies at its core.

[2] The fact that this kind of worship is *Babel* can be seen in the many places where the Word describes Babel [Babylon]. Daniel contains one example in the statue that Nebuchadnezzar, king of Babylon, saw in a dream. Its head was gold; its chest and arms, silver; its belly and thighs, bronze; its legs, iron; its feet, part iron and part clay. The statue symbolizes the fact that from true worship there finally evolved the kind of worship called Babylon, and that is why a stone cut out of a rock crushed the iron, bronze, clay, silver, and gold. (See Daniel 2:31, 32, 33, 44, 45.) The statue of gold that Nebuchadnezzar, king of Babylon, set up, and that the people worshiped, was also nothing else (Daniel 3:1–end). Likewise the fact that the king of Babylon drank wine with his nobles out of the golden vessels from Jerusalem's temple, that they praised gods made of gold, silver, bronze, iron, and stone, and that this resulted in the handwriting on the wall (Daniel 5:1–end). Then there was the command by Darius the Mede that he be revered as god (Daniel 6:1–end); and there were the beasts that Daniel saw in a dream (Daniel 7:1–end), and likewise the beasts and Babylon in John's Book of Revelation.

[3] The fact that this kind of worship is symbolized and represented is clear to see not only in Daniel and John but also in the prophets. In Isaiah:

> Their faces are faces aflame. The stars of the heavens and their constellations do not shed their light. The sun has been shadowed over in its entrance, and the moon does not radiate its light. Tsiyim lie down there, and their houses are filled with ochim, and daughters of the owl live there, and satyrs leap there, and iyim answer in its palaces, and serpents in its pleasure halls. (Isaiah 13:8, 10, 21, 22)

This passage is talking about *Babylon* and describing the inner content of this kind of worship. It does so through the faces aflame (cravings), the failure of the stars (individual religious truths) to shine, the overshadowing of the sun (sacred love), the failure of the moon (religious truth as a whole) to radiate, and the tsiyim, ochim, daughters of the owl, satyrs, iyim, and serpents (inward aspects of worship) because these properties characterize self-love. So in John (Revelation 17:5), *Babylon* is also called the mother of obscenities and abominations. And the same author calls it "a dwelling place for serpents, and a prison for every unclean spirit, and a prison for every unclean and loathsome bird" (Revelation 18:2). When such attributes lie at the core, obviously no religious goodness or truth can exist, and the good effects of love and the true ideas of faith retreat as those attributes invade. In Isaiah 21:9 they are also called carved images of the Babylonian gods.

[4] The fact that self-love (arrogant self-dependence) is what pervades self-worship, or actually constitutes self-worship, is plain to see in Isaiah:

> Prophesy this parable over the *monarch of Babylon:* You have said in your heart, "I will scale the heavens; I will raise my throne above the stars of God and sit on the mountain of assembly, on the flanks of the north. I will climb above the loftiest parts of the cloud; I will become like the Highest One." Nevertheless, you will be thrown down to hell. (Isaiah 14:4, 13, 14, 15)

In these verses, clearly, Babylon is one who wishes to be worshiped as a god; in other words, it is self-worship. [5] In the same author:

> Go down and sit in the dirt, virgin *daughter of Babylon;* sit on the earth. There is no throne, *daughter of the Chaldeans.* You trusted in your wickedness; you said, "There is no one to see me." Your wisdom and your knowledge turned you away. You said in your heart, "I am, and there is no one else like me." (Isaiah 47:1, 10)

In Jeremiah:

> Here now, I am against you, ruinous mountain, ruining the whole earth; and I will stretch my hand out over you and roll you down from the rocks and make you a mountain aflame. If *Babylon* climbs into the heavens, and if it fortifies its lofty stronghold, destroyers will come to it from me. (Jeremiah 51:25, 53)

This too shows that Babylon is self-worship.

[6] Jeremiah describes the fact that they have no light of truth—none of the truth that faith espouses—but pure darkness:

> The word that Jehovah has spoken against *Babylon,* against the *land of the Chaldeans:* "A nation from the north will come up over them. It will make their land a desolation, and nothing will live in it; from human to animal they will move off, they will leave." (Jeremiah 50:1, 3)

The north stands for darkness, or lack of truth. No human and no animal stands for a lack of goodness.

For more on Babylon, see below at verse 28, where it speaks of Chaldea [§1368].

Jehovah muddled the language of the whole earth symbolizes conditions in this ancient church, in that inward worship started to die out. **1327** This can be seen from the fact that it refers to the language of the whole earth rather than the language of the people who started to build the city and the tower, as it did before in verse 7. *The language of the whole earth* symbolizes conditions in the church, since the *earth* is the church, as already demonstrated, in §§662, 1066.

This is how the case was with the churches that followed the Flood: There were three of these churches, and they are specifically mentioned in the Word. They were the first ancient church, named for Noah; the second, named for Eber; and the third, named for Jacob and later for Judah and Israel.

[2] In regard to the first, referred to as Noah, it was like a parent to the churches that followed. It was also more unblemished and innocent than they, as churches usually are in their beginnings. This can be seen from the first verse of the present chapter, which says that they had one language, or in other words, one doctrine: the universal recognition of charity as essential.

But with the passage of time, the first church started to backslide, as churches do. The main cause was that many of the people in it began to redirect others' worship to themselves, so as to make themselves more important than anyone else. This too can be seen above, in verse 4, since they said, "*Let us* build ourselves a city and a tower with its head in the sky, and *let us* make ourselves a name." People of this type in the church could not help acting as a kind of fermenting agent, or as firebrands. When sacred things were in imminent danger of being profaned by their contagion (as discussed in §§571, 582), conditions in this church changed, by the Lord's providence. The church's inward worship died out and its outward worship remained, which is symbolized here by Jehovah's *muddling the language of the whole earth.*

This also demonstrates that the kind of worship called Babel was prominent not in the first ancient church but in the time of the later churches, when human beings began to be worshiped as gods, especially after they died. That is why the non-Jewish nations had so many gods.

[3] The point in allowing internal worship to die out and external worship to remain was to prevent profanation. The profanation of what is holy carries eternal damnation with it. No one is capable of profaning anything holy except those who possess a knowledge of the faith and

acknowledge what they know. People who do not have the knowledge cannot profess it, let alone profane it. Deeper dimensions are what can be profaned, because they have a holiness to them, which shallower dimensions do not.

The situation resembles that of people who do evil things but do not think evil thoughts. They cannot be held to account for the evil they do, just as those who unintentionally do wrong cannot, and likewise those who lack rationality. So people who do not believe in life after death but do engage in outward devotions cannot profane anything that has to do with eternal life, because they do not believe in eternal life. The case is different with those who do know of and acknowledge it.

[4] This is also why we are allowed to live lives of indulgence and self-gratification—which lead us to disengage from deeper concerns—rather than come into the knowledge and acknowledgment of those deeper realities and profane them. For the same reason Jews today are permitted to immerse themselves in greed, so that they will therefore be all the more unlikely ever to acknowledge deeper realities. Their nature is such, after all, that if they acknowledged these things they could not help profaning them. Nothing distracts a person more from deeper concerns than greed, since this is the lowest earthly appetite. Many people in the church are in a similar situation, and those in lands outside the church are too. The latter (non-Christians) are the least capable of all of committing profanation.

This, then, is the reason the present verse says that Jehovah muddled the language of the whole earth. It is also the reason these words mean that the status of the church changed, in that its worship became superficial and devoid of any inward devotion.

[5] The captivity in Babylon into which the Israelites and later the Jews were carried off had a similar representation and symbolism. Jeremiah deals with it this way:

And there will be a nation and kingdom that have not served *Babylon's* king, and those who have not put their neck into the yoke of *Babylon's* king. With sword and famine and contagion I will exact punishment on that nation, until I finish them off with my hand. (Jeremiah 27:8 and following verses)

To serve Babylon's king and put one's neck into his yoke is to be stripped of all knowledge and acknowledgment of the goodness and truth that faith embraces. So it is the loss of inward worship. [6] This is even more evident elsewhere in the same prophet:

> This is what Jehovah has said to all the people in this city: "Your sisters and brothers who have not gone out with you into captivity—" This is what Jehovah Sabaoth has said: "Look, now, I am sending sword, famine, and contagion on them, and I will make them like revolting figs." (Jeremiah 29:16, 17)

Staying in the city and not going out to Babylon's king represented and symbolized those who had a knowledge of deeper things (religious truths) and profaned them. The passage says that sword, famine, and contagion—the penalties for profanation—would be sent on them and that they would become like revolting figs.

[7] Babylon symbolizes those who rob others of all their ability to know and acknowledge the truth, and this representation and symbolism appears in the following words from the same prophet:

> All Judah I will give into the hand of *Babylon's* king, and he will carry them off into *Babylon* and strike them with the sword. And I will give all the wealth of this city and all its toil and everything precious in it and all the treasures of Judah's kings—I will give it into the hand of their enemies, and they will plunder it all and seize it. (Jeremiah 20:4, 5)

At an inner level all the wealth, all the toil, every precious thing, and all the treasures of Judah's kings symbolize religious knowledge. [8] In the same author:

> I will bring the king of *Babylon* (and the clans of the north) over this land and over its residents and over all these nations all around. And I will exterminate them and turn them into a ruin and a hissing and eternal wastelands. And this whole land will become a wasteland. (Jeremiah 25:9, 11)

These verses use Babylon as an image for the way the deeper aspects of faith—inner worship, in other words—are wiped out. Anyone who embraces self-worship is devoid of religious truth, as shown above [§§1321, 1326:6]. Such a person destroys and devastates everything that is true and leads it into captivity. So Babylon is also called a ruinous mountain (Jeremiah 51:25). In addition, see previous remarks about Babylon in §1182.

1328   The fact that *and from there Jehovah scattered them over the face of the whole earth* means that inward worship became nonexistent can be seen from the symbolism of *being scattered* as evaporating. The direct reference in "being scattered over the face of the whole earth" is to the people who wanted to build the city of Babel. At the same time, though, since they are people who rob others of all ability to know the truth (as I said), these words symbolize being deprived of inward worship. The one is a consequence of the other. It is the consequence that is meant here, because the words appear for the third time.

The fact that the first ancient church was stripped of what it knew about truth and goodness can be seen from the fact that most of the nations composing that church became idolatrous, although they retained a certain sort of outward worship.

Idolatrous people outside the church meet with a much better fate than the same kind of people inside the church. The former are outward idolaters; the latter are inward idolaters. That the fate of the former is better becomes clear from the Lord's words in Luke 13:23, 28, 29, 30 and Matthew 8:11, 12.

This, then, is the reason that conditions in the first ancient church changed.

1329   Genesis 11:10. *These are the births of Shem: Shem was a son of one hundred years, and he fathered Arpachshad, two years after the flood.*

These are the births of Shem, symbolizes developments in the second ancient church; *Shem* is inward worship in general. *One hundred years* symbolizes the state of that church in the beginning. *Arpachshad* was a nation by that name, and it symbolizes secular knowledge. *Two years after the flood* means the second church after the Flood.

1330   The symbolism of *these are the births of Shem,* as developments in the second ancient church is established by the symbolism of births as the origin and development of doctrinal matters and forms of worship. This symbolism was mentioned before, at §1145.

Births here and elsewhere in the Word are simply phenomena in the church and consequently are matters of doctrine and worship. The Word's inner meaning involves nothing else. So when a church is born, the text says that its births are such and such. When the earliest church was born, for instance, Genesis 2:4 said, "These are the *births* of the heavens and the earth." Again, when the other churches that came after that one but before the Flood were born, Genesis 5:1 said, "This is the book of the *births.*" Likewise with the churches after the Flood, of which there were three: a first, called Noah; a second, named for Eber; and a third, named for Jacob and later for Judah and Israel. When the previous chapter describes the first of these churches, it starts the same way, at verse 1: "These are the *births* of Noah's sons." This second church, named for Eber, is described in similar words in the present verse: "These are the *births* of Shem." And verse 27 of the present chapter says of the third, "These are the births of Terah." So the core meaning of births is the origin and development of the church's doctrinal matters and forms of worship that are being described.

The reason that the births of this second church are credited to *Shem,* or in other words, that the church is described as starting with Shem, is that he symbolizes inward worship. Here he symbolizes the inward worship of this church. The implication is not that the inward devotions of this church were like those symbolized by Shem in the last chapter. It is just that these were the inward devotions of this particular church.

The fact that *Shem* is inward worship in general is now apparent from the above. The nature of inward worship in this church reveals itself in the names of those listed after Shem. To be precise, that worship was an intellectual exercise, as the different numbers of years involved prove, once they are examined and explained.

1331

One hundred years symbolizes the state of that church in the beginning. This is established by earlier statements and evidence about the symbolism of numbers and years as periods and conditions (or states), in §§482, 487, 488, 493, 575, 647, 648, 755, 813, 893. But explaining the identity and nature of the states symbolized by one hundred years and by the numbers of years in the rest of the chapter would take too long. Besides, it is quite complicated.

1332

The fact that *Arpachshad* was a nation by that name, and that it symbolizes secular knowledge, was mentioned in the last chapter at [verse 22, §§1223–1224, 1226–1227, 1230; and] verse 24, §1236.

1334

The symbolism of *two years after the flood* as the second church after the Flood can be seen from the fact that in the Word a year symbolizes a whole period, whether short or long, fewer years or more, as do a day and a week. In fact these units of time even symbolize the abstract idea of a period. This is visible in the passages quoted above at §§488 and 893. The same holds true here; *two years after the flood* symbolizes the church's second period, which began when this second church started.

1335

Genesis 11:11. *And after Shem fathered Arpachshad he lived five hundred years; and he fathered sons and daughters.*

1336

After Shem fathered Arpachshad he lived five hundred years is a symbol for the length of time it lasted and its state; here as before *Shem* symbolizes internal worship in general, while *Arpachshad* symbolizes secular learning. *And he fathered sons and daughters* symbolizes doctrinal matters.

1337 There is no need to prove this symbolism. It is evident from the symbolism of the same items as discussed earlier.

All that needs to be said is that internal worship in this church was merely an intellectual exercise. So it was an exercise of the love that can be called a love of truth, because at the start of this church hardly any charity was left. Consequently not much faith—which comes only from charity—remained either. This follows logically from explanations just above about the city and Tower of Babel and specifically the fact that Jehovah muddled the language of the whole earth (verse 9).

1338 The symbolism of *fathering sons and daughters* as doctrinal matters can be seen from the symbolism of offspring above at §§264, 489, 490, 491, 533.

1339 Genesis 11:12. *And Arpachshad lived thirty-five years and fathered Shelah.*

Arpachshad lived thirty-five years symbolizes the start of the second phase of this church, and it also symbolizes the second phase itself; *Arpachshad* here as before symbolizes secular knowledge. *And fathered Shelah* symbolizes what developed out of it; *Shelah* was a nation by that name, and it symbolizes the effect of that knowledge.

1340 This symbolism too needs no proof here. The fact that Shelah was a nation by that name and that it symbolizes the effect of secular knowledge was stated earlier, at verse 24 of the last chapter [§§1235, 1237].

1341 Genesis 11:13. *And after Arpachshad fathered Shelah he lived four hundred three years, and he fathered sons and daughters.*

After Arpachshad fathered Shelah he lived four hundred three years is a symbol for the length of time it lasted and its state; here as before *Arpachshad* symbolizes secular learning and *Shelah* symbolizes the effect of that learning. *And he fathered sons and daughters* symbolizes doctrinal matters.

1342 Genesis 11:14. *And Shelah lived thirty years and fathered Eber.*

Shelah lived thirty years symbolizes the start of the third phase; *Shelah* here as before symbolizes the effect of secular learning. *And fathered Eber* symbolizes what developed out of it; *Eber* was a nation, called the Hebrew nation after its forefather Eber, and it symbolizes this second ancient church's worship in general.

1343 The fact that *Eber* was a nation, called the Hebrew nation after its forefather, and that it symbolizes this second ancient church's worship in general, can be seen from the Word's narrative parts, which mention the Hebrew nation in many places. Since a new form of worship began with that nation, everyone who worshiped in a similar way was called Hebrew. Their worship was like the type of worship later restored among Jacob's descendants. Its leading characteristic was its practice of referring to its God as Jehovah and offering sacrifices.

With one heart the earliest church acknowledged the Lord and called him Jehovah, as can be seen from the early chapters of Genesis and other places in the Word. The ancient church (the church that followed the Flood)—and especially the individuals in it whose worship had depth and who were called Shem's children—also acknowledged the Lord and called him Jehovah. The rest, who engaged in shallow worship, acknowledged and worshiped Jehovah as well. But that church's inward worship eventually turned shallow and, even worse, idolatrous, and each nation began to have its own god that it worshiped. Then the Hebrew nation kept the name of Jehovah and used that name for their God, which distinguished them from the other nations.

[2] Jacob's descendants in Egypt lost not only their outward form of worship but also the knowledge that their God was called Jehovah. Even Moses himself did. So first of all they were informed that Jehovah was the God of the Hebrews, the God of Abraham, Isaac, and Jacob, as the following words in Moses show:

> Jehovah said to Moses, "You shall go in—you and the elders of Israel—to the king of Egypt and say to him, *'Jehovah, God of the Hebrews,* has come to meet us; and now let us go, please, on a journey of three days into the wilderness and *sacrifice to Jehovah our God.'"* (Exodus 3:18)

In the same author:

> Pharaoh said, "Who is *Jehovah* that I should listen to his voice, to send Israel away? I do not know *Jehovah* and will not send Israel away, either." And they said, "The *God of the Hebrews* has come to meet us. Please let us go a journey of three days into the wilderness, and let us *sacrifice to Jehovah our God."* (Exodus 5:2, 3)

[3] The following words in Moses show that along with losing their form of worship, Jacob's descendants in Egypt also lost the knowledge of Jehovah's name:

> Moses said to God, "But when I come to the children of Israel and tell them, 'The God of your fathers has sent me to you,' and they say to me,

'What is his *name?'*—what should I tell them?" And God said to Moses,
"*I Am Who I Am."* And he said, "This is what you shall say to the children
of Israel: 'I Am has sent me to you.'" And God said further to Moses,
"This is what you shall say to the children of Israel: '*Jehovah, the God of
your ancestors*—the God of Abraham, the God of Isaac, and the God of
Jacob—has sent me to you.' This is *my name* forever." (Exodus 3:13, 14, 15)

[4] This makes it clear that Moses too did not know, and that Jacob's
descendants were distinguished from all others by use of the name Jehovah,
God of the Hebrews. That is why Jehovah is called God of the Hebrews in
other places as well:

> "You shall say to Pharaoh, '*Jehovah, God of the Hebrews,* has sent me to
> you.'" (Exodus 7:16)

> "Go in to Pharaoh and speak to him: 'This is what *Jehovah, God of the
> Hebrews,* has said.'" (Exodus 9:1, 13)

> Moses went in—as did Aaron—to Pharaoh, and they said to him,
> "This is what *Jehovah, God of the Hebrews,* has said." (Exodus 10:3)

In Jonah:

> I am a *Hebrew,* and I fear *Jehovah,* God of the heavens. (Jonah 1:9)

In Samuel as well:

> The Philistines heard the sound of shouting. They said, "What is the
> sound of this great shouting in the camp of the *Hebrews?"* And they
> realized that the ark of *Jehovah* had come to the camp. The Philistines
> said, "Alas for us! Who will free us from the hand of these *majestic
> gods?* These are the *gods* that struck the Egyptians with every plague in
> the wilderness. Turn into men, Philistines, or you will be slaves to the
> *Hebrews."* (1 Samuel 4:6, 8, 9)

Here too it is evident that the nations were identified by their gods, whom
they would name, and that the Hebrew nation was identified with Jehovah.
    [5] The fact that sacrifices constituted the other essential feature of
worship in the Hebrew nation is evident in the passages quoted above—
Exodus 3:18 and 5:2, 3. Consider too that the Egyptians abhorred the
Hebrew nation on account of this ritual, as can be seen from the following in Moses:

> Moses said, "It is not right to do so, because we would be *sacrificing
> what the Egyptians abhor to Jehovah our God.* Look, were we to *sacrifice*

what the Egyptians find abhorrent in their eyes, wouldn't they stone us?"
(Exodus 8:26)

So the Egyptians loathed the Hebrew nation, and loathed it so much
that they also refused to eat bread with Hebrews (Genesis 43:32). This
too shows that Jacob's descendants included not only the Hebrew nation
but all nations that practiced this type of worship. That is also why the
land of Canaan was called the land of the Hebrews in Joseph's time:

Joseph said, "I was stolen from the *land of the Hebrews.*" (Genesis 40:15)

[6] Much evidence indicates that sacrifice existed among idolaters in the
land of Canaan, since people there sacrificed to their own gods—baals
and others. In addition, consider Balaam, who was from Syria, where
Eber lived, or in other words, where the Hebrew nation came from before
Jacob's descendants entered into the land of Canaan. Balaam not only
offered sacrifices but also called his God Jehovah. (Numbers 23:7 shows
that Balaam was from Syria, where the Hebrew nation originated. Numbers 22:39, 40 and 23:1, 2, 3, 14, 29 show that he offered sacrifices. Numbers
22, verse 18 and other verses there show that he called his God Jehovah.)

Genesis 8:20 says that Noah offered burnt offerings to Jehovah, yet
this is not a true but rather a made-up story, because burnt offerings
symbolized the holiness of worship; see the sections where that verse is
discussed [§§919–923].

These remarks now demonstrate what Eber—that is, the Hebrew
nation—symbolizes.

Genesis 11:15. *And after Shelah fathered Eber he lived four hundred*
three years; and he fathered sons and daughters.   **1344**

After Shelah fathered Eber he lived four hundred three years is a symbol for the length of time it lasted and its state; *Shelah* here as before
symbolizes the effect of secular knowledge, and *Eber* here has the same
symbolism he had before—the worship of that church, in general. *And*
he fathered sons and daughters symbolizes doctrinal matters.

Genesis 11:16. *And Eber lived thirty-four years and fathered Peleg.*   **1345**

Eber lived thirty-four years symbolizes the start of a fourth phase in
this church; *Eber* here as before symbolizes the worship of the church,
in general. *And fathered Peleg* symbolizes what developed out of it; *Peleg*
was a nation named after its forefather Peleg, and it symbolizes external
worship.

The fact that Peleg symbolizes external worship here follows from
the series of developments in worship and so from Peleg's lineage. At

verse 25 of the last chapter [§§1240, 1242] he had a different symbolism. This was because of the meaning of his name—that in his days the land was divided—and because in that passage it was he and his brother Joktan together who represented that church.

1346 Genesis 11:17. *And after Eber fathered Peleg he lived four hundred thirty years; and he fathered sons and daughters.*

After Eber fathered Peleg he lived four hundred thirty years is a symbol for the length of time it lasted and its state; *Eber* and *Peleg* have the same symbolism here as before. *And he fathered sons and daughters* symbolizes doctrinal matters—that is, matters of ritual.

1347 Genesis 11:18. *And Peleg lived thirty years and fathered Reu.*

Peleg lived thirty years symbolizes the start of a fifth phase; *Peleg* has the same symbolism here as before. *And fathered Reu* symbolizes what developed out of it; *Reu* was a nation named after its forefather Reu, and it symbolizes worship that is even shallower.

1348 Genesis 11:19. *And after Peleg fathered Reu he lived two hundred nine years; and he fathered sons and daughters.*

After Peleg fathered Reu he lived two hundred nine years is a symbol for the length of time it lasted and its state; *Peleg* and *Reu* have the same symbolism here that they had before. *And he fathered sons and daughters* symbolizes ritual.

1349 Genesis 11:20. *And Reu lived thirty-two years and fathered Serug.*

Reu lived thirty-two years symbolizes the start of a sixth phase; *Reu* has the same symbolism here as before. *And fathered Serug* symbolizes what developed out of it; *Serug* was a nation named after its forefather Serug, and it symbolizes worship that stays on the surface.

1350 Genesis 11:21. *And after Reu fathered Serug he lived two hundred seven years; and he fathered sons and daughters.*

After Reu fathered Serug he lived two hundred seven years is a symbol for the length of time it lasted and its state; *Reu* and *Serug* have the same symbolism here as before. *And he fathered sons and daughters* symbolizes the rituals of that kind of worship.

1351 Genesis 11:22. *And Serug lived thirty years and fathered Nahor.*

Serug lived thirty years symbolizes the start of a seventh phase in this church; *Serug* has the same symbolism here as before. *And fathered Nahor* symbolizes what developed out of it; *Nahor* was a nation named after its forefather Nahor, and it symbolizes worship verging on idolatry.

1352 Genesis 11:23. *And after Serug fathered Nahor he lived two hundred years; and he fathered sons and daughters.*

After Serug fathered Nahor he lived two hundred years is a symbol for the length of time it lasted and its state; *Serug* and *Nahor* have the same symbolism here as before. *And he fathered sons and daughters* symbolizes the rituals of that worship.

Genesis 11:24. *And Nahor lived twenty-nine years, and he fathered Terah.*

1353

Nahor lived twenty-nine years symbolizes the start of an eighth phase in this church; *Nahor* here as before symbolizes worship verging on idolatry. *And he fathered Terah* symbolizes what developed out of it; *Terah* was a nation named after its forefather Terah, and it symbolizes idolatrous worship.

Genesis 11:25. *And after Nahor fathered Terah he lived one hundred nineteen years; and he fathered sons and daughters.*

1354

After Nahor fathered Terah he lived one hundred nineteen years is a symbol for the length of time it lasted and its state; *Nahor* here as before symbolizes worship verging on idolatry; *Terah* symbolizes idolatrous worship. *And he fathered sons and daughters* symbolizes idolatrous ritual.

Genesis 11:26. *And Terah lived seventy years, and he fathered Abram, Nahor, and Haran.*

1355

Terah lived seventy years symbolizes the start of a ninth and last phase; *Terah* here as before symbolizes idolatrous worship. *And he fathered Abram, Nahor, and Haran* symbolizes all that developed out of it; *Abram, Nahor,* and *Haran* were real people, and nations were named after them too, whose members were idolaters.

The symbolism of *Terah* as idolatrous worship can be seen from the developments described from verse 20 to this point.

1356

This second ancient church degenerated from a certain inward worship and was adulterated, till in the end it became idolatrous. Churches tend to do this, by shifting away from their deeper dimensions toward shallow ones, ending at last in purely superficial concerns, having obliterated any deeper ones. This church followed the same course, to the point where the majority of its people did not acknowledge Jehovah as God but worshiped other gods. This can be seen in Joshua:

Joshua said to all the people, "This is what Jehovah, God of Israel, has said: 'Your ancestors lived across the river ages ago—*Terah,* father of *Abraham* and father of *Nahor*—and *served other gods.'*" (Joshua 24:2)

"Now fear Jehovah and serve him in integrity and truth; and take away the *gods* that *your ancestors served* across the river and in Egypt and serve

Jehovah. And if it is bad in your eyes to serve Jehovah, choose for your-selves today whom you would serve, whether it is the *gods that your ancestors* who were across the river *served* or the gods of the Amorites." (Joshua 24:14, 15)

This demonstrates plainly that Terah, Abram, and Nahor were idolaters.

[2] The fact that *Nahor* was a nation that practiced idolatrous wor-ship can be seen from Laban the Syrian, who lived in Nahor's city and worshiped the images or teraphim that Rachel stole (Genesis 24:10; 31:19, 26, 32, 34). Abraham had one god, Nahor another, and their father Terah another, as Genesis 31:53 shows. In Moses it is also said explicitly of Abram that Jehovah was not known to him:

I, Jehovah, appeared to Abraham, Isaac, and Jacob as God Shaddai, and *by my name "Jehovah" I was not known to them.* (Exodus 6:3)

Such evidence makes it clear how far this church, as it existed in this nation, strayed into the idolatrous worship symbolized by Terah. (And since that worship is symbolized by Terah, it is also symbolized by Abram, Nahor, and Haran.)

1357   There are three universal categories of idolatry. The first is love for ourselves, the second is love of worldly advantages, and the third is love of sensual pleasure. All idolatrous worship has one or another of these for its goal. The worship of idolaters has no other goal because idolaters do not know or care about eternal life and even deny its existence.

These three types of idolatry are symbolized by the three sons of Terah.

1358   The fact that *Abram, Nahor,* and *Haran* were real people, and that nations were named after them, whose members were idolaters, can be seen in the Word's narrative parts. The truth of this in respect to Nahor has already been demonstrated [§1356:2], since his city was actually called the city of Nahor (Genesis 24:10). In that day, cities were nothing but a number of clans living in the same place, and a collection of clans was a nation.

Many non-Jewish nations were born from Abraham, as can be seen not only from the descendants of Ishmael, or the Ishmaelites, but also from the descendants of the numerous children he had by his wife Keturah, who are named in Genesis 25:1, 2, 3, 4.

1359   Genesis 11:27. *And these are the births of Terah: Terah fathered Abram, Nahor, and Haran. And Haran fathered Lot.*

These are the births of Terah symbolizes the origins of and various developments in the idolatry from which the representative church arose. *Terah* was a son of Nahor, and Terah was also a nation named after its forefather Terah; he symbolizes idolatrous worship. *Abram, Nahor,* and *Haran* were sons of Terah, and they were also nations named after those men as their forefathers; here they symbolize the idolatrous forms of worship that resulted. *Lot* also gave rise to two nations of idolaters.

These are the births of Terah symbolizes the origins of and various developments in the idolatry from which the representative church arose. The symbolism of *births* as origins and developments was demonstrated earlier in this chapter, at verse 10 [§1330]. The object of discussion at this point is the third church that came after the Flood. This church arose when the second one (described from verse 10 up to here) turned idolatrous with Terah. It has been shown that Terah, Abram, Nahor, and Haran were idolaters, not to mention the nations that came from them, such as the Ishmaelites, Midianites, and others of Abram's descendants. In addition there were Nahor's descendants in Syria, and also the Moabites and Ammonites, who were offspring of Lot.

1360

Idolatry turned the church into a representative religion, but no one can see this without knowing what it means to be representative. What was represented in the Jewish religion and what is represented in the Word are the Lord and his kingdom and therefore the heavenly qualities of love and the spiritual properties of faith. These and many other things related to them are what is being represented, as is everything having to do with religion.

1361

The things that represent them are either people or various objects that exist in the world or on earth—in short, everything that is perceptible to the senses. In fact there is hardly any perceptible thing that cannot serve a representative role.

A general rule of representation, however, is that it implies nothing about the person or thing that does the representing, only about the phenomenon represented. [2] For example, every monarch, no matter who it was—in Judah or Israel, even in Egypt and elsewhere—was able to represent the Lord. The monarchy itself of these people was representative. So the Lord could be represented by the worst sovereign of all, such as the pharaoh who set Joseph up over the land of Egypt, or Nebuchadnezzar in Babylon (Daniel 2:37, 38), or Saul, or the other monarchs of Judah and Israel, whatever they were like. Their actual anointing (because of which they were referred to as "Jehovah's anointed") involved this representation.

All the priests without exception similarly represented the Lord. Priesthood itself is representative. Priests who were evil and impure represented the Lord as well, because with representative roles there is no implication concerning the character of the actual person.

Not only people played a representative role but animals too, such as all the sacrificial ones. Lambs and sheep represented heavenly qualities; pigeons and turtledoves represented spiritual ones. Rams, he-goats, young cattle, and adult cattle did too, but the heavenly and spiritual qualities they represented were of a lower order.

[3] What is more, not only animate beings played a representative role, as noted, but inanimate objects too. Examples are the altar and even the altar stones, the ark and the tabernacle with all that was in it, the Temple with all that was in it as well (as anyone can recognize), and so the lamps, the loaves of bread, and Aaron's garments.

And not only were these items representative but all the rituals of the Jewish religion were too.

In the ancient churches, [which were steeped in symbolism,] symbolic items included all the objects of the senses, such as mountains and hills; valleys, plains, rivers, brooks, springs, and wells; groves of trees; trees in general; and every tree in particular, to the point where each individual tree meant something specific. Later, when the symbolic church ended, such objects became representative. These remarks show what "representative objects" means.

Again, not only humans—without regard to their identity or character—but also animals and inanimate objects were capable of representing heavenly and spiritual attributes (that is, attributes of the Lord's kingdom in the heavens and of the Lord's kingdom on earth). And from this, one can deduce what a representative church is.

[4] Because of the way the representative relationship worked, any activity that met the requirements laid down for ritual appeared holy in the eyes of spirits and angels. This was true, for instance, when the high priest washed with water, wore the priestly garb as he ministered, and stood in front of the burning lamps. It did not matter what he was like, even if he was extremely impure and an idolater at heart. The same was true for the other priests as well. To repeat, when it comes to representative items, they imply nothing about the actual person, only about the quality itself that is being represented, in complete isolation from the person. The quality is just as separate from the person as it was from the adult cattle, young cattle, and lambs that were sacrificed, or from the blood that was poured out around the altar, or from the altar itself, and so on.

[5] This representative religion was established after all inward worship had died out and become not merely shallow but even idolatrous. It was established in order to maintain some connection between heaven and earth, or rather between the Lord and humankind through heaven. This occurred after the bond created by the deeper elements of worship had broken. However, the nature of this connection created only by representative elements will be told later [§§3478–3480, 4311, 8588:5–6, 8788, 9457, 9481, 10500], by the Lord's divine mercy.

Representative meanings do not start till the next chapter, but each and every detail from there on is purely representative. The present verse deals with the circumstances of the forefathers before some of them (and their descendants) came to serve representative roles. The fact that they practiced idolatrous worship is shown above [§1358].

Terah was a son of Nahor, and Terah was also a nation named after its forefather Terah; he symbolizes idolatrous worship. This was shown earlier [§§1353–1357].

1362

The fact that Terah was a nation can be seen from the acknowledgment by the nations springing from his sons that he was their ancestor. This is what Jacob's offspring—the Judeans and Israelites—did, just as the Ishmaelites, Midianites, and others acknowledged Abram, and just as the Moabites and Ammonites acknowledged Lot. Admittedly, those nations were named not for these ancestors but for the ancestors' children. But still when all the people acknowledge a common ancestor and call themselves that ancestor's offspring (the children of Terah, for instance, or the children of Abraham, or the children of Lot), each of the ancestors symbolizes a nation in a broad sense. That is what Terah, Abram, Nahor, and Lot symbolize here, since they are the trunks or roots of various nations. The case is similar with Jacob's offspring; all of them were named for his twelve sons, yet they are still called Jacob and Israel. They are also called the seed and children of Abraham (John 8:33, 39).

Abram, Nahor, and *Haran* were sons of Terah, and they were also nations named after those men as their forefathers; here they symbolize idolatrous forms of worship. This can be seen from evidence offered above [§1358] and also from the fact that Terah (whose children they were) symbolizes idolatry.

1363

Just what types of idolatrous cult are symbolized here by Terah's three sons and later by Lot (Haran's son) can be determined by examining the different kinds of idolatrous cults. There are four kinds in general, each one deeper than the next. The three deeper levels are like the children of one parent; the fourth is like a child of the third.

There are inward and outward types of idolatrous worship. The inward types are those that damn us, while the outward types do not. The deeper a form of idolatrous worship goes, the more it condemns us; the shallower it is, the less it condemns us. [2] Inward idolaters do not acknowledge God but adulate themselves and the world; all their cravings serve as their idols. Outward idolaters, however, can acknowledge God, even though they do not know who the God of the universe is.

Internal idolaters are recognized by the life they have acquired for themselves; the further their life diverges from a life of charity, the deeper their idolatry goes. External idolaters are recognized only by their worship; even though they are idolaters, they can still live a life of charity.

Inward idolaters are capable of profaning holy things, but outward idolaters are not. Outward idolatry is tolerated, then, to keep people from profaning holy things, as indicated by earlier remarks, at §§571, 582, and above at verse 9, §1327.

1364 The fact that *Lot* gave rise to two nations of idolaters can be seen from the two sons he had by his daughters (Genesis 19:37, 38), Moab and Ammi, from whom the Moabites and Ammonites came. The fact that they were idolaters is evident from the Word. Lot is mentioned here as the father of the idolatrous cults symbolized by Moab and Ammi.

1365 Genesis 11:28. *And Haran died in the presence of Terah, his father, in the land of his birth, in Ur of the Chaldeans.*

Haran died in the presence of Terah, his father, in the land of his birth, in Ur of the Chaldeans, means that deeper worship was obliterated and became purely idolatrous. *Haran* symbolizes deeper idolatrous worship; *Terah, his father,* symbolizes idolatrous worship in general, as before; *the land of his birth* symbolizes the source from which it developed. *Ur of the Chaldeans* symbolizes outward worship that involves falsities.

1366 *Haran died in the presence of Terah, his father, in the land of his birth, in Ur of the Chaldeans,* means that deeper worship was obliterated and became purely idolatrous. This can be seen from the symbolism of Haran, Terah, birth, and Ur of the Chaldeans, and by the fact that Haran is said to have died in the presence of Terah, his father.

In respect to the obliteration or annihilation of deeper worship, the fact of the matter is that the church cannot emerge anew in any nation until it has been so thoroughly devastated that no trace of evil or falsity remains in its inward worship. As long as evil lingers in the church's inward worship, it blocks off the good impulses and true concepts that constitute the church's inward worship, because as long as evil and falsity remain, nothing good or true can be received.

This fact is illustrated by people who have been born into some heresy and have confirmed themselves in its falsities to the point of total conviction. It is hard if not impossible for them to reach a point where they can accept true ideas that run counter to their falsities. The case is different, though, with non-Christians who have no idea what the truth of the faith is and yet live a life of neighborly love. (This was the reason that the Lord's church could not be restored among Jews but only among non-Jews who lacked all knowledge of the faith.) The former completely obscure the light of truth with their falsities and in this way blot it out. The latter do not, because they do not know what the truth of the faith is, and what they do not know they also cannot obscure or blot out.

[2] Since a new church was now to be restored, a group was selected to have the good impulses and true ideas of faith planted in them. Those selected were people in whom all knowledge of religious goodness and truth had been wiped out and who had outwardly become idolaters, like the surrounding nations.

Terah and Abram were people of this kind, as shown above [§§1356, 1363]. They worshiped other gods and did not know Jehovah, so they also did not know about the goodness and truth of the faith. As a result, they had become better suited to receiving the seed of truth than others in Syria who still retained some knowledge. (Balaam's existence demonstrates that the knowledge remained with some people; he was from Syria and not only worshiped Jehovah but also conducted sacrifices and was a prophet as well.)

These, now, are the contents of the present verse—inward worship was obliterated and became purely idolatrous.

The symbolism of *Haran* as deeper idolatrous worship and that of **1367**
Terah as idolatrous worship in general has been stated and illustrated before [§§1356, 1363]. The fact that *the land of his birth* symbolizes the source and that their idolatrous worship developed from it is established by the symbolism of birth as origins and developments, discussed earlier, at verses 10 and 27 [§§1330, 1360].

The symbolism of *Ur of the Chaldeans* as outward worship that involves **1368**
falsities can be seen from the symbolism of Chaldeans in the Word.

It was shown above at verse 9 that Babel symbolizes worship that has evil inside it [§1326]. *Chaldea*, on the other hand, symbolizes worship that has falsity inside it. Babel, then, symbolizes worship that has nothing good inside it, while Chaldea symbolizes worship that has nothing true inside. Worship that has nothing good and nothing true inside is worship that has a profane, idolatrous quality inside. The fact that

Chaldea symbolizes this kind of worship in the Word can be seen from the following places. In Isaiah:

> Look: the *land of the Chaldeans!* This people is not. Assyria founded [the land] among tsiyim. They will erect their spy towers; [the Chaldeans] will raise up their palaces. [Assyria] will make it a ruin. (Isaiah 23:13)

The land of Chaldeans who were not a people stands for falsity. "Assyria founded it" stands for the fact that rationalizations laid the foundation. The spy towers stand for delusions. In the same author:

> This is what Jehovah, your Redeemer, the Holy One of Israel, has said: "Because of you I have sent to *Babylon* and thrown down the bars of the gates, all of them, and the *Chaldeans,* in whose ships there is shouting." (Isaiah 43:14)

Babylon stands for worship that has evil deep inside. The Chaldeans stand for worship that has falsity deep inside. The ships are a knowledge of truth, but knowledge that has been perverted. [2] In the same author:

> Sit silent and go into the dark, *daughter of the Chaldeans,* because you will no longer be called an overseer of kingdoms. I was enraged with my people. I profaned my inheritance and gave them into your hand. These two things will come to you suddenly on one day: loss of children and widowhood together. To their full extent they will come over you, because of the abundance of your sorceries and because of the scope of your spells. (Isaiah 47:5, 6, 9)

It is evident here that Chaldea is the profanation of truth, which is referred to as sorceries and spells. In the same author:

> Leave *Babylon;* flee from the *Chaldeans.* (Isaiah 48:20)

This stands for running from the profanation of anything good or true in worship. In Ezekiel:

> Make known to Jerusalem its abominations. Your father is an Amorite and your mother a Hittite. You whored with the sons of Egypt. You whored with the sons of Assyria. Therefore you multiplied your whoredom all the way into the *land of Chaldea.* (Ezekiel 16:2, 3, 26, 28, 29)

This speaks of the Jewish religion in particular. The sons of Egypt stand for facts. The sons of Assyria stand for rationalizations. The land of Chaldea, to which Jerusalem spread its increasing whoredom, stands for the profanation of truth. Anyone can see that Egypt, Assyria, and Chaldea do not mean different lands and that the passage is not talking about whoredom at all. [3] In the same author:

> Oholah whored and doted on her lovers, the neighboring Assyrians, and her whorings from [her time in] Egypt she did not abandon. She added to her whorings and looked at men, a portrayal on the wall, images of *Chaldeans* painted in vermilion, sashes girdling their hips, floppy dyed turbans on their heads, all of them appearing to be leaders, looking like the *sons of Babylon, Chaldeans,* in the *land of their birth.* She lusted for them at one glance of her eyes and sent messengers for them to *Chaldea.* The *sons of Babylon* defiled her through their whorings. (Ezekiel 23:5, 8, 14, 15, 16, 17)

The Chaldeans are called sons of Babylon, who stand for the presence of profaned truth in worship. Oholah stands for the spiritual church, which is called Samaria [Ezekiel 23:4]. [4] In Habakkuk:

> I am rousing the *Chaldeans,* a nation bitter and hasty, invading the breadth of the land to take possession of dwellings that are not theirs. Terrifying and fearsome [is that nation], and from itself alone do its judgment and its superiority issue. Its horses are nimbler than leopards, and its eyes are [nimbler] than wolves at evening. And in all directions its riders spread, and its riders approach from a distance; they fly forward like an eagle darting in to eat. The whole [nation] comes intent on violence. Its breathless desire faces eastward. (Habakkuk 1:6, 7, 8, 9)

This passage depicts the nation of Chaldea through many representative images symbolizing the profanation of truth in worship. [5] Two entire chapters in Jeremiah (chapters 50 and 51) also describe Babylon and Chaldea, and they make it quite clear what each symbolizes: Babylon symbolizes the profanation of heavenly qualities in worship and Chaldea the profanation of spiritual qualities in worship.

These quotations show, then, what Ur of the Chaldeans symbolizes: external worship that has something profane and idolatrous deep inside. The worship of the Chaldeans was actually like this too, as I was permitted to learn from the Chaldeans themselves.

Genesis 11:29. *And Abram and Nahor took themselves wives; the name of Abram's wife was Sarai, and the name of Nahor's wife was Milcah daughter of Haran (the father of Milcah and the father of Iscah).*

1369

Abram and Nahor took themselves wives and the name of Abram's wife was Sarai, and the name of Nahor's wife was Milcah daughter of Haran (the father of Milcah and the father of Iscah) symbolizes evil and falsity wedded in idolatrous worship—a union that resembles these marriages. The husbands symbolize different kinds of evil and the wives symbolize different kinds of falsity.

1370   Explaining why this is the symbolism would take too long, since the different kinds of idolatry and the ways they developed would have to be discussed in the process. The only way to recognize different kinds of idolatry is by their opposites. More precisely, the only way to recognize them is from the profanation of such things as the heavenly attributes and spiritual attributes of love; rational thoughts that spring from these attributes; and, lastly, facts. The ways in which each of these things is profaned are themselves the general categories and specific types of idolatry. The cults of various idols, which are external idolatries, are not categories of idolatry, however. These cults can be linked with affections for goodness and truth. So they can be linked with charity, as they are among nations that live lives of mutual kindness. Deeper forms of idolatrous worship are what the outwardly idolatrous cults in the Word symbolize.

The births and generations of these idolatries, and their marriages (which are marriages of evil and falsity), mirror exactly the relationships and marriages described in verse 27 and the current verse.

1371   Genesis 11:30. *And Sarai was infertile; she had no offspring.*

Sarai was infertile; she had no offspring, means that evil and falsity would no longer reproduce themselves.

1372   This symbolism is established by that of *infertility,* discussed elsewhere [§§3286, 9325]. Sons and daughters symbolize truth and goodness or, in an opposite sense, evil and falsity, as already demonstrated [§§264, 489–491, 568]. So infertility symbolizes the fact that the evil and falsity of idolatrous worship would no longer reproduce themselves.

1373   Genesis 11:31. *And Terah took Abram his son and Lot son of Haran (son of his son) and Sarai his daughter-in-law (wife of his son Abram), and they went out with them from Ur of the Chaldeans to go into the land of Canaan. And they came all the way to Haran and stayed there.*

These words mean that people who practiced idolatrous worship were taught about the heavenly and spiritual aspects of faith, so that a representative church could therefore come into existence.

1374   This symbolism can be seen from the remarks above and by others to come in the next chapter.

Genesis 11:32. *And the days of Terah were two hundred five years; and* **1375**
Terah died in Haran.

The days of Terah were two hundred five years is a symbol for the
length of time the idolatrous worship meant by Terah lasted and its state.
And Terah died in Haran symbolizes the end of idolatry and the beginning of a representative church started by Abram.

Location and Place in the Other Life; Distance and Time There as Well (Continued)

I have often talked with spirits about the idea they have of place and **1376**
distance. "They're not real," I tell them, "but only look as though they
were. On the contrary, space and distance are just changes in the state
of your thoughts and feelings, which make themselves visible this way
in the world of spirits. There is no such appearance in heaven, among
angels, since they have no concept of space and time, only of state."

Spirits who have physical and earthly ideas clinging to them do not
grasp this, though. They believe that the situation really is exactly as they
see it. It is almost impossible to lead spirits like this to believe anything but
that they are still living in their bodies. They refuse to be convinced that
they are spirits. So they are almost completely unwilling to hear that any
kind of appearance or fallacy exists, preferring to live in their illusions. In
this way they shut themselves off from understanding and acknowledging
anything true or good that is too far removed from their misconceptions.

They have been shown over and over that a change of location is
nothing more than a visible manifestation or else a trick of the senses.
Changes of location in the other world are of two kinds, you see. One,
described earlier [§1276], involves the fact that all spirits and angels keep
their same place in the universal human at all times, which is a visible
manifestation. The other involves the fact that spirits can appear in a
place when they are not really there, which is an illusion.

The fact that location, change of location, and distance in the world **1377**
of spirits are appearances was clarified for me in the following way: All
souls and spirits whatsoever, from the beginning of creation, appear
in their own position at all times and never change place except when

conditions inside them change. As conditions inside them change, their relative location and distance alter too. Each spirit has a general, governing state, though, and the particular and the highly specific states still relate to the general one. For this reason, all spirits return to their position after such changes.

1378   I have learned, both by talking with angels and by personal experience, that spirits as spirits are not in the place they appear to be, so far as the organic substances composing the [spiritual] bodies they have are concerned. They can be very far off and still appear in that place. I realize that people who allow illusions to fool them will not believe this, but it is still the fact of the matter.

I illustrated this to spirits who would not believe anything they could not see with their eyes (even if it was merely an illusion) by the fact that something similar happens with human beings in the world. Take the sound in your ear of another person talking. If you did not know better—from practice gained since infancy in learning to tell sounds apart, and from seeing the distance—you would inevitably believe that the speaker was close to your ear. Long-distance vision is similar. If you did not know better because of seeing what intervenes, or calculate the distance on the basis of previous knowledge, you would believe a remote object to be right in front of your eyes. How much more so with spirits' speech, which is inner speech, and their eyesight, which is inner sight! [2] Moreover I said that it was no grounds for doubt, still less for denial, to say that such and such does not appear that way to your senses and that you cannot perceive it to be so, when manifest experience dictates otherwise. There are many things in the physical world that run contrary to the illusions of the senses but are accepted because of lessons taught by visual experience. An example is the act of sailing around the world. People who allow illusions to mislead them would believe that ship and sailor would both fall off when they reached the opposite side, and that people on the other side of the world could not possibly stand on their feet.

The same is the case with this fact and many others in the next life that contradict sensory illusions and yet are true, such as the notion that we do not have life on our own but only from the Lord, and so on and so on.

With these arguments and others I was able to convince doubting spirits to believe that the situation was as described.

1379   These remarks also show that when spirits walk or move around or go from one place to another—a frequent sight—it is nothing but a change of state. That is, it appears in the world of spirits as a change of location but in heaven as a change of state. In this it resembles many other objects and events that have a representative meaning and that display themselves in visible form there. These will be discussed later [§§1619–1633, 1641:2, 1643, 1764], with the Lord's divine mercy.

Location, change of location, and distance in the other life are illusory **1380** too, as I was able to see by this fact: In fantasy, spirits can instantly be swept up high—extremely high—and in the same moment down low. They can also be carried seemingly from one end of the universe to the other. In fact witches and warlocks in the other world can use fantasy to trick you into believing they are in one place and at the same time in another too, or even in many places. They pretend to be everywhere at once.

People who were ambitious during bodily life and people who were deceitful often appear overhead, and yet they are in a hell under the feet. As soon as they are stripped of their conceit, they tumble into their hell, as I was shown.

This is not a manifestation but an illusion. As noted [§§1376–1377], there are two kinds of change in location: the way all spirits and angels have of keeping to their place at all times is a visible manifestation, while their habit of showing up in a place when it is not their proper place is an illusion.

Souls and spirits who have not yet been allotted a permanent posi- **1381** tion in the universal human travel to different places, now here, now there; now they appear on one side and now on another; now up, now down. They are called roaming souls or spirits and resemble fluids in the human body that travel from the stomach, at one moment into the head, at another to other places, and remain on the move. That is how these spirits act before they arrive at their designated place—a place suited to their overall state. It is their state that changes and wanders in this way.

People on earth cannot help confusing God's infinity with infinity of **1382** space, and since their only idea of spatial infinity is that it is nothing—which is true—they also fail to believe in the divine infinity.

The case is the same with divine eternity. People cannot understand it except in terms of eternal time. But it is still presented as a temporal phenomenon with those who are caught up in the concept of time.

A true picture of God's infinity is instilled into angels by the consideration that they can come into the Lord's presence in a split second, without any intervening space or time, even if they should be at the ends of the universe. A true picture of God's eternity is instilled by way of the idea that the passing of thousands of years seems like no time to them; it is almost as if they had lived for just a moment. And both concepts come by way of the idea that in their present they have both past and future. For this reason, they do not worry about events that are yet to come. They never think about death but only about life.

Thus for them, every present moment contains the Lord's eternity and infinity.

Genesis 12

The Ability of Spirits and Angels to Perceive Things; Auras in the Other Life

AMONG the amazing things in the other life are perceptions, of which there are two kinds. One exists with angels: they perceive what is true and good, what comes from the Lord and what from themselves, and what the source and nature of their thoughts, words, and deeds is, when these come from themselves. The other kind is one that is common to everyone—to angels at the peak of perfection and to spirits according to their quality: as soon as another person approaches, they know what that person is like.

Let us turn to the first kind, the kind angels have—their ability to tell what is true and good, what comes from the Lord, what comes from themselves, and what the source and nature of their thoughts, words, and deeds is, when these come from themselves.

I was allowed to talk with the descendants of the earliest church about their ability to perceive. They said they did not and could not think anything on their own or will anything on their own. With each and every thought or impulse, they said, they can tell what comes from the Lord and what comes from somewhere else. They perceive not only how much is from the Lord and how much is seemingly from themselves but also (when it does seem to originate in themselves) where it comes from. That is, they perceive which angels it comes from, what those angels are like, what all their different thoughts are, and so what the various influences are, along with countless other factors.

Perceptions of this kind come in many varieties. Heavenly angels, who love the Lord, perceive goodness, and this enables them to perceive everything that is a matter of truth. Since they perceive truth from the standpoint of what is good, they do not allow any discussion of truth (let alone argument about it) but say yes or no. Spiritual angels, on the other hand, who also have perception (though not the kind heavenly angels have), do talk about truth and goodness. They still perceive things, but they perceive them in many different ways, because this kind of perception has countless variations. The variations have to do with perceiving whether the Lord wills a thing or accepts it or tolerates it—which are quite different from each other.

1385   There are spirits belonging to the region of the skin (particularly the squamous layer) who want to argue everything. They do not perceive what is good or true, and in fact the more they argue, the less they perceive it. They identify wisdom with sophistry, which they count on to make them seem wise. I told them that the role of angelic wisdom is to perceive whether a thing is good or true without sophistic reasoning, but they cannot grasp the possibility that this kind of perception exists. They are the same people that used the academic and philosophical disciplines during bodily life to cast confusion over truth and goodness and as a result seemed to themselves to be more knowledgeable than others. (They had not started with any valid assumptions taken from the Word.) Consequently, they do not have much common sense.

1386   As long as spirits imagine that they lead themselves, and that they think for themselves and gain knowledge, intelligence, and wisdom for themselves, they cannot have perception. Instead they consider perception to be stuff and nonsense.

1387   Several times I have talked about perception with people in the next life who while they were living in the world had imagined they could investigate and understand any subject. "Angels," I said, "perceive that they think and speak and that they will and act from the Lord."

The people I was talking to, though, could not comprehend what perception was. They thought that if everything were the result of outside influence like this, it would rob them completely of life, because it would mean never thinking for themselves, never thinking independently—which for them was life. It would mean that someone else was thinking for them and not they themselves. So they would be mere instruments, devoid of life.

"The difference in quality of life between having perception and not having it," I pointed out, "is like night and day. You first start to live your own life when you receive this perception, because you then live from the Lord. You then enjoy a sense of individuality as well, which comes to you replete with every happiness and joy."

From plentiful experience, I also illustrated for them how perception works, and they then acknowledged that it was possible. After a while, though, they again forgot, doubted, and denied. This showed me how hard it is for people to grasp what perception is.

The second kind of perception, as already mentioned [§1383], is one **1388** that is common to everyone—to angels at the peak of perfection and to spirits according to their quality. As soon as another person approaches, they know what that person is like, even if the person says nothing. It reveals itself instantaneously, by a sort of inspiration that is most amazing. Good spirits are recognized not only for the type of goodness they have but also for the type of belief. When they talk, it comes through in every word. Evil spirits are recognized for their wickedness and unbelief, and when they talk, it comes through in every word. The clues are so plain as to be unmistakable.

Something similar can be seen with people on earth. They too can sometimes tell what others are thinking from the gestures, facial expression, and speech of those others, even when their words contradict it. This skill in humans is an innate one whose origin can be traced to a character trait in spirits that grants them the same ability, and so to an individual's own spirit and its communication with the world of spirits. This shared perception originates in the Lord's wish that all blessings spread contagiously and that everyone enjoy mutual love and grow happy as a result. That is why this type of perception also prevails everywhere among spirits.

Souls that had arrived in the other life once expressed their surprise **1389** to find that another person's thoughts are communicated in this way. They were also amazed that they could instantly tell not only what kind of character that other person had but also what the person's beliefs were.

I told them that spirits receive abilities far superior once they separate from their bodies. During physical life, objects of the senses have an impact on us, as do fantasies built out of the impressions those objects leave on our memory, not to mention worries about the future; various cravings aroused by external stimuli; concern over food, clothes, housing, and children; and so on. People in the other life never think about any of these things. When such thoughts are set aside as obstacles and barriers, together with bodily desires connected to the coarser sensations, people cannot help being in a more ideal condition. Their former abilities remain but become much more perfect, lucid, and free. This is especially true with people who have lived lives of charity and faith in the Lord, and of innocence. Their capacities are heightened tremendously over the ones they had in the body, until finally their gifts match those of angels in the third heaven.

1390   It is not only the feelings and thoughts of others that are shared but their knowledge as well. So widely is knowledge shared that each spirit thinks he or she already knows what the next spirit knows, even if the first spirit had previously known nothing about the subject. Everything that others know about accordingly becomes common property. Some spirits retain the knowledge, some do not.

1391   Spirits share these things with each other in conversation and through mental images accompanied by visual representations. The images that compose their thoughts also take visible form, you see, which allows everything to be presented in full detail. Spirits can depict more through a single mental image than they can express in a thousand words. Angels even perceive what lies behind the image, what feeling is connected with it, where that feeling comes from, what the purpose of it is, and many other inner aspects.

1392   It is also common in the other world for one person to communicate pleasure and happiness in a remarkable way by actually passing them on to a number of others, who are as much affected by them as the original person. The communication takes place without any lessening of the feelings in the person who shares them to begin with.

I too was given the opportunity to share my pleasure with others by transferring it to them.

You can imagine, then, what kind of happiness exists in people who love their neighbor more than themselves and want nothing more than to spread their happiness to others. Their attitude traces its origin to the Lord, who communicates happiness to angels in the same way.

When people share happiness, they are constantly passing it along in the way just described, but they do so without reflecting on their active role in the process and without making a conscious, deliberate decision to engage in it.

1393   Another astonishing way happiness spreads is through extraction—a process whose nature cannot be grasped by people on earth. Harsh, disturbing elements are removed in an instant, and in the process, something pleasing and happy is presented, with nothing to block it. Once any hindrances are removed, angels stream in and communicate their joy.

1394   Since perception allows one person to see immediately what kind of love and belief another has, people come together in communities insofar as they harmonize, and separate insofar as they conflict. The process is so precise that not the smallest variation fails either to divide or to unite. As a result, communities in the heavens have distinctive characters—as distinct as anyone could possibly imagine. The differences depend on variations in love for the Lord and faith in him, which are countless. From this comes the form of heaven, which is such that it resembles a single human. That form is constantly being perfected.

A wealth of experience has taught me how this kind of perception works, but recounting all of it would take too long. **1395**

Many times I have heard swindlers talking and perceived not only the presence of fraud but also its nature and the nature of the malice behind it. It is as if an image of their duplicity dwells in every sound they utter. In addition, I have perceived whether the fraud was invented by the speaker or by others talking through the speaker.

It is the same with people who hate. One can see right away the character of their hatred and the factors that go into it, which are more numerous than you could ever be persuaded to believe. When the victims of their hatred are present in person, it creates a pitiable situation for the haters, since whatever thoughts they had entertained or plots they had hatched against the person stand out in plain view.

A certain spirit who wanted to take credit for the deeds he had done and the doctrines he had taught while living in the world went off toward the right and came upon some people who were not like him. In order to attach himself to them, he said that he was a nobody and would like to serve them, but they had been sensing what he was like from the moment he approached them, while he was still far away. Their immediate answer was that he was not the kind of person he said; he wanted to be important and consequently would not be able to get along with them, since they were not. Embarrassed by this, he left, amazed that they could tell from such a distance. **1396**

Since their sensitivities are so acute, evil spirits cannot go near any environment or community inhabited by good spirits, who love each other. Let the good spirits just approach and the evil ones begin to suffer, complaining and crying. **1397**

A certain evil spirit was brash and bold enough to force his way into a community that lay at the very threshold of heaven. The instant he arrived, he found he could hardly breathe and sensed that he stank like a corpse, so he slipped back down.

There were quite a few spirits around me who were not good. An angel came, and I saw that the spirits could not bear his presence, since **1398** the nearer he came, the farther away they went. I was surprised but was able to see that they could not linger in the aura that he carried with him. This too showed me, as other experiences have done, that one angel can drive away tens of thousands of evil spirits, since evil spirits cannot abide an atmosphere of mutual love.

Still, I could tell that his aura was being moderated by his associations with others. If it had not been, all the spirits would immediately have scattered.

This once again shows clearly what kind of perception exists in the other life, and it shows how people join together and separate in response to their perceptions.

1399   All spirits have contact with the inner heaven and the inmost (although they are unaware of it); otherwise they could not live. Their inner nature is recognized by angels, who are awake to deeper dimensions, and the Lord also governs them through angels. So their inner characteristics become common knowledge in heaven, as their outer ones do in the world of spirits.

These inner communications adapt each of them for some useful role, and they are drawn to that role without realizing it.

The situation with people on earth is the same. We too communicate through angels with heaven—in complete ignorance of the fact that we do—because otherwise we could not live. (The influence heaven has on our thinking is merely the outermost effect of that interaction.) Such contact is the source of all our life, and it regulates everything we try to do in life.

1400   For more on perception and the auras that perception generates, see the end of the present chapter [§§1504–1520].

Genesis 12

1. And Jehovah said to Abram, "Go your way from your land and from your birth[place] and from your father's house to the land that I show you.

2. And I will make you into a great nation and bless you and make your name great, and you will be a blessing.

3. And I will bless those who bless you, and the one who curses you I will curse, and in you all the clans of the ground will be blessed."

4. And Abram went, as Jehovah had spoken to him, and with him went Lot. And Abram was a son of seventy-five years when he left Haran.

5. And Abram took Sarai his wife, and Lot his brother's son, and all their gain that they had gained, and [every] soul that they had made in Haran, and they left to go into the land of Canaan. And they came into the land of Canaan.

6. And Abram passed through the land, all the way to the place of Shechem, all the way to the oak grove of Moreh. (And the Canaanite was then in the land.)

7. And Jehovah was seen by Abram and said, "To your seed I will give this land." And there he built an altar to Jehovah, who had been seen by him.

8. And he moved from there onto a mountain to the east of Bethel and spread his tent; Bethel was toward the sea and Ai toward the east. And there he built an altar to Jehovah and called on Jehovah's name.

9. And Abram traveled, going and traveling toward the south.

10. And there was famine in the land; and Abram went down into Egypt to reside as an immigrant there, because the famine was heavy in the land.

11. And it happened when he came near entering Egypt that he said to Sarai his wife, "Consider, please; I know that you are a woman beautiful to see.

12. And it will happen when the Egyptians see you that they will say, 'This is his wife,' and kill me and keep you alive.

13. Please say you are my sister, in order that it may go well for me on account of you and that my soul may live because of you."

14. And it happened when Abram came into Egypt that the Egyptians saw the woman, that she was very beautiful.

15. And Pharaoh's officers saw her and praised her to Pharaoh; and the woman was taken to Pharaoh's house.

16. And he was good to Abram on her account, and Abram had flock and herd, and male donkeys and male servants, and female servants and female donkeys, and camels.

17. And Jehovah struck Pharaoh—and his household—with great plagues because of this word of Sarai, Abram's wife.

18. And Pharaoh called Abram and said, "What is this you have done to me? Why didn't you point out to me that she was your wife?

19. Why did you say, 'She is my sister'? And I would have taken her for my woman. And now look: your wife; take her and go."

20. And Pharaoh gave orders concerning Abram to his men, and they sent him away, and his wife, and all that he had.

Summary

1401 TRUE history begins here. All the elements are representative, and the individual words are symbolic.

Everything said about Abram in this chapter represents the Lord's state from childhood to adolescence.

The Lord was born the same as any other human, so he also advanced from a murky state to one of greater clarity. Haran is the first phase, which is dark; Shechem is the second; the oak grove of Moreh is the third; the mountain from which Bethel was toward the sea and Ai was toward the east is the fourth; going from there southward into Egypt is the fifth.

1402 Everything said about Abram's stay in Egypt represents and symbolizes the Lord's early education. Abram is the Lord; Sarai as his wife is truth that needs to be connected to something from heaven; Sarai as his sister is intuitive truth; and Egypt is secular knowledge.

The chapter describes the Lord's progress from superficial facts all the way to heavenly truth. This progression followed the divine plan calling for the Lord's human quality to be united with his divine quality and for the Lord to become at the same time Jehovah.

Inner Meaning

1403 FROM the first chapter of Genesis up to this point, or rather up to Eber, the story elements were not true history but were made up, and on an inner level they symbolized heavenly and spiritual matters. In the current chapter, and in those to come, the narrative details are not made up but are truly historical details. On a deeper level they too symbolize heavenly and spiritual matters, as anyone can see simply by considering that it is the Lord's Word.

In these genuinely historical parts, every single statement and word **1404** symbolizes something radically different in the inner meaning than in the literal meaning, but the historical elements themselves are representative.

Abram, the first to be chronicled, broadly represents the Lord and more narrowly represents the heavenly self. Isaac, who comes next, likewise represents the Lord generally but the spiritual self specifically. Jacob too represents the Lord generally, and specifically he represents the earthly self. So the three of them represent properties of the Lord, of his kingdom, and of the church.

The nature of the inner meaning, though, as has been transparently **1405** demonstrated already [§§64, 647, 813, 1143], requires that each and every particular be understood separately from the literal meaning, as if the literal meaning did not exist. The soul and life of the Word is in the inner meaning, and it does not reveal itself unless the literal meaning vanishes, so to speak.

That is how angels—enabled by the Lord—perceive the Word when we on earth are reading it.

The summary prefacing this chapter [§§1401–1402] indicates what **1406** the historical events in it represent. The symbolism of the sentences and words will become clear in what follows, where they are explained.

Genesis 12:1. And Jehovah said to Abram, "Go your way from your land **1407** *and from your birth[place] and from your father's house to the land that I show you."*

The events of this verse and later ones happened as written, but the historical facts are representative and the words are all symbolic. In an inner sense, *Abram* means the Lord, as noted above. *Jehovah said to Abram* symbolizes a first realization. *Go from your land* symbolizes the bodily and worldly concerns that he would withdraw from. *And from your birth[place]* symbolizes bodily and worldly concerns that were relatively superficial. *And from your father's house* symbolizes ones that were deeper. *To the land that I show you* symbolizes spiritual and heavenly traits that would be presented to view.

The events of this verse and later ones happened as written, but the **1408** historical facts are representative and the words are each symbolic.

This is true of all the narrative parts of the Word—not only the books of Moses but Joshua, Judges, Samuel, and Kings as well. Nothing but history appears in any of them. Yet although the literal meaning is a history, the inner meaning holds the mysteries of heaven, which lie hidden there. These mysteries can never be seen, as long as we train our mind's eye on the historical details; they are not unveiled until we withdraw our minds from the literal meaning.

The Lord's Word is like a body with a living soul. Anything having to do with the soul remains invisible—to the point that we scarcely believe we even have a soul, let alone that it lives on after death—as long as the body monopolizes our thinking. As soon as concern for our person ebbs from our minds, though, qualities of the soul and of life reveal themselves. That is why everything connected with our body has to die before we can be born anew or regenerate. Not only that, the body itself also has to die, so that we can enter heaven and behold heavenly sights.

[2] The case with the Lord's Word is the same. Its "body" is the contents of the literal meaning, and as long as we fix our minds on those, we see nothing deeper. When they "die," though, [the deeper content] first stands out in plain sight.

Still, the features of the literal sense are like those things in us that belong to the body. Specifically, they are like facts that we glean from our sense impressions and retain in our memory. These are general containers that hold deeper levels inside. You can see from this that containers are one thing, the vital concepts contained within them are another. The containers are earthly; their vital contents are spiritual and heavenly. So also with the historical passages of the Word, and with the individual words there as well. They are general containers that are earthly and even physical, and they hold spiritual and heavenly features. The latter never enter our field of vision except through the inner meaning.

[3] Anyone can see this merely from the consideration that the Word often speaks in accord with appearances and even in accord with illusions of the senses. It says, for instance, that the Lord feels anger, punishes people, curses them, kills them, and so on, when in fact the inner meaning says the opposite—that the Lord never feels anger or punishes people, let alone cursing or killing them. Yet it does not hurt people to believe in simplicity of heart that the Word is just what they take it to be in the letter, as long as they live lives of neighborly love. The reason it does no harm is that the Word teaches nothing but the need for each of us to live in charity with our neighbor and to love the Lord above all. People who do this have deeper dimensions inside, so any illusions they acquire from the literal meaning are easily dispelled.

1409 The idea that the historical facts are representative but the words are each symbolic can be seen from previous remarks and illustrations in §§665, 920, and 1361 concerning representation and symbolism. Since the representative narrative begins here, let me give a further, brief explanation.

The people of the earliest church, which had a heavenly character, regarded every earthly, worldly, or bodily thing that ever presented itself to their senses as a dead object only. But each and every item in the world presents some image of the Lord's kingdom and so of heavenly and spiritual attributes. As a result, when they observed those objects, or encountered them by some other sense, their thoughts centered not on the objects but on aspects of heaven and of the spirit and came not from the objects but through them. So for them, dead objects were alive.

[2] The symbolic meanings of these items were received from their lips by the next generation, which gathered such meanings together and made doctrinal precepts out of them. Collectively, these formed the Word of the ancient church, after the Flood. Such precepts taught the people of the ancient church in a symbolic way, because they were both a means by which those people learned inward lessons, and the source of their thoughts about heavenly and spiritual matters.

This knowledge started to die out, however, so that people had no idea what such objects symbolized, and they began to make them sacred—though they were worldly and temporal things—and to worship them, without any thought of their symbolism. Then those same objects became representative. Such was the origin of the representative church, which commenced with Abram and was later established among Jacob's descendants.

From all this you can see that representation rose out of the symbolism of the ancient church and that the symbolism of the ancient church rose out of the heavenly ideas of the earliest church.

[3] The nature of representation can be seen from the Word's histories. There, all the deeds of these patriarchs—Abram, Isaac, and Jacob—and later of Moses, the Judges, and the monarchs of Judah and Israel, are nothing if not representative.

In the Word, as noted [§1402], *Abram* represents the Lord, and because he represents the Lord, he also represents the heavenly self; Isaac too represents the Lord, and therefore the spiritual self; and Jacob as well represents the Lord, and therefore an earthly self corresponding to the spiritual self.

[4] The situation with regard to representation, though, is that it implies nothing about the character of the person but only about the

phenomenon that the person represents. All the monarchs of Judah and Israel represented the Lord's sovereignty, no matter what they were like, and all the priests represented the Lord's priesthood, no matter what they in turn were like. So bad ones and good ones alike were able to represent the Lord and the heavenly and spiritual qualities of his realm. As stated and proved already [§§665, 1361], the representative meaning is completely separate from the person.

This, then, is why all the historical sections of the Word are representative. Since they are representative, it follows that all the words there are symbolic. That is, they mean something different in an inner sense than in the literal sense.

1410   *Jehovah said to Abram* symbolizes a first realization. The situation is this: The recorded fact is representative, but the actual words are symbolic. The ancient church's method of expression was such that when a thing was true, they would say, "Jehovah said," or "Jehovah spoke," meaning that it was so, as shown before [§§630, 708, 926, 1020, 1037].

After symbolism turned into representation, Jehovah (or the Lord) really did speak with people, and then when it says that *Jehovah said* something or that *Jehovah spoke* with someone, it has the same meaning as it did earlier. The Lord's words in the historical parts entail much the same thing that his words in the fictional parts do. The only difference is that the authors of the latter make up what seems to be a true story, while the authors of the former do not make it up.

This clause, then—"Jehovah said to Abram"—symbolizes nothing else than a first realization. In the ancient church, for instance, when people realized that a thing was so, because either conscience or some other inner voice or their Scriptures told them it was, they too said, "Jehovah said."

1411   The symbolism of *go from your land* as the bodily and worldly concerns that he would withdraw from can be seen from the symbolism of *land,* which varies, depending on the person or thing with which it is associated. Take the first chapter of Genesis, and other places, where land also symbolizes our outer self (§§82, 620, 636, 913). The reason it means bodily and worldly concerns here is that these concerns belong to the outer self.

Strictly speaking, a land means the land itself, or an area, or a country. It is also an inhabitant there, or else the people itself or the nationality itself that lives in that land. So the name of a land means not only a people or nationality, in a broad sense, but also an inhabitant, in a narrow sense. When a land is associated with a single inhabitant, the symbolism depends on the reason for the association. Here the reference is to bodily and worldly matters because the land of birth that Abram was to leave was an idolatrous one. So the narrative here says that he was going to leave that land, but the representative meaning is that he would withdraw from the preoccupations of the outer self; in other words, superficial concerns would not conflict or interfere. And since this is about the Lord, the meaning is that superficial aspects would actually harmonize with deeper ones.

And from your birth[place] symbolizes bodily and worldly concerns that were relatively superficial, while *and from your father's house* symbolizes ones that were deeper. This can be seen from the symbolism of *birth* and from that of a *father's house.* **1412**

We concern ourselves with our body and the world on shallower and deeper levels. Shallower matters really do belong to the body; they are physical pleasures and sensory experiences. The deeper ones are emotions and factual knowledge. These are the things symbolized by Abram's *birth* and by his *father's house.* Much evidence can confirm the claim that this is the symbolism, but since it can be seen from the series of ideas and from an examination of the subjects dealt with on an inner level, there is no need to spend time proving it.

The symbolism of *to the land that I show you* as spiritual and heavenly traits that would be presented to view is established by the symbolism of the *land* (§§662, 1066). Here it is established by the symbolism of the land of Canaan, which represents the Lord's kingdom, as can be seen from many places in the Word. This is why the land of Canaan is called the Holy Land, and the heavenly Canaan. Because it represented the Lord's kingdom, it also represented and symbolized spiritual and heavenly qualities of the Lord's kingdom and, here, of the Lord himself. **1413**

Because this speaks of the Lord, it contains more hidden wisdom than could ever be thought or expressed. In an inner sense it is talking about the Lord's first state, when he was born. This state is a deep mystery, so it cannot be explained intelligibly. All that can be said is that although he was conceived by Jehovah, he was otherwise like any other person. He was born to a woman, a virgin, and by birth to her he acquired weaknesses like those of any ordinary person. Such weaknesses arise from the body, and the current verse says he would withdraw from them so that heavenly and spiritual entities could be presented to his view. **1414**

There are two heredities that we acquire by birth, one from our father and the other from our mother. The Lord's heredity from his Father was divinity, but his heredity from his mother was human frailty. This frailty, which we all acquire by inheritance from our mothers, is something corporeal that disintegrates when we are being reborn. What we receive from our fathers, though, remains forever, and the Lord's heredity from Jehovah, as noted, was divinity.

Another secret is that the Lord's humanity also became divine. In him alone, everything belonging to his body corresponded to something divine, with exquisite or infinite perfection. This led to union between his physical elements and his divinely heavenlike attributes, and between his sensory experiences and his divinely spiritual attributes. So he is the complete and perfect human, and the only human.

1415   Genesis 12:2. *"And I will make you into a great nation and bless you and make your name great, and you will be a blessing."*

I will make you into a great nation symbolizes a kingdom in the heavens and on earth; it is called a *great nation* because of what is heavenly and good about it. *And bless you* symbolizes the way heavenly things reproduce themselves and spiritual things multiply. *And make your name great* symbolizes glory. *And you will be a blessing* means that absolutely everything is from the Lord.

1416   The symbolism of *I will make you into a great nation* as a kingdom in the heavens and on earth can be seen from the symbolism of a *nation*. In an inner sense a nation is the heavenly quality of love and the good that comes out of it, so it is everyone everywhere who has the heavenly gift of love and charity. Here, because the subject in an inner sense is the Lord, it means *every* heavenly quality and *all* the resulting good. So it is the Lord's kingdom, which exists in people who have love and charity in them.

In the highest sense, the Lord himself is a great nation, because he is heavenliness itself, and goodness itself, since all the good growing out of love and charity comes from him alone. As a result, the Lord also is his actual kingdom; that is, he is the all in all of his kingdom, as every angel in heaven acknowledges. This shows, then, that "I will make you into a great nation" symbolizes the Lord's kingdom in the heavens and on earth.

[2] Passages illustrating the symbolism of a nation and of "the nations" and quoted in §§1258, 1259, also demonstrate that wherever the discussion centers on the Lord and on the heavenly aspects of love, a nation in an inner sense symbolizes the Lord and everything that is heavenly. The

following quotations offer further confirmation. Concerning Abraham, in a later passage:

> No longer will your name be called Abram, but your name will be Abraham, because I have made you father of an abundance of *nations.* (Genesis 17:5)

From Jehovah's name came the word particle *h* in *Abraham,* because of Abraham's representation of Jehovah, or the Lord. Likewise concerning Sarai:

> You shall not call her name Sarai, but Sarah is her name. And I will bless her and also give you a son from her. So I will bless her, and she will become *nations;* monarchs of various peoples will come from her. (Genesis 17:15, 16)

The nations stand for the heavenly qualities of love, while the monarchs of various peoples stand for the spiritual aspects of faith that develop out of those qualities, both of which are the Lord's alone. [3] Again, concerning Jacob:

> "Your name will no longer be called Jacob, but Israel will be your name"; and [God] called his name Israel. And God said, "I am God the Thunderer. Grow and multiply! A *nation* and a throng of *nations* will develop out of you, and monarchs will come from your genitals." (Genesis 35:10, 11)

Israel stands for the Lord. Some people realize that he is Israel in the highest sense, and since he is, obviously the nation and throng of nations, and the monarchs from his genitals, are the heavenly and spiritual qualities of love. Consequently they are also the people who possess the heavenly and spiritual qualities of love. Concerning Ishmael, Abram's son by Hagar:

> The slave's son—I will make him into a *nation,* since he is your seed. (Genesis 21:13, 18)

For Ishmael's representation, see the explanation given at that verse. "Abram's seed" is the actual love whose presence allows the word *nation* to be used in connection with Ishmael's birth. [4] The fact that a nation symbolizes the heavenly attributes of love can be seen in Moses:

> If you listen closely to my voice and keep my pact, you will be a personal possession to me, out of all the peoples, and you will be a *kingdom of priests* and a *holy nation* to me. (Exodus 19:5, 6)

The kingdom of priests, which is the Lord's kingdom in the heavens and on earth, is explicitly being called a holy nation. Reference to the Lord's kingdom on the basis of his kingship, however, has to do with the spiritual attributes of love, and this kingdom is called a holy people. So "monarchs from his genitals," as in the quotation above, are spiritual entities. In Jeremiah:

> "If these statutes depart from before me," says Jehovah, "the seed of Israel will also cease to be a *nation* before me all its days." (Jeremiah 31:36)

The seed of Israel stands for the heavenly quality of neighborly love, and when this ceases, it is no longer a nation before the Lord. [5] In Isaiah:

> The people walking in darkness have seen great light. You have multiplied the *nation*. (Isaiah 9:2, 3)

This is talking about the church among non-Jewish nations in particular and about everyone in general who lives without knowledge but with love for others. These people are a nation, because they belong to the Lord's kingdom. In David:

> . . . so that I can see the good of your chosen people; so that I can rejoice in the joy of your *nation;* so that I can boast of your inheritance. (Psalms 106:5)

The nation clearly stands for the Lord's kingdom.

The symbolism of a nation as the heavenly quality of love, and the good that comes of it, rose out of a certain way of seeing things: The people of the earliest church were divided into households, clans, and nations and this was their model for the Lord's kingdom. Since it was their model for the Lord's kingdom, it was their model for the nature of heaven itself. From this point of view rose the symbolism, and from the symbolism rose the representation.

1417 The fact that it is called a *great nation* because of what is heavenly and good about it is established by the remarks and illustrations just offered and from others above at §1259.

From this you can see what the church among "the nations" (non-Jews) properly is.

1418 *And bless you* symbolizes the way heavenly things reproduce themselves and spiritual things multiply, as can be seen from the symbolism in the Word of *blessing,* discussed just below [§§1420, 1422].

The symbolism of *and make your name great* as glory can be seen **1419** without an explanation.

On the surface, *making a name* implies something worldly, as does glory, but in an inner sense it implies something heavenly. The heavenly equivalent is not the effort to become greatest but to become least, the servant of all, as the Lord said in Matthew:

> It shall not be this way among you, but anyone among you who wants to become great will have to be your attendant. And anyone who wants to be first will have to be your slave. Just as the Son of Humankind did not come to be served but to serve others, and to give his soul as a ransom for many. (Matthew 20:26, 27, 28; Mark 10:43, 44, 45)

[2] What makes love heavenly is not the desire to have anything for ourselves but to share with everybody; so it is the desire to give everything that is ours to others. This is the essence of heavenly love. Because the Lord is love itself, or the essence and living power of the love that everyone in heaven has, he wants to give everything that is his to the human race. That is what is symbolized by his declaration that the Son of Humankind had come to give his soul as a ransom for many people.

This demonstrates that the inner meaning of a name and glory is something entirely different from the surface meaning. Anyone in heaven who is obsessed with becoming big and important is rejected, because this goes against the essence and vitality of heavenly love, as given by the Lord.

From this it also follows that nothing is more opposed to heavenly love than self-love. See more on this, from experience, in §§450, 452, 952.

The fact that *and you will be a blessing* means that absolutely every- **1420** thing is from the Lord can be seen from the symbolism of a *blessing*. The word *blessing* is used for all kinds of benefits—personal, worldly, and earthly benefits in the superficial sense, and spiritual and heavenly benefits in a deeper sense. To be a blessing is to be one from whom everything good comes, one who gives us all those benefits, which could never be said of Abram. This too provides evidence that Abram represents the Lord, since the Lord alone is a blessing. The case is the same with later statements regarding Abraham, such as:

> Abraham shall unquestionably become a great and populous *nation,* and all the *nations* of the earth will be *blessed* in him. (Genesis 18:18)

Regarding Isaac:

> All the *nations* of the earth will be *blessed* in your seed. (Genesis 26:4)

Regarding Jacob:

> All the clans of the earth will be *blessed* in you and in your seed. (Genesis 28:14)

Anyone can see that nations cannot be—and have not been—blessed in Abraham, Isaac, and Jacob or in their seed but in the Lord. David says so openly:

> His name will exist forever; before the face of the sun, the name of [a monarch's] son will be his, and all *nations* will be *blessed* in him. (Psalms 72:17)

This is about the Lord. In the same author:

> You will appoint him to be eternal *blessings*. (Psalms 21:6)

This too is about the Lord. In Jeremiah:

> The *nations* will be *blessed* in him, and of him they will boast. (Jeremiah 4:2)

All this now indicates that a blessing symbolizes the Lord. It also shows that when he is called a blessing, the meaning is that from him come all heavenly and spiritual qualities, which are the only good things there are; and since they are the only good things, they are the only true things. As a consequence, to the extent that earthly, worldly, and personal benefits contain heavenly and spiritual benefits, they actually are beneficial, and actually are blessings.

1421 Genesis 12:3. *"And I will bless those who bless you, and the one who curses you I will curse, and in you all the clans of the ground will be blessed."*

I will bless those who bless you means that all happiness belongs to those who acknowledge the Lord in their hearts. *And the one who curses you I will curse* means that unhappiness is the lot of those who do not acknowledge him. *And in you all the clans of the ground will be blessed* means that everything true and good comes from the Lord.

1422 *I will bless those who bless you* means that all happiness belongs to those who acknowledge the Lord in their hearts. This can be seen from the symbolism of a *blessing* as involving absolutely all gifts from the Lord, both those that are good and those that are true, and accordingly heavenly, spiritual, earthly, worldly, and personal benefits. And because a blessing in a comprehensive sense encompasses all those gifts, you can see what it symbolizes in each instance from the story line [at Genesis 12:3], since the symbolism depends on context. It stands to reason, then, that "I will bless those who bless you" means that all happiness belongs to those who acknowledge the Lord in their hearts, since in an inner sense the discussion here centers on the Lord, as noted [§§1401–1402].

[2] Among the ancients, blessing Jehovah (the Lord) was a customary way of speaking, as the Word reveals. In David, for example:

> In your assemblies, *bless God; [bless] the Lord* from the fountain of Israel. (Psalms 68:26)

In the same author:

> Sing to Jehovah; *bless his name!* Spread the good news of his salvation from day to day! (Psalms 96:2)

In Daniel:

> In a vision at night, the secret was revealed. So Daniel *blessed the God of the heavens* and said, "*A blessing on the name of God himself* from age to age, because wisdom and might are his." (Daniel 2:19, 20)

We also read of Zechariah and Simeon that they *blessed* God (Luke 1:64; 2:28). In these passages it is clear what blessing the Lord is: singing to him, spreading the good news of his salvation, proclaiming his wisdom and might, and so confessing and acknowledging the Lord with all our heart. People who do this cannot help being blessed by the Lord; that is, they cannot help receiving gifts that are blessings, or in other words, heavenly, spiritual, earthly, worldly, and personal good. These things are good, and produce happiness, when they come in this order.

[3] As it was common for people to speak in terms of blessing Jehovah (the Lord) or being blessed by him, it was also a common turn of speech to say, "*A blessing on Jehovah.*" In David, for instance:

> *A blessing on Jehovah,* because he has heard the voice of my prayers. (Psalms 28:6)

In the same author:

> *A blessing on Jehovah,* because he has made his mercy to me extraordinary. (Psalms 31:21)

In the same author:

> *A blessing on God,* who has not cast my prayers aside or cast his mercy away from me. (Psalms 66:20)

In the same author:

> *A blessing on Jehovah God,* the God of Israel, working miracles alone. And *a blessing on* his glorious *name* forever; and with his glory all the earth will be filled. (Psalms 72:18, 19)

In the same author:

> *A blessing on you, Jehovah;* teach me your statutes. (Psalms 119:12)

In the same author:

> *A blessing on Jehovah,* my rock, teaching my hands. (Psalms 144:1)

In Luke:

> Zechariah, filled with the holy spirit, prophesied, saying, "*A blessing on the God of Israel,* because he has visited his people and secured their deliverance." (Luke 1:67, 68)

1423   *And the one who curses you I will curse* symbolizes the unhappiness of those who do not acknowledge him. This can be seen from the symbolism of *cursing* and *being cursed* as turning ourselves away from the Lord (shown before, in §§245, 379) and so as failing to acknowledge him. Those who do not acknowledge him turn away. So cursing here involves all traits opposed to the ones implied by a blessing.

1424   *And in you all the clans of the ground will be blessed* means that everything good and true comes from the Lord. This can be seen from the symbolism of *blessing,* treated of in this verse and the last [§§1420, 1422], and from the symbolism of the *clans of the ground* as everything good and true.

In the Word, the symbolism of *clans* is like that of nations and also of peoples, since the Word refers to both nations and peoples as clans and speaks of "clans of the nations" and "clans of the peoples" [1 Chronicles 16:28; Psalms 22:27; 96:7]. Nations symbolize goodness, as shown, and peoples symbolize truth, as also shown (§1259). So clans symbolize both goodness and truth (§1261).

The reason they are called clans of the *ground* is that everything good and true is part of a loving faith, which is a feature of the church. The symbolism of the ground as the church and therefore as faith within the church has already been shown, at §566.

Genesis 12:4. *And Abram went, as Jehovah had spoken to him, and with him went Lot. And Abram was a son of seventy-five years when he left Haran.* **1425**

Abram, as noted, represents the Lord's human quality. *And Abram went, as Jehovah had spoken to him,* symbolizes progress toward divine characteristics. *And with him went Lot* symbolizes the senses; *Lot* represents the Lord as a sensory, physical being. *And Abram was a son of seventy-five years* means that he did not yet have much divinity. *When he left Haran* symbolizes a shadowy state for the Lord.

The representation of *Abram* as the Lord's human quality can be seen from details describing Abram [§1401]. Later on he represents both the human and the divine quality of the Lord, but at that point he is called Abraham. **1426**

From the first verse to the present one, the contents represent and symbolize the Lord's first realization that he would clothe himself in heavenly properties and so in divine ones. The steps his human quality took toward becoming divine start here.

The symbolism of *and Abram went, as Jehovah had spoken to him,* as progress toward divine characteristics can be seen from the remarks just made. **1427**

And with him went Lot symbolizes the senses; *Lot* represents the Lord as a sensory, physical being. This can be seen from Lot's representation in what follows, where the discussion focuses on him in his separation from Abram and in his rescue by angels [§§1547, 2324]. (Later, after his separation from Abram, Lot takes on another representation, as will be described below [§2324], the Lord in his divine mercy willing.) **1428**

Clearly the Lord was born like any other person to a human mother— a virgin one—and had senses and a physical presence like other people's. He was not like others, though, in this: the sensory, physical component in him eventually united with heavenly attributes and became divine. Lot represents what belonged exclusively to the Lord's body and senses or, to say the same thing, the Lord's sensory, physical self as it was when he was a youth, not as it came to be when united with his divinity by means of heavenly qualities.

The fact that *and Abram was a son of seventy-five years* means that he did not yet have much divinity can be seen from the symbolism of *five* as a little and of *seventy* as holiness. The symbolism of five as a little was illustrated above in §649 and that of seventy (or seven) as holiness in §§395, 433, 716, 881. Since the number seventy is mentioned in connection with the Lord here, it symbolizes divine holiness. **1429**

Previous statements and proofs regarding years and numbers (§§482, 487, 493, 575, 647, 648, 755, 813) show that on a deeper level, the numbers counting Abram's years have a different meaning [than the literal one]. The same conclusion is indicated by the fact that the Word contains not so much as a syllable or even a mark that lacks an inner meaning. It would never have been mentioned that Abram was then [a son] of seventy-five years if this had not involved spiritual and heavenly matters, and in fact the event would not have occurred at that particular stage of his life. The presence of a deeper meaning can also be seen from other numbers measuring both years and concrete objects in the Word.

1430   The symbolism of *when he left Haran* as a shadowy state for the Lord, like that which we experience in youth, can be seen from the symbolism of *Haran* in verses 31, 32 of the previous chapter, Genesis 11. Terah was first to come to Haran, with Abram, and that is where Terah, Abram's father, died. The symbolism can also be seen from later passages describing Jacob's journey to Haran, where Laban was (Genesis 27:43; 28:10; 29:4 [§§3612, 3691]).

Haran was an area where worship was superficial and—in the case of Terah, Abram, and Laban—even idolatrous. But it does not mean the same thing deep down as it does on the surface; all it means is something that is vague. When the surface meaning develops into a deeper meaning, the notion of idolatry does not remain but is erased. Compare the way mountains gave rise to the thought of holy love (§795); when the inner meaning develops out of the surface meaning, first the image of a mountain disappears and the idea of height remains, and then holiness is represented by the height. It is the same with all other images.

1431   Genesis 12:5. *And Abram took Sarai his wife, and Lot his brother's son, and all their gain that they had gained, and [every] soul that they had made in Haran, and they left to go into the land of Canaan. And they came into the land of Canaan.*

And Abram took Sarai his wife symbolizes goodness with truth connected to it. *Abram,* as noted [§1402], means the Lord, and here it means when he was young; *Sarai his wife* means truth. *And Lot his brother's son* symbolizes truth gained through the senses, that is, the first kind of truth instilled in the youth. *And all the gain that they had gained* symbolizes everything that can be identified as sensory truth. *And [every] soul that they had made in Haran* symbolizes all the essential vitality that is possible in this shadowy state. *And they left to go into the land of Canaan* means that by these means he would press on all the way to the heavenly aspects of love. *And they came into the land of Canaan* means that he arrived at the heavenly aspects of love.

The symbolism of *and Abram took Sarai his wife* as goodness with truth connected to it can be seen from the symbolic meaning in the Word of a human and his wife, given in §915. So in an inner sense here the one thing Sarai means is truth. **1432**

Absolutely everything in us features something equivalent to a marriage. Never could there be an element so tiny as to lack that image of a marriage, whether in our outer self or our inner self, with all that either encompasses. Every single thing comes into existence and remains in existence because of the Lord and because of the union (the marriage, essentially) between his human quality and his divine quality; and also because of the bond—the heavenly marriage, in other words—between both of those qualities and his kingdom in the heavens and on earth. Here, where truth attached to goodness in the Lord needed to be represented, it could only be represented by Abram's wife, since it could only be represented by historical details involving Abram.

Concerning the fact that absolutely everything contains the equivalent of a marriage, see above in §§54, 55, 718, 747, 917.

Abram means the Lord, and here it means when he was young, while *Sarai his wife* means truth, as the discussion shows. **1433**

The symbolism of *and Lot his brother's son* as truth gained through the senses, that is, as the first kind of truth instilled in the Lord as a youth, can be seen from the following: *Lot* symbolizes the senses, as mentioned in the last verse. A *son* symbolizes truth, as described earlier, in §§264, 489, 491, 533. And a *brother* is also religious truth, §367. So Lot here is truth gained through the senses. **1434**

The inner sense implies nothing about the people or the words involved; it concerns itself only with their symbolism. In heaven, they do not know who Lot is but what quality he represents. They do not know what a son is but what a spiritual condition resembling that of a son is. And they do not know what a brother is except from the kind of brotherhood that exists in heaven.

[2] To turn to the subject of truth gained through the senses, it is the first kind of truth that instills itself, because our powers of judgment reach no deeper in youth. Sensory truth is the vision of all earthly and worldly things as the creation of God; of each and every object as having a purpose; and of each and every object as displaying an image of God's kingdom. This sensory truth is infused only in heavenly people,

and since only the Lord was a heavenly person, these sensory truths and others like them filtered in early in his youth. This prepared him for receiving heavenly truth.

1435   The symbolism of *and all the gain that they had gained* as everything that can be identified as sensory truth can be seen from the discussion.

Gain is the term for every fact on which we base our thinking. In our capacity as humans, we cannot entertain any fragment of thought without acquired facts. The concepts that compose our thinking are founded on facts, which enter through our senses and print themselves on our memory. So facts are containers for spiritual material, while feelings that rise out of positive types of bodily pleasure are containers for heavenly material. All of these are called "gain," and specifically gain acquired in Haran, which symbolizes the dim kind of state that characterizes children up till adolescence.

1436   The symbolism of *and [every] soul that they had made in Haran* as all the essential vitality that is possible in this shadowy state can be seen from the following: A *soul* symbolizes essential vitality, and *Haran* symbolizes a shadowy state, as described at the previous verse.

Strictly speaking, a *soul* symbolizes what is alive in us and so our life itself. It is not our body that lives but our soul; our body receives life through our soul. Our actual life force, or actual vitality, comes from heavenly love. Nothing living can possibly exist unless it derives from that source. So a soul here symbolizes a goodness whose living quality comes from heavenly love. This kind of goodness is genuinely essential and alive.

On the literal level, a soul here means every person and every animal that was alive and that they had acquired for themselves, but in an inner sense what it means is an essential vitality.

1437   The meaning of *they left to go into the land of Canaan* as the fact that by these means he would press on all the way to the heavenly aspects of love can be seen from the symbolism of the *land of Canaan*. The land of Canaan represents the Lord's kingdom in the heavens and on earth, as the Word reveals in many places. The reason for the connection is that the land of Canaan saw the establishment of the representative church, in which everything in general and particular represented the Lord and the heavenly and spiritual elements of his kingdom. It was not just their rituals that had a representative meaning but everything connected with ritual as well—the people who ministered, the tools of their ministry, and the places where they carried it out. Because the representative church was there, the land was called the Holy Land, even though it was anything but holy, since profane idolaters lived there. This, then, is why the land of Canaan here and in what follows symbolizes the heavenly qualities of love. The heavenly qualities of love are all that the Lord's kingdom contains and all that it comprises.

The fact that *and they came into the land of Canaan* means that he **1438** arrived at the heavenly aspects of love is established by the remarks just made about the land of Canaan. This passage describes how the Lord in his early life—specifically, from birth to adolescence—arrived at the heavenly aspects of love.

The heavenly aspects of love are the true essentials; everything else develops out of them. These were the first things of all to be instilled in the Lord, because everything else then germinated from them like plants sprouting from their seed. In the Lord, because he was born of Jehovah, the seed itself was heavenly. For the same reason, he was the only being in whom this seed was ever sown.

No humans that have ever lived have any other seed sown in them than some foul, hellish germ that is the carrier and source of their selfhood; and this they inherit from their father, as everyone knows. So unless we receive from the Lord a new seed and new selfhood, that is, a new will and a new intellect, we are inevitably doomed to hell. Hell is what we must be withdrawn and constantly withheld from by the Lord, and this means all of us: people on earth, spirits, and angels.

Genesis 12:6. *And Abram passed through the land all the way to the* **1439** *place of Shechem, all the way to the oak grove of Moreh. (And the Canaanite was then in the land.)*

Abram passed through the land all the way to the place of Shechem symbolizes the Lord's second state, when the heavenly qualities of love symbolized by *Shechem* would appear to him. *All the way to the oak grove of Moreh* symbolizes his third state: the dawn of perception, which is the *oak grove of Moreh. And the Canaanite was then in the land* symbolizes the evil in his outer self that he inherited from his mother.

The symbolism of *Abram passed through the land all the way to the* **1440** *place of Shechem* as the Lord's second state, when the heavenly qualities of love would appear to him, can be seen from remarks above and from the overall scheme. The remarks above include the fact that he would press on all the way to the heavenly aspects of love and that he arrived at them, symbolized by "they left to go into the land of Canaan" and "they came into the land of Canaan." The overall scheme indicates that after he continued on to heavenly qualities and reached them, they became visible to him. Heavenly traits contain the soul's true light, because they contain divinity itself, that is, Jehovah himself. And since the Lord was going to unite his human essence to his divine essence when he arrived at heavenly qualities, it was inevitable that Jehovah would appear to him.

1441   The symbolism of *Shechem* as these qualities can also be seen from the consideration that Shechem is the first stopping place in the land of Canaan as you come from Syria, or Haran. Because the land of Canaan symbolizes love's heavenly aspects, it stands to reason that Shechem symbolizes the first disclosure of heavenly attributes. When Jacob returned from Haran to the land of Canaan, he too came to Shechem, as these verses show:

> Jacob traveled to *Succoth* and built himself a house, and for his livestock he made shelters; so he called the name of the place Succoth. And Jacob came to Salem (the city of *Shechem,* which is in the land of Canaan) when he came from Paddan-aram, and he camped in front of the city and raised an altar there. (Genesis 33:17, 18, 19, 20)

Here again Shechem symbolizes first light. [2] In David:

> God has spoken in his holiness: "I will exult. I will cleave *Shechem,* and the valley of *Succoth* I will measure out. I own Gilead, and I own Manasseh, and Ephraim is the strength of my head. Judah is my lawgiver. Moab is my washbasin. On Edom I will set my shoe; over Philistia I will trumpet." (Psalms 60:6, 7, 8; 108:7, 8, 9)

Shechem has a similar kind of symbolism here too. These prophetic words of David's clearly illustrate the fact that names, including that of Shechem, have no meaning but a symbolic one; otherwise the prophecy would be hardly anything besides a conglomeration of names.

Shechem became a city of refuge (Joshua 20:7) and a city of priests as well (Joshua 21:21), and a pact was struck there (Joshua 24:1, 25). These facts involve something similar.

1442   The symbolism of *all the way to the oak grove of Moreh* as the dawn of perception can also be seen from the course of progress here. It is plain that as soon as Jehovah appeared to the Lord in his heavenly aspects, the Lord acquired perception. All perception results from heavenly traits.

(Earlier sections—104, 202, 371, 483, 495, 503, 521, 536, 865—have defined perception and shown what it is.)

The Lord gives perception to everyone who arrives at heavenly qualities. Those who became heavenly people, as members of the earliest church did, all received perception (as demonstrated before, in §§125, 597, 607, 784, 895). Those who become spiritual people—that is, who receive from the Lord the gift of neighborly love—have something analogous to perception. Or they hear the voice of conscience, which speaks more or less clearly, depending on the extent to which they become heavenly in their love for others. This is an inherent result of loving others in a heavenly way, since the Lord is present only in the heavenly aspects of charity, which also reveal him to our eyes. How much more true this was for the Lord, who developed from being an infant into being Jehovah, and who was joined and united with Jehovah to the point of being one with him.

In regard to the fact that the *oak grove of Moreh* is the dawn of perception, this is the situation: In us we have capacities for true understanding, for rationality, and for knowing facts. Capacities for true understanding are at the center, rational abilities are less central, and factual knowledge is on the outside. These abilities, in this arrangement, are called our spiritual assets.

1443

In heavenly people, the ability to understand is compared to a garden filled with all kinds of trees. Rational capacities are compared to a forest of cedar and so on—the kind of trees in Lebanon. But facts are like oak groves, since they resemble the tangled branches that oaks have. The trees themselves symbolize perceptions. The trees on the east in the Garden of Eden, for instance [Genesis 2:8, 9], symbolize the deepest perceptions, or those that comprise true understanding, as already shown (§§99, 100, 103). The trees in Lebanon's forest symbolize perceptions that are less deep, or the perception of rational concepts. The trees found in an oak grove, though, symbolize more superficial perceptions, or the perception of facts, which belong to the outer self. That is why the oak grove of Moreh symbolizes the dawn of perception in the Lord, since he was still young and did not yet have spiritual assets inside him.

In addition, the oak grove of Moreh was where the children of Israel first arrived after crossing the Jordan and saw the land of Canaan. Moses speaks of it this way:

> You shall give the blessing on Mount Gerizim and the curse on Mount
> Ebal. Are they not across the Jordan, beyond the path of the sunset, in

the land where the Canaanite lives in the plain opposite Gilgal, beside the *oak groves of Moreh?* (Deuteronomy 11:29, 30)

This too symbolizes the beginning of perception, since the entry of the children of Israel represents the entry of the faithful into the Lord's kingdom.

1444   The symbolism of *and the Canaanite was then in the land* as the evil in his outer self that he inherited from his mother can be seen from statements already made about the Lord's heredity [§1414]. He was born like the rest of us and carried with him different kinds of evil that he had received from his mother, which he fought against and completely overcame. As people generally realize, the Lord underwent and endured heavy spiritual trials. (With the Lord's divine mercy, these will be discussed later [§§1573:4, 1659:2, 1661, 1663, 1668, 1690, 1692, 1787, 1812–1813, 1820:5].) In fact he fought alone, with his own might, against all of hell; that is how severe his trials were.

No one can undergo spiritual crisis unless something bad clings to the person. No one devoid of evil can suffer the least tribulation. Evil is what hellish spirits stir up. [2] The Lord had no actual evil, no evil of his own, as all the rest of us do. What he had was evil inherited from his mother, which in the present verse is called the *Canaanite then in the land.* For more on this, see the remarks above at verse 1, §1414. To review, we are born with two heredities, one from our father and the other from our mother. Our heredity from our father lasts forever; that from our mother is dissolved by the Lord when we are being reborn. The Lord's heredity from his father, though, was divine, while his heredity from his mother was evil. The latter is the subject of the current verse and is what enabled him to be put to the test. (For mention of his trials, see Mark 1:12, 13; Matthew 4:1; Luke 4:1, 2.) But again, he had no actual evil, no evil of his own. Nor did any of his mother's evil heredity remain after he had overthrown hell through his trials, which is why it says here that it was *then,* that is, that the Canaanite was *then* in the land.

[3] The Canaanites were people who lived along the sea and the shores of the Jordan, as is evident in Moses:

When the scouts returned, they said, "We came into the land to which you sent us, and in fact it was flowing with milk and honey, and this is its fruit. But a strong people is living in the land, and the cities are fortified and very big, and we saw the offspring of Anak there. Amalek lives in the south; and the Hittite and the Jebusite and the Amorite live on the mountain, and *the Canaanite lives along the sea and along the shores of the Jordan.*" (Numbers 13:27, 28, 29)

The fact that the Canaanites lived along the sea and the shores of the Jordan consequently symbolized evil in a person's outer self—the kind of evil we inherit from our mother—since the sea and the Jordan were outer borders. [4] Zechariah also yields evidence that a Canaanite symbolizes this kind of evil:

No longer will there be a *Canaanite* in the house of Jehovah Sabaoth on that day. (Zechariah 14:21)

This refers to the Lord's kingdom and symbolizes the fact that the Lord has completely conquered the evil meant by a Canaanite and banished it from his kingdom.

All types of evil are symbolized by the idolatrous nations in the land of Canaan, including the Canaanites proper, in such places as Genesis 15:19, 20, 21; Exodus 3:8, 17; 23:23, 28; 33:2; 34:11; Deuteronomy 7:1; 20:17; Joshua 3:10; 24:11; Judges 3:5. What particular evil each nation symbolizes will be told elsewhere, by the Lord's divine mercy.

Genesis 12:7. *And Jehovah was seen by Abram and said, "To your seed I will give this land." And there he built an altar to Jehovah, who had been seen by him.* **1445**

Jehovah was seen by Abram means that Jehovah appeared to the Lord while he was still young. *And said, "To your seed I will give this land,"* means that those who believed in him would receive heavenly gifts. *And there he built an altar to Jehovah, who had been seen by him,* symbolizes the time when he first worshiped his Father with a heavenly kind of love.

The meaning of *Jehovah was seen by Abram* as the fact that Jehovah appeared to the Lord while he was still young is established by the foregoing remarks and simply by Abram's representation of the Lord. It can also be seen from the course of progress; he acquired heavenly traits and then perception, from which it follows that Jehovah appeared to him. **1446**

The fact that *he said, "To your seed I will give this land,"* means that those who believed in him would receive heavenly gifts can be seen from the symbolism of *seed* and from the symbolism of *land. Seed* symbolizes belief in the Lord, as shown earlier, in §§255, 256. *Land* symbolizes heavenly attributes, as also shown above, at verse 1 of this chapter [§1413] and in §§620, 636, 662, 1066 as well. **1447**

On the literal plane, Abram's seed means his descendants by Jacob's line, while the land means the actual land of Canaan. This land was to be given to them as a possession to enable them to represent heavenly and spiritual facets of the Lord's kingdom and church. It was also given to them to enable a representative church to be established among them, and because the Lord was to be born there. On an inner level, however, seed symbolizes nothing but belief in the Lord, while land symbolizes nothing but heavenly qualities. Here, the meaning is that those who believed in him would receive heavenly gifts.

It has been said many times before what believing in the Lord means.

1448   The symbolism of *and there he built an altar to Jehovah, who had been seen by him,* as the time when he first worshiped his Father with a heavenly kind of love can be seen from the symbolism of an altar as the main representative object used in worship (§921).

1449   Genesis 12:8. *And he moved from there onto a mountain to the east of Bethel and spread his tent; Bethel was toward the sea and Ai toward the east. And there he built an altar to Jehovah and called on Jehovah's name.*

He moved from there onto a mountain to the east of Bethel symbolizes the Lord's fourth state as a youth, which would involve development in the heavenly aspects of love; these are what the *move onto a mountain to the east of Bethel* is. *And spread his tent* symbolizes the holy attributes of faith. *And Bethel was toward the sea and Ai toward the east* means that his state would still be confused. *And he built an altar to Jehovah* symbolizes his outward worship of his Father in that state. *And called on Jehovah's name* symbolizes his inward worship of his Father in that state.

1450   The fact that *he moved from there onto a mountain to the east of Bethel* symbolizes the Lord's fourth state as a youth can be seen from what comes above and below and so from the course of progress being described as well. Following that course, the Lord absorbed the heavenly aspects of love first of all, starting in infancy. The heavenly aspects are love for Jehovah, love for one's neighbor, and the innocence that marks both. Absolutely everything else flows from those attributes, which function as the actual fountains of life, since nothing else is more than a branch of that stream.

These heavenly traits are infused in us principally at the stage of childhood, from infancy up to adolescence. They are not infused along with any knowledge, because they filter in from the Lord and affect us before we have any idea what love is, or what an emotion is, as can be seen from the state of babies and then of children. In us such traits are called a remnant, and the Lord instills it in us and stores it away for use at later stages of our life. This remnant has been discussed several times before; for more on it, see §§468, 530, 560, 561, 660, 661.

Since the Lord was born like any other person, he was also led into heavenly capacities in orderly stages, from childhood to adolescence, and later into knowledge. The nature of the knowledge that he had is depicted in the current verse and is represented below by Abraham's stay in Egypt.

The fact that *moving onto a mountain to the east of Bethel* symbolizes development in the heavenly aspects of love is established by the following: A *mountain* symbolizes what is heavenly, as shown in §§795, 796. The *east* symbolizes Jehovah himself—who is the true east—and specifically his love, as also shown, in §101. And *Bethel* symbolizes knowledge of heavenly qualities.

1451

Heavenly attributes are instilled in a person both without any accompanying knowledge and with it—the former from infancy to adolescence (as noted just above), but the latter from adolescence to a time of full maturity.

Because the Lord was to advance into the knowledge of heavenly matters—knowledge symbolized by Bethel—the present verse says, "He moved from there onto a mountain to the east of Bethel."

The symbolism of *and spread his tent* as the holy attributes of faith can be seen from the symbolism of a *tent* as the holy quality of love and consequently the holy quality of the faith that comes of love, as shown before, in §414. Abram's *spreading* of the tent there means that [faith] now took its start.

1452

Bethel was toward the sea and Ai toward the east means that his state would still be confused, specifically in respect to the knowledge of heavenly and spiritual affairs. It is one thing to acquire heavenly qualities and another to acquire knowledge of them. Children and young people are more immersed in heavenly matters than adults are, because they have love for their parents, love shared with peers, and innocence. Adults, on the other hand, are more caught up in knowledge about these things than children and young people are, even though most of them do not display heavenly kinds of love.

1453

Until we learn about the properties of love and faith, we live in dim conditions, so far as knowledge goes. Such conditions are portrayed here by the fact that Bethel was toward the sea (the west) and Ai toward the east. *Bethel*, as noted [§1451], symbolizes the knowledge of heavenly matters. *Ai,* though, symbolizes the knowledge of worldly matters. When the former knowledge is dim, it is said to be on the west, because in the Word, the west symbolizes obscurity. When the latter knowledge is clear, it is said to be on the east, because the east is brighter than the west. There is no need to prove this symbolism of west and east, since anyone can see it without proof.

[2] The symbolism of *Bethel* as the knowledge of heavenly things can be seen from other passages in the Word that mention Bethel. In the next chapter, Genesis 13, for example:

> Abram went on his journeys from the south all the way to *Bethel,* all the way to the place where his tent had been at the start, between *Bethel* and *Ai,* to the place of the altar that he had made there. (Genesis 13:3, 4)

"On his journeys from the south to Bethel" in this passage symbolizes an advance into the light of knowledge, which is why it does not say here that Bethel was on the west and Ai on the east. As regards Jacob, when he saw the ladder:

> He said, "This is nothing but the *house of God,* and this the gate of heaven." And he called the name of this place *Bethel.* (Genesis 28:17, 19)

Here too Bethel symbolizes a knowledge of heavenly things. We ourselves are "Bethel"—which means "God's house"—and the "gate of heaven" when we achieve the heavenly qualities we have learned about. While we are being reborn, the knowledge of spiritual and heavenly qualities initiates us into the process; but when our rebirth is complete, our initiation is complete, and the spiritual and heavenly attributes we have learned about become ours. Later on:

> God said to Jacob, "Rise; go up to *Bethel* and live there. Make there an altar to God, who appeared to you." (Genesis 35:1, 6, 7)

Here again Bethel symbolizes knowledge. [3] The ark of Jehovah was in *Bethel,* and the children of Israel would go there and ask Jehovah questions (Judges 20:18, 26, 27; 1 Samuel 7:16; 10:3), which has a similar symbolism. So does the fact that the king of Assyria sent [to Samaria] one of the priests he had carried off from Samaria, and that this priest settled in *Bethel* and *was teaching them how to fear Jehovah* (2 Kings 17:27, 28). In Amos:

> Amaziah said to Amos, "Seer, go, flee into the land of Judah and eat bread there, and there you are to prophesy. And at *Bethel* you must not

continue to prophesy anymore, because it is a royal sanctuary, and it is a house for the kingdom." (Amos 7:12, 13)

[4] After Jeroboam desecrated Bethel (1 Kings 12:32; 13:1–8; 2 Kings 23:15), it took on the opposite representation. Examples may be seen in Hosea 10:15; Amos 3:14, 15; 5:5, 6, 7.

The symbolism of *Ai* as the knowledge of worldly things can also be proved by narrative and prophetic passages in the Word—in Joshua 7:2; 8:1–28; Jeremiah 49:3, 4.

The symbolism of *and he built an altar to Jehovah* as his outward worship of his Father in that state can be seen from the symbolism of an altar as the main representative object used in worship (§921).

1454

The symbolism of *and called on Jehovah's name* as his inward worship of his Father in that state can be seen from the symbolism of calling on Jehovah's name (§440). Anyone can see that building an altar to Jehovah is outward worship, while calling on Jehovah's name is inward.

1455

Genesis 12:9. *And Abram traveled, going and traveling toward the south.*

1456

Abram traveled, going and traveling, symbolizes further advancement. *Toward the south* means into goodness and truth and so into a condition in which inner things would be clear.

The symbolism of *And Abram traveled, going and traveling,* as further advancement can be seen from the symbolism of *going and traveling.* Among the ancients, journeys, travels, and immigration had no other meaning, so in the Word as well they have no other symbolism on an inner level.

1457

This is where the Lord's advances into knowledge begin.

Like any other person, the Lord also learned by instruction. Luke demonstrates this:

The child *grew* and became strong in spirit. He was in the wastelands up to the day of his presentation to Israel. (Luke 1:80)

In the same author:

The child *grew* and became strong in spirit and *was filled with wisdom;* and [God's] favor was on him. (Luke 2:40)

In the same author:

Joseph and Jesus' mother, after three days, found him in the Temple, sitting in the middle of the teachers and *listening to them* and *asking*

them questions; everyone listening to him was astounded at his understanding and his answers. Seeing him, [Joseph and Mary] were amazed,
but he said to them, "Why did you search for me? Didn't you know
that I have to see to my Father's business?" (Luke 2:46, 47, 48, 49)

Verse 42 of the same chapter says that he was then twelve years old. In
the same author:

After that, Jesus *advanced in wisdom* and age and in favor with God
and humankind. (Luke 2:52)

1458   The fact that *toward the south* means into goodness and truth and
so into a condition in which inner things would be clear can be seen
from the symbolism of the *south,* or noonday light. The symbolism of
the south as a stage of clarity comes from this: In the other life there are
no compass directions, just as there are no times and seasons, but only
the conditions symbolized by directions and time periods. The state of
our ability to understand things resembles conditions at different times
of day and seasons of the year and also in different quarters of the globe.
A day goes through the stages of evening, night, morning, and midday; a
year goes through those of fall, winter, spring, and summer; and conditions in the four quarters are those of the sun in the west, north, east, and
south. Similar to these conditions are the states of our ability to understand. In heaven, amazing to say, the people on whom the light shines
are those who enjoy a condition of wisdom and understanding, and it
shines in perfect accord with that condition. Those who enjoy the highest state of wisdom and understanding have the greatest light. Wisdom
there, however, is a matter of love and charity, while understanding there
is a matter of faith in the Lord. The other world has a kind of light
to which the light of the world can hardly be compared, as a wealth of
experience has shown me. (I will have more to say about these experiences below [§§1521–1534, 1619–1625], with the Lord's divine mercy.)
And because such a correspondence exists in heaven between light and
matters of understanding, here and elsewhere in the Word that is truly
what the south means.

The south here symbolizes understanding, which is acquired by
means of religious knowledge. Religious concepts are heavenly and spiritual truths, which are just so many rays of light in heaven and which the
light also makes visible, as noted. Because the Lord was now to soak up

knowledge, so that he could become the actual light of heaven even in respect to his human nature, the present verse says that he traveled, going and traveling toward the south.

[2] The fact that the south symbolizes these things can be seen from similar passages in the Word, as in Isaiah:

> I will say to the north, "Hand them over!" and to the *south,* "Do not hinder them! Bring my sons from far away and my daughters from the end of the earth." (Isaiah 43:6)

The north stands for people who lack knowledge; the south, for people who possess it. Sons stand for truth and daughters for goodness. In the same author:

> If you bring out your soul for someone starving and satiate an afflicted soul, in the shadows your *light* will rise, and your darkness will be like *midday.* (Isaiah 58:10)

Bringing out your soul for someone starving and satiating an afflicted soul stands for good deeds inspired by neighborly love, in general. "In the shadows your light will rise" stands for the fact that [people who do such deeds] have an intelligent understanding of truth, while "your darkness will be like midday" stands for the fact that they have a wise appreciation of goodness; midday, or the south, symbolizes goodness on account of its warmth, and truth on account of its brightness. [3] In Ezekiel:

> In visions of God, he brought me to the land of Israel and put me on a mountain which was very tall and on which there was something like the structure of a city on the *south.* (Ezekiel 40:2)

This is about a new Jerusalem, or the Lord's kingdom, which is said to be on the south because it has the light of wisdom and understanding. In David:

> Jehovah will present your virtue as a *light* and your integrity as the *midday.* (Psalms 37:6)

In the same author:

> You will not be afraid of the horror at *night,* of the arrow [that] might fly by *day;* of contagion [that] will walk in the *dark,* of destruction [that] ravages at *midday.* (Psalms 91:5, 6)

Not being afraid of the destruction that ravages everything at midday stands for not being afraid of the damnation that befalls people who have knowledge and pervert it. In Ezekiel:

> Child of humankind, turn your face toward the *south* and loose a shower [of words] to the *south* and prophesy to the forest of the *south* field. And you are to say to the forest of the *south,* "All faces from *south* to north will be burned in [the flame]." (Ezekiel 20:46, 47)

The forest of the south stands for people who have the light of truth but put it out; so it stands for people like this in the church. [4] In Daniel:

> From one of [the goat's horns] one small horn went out and grew quite a bit toward the *south* and toward the sunrise and toward the ornament [of Israel], and it grew right to the army of the heavens. (Daniel 8:9, 10)

This stands for individuals who attack what is good and true. In Jeremiah:

> Give glory to Jehovah your God before he brings darkness and before your feet stumble on the dusky mountains; and you will wait for light, and he will turn it into the shadow of death, he will turn it into blackness. The *cities of the south* will be closed, and there will be no one to open. (Jeremiah 13:16, 19)

The cities of the south stand for knowledge of truth and goodness. In Obadiah:

> The deportees of Jerusalem who are in Sepharad will inherit the *cities of the south.* (Obadiah verse 20)

The cities of the south again stand for truth and goodness and so for the truth and goodness they actually inherit. The topic here is the Lord's kingdom.

[5] As I said, "Abram traveled, going and traveling toward the south," symbolizes the Lord's advance into goodness and truth and so into a condition in which inner things were clear. The case with this is that knowledge is what opens up a line of sight to heavenly and spiritual entities. Knowledge opens a path leading from the inner self to the outer, which contains receiving vessels—as many receiving vessels as concepts concerning goodness and truth. Heavenly things flow into these concepts as their proper vessels.

1459   Genesis 12:10. *And there was famine in the land; and Abram went down into Egypt to reside as an immigrant there, because the famine was heavy in the land.*

There was famine in the land symbolizes the scarcity of knowledge that still affected the Lord when he was young. *And Abram went down into Egypt to reside as an immigrant* means being taught concepts from the Word; *Egypt* is the knowledge of those concepts, while *residing as an immigrant* is being taught. *Because the famine was heavy in the land* symbolizes a severe shortage in his outer self.

The symbolism of *there was famine in the land* as the scarcity of knowledge that still affected the Lord when he was young can be seen from remarks above. In our youth, the knowledge we have never comes from inside but from the objects of the senses, especially from what we hear. As noted [§1458:5], our outer self contains receiving vessels, which are called vessels of memory. Knowledge forms these vessels, as anyone can see, and does so under the influence and with the help of the inner self. So knowledge is learned and planted in the memory to the extent that the inner self exerts an influence. This was true for the Lord too, when he was young, because he was born like the rest of us and was taught like the rest of us. His inner capacities, however, were heavenly ones, which adapted the vessels so that they could receive knowledge, and so that the various points of knowledge could then become vessels for receiving divinity. His inner aspects were divine ones from Jehovah, his Father; his outer aspects were human ones from Mary, his mother.

This demonstrates that in the Lord, just as in other people, the outer self suffered a shortage of knowledge in his youth.

[2] The symbolism of a *famine* as a scarcity of knowledge can be seen in other passages of the Word. In Isaiah, for example:

> The work of Jehovah they do not examine, and the product of his hands they do not see. Therefore my people will go into exile because they lack *knowledge*. And their nobility will be victims of *famine;* and their multitude will be parched with thirst. (Isaiah 5:12, 13)

Victims of famine stand for a dearth of heavenly knowledge; a multitude parched with thirst stands for a dearth of spiritual knowledge. In Jeremiah:

> They lied against Jehovah and said, "He does not exist, and evil will not come on us, and *sword* and *famine* we will not see. And the prophets will become wind, and no word will come to them." (Jeremiah 5:12, 13)

Sword and famine stand for being deprived of the knowledge of truth and goodness. The prophets stand for people who teach but do not have "the word" in them. Passages throughout the Word show that being devoured by sword and famine is being deprived of the knowledge of truth and goodness. They also show that sword and famine are purgative; a sword is that which purges our spiritual elements, while famine is that which purges our heavenly elements. Examples are Jeremiah 14:13, 14, 15, 16, 18; Lamentations 4:9; and so on. [3] Ezekiel contains another example:

> And more *famine* I will bring on you, and I will break the staff of bread for you. And I will send *famine* on you, and the evil wild animal, and they will bereave you; and a *sword* I will bring on you. (Ezekiel 5:16, 17)

Famine stands for being bereft of heavenly knowledge, or of the knowledge of what is good. The result is falsity and evil. In David:

> And [Jehovah] called down a *famine on the land;* the whole staff of bread he broke. (Psalms 105:16)

Breaking the staff of bread stands for being deprived of heavenly nourishment. For good spirits and angels, no other bread sustains life than the knowledge of what is good and true, and goodness and truth itself. This fact leads to the inner-level symbolism of famine and bread. In the same author:

> He has *satisfied* the longing soul, and the *starving* soul he has filled with good [food]. (Psalms 107:9)

The starving soul stands for people who desire knowledge. In Jeremiah:

> Lift the palms of your hands over the soul of your children, who faint with *hunger* at the head of all your streets. (Lamentations 2:19)

Hunger stands for a lack of knowledge, and streets for truth. In Ezekiel:

> They will live securely, and no one to terrify them. And I will raise a sapling up for them, for a name, and they will no longer be devoured by the *famine in the land.* (Ezekiel 34:28, 29)

This stands for the fact that they will no longer be deprived of the knowledge of goodness and truth. [4] In John:

> They will no longer *starve* and no longer thirst. (Revelation 7:16)

This is speaking of the Lord's kingdom, whose inhabitants enjoy a wealth of all heavenly knowledge and benefits (no starving) and a wealth of spiritual knowledge and truth (no thirst). The Lord likewise said in John:

> I am the bread of life; *no one* who comes to me will *starve* and no one who believes in me will ever *thirst.* (John 6:35)

In Luke:

> Fortunate are those of you who *starve* now, because you will be *satisfied*. (Luke 6:21)

In the same author:

> The *starving* he has filled with good [food]. (Luke 1:53)

This passage speaks of heavenly good and the knowledge of that good. The symbolism of famine as a scarcity of knowledge is mentioned openly in Amos:

> Watch! The days are coming, and I will send *famine into the land;* not *starvation* for bread, and not thirst for water, but for hearing Jehovah's words. (Amos 8:11, 12)

The fact that *and Abram went down into Egypt to reside as an immigrant* means being taught concepts from the Word can be seen from the symbolism of *Egypt* and of *residing as an immigrant.* The symbolism of Egypt as the knowledge of those concepts, and the symbolism of residing as an immigrant as being taught, comes directly below. **1461**

The passages in Luke quoted at the last verse (verse 9, §1457) make it clear that while he was young, the Lord was taught like any other person. So do the remarks directly above concerning the outer self, which cannot be reduced into correspondence and agreement with the inner self except through knowledge. One's outer self is body-centered and sense-oriented and cannot absorb anything heavenly or spiritual unless, like soil, it has seeds of knowledge planted in it. In those seeds of knowledge, heavenly influences can find their receiving vessels. The knowledge, however, has to be from the Word. Knowledge from the Word is such that it offers access to the Lord himself. The Word itself, after all, comes from the Lord by way of heaven and in each and every detail contains life from the Lord, despite appearances to the contrary in its outward aspect. From this you can see that when he was young, the Lord did not want to be indoctrinated with any other kind of knowledge but knowledge of the Word, which, again, gave him open access to his Father, Jehovah himself, with whom he was to unite and become one. He had all the more reason for his reluctance in the fact that the Word says nothing that does not have to do with him at its deepest levels and that did not first come from him. (His human nature was only an addition to his divine nature, which has existed from eternity.)

1462   *Egypt* in relation to the Lord is the knowledge of those concepts, but in relation to all other people, it is factual knowledge in general. This is established by the symbolism of Egypt in the Word, dealt with several times before, particularly in §§1164, 1165. The ancient church existed in Egypt, among many other places (see §1238), and during the time the church lasted there, the arts and sciences flourished. Egypt, consequently, symbolized scholarly learning. Eventually, though, its people wanted to use their expertise to pry into religious mysteries; they wanted to rely on their own powers in examining whether various divine secrets were true. When that happened, magic came into being, and Egypt then symbolized scholarship that twists the truth, which gives rise to falsity, which in turn gives rise to evil. This symbolism can be seen in Isaiah 19:11.

[2] Egypt symbolizes useful kinds of knowledge, so in the present verse it symbolizes the knowledge of concepts that can serve as vessels for what is heavenly and spiritual. The following places in the Word bear this out. In Isaiah:

> They led *Egypt*—the cornerstone of the tribes—astray. (Isaiah 19:13)

Egypt is being called the cornerstone of the tribes, which was to serve as a support for the tenets of faith symbolized by the tribes. In the same author:

> On that day there will be five cities in the land of *Egypt* speaking the tongue of Canaan and swearing to Jehovah Sabaoth. Each will be called "Ir heres." On that day there will be an altar to Jehovah in the middle of the land of *Egypt* and a pillar to Jehovah along its border, and it will serve as a sign and as a witness to Jehovah Sabaoth in the land of *Egypt*. For they will cry out to Jehovah because of their oppressors, and he will send them a deliverer and chieftain, who will rescue them. And Jehovah will become known to *Egypt,* and the *Egyptians* will recognize Jehovah on that day. And they will offer sacrifice and minha and swear an oath to Jehovah and fulfill it. And Jehovah will strike *Egypt*—strike, and heal. And they will return to Jehovah, and he will be prevailed on by their prayers and heal them. (Isaiah 19:18, 19, 20, 21, 22)

This treats of Egypt in a good sense, as standing for people who possess facts, or earthly truths, that act as containers for spiritual truths. [3] In the same author:

> On that day there will be a path from *Egypt* to Assyria, and Assyria will come into *Egypt* and *Egypt* into Assyria; and the *Egyptians* will serve Assyria. On that day Israel will be third to *Egypt* and Assyria, a blessing

in the middle of the earth, whom Jehovah Sabaoth will bless, saying,
"A blessing on my people *Egypt* and on the work of my hands, Assyria,
and on my inheritance, Israel!" (Isaiah 19:23, 24, 25)

In this passage Egypt symbolizes a knowledge of earthly truth; Assyria
symbolizes the power of reason, or rational ideas; and Israel symbolizes
spiritual matters. These follow one after the other, which is why it says
that on that day there will be a path out of Egypt into Assyria and that
Israel will be third to Egypt and Assyria. [4] In Ezekiel:

> Fine linen with embroidery from *Egypt* was what you spread out to
> serve you as a banner. (Ezekiel 27:7)

This is about Tyre, which symbolizes the possession of religious knowledge. Fine linen with embroidery stands for truths in the secular disciplines that perform a service. Secular facts, since they belong to the outer
self, ought to serve the inner self. In the same author:

> This is what the Lord Jehovih has said: "At the end of forty years, I will
> gather *Egypt* from the peoples where they have been scattered, and I
> will bring *Egypt* back from captivity." (Ezekiel 29:13, 14)

These words—that they would be gathered from the peoples and brought
back from captivity—stand for something similar, and they are said of
Judah and Israel in a number of places. In Zechariah:

> And it will happen that whoever does not go up from the clans of the
> earth to Jerusalem to worship the King, Jehovah Sabaoth, on them
> there will be no rain. And if the clan of *Egypt* does not go up and does
> not come, . . . (Zechariah 14:17, 18)

This too speaks in a good sense of Egypt, which means something similar.

[5] Egypt's symbolism as learning, or human wisdom, is visible in
Daniel too, where the knowledge of heavenly and spiritual subjects is
called the "hidden treasures of gold and silver" and also the "desirable
things of *Egypt*" (Daniel 11:43). And of Solomon it is said that:

> His wisdom multiplied beyond the wisdom of all the children of the
> east and beyond all the *wisdom of the Egyptians*. (1 Kings 4:30)

The house that Solomon built for the daughter of Pharaoh had the same
representation (1 Kings 7:8 and following verses).

[6] The fact that the Lord was taken to Egypt as a child also has no
other symbolism than [the journey of] Abram does here. In addition, it

allowed the Lord to fulfill all that had been represented concerning him.
The relocation to Egypt of Jacob and his offspring also represented nothing else in the deepest sense than the Lord's earliest instruction in knowledge from the Word, as is evident in the following passages. This is what
we find in Matthew concerning the Lord:

> An angel of the Lord appeared in a dream to Joseph, saying, "When
> you have woken, take the boy and his mother and escape into *Egypt,*
> and be there until I say." Waking up, he took the boy and his mother
> by night and retreated into *Egypt* and was there until Herod's death, so
> that there would be a fulfillment of the saying by the prophet when he
> said, "Out of *Egypt* I called my child." (Matthew 2:13, 14, 15, 19, 20, 21)

Hosea speaks of the same event this way:

> When Israel was a boy, I doted on him, and out of *Egypt* I called my
> child. (Hosea 11:1)

This shows that Israel as a boy means the Lord and that the words *out of
Egypt I called my child* mean instruction of him when he was young. [7] In
the same author:

> Through a prophet Jehovah brought Israel up out of *Egypt,* and through
> a prophet [Israel] was kept safe. (Hosea 12:12, 13)

Here too Israel means the Lord. A prophet symbolizes a teacher and
accordingly the teaching of religious concepts. In David:

> God Sabaoth, bring us back and make your face shine, and we will
> be saved. You have caused a grapevine to travel from *Egypt;* you have
> driven away the nations and planted it. (Psalms 80:7, 8)

This too is about the Lord, who is being called a grapevine from Egypt
because of the religious concepts he was learning.

1463   The fact that *residing as an immigrant* means being taught can be seen
from the symbolism of *immigrating* in the Word as being taught. This
symbolism comes about because in heaven, residing in a foreign land and
immigrating—in other words, moving from one place to another—is
simply a change in condition, as shown earlier (§§1376, 1379). So every
time the Word speaks of traveling, immigrating, or moving from place to
place, the one thing that comes to an angel's mind is the kind of change in
condition that angels experience. Changes of state can be either changes

in one's way of thinking or changes in one's feelings. Changes in the state of one's thinking are new concepts. In the world of spirits, these changes result from instruction, and since the people of the earliest church were in contact with heaven and its angels, a consequence was that traveling meant exactly that to them. So here the fact that Abram went down into Egypt to reside as an immigrant does indeed symbolize instruction of the Lord. [2] The journey of Jacob and his offspring into Egypt means much the same. In Isaiah, for instance:

> This is what the Lord Jehovih has said: "My people *went down to Egypt* in the beginning to *stay as immigrants,* and Assyria for no reason oppressed them." (Isaiah 52:4)

Assyria here stands for specious logic.

In the Jewish church, for the same reason, people who were being taught were called *immigrants residing* in their midst, and by command they were to be treated the same as the native-born (Exodus 12:48, 49; Leviticus 24:22; Numbers 15:13, 14, 15, 16, 26, 29; 19:10). Ezekiel speaks of them this way:

> You shall divide this land for yourselves according to the tribes of Israel. And it will happen that you shall divide it by lot as an inheritance for yourselves and for the *immigrants residing* in your midst, and they shall be to you as the native-born among the children of Israel. Along with you they shall cast a lot for an inheritance in the middle of the tribes of Israel. And it will happen that, in the tribe that an *immigrant* is *residing* with, there you shall give [the immigrant] an inheritance. (Ezekiel 47:21, 22, 23)

This is about a new Jerusalem, or the Lord's kingdom. The immigrants residing in the land mean people who allow themselves to be instructed, and consequently they mean religious outsiders. Evidence that immigrants stand for people who are being taught may be seen in the statement that whatever tribe an immigrant was living with, that was where the immigrant was to receive an inheritance; tribes stand for tenets of the true faith.

[3] Immigrating also has the same symbolism as traveling and settling. Traveling symbolizes the customs and pattern of a life, while settling somewhere symbolizes living one's life, as mentioned earlier, in §1293. So the land of Canaan is also referred to as the land of Abraham's, Isaac's, and

Jacob's travels (in Genesis 28:4; 36:7; 37:1; Exodus 6:4). And Jacob said to Pharoah:

> The days of the years of my *travels:* Few and evil have been the days of the years of my life, and they have not overtaken the days of the years of the life of my forebears, in the days of their *travels.* (Genesis 47:9)

Travels here stand for the way we live and what we are taught.

1464 The symbolism of *because the famine was heavy in the land* as a severe shortage in his outer self can be seen from the symbolism of *famine* above in this verse [§1460].

This verse holds too many secrets to list briefly. The Lord's capacity to learn outstripped any other individual's, but since unlike other people he needed to be taught heavenly knowledge before spiritual, the message applies to him. Another reason it applies is that his external self contained evil he inherited from his mother, which he would have to fight and overcome. Not to mention countless other secrets.

1465 Genesis 12:11. *And it happened when he came near entering Egypt that he said to Sarai his wife, "Consider, please; I know that you are a woman beautiful to see."*

And it happened when he came near entering Egypt means when he started to learn; *Egypt,* as noted, means the knowledge of religious concepts. *That he said to Sarai his wife* means that these were his thoughts about the truth to which heavenly qualities are attached; *Sarai his wife* is truth connected to the heavenly capacities the Lord had inside him. *Consider, please; I know that you are a woman beautiful to see,* means that truth from a heavenly source is appealing.

1466 The fact that *and it happened when he came near entering Egypt* means when he started to learn can be seen from the symbolism of *Egypt* as the knowledge of religious concepts. When someone is said to approach this, it cannot mean anything else.

1467 The fact that *Egypt* is the knowledge of religious concepts can be seen from the remarks and illustrations concerning Egypt at the last verse [§1462].

1468 *That he said to Sarai his wife* means that these were his thoughts about the truth to which heavenly qualities are attached, as can be seen from the symbolism of *Sarai* when she is called a *wife.* What a *wife* actually means in the Word's inner sense is truth united with goodness, because the bond between truth and goodness is no different than a marriage. When the Word speaks of a husband by name, he symbolizes what is good and his wife symbolizes truth. When it does not name the husband but calls him a man, however, he symbolizes truth and his wife symbolizes what is good. The Word is consistent in this respect, as was noted earlier, at §915. Because Abram is mentioned by name in this chapter, Sarai his wife symbolizes truth. So saying something to Sarai his wife, in an inner sense, is thinking such and such about the truth to which heavenly qualities are united.

It is historically true that Abram spoke this way to his wife when he set out for Egypt, but as mentioned already, all the historical events of the Word are representative, while all the words are symbolic [§§1401–1409]. What was recorded was confined to the events, sequence, and wording that would express those secrets in an inner sense.

The fact that *Sarai his wife* is truth connected to the heavenly capacities the Lord had inside him is established by the statements just made concerning Sarai as a wife.

1469

The reason I say truth connected to heavenly capacities is that the Lord already had all truth inside him—a heavenly quality carries truth with it; the one is as inseparable from the other as light is from a flame—but it was hidden in his inner self, which was divine. Secular and religious knowledge, which he gained by study, are not truth but only vessels for receiving truth. The things we have in our memory are anything but truth, even if truth is attributed to them. Instead, they function as vessels that *hold* truth. The Lord had to form or rather open up these vessels by being instructed in concepts from the Word. The goal was not only to infuse heavenly characteristics into those concepts but also to make the concepts themselves heavenly and therefore divine. The Lord united his divine nature to his human nature so that his human nature would also become divine.

The fact that *consider, please; I know that you are a woman beautiful to see,* means that truth from a heavenly source is appealing can be seen from the symbolism of a *woman beautiful to see.* All truth that is heavenly, or that develops out of something heavenly, is blissful for our inner self and appealing to our outer self, and that is exactly how heavenly angels perceive truth. The situation is wholly different, though, when truth is not from a heavenly source.

1470

There are two kinds of happiness in a person's inner self and two kinds of pleasure corresponding to them in the outer self; one is associated with goodness and the other with truth. Heavenly happiness and pleasure come from goodness; spiritual happiness and pleasure come from truth. It is common knowledge that truth itself brings happiness and pleasure, but the happiness and pleasure are quintessential when they come from a heavenly origin. Their presence renders the truth itself heavenly as well, and then it is called heavenly truth. It bears a resemblance to sunlight in the spring, which enfolds in itself a warmth that makes all the vegetation on earth grow and gives them something almost like animal life. This heavenly kind of truth is beauty itself, and it is what is here called a woman beautiful to see.

Any additional secrets wrapped up in this clause will come out in what follows.

1471   Genesis 12:12. *"And it will happen when the Egyptians see you that they will say, 'This is his wife,' and kill me and keep you alive."*

And it will happen when the Egyptians see you symbolizes the study of religious concepts; what is being depicted is the turn that study takes when the people who engage in it see heavenly concepts. *That they will say, 'This is his wife,'* means that they will call such concepts heavenly. *And kill me and keep you alive* means that they would not care about heavenly things but only about the knowledge itself, which they would steal.

1472   *And it will happen when the Egyptians see you* symbolizes the study of religious concepts; what is being depicted is the turn that study takes when the people who engage in it see heavenly concepts. This is evident from the symbolism of *Egypt* as the study of religious concepts, which has been demonstrated already [§§1164–1165, 1194–1195, 1462]. From this you can tell what "if the Egyptians see" means: that the character of this study is depicted in the present verse. Such a characteristic is inherent in the knowledge of religious concepts and is an earthly element of it. It asserts itself in young people when they are just starting to learn; the loftier a subject is, the more they want to know about it. When they hear that a subject has heavenly or divine implications, they are still more eager. But the thrill involved is an earthly one and rises out of a craving that belongs to the outer self.

In people other [than the Lord], this craving causes them to find pleasure only in the bare study of religious knowledge, without any other goal. The reality is that the study of such knowledge is merely a kind of tool designed to fulfill a use. To be specific, the knowledge is intended to serve as a vessel for heavenly and spiritual entities. When it serves this purpose, then it first comes into use, and all the pleasure it provides comes from the use of it.

[2] Anyone who pays attention can see that in itself a store of religious knowledge is just a means for becoming rational, then spiritual,

and at last heavenly. The knowledge can then bring our outer being into contact with our inner being, and when this happens, our study of it has served its true purpose. The inner self, after all, concerns itself only with that which is useful. For the same reason, the Lord imparts the pleasure that youth and early adulthood discovers in learning things. When we start to put our delight in bare learning, however, it is a bodily desire that carries us away. Insofar as it carries us away—insofar as we find pleasure in mere learning—so far we remove ourselves from heaven, and so far the facts we know shut themselves off from the Lord, to partake of the material world. On the other hand, insofar as we acquire facts for some useful purpose—for the sake of human society, of the Lord's church on earth, of the Lord's kingdom in the heavens, or (most especially) of the Lord himself—so much more do they open up. Angels possess all religious knowledge, and their knowledge is so broad that hardly one part in ten thousand can be passed on to people on earth in an entirely comprehensible way. Yet knowledge itself counts for nothing with angels, compared to the use it can serve.

[3] These considerations indicate what is meant by the words "When the Egyptians see you, they will say, 'This is his wife,' and kill me and keep you alive."

The Lord realized all this when he was young and thought along these lines, which is why I explain the phrase as I do: knowledge is inherently such that if the Lord had been carried away by the naked desire for learning religious concepts, he would have grown indifferent to any heavenly dimensions and cared only for the knowledge itself. And he would then have been robbed of this knowledge by the craving to acquire it.

I will have more to say on this below.

That they will say, 'This is his wife,' means that they will call such concepts heavenly. This can be seen from the symbolism of a *wife* as truth connected to heavenly qualities and so from the symbolism of *this is his wife* as something heavenly. **1473**

The fact that *and kill me and keep you alive* means that they would not care about heavenly things but only about the knowledge itself can be seen from the remarks just made. **1474**

[2] Genesis 12:13. *"Please say you are my sister, in order that it may go well for me on account of you and that my soul may live because of you."*

Please say you are my sister symbolizes intuitive truth, which is a *sister*. *In order that it may go well for me on account of you* means that what was heavenly could not be abused in that case. *And that my soul may live because of you* means that what was heavenly could be preserved in that case.

1475
The symbolism of *please say you are my sister* as intuitive truth, which is a *sister,* can be seen from the symbolism of a sister as intuitive truth, when heavenly truth is a wife. More will be said about this symbolism below.

The situation is this: Secular knowledge by its very nature wants nothing more than to thrust itself into heavenly affairs and explore them, but this goes against proper procedure, since it means doing violence to heavenly matters. The proper procedure is for a heavenly idea to insert itself by means of a spiritual idea into our rational thinking and by means of this into some fact that we know, and to fit the fact to its purposes. If this procedure is not followed, no wisdom is at all possible.

This verse again holds secrets about the way the Lord's Father taught him in a completely orderly way. Consequently it also holds secrets about the way his outer self united with his inner, that is, the way his outer self became divine, just like his inner self, so that he became Jehovah in regard to both of his essential qualities. This was accomplished through religious concepts, which are a means. Without these concepts as a means, a person's outer self could not even become human.

1476
The fact that *in order that it may go well for me on account of you* means that what was heavenly could not be abused in that case can be seen from statements above. The proper sequence, as already mentioned several times, is for the heavenly dimension to flow into the spiritual one, and the spiritual one into the rational one, and the rational one into the dimension of factual knowledge. When this order is followed, then the heavenly dimension adapts the spiritual one to its purposes, the spiritual adapts the rational, and the rational adapts the factual. The realm of factual knowledge in general then becomes the outermost vessel. Or, what is the same, facts individually and in their details become the outermost vessels, corresponding to rational ideas; rational ideas become vessels corresponding to spiritual ideas; and spiritual ideas become vessels corresponding to heavenly ideas. When this pattern is followed, the heavenly dimension cannot be abused. Otherwise it *is* abused.

Since the present verse in an inner sense deals with the Lord's education, it describes how he advanced.

1477
That my soul may live because of you means that what was heavenly could be preserved in that case, as indicated by the symbolism of a *soul* as something heavenly. The heavenly element is the soul itself, since it is life itself. This shows what "that my soul may live because of you" symbolizes.

What follows will demonstrate that heavenly qualities, or divine ones, were not attached to the Lord so as to unite into a single essence [with his human qualities] until after he had suffered spiritual trials and by that means rid himself of the evil he had inherited from his mother. How his heavenly core remained unharmed and how it was instead preserved is portrayed in the current and following verses.

Genesis 12:14. And it happened when Abram came into Egypt that the Egyptians saw the woman, that she was very beautiful. **1478**

It happened when Abram came into Egypt means when the Lord began to be taught. *That the Egyptians saw the woman, that she was very beautiful,* means that by its very nature the study of religious knowledge is pleasing for its own sake.

The fact that *it happened when Abram came into Egypt* means when the Lord began to be taught is established by the representation of *Abram* in an inner sense as the Lord when he was young. It is also established by the symbolism of *Egypt* as the study of religious knowledge, which was demonstrated above at verse 10 of this chapter [§1462]. It stands to reason, then, that coming into Egypt is being taught. **1479**

That the Egyptians saw the woman, that she was very beautiful, means that the study of religious knowledge is pleasing for its own sake. This can be seen from remarks above at verse 11 showing that the study of knowledge is like this in our youth. **1480**

It is more or less intrinsic to factual knowledge (because it is intrinsic to human beings) that at the very start we take pleasure in it for no other purpose than that of knowing. Each of us is like this. Our spirit finds intense delight in knowing—so intense that there is hardly anything we prefer. Factual knowledge is food for the spirit, which is sustained and refreshed by it, just as our outer self is sustained and refreshed by earthly food. This food for our spirit is something that is communicated to our outer self to enable it to adapt to the inner self.

[2] The different types of this food, though, arrange themselves in a hierarchy: Heavenly food is every benefit of love and charity received from the Lord. Spiritual food is every true tenet of faith. These two types of food are what an angel lives on. From them comes a kind of food that is also heavenly and spiritual but angelic in a lower degree, and this is the food that an angelic spirit lives on. From this too comes an even more humble type of heavenly and spiritual food, which has to do with reason and therefore with factual knowledge. It is the food that good spirits live on. In last place comes food for the body, which is our proper

food during bodily life. These types of food correspond to each other in a miraculous way.

This too shows why and how academic studies can provide their own satisfaction. They resemble appetite and the sense of taste. So the meals we eat on earth correspond to facts in the world of spirits, and appetite and taste themselves correspond to a craving for education. This can be seen from my experiences, discussed later [§§4791–4795, 4801], the Lord in his divine mercy willing.

1481   Genesis 12:15. *And Pharaoh's officers saw her and praised her to Pharaoh; and the woman was taken to Pharaoh's house.*

Pharaoh's officers saw symbolizes the main commandments, which are *Pharaoh's officers. And praised her to Pharaoh* means that these would please him. *And the woman was taken to Pharaoh's house* means that they would capture his fancy.

1482   *Pharaoh's officers saw* symbolizes the main commandments, which are *Pharaoh's officers,* as can be seen from the symbolism of officers and of Pharaoh. In the Word, in both the narrative and prophetic parts, *officers,* or chiefs, symbolize things that are most important. And *Pharaoh* symbolizes the same thing as Egypt. The present verse refers to Egypt or Pharaoh in the best sense because it uses both to portray the study of religious knowledge—the first study that the Lord took up in his youth.

The fact that they were the main commandments from the Word can be seen from the symbolism of these things on an inner level.

Much evidence confirms that in the Word, Pharaoh symbolizes the same thing as the whole of Egypt, just as the monarchs of other kingdoms mentioned by name symbolize the same thing as the names of the kingdoms themselves.

Officers, though, symbolize the primary elements in those kingdoms. In Isaiah, for instance:

> Stupid are the *chieftains* of Zoan, the sage advisors of Pharaoh. How can you say to Pharaoh, "I am the offspring of sages, the offspring of the monarchs of old"? The *chieftains* of Zoan have become fools; the *chieftains* of Noph have been deceived. (Isaiah 19:11, 13)

The chieftains of Zoan and Pharaoh's sage advisors stand for the most important facts we learn. And since wisdom flourished early in Egypt, as noted before [§§130, 1462], Egypt is referred to as the offspring of sages and the offspring of the monarchs of old.

Officers or chieftains stand for primary things in many other passages of the Word as well.

The fact that *they praised her to Pharaoh* means that these would **1483** please him can be seen without explanation.

The fact that *the woman was taken to Pharaoh's house* means that they **1484a** would capture his fancy can be seen from the symbolism of a *woman* and of a *house*. A *woman* symbolizes truth—here, the truth contained in scholarly learning, whose pleasures captivated the Lord in his youth. The pleasures of truth are those that come from truth intuitively known (symbolized by a sister). A *house* symbolizes qualities in us, especially qualities of our will, as shown earlier, in §710. So here it symbolizes what we fancy, or what we love to know and learn.

Genesis 12:16. *And he was good to Abram on her account, and Abram* **1484b** *had flock and herd, and male donkeys and male servants, and female servants and female donkeys, and camels.*

He was good to Abram on her account means that the number of facts the Lord knew multiplied. *And Abram had flock and herd, and male donkeys and male servants, and female servants and female donkeys, and camels,* symbolizes all the general categories of fact.

And he was good to Abram on her account means that the number of **1485** facts the Lord knew multiplied, as can be seen from the symbolism of *being good* to anyone as enriching that person.

It is the secular knowledge symbolized by Pharaoh that is being said to have benefited Abram, or in other words, to have benefited the Lord when he was young. What is more, it benefited him *on her account,* that is, on account of intuitive truth, which he desired. The desire for truth was what enriched him.

The fact that *and flock and herd, and male donkeys and male servants,* **1486** *and female servants and female donkeys, and camels,* symbolize all the general categories of fact can be seen from the symbolism of all these in the Word. It would take too long to demonstrate the specific symbolism of each, though—of flock and herd, of male donkeys and male servants, of female servants and female donkeys, and of camels. Each has its own symbolism. As a group, they symbolize all facets of the study of religious knowledge and secular fact. Facts, viewed in themselves, are the male donkeys and servants. The satisfaction they yield are the female servants and donkeys. The camels are general knowledge whose purpose is to serve. The flock and herd are what we possess. And this applies throughout the Word.

Nothing whatever in our outer self is anything but a servant; it exists only to serve our inner self. This is true of all the facts we know, since they belong exclusively to our outer self. After all, they have been collected from earthly and worldly sources through our senses in order to serve our intermediate or rational self, so that this can serve our spiritual self, so that this can serve our heavenly self, so that this can serve the Lord. So they arrange themselves in subordination to one another, the most outward elements ranking below the more inward ones in succession and therefore each and every one of them in order below the Lord.

Facts, as a result, are the final foundation on which the inner layers rest in sequence. And as they are the final foundation, they are inherently more subservient than the other levels. Anyone can see what role facts are capable of filling; all you have to do is reflect on it, or ask yourself what use they are. When you ponder their function in this way, you can grasp what the quality of that function is. Every bit of factual information has to exist for some purpose, and this is the service it performs.

[2] Genesis 12:17. *And Jehovah struck Pharaoh—and his household—with great plagues because of this word of Sarai, Abram's wife.*

Jehovah struck Pharaoh with great plagues means that facts were destroyed. *And his household* symbolizes the facts he had collected. *Because of this word of Sarai, Abram's wife,* means because truth needs to be connected with something heavenly.

1487   *Jehovah struck Pharaoh with great plagues* means that facts were destroyed, as can be seen from the following: *Pharaoh* symbolizes learning in general and consequently the facts learned. And *being struck with plagues* symbolizes being destroyed.

This is how it is with facts: While we are young we accumulate them for the sole purpose of knowing them. In the Lord's case, the motivation was the pleasure he felt in truth and the love he had for it.

The facts we collect in youth are very plentiful, but the Lord organizes them properly so that they can serve a use; they enable us first to think, then to figure out how we can put facts to use, and finally to become embodiments of usefulness ourselves. (This happens when our life itself consists in being useful, when our life is one of useful activity.) These functions are performed by the facts we absorb in our youth. Without facts, our external self could never unite with our inner self and in the process become truly useful. Some people do come to embody usefulness; in other words, they view everything in terms of its use and direct all their action toward a useful goal. Perhaps they do not reflect explicitly on the question of usefulness, but still they do so tacitly, by second nature. With these people, factual knowledge has filled its first function, which is to make them rational, and the facts are then destroyed, because they no longer have a purpose; and so on from there.

This is what the present verse means when it says that Jehovah struck Pharaoh with great plagues.

The symbolism of *and his household* as the facts he had collected can be seen from the symbolism of a house or *household* here as facts that are being collected. Accumulating facts and using them to construct or "build" an outer self is much like building a house. Accordingly, houses and the building of houses have this same symbolism throughout the Word, as in Isaiah:

> I am creating new heavens and a new earth. They will *build houses* and inhabit them. And they will plant vineyards and eat the fruit of them. They will not *build,* and another inhabit. (Isaiah 65:17, 21, 22)

A house here is a place where there is wisdom and understanding and so where goodness and truth are known, since it is talking about the Lord's kingdom—that is to say, about new heavens and a new earth. In Jeremiah:

> *Build houses* and live in them; and plant gardens and eat their produce. (Jeremiah 29:5)

The meaning is the same. In David:

> Happy is the man who fears Jehovah; in Jehovah's commandments he takes great pleasure. Wealth and riches are in his *house,* and his virtue will be standing forever. (Psalms 112:1, 3)

The wealth and riches stand for the wealth and riches of wisdom and understanding and so for religious concepts, which are "in his house," that is, inside the person.

[2] Houses with an opposite meaning come up in Zephaniah:

> I will exact punishment on those who say, "Jehovah has not done good and has not done evil." And their riches will become plunder, and their *houses* a ruin; and they will *build houses* and not live in them, and plant vineyards and not drink the wine. (Zephaniah 1:12, 13)

In Haggai:

> "Go up onto the mountain and bring wood and *build a house.* To look for much . . . ! And here, it became little. And you brought it into [your] *house* and I blew it away. Why?" says Jehovah. "Because of my *House,* which has been deserted, while you go running each to your

own *house.* Therefore the heavens above you have been shut off from their dew." (Haggai 1:8, 9, 10)

A house here stands for facts from which we produce falsity by means of twisted logic. In Isaiah:

> Doom to those attaching *house* to *house;* field to field they bring together, until there is no room and you live alone in the middle of the land. If many *houses* are not made desolate—large ones, and good—without any inhabitant, . . . ! Jehovah's vineyard is the *house* of Israel. (Isaiah 5:7, 8, 9)

Here too the house stands for facts from which we produce falsities. In Amos:

> Look! Jehovah is issuing commands, and he will strike the large *house* with cracks and the small *house* with crevices. Will horses run on rock? Will anyone plow it with oxen? For you have transformed integrity into poison, and the fruit of justice into wormwood. (Amos 6:11, 12)

The house again stands for falsity and the evil that falsity gives rise to; horses stand for skewed logic; integrity stands for truth that is transformed into poison; and the fruit of justice stands for virtues that are transformed into wormwood.

[3] Throughout the Word, then, houses stand for human minds, which ought to hold understanding and wisdom. Pharaoh's house here stands for the facts on which understanding and therefore wisdom are based. The house that Solomon built for Pharaoh's daughter (1 Kings 7:8 and following verses) also has the same symbolism. Since houses stand for our minds, which contain understanding and wisdom, and which also contain the emotions that belong to our will, the symbolism of a house in the Word is broad. The particular symbolism can be deduced from the context in which it is mentioned. People themselves are also called houses.

1489   *Because of this word of Sarai, Abram's wife,* means because truth needs to be connected with something heavenly. This can be seen from the symbolism of a *wife,* and so of *Sarai the wife,* as truth that needs to be connected with something heavenly, discussed above at verse 12 [§1473].

The situation is that unless facts—which filled a purpose when we were young—are destroyed and obliterated as we become rational, truth can never be wedded to any heavenly quality. Those first facts, for the most part, are earthly, bodily, and worldly in their purpose. Even though the commandments that we absorb as young people are divine, we cannot form any notions about them except on the basis of facts like those. As long as the lowly facts from which we form our ideas cling to us, then, our minds cannot be lifted up.

It was the same in the Lord's case, because he was born like any other person and had to be taught like any other person, although his progress followed a divine plan, whose nature has been discussed. The present story of Abram in Egypt depicts the divine plan by which the Lord's outer self was united with his inner self so that his outer self too would become divine.

Genesis 12:18. *And Pharaoh called Abram and said, "What is this you have done to me? Why didn't you point out to me that she was your wife?"*   **1490**

And Pharaoh called Abram means that the Lord remembered. *And said, "What is this you have done to me?"* means that it caused him anguish. "*That she was your wife*" means when he realized that it would not be right for him to have any truth but truth that was wedded to something heavenly.

The meaning of *Pharaoh called Abram* as the fact that the Lord remembered can be seen from the symbolism of Pharaoh as secular learning. Secular knowledge itself, or the facts themselves that the Lord drank in when he was young, are being called *Pharaoh* here. As a result, it is factual knowledge itself that addresses the Lord in this way, or rather it is Jehovah speaking through factual knowledge. The reader can see from this that the present clause means that the Lord remembered. Awareness comes through the facts we learn and so through Pharaoh, who symbolizes secular knowledge, as noted.   **1491**

The fact that *he said, "What is this you have done to me?"* means that it caused him anguish can be seen from the outrage itself with which the words are said. The anguish, then, is explicitly voiced in these words. The inner meaning is such that the actual emotion implicit in the words is what makes up the inner meaning. The literal words themselves are not noticed; it is as if they did not exist. The feeling present in the words is anger on the part of secular knowledge, so to speak, and grief on the part of the Lord—grief to know that the facts he had learned with such satisfaction and pleasure would be destroyed in this way. His predicament resembled that of babies who love something that their parents can see is dangerous for them; removing the object makes the baby cry.   **1492**

That she was your wife means that it would not be right for him to have any truth but truth that was wedded to something heavenly. This can   **1493** be seen from the symbolism of a *wife* as truth that needs to couple with something heavenly, as discussed above at verse 12 [§1473]. Again, what is depicted here is the plan by which the Lord advanced into understanding and from understanding into wisdom so that he would become wisdom itself throughout—in regard to his human quality as well as his divine.

1494   Genesis 12:19. *"Why did you say, 'She is my sister'? And I would have taken her for my woman. And now look: your wife; take her and go."*

Why did you say, "She is my sister"? means that at the time he was not aware of possessing anything but intuitive truth. *And I would have taken her for my woman* means that in his ignorance he could have abused the truth that was to be wedded to a heavenly quality. *And now look: your wife; take her and go,* means that the truth would be wedded to a heavenly quality.

1495   *Why did you say, "She is my sister"?* means that at the time he was not aware of possessing anything but intuitive truth. This can be seen from the symbolism of a *sister* as intuitive truth, and from the fact that [Abram] *said* these words, as verse 13 shows. This was done so that the heavenly aspect would not be damaged but preserved.

This evidence indicates that when the Lord was young and learning factual information, at the very first he fully believed that facts existed only for the sake of his intellectual side; that is, that they existed only to enable him to recognize truth. Later he discovered that their real purpose was to enable him to reach heavenly goals. Things were done this way in order to prevent the abuse of heavenly attributes and to promote their welfare instead.

While we are learning, we progress from facts to rational truth, then to truth known through higher intuition, and finally to heavenly truth, symbolized here by a wife. If we go from facts and rational truth directly to heavenly truth, rather than by means of intuitional truth, we do harm to what is heavenly. This is because truth that we arrive at by reasoning, on the basis of facts, has no link with heavenly truth except through intuitive truth, which stands in between. Definitions of heavenly truth and intuitive truth appear directly below [§1496].

[2] To show what the case is here, I need to say something about proper order. The proper order is for the heavenly dimension to act on the spiritual dimension and adapt it to its own purposes. The spiritual dimension should act on the rational and adapt this to its own purposes. And the rational dimension should act on the factual and adapt this to its own purposes.

This is indeed the pattern that we follow in childhood, when we are learning, but the appearance is exactly the opposite: we seem to proceed from facts to rational thinking, from this to spiritual ideas, and finally to heavenly concepts. This is the way it appears because this is how a path to the heavenly plane—the deepest plane—opens up. All instruction is simply an opening of the path. To the extent that the path opens (or to put it another way, to the extent that the receiving vessels open), these entities flow into one another in sequence, as noted: rational ideas derived from ideas that are simultaneously heavenly and spiritual flow [into facts]; then heavenly-spiritual ideas flow into rational ones; and heavenly ideas flow into heavenly-spiritual ones. The higher types of concept are constantly striking our minds, and they also prepare and form for themselves appropriate vessels, which are then opened up. As evidence, consider this: facts and logic are inherently dead, and any appearance that they are alive comes from a deeper life force that flows into them.

[3] Anyone can see the same thing clearly from our ability to think or form a judgment. All the secret skills belonging to the art and science of analytic thinking lie buried in these two abilities, and there are so many skills that not even one in a million can be probed exhaustively. And this is so not only for an adult but even for young people; all their thoughts and all their words are full of such mysteries, although no one, not even the smartest person, is aware of it. We would never have such hidden skills if the heavenly and spiritual entities that lie deep inside us were not striking our minds, flowing in, and producing all these effects.

I would have taken her for my woman means that in his ignorance he could have abused the truth that was to be wedded to a heavenly quality, as can be seen from the remarks just above and from earlier remarks at verse 13 [§§1475–1476]. **1496**

In regard to the idea that truth would be wedded to something heavenly, the case is this: Viewed in itself, the truth that we learn when we are young is just a vessel designed for the infusion of a heavenly essence. Truth has no life on its own, only from the heavenly dimension that enters into it. The heavenly dimension is love and charity; this is the source of all truth. And since all truth comes from this source, truth is nothing but a kind of vessel.

Truth also plainly displays itself as a vessel in the other world. In that world, people never regard truth from the viewpoint of truth but from that of the life within it. In other words, they regard it from the viewpoint of heavenly traits, which are traits of love and charity within the truth. These traits cause truth to be heavenly and to be called heavenly truth.

This evidence now shows what intuitive truth is. It also demonstrates that for the Lord, intuitive truth opened the path to heavenly qualities.

Factual truth, rational truth, and intuitive truth are three separate things, which come one after the other. Factual truth is the product of secular knowledge. Rational truth is factual truth logically proved. Intuitive truth is truth united to an inner perception that the thing is so. The Lord received this kind of truth while he was still young, and in him it opened the path to heavenly qualities.

1497   *Now look: your wife; take her and go,* means that the truth would be wedded to a heavenly quality. This can be seen from the symbolism of a *wife* as truth that needs to be united with something heavenly—a symbolism demonstrated earlier, at verses 11 and 12 [§§1468–1469, 1472–1473]—and from the statements just above.

1498   Genesis 12:20. *And Pharaoh gave orders concerning Abram to his men, and they sent him away, and his wife, and all that he had.*

Pharaoh gave orders concerning Abram to his men, [and they sent him away,] means that the facts the Lord knew deserted him. *And his wife* means that the same thing happened to the truth that was united with heavenly traits. *And all that he had* symbolizes everything related to heavenly truth.

1499   *Pharaoh gave orders concerning Abram to his men, [and they sent him away,]* means that the facts the Lord knew deserted him. This can be seen from the symbolism of *Pharaoh* as scholarly learning and from the symbolism of *men* as properties of the intellect (a symbolism demonstrated earlier, at §158). Here, because the men are mentioned in connection with Pharaoh, or learning, they symbolize intellectual things that are relevant to education.

To say more about the way the facts the Lord knew deserted him: When heavenly attributes form a bond with truth known through intuition, and that truth becomes heavenly, anything that is superfluous automatically disappears. This is an intrinsic feature of heavenly things.

1500   *His wife* means that the same thing happened to the truth that was united with heavenly traits; that is to say, the facts he knew deserted this truth. This can be seen from the symbolism of a *wife* as truth united to what is heavenly (mentioned above) and also from the remarks just made. Useless facts leave when heavenly concepts arrive, just as foolish ones do when wisdom arrives. They are like shells or scales that slough off spontaneously.

The symbolism of *all that he had* as everything related to heavenly truth now follows from the above.

These remarks now make it clear that Abram's stay in Egypt simply represents and symbolizes the Lord, and specifically the education he received when he was young. The following saying of Hosea's offers further confirmation:

> Out of Egypt I called my child. (Hosea 11:1; Matthew 2:15)

Still further confirmation appears in the following words in Moses:

> The residence of the children of Israel who resided in Egypt: four hundred thirty years. And it happened at the end of four hundred thirty years—and it happened on that same day—that all the armies of Jehovah left the land of Egypt. (Exodus 12:40, 41)

These years were counted not from the time of Jacob's entry into Egypt but from that of Abram's stay there, from which time four hundred thirty years had passed. So the child out of Egypt referred to in Hosea 11:1 symbolizes the Lord, in an inner sense.

Still further confirmation comes from the fact that in the Word, the sole function of "Egypt" is to symbolize scholarly learning, as shown in §§1164, 1165, 1462.

[2] The presence of these secrets can also be seen from the fact that similar things are said of Abram—that he called his wife his sister—during his stay in Philistia (Genesis 20:1–end). Similar things are said of Isaac as well—that he called his wife his sister—when he too stayed in Philistia (Genesis 26:6–13). These stories, involving almost the same circumstances, would never have been recounted in the Word if the kind of secrets mentioned had not lain hidden in them.

What is more, this is the Lord's Word, which has no life whatsoever in it if it does not contain an inner meaning that focuses on him.

[3] The secrets that lie buried here (and in the stories about Abram and Isaac in Philistia) tell how the Lord's human quality came together with his divine quality. Or, to say the same thing another way, they tell how the Lord became Jehovah down to his human nature as well. They also reveal that the process started when he was young, which is the subject here.

In addition, these verses involve much more hidden information than anyone could ever believe. The amount that can be expressed, however, is so small that it hardly amounts to anything. Besides the deep mysteries concerning the Lord, the chapter also includes secrets about our own education and rebirth as heavenly people, and about our education and rebirth as spiritual people. It deals with those processes as they occur not only in the individual specifically but also in the church generally. Then too it contains secrets about the education of children in heaven. In short, it describes the instruction of everyone who is becoming the Lord's image and likeness. These things show only in the inner meaning, not in the literal meaning, since the historical details overpower and eclipse them.

Perception and Auras in the Other Life (Continued)

1504 IN the other life, as mentioned [§§1388, 1396], one individual recognizes another's character as soon as that other approaches, even if she or he says nothing. This experience reveals the fact that our inward reaches are somehow active (although we are unaware of it) and that their activity enables others to perceive what kind of spirit we are. I was able to see the truth of this by observing that the aura of this activity not only radiates far and wide but sometimes (when the Lord allows) makes itself perceptible in various ways.

1505 In addition, I learned how we acquire these auras, which become so tangible in the other world. To put it in comprehensible terms, take the example of people who have formed an opinion of themselves as superior to others. They eventually develop the habit and the instinct, so to speak, of focusing on themselves whenever they see other people or talk to them, wherever they go. They do so consciously at first and then unconsciously, so that they themselves become blind to it. Still, the habit governs every one of their gestures and words, just as it governs every one of their feelings and thoughts. This is something we are capable of noticing in others. Such a trait is what creates an aura in the next life, and others perceive the aura, but no more often than the Lord allows.

[2] The same is true with other attitudes as well. As a result, there are as many auras as there are moods and combinations of mood, which are

countless. Our aura is like an image of ourselves projected outside us. In fact it is an image of everything inside us. What presents itself to view or to perception in the world of spirits, however, is only a general approximation. In heaven, on the other hand, our character is recognized in a more specific way. No one but the Lord, though, knows what we are like down to the smallest details.

Let me relate several experiences illustrating the nature of auras.

1506

A certain spirit I had known and talked to when he lived in his body later appeared many times in the company of evil spirits. Because he had a high opinion of himself, he had developed an air of superiority to others. And because he was like this, the other spirits suddenly fled, so that none but he could be seen. He then filled up his whole environment in all directions, and the atmosphere was one of concentration on himself. Soon afterward, abandoned by fellow members of his own community as well, he sank into another state. (Those in the other life who are deserted by the community in which they live seem to become half dead at first. At that point, the only thing that keeps them alive is the influence of heaven on their inward capacities.) Then he began to complain and to suffer.

Other spirits later told me that they could not stand to have him near, because he considered himself more important than anyone else. Eventually, having formed ties with a new community, he rose high up and consequently seemed to himself to be governing the universe all alone. (Those are the lengths to which self-love inflates our pride when left to itself.) Afterward he was thrown down among hellish spirits. Such is the lot that awaits those who consider themselves greater than others. More than any other love, self-love is opposed to mutual love, which is the life of heaven.

There was one person who in bodily life had viewed himself as greater and wiser than others, although in other respects he had been honorable enough, not holding other people in contempt on that account. Because he had been born to high position, however, he had developed an air of prestige and power.

1507

As such he came to me and for a long time said nothing. I noticed, though, that he was surrounded by a kind of fog, which drifted out from him and started to envelop other spirits and then to distress them. Speaking to me from inside it, they said that they could not possibly stay there, that they were being robbed of all freedom, so that they did not dare to say anything. He too began to talk and addressed them, calling them his children and at various times instructing them, but always with the authority that he had acquired.

This experience showed me what an aura of personal power is like in the other world.

1508 I had many opportunities to observe that people who had been endowed with the highest positions in the world inevitably took on an air of authority as a result. Consequently they were unable to hide it or cast it off in the other life. In the ones who have received the gift of faith and of love for others, the air of authority combines in a miraculous way with one of benevolence, so that it disturbs no one. In fact well-mannered spirits also offer them a kind of corresponding deference. The atmosphere they give off is not a dictatorial one; it is just an aura natural to them, because they were born that way. Since they are good, and since they work at shedding that aura, after a certain amount of time they succeed.

1509 For several days I had with me the kind of spirits who had not concentrated at all on the good of society when they lived in the world but on themselves. They had been useless, so far as political office goes, and their only goal had been to live sumptuously, wear glamorous clothes, and grow rich. They were used to putting up pretenses; to finding means of worming their way in everywhere by various kinds of flattery; and to vying for office with the sole purpose of making themselves visible and taking charge of their overlord's resources. Anyone engaged in any serious kind of work they regarded with contempt. They had been courtiers, I perceived.

The effect they had was to sap me of all my energy and to make it burdensome for me to act on or think about anything worthwhile, anything true or good—so terribly burdensome that in the end I hardly knew what to do.

When spirits like this come among other spirits, they infect them with a similar sluggishness. In the other life, they are useless members of society and are rejected wherever they go.

1510 Every spirit and to a greater extent every community of spirits has its own aura, formed from and given off by the assumptions and self-deceptions that it has adopted. (Demons have an aura formed by their longings.)

By its inherent nature, when one person's aura of assumptions and self-deceptions influences another person, it makes truth appear to be false. It also stirs up all kinds of supportive ideas, so that it convinces the person to accept falsity as true and evil as good. [2] (This fact made it clear to me how easily we can become entrenched in falsity and evil, unless we believe the truth that comes from the Lord.) Such auras are denser or thinner, depending on the nature of the falsities.

These auras are completely out of harmony with the auras of spirits who subscribe to the truth. If the two kinds of aura come near each other, war breaks out. If the atmosphere of falsity is permitted to win, the good spirits come into times of trial and anguish.

I also perceived an atmosphere of disbelief, in which people accept nothing that is said and scarcely even what is in plain sight. And I perceived the atmosphere of those who believe nothing but what they can grasp with their senses.

[3] In addition, I saw someone dressed in dark clothing sitting near a mill, apparently milling flour. At his side appeared a little mirror. Later I saw certain products of his disordered imagination, which were surprisingly wispy. I wondered who he was, but he came to me and said that he was the person sitting by the mill and that he had possessed the idea that absolutely everything was simply a hallucination and nothing was real, which is why he ended up in this position.

Much experience has taught me to recognize—and to recognize as clearly as I recognize anything—that spirits who are caught up in falsity influence our thinking and thoroughly convince us that falsity is true. We cannot see it any other way, and this results from their aura.

Demons too, who are immersed in evil, influence our will in this way and cause evil to seem utterly good. We cannot feel it any other way, and this again results from their aura.

I have had a thousand opportunities to perceive clearly the influence of each group, to tell who it came from, how angels working for the Lord removed the effects, and many other details besides, which cannot well be listed individually.

From this I could see two things with such certainty that nothing has ever seemed more certain to me. One is where the falsity and evil in us come from. The other is the fact that false assumptions and the desire for evil give rise to these auras that stay with us after physical life has ended and that display themselves so openly.

When hallucinatory auras present themselves to view, they look like clouds, thicker or thinner according to the nature of the hallucination. There is a kind of foggy crag under the left foot in the region of the pre-Flood people, and they spend their lives beneath it. Its fogginess is due to their hallucinations and keeps them at a distance from everyone else in the other world.

People who have lived lives of hatred and revenge give off auras of a type that causes fainting and induces vomiting. These auras are essentially poisonous. They are usually tested for their toxicity and density by means of a kind of dusky blue strip. As these strips disappear, the aura also shrinks.

1513 One of those who are called lukewarm came to me, acting as though he had repented. It did not feel like a trick, although I would have thought that he was hiding something inside. But the spirits were saying that they could not stand to have him near, that they were feeling the same sensation you feel when you are about to vomit, and that he was one of those who needed to be spat out.

Later, he started saying unspeakable things and was unable to stop, no matter how much pressure was put on him not to talk that way.

1514 Auras also present themselves to the senses through odors, which spirits are much more keenly sensitive to than people on earth are. In fact auras correspond to smells, amazingly enough.

Some people have indulged in humbug, which has given them their character. When their aura is turned into a smell, it stinks like vomit.

Some have learned to speak elegantly in order to impress others with everything they say. When their aura takes on an odor, it resembles the smell of burnt bread.

Some have indulged in mere physical pleasure, without developing any neighborly love or any faith. Their aura smells like excrement.

The same is true of those who have carried out a life filled with adultery, although their stench is even worse.

[2] Some have lived lives of intense hatred and vengefulness and of cruelty. When their aura is turned into a smell, it reeks like a corpse.

The smell of rats wafts from those who have been disgustingly greedy.

The smell of bedbugs drifts from those who have persecuted the innocent.

These smells cannot be picked up by any earthly person except one whose inner senses have been opened to allow companionship with spirits.

1515 I perceived the aura of stench from a certain woman who later joined a group of sirens, and the stench emanated from her wherever she went for a period of several days. The spirits said that the reek was almost lethal, but still the woman herself did not smell it at all.

Sirens have essentially the same foul smell, since their inner depths are revolting, although their outer looks are mostly attractive and fetching. For more about them, see §831.

Surprisingly, sirens in the other world catch on quickly to everything there and see how things stand better than others do, even in regard to doctrinal matters. Their whole focus, however, is to turn what they learn into magic and seize power over others. They enter into good people's feelings by a pretense of virtue and truth, but their nature is nevertheless as described.

This shows that doctrine is worthless unless we become what it teaches us to become—that is, unless our goal is to use it in our lives. Besides, hellish spirits count among their number many people who displayed more skill at doctrinal questions than others. People who have lived a charitable life, though, are all in heaven.

I talked with some spirits about the sense of taste. They said they had no sense of taste but something else that allowed them to recognize flavor, which they compared to smell, although they could not describe it. **1516**

This recalled to my mind the fact that taste and smell come together in a third faculty, as can be seen from animals, which find their food by scent. The scent reveals to them whether a thing is their proper food and good for them.

I once smelled a wine smell and learned that it came from those who ingratiate themselves with others in a spirit of affability and bona fide love, so that their compliments also contain some truth. This fragrance has many variations and arises from an atmosphere of polished charm. **1517**

When heavenly angels are present with the body of a dead person who is to be revived, the smell of the body turns into a sweet fragrance, and once evil spirits smell it, they cannot come close. **1518**

When an aura of charity or faith is perceived as a smell, it yields intense pleasure. The smell is sweet, like the smell of flowers, of lilies, of different types of perfume, with unlimited variety. **1519**

An angel's aura can also be displayed visibly, as an atmosphere or nimbus, and these are so beautiful, so sweet, and so full of variety that they could never be described.

However, although I have been talking about the way a spirit's inner dimensions can be perceived through auras radiating from and generated by the spirit, and through smells too, it needs to be known that these indicators do not display themselves all the time. In addition, the Lord modifies them in various ways, to keep a spirit's character from lying open to others' view all the time. **1520**

Genesis 13

The Light in Which Angels Live

1521 EVERY sense but taste is much keener and richer in spirits and angels than it can ever be in people on earth, as has been made clear to me many times. Not only can angels see and interact with each other—finding their greatest happiness in mutual love, as they do—they also have more to see in their surroundings than you could ever believe. The world of spirits and the heavens are full of representative objects like the ones the prophets saw, and these objects are so awe-inspiring that anyone whose eyes were simply opened to gaze on them for a few hours could not help being dumbfounded.

The light in heaven is such that it outshines even the noonday light of our solar system by an unbelievable amount. The inhabitants of heaven do not receive any light from this world, however, because they are too high or too deep for the reach of that light. Truth is light from the Lord, who is their sun.

Even the noonday light of the world is like thick darkness to angels. When they have the opportunity to look at worldly light, it is as if they were looking at utter darkness; this I have learned from experience. This shows the difference between heaven's light and the world's light.

1522 I have seen the light that spirits and angels live in so many times that it no longer gives me pause, having become quite familiar to me. Citing all my experience would take too long, though, so let me relate just a few examples.

1523 I was taken into the dwellings of good spirits and angelic spirits several times in order to learn what their light was like. There I saw not only the spirits but the things surrounding them as well.

I also saw babies and mothers bathed in a light of the greatest possible brilliance and radiance.

1524 An intense flame dropped into view unexpectedly, powerfully dazzling not only my physical sight but also my inner vision. Soon a dark spot appeared, like a dusky cloud with something earthlike about it.

When I wondered about it, I was taught that the light among angels in heaven is just as bright compared to the light in the world of spirits. Although spirits also live in light, there is a comparable difference between the two. Like the light, the understanding and wisdom of angels is greater than that of spirits—and not just the understanding and wisdom but everything that comes from understanding and wisdom, such as speech, thought, joy, and gladness, because these correspond to the light. As a result, I was able to see how much more perfect angels are than people on earth, whose darkness is even greater than that of spirits.

I was shown the glow that those who belong to a certain inner region of the face live in. It was a glow beautifully dappled with rays of golden flame for the benefit of those who respond to what is good, and with rays of silvery light for those who respond to what is true. Sometimes they are also able to see the sky, but not the sky that appears to our eyes. To their eyes the sky is represented as being resplendent with tiny stars. **1525**

The reason there is such a difference in the level of light is that all good spirits in the first heaven, all angelic spirits in the second heaven, and all angels in the third—as a whole—are divided into heavenly ones and spiritual ones. The heavenly ones are those who love what is good; the spiritual ones are those who love what is true.

I was drawn away from trivial ideas anchored in the body so that my attention could be kept on spiritual ideas. Then there appeared the vivid gleam of a diamond-bright light, and this lasted fairly long. I cannot describe the light in any other way, because it resembled something diamondlike gleaming in each minuscule element. As long as I was kept in that light, I perceived all worldly and body-centered minutiae as being a long way below me. The experience taught me what a bright light people enjoy when they withdraw from matter-based thinking and immerse themselves in spiritual ideas. **1526**

I have seen the light that shines on spirits and angels so many other times as well that if all my experiences were to be recounted, they would fill pages and pages.

When it pleases the Lord, good spirits appear to others (and also to themselves) as shining stars whose radiance matches the quality of the spirits' charity and faith. Evil spirits, though, resemble little balls of coal fire. **1527**

Sometimes, among evil spirits, a life devoted to the fulfillment of one's sensual desires resembles a coal fire. This semblance of fire is what the vitality of the Lord's love and mercy turns into when it flows into them. The vital energy of their hallucinations, on the other hand, looks **1528** like the light that comes from such a fire—a dim light with no range whatever. When the living energy of mutual love approaches, the pseudo-fire is snuffed out and turns cold, while the weak light from it goes dark.

Evil spirits pass their lives in the dark. Astonishingly, some of them even love darkness and abominate light.

1529　　People know perfectly well in heaven—though not as well in the world of spirits—where such great light comes from: the Lord. Remarkably, in the third heaven the Lord appears to heavenly angels as a sun and to spiritual angels as a moon. There is no other source for their light. But the *amount* of light they enjoy depends on the amount of heavenliness and spirituality they have; and the *type* of light they enjoy depends on the type of heavenliness and spirituality. Consequently, the genuinely heavenly and spiritual quality of the Lord presents itself to the angels' outward sight in the form of light.

1530　　Anyone could have seen the truth of this from the Word—for instance, from the time when the Lord revealed himself to Peter, James, and John, since his face then shone like the sun and his clothes became like the light (Matthew 17:2). The only reason he appeared this way to them was that their inner eyes were open.

The prophets provide evidence for the same thing. In Isaiah, for example, where it deals with the Lord's kingdom in the heavens:

> The light of the moon will be like the light of the sun, and the light of the sun will be seven times as strong, like the light of seven days. (Isaiah 30:26)

And in a passage from John also dealing with the Lord's kingdom, which is called the New Jerusalem:

> The city has no need for the sun or the moon to shine in it, since God's glory lights it and its lamp is the Lamb. (Revelation 21:23)

In another place as well:

> Night will not exist there, and they will have no need for a lamp or sunlight, because the Lord God gives them light. (Revelation 22:5)

Additionally, when the Lord appeared to Moses, Aaron, Nadab, Abihu, and the seventy elders,

> They saw the God of Israel, under whose feet was something like a work of sapphire stone, and it looked like the substance of the sky for cleanness. (Exodus 24:10)

Since the Lord's heavenly, spiritual quality appears to angels' outward sight as a sun or moon, the sun in the Word symbolizes something
heavenly; the moon, something spiritual.

For proof to me that he appears before heavenly angels as a sun and **1531**
before spiritual angels as a moon, the Lord in his divine mercy opened my
inner eyes to look all the way into heaven. There I saw clearly a radiant
moon ringed by many smaller moonlets, whose combined light was almost
as strong as the sun's. As Isaiah said, "The light of the moon will be like the
light of the sun" (Isaiah 30:26). But a sight of the sun was not given to me.

The moon appeared out in front, toward the right.

Amazing sights can be seen by the Lord's light in heaven—so many **1532**
of them that they could never be listed. These sights consist of one scene
after another representing the Lord and his kingdom, resembling scenes
described by the prophets and by John in the Book of Revelation. There
are other symbolic objects as well. We cannot possibly see them with our
physical eyes, but as soon as the Lord opens our inner eyes—the eyes of
our spirit—similar sights can immediately present themselves to view.
The visions of the prophets were nothing more than the opening of their
inner eyes. This is what happened when John saw the golden lampstands
(Revelation 1:12, 13), the holy city as pure gold, and its light source like a
very precious stone (Revelation 21:2, 10, [11, 18]), not to mention much
in the prophets. These considerations teach not only that angels live in
the highest light but also that heaven contains countless marvels that no
one could ever believe.

Until my eyes were opened, I almost inevitably cherished the same **1533**
idea as others about the countless wonders that appear in the next world. I
thought that neither light nor the kind of phenomena light creates—to say
nothing of sensory powers—could possibly exist in the next world. This
thinking grew out of a delusion that the well-educated adopt concerning
immateriality, which they ascribe so broadly to spirits and to everything in
a spirit's life. Such a delusion could yield only one way to conceive of anything spiritual: that because it lacked matter, either it was too vague to be
grasped in any way or it was nothing at all. That is what "immaterial"
means, of course. The reality is diametrically opposed. If spirits were not
organic—and if angels were not made of organic substance—they would
not be able to speak or see or think.

In the other life, the most miraculous things present themselves to **1534**
the eyesight of spirits and angels, thanks to light radiating from its heavenly and spiritual origin in the Lord. These sights include parks, cities,

palaces, houses, the most beautiful kinds of atmosphere, and much else besides. See the continuation concerning light at the end of the present chapter [§§1619–1633].

Genesis 13

1. And Abram went up from Egypt—he and his wife and everything he had—and Lot with him, toward the south.

2. And Abram was very heavy with livestock, silver, and gold.

3. And he went on his journeys from the south all the way to Bethel, all the way to the place where his tent had been at the start, between Bethel and Ai,

4. to the place of the altar that he had made there in the beginning; and there Abram called on Jehovah's name.

5. And Lot too, who went with Abram, had flock and herd and tents.

6. And the land could not sustain them, to [allow them to] live together, because their gain was large and they could not live together.

7. And there was controversy between the herders of Abram's livestock and the herders of Lot's livestock. (And the Canaanite and the Perizzite were then living in the land.)

8. And Abram said to Lot, "Please, let us not have strife between me and you, and between my herders and your herders; because we are men who are brothers.

9. Is the whole land not before you? Please separate from me; if [you go] to the left, I will go right; if to the right, I will go left."

10. And Lot raised his eyes and saw the whole plain of the Jordan, that it was all well watered (before Jehovah had destroyed Sodom and Gomorrah), like the garden of Jehovah, like the land of Egypt as you come to Zoar.

11. And Lot chose for himself all the plain of the Jordan; and Lot set out from the east, and they separated, a man from his brother.

12. Abram lived in the land of Canaan, and Lot lived in the cities of the plain and pitched his tent as far as Sodom.

13. And the men of Sodom were very evil and sinful against Jehovah.

14. And Jehovah said to Abram, after Lot separated from him, "Please raise your eyes and look out from the place there where you are toward the north and toward the south and toward the east and toward the west,

15. because all the land that you see—to you I will give it, and to your seed forever.

16. And I will make your seed like the dust of the earth, in that if anyone can count the dust of the earth, your seed too will be counted.

17. Get up; walk through the land along its length and along its breadth, because to you I will give it."

18. And Abram pitched his tent, and he came and lived in the oak groves of Mamre, which is in Hebron; and there he built an altar to Jehovah.

Summary

THE present chapter deals with the Lord's outer self, which was to **1535** be united with his inner self. His outer self is his human quality; his inner self is his divine quality. The former is represented here by Lot and the latter by Abram.

What is described here is the state of the Lord's outer self as it was **1536** in his youth, when he first absorbed secular and religious knowledge. In other words, he pressed forward from that state more and more toward union with his inner self (verses 1, 2, 3, 4).

Quite a few obstacles to that union were still present in his outer **1537** self, however (verses 5, 6, 7), and yet he wanted to separate from them (verses 8, 9).

The Lord witnessed the outer self at its most beautiful, when united **1538** with the inner self. He also witnessed what it is like when not united to the inner self (verses 10, 11, 12, 13).

A promise that when the Lord's outer self united with his inner— **1539** when his human quality united with his divine quality—he would be given all authority (verses 14, 15, 16, 17).

The Lord's inner perception (verse 18).

Inner Meaning

TRUE history in the Word started in the last chapter, chapter 12, as **1540** noted [§§1020, 1283, 1401, 1403, 1408:1]. Up to that point—or rather up to Eber's story—it was fiction.

The continuing story of Abram here symbolizes the Lord, in an inner sense. Specifically, it symbolizes his early life and what this was like before his outer self united with his inner self to form a single entity, that is, before his outer self likewise became heavenly and divine.

The historical events are what *represent* the Lord; the actual words *symbolize* the things represented.

Because it is a history, though, readers cannot help fixing their attention on those events. This is especially true today, when few if any believe that an inner meaning exists, let alone that it permeates every single word. Perhaps they will still fail to acknowledge an inner sense, even when it has been so clearly demonstrated. Part of the reason may also be that the deeper meaning appears to depart so radically from the literal meaning that it can hardly be recognized. But the reader can see [that there is such a meaning] simply by considering the fact that the historical details cannot possibly be Scripture, since in isolation from any inner meaning they contain no more divinity than other stories do. The deeper sense is what makes the narrative divine.

[2] The inner meaning is the real Word, as much of revelation discloses. One example is the statement, "Out of Egypt I called my child" (Matthew 2:15), and there are many others besides. After his resurrection, the Lord himself also taught his disciples what it was that Moses and the prophets had written about him (Luke 24:27). In doing so, he showed them that nothing is written in the Word that does not focus on him, his kingdom, and the church. These are the spiritual and heavenly subjects of the Word. What the literal meaning contains is worldly, bodily, and earthly, for the most part, and could never constitute the Lord's Word.

Modern people are such that this dimension is all they perceive; what the spiritual and heavenly dimension is they scarcely know. Not so the people of the earliest church and the ancient church. Had they lived today and read the Word, they would have paid no attention to the literal meaning (which they would view as insignificant) but only to the deeper meaning. They are stunned that anyone could perceive the Word in any other way. For this reason, all the books of the ancients were written to express something different in an inner sense than in the literal sense.

1541   [Genesis 13:1.] *And Abram went up from Egypt—he and his wife and everything he had—and Lot with him, toward the south.*

These words and the following verses of the current chapter also represent the Lord in an inner sense; they continue to treat of his life from the time when he was a boy.

Abram went up from Egypt means that the Lord rose above facts, which deserted him. In an inner sense, *Abram* is the Lord—here, the Lord while still a youth; *Egypt* is factual knowledge here as before [§§1164–1165, 1462]. *He and his wife* symbolizes heavenly truth that the Lord then possessed. *And everything he had* symbolizes everything connected with heavenly attributes. *And Lot with him* symbolizes the senses. *Toward the south* means into heavenly light.

In their inner sense these words and the following verses of the current chapter also represent the Lord; they continue to treat of his life from the time when he was a boy. This can be seen from remarks and illustrations in the previous chapter and from what follows [§§1544, 1548, 1556, 1557, 1560]. Above all, it can be seen from the fact that this is the Lord's Word, that it has come down from him through heaven, and that as a result not the smallest part of a word has been written in it that does not involve secrets of heaven. Nothing derived from such a source could ever be otherwise.

1542

It has already been shown that the inner meaning has to do with the Lord's education when he was young [§§1402, 1459–1502].

There are two things in us that prevent us from becoming heavenly. One belongs to our intellectual side; the other, to our volitional side. The intellectual one is the useless facts that we soak up in youth and early adulthood. The volitional one is the gratification of our most cherished cravings. Both block us from attaining heavenly goals. They need to be shaken off first, and when they have been, then we can enter first into the light reflected by heavenly things and finally into heavenly light itself.

[2] Since the Lord was born like any other person, and needed to be taught like any other person, he too had to learn facts, a situation that was represented and symbolized by Abram's stay in Egypt. Superfluous knowledge eventually parted from him, and this was represented by verse 20 of the last chapter: "Pharaoh gave orders concerning Abram to his men, and they sent him away, and his wife, and all that he had." Sensual gratification—which the urges of our will lead us into, and which compose our sense-oriented (or most superficial) self—also disappeared from him. This is represented in the current chapter by Lot's separation from Abram, since Lot represents our sense-oriented side.

Abram went up from Egypt means that the Lord rose above facts, which took leave of him, as can be seen from the symbolism of *Abram,* in that he represents the Lord. It is also established by the symbolism of

1543

Egypt as factual knowledge, and by the symbolism of *going up.* "Going up" is the expression used when one rises up out of lower things (facts) toward higher things (heavenly qualities). So in the Word, going up from Egypt into the land of Canaan—an activity mentioned frequently—involves the same idea.

1544 In an inner sense, *Abram* is the Lord—here, the Lord while still a youth—and *Egypt* is factual knowledge. This has already been demonstrated.

1545 The symbolism of *he and his wife* as heavenly truth that the Lord then possessed can be seen from the symbolism of *him*—Abram—as the Lord. And because Abram symbolizes the Lord, he also symbolizes something heavenly in the Lord. Our humanness comes from the qualities we possess. The Lord's humanity was the result of heavenly qualities, because he was the only heavenly person who ever lived. He was heavenliness itself. So "Abram" and more especially "Abraham" mean heavenly traits.

The symbolism is also visible from that of a *wife* as truth attached to a heavenly quality, shown above at §1468.

The fact that it was heavenly truth, or truth from heavenly origins, can be seen from the mention of *him* first and of *his wife* second. Heavenly truth differs from truth that is heavenly. Heavenly truth originates in a heavenly quality, but truth that is heavenly originates with truth and is grafted onto heavenly qualities through religious knowledge.

1546 The symbolism of *and everything he had* as everything connected with heavenly attributes can now be seen from the above.

1547 The symbolism of *and Lot with him* as the senses was briefly pointed out above at §1428. Because the present passage discusses Lot in a specific way, the aspect of the Lord that he represents needs to be known. Pharaoh represented facts, which eventually sent the Lord away. *Lot,* though, symbolizes the sensory dimension, that is, the outer self and its pleasures, which are pleasures of the senses and are therefore our most superficial aspect. They tend to ensnare us when we are young and lead us away from goodness. After all, the more we indulge in the pleasures that rise out of our appetites, the more we are distracted from the heavenly qualities of love and charity. Self-love and materialism, which heavenly love can never harmonize with, permeate those pleasures. Pleasures perfectly consistent with heavenly values exist too, however, and they look the same on the outside (see a discussion of them above at §§945, 994, 995, 997). But pleasures that rise out of our cravings need to be controlled and purified, because they block the entry to heavenly regions. The current chapter deals with the latter kind of pleasures, not the former, under the image of Lot in his separation from Abram.

Here the message is that such pleasures were present, which is what "Lot was with him" means. Usually Lot symbolizes the outer self, though, as will become clear later [§1563].

The fact that *toward the south* means into heavenly light is established by the symbolism of the *south,* or noonday light, as a condition in which inner things are clear (discussed above at §1458). **1548**

There are two states that shine with heavenly light. The first is the one we enter in infancy. Most people recognize that little children have innocence and that they act in good and loving ways. These are heavenly traits, which the Lord first introduces us into, and he stores them up in us for use when we are older, and for use when we come into the other world. They are what are called the first remnant, described in many earlier places.

In the second state, we are introduced to spiritual and heavenly concepts by learning about them, and these concepts need to be grafted onto the heavenly gifts we have received since infancy.

In the Lord, those concepts were grafted onto his earliest heavenly gifts. From this he gained light, and the light is called "the south" here.

Genesis 13:2. *And Abram was very heavy with livestock, silver, and gold.* **1549**

Abram was very heavy with livestock symbolizes the good impulses with which the Lord then grew rich. *Silver* symbolizes true ideas. *And gold* symbolizes the good effects that result from truth.

The symbolism of *Abram was very heavy with livestock* as good impulses is established by the symbolism of *livestock* and of a flock as what is good. This was discussed earlier, in §§343 and 415. **1550**

The symbolism of *silver* as true ideas can be seen from the symbolism of silver as what is true. **1551**

The earliest people compared the goodness and truth in human beings to different metals. The deepest goodness or blessings, which are heavenly ones, resulting from love for the Lord, they compared to gold. The truth that rises out of these blessings they compared to silver. Lowlier benefits, on the other hand, or earthly blessings, they compared to bronze, while they compared lowlier kinds of truth to iron. What is more, they did not merely compare them to these metals, they also called them by the names of the metals. From this they also derived the practice of comparing different eras to the same metals and calling them the Golden, Silver, Bronze, and Iron Ages, in that order. The Golden Age was the era of the earliest church, a heavenly race. The Silver Age was the era of the ancient church, which was a spiritual race. The Bronze Age was the era of the next church, and the Iron Age followed it.

Similar things were symbolized by the statue Nebuchadnezzar saw in his dream,

> its head made of *fine gold,* its chest and arms of *silver,* its belly and thighs of *bronze,* and its shins of *iron.* (Daniel 2:32, 33)

The fact that they would come in this order, or that the different eras of the church had come in this order, can be seen in the same chapter of that prophet.

[2] The following passages show that wherever silver is mentioned in the Word, on an inner level it symbolizes truth, and in an opposite sense falsity. In Isaiah:

> For *bronze* I will bring in *gold,* and for *iron* I will bring in *silver;* and for wood, bronze; and for stones, iron. And I will make peace your property, and justice your taskmaster. (Isaiah 60:17)

The meaning of each metal is plain to see here. The passage deals with the Lord's Coming, his kingdom, and the heavenly church. "For bronze, gold" is heavenly good in place of earthly good. "For iron, silver" is spiritual truth in place of earthly truth. "For wood, bronze" is earthly good in place of good on the bodily plane. "For stones, iron" is earthly truth in place of truth on the plane of the senses. In the same author:

> Oh, everyone who is thirsty, come to the water, and whoever does not have *silver,* come, buy and eat! (Isaiah 55:1)

One who lacks silver is one who knows no truth and yet does the good deeds of neighborly love. Many people within the church and many nations outside it are like this. [3] In the same author:

> For me the islands will await, as will the ships of Tarshish, from the start, to lead your children from far away—their *silver* and their *gold* with them—to the name of Jehovah your God and to the Holy One of Israel. (Isaiah 60:9)

This treats specifically of a new church (or a church among non-Jews) and generally of the Lord's kingdom. Ships of Tarshish stand for religious knowledge, silver for true ideas, and gold for good impulses, which will lead us to the name of Jehovah. In Ezekiel:

> You took the articles of your finery—made of my *gold* and of my *silver,* which I had given to you—and made yourself images of a male. (Ezekiel 16:17)

The gold here stands for knowledge of heavenly attributes and the silver for knowledge of spiritual ones. In the same author:

> You were adorned in *gold* and *silver,* and your clothing was fine linen and silk and embroidery. (Ezekiel 16:13)

This is about Jerusalem, which symbolizes the Lord's church, whose finery is depicted this way. In the same author:

> How wise you are! Nothing secret has lain hidden from you. In your wisdom and in your understanding you have made yourself riches, and you have made *gold* and *silver* for your treasuries. (Ezekiel 28:3, 4)

This passage concerns Tyre. Clearly the gold mentioned in it is a wealth of wisdom and the silver is a wealth of understanding. [4] In Joel:

> My *silver* and my *gold* you have stolen, and my good, desirable things you have taken into your temples. (Joel 3:5)

This is about Tyre, Sidon, and Philistia. They symbolize religious knowledge, which is the gold and silver they took into their temples. In Haggai:

> Those who are the choice of every nation will come, and I will fill this House with glory. Mine is the *silver* and mine the *gold.* Greater will the glory of this later house be than that of the earlier. (Haggai 2:7, 8, 9)

This is about the Lord's church, with which the gold and silver are associated. In Malachi:

> He will sit smelting and refining *silver* and will purify the children of Levi. (Malachi 3:3)

This passage tells of the Lord's Coming. In David:

> Jehovah's words: pure words, *silver* smelted in a crucible of earth, melted seven times. (Psalms 12:6)

Silver purified seven times stands for divine truth. When the children of Israel left Egypt, they were given this command:

> Seek—a woman from her neighbor, and from her houseguest—*articles of silver* and *articles of gold* and clothes, and place them on their sons and on their daughters, and plunder the Egyptians. (Exodus 3:22; 11:2, 3; 12:35, 36)

Anyone can see that the children of Israel would never have been told to rob and plunder the Egyptians in this way if such actions had not represented something hidden. What hidden meaning they represented can be deduced from the symbolism of silver, gold, clothes, and Egypt. Obviously it all represented something similar to Abram's heaviness here in silver and gold brought from Egypt.

[5] Just as silver symbolizes truth, in the opposite sense it symbolizes falsity, because people whose thinking is false consider falsity true, and this too can be seen in [Moses and] the prophets. In Moses:

> You shall not covet the *silver* and *gold* of the nations or take it for yourself; otherwise you might be ensnared by it, because it is an abomination to Jehovah your God. You shall utterly detest it. (Deuteronomy 7:25, 26)

The gold of the nations stands for evil and their silver for falsity. In the same author:

> You shall not make gods of *silver* beside me; and gods of *gold* you shall not make for yourselves. (Exodus 20:23)

These words mean nothing at all in the inner sense if they do not mean false notions and corrupt desires; false notions are gods of silver, and corrupt desires are gods of gold. In Isaiah:

> On that day they will each repudiate their *silver idols* and their *gold idols* that your hands made for you—a sin. (Isaiah 31:7)

Silver idols and gold idols stand for something similar. "Your hands made them" stands for the fact that they originate in self-centeredness. In Jeremiah:

> They are becoming foolish and growing stupid. Their education in worthless things is a piece of wood. *Silver* beaten thin is brought from Tarshish and *gold* from Uphaz, the work of the artist and of the metal-smith's hands; blue-violet and red-violet fabric is their clothing—all of them the work of the wise. (Jeremiah 10:8, 9)

Obviously, these words have a similar meaning.

1552   The symbolism of *and gold* as the good effects that result from truth can be seen from the symbolism of gold as heavenly good, or the good that comes of wisdom and love. This is established by the proofs just above and by remarks earlier at §113. The fact that in this verse it means good effects resulting *from truth* follows from the message of the last chapter: that the Lord united intuitive truth with heavenly qualities [§§1495–1497].

Genesis 13:3. *And he went on his journeys, from the south all the way to Bethel, all the way to the place where his tent had been at the start, between Bethel and Ai.* **1553**

He went on his journeys means according to plan. *From the south all the way to Bethel* means from the light of understanding into the light of wisdom. *All the way to the place where his tent had been before* means to the holy traits that existed before he became steeped in knowledge. *Between Bethel and Ai* here as before symbolizes heavenly and worldly categories of knowledge.

He went on his journeys means according to plan, as can be seen from the symbolism of *journeys* or travels as further progress (discussed in §1457). Since the progress followed a plan, the journeys here have this meaning and no other. **1554**

From infancy, the Lord advanced toward heavenly goals and reached them exactly according to the divine plan. The nature of this plan is depicted by Abram on an inner level.

Everyone that the Lord creates anew also follows such a plan, although it differs from person to person, depending on the individual's nature and bent of mind. What plan an individual is following while being reborn, though, is not known to a single soul (not even to angels, except in a shadowy way) but only to the Lord.

From the south all the way to Bethel means from the light of understanding into the light of wisdom. This is established by the symbolism of the *south* as the light of understanding or, to put it another way, as a condition in which inner things are clear (dealt with earlier, in §1458), and by the symbolism of *Bethel* as heavenly light rising out of religious knowledge (dealt with earlier, in §1453). **1555**

The light we gain through knowledge of faith's true concepts and good actions is called the light of understanding, whereas the light of wisdom is part and parcel of life and is gained from life. The light of understanding relates to our intellectual side, or our intellect, while wisdom's light relates to our volitional side, or our life.

[2] Few if any know how we are led to true wisdom. Understanding is not wisdom but leads to wisdom, since to understand what is true and good is not to *be* true or good. To be wise *is* to be so. Wisdom is exclusively a question of the way we live, of actually being wise. Wisdom, or in other words, life, is what secular and religious knowledge introduces us into.

We each have two sides: intellect and will. The will is the first part; the intellect comes second. The kind of life we have after death depends on our volitional side, not our intellectual side. From infancy through adolescence the Lord forms our will by instilling innocence in us and goodwill toward our parents, caretakers, and playmates, and by other means that we are unaware of. These are heavenly attributes. If these heavenly attributes were not first instilled in us as babies, children, and youths, we could never become human. That is how the first level is formed.

[3] We are not human, however, unless also equipped with an intellect. The will alone does not make us human, but intellect together with will. Moreover, we cannot develop an intellect without both secular and religious knowledge. As a result, we need to absorb this knowledge by degrees, beginning in childhood. That is how the second level is formed.

When the intellectual side has received an education in both kinds of knowledge, especially the knowledge of truth and goodness, then we can first be reborn. And when we are being reborn, the Lord uses that knowledge to graft true ideas and good impulses onto the heavenly gifts we have received from him since infancy. In this way our intellectual abilities fuse with our heavenly gifts. When the Lord has united the two in this way, we receive the gift of love for others—a product of conscience—and start to act on it. This is how we first receive new life, which comes gradually. The light we enjoy in this new life is called wisdom, which now plays the leading role and overshadows any mere ability to understand. That is how the third level is formed.

If we become this kind of person during bodily life, in the next life we are constantly being perfected.

This indicates what the light of understanding is and what the light of wisdom is.

1556 *All the way to the place where his tent had been before* means to the holy traits that existed before he became steeped in knowledge. This can be seen from the symbolism of a *tent* as holy attributes of faith (dealt with previously at §§414, 1452) and from the remarks just above.

Consequently, it means that the Lord returned to the heavenly qualities he possessed before he had absorbed factual and religious knowledge, as can be seen from the words of the last chapter: "And Abram moved from there onto a mountain to the east of Bethel and spread his tent" (verse 8 [§§1450–1455]). This was before he set out for Egypt, that is, before the Lord became steeped in factual and religious knowledge.

1557 *Between Bethel and Ai* symbolizes heavenly and worldly categories of knowledge. This can be seen from the symbolism of *Bethel* as the light of wisdom, coming by way of religious knowledge (§1453), and from the symbolism of *Ai* as the light shed by worldly knowledge (also mentioned in §1453).

The discussion in §1453 shows what kind of state the Lord was then in: a youthful one, which is such that worldly concerns are present. Worldly concerns cannot be dispelled until truth and goodness are grafted onto our heavenly qualities by means of knowledge. We cannot possibly distinguish between heavenly and worldly values until we learn to recognize what belongs to heaven and what to the world. Knowledge brings a vague, general idea into clear focus, and the clearer the idea becomes as a result of knowledge, the more easily we can isolate worldly influences.

[2] But that youthful state is still holy, because it is innocent. Ignorance is completely incapable of doing away with holiness as long as innocence is present within it, since holiness makes its home in ignorance that is innocent. In any human being but the Lord, holiness can dwell only in ignorance; if it does not dwell in ignorance, it is not holy. Even among the angels themselves, who enjoy the greatest possible light from understanding and wisdom, holiness resides in ignorance. They recognize and admit that they know nothing on their own, that anything they do know comes from the Lord. They also recognize and admit that all their learning, their understanding, and their wisdom is nothing compared to the Lord's infinite knowledge and therefore that theirs is ignorance. If we fail to acknowledge that what we do not know amounts to infinitely more than what we do know, we cannot experience the holy ignorance of the angels.

[3] Holy ignorance does not consist in knowing less than other people but in admitting that we know nothing on our own and that the things we do not know infinitely outnumber the things we do know. It consists especially in acknowledging that facts and intellectual pursuits are far less important than heavenly concerns; in other words, what we understand is far less important than how we live.

As for the Lord, because he was going to unite his human aspects to his divine ones, he advanced according to the ordained plan and now arrived at the type of heavenly state he had experienced in his youth. Worldly concerns are present in this state too. He moved on from there into a more heavenly state and finally into the heavenly state experienced in infancy, in which he fully united his human and divine natures.

Genesis 13:4. *To the place of the altar that he had made there in the beginning, and there Abram called on Jehovah's name.*

1558

To the place of the altar symbolizes sacred elements of worship. *That he had made there in the beginning* means adopted by him when he was young. *And there Abram called on Jehovah's name* symbolizes inward worship in that state.

1559   The symbolism of *to the place of the altar* as sacred elements of worship can be seen from the symbolism of an *altar* as the main representative object in worship, discussed in §921.

1560   *That he had made in the beginning* means adopted by him when he was young, as can be seen from the discussion of verse 8 of the previous chapter [§§1450–1455]. The present verse says "in the beginning" and the last verse said "at the start" because this was before the Lord had been trained in secular and religious knowledge. A start means every phase we pass through before education. Once we commence our education, it is called a beginning.

1561   The symbolism of *and there Abram called on Jehovah's name* as inward worship in that state is established by the symbolism of *calling on Jehovah's name,* dealt with before, in §§440, 1455. The reason this verse mentions an altar and invocation of Jehovah's name, just as Genesis 12:8 did, is that the two phases are similar. The difference is that the present phase has more light to it than the previous one. Knowledge grafted onto the earlier phase, as described [§§1458, 1548], adds clarity to it.

When truth and goodness are connected through knowledge to the earlier, heavenly quality, its resulting active power is depicted in this way. Worship itself is simply action emerging from the heavenly character within. The heavenly core could never exist without activity. Worship is the first act that it emerges into, because that is how it expresses itself, since it senses joy in worship. Every good deed of love and charity is the essence itself of the active power.

1562   Genesis 13:5. *And Lot too, who went with Abram, had flock and herd and tents.*

And Lot too, who went with Abram, symbolizes the outer self that the Lord had. *Had flock and herd and tents* symbolizes that which the outer self has in abundance. *Flock and herd* are the possessions of the outer self, while *tents* are the worship practiced by the outer self, all of which separated itself from his inner self.

1563   The symbolism of *and Lot too, who went with Abram,* as the outer self that the Lord had can be seen from the representation of *Lot* as the sensory self or, what is the same, the outer self.

We each have an inward part and an outward part or, to put it another way, an inner self and an outer self, as everyone in the church knows; for more, see above at §§978, 994, 995, 1015.

The outer self receives its life chiefly from the inner self, that is, from its spirit, or soul. This is the origin of its actual life force as a general whole. That force cannot be received by the outer self in a detailed or distinct way unless there is an opening of its organic vessels, which are necessary for reception of the specific influences from the inner self, down to the most minute. These organic vessels necessary for reception are not opened up except by means of the senses—mainly hearing and sight. When they do open, the inner self can enter in with its specific and minute details. Those vessels are opened by means of the senses through facts and religious knowledge (properties of the intellect), and also through appetites and pleasures (properties of the will).

[2] The plain and inevitable consequence is that the outer self will then be infiltrated by secular and religious concepts incompatible with spiritual truth and by appetites and pleasures incompatible with heavenly goodness. All the ones that focus on personal, worldly, and earthly rewards as their goals fall into this category. When we focus on them as our goals, they drag our outer self out toward the surface and downward. In this way they distance the outer self from the inner. If these distractions are not first dispelled, the inner self cannot possibly come into harmony with the outer self, so before the inner self can come into harmony with the outer self, such things must first be put aside.

The fact that they were put aside or separated in the Lord is represented and symbolized by Lot's separation from Abram.

The symbolism of *he had flock and herd and tents* as that which the outer self has in abundance can be seen from the symbolism of *flock, herd,* and *tents,* discussed directly below. Here they symbolize the possessions of the outer self, because Lot, again, represents the Lord's outer self.

1564

The outer self harbors two kinds of traits: those compatible with the inner self and those incompatible. The flock, herd, and tents here symbolize incompatible traits, as indicated by the words that follow in verse 7: "And there was controversy between the herders of Abram's livestock and the herders of Lot's livestock."

The fact that *flock and herd* are the possessions of the outer self can be seen from the symbolism of *flock* and *herd* as goodness, treated of in §§343 and 415. Here, though, they symbolize things that need to detach,

1565

or nongoodness, since they are depicted as belonging to Lot, who separated from Abram. The fact that flock and herd are nongoodness as well can be seen from the following passages in the Word. In Zephaniah:

> I will destroy [everything] in you, so that you are without inhabitant; and the region of the sea will consist of dwellings excavated for shepherds and folds for the *flock.* (Zephaniah 2:5, 6)

In Jeremiah:

> In you I will scatter shepherd and *flock,* and in you I will scatter the farmer and the farmer's yoked team. (Jeremiah 51:23)

In the same author:

> Go up to Arabia and lay waste to the children of the east. [Others] will take their *tents* and their *flocks.* (Jeremiah 49:28, 29)

1566   *Tents* are the worship practiced by the outer self, which separated from inward [worship]. This can be seen from the symbolism of a *tent* as the holiness of worship (§414) and from the representation of Lot as the outer self, which is portrayed as having "tents," or worship. In the opposite sense, tents symbolize worship that is not holy, as can also be seen from the following places in the Word. In Hosea:

> The nettle will inherit them, the bramble will be in their *tents.* (Hosea 9:6)

In Habakkuk:

> I saw the *tents* of Cushan; the tent curtains of Midian's land shook; against the rivers Jehovah raged. (Habakkuk 3:7, 8)

In Jeremiah:

> Shepherds and their flocks will come to the daughter of Zion. They will fix their *tents* opposite her all around. They will each graze their space. (Jeremiah 6:3)

In David:

> He struck every firstborn in Egypt, the beginning of their strength in the *tents* of Ham. (Psalms 78:51)

In the same author:

> I have chosen to stand at the threshold in the house of my God rather than reside in *tents* of ungodliness. (Psalms 84:10)

Genesis 13:6. *And the land could not sustain them, to [allow them to]* **1567** *live together, because their gain was large and they could not live together.*

The land could not sustain them, to [allow them to] live together, means that different aspects of his deeper, heavenly dimension could not coexist with those things. *Because their gain was large and they could not live together* means that the gains of his inner self were incompatible with gains of his outer self.

The land could not sustain them, to [allow them to] live together, means **1568** that different aspects of his deeper, heavenly dimension could not coexist with those things, that is, with the things that Lot symbolizes here. To repeat, Abram represents the Lord—here, his inner self. Lot, though, represents his outer self—here, elements that needed to be separated from his outer self, since inward elements could not live together with them.

The outer self has many characteristics that the inner self *can* live with. Positive emotions and the pleasures and gratifications that rise out of them are an example, because they are effects of the inner self's good qualities and of its joys and blessings. When they are the effects of these things, they correspond to them perfectly, and then the inner rather than the outer self lays claim to them. After all, an effect results not from an effect but from an efficient cause, as is recognized. For example, when neighborly love shines out from the face, it is not the face that is responsible but the love lying within and so shaping the face and causing the effect. Again, the innocence present in the expression and gestures of little children and so in the games they play with each other is attributable not to their expression or gestures but to the innocence flowing in through their soul from the Lord. So these are effects. The same is true in all other cases. The logical conclusion, then, is that the outer self contains many elements that can live together or harmonize with the inner self.

[2] On the other hand, there are also many elements that are out of harmony, or that the inner self cannot live with. Take everything that wells up out of self-love and materialism. Anything from that source focuses on oneself and the world as its goal. With this goal the heavenly impulses of love for the Lord and love for one's neighbor are incompatible. The latter look to the Lord, and to his kingdom and everything belonging to him, as their goal.

Self-love and materialism look either out toward the surface or downward for their aims. Love for the Lord and love for our neighbor, though, look inward or upward for their aims. This leads to the conclusion that they clash too sharply ever to coexist.

[3] To learn what creates correspondence and agreement between your outer self and your inner, and what creates discord, simply consider what aims predominate, or to put it another way, what type of love predominates. (The different kinds of love we have are aims, since whatever we love is what we focus on as our aim.) From this you will see what kind of life you presently have, and what kind of life you will have after death. The goals or—what is the same—the types of love that predominate are what shape our life. No one's life is ever anything else.

If elements that clash with eternal life (in other words, with spiritual and heavenly life, which is eternal life) are not put aside during bodily life, they will have to be put aside in the other world. If they cannot be put aside, we cannot help being unhappy forever.

[4] The reason for saying these things is to show that the outer self has traits that are compatible with the inner self and traits that are incompatible, and that compatible traits can never coexist with incompatible ones. They also show that compatible elements in the outer self come from the inner self, or rather from the Lord through the inner self, like a face that beams with charity—a face of charity—or like the innocence in a child's expression and gestures, as noted. Incompatible elements, though, belong to us and our demand for self-governance. This clarifies what it means that the land could not sustain them, to [allow them to] live together.

In an inner sense, this verse deals with the Lord, and since it deals with the Lord, it also deals with every likeness and image of him. To specify, it speaks of his kingdom, the church, and every person in his kingdom or church. So it depicts the way things stand with us humans. The way things stood with the Lord—before he had completely overcome evil (the Devil and hell) by his own might and in so doing become heavenly, divine, and Jehovah even in regard to his human quality—depends on what phase he was in.

1569 *Because their gain was large and they could not live together* means that the gains of his inner self were incompatible with gains of his outer self, as is established by the discussion just above.

1570 Genesis 13:7. *And there was controversy between the herders of Abram's livestock and the herders of Lot's livestock. (And the Canaanite and the Perizzite were then living in the land.)*

There was controversy between the herders of Abram's livestock and the herders of Lot's livestock means that his inner self and his outer did not agree; the *herders of Abram's livestock* are heavenly values, while the *herders of Lot's livestock* are the values of the senses. *And the Canaanite and the Perizzite were then living in the land* symbolizes evil and falsity in his outer self.

There was controversy between the herders of Abram's livestock and the **1571** *herders of Lot's livestock* means that his inner self and his outer did not agree. This can be seen from the symbolism of *livestock herders* as people who teach and consequently as elements of worship, as anyone can recognize. As a result, there is no need to take time proving it from the Word.

This clause looks back to the things called "tents" above in verse 5, which symbolize worship, as pointed out there [§1566]. The words of the last verse, verse 6, allude to the things called "flock and herd" in verse 5, which are possessions, or "gain," as also pointed out there [§1565].

Because the subject here is worship, specifically the worship of the Lord's inner self and that of his outer self, and because these did not harmonize yet, the present verse says that *there was controversy between* the herders. *Abram* represents his inner self and *Lot* his outer self.

Worship especially, and in fact each individual aspect of worship, reveals the existence and nature of any variance between our inner and outer selves. When our inner self wants to focus on the purposes of God's kingdom in its worship, and our outer self wants to focus on the world's purposes, dissension arises and reveals itself in our worship. In fact even the smallest disagreement is noticed in heaven.

These are the concepts symbolized by the friction between the herders of Abram's livestock and the herders of Lot's livestock.

The reason is also added: that the Canaanite and the Perizzite were present in the land.

The *herders of Abram's livestock* are heavenly values, which belong **1572** to the inner self, while the *herders of Lot's livestock* are the values of the senses, which belong to the outer self, as established by the foregoing remarks.

By heavenly values, which are the herders of Abram's livestock, I mean heavenly values in worship, which belong to the inner self. The herders of Lot's livestock mean sensual values in worship, which belong to the outer self—values that are not compatible with the heavenly values of worship belonging to the inner self. What the case with these things is can be seen from previous explanations.

And the Canaanite and the Perizzite were then living in the land sym- **1573** bolizes evil and falsity in the Lord's outer self, as can be seen from the following: The *Canaanite* symbolizes evil in his outer self, inherited from his mother, as dealt with earlier, in §1444. And the *Perizzite* symbolizes falsity coming out of that evil, to be dealt with below [§1574].

His outer self contained evil inherited from his mother, as noted before; see §§1414 and 1444. It follows that falsity came out of this evil. Wherever there is inherited evil, there is also falsity. The one gives birth to the other. But evil cannot give birth to falsity until we have absorbed secular and religious knowledge. Evil has no other object it can act on or influence but these kinds of knowledge. So the evil that exists on our volitional side turns into falsity on the intellectual side. As a result, since this falsity in the Lord was spawned by his heredity, it too was inherited, unlike falsity that develops out of [consciously adopted] false premises. But it was located in his outer self, and his inner self could see that it was false.

[2] Because the Lord inherited evil from his mother before he was trained in secular and religious knowledge—before Abram emigrated to Egypt—verse 6 of the last chapter says that the Canaanite was in the land, but it does not say that the Perizzite was. Here, however, after he had absorbed both kinds of knowledge, it says that the Canaanite and the Perizzite were living in the land, which shows that a Canaanite symbolizes evil and a Perizzite falsity.

It also shows that mention of the Canaanite and Perizzite forms no part of a story line, since nothing above or below deals with them; and the same is true in verse 6 of the last chapter, which mentions a Canaanite. This makes it plain that the verse contains some kind of secret that can be known only from the inner meaning.

[3] Anyone might be astonished to hear that the Lord had evil inside him inherited from his mother, but since the present verse says so openly, and the inner sense is talking about the Lord, no one can doubt that it was so.

One human being could never be born to another without inheriting evil from him or her. But the evil we inherit from our father and the evil we inherit from our mother are very different. The evil we inherit from our father lies deep within and remains forever, because it can never be rooted out. This was not true of the Lord, because he was the son of his Father Jehovah and was therefore divine or Jehovah on the inside. The evil we inherit from our mother, conversely, belongs to our outer self. This evil was present in the Lord, and it is called the Canaanite in the land, while the falsity that develops from it is called a Perizzite.

The Lord, then, was born like any other person and had weaknesses like any other person.

[4] The fact that he underwent spiritual trials provides clear evidence that he inherited evil from his mother. No one who is free of evil can ever be tempted; it is the evil in us that is the source and means of our trials.

The Lord *was* tested and underwent trials so severe that no one could ever endure even a millionth of what he went through. He endured them alone and completely overcame evil (or the Devil and the whole of hell) by his own power. These things too are evident.

Luke says the following about the Lord's trials:

> Jesus was led in the spirit into the desert, where he was tested for forty days by the Devil, so that he did not eat during those days. But after the Devil had finished all his testing [of Jesus], he left Jesus alone for a while. So Jesus returned in the strength of the spirit into Galilee. (Luke 4:1, 2, 13, 14)

[5] And Mark says this:

> The spirit forced Jesus out into the wilderness, and he was in the wilderness forty days, where he was tested; and he was with the animals. (Mark 1:12, 13)

The animals symbolize hell. Furthermore, he was tested to the point of death, so that he sweated drops of blood:

> And when he was in agony, he prayed more intensely. And his sweat became as drops of blood falling on the ground. (Luke 22:44)

[6] No devil can ever put an angel to the test. As long as the angel remains in the Lord, evil spirits cannot even approach at a distance without being seized immediately by horror and terror. Much less could hell have approached the Lord if he had been born divine, free of any evil clinging to him from his mother.

[7] It is a common saying among preachers that the Lord also bore the wickedness and evil of the human race. But it would be impossible to draw wickedness and evil off into himself except by way of heredity. Divinity is not susceptible to evil.

In order to conquer evil by his own strength, therefore—which no human ever was or ever will be able to do—and become the sole embodiment of uprightness, the Lord wished to be born like any other person.

Otherwise being born would have been of no use to the Lord. He could have taken on a human identity without birth, as he sometimes did when appearing to the earliest church and to the prophets as well. In order to clothe himself also in evil that he could fight against and overthrow, however, he did come into the world, and by this means he would unite the divine nature to the human nature in himself.

[8] The Lord had no actual evil, or evil of his own, however, as he also says in John:

> Which one of you will denounce me for sin? (John 8:46)

These remarks now demonstrate clearly what it means when it says just above that there was controversy between the herders of Abram's livestock and the herders of Lot's livestock; the reason was that the Canaanite and the Perizzite were living in the land.

1574   The symbolism of a *Canaanite* as evil in his outer self, inherited from his mother, was shown above at §1444. The symbolism of a *Perizzite* as falsity coming out of that evil, though, can be seen from other passages in the Word mentioning a Perizzite. Concerning Jacob, for instance:

> Jacob said to Simeon and to Levi, "You have caused me trouble, making me stink with the inhabitant of the land—with the *Canaanites* and with the *Perizzites*—and my numbers are few; and they will gather against me and strike me, and I will be destroyed, I and my household." (Genesis 34:30)

Here too a Canaanite symbolizes evil, and a Perizzite, falsity. [2] In Joshua:

> Joshua said to Joseph's children, "If you are a numerous people, go up into the forest, and you are to carve out [a place] for yourself there in the land of the *Perizzite* and the *Rephaim,* if Mount Ephraim is too narrow for you." (Joshua 17:15)

The Perizzites symbolize falsity as a premise, while the Rephaim symbolize falsity as a conviction. These they were to annihilate, because in an inner sense Mount Ephraim is the capacity for understanding. [3] In Judges:

> After Joshua's death, the children of Israel asked Jehovah a question, saying, "Who will go up to the *Canaanites* for us at first, to fight against them?" And Jehovah said, "Judah will go up. See? I've given the land into his hand." And Judah said to Simeon his brother, "Go up with me into my allotment and we'll fight against the *Canaanite,* and I, yes

I, will go with you into your allotment." And Simeon went with him, and Judah went up, and Jehovah gave the *Canaanite* and the *Perizzite* into their hand. (Judges 1:1, 2, 3, 4, 5)

Judah too represents the Lord's heavenly qualities, while Simeon represents the spiritual qualities in him, which sprang from the heavenly ones. The Canaanite is the evil and the Perizzite is the falsity that he overcame. This was a divine answer, or prophecy, which should be understood in this way.

Genesis 13:8. *And Abram said to Lot, "Please, let us not have strife between me and you, and between my herders and your herders; because we are men who are brothers."*

1575

Abram said to Lot means that this is what his inner self said to his outer self. *Please, let us not have strife between me and you, and between my herders and your herders* means that there should be no discord between the two. *Because we are men who are brothers* means that in and of themselves they were unified.

Abram said to Lot means that this is what his inner self said to his outer self, as is established by the representation here of *Abram* as his inner self and from the representation of *Lot* as the outer self that needed to be separated. The reason Abram represents the inner self is that he is being seen in relation to Lot, who is the part of the outer self that needed to be separated.

1576

The outer self, as noted, contains attributes that harmonize and attributes that clash [§§1547, 1563–1564, 1568]. Those that clash are Lot, here, so those that harmonize are Abram—even the ones in the outer self, since they form a unit with the inner self and belong to the inner self.

Please, let us not have strife between me and you means that there should be no discord between the two, as can be seen from previous statements.

1577

The subject of the harmony or union between the inner and the outer self involves more secrets than can ever be told. The inner and outer selves in any individual never become one, and never have been or will be able to. They can do so only in the Lord, which is why he came into the world.

When we have been reborn, it seems as though they exist united in us, but they are the Lord's. Anything harmonious is the Lord's, whereas anything discordant is ours.

[2] The inner self has two elements: a heavenly one and a spiritual one. These two elements form a single whole when the spiritual element

comes from the heavenly one. To put the same thing another way, the inner self has two elements: goodness and truth. These two elements form a single whole when truth comes from goodness. Or to put it yet another way, the inner self has two elements: love and faith. These two elements form a single whole when faith comes from love. Or to put it yet again another way, the inner self has two elements: will and intellect. These two elements form a single whole when the intellect comes from the will.

The situation here can be grasped still more plainly by comparison with light from the sun. If light from the sun holds both warmth and illumination, as it does in springtime, it causes everything to grow and flourish. But if light from the sun holds no warmth, as it does in wintertime, it causes everything to droop and die.

[3] This shows what constitutes the inner self; what constitutes the outer self is evident as a consequence. Everything in the outer self is earthly. Our outer self is actually the same thing as our earthly self. Our inner self is said to unite with our outer self when the heavenly-spiritual dimension of the inner self exerts an influence on the earthly dimension of the outer self, causing them to join forces. The earthly dimension too becomes heavenly and spiritual as a result, but on a lower plane. Or, what is the same, the outer self too becomes heavenly and spiritual as a result, but in a more superficial way.

[4] The inner self and outer self are absolutely distinct from each other, because heavenly and spiritual stimuli are what affect the inner self, but earthly stimuli are what affect the outer self. However, even though they are distinct, they still become one, which they do when the heavenly-spiritual dimension of the inner self acts on the earthly dimension of the outer self and organizes it as its own.

Only in the Lord did the inner self become one with the outer. They have not become one in any other person except to the extent that the Lord has united and is uniting them. Love and charity, or goodness, is the only thing that unifies, and no love or charity at all—no goodness—exists unless it comes from the Lord.

This kind of union is what is aimed at in Abram's words here: "Please, let us not have strife between me and you, and between my herders and your herders; because we are men who are brothers." [5] The case with the words *between me and you, and between my herders and your herders* is this: The inner self has two aspects, heavenly and spiritual, that form a unit, as noted. Just as the inner self has these aspects, the outer self does too. Its heavenly aspect is called earthly good, and its spiritual aspect is called earthly truth. *Let us not have strife between me and you* has to do with what is good, that is, with preventing good in the inner self from parting ways with good in the outer self. *Let us not have strife between my herders and your herders* has to do with truth, that is, with preventing truth in the inner self from parting ways with truth in the outer self.

We are men who are brothers means that in and of themselves they [1578]
were unified, as can be seen from the symbolism of a *man who is a brother* as unity, specifically the union of goodness and truth.

Genesis 13:9. *"Is the whole land not before you? Please separate from me:* [1579]
if to the left, I will go right, and if to the right, I will go left."

Is the whole land not before you? symbolizes every benefit. *Please separate from me* means that nothing good can appear unless discordant factors cease to exist. *If to the left, I will go right, and if to the right, I will go left* symbolizes separation.

The symbolism of *Is the whole land not before you?* as every benefit [1580]
can be seen from the symbolism of *land* in a good sense—here, the land of Canaan—as something heavenly and so as something beneficial (discussed above at §§566, 620, 636, 662).

The inner self addresses the outer here, but what it addresses are the features of the outer self that clash. This is a common occurrence among people who notice in themselves some evil from which they want to separate, as they do in times of spiritual trial and battle. As those who have been through such trials and battles realize, they notice discordant elements inside themselves that they cannot get away from as long as the fight continues. Nevertheless they do still long to get away—so fervently, sometimes, that they grow angry with the evil and try to expel it. This is what is symbolized here.

Please separate from me means that nothing good can appear unless [1581]
discordant factors cease to exist. This can be seen from the remarks just above: that the inner self wants discordant factors in the outer self to *separate* because none of the benefits that constantly flow in from the inner self (or rather from the Lord through the inner self) can appear until those factors leave.

In regard to separation, we need to see that it is not a separation but a muting. In no one but the Lord can the evil in the outer self be entirely removed. Once we have acquired any, it remains. When it quiets down, though, it seems to go away, since it seems nonexistent. It does not quiet down to this point unless the Lord quiets it for us, but when it does, then good things first flow in from the Lord and affect our outer self.

This is the stage that the angels have reached. For all they can see, evil has separated from them, but in reality their situation is merely one of being withheld from evil and so one in which evil is muted to the point where it seems nonexistent. It is a mirage, then, and this the angels realize when they reflect on it.

1582   *If to the left, I will go right, and if to the right, I will go left,* symbolizes separation, as can be seen from the symbolism of *right and left.* Right or left is just relative direction. It is not a fixed quarter or a fixed place, as is evident from the fact that both east and west, both south and north can be on the right or the left, depending on the direction a person faces. The same is true of a location. The land of Canaan too could not have been described as being to the right or to the left except in a relative way.

Wherever the Lord is, that is the center; right and left are determined by it. The same was true of Abram, who represented the Lord. Whether he had gone off in one direction or the other, the representation would have stayed with him. The same was also true of the land; it would have been all the same, for instance, whether Abram had lived in the land of Canaan or elsewhere. Compare the situation of the highest ranking person at a table. The place where such a person sits is the head, and the other places are on the right or left accordingly. So speaking of going right or left was a standard way of expressing a choice, and it symbolized separation.

1583   Genesis 13:10. *And Lot raised his eyes and saw the whole plain of the Jordan, that it was all well watered (before Jehovah had destroyed Sodom and Gomorrah), like the garden of Jehovah, like the land of Egypt as you come to Zoar.*

And Lot raised his eyes means that his outer self was enlightened by his inner self. *And saw the whole plain of the Jordan* symbolizes the goodness and truth that existed in his outer self. *That it was all well watered* means that they are able to grow there. *Before Jehovah had destroyed Sodom and Gomorrah* symbolizes the outer self as destroyed by evil cravings and false or distorted convictions. *Like the garden of Jehovah* symbolizes the rational ideas of the outer self. *Like the land of Egypt as you come to Zoar* symbolizes facts acquired as a result of the desire for what is good.

The symbolism here is that the Lord witnessed his outer self at its most beautiful, when united with his inner self.

1584   *Lot raised his eyes* means that his outer self was enlightened by his inner self. This can be seen from the meaning of *raising one's eyes* as seeing and in an inner sense as perceiving. Here it means being enlightened, because it is said of *Lot,* or the outer self. When the outer self perceives what its own quality is when united with the inner self—in other words, when it is at its most beautiful—it is being enlightened by the inner self. It is experiencing divine vision, which is the topic of discussion here. No one can doubt that when the Lord was young his outer self often enjoyed this divine power of sight, because he alone was to unite his outer self with his inner. (His outer self was his human quality, but his inner self was his divine quality.)

And saw the whole plain of the Jordan symbolizes the goodness and truth that existed in his outer self, as can be seen from the symbolism of a *plain* and the *Jordan.* In an inner sense, the plain surrounding the Jordan symbolizes the outer self, with everything in it that is good or true.

1585

The reason the Jordan basin symbolizes these things is that the Jordan was a boundary for the land of Canaan. As previous remarks have shown, the land of Canaan symbolizes the Lord's kingdom and church, and specifically its heavenly and spiritual attributes [§§1, 566–567, 585, 620, 662, 1413, 1437, 1441], which is why it is also called the Holy Land and the heavenly Canaan. And since it symbolizes the Lord's kingdom and church, in the highest sense it symbolizes the Lord himself, who is the all-in-all of his kingdom and church. [2] As a consequence, everything in the land of Canaan carried a representative meaning. Sites in the middle of the land—its most central parts, in other words—represented the Lord's inner self. Mount Zion, for instance, represented his heavenly qualities, and Jerusalem, his spiritual ones. More distant locations represented traits more remote from internal ones. The most distant points—the borders—represented his outer self. Canaan had many borders; in general they were the two rivers of the Euphrates and the Jordan, and the sea as well. So the Euphrates and the Jordan represented his outward aspects. Here, then, the Jordan basin symbolizes—just as it represents—all the properties of his outer being. The case is similar when the land of Canaan stands for the Lord's kingdom in the heavens; similar when it stands for the Lord's church on earth; similar when it stands for the individual member of his kingdom or church; similar when it stands abstractly for the heavenly attributes of love; and so on.

[3] This is why almost all the cities and in fact all the mountains, hills, valleys, rivers, and other features of the land of Canaan played a representative role.

Because the river Euphrates was a boundary, it represented the sense impressions and facts that belong to the outer self, as shown earlier, in

§120. The Jordan and the Jordan plain did too, as the following passages demonstrate. In David:

> My God, my soul is bowing down upon me. Therefore I will remember you from the *land of Jordan,* and [I will remember] the Hermons from the little mountain. (Psalms 42:6)

The land of Jordan here stands for something lowly and accordingly something remote from heavenly qualities, like our superficial traits, which are remote from our deep ones.

[4] The children of Israel crossed the Jordan when they entered the land of Canaan, and at their crossing the river parted. This also represented entry to the inner self through the outer, and an individual's entry into the Lord's kingdom as well, among other things (Joshua 3:14–end; 4:1–end).

Because our outer self constantly attacks our inner self and tries to gain control over it, "the boast of the Jordan," or "the swelling pride of the Jordan," became a standard phrase among the prophets. In Jeremiah, for instance:

> How will you prove yourself the equal of horses? And in a land of peace you are smug; but how do you behave in the *swelling pride of the Jordan?* (Jeremiah 12:5)

The swelling pride of the Jordan stands for aspects of our outer self that rise up and try to dominate our inner self, as attempts at rationalization (the horses here) and a consequent smugness do. [5] In the same author:

> Edom will become a ruin. Look: like a lion he will go up from the *boast of the Jordan* to the dwelling of Ethan. (Jeremiah 49:17, 19)

The boast of the Jordan stands for pride lifted up by our outer self against the goodness and truth of our inner self. In Zechariah:

> Howl, fir tree, because the cedar has fallen, because the majestic ones have been ravaged; wail, oaks of Bashan, because the walled forest has come down. The sound of the wailing of the shepherds, because their majesty has been ravaged! The sound of the roaring of young lions, that the *boast of the Jordan* has been ravaged! (Zechariah 11:2, 3)

Numbers 34:12 shows that the Jordan was a boundary of the land of Canaan, and Joshua 15:5 shows that it was the eastern border of the land of Judah.

That it was all well watered means that they (goodness and truth) are able to grow there, as is established by the symbolism of *well-watered* ground; see above at §108. **1586**

Before Jehovah had destroyed Sodom and Gomorrah symbolizes the outer self as destroyed by evil cravings and false or distorted convictions. This can be seen from the symbolism of *Sodom* as evil cravings and from the symbolism of *Gomorrah* as distorted convictions. These two are what destroy our outer self and divide it from our inner self. These two were also what destroyed the earliest church before the Flood. Cravings for evil belong to the will, and distortions adopted as convictions belong to the intellect, and when the two of them take over, our whole outer self is destroyed. Once destroyed, it also detaches from our inner self; not that our soul, or spirit, separates from the body, but that the goodness and truth coming from our soul or spirit does. Then goodness and truth no longer influence us except in a distant way. (I will say more about this influence elsewhere, by the Lord's divine mercy.) **1587**

The Lord came into the world because the outer self in the human race had been ruined in this way and its link with the inner self (that is, with goodness and truth) had been broken. He came into the world, then, to join and unite his outer self with his inner, or in other words, to join and unite his human quality with his divine.

The present verse describes the character of the outer self when united to the inner, at least before Jehovah had destroyed Sodom and Gomorrah: it was like the garden of Jehovah, like the land of Egypt as you come to Zoar.

Like the garden of Jehovah symbolizes the rational ideas of the outer self. This can be seen from the symbolism of *Jehovah's garden* as intelligence (discussed in §100) and so as the rational plane, which is midway between the inner self and the outer. The rational plane is the same thing as the intelligence of the outer self. **1588**

The term *garden of Jehovah* is used when our rational mind is heavenly, or when it comes from a heavenly origin, as it did in the people of the earliest church. Isaiah speaks of it this way:

> Jehovah will comfort Zion, he will comfort all its wastelands, and he will make its wilderness like Eden and its desert like a *garden of Jehovah*. Joy and gladness will be found in it; acclamation and the voice of song. (Isaiah 51:3)

The term *garden of God,* on the other hand, is used when our rational mind is spiritual, or when it comes from a spiritual origin, as it did in the people of the ancient church. Ezekiel speaks of it this way:

> You were full of wisdom and perfect in beauty in Eden, the *garden of God.* (Ezekiel 28:12, 13)

Human rationality is compared to a garden because of a representative type of garden that appears in heaven. Human rationality is what presents itself in this way and no other, when something heavenly and spiritual from the Lord acts on it. In fact it even presents the sight of lush parks whose magnificence and beauty exceed anything the human imagination can invent. This is the effect that results when heavenly-spiritual light flows in from the Lord, as mentioned before in §§1042, 1043. It is not the pleasures and beauties themselves of these parks that touch the heart but the heavenly-spiritual entities alive inside them.

1589   *Like the land of Egypt as you come to Zoar* symbolizes facts acquired as a result of the desire for what is good, as the following symbolism indicates: *Egypt* (which is discussed in §§1164, 1165 and which is treated in a good sense in §1462) symbolizes factual knowledge. And *Zoar* symbolizes the desire for what is good. The city of Zoar was not far from Sodom, and it was where Lot escaped to when angels rescued him from the conflagration of Sodom, as reported in Genesis 19:20, 22, 30. Zoar is also mentioned in Genesis 14:2, 8; Deuteronomy 34:3; Isaiah 15:5; Jeremiah 48:34. Here too it symbolizes desires; and since it symbolizes the desire for what is good, in the opposite sense (which is the usual sense) it also symbolizes the desire for what is evil.

[2] Our outer self has three components: rationality, the facts we know, and our physical senses. Rationality lies within, knowledge is more superficial, and the physical senses form the surface. Rationality is what connects our inner and outer selves, and the nature of that connection depends on the nature of our rationality. (The physical senses here are sight and hearing.)

Our rational capacity, though, is worthless by itself, if our feelings or desires do not flow into it, activate it, and bring it to life. It follows, then, that the quality of our rational capacity mirrors the quality of our feelings. When a desire for goodness flows into our rational mind, it turns into a desire for truth there. The opposite happens when a desire for evil enters. And since the facts we know put themselves at the disposal of our

rational mind and serve as tools for its use, it also follows that our feelings act on the facts we possess and arrange them in some kind of order.

Nothing in our outer self ever shows any life except emotion. Positive emotions come down from the heavenly plane, or in other words,
from heavenly love, which bestows life on everything it touches. It even
brings life to negative emotions, or corrupt desires. [3] A loving goodness
constantly flows in from the Lord, and it flows through the inner self
into the outer. People under the sway of negative emotions or corrupt
desires pervert that goodness, but the life that comes with it still remains.

To understand this, look at the way physical objects receive the sun's
rays, by way of comparison. Some objects—diamonds, rubies, hyacinths,
sapphires, and other precious stones, for instance—take the light very
beautifully and turn it into gorgeous colors. Others do not but turn it
into hideous colors instead. Another illustration is the very character of
different people; some welcome the kindnesses of others with open arms,
but some turn those kindnesses to evil.

All of this indicates what factual knowledge acquired as a result of
the desire for goodness is—this being what "the land of Egypt as you
come to Zoar" symbolizes—when the rational mind is like a garden of
Jehovah.

The symbolism here is that the Lord witnessed his outer self at its **1590**
most beautiful, when united with his inner self. This can be seen from
the deeper meaning, in which Abram represents the Lord's inner self,
and Lot his outer self.

The beauty of the outer self when united to the inner self cannot be
described because it does not occur in any other human being than the
Lord. Any such beauty that does occur in a person or angel comes from
the Lord. It can be seen in the image of the Lord's outward self as this
appears in the heavens (see §§553, 1530), but only to a very small degree.

The three heavens are images of the Lord's outer being, and their
beauty cannot be described in any way that will present a true, comprehensible idea of it to anyone. Just as everything in the Lord is infinite, so
everything in heaven is limitless. Heaven's boundlessness is an image of
the Lord's infinity.

Genesis 13:11. *And Lot chose for himself all the plain of the Jordan; and* **1591**
Lot set out from the east, and they separated, a man from his brother.

Lot chose for himself all the plain of the Jordan symbolizes the outer
self and its character. *And Lot set out from the east* symbolizes those traits

in the outer self that withdraw from heavenly love. *And they separated, a man from his brother,* means that those things separate.

1592 The symbolism of *Lot chose for himself all the plain of the Jordan* as the outer self and its character is established by the symbolism of the *plain of the Jordan* as the outer self (discussed at the last verse [§1585]).

The beauty of the outer self when united with the inner self is depicted in the previous verse, but its ugliness when disconnected is depicted in this verse and the next two.

1593 The symbolism of *and Lot set out from the east* as those traits in the outer self that withdraw from heavenly love can be seen from the symbolism of the *east* as the Lord and so as every heavenly quality (discussed earlier, at §101). Since the east symbolizes the Lord, it follows that the east here means his inner self, which was divine. So *Lot's setting out from the east* here symbolizes the fact that his outer self withdrew from his inner.

1594 It follows from this that *they separated, a man from his brother,* means that those things separate. It was said above at verse 8 what a *man who is a brother* is, namely, unity [§1578]. So *separating themselves, a man from his brother,* is division.

People do not know what divides the outer self from the inner, and the reasons are many. One is that they do not realize (or if they have heard, do not believe) that any inner self exists. Another is that they do not realize (or if they have heard, do not believe) that self-love and its desires are what divide; so do materialism and its desires, although not as much as self-love.

[2] The reason they do not realize (and if they have heard, do not believe) that any inner self exists is that they live enmeshed in their body and senses, which can never glimpse anything deeper. Inner qualities can see what is more superficial, but superficial qualities can never see what is deeper. Take sight as an example. Our inner eye can see what our outer eye sees, but our outer eye could never see what our inner eye does. Again, true understanding and rationality can perceive the existence and nature of bare facts, but the reverse is not true.

Another reason is that they do not believe in a spirit that separates from the body when people die. They barely believe in any inner life at all, which they call the soul. When people who focus on their senses and body think about the separation of the spirit from the body, it strikes them as impossible, because they locate life in the body. They confirm themselves in this view by the argument that brute animals too are alive and yet do not live on after death, and by many other arguments as well. They adopt all these attitudes because they live enmeshed in their body and senses, and this kind of life, regarded in itself, is almost exactly the same as the life of brute animals. The only difference is that people are capable of thinking and of reasoning about subjects that come up; and yet they do not then reflect on this advantage they have over animals. [3] But this is not the main factor dividing the outer self from the inner, because most people succumb to such disbelief—the best-educated more than the simple.

The chief divisive factor is self-love; materialism too, but not so much as self-love. The reason people are unaware of this is that they live lives devoid of neighborly love, and when they do, they are incapable of seeing that a life of self-love and self-centered cravings is as contrary to heavenly love as it is. In addition, self-love and its cravings then harbor a burning flame that yields pleasure, which touches their life so powerfully that they can scarcely believe it does not constitute eternal happiness itself. As a result, many of them also consider eternal happiness to consist in becoming influential after the life of the body ends, and being waited on by others, even by angels. This despite the fact that they have no interest themselves in serving anyone, unless for the ulterior, selfish motive of having others serve them. They say at the time that they want to serve only the Lord, but this is a lie, because people motivated by self-love want even the Lord to serve them, and the less it happens, the further they withdraw. In their heart, then, they carry the desire to become the Lord themselves and to rule the whole universe. Since most—or rather all—people are like this, you can imagine what kind of reign that would be! Would it not be the government of hell, where each person loves herself or himself more than any other? Such is the inherent character of self-love. All this evidence reveals the nature of self-love. So does the fact that self-love conceals within itself hatred against anyone who does not submit to us as a slave, and that because it conceals hatred, it also conceals vengefulness, cruelty, deceit, and many other unspeakable evils.

[4] Mutual love, however—which is the only heavenly love—consists in not merely saying but admitting and believing that we ourselves are extremely unworthy; that we are vile, disgusting creatures whom the Lord in his infinite mercy is always withdrawing and withholding from hell, although we are always attempting and even begging to throw ourselves headlong into it. The reason we need to admit and believe this is that it is true. We are asked to admit and believe it not because the Lord or any

angel wants us to surrender; the aim is to prevent us from puffing up with pride despite the fact that we are like this. It would be like hearing dung claim to be pure gold, or a fly in an outhouse claim to be a bird of paradise. So the more we admit and believe that we are what we are, the more we back away from self-love and self-centered desires and shudder at ourselves. The more we do this, the more we receive heavenly love from the Lord—that is, mutual love, which is the desire to serve everyone. These are the people meant by the least who become the greatest in the Lord's kingdom (Matthew 20:26, 27, 28; Luke 9:46, 47, 48).

[5] This evidence shows what the chief means of dividing the outer self from the inner is: self-love. It also shows that the chief means of uniting the outer self to the inner is mutual love, which is absolutely impossible to acquire until self-love withdraws. The two are, after all, diametrically opposed.

Our inner self is simply mutual love. Our actual spirit, or soul, is our intermediate self, which lives on after death. It is organic, since it is linked to our body while we live in the world. This intermediate self, this soul or spirit of ours, is not our inner self, but the inner self is present within it when mutual love is present. The qualities of the inner self are the Lord's, so that our inner self can be said to *be* the Lord. But as long as angels, or human beings, live a life of mutual love, the Lord gives them a heavenly sense of autonomy, so that for all they can tell they are doing good on their own. As a consequence, the inner self is attributed to them as if it was theirs. However, those who love one another admit and believe that no goodness or truth is theirs but that all of it is the Lord's. The ability to love another as themselves (and more especially to love another more than themselves, if they resemble angels) is a gift from the Lord, as they also admit and believe. This gift and its blessings retreat from their grasp the more they retreat from acknowledging that it is the Lord's.

1595   Genesis 13:12. *Abram lived in the land of Canaan, and Lot lived in the cities of the plain and pitched his tent as far as Sodom.*

Abram lived in the land of Canaan symbolizes the inner self and its focus on the heavenly attributes of love. *And Lot lived in the cities of the plain* symbolizes the outer self and its focus on facts. *And pitched his tent as far as Sodom* means extending to the point of corrupt desire.

1596   The symbolism of *Abram lived in the land of Canaan* as the inner self and its focus on the heavenly attributes of love is established by the symbolism of the *land of Canaan* as the heavenly attributes of love, discussed several times already.

The symbolism of *and Lot lived in the cities of the plain* as the outer self and its focus on facts can be seen from the representation of *Lot* as the outer self and from the symbolism of a city or *cities* as doctrinal tenets. Doctrinal teachings in and of themselves are nothing but facts, when they are portrayed as belonging to the outer self, once this has separated from the inner. The symbolism of cities as tenets of doctrine, both true and false, was shown above in §402.

1597

And pitched his tent as far as Sodom means extending to the point of corrupt desire. This is established by the symbolism of *Sodom* as such desire (mentioned above at verse 10 [§1587]).

1598

These words correspond to those in verse 10 above saying that the plain of the Jordan was all well watered like the garden of Jehovah, like the land of Egypt as you come to Zoar. The subject there was the outer self when it has become one with the inner self, and "the land of Egypt as you come to Zoar" symbolized facts acquired as a result of positive emotions. Lot's settling in the cities of the plain and pitching his tent as far as Sodom here symbolizes the outer self when it has *not* become one with the inner, and the cities symbolize facts acquired as a result of negative emotions, or of corrupt desires. Verse 10 portrayed the beauty of the outer self when united with the inner, but the present verse depicts its ugliness when not united. The next verse goes even further by saying, "And the men of Sodom were very evil and sinful against Jehovah."

Anyone can see how ugly the outer self is when separated from the inner by considering the remarks on the leading role played by self-love and self-centered cravings in dividing the two [§1594]. The beauty of the outer self when united with the inner is equaled by its ugliness when divided. The outer self regarded in itself exists for no purpose but to serve the inner self; it is a kind of tool for converting goals into useful efforts and embodying those efforts in an effect, bringing everything to perfect completion. The opposite happens when the outer self detaches from the inner and aims to serve itself alone or, even worse, to control the inner self. This course of action is inspired chiefly by self-love and its desires, as shown [§§1568:2, 1594:3–5].

Genesis 13:13. *And the men of Sodom were very evil and sinful against Jehovah.*

1599

The men of Sodom were very evil and sinful against Jehovah symbolizes the point of corrupt desire to which facts extended.

The symbolism of *the men of Sodom were very evil and sinful against Jehovah* as the point of corrupt desire to which facts extended can be seen from the following: *Sodom* symbolizes corrupt desire, or cravings, as

1600

mentioned previously [§§1587, 1598]. And *men* symbolize intellectual and rational matters; here they symbolize facts, because they are attributed to the outer self separated from the inner. The symbolism of men as intellectual or rational matters has also been demonstrated before, in §§265, 749, 1007.

Facts are said to extend to the point of corrupt desire when our only goal in learning them is to gain prestige, rather than to use them to help us become good. All facts exist for this purpose: to enable us to become rational and therefore wise, and in this way serve the inner self.

1601   Genesis 13:14. *And Jehovah said to Abram, after Lot separated from him, "Please raise your eyes and look out from the place there where you are toward the north and toward the south and toward the east and toward the west."*

Jehovah said to Abram means this is the way Jehovah talked to the Lord. *After Lot separated from him* means when the cravings of his outer self had been put aside so as not to get in the way. *Please raise your eyes and look out from the place there where you are* symbolizes the Lord's state at that time, from which he could perceive what was to come. *Toward the north and toward the south and toward the east and toward the west* symbolizes absolutely everyone in the universe.

1602   *Jehovah said to Abram* means this is the way Jehovah talked to the Lord, as can be seen from the inner sense of the Word, in which *Abram* means the Lord. It can also be seen from the actual state he was then in, which is depicted here. The state was one in which superficial traits that would get in the way were put aside, and it is symbolized by the words "after Lot separated from him."

The Lord's inner being was divine, because he was born of Jehovah. So naturally when there were no obstacles on the part of his outer self, he saw the whole future.

The reason this presented itself at the time as speech by *Jehovah* is that the viewpoint was that of his outer self. In regard to his inner self, he was one with Jehovah, as the Lord himself teaches in John:

> Philip said, "Show us the Father." Jesus said to him, "After all the time I've spent with you, don't you know me, Philip? Whoever sees me sees the Father. How then can you say, 'Show us the Father'? Don't you believe that I am in the Father and the Father is in me? Believe me that I am in the Father and the Father is in me." (John 14:6, 8, 9, 10, 11)

1603   *After Lot separated from him* means when the cravings of his outer self had been set aside so as not to get in the way. This is established by the representation of *Lot* as his outer self and by the previous statement that Lot separated himself—that is, impediments separated themselves. When they had been put aside, his inner self (Jehovah) became unified with his outer self (the Lord's human quality). Outward traits are the only incompatible elements, the elements described as blocking the inner self from integrating with the outer self when acting on it [§§1547, 1563:2, 1568, 1581, 1594]. The outer self is only a kind of tool or organ, in itself devoid of life, that receives life from the inner self. When it does, it appears as if it contains inherent life.

[2] In the Lord, however, even the organic parts of his human nature received life, after he had purified them by ridding himself of the evil he had inherited. Just as the Lord's inner being was life itself, then, his outer being too became life itself. This is what his attainment of glory means in John:

> Jesus says, "Now the Son of Humankind has gained glory, and God has gained glory in him. If God has gained glory in him, God will also make him glorious in his own self, and will make him glorious immediately." (John 13:31, 32)

In the same author:

> Father, the hour has come; give glory to your Son, so that your Son may also give glory to you. Now therefore make me glorious—you, Father, in your own self—with the glory that I had in you before the world existed. (John 17:1, 5)

In the same author:

> Jesus said, "Father, make your name glorious." So a voice went out from heaven: "I both have made it glorious and will again make it glorious." (John 12:28)

Please raise your eyes and look out from the place there where you are **1604** symbolizes the Lord's state at that time, [from which he could perceive what was to come]. This is established by the symbolism of *raising one's eyes and seeing,* which means being enlightened and perceiving (discussed above at verse 10 [§1584]), and by the inner-level symbolism of a *place* as a state or condition. (Sections 1274, 1376, 1377, 1378, 1379 showed that what a place means is a state.)

The symbolism of *toward the north and toward the south and toward* **1605** *the east and toward the west* as absolutely everyone in the universe can be seen from the meaning of these directions. North, south, east, and west each symbolize something of their own in the Word. The *north* symbolizes people outside the church, that is, people who are in the dark as far as truths of the faith go; it also symbolizes the darkness inside a person. The *south,* on the other hand, symbolizes people in the church, that is, people who are in the light as far as religious knowledge goes; likewise it symbolizes the light itself. The *east* symbolizes people who have gone before, and heavenly love too, as shown before. The *west,* on the other hand, symbolizes people yet to come, and likewise people lacking love. What each symbolizes can be seen from the running thread of the inner meaning.

When all the directions are mentioned, however, as north, south, east, and west are here, they symbolize everyone now alive in the whole inhabited world, and in addition those who have gone before and those yet to come. They also symbolize different states of love and faith in the human race.

1606   Genesis 13:15. *"Because all the land that you see—to you I will give it, and to your seed forever."*

Because all the land that you see—to you I will give it symbolizes the kingdom of heaven and the fact that it would be the Lord's. *And to your seed forever* symbolizes the people who would believe in him.

1607   *Because all the land that you see—to you I will give it* symbolizes the kingdom of heaven and the fact that it would be the Lord's. This can be seen from the symbolism of the *land*—here the land of Canaan, since it says *the land that you see*—as the kingdom of heaven. The land of Canaan represented the Lord's kingdom in the heavens (heaven) and his kingdom on earth (the church), a symbolism that has been discussed several times earlier [§§1, 115, 620, 1025:4, 1066, 1413, 1437, 1585].

Many places in the Word indicate that the Lord was given a kingdom in heaven and on earth. In Isaiah, for example:

> A child has been born, a son has been given to us, and sovereignty will be on his shoulder; and his name will be called Miraculous, Counselor, God, Hero, Eternal Father, Prince of Peace. (Isaiah 9:6)

In Daniel:

> I was seeing in visions at night, and there! In the clouds of the heavens, it was as if the Son of Humankind was coming. And he came to the Ancient One, and they brought him before the [Ancient One]. And he was given power to rule, and glory, and kingship; and all peoples,

nations, and tongues will serve him. His ruling power is eternal power that will not pass away, and his kingship one that will not perish. (Daniel 7:13, 14)

The Lord himself also says this; in Matthew:

Everything has been turned over to me by my Father. (Matthew 11:27; and Luke 10:22)

In another place in Matthew:

Authority in heaven and on earth has been given to me. (Matthew 28:18)

In John:

You have given your Son authority over all flesh, so that to all that you have given him he may give eternal life. (John 17:2, 3)

The same thing is meant by sitting on his right side, as in Luke:

From this time now, the Son of Humankind will be sitting on the right side of God's strength. (Luke 22:69)

[2] All authority in the heavens and on earth was given to the Son of Humankind, but it is important to realize that the Lord had authority over everything in the heavens and on earth before he came into the world. He was God from eternity, and Jehovah, as he himself clearly says in John:

Now make me glorious—you, Father, in your own self—with the glory that I had in you before the world existed. (John 17:5)

And in the same author:

Truly, truly, I say to you: before Abraham existed, I existed. (John 8:58)

After all, he was Jehovah and God to the people of the earliest church (the church before the Flood) and was visible to them. He was also Jehovah and God to the ancient church (the church after the Flood). And he was the one whom all the rituals of the Jewish religion represented and whom the Jews would worship. The reason he says that all authority in heaven and on earth was given to him, as if it was then happening for the first time, is that "Son of Humankind" means his human quality. Once this quality had become one with his divine quality, it too was Jehovah and at that same time possessed authority. This could never have happened before he had acquired his glory—that is, before his human nature had also come to have life in itself, through union with his divine nature, and so had likewise become divine, had become Jehovah. He says so in John:

> Just as the Father has life in himself, he has also granted the Son to have life in himself. (John 5:26)

[3] His human nature, or outer self, is also what Daniel calls Son of Humankind in the passage quoted above; and Isaiah in the passage quoted refers to it with the words "A child has been born and a son has been given to us."

He now saw and was promised that he would be given the kingdom of heaven and all power in the heavens and on earth, which is symbolized by the words "All the land that you see—to you I will give it, and to your seed after you forever." This was before his human quality had become one with his divine quality, which happened when he completely overcame the Devil and hell. That is to say, it happened when he rid himself of all evil—the only incompatible element—by his own power and his own strength.

1608   The symbolism of *and to your seed forever* as the people who would believe in him can be seen from the symbolism of *seed* as faith, specifically the faith that comes of charity, as discussed earlier, in §§255, 256, 1025.

The Lord's own words in John make it plain that it was his seed—people believing in him—who would be given the kingdom of heaven:

> The Father loves the Son and has given everything into his hand. Those who believe in the Son have eternal life; but those who do not believe in the Son will not see life. (John 3:35, 36)

[2] And in the same author:

> As many as did accept him, to them he gave the power to be God's children, to those believing in his name, not from blood or from the flesh's will or from a man's will. (John 1:12, 13)

These words show what faith is, or belief in the Lord: it exists in people who accept and believe in him not because of the flesh's will or because of a man's will. The will of the flesh means something opposite to love and charity, since flesh symbolizes such an opposite (§999); and a man's will means something opposite to the faith that comes of love or charity, which is what a man symbolizes. The flesh's will and a man's will are what divide, but love and the faith that comes of love are what unite. So people who have love and the faith that comes of love are the ones born of God, and because they are born of God, they are called God's children. They are also his seed who will inherit the kingdom of heaven, as symbolized by the words of the present verse: "All the land that you see I will give to you and to your *seed* forever."

[3] Anyone willing simply to think about it is capable of seeing that the kingdom of heaven cannot be given to people whose faith is devoid of charity, that is, people who say they have faith and yet hate their neighbor. This kind of faith cannot have any life in it, since hatred—hell, in other words—constitutes its life. Hell consists of pure hatred—not the kinds of hatred that we inherit, but the kinds that we secure for ourselves by the way we actually live.

Genesis 13:16. *"And I will make your seed like the dust of the earth, in that if anyone can count the dust of the earth, your seed too will be counted."*   **1609**

I will make your seed like the dust of the earth means multiplying beyond measure. *In that if anyone can count the dust of the earth, your seed too will be counted,* means a positive assertion.

I will make your seed like the dust of the earth means multiplying   **1610** beyond measure, as can be seen without explanation. This verse says that his seed would be made like the *dust of the earth;* other passages in the Word say "like the sand of the sea," or "like the stars of the heavens." Each has its own particular symbolism. The dust of the earth has to do with heavenly qualities, because the earth symbolizes the heavenly aspect of love, as shown earlier [§§620, 1413, 1437, 1585]. The sand of the sea has to do with spiritual qualities, because the sea symbolizes the spiritual aspect of love, as also shown. "Like the stars of the heavens" symbolizes both, in a higher degree. Because these items are incapable of being counted, it became customary to use them to express the idea of immeasurable reproducing and multiplying.

[2] The multiplying of the *seed*—the faith that comes of love, or love itself—beyond measure symbolizes the Lord in the highest sense. Specifically, it symbolizes his human quality, because the Lord's human quality is called the "seed of a woman," as discussed in §256. And since the Lord's human quality is meant, multiplication beyond measure means infinite heavenliness and spirituality.

On the other hand, when seed symbolizes the faith that comes of charity (or charity itself) in the human race, the meaning is that the seed in each individual who lives a life of charity would multiply beyond measure. This actually happens in the other world to everyone who lives a life of neighborly love. Charity and the faith that results from charity, along with happiness, increase so abundantly in such people that it can be depicted only by something immeasurable and inexpressible.

When seed symbolizes the human race itself, its multiplication in the Lord's kingdom is again beyond measure and comes not only from people inside the church and their children but also from people outside the church and their children. As a result, the Lord's kingdom, or heaven, is immeasurable, as will be discussed elsewhere, the Lord in his divine mercy willing.

1611   Genesis 13:17. *"Get up; walk through the land along its length and along its breadth, because to you I will give it."*

Get up; walk through the land, means in order to see the whole kingdom of heaven. *Along its length and along its breadth* symbolizes its heavenly aspect and its spiritual aspect. *Because to you I will give it* means that it would be his.

1612   *Get up; walk through the land,* means in order to see the whole kingdom of heaven, as can be seen from the symbolism of *land* as the kingdom of heaven, dealt with several times before [§§1, 115, 1413, 1437, 1585].

On the literal level, *getting up and walking through* the land is scouting it out to see what it is like. So on an inner level, where land (that is, the land of Canaan) symbolizes God's kingdom in the heavens (or heaven) and God's kingdom on earth (or the church), it means having a thorough view. It also means perceiving.

1613   *Along its length and along its breadth* symbolizes the heavenly aspect and the spiritual aspect, or to put it another way, what is good and what is true. (For the symbolism of *length* as something good and of *breadth* as something true, see the remarks above at §650.) The reason for this meaning is that land symbolizes the kingdom of heaven or the church, neither of which can be said to have length or breadth. They have only the equivalents of length and breadth, or in other words, something that corresponds to these—namely, goodness and truth. The heavenly aspect or goodness is primary, so it is compared to length, but the spiritual aspect or truth is secondary, so it is compared to breadth.

[2] The fact that breadth is truth stands out fairly clearly in the prophetic portions of the Word. In Habakkuk, for instance:

> I am raising up the Chaldeans, a nation bitter and swift, *walking through the breadth of the land.* (Habakkuk 1:6)

The Chaldeans stand for people whose thinking is distorted. Walking through the breadth of the land stands for destroying truth, since it is the Chaldeans who are said to do it. In David:

> Jehovah, you did not shut me up in the hand of my enemy; you made my feet stand in a *broad place*. (Psalms 31:8)

Standing in a broad place means standing on the truth. In the same author:

> In tight-bound anguish have I called on Jah; he answers me with *broad liberality*. (Psalms 118:5)

Answering with broad liberality stands for answering truly. In Hosea:

> Jehovah will pasture them like a lamb, in a *broad place*. (Hosea 4:16)

Pasturing an animal in a broad place stands for teaching truth. [3] In Isaiah:

> Assyria will go through Judah, he will flood in and pass over, he will reach all the way to their neck, and the spread of his wings will be the fullness of the *land's breadth*. (Isaiah 8:8)

Assyria stands for sophistry that will flood the land, or in other words, the church. His wings stand for arguments that lead to falsity. The full breadth stands for being full of falsity, or of ideas that oppose truth.

Since the length of the land symbolized goodness and its breadth symbolized truth, the New Jerusalem is described as having been measured and lying square, its *length* being as great as its *width* (Revelation 21:16). From this anyone can see that the sole meaning of length and width is [goodness and truth], since the New Jerusalem is purely and simply the Lord's kingdom in the heavens and on earth.

Once upon a time the inner-level symbolism of things made it common for people to speak of heavenly and spiritual qualities in terms of phenomena found on earth, such as length and breadth. Height and depth likewise form a part of modern everyday language when the subject is wisdom.

The meaning of *because to you I will give it* as the fact that it would be **1614** his can be seen without explanation.

Certain points that have been demonstrated many times show that the "land"—the kingdom of heaven—is the Lord's alone: specifically, that no one else is the Lord of heaven [§§14, 15, 300, 458, 548:1, 1607], and since he is the Lord of heaven, he is also the Lord of the church [§§768:3,

1585:1, 1607]. It can also be seen from the fact that everything heavenly or spiritual (everything good or true) comes from the Lord alone, with the result that the Lord is the all-in-all of his heaven—so much so that anyone who fails to see goodness and truth as coming from the Lord ceases to be in heaven. Such is the prevailing atmosphere throughout heaven. Such is the soul of heaven as well, and such is the life force that flows into everyone who cultivates goodness.

1615   Genesis 13:18. *And Abram pitched his tent, and he came and lived in the oak groves of Mamre, which is in Hebron; and there he built an altar to Jehovah.*

Abram pitched his tent, and he came and lived in the oak groves of Mamre, which is in Hebron, means that the Lord arrived at a still deeper perceptive ability; this is his sixth phase. *And there he built an altar to Jehovah* symbolizes worship in that phase.

1616   *Abram pitched his tent, and he came and lived in the oak groves of Mamre, which is in Hebron,* means that the Lord achieved a still deeper perceptive ability, as can be seen from the symbolism of *pitching a tent* (in the sense of setting a tent up in a series of locations) as uniting. A *tent* means the holiness of worship, as shown before in §§414, 1452, and this is what unites the outer self to the inner. The meaning can also be seen from the symbolism of an *oak grove* as perception, as discussed above in §§1442, 1443. Those sections dealt with the oak grove of Moreh, which is the dawn of perception. The present verse, though, speaks of the oak groves of Mamre, in the plural, and they symbolize increasing perception—that is, deeper perception. This perception is referred to as the "oak groves of Mamre, which is in Hebron." *Mamre* is mentioned elsewhere too, as for example in Genesis 14:13; 18:1; 23:17, 18, 19; 35:27. So too is *Hebron:* Genesis 35:27; 37:14; Joshua 10:36, 39; 14:13, 14, 15; 15:13, 54; 20:7; 21:11, 13; Judges 1:10, 20; and in other places. What they symbolize there will be seen in the relevant places, by the Lord's divine mercy.

[2] To expand on the symbolism of the "oak groves of Mamre, which is in Hebron" as a still deeper ability to perceive: The more the attributes of the outer self unite with the heavenly qualities of the inner self, the more perception grows and deepens. Union with heavenly qualities yields perception. This is because the heavenly attributes of love for Jehovah contain the actual living energy of the inner self. To put the same thing another way, the heavenly attributes of love—or in other words, heavenly love itself—contain Jehovah's presence. His presence is

not perceived in the outer self until union is achieved. All perception comes from union.

[3] The inner meaning here reveals how matters stood with the Lord: His outer self (his human nature) united with his divine nature more and more as the religious knowledge he possessed multiplied and reproduced itself. No individual, so far as he or she is human, can be united to Jehovah (that is, the Lord) except through religious knowledge, because it is this knowledge that makes a person human. This was true for the Lord too, because he was born like any other person and was taught the same way as any other person. Heavenly values, however, were constantly being infused into the religious concepts he had learned, which acted as receiving vessels. These concepts, then, were constantly being made into vessels for receiving heavenly qualities and were themselves made heavenly as well.

So the Lord made continuous progress toward the heavenly condition of early childhood. [4] As I have said before, the heavenly aspects of love are instilled in us from infancy up until adolescence [§§430, 561, 1438, 1450–1451, 1453:1, 1472, 1495–1496, 1548, 1555:2, 1557]—even into early adulthood, depending on the kind of person we are. During that time and later, we are trained in knowledge both secular and religious. If we are the kind of people who can be reborn, heavenly dimensions—aspects of love and charity—fill out both kinds of knowledge. In this way the knowledge is grafted onto the heavenly gifts that we have received from infancy up till adolescence and early adulthood. In the process, our outward self unites with our inward self. First the knowledge is grafted onto the heavenly gifts we received as young adults, next onto those we received throughout adolescence, and finally onto those we received in early childhood. Then we become little children, of whom the Lord said, "To such belongs the kingdom of God" [Mark 10:14; Luke 18:16]. The Lord alone does the grafting, so nothing heavenly exists or can exist in us that does not come from the Lord and belong to the Lord.

[5] The Lord, however, did all this by his own power—united his outer self to his inner, filled his knowledge with heavenly dimensions, and grafted this knowledge onto his heavenly gifts. Moreover, he did so according to the divine plan; first he grafted the knowledge onto the heavenly gifts received in adolescence, then onto those received at the age between childhood and adolescence, and finally onto those he received in his childhood. By these means he caused his human nature as well to become innocence itself and love itself, the source of all innocence and all love in the heavens and on earth.

This kind of innocence is true childhood, because it is also wisdom. A child's innocence is useless, though, unless religious knowledge turns it into the innocence of wisdom, so children in the other life are trained in such knowledge.

Because the Lord grafted this knowledge onto his heavenly gifts, he had perception, since all perception comes from union, as noted. Perception dawned in him when he grafted on the facts he had learned in youth, and this dawn of perception is symbolized by the oak grove of Moreh. It evolved (as described in the current verse) into a deeper kind when he grafted religious knowledge on, and this kind of perception is symbolized by the oak groves of Mamre, which is in Hebron.

1617   The fact that this is his sixth phase can be seen from the contents of the last chapter [§1401].

1618   The symbolism of *and there he built an altar to Jehovah* as worship in that phase is established by the symbolism of an *altar* as that which represents all worship in general, discussed earlier at §921.

In an inner sense, worship means all union achieved through love and charity. We worship constantly when we have love and charity; outward worship is merely an effect. Angels worship in this way, so they have a perpetual Sabbath. As a result, the Sabbath at a deeper level also symbolizes the Lord's kingdom.

While we are in the world, however, we really ought to worship outwardly as well. External worship stirs deeper dimensions, and it maintains the holiness of our external acts so that deeper elements can influence us. What is more, we absorb knowledge during worship and undergo preparation for accepting heavenly qualities. We also receive unconsciously the gift of holy states that the Lord preserves for our use in eternal life. Every state of our life returns in the other world.

The Light in Which Angels Live (Continued); Their Magnificent Gardens and Their Dwellings

1619   WHEN we gain access to inward sight (the sight of our spirit), we see the objects of the other world, which could never be presented to the sight of our physical eyes. This is exactly what the visions of the prophets were.

In heaven, as noted [§1532], there are constant symbolic representations of the Lord and his kingdom. In fact every single thing the angels see represents and symbolizes something. This is the source of representation and symbolism in the Word, because the Word comes by way of heaven from the Lord.

There are more objects to be seen in the world of spirits and heaven than can be listed. As the present subject is light, let me tell about the things that arise directly out of the light, such as atmospheres, parks, rainbows, palaces, and houses. With their outward eyes, spirits and angels see these items as being so radiant and alive, so perceptible to all their senses, that they declare them to be real and the objects of the world to be unreal by comparison.

1620

I start with the atmospheres that the blessed live in, which are made of light, because they rise out of the light there. The number of different kinds cannot be counted, and they are so beautiful and pleasant that they cannot be described. There are diamondlike atmospheres that flash in all their most minuscule elements, as if they were made of diamond pellets. There are atmospheres that resemble the gleam of all kinds of gems. There are atmospheres seemingly made of translucent pearls glowing from within, streaking the air with the most brilliant colors. There are atmospheres afire with gold, it seems, or with silver, or with diamondlike gold and silver. There are atmospheres composed of multicolored flowers so small they cannot be seen; countless variations on this type of atmosphere fill the heaven where small children live. In fact one even sees atmospheres composed of what seem to be children at play, again at a size that is too small to see but that can be perceived, although only by the deepest power of thought. This gives young children the idea that everything around them is alive and is part of the Lord's stream of life—a thought that gladdens them to the core.

1621

There are many other kinds of atmosphere besides, because the variations are beyond number and also beyond description.

To turn now to the magnificent gardens: they are breathtaking. Huge parks containing every kind of tree come into view, so beautiful and so charming that they defy all power of imagination. They are presented to the inhabitants' outward sight in such a living way that not only are they seen, they are also perceived in all their detail much more vividly than anything our physical eyesight discerns on earth.

1622

To remove any doubts I might have on the subject, I was taken there (the place is in front, at an angle slightly above the right eye, where people who live the life of paradise are located), and I saw. Absolutely everything appears in its loveliest springtime and its loveliest bloom, with stunning magnificence and variety. Every single object is alive with representation, since nothing exists there that does not represent or symbolize something heavenly or spiritual. So the sights not only please the eyes but also cheer the mind.

[2] Some souls newly arrived from the world once expressed doubt—because of principles they had adopted while still alive—that similar things could exist in the other world, where there is neither wood nor stone. They were taken up to that place and spoke to me from there. Stupefied, they said that it was indescribable, and that they could never find a mental picture to represent its indescribability. Exhilaration and happiness shone out from every particle, they said, with unending variety.

For the most part, souls being introduced to heaven are taken first of all to the paradisal gardens. Angels look at such things with very different eyes, however. It is not the actual gardens that delight an angel but the things they represent, and so the heavenly and spiritual realities behind them.

The earliest church had its paradisal gardens from this source.

1623 As for rainbows, there is a kind of iridescent heaven, in which the whole atmosphere seems to be made of tiny rainbows, one after another. The people who live there belong to the region of the inner eye and are stationed off to the right, out in front and a little bit up above. The entire atmosphere there—all the air—consists of these gleams of light and therefore radiates out of each individual "beacon," so to speak.

A much larger rainbow (compounded of similar smaller ones that are exquisite miniatures of the big one) forms a gorgeous belt around the outside.

Each color, then, consists of many, many rays, so that millions of rays make up a single, all-inclusive rainbow visible to the eye. The rainbow is a modification of the points of light, a modification produced by the heavenly and spiritual forces that create the rainbow and in the process present before the observer's eyes a picture full of representative meaning.

There is no limit to the different types and varieties of rainbows, several of which I was privileged to see. To grasp in some measure the kind of variation they display, and to see how very many rays of light go into a single visible one, let me describe just one or two.

1624 Once a large-scale rainbow appeared before me so that I could learn from it what rainbows are like at the smallest scale. There was a brilliant white light with a kind of belt about it. At the core of the belt was something dim and earthlike surrounded by a bright radiance. The radiance was dappled and broken up by another kind of light containing golden starlike sparkles. Other changes occurred when flowers of different colors entered into the bright radiance—colors produced not by white light but by a fiery kind of light. All of it represented heavenly and spiritual qualities.

In the other world, all visible colors represent something heavenly or spiritual. Colors that partake of fire represent aspects of love and of a desire for what is good. Colors that partake of white light represent aspects of faith and of a desire for truth. All colors in the next life come from these sources and therefore gleam so brilliantly that colors in this world cannot be compared to them. There are also colors that have never been seen in the world.

A rainbow shape with something grasslike and green at its center also appeared, and I sensed a kind of sun off to the side, out of sight, gleaming, and giving off a light so bright that it cannot be described. At the edges were the most beautiful variations of color possible, in a luminescent, pearly field.

1625

These and other experiences showed me what a rainbow is like in its smallest components. They also showed me that there is no end to the number of variations, which depend on neighborly love and the resulting faith in an individual who sees them represented. That individual in turn looks like a rainbow to others when presented to their view in all her or his beauty and glory.

In addition to these wonders of paradise, one also sees cities full of splendid mansions, one after another, gleaming with color, beyond the skill of any architect to create. Not surprisingly, cities like them appeared to the prophets as well, when their inner eyes were open; and these cities were as plain to see as any that could exist in the world. The New Jerusalem appeared to John, for instance, and he described it in these words:

1626

> He took me away *in spirit* onto a mountain big and high and showed me the great city, Jerusalem the Holy, having a wall big and high, having twelve gates. The structure of the wall was jasper, and the city was pure gold, like golden glass. The foundations of the wall were adorned with every precious stone. The first foundation was jasper, the second sapphire, the third chalcedony, the fourth emerald, the fifth sardonyx, the sixth sard, the seventh chrysolite, the eighth beryl, the ninth topaz, the tenth chrysoprase, the eleventh hyacinth, the twelfth amethyst. (Revelation 21:10, 12, 18, 19, 20)

The prophets also describe the new Jerusalem.

Sights like these in countless numbers appear to angels and angelic spirits in broad daylight, and surprising to say, the angels and spirits perceive them with all their senses. This will never be believed by anyone who has blotted out all spiritual thinking by means of the terms and definitions used in human philosophy and by argumentation—yet it is absolutely true. The fact that the saints saw them so many times could have convinced such people that it is true.

1627   In addition to cities and mansions, I was sometimes able to see decorative elements, such as those that appear on stairways and main doors. These elements moved as if they were alive, and changed with ever fresh beauty and symmetry. I learned that such changes can keep going indefinitely, one after another, even to eternity, and there is a constantly renewed harmony among the variations, formed by the very sequence of changes itself. These were only the least of their wonders, I heard.

1628   All angels have their own houses to live in—magnificent houses. While there, I saw them several times, with astonishment, and spoke with the angels in them. They are so clear to see, so visible, that nothing could be more so. Houses on earth are almost nothing by comparison. Angels also call earthly dwellings lifeless and unreal but their own dwellings alive and genuine, because they come from the Lord. The architecture is such that it is the source of the art itself, with unending variety.

They said that if they were given all the palaces in the whole inhabited world, they would not exchange their own for them. Anything made of stone, brick, or plank seems dead to them, but anything from the Lord, or from life and light itself, is alive. Such materials are all the more alive because angels experience them with the full range of senses, since objects there are perfectly suited to the senses of spirits and angels. Objects in the light of the sun's realm are not the least bit visible to spirits' eyes. To the senses we have in our bodies, though, stone and wood are well suited. What is spiritual responds to what is spiritual, and what is physical responds to what is physical.

1629   The houses of good spirits and angelic spirits usually have porticoes, or long entryways, vaulted and sometimes doubled, where they walk. The walls of the walkways are formed in many different ways and are graced with flowers and flower garlands woven in an extraordinary manner, not to mention other kinds of decoration that change and replace one another, as noted. These details appear to them in brighter light at one time, in weaker light at another, but always offering profound pleasure.

Their houses also turn more beautiful as the spirits grow in perfection. When the houses are undergoing change, something representing a window appears at the side and widens, and the inside grows darker. A piece of starry sky appears, as does a kind of cloud, which is a sign that their houses are changing into even more enchanting ones.

Spirits are quite disgusted by the poor opinion people have of the life that spirits and angels enjoy. They are upset to know that we imagine them as existing in a dim, obscure state (which would have to be awfully grim) and inhabiting a kind of vacuum or void. The truth is that they have the greatest possible light, enjoy every benefit available to each of the senses, and feel it very deeply. `1630`

There were also some souls just come from the world who brought with them (from assumptions they had adopted there) the idea that such vitality was not possible in the other world. As a result, they were taken into angel homes, where they talked with the angels and saw what was there. When they returned, they kept saying, "I can see it's true!" "Those things are real!" "I would never have believed this during life in the body. I never *could* have." They said that these have to be some of the most amazing things that exist, but no one believes in such things because no one understands them. Just because they do not understand it—and this is something they are told—they should not doubt it, since it is a matter to be experienced by the senses (the inner senses, at any rate). After all, if we believed only what we could grasp, we would not believe in anything on the inner level of the physical world, let alone anything having to do with eternal life.

That is what produces the insanity of our era.

Some people have been rich during bodily life and lived in stately mansions, identifying their heaven with these advantages and cheating others out of their possessions by various ruses, without conscience and without compassion. When they come into the other life, they are first introduced into exactly the same kind of life they had lived in the world (as noted before [§943].) Sometimes they are even allowed at this point to live in mansions, just as they had in the world, since at first everyone in the other life is welcomed as a guest and a newcomer. In order to avoid exposing the inner depths and life goals of these people as yet, angels show them every favor and kindness, on behalf of the Lord. But the scene changes. The mansions gradually fade and turn into huts, which degenerate further and further until they finally disappear. Then the owners wander around like beggars and ask to be taken in, but because they are what they are, society rejects them. In the end they come to resemble excrement, and a cloud smelling like [rotten] teeth wafts from them. `1631`

1632   With angels I have discussed representations and the fact that nothing in the plant kingdom on earth fails to represent the Lord's kingdom
in some way. They have said that every pretty and attractive specimen
of the plant kingdom comes from the Lord by way of heaven; and since
the Lord's heavenly and spiritual forces act on the physical world, they
actually take on a visible form. That is where the soul or life of plants
comes from, and it is the reason that they represent something. As this is
unknown in the world, it is called a heavenly secret.

1633   I also learned in depth about the nature of the inflow into the life
force of animals, a force that dissipates entirely after they die. This will
be discussed later, with the Lord's divine mercy.

Genesis 14

The Way Spirits and Angels Talk

THE Lord's Word makes it clear that many people used to talk with
spirits and angels, and that they heard and saw much in the other
world, but that heaven was later shut, so to speak. It was closed so tightly
that today hardly anyone believes spirits and angels exist, let alone that
anyone can talk with them. To most people's way of thinking, speech
with invisible beings (whose existence they deny at heart) is impossible.

1634

In the Lord's divine mercy, however, I have been granted the almost
continuous opportunity for several years now to hold conversations with
them and to go among them as one of them. Let me report here, then, what
I have had the privilege of learning about the way they talk to each other.

When spirits talked to me, I heard them as clearly and distinctly as
the people I speak with on earth. In fact when I talked with spirits while
surrounded by people, I noticed that I could hear the spirits just as audi-
bly as the people—so much so that the spirits sometimes had trouble
believing they could not be heard by my companions. There was no difference whatever in the sound.

1635

But since spirits' speech stimulates the ear's inner organs in a different way than conversation with other people does, it was inaudible to
everyone but me, in whom those organs were open, by the Lord's divine
mercy. Human speech enters through the ear along an external route,
by means of the air. The speech of spirits enters not by the ear or the air
but by an inner way. It reaches the same organs inside the head (in the
brain), which is why it sounds the same.

The following example made it clear to me how hard it is to convince people that spirits and angels exist, let alone that anyone can talk to
them. There was a group of spirits I had known when they lived in the
body who had been among the better-educated. (I have spoken with
almost all those I had known during their physical lives—with some for
several weeks and with some for a year—exactly as though they were living in their bodies.) They were once led into the same patterns of thought

1636

they had had when they lived in the world—an easy change to accomplish in the other life. The question was then suggested to them, "Do you believe anyone can talk to spirits?" "You would have to be deluded to believe such a thing," they said then, in that condition, and doggedly continued to assert their opinion. The experience showed how difficult it is to convince anyone that any speech between people and spirits is possible. The reason for the difficulty is that people do not believe in the existence of spirits, let alone in their own future arrival among spirits after death. This disbelief afterward shocked even the spirits themselves. Yet they were some of the better-educated and had often spoken publicly about the next life, and about heaven and angels. One would have assumed that the idea was very familiar to them as a simple fact, especially from the Word, where it comes up frequently.

1637   One of the amazing things that happen in the other life is that when spirits talk to us humans, they do so in our native language. They speak it as easily and fluently as if they had been born in the same land and raised with the same language, whether they come from Europe or the Near East or some other part of the globe. So do those who lived thousands of years earlier, before the language even existed. In fact spirits have no idea that the speech they use with us is not their own native tongue. They use our secondary languages too, but beyond these, they are not capable of producing one syllable of another language, unless the Lord gives it directly to them. Even babies who die before they have really learned any language at all talk this way.

[2] The reason, though, is that the language that spirits are familiar with is composed not of words but of thoughts. This language is common to all tongues. When spirits are present with a person on earth, their individual thoughts fall into words the person knows. The thoughts agree with and adapt to those words so perfectly that the spirits have no notion that the actual words are not their own. They fully believe they are speaking their own language, when it is really the person's language they are speaking. I have discussed these matters with spirits a number of times.

All souls receive this gift as soon as they enter the other world. They can understand the speech of everyone in the whole family of nations, just as though they had been born in those nations, because they sense whatever a person is thinking. Not to mention other talents in which they excel even more dramatically.

That is why it happens after physical death that souls can converse and interact with everyone, no matter what the individual's region or language was.

The words they use—that is, the words they stir up or retrieve from our memory and presume to be their own—are well chosen, clear, meaningful, distinctly enunciated, and relevant. Surprising to say, the spirits are smarter and faster at choosing words than we are ourselves. As a matter of fact (and this has been demonstrated to me), they grasp a word's various shades of meaning and apply them immediately, without any forethought. The reason, again, is that the thoughts composing their language flow only into suitable words. **1638**

The situation is almost the same as the times when we speak without thinking about the words and focus solely on the meaning of the words. Under those circumstances, our thought falls quickly and easily into phrasing that accords with our meaning. It is the inner meaning that produces the words. The same kind of inner meaning, but even more subtly nuanced and refined, is what the language of spirits consists in, and by it we communicate with them, although we are unaware of it.

Verbal speech, as I said, is characteristic of people on earth and, to be specific, of their physical memory. Speech composed of thoughts, however, is the speech of spirits and, to be specific, of inner memory, which is the memory of the spirit. We are not aware that we have the latter kind of memory, because the memory of trivia belonging to the material world—physical memory—seems all-important and overshadows the inner memory. The reality, though, is that without the inner memory characteristic of our spirit, we are completely incapable of thought. **1639**

I have often used my inner memory in talking with spirits, which is to say that I have used their own language; that is, I have spoken by means of thought. The universality of the language and its richness can be seen from the fact that each word contains a whole concept of tremendous reach. As we know, it can take some time to lay out the thought behind a single word, still more the thought behind a single topic, and more yet the thought behind a constellation of topics, even if these can be brought together into a single, simple-looking composite. These considerations give some clue to the kind of speech that spirits naturally use with each other and what type of speech it is that links us to spirits.

Not only was I able to hear clearly what the spirits were saying to me, I could also tell just where they were at the time—above my head or below, on my right side or my left, at my ear, somewhere else near my body or perhaps inside it, at such and such a distance far or near. I could tell where they were because they spoke to me from the various places or locations they were in, which were determined by their position in the universal human, or in other words, by their state of mind. **1640**

[2] I was also allowed to perceive when they came and went, where they were going and for how long, whether they were many or few, and so on.

From their speech I could tell what they were like, too, since their speech (like their aura) reveals clearly what their turn of mind and their character is, and what opinions and attitudes they hold as well. If they are deceitful, for instance, then when they talk, the general and specific type of their deceit can be detected in every word and thought, even if they are not lying at the moment. The same is true of all other vices and obsessions. These are so obvious that there is no need for lengthy investigation; an image of each is present in every word and thought.

[3] It is also possible to sense whether the thinking behind their words is closed- or open-minded, and what part comes from that individual, from other individuals, or from the Lord. It works almost the same as with the faces of people on earth, in which we can usually recognize pretense, fraud, gladness, cheer (real or fake), true friendship, shyness, or insanity, even if the person does not talk. Sometimes the same thing shows up in the tone of voice. Why not in the other life, then, where perception is far more sensitive?

In fact before spirits speak, their thought alone reveals what they are about to say, since thought is communicated more quickly and readily than speech.

1641   In the next life, spirits converse with each other the same way we do on earth. Good spirits engage in the intimate conversation of loving friends, as I have witnessed many times. They use their customary speech, which enables them to express more in a minute than we could over the course of an hour. As noted, their language is universal, common to all tongues, because it uses ideas—the rudiments of all words—as its medium. They discuss things with such acumen and insight, pursuing so many well-constructed, persuasive lines of reasoning that if people knew about it they would be dumbfounded. Spirits link opinion and feeling, which lends animation to their speech.

[2] Sometimes spirits employ representations as well—an appeal to the eye and so to living experience. Take for example a discussion of shame and the question of whether it can exist apart from reverence. People on earth cannot settle the matter without endless argument involving various proofs and examples, and even then the issue remains in doubt. Spirits, on the other hand, take only a minute. They run in order through the various ways in which shame affects us and then the ways in which reverence does, noticing points of agreement and disagreement. These

they also observe in visual representations connected to their speech. From the evidence, they instantly arrive at a conclusion, which rises spontaneously out of the harmony thus imposed on conflicting ideas. All other subjects are dealt with in the same way.

Our souls take up this ability immediately after death. Good spirits like nothing better at that time than to teach uninformed newcomers.

[3] The spirits themselves are unaware—unless the Lord inspires them to reflect on it—that they speak such an exalted language among themselves or that they enjoy such an outstanding gift. This way of speaking is natural for them, and by then it is ingrained. Their situation is like that of people who fix their minds on the meaning of a message and not on the words or form of expression: if they do not reflect on it, they sometimes do not even know what language is being used.

This, then, is the way spirits talk; but the speech of angelic spirits **1642** is even more universal and perfect, and the speech of angels still more so. There are three heavens, as noted before [§§459, 684]. Good spirits inhabit the first, angelic spirits the second, and angels the third. Perfection increases as it rises, so that superficial elements have almost the same relation to deeper ones as hearing (to illustrate by comparison) has to sight, and sight has to thought. What the ear can absorb from speech in an hour can be presented to the eye in a minute—a panorama of fields, mansions, and cities, for instance. And what the eye takes many hours to observe, the thought can grasp in a minute. The speech of spirits bears the same ratio to that of angelic spirits, and the speech of angelic spirits to that of angels. Angelic spirits incorporate more clear, distinct concepts into one idea, spoken or thought, than spirits cover in several thousand; and angels outdo angelic spirits to the same degree. How must it be with the Lord, then, the source of all the life in our feelings, thoughts, and speech, the one who alone is the Message and the Word?

The speech of angelic spirits defies comprehension. To say just a few **1643** words about it—but only about the representative kind—it presents the actual subject matter in a representative form. This form is a remarkable one drawn from the objects of the senses, and the sweetest, most beautiful images vary it in countless ways. A continuous stream of emotions rising out of the happiness of mutual love flows in from the Lord through the next higher heaven, making absolutely everything seem to come alive. Every single topic of discussion is exhibited in this way, in unbroken series of images. To describe just one representative image from any series intelligibly would be impossible.

These are the influences that affect the thinking of [good] spirits, but the spirits are unaware of those influences except as a general something-or-other flowing in and affecting them. They lack a distinct perception of details that angelic spirits perceive quite clearly.

1644 There are many evil spirits who are not wholly superficial. They too do not talk the way [good] spirits do but likewise focus on the fundamental assumption behind an idea, so they are more subtle than [good] spirits. Their numbers are large. They are completely separate from angelic spirits, whom they cannot even begin to approach. These evil, subtler spirits also link their own ideas in an abstract way to objects [of the senses] and to subjects [of discussion], but only to impure ones. Within those objects and subjects, they create for themselves a variety of images, uniformly foul, in which they wrap their ideas. They resemble idiots.

Their manner of speech was described to me, and also represented as a heap of filthy garbage overflowing its container. The intellectual element of it was presented as the backside of a horse whose forequarters could not be seen. (In the world of spirits a horse represents the intellect.)

The speech of angelic spirits, in contrast, was represented by a virgin tastefully clothed, charmingly dressed, wearing a beautiful whitish garment neatly gathered to a kind of bodice.

1645 Angels' speech, however, defies description. It is far superior to the speech of spirits, since it surpasses that of angelic spirits, and is positively unintelligible to us in every way as long as we are living in the body. Spirits in the world of spirits cannot even form a notion of it for themselves, since it lies beyond the reach of their thoughts.

The speech of angels does not involve mental images representing the subject matter, as with spirits and angelic spirits. Instead, angels speak in terms of purpose and therefore of usefulness, which are the first and most important elements of any subject. Into these they weave their angelic thoughts, which take on endlessly new and different forms. A mutually loving goodness from the Lord touches each and every word with an inner delight and happiness, while the truth of a faith inspired by mutual love gives it beauty and tremendous appeal. Purpose and consequent use are like containers that are extraordinarily pliable, subject in the most pleasurable way to unending variation, manifested in heavenly and spiritual forms we cannot possibly comprehend. The Lord holds angels in these thoughts because his kingdom is exclusively a kingdom of purpose and usefulness.

As a result, the angels present with us pay no attention to anything but purpose and use, and they elicit nothing else from our thoughts.

Nothing else matters to them—whether it belongs to the mental or material world—because it is far beneath their sphere of interest.

In the world of spirits (to the inner eye, in other words), angels' speech sometimes appears as the flickering of a light or of a radiant flame. The appearance differs, depending on the state of emotion embodied in their words. It is only the most general emotional components of their speech, rising out of countless individual feelings, that are presented in this way.

1646

The speech of heavenly angels is different from that of spiritual angels, and it is even more impossible to describe or explain. Heavenly good as a motive is what they apply their thinking to, and consequently they have true happiness. Amazing to say, their speech is much fuller, because they sit at the spring or source from which the living energy of thought and speech flows.

1647

Good spirits and angelic spirits have a way of speaking all together in large numbers, particularly in circle choirs or choruses. (I will have more to say on these later [§§2294, 2595–2596, 3350–3351, 3893, 5173:1, 5181–5183, 8115], with the Lord's divine mercy.) Their choral speech I have heard quite often. It has a rhythmic flow to it. They do not think at all about the words or concepts, which their meaning pours into without effort. No words or concepts that complicate the sense or distract the listener ever inject themselves. Neither do any that have an artificial feel, or that seem to them to display a vain, self-flattering elegance. Such faults would immediately disturb them. They never fixate on a word but consider only the meaning. Words are the natural consequences of the meaning itself. The spirits end in unison, and usually a single unison. When the ending is more elaborate, intonation carries them from one unison to the next.

1648

These traits arise from the fact that the spirits think and talk in concert. So they have a smooth-flowing style of speech that results from the interconnections in their community and the unanimity of it. This was the style of ancient songs, and it is the style of the Psalms of David.

Surprisingly, this manner of speech—with a cadence that imitates the rhythm and music of a song—is natural for spirits. It is the way they talk among themselves, even though they are unaware of doing so. Souls take up the habit of speaking this way right after death. I too was introduced to it, and eventually it became familiar to me.

1649

The reason spirits talk this way is that they speak in concert as a community, although they usually do not realize they are doing so. This indicates clearly that all spirits are divided into communities, and that all things are therefore divided into something analogous to communities.

1650   For more on the way spirits talk and how it varies, see the end of the present chapter [§§1757–1764].

Genesis 14

1. And it happened in the days of Amraphel, king of Shinar; Arioch, king of Ellasar; Chedorlaomer, king of Elam; and Tidal, king of Goiim,

2. that they made war with Bera, king of Sodom; and with Birsha, king of Gomorrah; Shinab, king of Admah; and Shemeber, king of Zeboiim; and the king of Bela (which is Zoar).

3. All the latter gathered together to the valley of Siddim (that is, the salt sea).

4. For twelve years they served Chedorlaomer, and in the thirteenth year they rebelled.

5. And in the fourteenth year came Chedorlaomer and the kings who were with him, and they struck the Rephaim in Ashteroth-karnaim, and the Zuzim in Ham, and the Emim in Shaveh-kiriathaim,

6. and the Horites on their mountain (Seir), all the way to El-paran, which is up in the wilderness.

7. And they turned back and came to En-mishpat (that is, Kadesh) and struck every field of the Amalekites, and also the Amorite living in Hazazon-tamar.

8. And the king of Sodom, and the king of Gomorrah, and the king of Admah, and the king of Zeboiim, and the king of Bela (which is Zoar) went out and marshaled the battle with them in the valley of Siddim—

9. with Chedorlaomer, king of Elam; and Tidal, king of Goiim; and Amraphel, king of Shinar; and Arioch, king of Ellasar; four kings against five.

10. And the valley of Siddim was pit after pit of tar, and the king of Sodom and [the king] of Gomorrah fled and fell there, and the rest fled into the mountain.

11. And [the four] took all the resources of Sodom and Gomorrah, and all their food, and went away.

12. And they took Lot and his property—the son of Abram's brother—and went away; and he had been living in Sodom.

13. And an escapee came and told Abram the Hebrew, and he was living in the oak groves of Mamre the Amorite, brother of Eshcol and brother of Aner; and these were men bound by a pact with Abram.

14. And Abram heard that his brother had been captured, and he mustered his trainees, offspring of his household, three hundred eighteen of them, and pursued all the way to Dan.

15. And he divided [his forces] against [the enemy] by night, he and his servants, and struck them and pursued them all the way to Hobah, which is to the left of Damascus.

16. And he brought back all the property; and Lot his brother and his property he also brought back, and also the women and the people.

17. And the king of Sodom went out to meet him, after he returned (from striking Chedorlaomer and the kings who were with him) to the valley of Shaveh, that is, the king's valley.

18. And Melchizedek, king of Salem, brought out bread and wine; and he was a priest to God the Highest.

19. And he blessed him and said, "A blessing on Abram from God the Highest, possessor of the heavens and the earth.

20. And a blessing on God the Highest, who has delivered your enemies into your hand." And [Abram] gave him a tenth of everything.

21. And the king of Sodom said to Abram, "Give me the souls, and the property take for yourself."

22. And Abram said to the king of Sodom, "I have lifted my hand to Jehovah, God the Highest, possessor of the heavens and the earth:

23. 'From the string of a shoe even to its strap, if I should take anything that is yours, . . . !' To prevent you from saying, 'I have made Abram rich.'

24. Excepting only what the young men have eaten, and the share of the men who went with me—Aner, Eshcol, and Mamre; these shall take their share."

Summary

THIS chapter deals with the spiritual battles the Lord fought, which the wars depicted in the chapter represent and symbolize.

1651

1652   The goodness and truth present in his outer self—which merely appeared to be good and true—were the weapons the Lord used during his youth in his combat against evil and falsity. The kings named in verse 1 symbolize apparent goodness and truth, while those named in verse 2 symbolize the evil and falsity he fought against. The latter were unclean (verse 3).

1653   The evil and falsity that he battled did not show up at all until it erupted during his adolescence, as symbolized by the kings' service to Chedorlaomer (verse 4).

1654   At that point the Lord defeated and thoroughly conquered every variety of false persuasion—the Rephaim, Zuzim, Emim, and Horites (verses 5, 6). He then did the same to the outright falsity and evil meant by the Amalekite and Amorite (verse 7), and afterward to all other falsity and evil, meant by the kings mentioned in verses 8, 9, 10, 11.

1655   Apparent truth and goodness, which are not intrinsically true or good, seized control of his outer self (verse 12). His rational self (Abram the Hebrew) perceiving this, rescued and freed it (verses 13, 14, 15, 16).

1656   After these conflicts, evil and falsity surrendered (verse 17).

1657   The Lord's deepest self within his intermediate self (his divinity within his rationality) is Melchizedek, and it blessed him after his struggles (verses 18, 19, 20). The tenth part is the remnant, or the states of goodness and truth remaining with him from those struggles (verse 20).

1658   The evil and hellish spirits he had conquered begged for their lives; they did not care about anything else. The Lord, however, took nothing from them, because their evil and falsity lent him no strength. Still, he did give good spirits and angels power over them. (All of which is symbolized by the contents of verses 21, 22, 23, 24.)

❀❀❀❀❀❀❀❀❀❀❀❀❀❀❀❀❀❀❀❀❀❀❀❀❀❀❀❀

Inner Meaning

1659   THE contents of this chapter do not look as though they could represent anything. All the chapter talks about is the wars among a number of kings, Abram's rescue of Lot, and finally Melchizedek, so it reads as if it did not have a single heavenly secret buried inside. Still, in the inner meaning, these elements of the story (like all the others) conceal the deepest secrets possible, which follow on in an unbroken chain from those above and lead in an unbroken chain to those below.

[2] The earlier parts spoke of the Lord and his education, and of his outer self, which needed to unite with his inner self by means of knowledge both secular and religious. As noted, though, his outer self harbored obstacles to the union, as a result of his maternal heredity [§§1414, 1444, 1573, 1601–1603]. What interfered had to be thrust out through combat and times of trial before his outer self could become one with his inner, or in other words, before his human quality could become one with his divine. The present chapter therefore discusses those struggles, which the inner sense represents and symbolizes through the wars here described.

Within the church it is known that Melchizedek represented the Lord and as a result that when the subject is Melchizedek the inner sense speaks of the Lord. A further conclusion, logically, is that not only what is said of Melchizedek but everything else too has a representative meaning. After all, not a syllable could have been written in the Word which did not come down from heaven and in which angels consequently do not see heavenly dimensions.

[3] In the earliest times, too, wars represented many things. The people of those times called them *Jehovah's Wars,* and the sole purpose of the term was to symbolize the struggles of the church and of the people in the church, or in other words, to symbolize the spiritual trials of those people. Spiritual trials are nothing but our battles and wars against the evil in us, so they are fights against the Devil's crew, which stirs up the evil and tries to destroy religion and religious people.

The wars mentioned in the Word have no other meaning, as is obvious from the consideration that the Word cannot treat of anything but the Lord, his kingdom, and the church. This is because it is divine rather than human and accordingly has to do with heaven rather than the world. So the wars of the literal story can mean nothing else in an inner sense. You will be able to see this better below.

Genesis 14:1, 2. *And it happened in the days of Amraphel, king of Shinar; Arioch, king of Ellasar; Chedorlaomer, king of Elam; and Tidal, king of Goiim, that they made war with Bera, king of Sodom; and with Birsha, king of Gomorrah; Shinab, king of Admah; and Shemeber, king of Zeboiim; and the king of Bela (which is Zoar).* **1660**

It happened in the days of Amraphel, king of Shinar; Arioch, king of Ellasar; Chedorlaomer, king of Elam; and Tidal, king of Goiim, symbolizes just so many different categories of apparent goodness and truth (which are

not good or true in and of themselves) in the Lord's outer self; each of
the kings and each of the nations symbolizes some variety of such goodness and truth. *They made war with Bera, king of Sodom; and with Birsha,*
king of Gomorrah; Shinab, king of Admah; and Shemeber, king of Zeboiim;
and the king of Bela (which is Zoar), symbolizes just so many categories of
evil desire and distorted conviction that the Lord fought against.

1661　　*And it happened in the days of Amraphel, king of Shinar; Arioch, king of*
Ellasar; Chedorlaomer, king of Elam; and Tidal, king of Goiim, symbolizes
just so many different categories of apparent goodness and truth (which
are not good or true in and of themselves) in the Lord's outer self. This
can be seen from the inner-level symbolism of all these kings, as well as
from what follows. The subject is the Lord's combat with evil and falsity,
and here it is about his first struggle, which took place in his adolescence
and at the dawn of his adulthood. It was a struggle that he first faced and
underwent after he had been trained in both secular and religious knowledge. That is why the verse says that it happened in the days of these kings.

[2] None of us can possibly fight evil and falsity until we know how
to recognize them and consequently until we have been educated. We
do not know what evil is, still less what falsity is, until we come into
the capacities of intellect and judgment. That is the reason we do not
undergo spiritual trials until we reach adult age—the age of majority in
our case, of adolescence in the Lord's.

The very first weapons that any of us wield are the good impulses and
true concepts we have acquired by learning about them. These we use
as the basis and means for evaluating evil impulses and false concepts.
[3] When we first start to fight, we universally believe that the goodness and
truth we wield are our own; we take credit for them and also for the power
to resist. Such an attitude is acceptable, because at that point we are incapable of knowing any better. Until we have been reborn there is much
that we cannot possibly see clearly enough to say that we know, acknowledge, and believe it. We do not see that nothing good or true comes from
us, that everything good and true comes from the Lord, and that we have
no power of our own to resist anything evil or false. We do not realize
that evil spirits stir up the evil and falsity they flood us with. Still less do
we realize that evil spirits put us in touch with hell, or that hell exerts
as much pressure on us as the ocean does on each stone in a jetty—far too
much pressure for us ever to resist by our own strength. Still, since until
we regenerate we cannot help supposing the power is ours, we are allowed
to think this way and so to be introduced into the battles of spiritual crisis. Later on, though, we start to see the light.

[4] While we are at the stage of imagining that goodness and truth come from ourselves and that the strength to resist is ours, the goodness and truth with which we fight evil and falsity are neither good nor true, even though they seem to be so. An inflated sense of self lurks inside them, and we take credit for the victory. We pride ourselves on having conquered evil and falsity, when it is the Lord alone who fights and wins. No one can see the truth of this but those reborn through times of tribulation.

[5] The Lord was introduced into fearsome struggles against evil and falsity in his early adolescence, and at that time he too could not imagine any differently. This was partly due to the divine plan—that his human side be introduced to and united with his divine side through constant battles and victories. It was also due to the fact that the goodness and truth he used in the combat with evil and falsity belonged to his outer self. So the goodness and truth were not entirely divine, which is why they are called apparent goodness and truth. For all these reasons, his divine side kept introducing his human side into the struggle in such a way that it would win by means of its own power.

The secrets hidden in all this, however, are too manifold ever to describe. To put it briefly, the goodness and truth the Lord had that he used for weapons in his early battles were saturated with his mother's heredity. To the extent that his mother's heredity saturated them, they were not divine, but as he overcame evil and falsity they were gradually purified and became divine.

Each of the kings and each of the nations symbolizes a variety of such goodness or truth, as can be seen from their symbolism on an inner level in relation to the subject at hand. Each nation and each land has some definite though general symbolism, in both a positive and a negative sense. This general symbolism, however, adapts to the subject at hand. **1662**

Apparent goodness and apparent truth are symbolized by the names of the kings and the nations here, and much evidence exists to prove it, but it has been proved often enough before. Besides, so many names occur here that explaining the symbolism of each one individually would take too long.

They made war with Bera, king of Sodom; and with Birsha, king of Gomorrah; Shinab, king of Admah; and Shemeber, king of Zeboiim; and the king of Bela (which is Zoar), symbolizes just so many categories of evil desire and distorted conviction that the Lord fought against. This too can be seen from the symbolism of the kings and nations mentioned here, and from what follows as well. Again, explaining precisely **1663** which evil desire or distorted persuasion each of them symbolizes would take too long. The symbolism of *Sodom* and *Gomorrah,* of *Admah* and *Zeboiim,* and of *Zoar* has been touched on already [§§1212, 1589]. It is the most general or universal categories of evil and falsity that are symbolized on the inner level here, and they follow one another in order.

[2] The Lord underwent and suffered trials heavier than those of anyone else in the universe—the heaviest of all—but this is not well known from the Word, which merely notes that he was in the wilderness for forty days, where he was tested by the Devil [Matthew 4:1–2; Mark 1:12–13; Luke 4:1–2]. The actual trials that he then experienced are not described in more than a few words, but those few cover everything. In Mark 1:12, 13, for instance, it says that he was with the animals there, which symbolize the worst of the hellish mob. Subsequent details—that the Devil led him onto the spires of the Temple and onto a tall mountain—are nothing but images representing the terrible crises he faced in the wilderness [Matthew 4:3–11; Luke 4:3–13]. There will be more on this below, the Lord in his divine mercy willing.

1664   The *wars* here symbolize nothing else on an inner level than spiritual battles or trials, as stated above in the preliminaries [§§1651, 1659]. So do other battles mentioned in the Word, especially in the prophets. Human wars have no importance on the inner planes of the Word, since they are not spiritual or heavenly and the Word contains only what is spiritual and heavenly.

The following passages (and many others as well) point to the symbolism of wars in the Word as fights with the Devil or, to put it another way, with hell. In John:

> They are spirits of demons, working signs [of their intent] to go out to the monarchs of the earth and of the whole inhabited world, to gather them for the *war* on that great day of God Almighty. (Revelation 16:14)

Anyone can see that no other type of war on the great day of God Almighty is meant in this verse. [2] In the same author:

> The beast that comes up out of the abyss will make *war.* (Revelation 11:7)

The abyss here is hell. In the same author:

> The dragon was enraged against the woman and went off to make *war* with the rest of her seed—those who were keeping God's commands and who possess Jesus Christ's testimony. (Revelation 12:17)

It was granted to [the beast] to make *war* with the godly. (Revelation 13:7)

All these wars are the kinds of fights we face in times of trial. The *wars* of the southern and northern monarchs and so on in Daniel 10 and 11 have no other meaning. Neither do the things said of Michael in Daniel 10:13, 21; 12:1; Revelation 12:7. [3] The other prophets also provide evidence that wars symbolize nothing else. In Ezekiel, for example:

> You have not gone up into the breaches or built a wall for the house of Israel, to stand fast in *war* on the day of Jehovah. (Ezekiel 13:5)

This is addressed to the prophets. In Isaiah:

> They will beat swords into hoes and their spears into scythes; nation will not lift sword against nation, and they will not learn *war* anymore. (Isaiah 2:4)

It is obvious here that no other kind of war is meant, and as a result that the weapons mentioned in the Word—swords, spears, shields, and so on—truly do mean the implements of such war. [4] In the same author:

> Bring water to meet the thirsty, you who live in the land of Tema; approach the wanderers with bread for them; for they will wander in the face of swords, in the face of an outstretched sword and of a strung bow and of the weight of *war*. (Isaiah 21:14, 15)

In Jeremiah:

> Shepherds and their flocks will come to the daughter of Zion. They will fix their tents near her all around. They will each graze their space. Consecrate *war* against her. Rise and let us go up at noon. (Jeremiah 6:3, 4, 5)

No other war is meant here, because it is a war against the daughter of Zion, that is, against the church. [5] In the same author:

> In what way have they not abandoned the city of praise, the city of my joy! Therefore its youths will fall in its streets and all the *men of war* will be cut off on that day. (Jeremiah 49:25, 26)

The city of praise and joy stands for attributes of the church. The men of war stand for people who put up a fight. [6] In Hosea:

> I will strike a pact with them on that day—with the wild animal of the field, and with the bird in the heavens and the creeping animal

of the ground. And bow and sword and *war* I will break off from the
earth, and I will make them lie down securely. (Hosea 2:18)

Again, just as war stands for personal struggles, the different weapons
here stand for the implements of that spiritual struggle, which are broken
when our obsessions and distorted thinking die down and we come into
a time of peace and quiet. [7] In David:

> Observe the works of Jehovah, who makes wastelands on the earth,
> stopping *wars* all the way to the end of the earth. The bow he breaks,
> and he lops off the spear; chariots he burns with fire. (Psalms 46:8, 9)

Likewise. In the same author:

> In Salem is God's dwelling place, and his abode is in Zion. There he
> broke the bow's flaming arrows, the shield, and the sword—and *war*.
> (Psalms 76:2, 3)

Because priests represented the Lord, who does all the fighting for us,
their function is described as *military service* in Numbers 4:23, 35, 39, 43, 47.

[8] We do not see that Jehovah alone—the Lord—fights and overcomes the Devil in us during our spiritual struggles, and yet it is the
unchanging truth. Evil spirits cannot lift a finger against us without permission, and angels cannot ward off the least threat except by the Lord's
power. So the Lord alone is the one who carries the weight of every battle
and wins. This was represented in various places by the wars the children
of Israel waged against the surrounding nations. The statement that the
Lord is the only one to do this also appears in Moses:

> Jehovah your God, walking in front of you, *he will fight* for you. (Deu-
> teronomy 1:30)

In the same author:

> Jehovah your God is walking with you, to *fight* for you with your ene-
> mies to save you. (Deuteronomy 20:4)

Joshua contains such statements as well, as in 23:3, 5. [9] All the wars
there against the idolatrous residents of the land of Canaan represented
battles carried on with hell by the Lord and therefore by his church and
people in his church. This idea accords with the following words in
Isaiah, too:

> As the lion roars—and the young lion—over its prey, when an abun-
> dance of shepherds race up against it, by whose voice [the lion] is not

dismayed and by whose commotion it is not distressed; so Jehovah Sabaoth will come down to *do battle* on Zion's mountain and on its hill. (Isaiah 31:4)

[10] So Jehovah (the Lord) is also called a man of war, as in Moses:

Jehovah is a *man of war;* Jehovah is his name. (Exodus 15:3)

In Isaiah:

Jehovah will go forth as a hero; as a *man of wars* he will rouse his zeal. He will shout, even bellow; over his enemies he will prevail. (Isaiah 42:13)

That is why many activities of war are also attributed to the Lord, like the shouting and bellowing here. [11] Spirits and angels appear as men of war too, when they are representing [the Lord]. In Joshua, for instance:

Joshua raised his eyes and looked, and here, now, a man standing opposite him, and *his sword was unsheathed in his hand.* He said to Joshua, "I am the *leader of Jehovah's army."* And Joshua fell on his face to the earth. (Joshua 5:13, 14)

The scene appeared this way because it was representative. So Jacob's descendants called their wars *Jehovah's wars.* [12] The ancient churches did the same, since they had books likewise named *Jehovah's Wars,* as is evident in Moses:

It is said in the book *Jehovah's Wars . . .* (Numbers 21:14, 15)

These wars were written about in the same way as the wars mentioned in the current chapter, but they were purely symbolic of the church's battles. This method of writing was well known in ancient times because the people of that day were deeper and their thinking loftier.

Genesis 14:3. *All the latter gathered together to the valley of Siddim (that is, the salt sea).*   **1665**

All the latter gathered together to the valley of Siddim means that they had unclean desires. *That is, the salt sea,* symbolizes the rank falsities that resulted.

They all gathered together to the valley of Siddim means that they had unclean desires. This can be seen from the symbolism of the *valley of Siddim,* portrayed below in verse 10 as "pit after pit of tar," or a place full of tar pits, which symbolize foul and unclean desires (§1299). The meaning can also be seen from this: that Sodom, Gomorrah, Admah, and Zeboiim symbolized evil cravings and distorted persuasions, which are inherently unclean.   **1666**

Anyone in the church can see that they are unclean, and in the next world it is literally visible that they are so. Spirits who embrace such things love nothing better than to play out their lives in the midst of standing water, mud, and excrement; their very nature carries such an environment with it. Filth like this wafts perceptibly from them when they go near the realm of good spirits, especially when they feel like harassing those spirits—in other words, like gathering to attack them. Such evidence shows what the valley of Siddim is.

[2] *That is, the salt sea,* symbolizes the rank falsities that resulted. This can be seen from the symbolism of the *salt sea,* which is essentially the same as that of the Siddim valley (since it says, "the valley of Siddim, that is, the salt sea"). The reason the phrase is added, despite having the same symbolism, is that the salt sea symbolizes the false notions that gush out of our corrupt desires. Not one such desire exists that does not produce distortions. The driving energy of our appetites can be compared to a coal fire, and falsity, to the feeble light it yields. Just as fire cannot burn without glowing, our cravings cannot burn without producing falsity. Every craving is tied up with some foul love, since what we love we crave; that is why it is called a craving. The craving itself is an arm of our love. Whatever promotes or agrees with that unsavory love is called falsity. This goes to show why "the salt sea" was added to "the valley of Siddim" here.

[3] Because our appetites and false notions are what devastate us spiritually, or strip us of all the living energy of love for what is good and all devotion to truth, devastation is depicted in many places as salt barrens. In Jeremiah, for example:

> Those who use flesh as their arm will be like a naked shrub in the desert and will not see when something good comes. And they will settle in the *parched places* in the wilderness—a *salty land,* and one that is not inhabited. (Jeremiah 17:[5], 6)

In Ezekiel:

> It has its marshes and its swamps, and they are not being cured; they will be given over to *salt.* (Ezekiel 47:11)

In David:

> Jehovah makes rivers into a desert, and outlets of water into a dry gulch, a *land of fruit into a salty land,* because of the wickedness of those living in it. (Psalms 107:33, 34)

In Zephaniah:

> Moab will be like *Sodom,* and the children of Ammon like *Gomorrah:* a place abandoned to nettle, and a *salt pit,* and a ruin forever. (Zephaniah 2:9)

[4] In Moses:

> *Sulfur* there will be, and *salt;* the whole land will be a conflagration. It will not be sown and will not sprout, and no grass will come up in it, as in the overthrow of *Sodom* and *Gomorrah, Admah* and *Zeboiim.* (Deuteronomy 29:23)

Sulfur and salt and the conflagration of the whole land stand for devastation of good impulses and true thoughts. Sulfur stands for the devastation of anything good, salt for the devastation of anything true, since heat and salt destroy the land and its produce in the same way that ardent craving destroys what is good and distorted thinking destroys truth.

As salt symbolized devastation, it was customary for people to sow with salt the cities they had destroyed, so that they could not be rebuilt. An example appears in Judges 9:45.

Salt can also be taken in the opposite sense, as meaning a fertilizer and a flavoring.

[5] Genesis 14:4. *For twelve years they served Chedorlaomer, and in the thirteenth year they rebelled.*

For twelve years they served Chedorlaomer means that evil and falsity did not show up in his youth; rather they were subservient to apparent goodness and truth. *And in the thirteenth year they rebelled* symbolizes the threshold of his trials in youth.

For twelve years they served Chedorlaomer means that evil and falsity did not show up in his youth; rather they were subservient to apparent goodness and truth. This is established by the representation and symbolism of *Chedorlaomer* and of those who served him, discussed above at verse 1. It can also be seen from the symbolism of the number *twelve.*

Chedorlaomer, along with those named above in verse 1, symbolizes apparent goodness and truth in the Lord; so he symbolizes the Lord's outer self in regard to apparent goodness and truth. The rest of the chapter makes it clear that Chedorlaomer here stands for all the kings mentioned in verse 1 as a group. So does the fact that he was the king of Elam, the symbolism of which was dealt with earlier [§1228], as being the faith that grows out of love for others, or out of charity. It symbolizes both truth and goodness here, then, since faith and all that goes with

1667

faith consists entirely of truth, while charity and all that goes with charity consists of goodness.

[2] Here, however, it is the goodness of childhood, which may appear good but is not, as long as inherited evil pollutes it. It is the product of a selfishness and materialism that are embedded in and attached to it. Whatever results from self-love and materialism during childhood appears to be good. It is *not* good, but should still be called good when it appears in children or adolescents who do not yet know what real goodness is. Ignorance excuses them, and innocence makes it seem good. The situation changes, though, when we learn to recognize right and wrong. The kind of goodness and truth that exist in a youth not yet educated is symbolized by Chedorlaomer.

[3] The fact that they served *twelve years* symbolizes the whole period of this type of goodness and truth. On an inner level, twelve symbolizes every aspect of the faith that belongs to charity, or the faith that grows out of charity (just as Elam did at Genesis 10:22 [§1228]). As long as this kind of goodness and truth is present in us—whether it is during our youth or at any other stage in our life—evil and falsity can achieve nothing. In other words, evil spirits do not then dare to do anything or to inflict any harm, as is fairly clear from children, well-intentioned young people, and the simplehearted; even if evil spirits (the worst of the Devil's crew) are present with such a person, they cannot do anything. They are enslaved, which is what is symbolized here by the twelve years that they served Chedorlaomer.

[4] The reason they are then enslaved and subservient is that the person has not yet acquired an aura of self-interest and falsity. Evil spirits and demons are not allowed to act on us unless they act on the traits we have chosen for ourselves by the way we live. They are forbidden to act on the traits we have merely inherited. Until we acquire these auras, then, evil spirits serve us. As soon as we do acquire them, on the other hand, evil spirits pour into us and attempt to control us. This is because they are then in their element, and they find a kind of pleasure in it—a pleasure that is the core of their life. Where the carcass is, there are the eagles [Matthew 24:28; Luke 17:37].

1668   *And in the thirteenth year they rebelled* symbolizes the threshold of his trials in youth, as can be seen from the symbolism of the *thirteenth year* and of *rebelling*.

The *thirteenth year* is right between the twelfth and fourteenth. The symbolism of twelve has already been given, and the symbolism of fourteen appears below. The point halfway between times free of trial and times full of trial is thirteen.

The symbolism of *rebelling* can be seen from its use in relation to the evils (or evil spirits) present in us when they are enslaved and subservient but then start to rise up and make trouble. [2] The extent of rebellion by our evils (or the evil spirits) depends on the extent to which we justify any evil or falsity in ourselves, despite our desire to dedicate ourselves to goodness and truth. To put it another way, their rebellion depends on the extent to which corrupt desires and false ideas worm their way into our good impulses and true ideas. Corrupt desires and false ideas are what evil spirits place their life in; good impulses and true ideas are what angels put their life in. This gives rise to trouble and conflict. It arises in everyone who has a conscience, and it arose even more intensely in the Lord when he was young, since he had an innate perception [of right and wrong]. Those who have conscience sense the trouble and conflict as a dull ache, but those who have perception feel it as a sharp pain; and the deeper their perception, the sharper the pain. This suggests how much worse the Lord's trials were than ours, since he had interior and inmost perception.

Genesis 14:5. *And in the fourteenth year came Chedorlaomer and the kings who were with him, and they struck the Rephaim in Ashteroth-karnaim, and the Zuzim in Ham, and the Emim in Shaveh-kiriathaim.* 1669

In the fourteenth year symbolizes his first trial. *Came Chedorlaomer* symbolizes apparent goodness in his outer self. *And the kings who were with him* symbolizes apparent truth linked with that goodness. *And they struck the Rephaim in Ashteroth-karnaim, and the Zuzim in Ham, and the Emim in Shaveh-kiriathaim* symbolizes persuasive lies, or rather the hells that do the persuading, which the Lord defeated thoroughly.

The symbolism of *in the fourteenth year* as his first trial can be seen from the symbolism of *fourteen,* or the end of a second "week," as discussed at §728, where a period of seven days, or one week, symbolizes the beginning of a person's trials. A period of fourteen days, or two weeks, has the same symbolism. The number here is fourteen because it looks back to the twelve of the previous verse, which meant the period of youth, as noted. 1670

The symbolism of *came Chedorlaomer* as apparent goodness in his outer self is established by the symbolism of *Chedorlaomer* (discussed at the last verse) as apparent goodness and truth. Here he symbolizes only 1671 goodness because the text adds "and the kings who were with him," and these symbolize truth.

1672   The symbolism of *and the kings who were with him* as apparent truth linked with that goodness can be seen from the symbolism of *kings* in the Word. In the narrative and prophetic parts of the Word, monarchs, kingdoms, and peoples symbolize truth and everything connected with truth, as a great deal of evidence can confirm. The Word carefully distinguishes between a people and a nation; a people symbolizes truth, and a nation, goodness, as shown previously, in §§1259, 1260. Peoples are said to have monarchs; nations for the most part are not. Before the children of Israel agitated for kings, they were a nation and represented goodness, or a heavenly quality. After they sought and received a king, they became a people and represented not goodness (or a heavenly quality) but truth (or a spiritual quality). This was the reason it counted against them as a flaw (1 Samuel 8:7–end). I will have more to say on this elsewhere, with the Lord's divine mercy.

Because the text here mentions Chedorlaomer and adds "the kings who were with him," both goodness and truth are symbolized—goodness, by Chedorlaomer; truth, by the kings. But the nature of that goodness and truth at the threshold of the Lord's trials has been described above [§1661].

1673   *And they struck the Rephaim in Ashteroth-karnaim, and the Zuzim in Ham, and the Emim in Shaveh-kiriathaim* symbolizes persuasive lies, or rather the hells that do the persuading, which the Lord defeated thoroughly. This can be seen from the symbolism of the *Rephaim, Zuzim,* and *Emim.* They are the same type of being as the Nephilim mentioned in Genesis 6:4, who symbolize false persuasions, or delusions. Or rather they symbolize those whose delusions about their own importance and superiority caused them not to value anything holy or true, and who infused false thinking with perverse cravings. This symbolism was more than amply demonstrated at that verse (see §581 and the verses quoted there: Numbers 13:33; Deuteronomy 2:10; Isaiah 14:9; 26:14, 19; Psalms 88:10).

The three nations here, along with the Horites on Mount Seir, symbolize various types of persuasive lies. There are many kinds, differentiated not only by the falsity involved but also by the appetite linked with or permeating them, or the appetite from which they spring and flow. People cannot possibly grasp what the different types of persuasive lie are like, when they only barely know that such a thing exists, or that such a thing as an evil craving exists. In the other life, though, such things are arranged into their different categories and subcategories along very clearly drawn lines.

[2] The people who lived before the Flood—particularly the ones called Nephilim—adopted the most dreadful lies as their convictions. These people were so bad that now in the other world, by the force of their persuasions, they rob the spirits they come across of any ability to think. The victims hardly feel as though they are still alive, let alone capable of thinking a valid thought. There is, as I have shown, a sharing of all thoughts in that world [§§315, 549, 969, 1390–1391], so when a force as persuasive as this exerts an influence, it inevitably kills off all power of thought in others.

This was the type of unspeakable nations the Lord fought and defeated in his early youth. Had he not done so through his coming into the world, no one would be left on the planet today, because the Lord governs all of us by means of spirits.

At the present time, these people's fantasies create around them a kind of foggy crag that they are always trying to break free from, without success. (For more information, see §§1265–1272 and many earlier sections.) They and others like them are meant by Isaiah:

> The dead will not live, the *Rephaim* will not rise, because you inflicted punishment on them and destroyed them and wiped out all memory of them. (Isaiah 26:14)

And in David:

> Will you do a miracle for the dead? Will the *Rephaim* arise, will they acclaim you? (Psalms 88:10)

The dead here mean not the dead but the damned.

[3] Some people today (especially those from the Christian world) also have delusions, but their delusions are not as horrendous as those of the pre-Flood people. A convinced belief in falsity can involve both our voluntary and our intellectual sides, as it did in the people who lived before the Flood and in those meant here by the Rephaim, Zuzim, and Emim. When it involves only our intellectual side, however, and rises out of false premises that we confirm in our own mind, it is a very different thing. This kind of conviction is not as strong or as lethal as that of the former people, but in the next life it still troubles other spirits a great deal and in some measure deprives them of the ability to think.

In people on earth, spirits who hold this kind of conviction stimulate only those ideas that tend to support falsity. They leave us incapable of seeing falsity as anything but true, and evil as anything but good. Their aura is what does it. As soon as angels call up any hint of truth, these spirits choke and smother it.

[4] We can tell whether such spirits control us simply by this: If we consider the truth of the Word to be false, if we have proved this to ourselves so firmly that we are blind to any other way of thinking, we can be fairly certain such spirits are present with us and dictating to us. Again, when we convince ourselves that our own personal advantage is good for everyone, when we feel that nothing contributes to the larger good unless it also contributes to our own profit, the evil spirits with us offer so many confirmations that we cannot see otherwise. People who identify all self-interest with the common good (or disguise it as the common good) do the same in the other life with the common good there.

Constant, living experience has taught me to recognize that this is what spirits' influence on us is like.

1674   Genesis 14:6. . . . *and the Horites on their mountain (Seir), all the way to El-paran, which is up in the wilderness.*

The Horites on their mountain (Seir) symbolize persuasive lies that result from self-love. *All the way to El-paran, which is up in the wilderness,* symbolizes the extent of them.

1675   The symbolism of *the Horites on their mountain (Seir)* as persuasive lies that result from self-love can be seen from the symbolism of the *Horites* and of *Seir.*

To turn to the *Horites,* they were people inhabiting Mount Seir, as indicated by Genesis 36:8, 20, and following verses, which mention Esau, who is also called Edom. In a positive sense, Esau (Edom) symbolizes and at the same time represents the Lord's human quality. Much evidence in both the narrative and the prophetic parts of the Word demonstrates this, as will be discussed later [§§3300, 3302, 3322, 3599, 4241, 4641], with the Lord's divine mercy. Because the Horites represented people who persuade themselves of falsity, and because representations in those days had tangible reality, the occasion on which Esau's descendants drove the Horites off Mount Seir represents the same thing [as the present verse]. [2] In Moses' words:

> This too is considered the land of the *Rephaim.* The *Rephaim* lived in it before, and the Ammonites call them Zamzummim—a people large and numerous and tall as the Anakim. And Jehovah destroyed [the

Rephaim] from before [the Ammonites]—and they took possession of
them and lived [there] in place of them—as he did for the *children of
Esau* living in *Seir,* in that he destroyed the *Horites* from before them,
and they took possession of them and lived [there] in place of them.
(Deuteronomy 2:20, 21, 22)

These details represent and symbolize the same thing as those given concerning Chedorlaomer here: that he and the kings with him struck the
Horites on Mount Seir. Chedorlaomer, as I said [§1667], represents the
goodness and truth the Lord had when he was young. As a consequence
he represents the Lord's human side in regard to the goodness and truth
he then had, which he used for demolishing persuasive falsities. That is, he
used this goodness and truth for crushing hells filled with the Devil's persuasive crew, hells that tried their hardest to destroy the world of spirits
and through it the human race by means of their convincing lies.

[3] Since Esau, or Edom, represented the Lord's human side, *Mount
Seir* (and Paran as well) represented attributes of his human side—
namely, the heavenly qualities of love. This can be seen from Moses'
blessing:

> Jehovah came from Sinai and dawned from *Seir* on them; he shone out
> from Mount *Paran* and came with the holy myriads. Out of his right
> hand came the fire of a law for them. Yes, he loves the peoples. (Deu-
> teronomy 33:2, 3)

The sole thing meant by "Jehovah dawned from Mount Seir and shone
out from Mount Paran" is the Lord's human nature. Anyone can see that
dawning from Mount Seir and shining out from Mount Paran has to do
not with mountains or their inhabitants but with divine matters. It symbolizes the heavenly qualities of the Lord's human nature and describes
Jehovah as dawning and shining out from this. [4] The symbolism of
Seir as the Lord's human side can be seen from the song of Deborah and
Barak in Judges:

> Jehovah, when you came out from *Seir,* when you marched from the *field
> of Edom,* the earth trembled, the heavens also showered; yes, the clouds
> showered water, mountains streamed down. This is Sinai, in the presence
> of Jehovah, the God of Israel. (Judges 5:4, 5)

The sole thing meant by coming out from Seir and marching from the
field of Edom is likewise the Lord's human side. [5] It is more obvious
still in the prophecy of Balaam, who was one of the children of the east,

or in other words, who came from Syria, where a remnant of the ancient church survived. The prophecy appears in Moses:

> I see him, but not yet; I view him, but he is not near. A star will rise out of Jacob, and a scepter will spring up from Israel. And *Edom* will be an inheritance, and an inheritance will *Seir* be for its enemies. (Numbers 24:17, 18)

Seeing him, but not yet, viewing him, although he is not near, is the Lord's arrival in the world. His human side is called a star that will rise out of Jacob, and it is also called Edom and Seir. Anyone can see that Edom and Seir would not be inherited. The statement that Seir would be the inheritance of its enemies, or the mountain of its enemies, is the same as the frequent insistence elsewhere that [Israel's] enemies be banished and their land taken [Exodus 34:24; Numbers 32:21; Deuteronomy 4:38; 6:18–19; 7:1, 17, 22; 9:1, 4–5; 11:23; 12:29; 18:12, 14; 19:1; 31:3; Joshua 23:9].

[6] Mount Paran, or El-paran—mentioned in the present verse—has the same symbolism as well, as can be seen from Habakkuk:

> God will come from Teman, and the Holy One from *Mount Paran;* selah. His majesty covered the heavens, and the earth was filled with his praise. (Habakkuk 3:3)

It is important to know, however, that the mountains and lands take their symbolism from the residents living there—from the Horites, when they lived there; from the people who displaced them, when they were driven out; from Esau, or Edom; and from others too. This is true of both meanings, positive and negative. In a positive sense they stand for the Lord's human nature and in a negative sense for self-love. The Lord's human nature is heavenly love itself. Self-love opposes heavenly love. So the Horites here symbolize persuasive lies rising out of self-love.

[7] Persuasive lies result from self-love and from materialism. Those resulting from self-love are extremely putrid; those resulting from materialism are not as bad. Those resulting from self-love stand opposed to heavenly kinds of love; those resulting from materialism oppose spiritual kinds of love. Those resulting from self-love carry with them an urge for absolute power. Loosen their restraints and they run wild, so much so that they seek to lord it over the whole universe—even over Jehovah, as shown before [§257]. Consequently persuasions of that type are never tolerated in the other life. Persuasions rising out of materialism, on the other hand, do not run as wild. They only drive us crazy with dissatisfaction over our lot, so that we strive vainly for heavenly joy and seek to take the belongings of

others for our own, with far less intent to control. But the differences between the two types of delusion are beyond counting.

All the way to El-paran, which is up in the wilderness, symbolizes the extent of those persuasions, as can be seen from the fact that the Horites were struck and fled that far. The wilderness of Paran is mentioned in Genesis 21:21; Numbers 10:12; 12:16; 13:3, 26; Deuteronomy 1:1.   **1676**

What *El-paran, which is in the wilderness,* symbolizes here is not very easy to explain. I can only say that the Lord's first victory over the hells that are symbolized by those nations did not yet reach any further. The lengths to which it did reach are symbolized by El-paran up in the wilderness.

[2] Those who have not received the opportunity to learn the secrets of heaven might imagine that there was no need for the Lord to come into the world in order to fight the inhabitants of the hells and to defeat and conquer them by letting himself be put to the test. He could have subdued them and shut them up in their hells simply by his divine omnipotence, such people might believe. Yet it is unshakably true that he did need to. Unraveling those secrets just in their general outlines would take a whole book, and it would take another to make enough room for rational arguments about such divine mysteries. Even then, human minds would still be unable (and for the most part unwilling) to comprehend them, no matter how well they were explained.

[3] It is enough to know and believe this eternal truth, since it *is* true: Had the Lord not come into the world to subdue and vanquish the hells by willingly undergoing trial, the human race would have perished. Human beings could not have been saved in any other way, not even those on our planet who lived in the days of the very earliest church.

Genesis 14:7. *And they turned back and came to En-mishpat (that is, Kadesh) and struck every field of the Amalekites, and also the Amorite living in Hazazon-tamar.*   **1677**

They turned back and came to En-mishpat (that is, Kadesh) means a continuation. *And struck every field of the Amalekites* symbolizes general categories of falsity. *And also the Amorite living in Hazazon-tamar* symbolizes general categories of the resulting evil.

The meaning of *they turned back and came into En-mishpat (that is, Kadesh)* as a continuation can be seen from what precedes and from what follows. The current theme is falsity and the evil in which it results. The Amalekite symbolizes falsity and the Amorite in Hazazon-tamar symbolizes the resulting evil.   **1678**

Kadesh symbolizes truth, but also disputes about truth. The theme here is falsity and the evil it results in, which the Lord overcame the first time he contended against it, so the present verse mentions *En-mishpat* *(that is, Kadesh),* since there was strife over the truth.

[2] The symbolism of *Kadesh* as truth under dispute is visible in Ezekiel, where the borders of the [visionary] holy land are defined:

> The southern side toward the south will be from *Tamar* all the way to the waters of Meriboth- [quarrels of] *kadesh,* the inheritance at the Great Sea, and [this will be] the southern side toward the south. (Ezekiel 47:19; 48:28)

The south stands for the light of truth. The boundary of the place, which means quarreling over truth, is called Kadesh. [3] *Kadesh* was also the place where Moses struck the rock from which water gushed, and the water was called Meribah from [a word meaning] quarrels (Numbers 20:1, 2, 11, 13). A rock symbolizes the Lord, as is known. Water, on the Word's inner plane, symbolizes what is spiritual, or truth. It is called the water of Meribah because of the strife over it. The fact that it was also called "the water of quarreling in Kadesh" is clear in Moses:

> You rebelled against what I said in the wilderness of Zin, in the quarreling of the congregation: that you should consecrate me with the water in view of them. This was the water of *quarreling in Kadesh* in the Wilderness of Zin. (Numbers 27:14; Deuteronomy 32:51)

Likewise *Kadesh* was where the scouts returned to from the land of Canaan and where [the people] murmured and bickered, not wanting to enter the land (Numbers 13:26).

[4] This evidence shows that *En-mishpat* (that is, Fountain of Judgment), or the Fountain of Mishpat (or Kadesh), symbolizes disputes over truth and so means a continuation.

Since the history here is real history and happened as described, it may seem as though such things could not be represented or symbolized by the places Chedorlaomer came to or by the nations he struck. But all the history in the Word—the places, the nations, the events—represents and symbolizes something, as is obvious from all the details in both the narrative and prophetic parts of the Word.

1679 *And struck every field of the Amalekites* symbolizes general categories of falsity, as can be seen from the representation and symbolism of the Amalekite nation. All the nations that lived in the land of Canaan represented categories of falsity and evil, as the following will establish, by the Lord's divine mercy. The *Amalekites* symbolized falsity and the *Amorites* *in Hazazon-tamar* symbolized the evil that springs from falsity. The fact that the Amalekites symbolized falsity that combats truth can be seen from mention made of them in Exodus 17:13–end; Numbers 13:29; 24:20; Deuteronomy 25:17, 18, 19; Judges 5:13, 14; 1 Samuel 15:1–end; 27:8; Psalms 83:7, 8.

[2] The Rephaim, Zuzim, Emim, and Horites mentioned in verses 5 and 6 symbolized persuasive lies rising out of evil cravings, or in other words, out of evil. In the present verse, though, the Amalekites and the Amorite in Hazazon-tamar symbolize falsity that results in evil. Falsity that springs from evil is one thing; falsity and the evil that springs from it is not the same. Falsity bubbles up either from cravings, which belong to the will, or from the assumptions we make, which belong to the intellect.

Falsity that results from cravings in the will is vile and does not easily allow itself to be uprooted, since it clings to our actual life. What we crave, that is, what we love, is our actual life. When we justify this life—this appetite, this love—in ourselves, all our justifications are falsities, and they are grafted onto our life. That is what happened with the people who lived just before the Flood.

[3] However, falsity developing from our assumptions, which belong to the intellect, cannot take very deep root in our volitional side. An example is false or heretical doctrines, which originate outside our will; we are indoctrinated in them from childhood on and later confirm them for ourselves as adults. As they are false, however, they cannot help producing bad effects in our lives. For instance, when people believe they earn salvation by doing good deeds and confirm themselves in this idea, the resulting evil is the sense of merit itself, along with self-righteousness and smugness. On the other hand, when people believe it is absolutely out of the question for their lives to be godly if they do not place merit in good works, the resulting evil is that they surrender to desire and pleasure and wipe out any trace of a godly life in themselves. It is similar in many other areas.

These are the types of falsity and resulting evil that form the theme of the present verse.

And also the Amorite living in Hazazon-tamar symbolizes general categories of the resulting evil. This can be seen from the remarks just above and from the representation and symbolism of *Amorites,* which are mentioned below in Genesis 15:16 [§1857].

In regard to the evil and falsity that the Lord fought, it needs to be known that they consisted of hellish spirits devoted to evil and falsity. In

1680

other words, they consisted of hells filled with evil and falsity, which were constantly plaguing the human race. Hellish spirits want nothing less than to destroy everyone, and nothing thrills them more than causing pain.

[2] In the other world, all spirits are divided up in this way: Those who wish evil on others are hellish or diabolical spirits, but those who wish well to others are good or angelic spirits. We can tell which group we are associating with, hellish or angelic. If we intend harm to our neighbors, think only evil thoughts about them, actually hurt them when we can, and enjoy doing so, we are associating with hellish spirits and become hellish spirits ourselves in the other life. If we have good intentions toward our neighbors, though, think only good thoughts about them, and actually do them good when we can, we are associating with angelic spirits and become angels ourselves in the other life. This is the sign. Examine yourself by this standard, if you want to know what you are like.

[3] To refrain from doing evil when one cannot or does not dare is worth nothing. It is also worthless to do good for selfish reasons. These are superficial efforts that we lay aside in the next world. In that world, we are what we think and what we intend. There are many who know how to speak well, from a lifetime of practice, but others sense immediately whether their mind or heart is in it. If not, they are sent away to join hellish spirits of their own kind.

1681   Genesis 14:8, 9. *And the king of Sodom, and the king of Gomorrah, and the king of Admah, and the king of Zeboiim, and the king of Bela (which is Zoar) went out and marshaled the battle with them in the valley of Siddim— with Chedorlaomer, king of Elam; and Tidal, king of Goiim; and Amraphel, king of Shinar; and Arioch, king of Ellasar; four kings against five.*

The king of Sodom, and the king of Gomorrah, and the king of Admah, and the king of Zeboiim, and the king of Bela (which is Zoar), went out symbolizes the evil and falsity that were in general control, as it did before. *And marshaled the battle with them* means that they attacked. *In the valley of Siddim* here as before symbolizes something unclean. *With Chedorlaomer, king of Elam; and Tidal, king of Goiim; and Amraphel, king of Shinar; and Arioch, king of Ellasar,* symbolizes truth and goodness in the [Lord's] outer self. *Chedorlaomer, king of Elam,* symbolizes truth; *Tidal, king of Goiim,* symbolizes goodness; and the others symbolize everything that results. *Four kings against five* symbolizes the unity of the truth and goodness and the disunity of the evil and falsity.

1682   *The king of Sodom, and the king of Gomorrah, and the king of Admah, and the king of Zeboiim, and the king of Bela (which is Zoar), went out* symbolizes the evil and falsity that were in general control.

This can be seen from remarks above at verse 2 concerning these kings, identifying them with evil cravings and false convictions [§1663]. At that point, these monarchs as a group symbolized all evil and all falsity or, to put it another way, evil cravings and false persuasions, which is why that verse said that war was made with them. Afterward the text deals with war against the Rephaim, Zuzim, Emim, and Horites, then against the Amalekite and Amorite, and finally against these same kings, named at the start. As a result, in the current verse they symbolize simply the prevailing evil and falsity, which are less serious.

The meaning of *marshaled the battle with them* as the fact that they attacked can be seen from the symbolism of marshaling a battle as making an assault, since verse 4 above says that they rebelled. These words also demonstrate that evil spirits are the ones who attack. The case is that the Lord never initiated a fight with any hell; the hells attacked him. This is also what happens to each of us when we are being tested, that is, when we fight evil spirits. With us, angels never mount an attack, but the evil, hellish spirits never stop attacking. Angels only deflect and defend against the attacks. This comes from the Lord, who never wants to hurt anyone or force anyone down into hell, not even the worst or most hostile of all his enemies. It is actually his enemies who hurt themselves and hurl themselves into hell. **1683**

This situation also follows from the nature of evil and the nature of goodness. Evil by its nature wants to wound everyone; goodness by its nature wants to hurt no one. The evil feel they are fully alive when they go on the offensive, because they are always wanting to destroy. The good feel they are fully alive when they are not attacking anyone but are taking advantage of the opportunity to help others by protecting them from evil.

The symbolism of *in the valley of Siddim* as something unclean can be seen from statements made above at verse 3 about the valley of Siddim and the salt sea [§1666]. **1684**

With Chedorlaomer, king of Elam; and Tidal, king of Goiim; and Amraphel, king of Shinar; and Arioch, king of Ellasar, symbolizes truth and goodness in the [Lord's] outer self, as can be seen from the symbolism of the same words in verse 1 of this chapter [§1661]. **1685**

[2] *Chedorlaomer, king of Elam,* symbolizes truth; *Tidal, king of Goiim,* symbolizes goodness; and the others symbolize everything that results. This is indicated by the change from verse 1 above in the order of their listing. Chedorlaomer, king of Elam, appeared in the third place there and appears in first place here, and Tidal, king of Goiim, appeared in fourth place there, in second here.

It is truth that is the first requirement for battle, because truth is the weapon we fight with. Truth enables us to recognize falsity and evil, so we never engage in these battles until we have absorbed secular knowledge and the knowledge of truth and goodness. *Chedorlaomer,* named first here, therefore symbolizes the truth possessed by the Lord. The same thing can be seen from the symbolism of *Elam* as the faith that develops out of a love for others, since this faith is the same thing as truth. The symbolism of Elam was illustrated earlier at Genesis 10:22 [§1228].

It follows that *Tidal, king of Goiim* (that is, of the nations), symbolizes goodness and that the other kings symbolize the further truth and goodness that result.

1686   *Four kings against five* symbolizes the unity of the truth and goodness and the disunity of the evil and falsity, as the symbolism of *four* and of *five* shows. *Four* symbolizes unity because it symbolizes pairings, just as two does when it has to do with a marriage between things, as noted at §720. *Five,* however, symbolizes disarray because it symbolizes a small amount, as illustrated at §649. All meanings depend on the subject under discussion.

1687   Genesis 14:10. *And the valley of Siddim was pit after pit of tar; and the king of Sodom and [the king] of Gomorrah fled and fell there, and the rest fled into the mountain.*

The valley of Siddim was pit after pit of tar symbolizes dirty lies and dirty cravings. *And the king of Sodom and [the king] of Gomorrah fled and fell there* means that those evils and falsities were conquered. *And the rest fled into the mountain* means that not all of them were; a *mountain* is self-love and materialism.

1688   *The valley of Siddim was pit after pit* (or full of pits) *of tar* symbolizes dirty lies and dirty cravings. This can be seen from the symbolism of *Siddim* as filth (discussed above at verse 3 [§1666]). It can also be seen from the symbolism of *pits* as lies and of *tar* as cravings. Lies are called pits here because of the dirty water these pits held, and cravings are called tar because of the foul, sulfurous smell in that water.

1689   *The king of Sodom and [the king] of Gomorrah fled and fell there* means that those evils and falsities were conquered. This is borne out by the symbolism of Sodom and Gomorrah as evil desires and distorted convictions—meanings dealt with earlier [§1663]. Here the kings of Sodom and Gomorrah stand for all the evil and falsity symbolized by the other kings as well. The meaning of the clause is also borne out by the symbolism of *fleeing* and *falling* as being conquered.

The rest fled into the mountain means that not all of them were con- **1690** quered, as can be seen without explanation from the fact that the ones who escaped survived.

The inner meaning speaks of the trials the Lord endured when he was young. Not a word is said about them in the New Testament Scriptures but only about his crisis in the wilderness (or just after he came out of the wilderness) and finally about his last crisis, which began in Gethsemane.

From his early youth up to the last hour of his life in the world, the Lord's life was one continuous struggle and one continuous victory, as many passages in the Old Testament Word indicate. The Lord's trials did not end with the test he faced in the wilderness, as these words in Luke show:

> After the Devil had finished all his testing [of Jesus], *he left Jesus alone for a while.* (Luke 4:13)

The same thing can be seen from the consideration that the Lord was tested up till his death on the cross and so till the last hour of his life in the world. This evidence makes it clear that the Lord's whole life in the world, from early youth on, consisted of constant trials and constant victories, the last of which occurred on the cross when he prayed for his enemies and so for everyone everywhere in the world.

[2] The Word's description of the Lord's life in the Gospels mentions none of his trials outside his final crisis, except for the one he faced in the wilderness. No more was revealed to the disciples. What was revealed seems so mild that it hardly amounts to anything, as far as the literal story goes; to speak and answer in that way is no trial. The fact is, though, that he was tested more severely than any human mind could ever grasp or believe. No one can know what a spiritual crisis is like except the person who has lived through one. The trial mentioned in Matthew 4:1–11; Mark 1:12, 13; and Luke 4:1–13 sums up all the Lord's trials, which consisted in his battling the self-love and materialism that filled the hells, out of love for the entire human race.

[3] All trials target the love we feel. The severity of the trial matches the nobility of the love. If love is not the target, there is no trial. To destroy a person's love is to destroy the core of that person's life, since love is life. The Lord's life was love for the whole human race, a love so great and good that it was pure, unalloyed love. He allowed this life of his to be attacked continuously, as noted [§§1661:5, 1676], from the dawn of his youth until his final moments in the world.

Love, which was the absolute core of the Lord's life, is symbolized by this:

> He was hungry, and the Devil said, "If you are the Son of God, say to this stone that it should become bread." And Jesus answered, "It is written, 'Humankind is not to live by bread alone but by every word of God.'" (Luke 4:2, 3, 4; Matthew 4:2, 3, 4)

[4] He fought against materialism and everything bearing its stamp, as symbolized by these words:

> The Devil led him up onto a tall mountain and showed him all the kingdoms of the inhabited world in a moment of time and said, "I will give you all this authority and the glory of these kingdoms, because it has been given to me, and I give it to anyone I want. If you will worship before me, then, they will all be yours." But answering him Jesus said, "Go back behind me, Satan! For it is written, 'You shall worship the Lord your God and him alone you shall serve.'" (Luke 4:5, 6, 7, 8; Matthew 4:8, 9, 10)

[5] He fought against self-love and everything bearing its stamp, as symbolized by these words:

> The Devil took him into the Holy City and stood him on a pinnacle of the Temple and said to him, "If you are the Son of God, throw yourself down, for it is written, 'He will command his angels concerning you, and on their hands they will carry you, to keep you from stubbing your foot against a stone.'" Jesus said to him, "Again it is written, 'You shall not test the Lord your God.'" (Matthew 4:5, 6, 7; Luke 4:9, 10, 11, 12)

His constant victory is symbolized by the statement that after his trial, "angels came close and tended to him" (Matthew 4:11; Mark 1:13).

[6] In short, the Lord was attacked by all the hells from early in his youth up to the very end of his life in the world, while he was continually routing, subduing, and vanquishing them. This he did purely out of love for the entire human race. Since his love was not human but divine, and the greater the love the harder the struggle, you can see how fierce his battles were and how savage on the part of the hells.

This is how it was, as I know for certain.

1691   The fact that a *mountain* is self-love and materialism can be seen from the symbolism of a mountain as discussed just below.

All evil and falsity spring from self-love and materialism. They have no other origin. Love for oneself and love of worldly advantages are the opposite of heavenly and spiritual love, and since they are the opposite, they are personified by people who work ceaselessly to destroy anything heavenly or spiritual in God's kingdom. Self-love and materialism give rise to all hatred, hatred to all vengefulness and cruelty, and vengefulness and cruelty to all deceit—in short, to all the hells.

[2] The symbolism in the Word of *mountains* as self-love and materialism is illustrated by the following passages. In Isaiah:

> The eyes of human pride will lower, and the loftiness of human beings will sink. The day of Jehovah Sabaoth will come over all the proud and lofty, over all the lofty *mountains,* and over all the tall *hills,* and over every *high tower.* (Isaiah 2:11, 12, 14, 15)

Clearly the lofty mountains stand for self-love and the tall hills for materialism. [3] In the same author:

> Every valley will be raised up, and every *mountain* and *hill* will be lowered. (Isaiah 40:4)

Here too they plainly stand for self-love and materialism. In the same author:

> I will devastate *mountains* and *hills,* and all their grass I will wither. (Isaiah 42:15)

Again the mountains stand for self-love and the hills for the love of worldly things. In Ezekiel:

> The *mountains* will be torn down, and the stairs will fall, and every wall will fall to the earth. (Ezekiel 38:20)

[4] In Jeremiah:

> Here now, I am against you, destroying *mountain,* destroying the entire earth; and I will stretch my hand out against you and roll you down from the *rocks* and make you a *mountain aflame.* (Jeremiah 51:25)

This describes Babylon and Chaldea, which symbolize self-love and love of worldly advantages, as shown before [§§1326, 1368]. In the Song of Moses:

> A fire has kindled in my anger, and it will burn all the way to the *lowest hell,* and it will consume the earth and its produce and torch the foundations of the *mountains.* (Deuteronomy 32:22)

The foundations of the mountains stand for the hells, as it explicitly says. The hells are called the foundations of the mountains because self-love and materialism reign supreme there and come from there. [5] In Jonah:

> Water surrounded me right to my soul; the abyss circled me; seaweed was bound onto my head. To the *excavations of the mountains* I went down. The poles of the earth lay above me forever; but you brought my life up out of the pit, Jehovah my God. (Jonah 2:5, 6)

These prophetic words depict the Lord's struggles against the hells as Jonah's ordeal in the belly of the huge fish. The same struggles are described in other Scripture passages as well, especially in David. Anyone in spiritual crisis is in hell. Being in hell has nothing to do with location and everything to do with state of mind.

[6] From the symbolism of mountains and towers as self-love and materialism we can deduce what it meant when the Devil took the Lord onto a tall mountain and onto the pinnacle of the Temple. It meant that he was being led into the very worst of his spiritual battles against love for himself and for the material world, or in other words, against the hells.

In the opposite sense (the usual one), mountains symbolize heavenly love and spiritual love, as demonstrated earlier in §§795, 796.

1692   Hardly anyone can see what the battles of spiritual crisis accomplish. They are the means for dissolving and shaking off evil and falsity. They are also the means by which we develop a horror for evil and falsity, and gain not only conscience but strength of conscience; and this is the way we are reborn. For that reason, people who are regenerating are thrust into combat and undergo terrible trials—if not during their physical lives, then in the other life, assuming they *can* regenerate. In consequence, the Lord's church is called the church militant.

The Lord alone relied on his own strength or power to endure his spiritual crises and the savage conflicts they entailed. The hells all besieged him, and he continually gained total victory over them.

[2] It is the Lord alone who does the fighting in people facing their own spiritual battles, and who conquers. By our own power, we cannot accomplish anything at all against evil, hellish spirits, because they band together with the hells in such a way that if one hell were overcome the next would rush in to fill the void. This would continue forever. They are like the ocean beating on the individual stones in a jetty. If it managed to open a chink or a tiny crack in the jetty, it would never stop until it had broken down and overflowed the entire structure, leaving not a

trace. That is how it would be if the Lord did not bear our battles by himself.

Genesis 14:11. *And [the four] took all the resources of Sodom and Gomorrah, and all their food, and went away.*

1693

They took all the resources of Sodom and Gomorrah means that [the hells] were stripped of the power to do evil. *And all their food* means that they were stripped of the power to think falsely. *And went away* means that this is how they were left.

They took all the resources of Sodom and Gomorrah means that [the hells] were stripped of the power to do evil, as the symbolism of *taking someone's resources* shows. On an inner level, the *resources of Sodom and Gomorrah* refer exclusively to evil and falsity. The resources here symbolize evil, and the food, falsity. The spiritual riches and wealth that good people have are actually the goodness and truth that the Lord gives them as a gift and enriches them with. So the riches and wealth that bad people have are actually the evil and falsity that they themselves have acquired. These are the things that wealth symbolizes in the Word.

1694

This evidence shows that taking the resources of Sodom and Gomorrah means stripping them of the power to do evil.

All their food means that they were stripped of the power to think falsely, as the symbolism of *food* shows. Previous sections (§§56, 57, 58, 680, 681) have explained what kind of heavenly, spiritual, and earthly-level food people enjoy in the other life. These types of food correspond to food for the body, so they are represented by food in the Word and are called food there. The food of evil and hellish spirits, however, is anything opposed to wisdom, understanding, and accurate knowledge; in other words, it is any falsehood. This food, surprisingly, sustains evil spirits. It sustains them because it is their life. Without the opportunity to slander or even blaspheme truth, they cannot survive. Even so, they are not free to think or speak any other falsehoods than those that rise out of what is bad in them; they are not free to tell lies that go against their own particular type of evil. That would be a misrepresentation. So far as their distortion of the truth grows out of their evil, it grows out of their life. Under these circumstances they are forgiven, because their nature is such that they would be incapable of surviving otherwise.

1695

[2] In regard to the idea that they are stripped of the power to do evil or think falsely, the case is this: When we are fighting our spiritual battles, evil spirits are permitted to dredge up every vice and falsehood we possess and to use them as weapons. When these spirits have been

overcome, though, they are no longer allowed to do so, because they instantly sense in us a strength of commitment to what is good and true. They have a keener perception of this strength than we do. When we commit ourselves to truth and goodness, the very air we project tells them right away how things stand, what type of response they are likely to receive, and so on. It is especially obvious with spiritually oriented people who have been reborn; they have just as many evil spirits with them as the unregenerate, but the spirits are under their control and serve them.

This is what I mean by saying that they were stripped of the power to do evil or think falsely.

1696   It can be seen without explanation that *they went away* means that [the hells] were left behind.

1697   Genesis 14:12. *And they took Lot and his property—the son of Abram's brother—and went away; and he had been living in Sodom.*

They took Lot and his property—the son of Abram's brother—and went away means that apparent goodness and truth (not good or true in itself) seized control of the Lord's outer self and everything in it. *And he had been living in Sodom* means the condition of [his outer self].

1698   *They took Lot and his property—the son of Abram's brother—and went away* means that apparent goodness and truth (not good or true in itself) seized control of the Lord's outer self and everything in it. This can be seen from the symbolism of *Lot* as the Lord's sensory or outward self, a symbolism already mentioned and discussed several times [§§1428, 1547, 1563]. Here specifically he symbolizes apparent goodness and truth in the Lord's outer self, which are being called the *property* of Lot. It has already been explained that this goodness and truth appeared good and true in the Lord's early youth, although they were not intrinsically so [§§1661, 1667]. They were gradually purified, and his spiritual trials were the means, as the remarks concerning such trials show [§§1652–1657, 1659, 1663–1664, 1692].

1699   The fact that *and he had been living in Sodom* means the condition of [his outer self] is established by the symbolism of Sodom.

1700   Genesis 14:13. *And an escapee came and told Abram the Hebrew, and he was living in the oak groves of Mamre the Amorite, brother of Eshcol and brother of Aner; and these were men bound by a pact with Abram.*

An escapee came and told Abram the Hebrew means that the Lord sensed things in his intermediate self; *Abram the Hebrew* is his intermediate self, linked to his inward or divine self. *And he was living in the oak groves of Mamre the Amorite* symbolizes the state of perception in his rational self. *[Mamre was] brother of Eshcol and brother of Aner, and these were men bound by a pact with Abram* symbolizes the state of his rational self (or its outward part) and the nature of its goodness and truth.

An escapee came and told Abram the Hebrew means that the Lord sensed things in his intermediate self, which can be seen from the symbolism of *Abram the Hebrew* as his intermediate self, united to his inward self. This will be discussed directly below. Because the inner meaning of these words has to do with the Lord, and because the historical events represent him, it is clear that *an escapee came and told* only means that the Lord sensed something.

1701

Our intermediate self senses what is going on in our outward self as if someone were reporting on it. The Lord was aware of everything that was happening and recognized clearly the nature and source of everything that emerged in him. If any evil monopolized the emotions of his outer self or any false idea monopolized his thinking, for instance, he inevitably knew what its nature was and where it came from. He could also tell exactly which evil spirits were stirring it up, and how, besides much else. These kinds of details and countless others are not hidden from angels and are only barely concealed from people on earth who have a heavenly type of perception. Still less would they escape the Lord.

The fact that *Abram the Hebrew* is his intermediate self, linked to his inward or divine self, can be seen from the symbolism of *Abram the Hebrew,* or in other words, from the epithet of *the Hebrew* here for Abram. In passages above and below that treat of Abram, he is not called a Hebrew, only here. So "Abram the Hebrew" represents and symbolizes something unique in the Lord. What it represents and symbolizes can be seen from the inner meaning. That is, "Abram the Hebrew" is the Lord's intermediate self linked to his inner, divine self, as can also be seen from the series of ideas in the inner meaning. The Word talks about Hebrews when something subservient (good or bad) is being symbolized. This will become visible from what follows [§1703]. The intermediate self is such that it serves the inner, divine self, so it is called Abram the Hebrew here.

1702

[2] Hardly anyone realizes what the intermediate self is, so it needs to be explained briefly. The intermediate self is midway between the inner self and the outer. The inner self communicates with the outer self by means of the intermediate self. Without that link, there could never be any communication. The heavenly dimension is separate from the earthly dimension and still more separate from the bodily dimension. Unless some intermediate agent existed to communicate through, the heavenly dimension could never act on the earthly, still less on the bodily dimension.

The intermediate self is what is called the rational self. This self, since it is in the middle, communicates with the deeper self (where goodness and truth itself lives) and with the shallower self (where evil and falsity lives). Its communication with the deeper self enables us to think about heavenly and spiritual concerns, or in other words, to look upward, which animals are unable to do. Its communication with the shallower self enables us to think about worldly and bodily concerns, or in other words, to look downward, almost exactly like animals, which have a similar focus on earthly matters. In short, the intermediate self *is* the rational self, which is spiritual or heavenly when it looks upward but animal-like when it looks downward.

[3] It is known that people are capable of seeing that they speak one way and think another; that they do one thing and will another; and that pretense and deceit exist. They can also see that reason or rationality exists, and that it lies deeper, since it can disagree [with the outer self]. And they can see that something exists inside a regenerating person that fights what exists on the outside. This inward thing that thinks differently and wills differently and fights is the intermediate self. It contains the conscience of a spiritual person and the perceptions of a heavenly person.

This intermediate self united to the inward, divine self in the Lord is what is being called Abram the Hebrew.

1703 The following places show that the Word describes subservient things as *Hebrews.* In Moses:

> When your *Hebrew* brother or sister is sold to you, that person shall also *serve* you six years, and in the seventh year you shall send him or her away free from beside you. (Deuteronomy 15:12)

The word *Hebrew* is used here because the subject is slavery. In Jeremiah:

> At the end of seven years, you shall each send away your *Hebrew* sister or brother who was sold to you and *served* you six years. (Jeremiah 34:9, 14)

Here too the word *Hebrew* is used because the subject is slavery. The children of Jacob are not called Hebrews anywhere else in the prophets. In Samuel:

> The Philistines were saying, "Strengthen yourselves and turn into men or you will be *slaves* to the *Hebrews* as they were *slaves* to you." (1 Samuel 4:9)

The same is true here. [2] In Moses:

> Jehovah said to Moses, "Go in to Pharaoh, and you are to speak to
> him: 'This is what Jehovah, God of the *Hebrews,* has said: "Send my
> people away so that they can *serve* me."'" (Exodus 9:1, 13; 10:3)

Here again it is because of their enslavement that they are called Hebrews.
Potiphar's wife concerning Joseph:

> She shouted out to the men of her household and said to them, "See?
> He has brought us a *Hebrew* man to mock us." (Genesis 39:14)

He is called a Hebrew because he was a slave there. The chief of the cup
bearers said to Pharaoh:

> With us was a young *Hebrew* man, the *slave* of the chief of the court-
> iers, and he interpreted our dreams for us. (Genesis 41:12)

In addition, Egyptians called the children of Israel *Hebrews* because they
were slaves, or in servitude, as is known (Exodus 1:15, 16, 19, and elsewhere).

And he was living in the oak groves of Mamre the Amorite symbolizes **1704**
the state of perception in his rational self. This can be seen from the symbolism of an oak grove and of the *oak groves of Mamre the Amorite,* dealt
with above, in §§1442, 1443, 1616.

[Mamre was] brother of Eshcol and brother of Aner, and these were men **1705**
bound by a pact with Abram symbolizes the state of his rational self (or of
its outward part) and the nature of its goodness and truth. This can be
seen from the symbolism of these men, which will be discussed below at
verse 24 where they come up again [§§1753–1754].

To put it briefly, Mamre, Eshcol, and Aner represent and symbolize
the angels present with the Lord during the battles of his early youth,
who were suited to the goodness and truth he then possessed. They are
named for the individual varieties of goodness and truth in him. Angels
in heaven never have any names; it is on the basis of their goodness and
truth that names are applied to them. Michael and other angels named in
the Word, for instance, never go by those names; the names are based on
the function they perform, whatever it is.

The same is true of Mamre, Eshcol, and Aner here, but in a representative way.

Genesis 14:14. *And Abram heard that his brother had been captured,* **1706**
and he mustered his trainees, offspring of his household, three hundred
eighteen of them, and pursued all the way to Dan.

Abram heard that his brother had been captured means that his intermediate self sensed what kind of state his outer self was in. *And he mustered his trainees, offspring of his household,* symbolizes the goodness in his outward self that was now free of slavery's yoke. *Three hundred eighteen of them* symbolizes the quality of that goodness. *And he pursued all the way to Dan* symbolizes the beginning of purification.

1707   *Abram heard that his brother had been captured* means that his intermediate self sensed what kind of state his outer self was in, as the following shows: *Abram* symbolizes the Lord's intermediate self linked with his inner, divine self, as mentioned in the last verse [§§1701–1702]. *Lot* symbolizes his outer self, as demonstrated earlier [§§1428, 1547, 1563, 1698]. And *hearing that his brother had been captured* means sensing what kind of state it was in. To be specific, apparent goodness and truth had seized control of it, as noted at verse 12 [§1698].

[2] This is the situation: The intermediate self meant by Abram the Hebrew sensed that the goodness and truth being used as weapons were not good and true except in appearance, and that they had seized control of the whole outward self symbolized by Lot, his brother's son. On perceiving this, the intermediate self purified that apparent goodness and truth (or rather the inner, divine self did so, by means of the intermediate self). How this could be done would be a complete mystery to anyone to whom it has not been revealed. After all, the way the inner self acts on the outer by way of the intermediate self is unknown, especially at this day, when few if any realize what the intermediate self is, let alone the inner self. For a description of the inward and intermediate selves, see just above at verse 13 [§1702]; [3] but here a short explanation of their interaction is needed.

In every individual, the inner self belongs to the Lord alone, because that is where he stores up the good impulses and true thoughts that he gives us as gifts from the time we are very small. These are the channel through which he acts on our intermediate, rational self, which in turn is the channel through which he acts on our outward self. In doing so, he makes it possible for us to think and to be human.

However, the stream of his influence from the inner self, acting on the intermediate self and through it on the external self, is of two kinds. Either he acts by heavenly means or he acts by spiritual means; to put the same thing another way, he acts either through goodness or through truth. When he operates by way of heavenly qualities, or good impulses, he acts only on those who have been reborn—those endowed with either perception or conscience. Accordingly, this influence comes either through perception or through conscience. So he cannot influence people by heavenly means unless they have love for him and charity for their neighbor. When the Lord operates by spiritual means, or by way of true ideas, he acts on every one of us. If he did not, we would be unable to think or talk. When by nature we pervert everything good and true, when we have no interest in heavenly or spiritual matters, then nothing heavenly, or good, influences us; the conduit for heavenly goodness closes. Yet what is spiritual, or true, does still influence us, and the conduit for such things is kept permanently open. From this you can see what the intermediate, rational self is.

[4] *Abram* here symbolizes the inner self within the intermediate self. When heavenly goodness from the inner self acts on the intermediate self, the inner self takes over the intermediate self and makes that self its own, although the intermediate self remains distinct from the inner. The same thing happens when the inner self acts through the intermediate self to influence the outward self; it then takes over the outward self as well and makes that self its own, although the outward self remains distinct from the intermediate.

That is what happened in this situation, where the Lord's inner self perceived in his intermediate self the conditions that existed for his outward self. His inward self saw that his outward self had been *captured,* that is, that it had been seized by apparent rather than actual goodness and truth, which were the weapons by which his outward self had fought so many enemies. When his inward self perceived this, it brought its influence to bear, reduced everything to order, and freed his outer self from what plagued it. In this way his inner self purified apparent goodness and truth; it changed them from apparent into actual goodness and truth, and so into goodness and truth allied with his inward, divine self. The means, as I said, was his intermediate self.

[5] In one respect the Lord was unlike any other person: his intermediate self was divine, so far as its heavenly goodness went, and was attached to his inner self from birth. His inner self along with this part of his intermediate self was Jehovah himself, his Father. In another respect, though, he resembled other people: his intermediate self was attached to his outward self, so far as its spiritual truths went, and thus was human. But this self too he made divine, or turned it into Jehovah, by fighting his spiritual battles under his own power and winning consistently.

The outer self is what is being called Lot. In a previous state he is referred to as Abram's nephew [Genesis 14:12], but in his current state, as *Abram's brother.* The outer self is described as a nephew when apparent truth and goodness seize control of it, but it is called a brother when real goodness and real truth do.

1708   *And he mustered his trainees, offspring of his household,* symbolizes the goodness in his outward self that was now free of slavery's yoke, as can be seen from the symbolism of Abram's *trainees* and the *offspring of his household.* In an inner sense, Abram's *trainees* or novices are the good qualities of the outer self that are capable of allying with the intermediate self. The *offspring of his household* in an inner sense is the fact that these same good qualities, and truths as well, were his own. This sentence holds more secrets than can be expressed, however. In particular it contains information about the way apparent goodness becomes real goodness after our spiritual struggles are over. It also reveals that this goodness is then capable of allying with the intermediate self and through this with the inward self and of becoming divine in the process. The Lord, you see, gradually joined his human nature to his divine nature, and he did so by fighting his spiritual battles and winning them, as noted [§§1659:2, 1661:5]. This goodness, which had become genuine, is what is being called Abram's trainees, or novices, because it was indeed newly trained. Because he accumulated it by his own power, it is called the offspring of his household.

1709   *Three hundred eighteen men* symbolizes the quality of that goodness, specifically the holiness of the struggle. The number eighteen involves this symbolism, and so does the number three hundred, because three and six are factors of both. *Three* symbolizes something holy, as shown in §§720, 901, and *six* symbolizes struggle, as shown in §§737, 900.

It is a historical fact that Abram mustered this many men, and yet it still represented something. So did every historical fact in the Word—in the five books of Moses, as well as in Joshua, Judges, Samuel, Kings, Daniel, and Jonah, in all of which the numbers likewise involve hidden meanings. Nothing was written in the Word that did not represent something. Otherwise it would not be the Word. Otherwise it would never have mentioned that Abram mustered 318 men, or that they were trainees and offspring of his household, and so on with many other details given in this chapter.

1710   The symbolism of *and he pursued all the way to Dan* as the state of his purification can be seen from the series of ideas in the inner meaning. Here, *pursuing* enemies is driving off the evil and falsity that coexisted with [apparent] goodness and truth and made them look good and true. So it means freeing and purifying them. *All the way to Dan* means to the farthest border of Canaan, so it means to the outermost limits of their

flight. Throughout the Word Dan can be seen to symbolize the farthest
borders or outermost limits of Canaan. In Samuel, for instance:

> . . . to transfer the kingship from the house of Saul, and to raise the
> throne of David over Israel and over Judah, from *Dan* all the way to
> Beer-sheba. (2 Samuel 3:10)

In the same author:

> The whole of Israel without exception shall be gathered from *Dan* all
> the way to Beer-sheba. (2 Samuel 17:11)

In the same author:

> David said to Joab, "Roam through all the tribes of Israel from *Dan* all
> the way to Beer-sheba." (2 Samuel 24:2, 15)

In Kings:

> Judah and Israel lived in safety, all of them under their own grape-
> vine and under their own fig tree, from *Dan* all the way to Beer-sheba.
> (1 Kings 4:25)

From these passages it is clear that Dan was the farthest border of
Canaan, and that Abram pursued his enemies that far—the enemies that
overran the goodness and truth of the Lord's outer self. Because Dan
was the border of Canaan, however, and was therefore inside Canaan, he
chased them even farther in order to rid the land of them completely—to
Hobah on the left of Damascus, as the next verse says. This is how he
accomplished the purification. In a holy sense the land of Canaan symbolizes the Lord's kingdom, as mentioned earlier [§§1, 620, 1413, 1437,
1585:1–2]. Consequently it symbolizes the heavenly effect of love, or that
which is good—chiefly goodness in the Lord.

Genesis 14:15. *And he divided [his forces] against [the enemy] by night,* **1711**
he and his servants, and struck them and pursued them all the way to Hobah,
which is to the left of Damascus.

He divided [his forces] against [the enemy] by night means the shadow
that the apparent goodness and truth were in. *He and his servants* symbolize the rational self and everything in the outer self that obeyed it.
And struck them symbolizes the rescue. *And pursued them all the way to*
Hobah, which is to the left of Damascus, symbolizes the extent.

He divided [his forces] against [the enemy] by night means the shadow **1712**
that the apparent goodness and truth were in, which can be seen from
the symbolism of *night* as shadowy conditions.

Conditions are said to be shadowy when we do not know whether a thing appears to be good and true or actually is good and true. Everyone who experiences apparent goodness and truth considers it genuinely good and true. The evil and falsity that lurk in apparent goodness and truth are what cast a shadow over it and make it appear real.

People who do not know any better cannot help seeing the good they do as their own and the truth they think as their own. The same applies to those who take credit for the good they do and feel that it makes them deserving. All the while they are unaware that the good is not good, even though it seems so, and that the sense of pride and personal merit they place in their deeds is an evil and a lie, which darkens and clouds their sight. The same applies in many other situations as well. [2] The type and amount of evil and falsity that lies hidden within can never be seen as clearly during physical life as in the next life. There it stands out just as plain to see as in broad daylight.

The situation is different, though, if we commit the error out of an ignorance that has not yet hardened. In that case, the evils and falsities are easily shaken off. But if we reinforce the belief that we can do good and resist evil under our own power, and that we earn salvation by doing so, this attitude clings. It turns good into evil and truth into falsity.

Still, the proper method is for us to do good as if on our own. We should not throw up our hands thinking, "If I can't do any good on my own, I ought to wait for direct inspiration; till then I should lie passive." This too is wrong. Instead we should do good as if we were doing it on our own, but when we reflect on the good we are doing (or have done), we ought to think, acknowledge, and believe that the Lord working in us is actually doing the good. [3] If we abandon all effort because of the kind of thinking mentioned, the Lord cannot work in us. He cannot act on those who rid themselves of every capacity for receiving the power to do good. It is like saying that you refuse to learn anything unless it comes to you as revelation. Or like saying that you refuse to teach anything unless the words are planted in your mouth. Or like refusing to try anything unless you can be propelled like an automaton. If this did happen, you would be still more resentful for feeling like an inanimate object. The reality is that what the Lord animates in us is that which seems to be ours. For instance, it is an eternal truth that life is not ours; but if it did not seem to be, we would have no life at all.

1713   The symbolism of *he and his servants* as the rational self and everything in the outer self that obeyed it can be seen from the following:

He, that is, Abram, symbolizes the intermediate self, discussed above [§§1702, 1707]. *Servants* symbolize things that obey.

Before the outer self has been freed and rescued, everything in it is called a *servant,* because all it does is obey the intermediate self. For example, the outer self has a supply of emotions and a supply of facts. The emotions grow out of something good in the intermediate self; the facts grow out of truth there. When the emotions and facts are forced to agree with the intermediate self, they are said to serve and obey it. So servants here mean nothing if they do not mean things in the outer self that obeyed.

The symbolism of *he struck them* as the rescue can be seen from the thread of the story, without explanation.

And pursued them all the way to Hobah, which is to the left of Damascus, symbolizes the extent, as can be seen from the symbolism of *Hobah, which is to the left of Damascus.* Where Hobah was no one knows, because it is not mentioned again in the Word. Damascus, however, was Syria's principal city, as 2 Samuel 8:5, 6 and Isaiah 7:8 show. The symbolism of Damascus is almost the same as that of Syria, which was discussed earlier at Genesis 10:22 [§1232]. Damascus is portrayed as the farthest border of the land of Canaan (although it lay beyond Dan), as in Amos:

> You took up Sikkuth, your king; and Kaiwan, your images, the star of your gods, whom you made for yourselves; and I will deport you beyond *Damascus.* (Amos 5:26, 27)

The border of the holy land (that is, the Lord's kingdom) toward the north is identified with the *border of Damascus* in Ezekiel 47:16, 17, 18; 48:1. In the present verse, when it says that they were struck and pursued all the way to Hobah, which is to the left of Damascus, it symbolizes the extent to which apparent goodness and truth were purified. However, unless the reader knows what that apparent goodness and truth were like, and what they needed to be purified of in order to become genuine, the proper meaning of Hobah on the left of Damascus here cannot be explained. It can only be said generally that they were purified.

Genesis 14:16. *And he brought back all the property; and Lot his brother and his property he also brought back, and also the women and the people.*

He brought back all the property means that the intermediate self restored everything in the outer self to its appropriate condition. *And Lot his brother and his property he also brought back* means the outer self and everything in it. *The women and the people* symbolize both the good impulses and the true ideas.

1717　*He brought back all the property* means that the intermediate self restored everything in the outer self to its appropriate condition, as can be seen from the symbolism of *bringing back all the property*. The *property* is that which Chedorlaomer and the kings with him took from their enemies, as told in previous verses. Chedorlaomer and the kings with him symbolized goodness and truth in the outer self. The property they acquired from their enemies was nothing else than the fact that these enemies were stripped of the power to do evil or think falsely. That is what is symbolized by the resources and all the food of Sodom and Gomorrah, which they took. For more on this, see above at verse 11 [§§1694, 1695].

[2] The situation here is such that it cannot be explained in a few words. In order to gain some notion of it, though, consider this: Those who fight spiritual battles and win acquire more and more power over evil spirits, or in other words, over the Devil's crew—so much power, finally, that the spirits do not dare to try anything. Every time such people win a victory, moreover, the Lord reorganizes the good impulses and true ideas they are using as weapons. So every time they win, their goodness and truth are purified; and the more they are purified, the more the heavenly qualities of love are instilled in their outer self and come into correspondence. This is what bringing back all the property symbolizes.

[3] Anyone who imagines that the outer self can be brought into correspondence without inward struggle is mistaken. Times of trial are the means for getting rid of evil and falsity and replacing them with goodness and truth. They are also the means for reducing the attributes of the outer self to obedience, so that the outer self can serve the intermediate self (the rational self) and through this the inner self (or rather the Lord working through the inner self).

No one can see that our times of trial produce these effects except people who have been reborn through their trials. Describing the process in even its most general outlines would be difficult, because it takes place without our awareness of the source or the method. It is, after all, the Lord's divine work.

1718　*And Lot his brother and his property he also brought back* means the outer self and everything in it. This is established by the symbolism of *Lot* as the outer self, as mentioned several times [§§1428, 1547, 1563, 1698].

Hardly anyone today knows what the outer self is, because people think that everything making up the outer self is connected with the body, such as its senses (touch, taste, smell, hearing, and sight), appetites, and pleasures. These constitute the *most* external self, however, which is purely physical.

The outer self proper is made up of facts in the memory, emotions belonging to the love that permeates us, the aspects of sensation that belong to our spirit, and the lower pleasures that are also the province of spirits. These compose what is strictly speaking our outer self. The evidence for this is that people in the other life (spirits, in other words) also have an outer self, an intermediate self, and consequently an inner self. The body is merely a kind of covering or shell that dissolves, allowing us truly to live and to improve in every way.

The symbolism of *the women and the people* as both the good impulses **1719** and the true ideas can be seen from the symbolism of wives and daughters as what is good (discussed before in §§489, 490, 491, 568, 915). Here, *women* stands in place of wives and daughters. It can also be seen from the symbolism of a *people* as truth (again, discussed before, at §§1259, 1260).

Genesis 14:17. *And the king of Sodom went out to meet him, after he* **1720** *returned (from striking Chedorlaomer and the kings who were with him) to the valley of Shaveh, that is, the king's valley.*

The king of Sodom went out to meet him means that evil and falsity surrendered. *After he returned from striking Chedorlaomer and the kings who were with him* symbolizes the deliverance and rescue of apparent goodness and truth. *To the valley of Shaveh, that is, the king's valley,* symbolizes the state at that point of the goodness and truth in the outer self.

The king of Sodom went out to meet him means that evil and falsity **1721** surrendered, as can be seen from this: The *king of Sodom* symbolizes the evil and falsity that had been fought, and *going out to meet* means surrendering.

It was part of the series of events that evil and falsity surrendered, and that is why the king of Sodom is mentioned here; but he is discussed below at verse 21 [§1740].

The symbolism of *after he returned from striking Chedorlaomer and* **1722** *the kings who were with him* as the deliverance and rescue of apparent goodness and truth can be seen from all that goes before. It can also be seen from the remarks above on Chedorlaomer and the kings who were with him [§§1671, 1672].

The symbolism of *to the valley of Shaveh, that is, the king's valley,* as **1723** the state at that point of the goodness and truth in the outer self can be seen from the symbolism of the *valley of Shaveh* and of *the king's valley.*

The *valley of Shaveh* symbolizes goodness in the outer self, and *the king's valley,* truth there.

The outer self is called a *valley* because it lies below. Anything that is more superficial is also lower, just as anything that is deeper is also higher.

The symbolism of a *king* as truth was mentioned earlier, in §1672.

1724 Genesis 14:18. *And Melchizedek, king of Salem, brought out bread and wine; and he was a priest to God the Highest.*

Melchizedek symbolizes the heavenly qualities of the Lord's intermediate self. *King of Salem* symbolizes the peaceful state of his intermediate plane, or his rational mind. *Brought out bread* symbolizes heavenly qualities and the refreshment they provide. *And wine* symbolizes spiritual qualities and the refreshment they provide. *And he was a priest* symbolizes holy love. *To God the Highest* symbolizes his inner self, which was Jehovah.

1725 The symbolism of *Melchizedek* as the heavenly qualities of the Lord's intermediate self can be seen from the symbolism of *Melchizedek* given just below. It can also be seen from what comes before and after.

I have already defined the inner self, intermediate self, and outer self sufficiently [§§3, 268, 857, 978, 1015, 1563, 1568, 1577, 1589:2, 1702, 1718]. I have also shown that the inner self acts through the intermediate self on the outer self. As noted, the inner self acts on the intermediate self either by heavenly or by spiritual means. It acts by heavenly means in anyone who has been reborn, that is, in those who live a life of love for the Lord and for their neighbor. It acts by spiritual means, though, in all people, whatever they are like, providing them with light from heaven—that is, with the ability to think, to speak, and to be human. For the discussion of this above, see §1707.

[2] The heavenly qualities of the intermediate self are all the different facets of heavenly love, as mentioned many times before. These heavenly qualities in the Lord's intermediate self (or rather his intermediate self in regard to these qualities) are called *Melchizedek.*

The Lord's inner being was Jehovah himself. When his intermediate self was purified after the battles of his spiritual struggle, it too became divine, became Jehovah. Likewise his outer self. But at the present point, in a time of spiritual conflict, not yet completely purified by spiritual battle, he is called Melchizedek—"king of sacred justice"—in relation to his heavenly attributes.

[3] The fact that this is so can also be seen in David, where the subject again is the Lord's spiritual battles, and where in the end the

heavenly qualities of his intermediate self are called Melchizedek. This is what David says:

> Jehovah said to my Lord, "Sit at my right till I have placed your foes as a stool for your feet. Jehovah will send a scepter of strength out from Zion. Rule in the midst of your foes. Yours is a willing people, on the day of your might, among sacred honors. Out of the womb from the dawn you receive the dew of your birth." Jehovah has sworn and will not go back on it: "You are a *priest forever* in accord with my word; [you are] *Melchizedek*." The Lord at your right struck monarchs on the day of his anger. (Psalms 110:1, 2, 3, 4, 5)

Like the present chapter, this has to do with the Lord's inward battles against the hells, as the individual words reveal. The Lord himself teaches that he is the one meant here (Matthew 22:43, 44, 45; Mark 12:36; Luke 20:42, 43, 44). Placing his foes as his footstool, ruling in the midst of his foes, a day of might, and *striking monarchs* on the day of his anger—all these symbolize inward struggles and victories.

The symbolism of *king of Salem* as the peaceful state of his intermediate plane, or his rational mind, can be seen from the symbolism of *Salem.* In the original language, Salem means peace and also wholeness, so it symbolizes a state of peace and a state of completion.

1726

A state of peace is the state of the Lord's kingdom. In that state the Lord's heavenly and spiritual blessings seem to be in their dawn and their springtime. Peace resembles dawn at the break of day and spring in the greening of the year. The dawn and the spring cause the senses and everything that touches them to be filled with joy and gladness. Each sensation draws its effect from the overall effect of the daybreak and the blooming of the year. It is the same with the peaceful state of the Lord's kingdom. In that state, every heavenly and every spiritual feature enjoys the flowering laughter of its springtime dawn—that is, its most genuine happiness. A state of peace affects every feature this way because the Lord is peace itself. That is what David meant by Salem:

> God is known in Judah; in Israel his name is great, and in *Salem* is his tabernacle, and his dwelling place is in Zion. (Psalms 76:1, 2)

While we are fighting our spiritual battles, the Lord from time to time grants us a time of peace and in this way revives us. A time of peace is symbolized here by Salem and soon after by the bread and wine as well, which symbolize heavenly and spiritual qualities, and so the condition of those qualities at peace. This condition is renewal itself.

1727 *Brought out bread* symbolizes heavenly qualities and the refreshment they provide; *and wine* symbolizes spiritual qualities and the refreshment they provide. This can be seen from the symbolism of *bread* as something heavenly (discussed in §§276, 680) and that of *wine,* and of a grapevine or vineyard, as something spiritual (discussed in §§1069, 1071). Because bread symbolizes heavenly elements, and wine, spiritual elements, they also became symbols in the Holy Supper.

Melchizedek's offer of bread and wine here has a symbolism similar to that of the Holy Supper because in the ancient church bread represented everything heavenly while wine represented everything spiritual. So here they represent the Lord himself, the source of everything heavenly and everything spiritual.

1728 *And he was a priest* symbolizes holy love, which can be seen from the symbolism of a *priest* in the Word.

Two roles are attributed to the Lord: king and priest. A monarch, or monarchy, symbolizes holy truth; a priest, or priesthood, symbolizes holy benevolence. Monarchy is divinely spiritual; priesthood is divinely heavenlike.

As sovereign, the Lord governs absolutely everything in the universe with divine truth; as priest he does so with divine benevolence.

Divine truth is the actual pattern for his entire kingdom, and all its laws are truths, or eternal realities. Divine benevolence is the vital essence itself of the pattern, and every bit of it is mercy. Both are attributed to the Lord. If divine truth were all there was, not a soul could be saved, since eternal truth damns everyone to hell. Divine benevolence, which is merciful, lifts everyone from hell to heaven.

This is what monarchs and priests represented in the Jewish church. It is also what Melchizedek represented as king of Salem and priest to God the Highest.

1729 *To God the Highest* symbolizes his inner self, which was Jehovah. This can be seen from the statement made several times above that the Lord's inner self is Jehovah himself [§§1475, 1573:3, 1602, 1707:5, 1725:2] and accordingly that the Lord is identical with Jehovah the Father, as he himself says in John:

"I am the way and the truth and life." Philip says, "Show us the Father." Jesus says to him, "After all the time I've spent with you, don't you

know me, Philip? Whoever has seen me has seen the Father. How then
can you say, 'Show us the Father'? Don't you believe that I am in the
Father and the Father is in me? Believe me that I am in the Father and
the Father is in me." (John 14:6, 8, 9, 10, 11)

[2] The Lord's human nature is what is called the Son of Humankind. At the end of his struggles and trials it united with his divine
nature, so that it too became Jehovah. In heaven, then, people recognize
no other Jehovah the Father than the Lord (see above, §15). Everything
about the Lord is Jehovah—not only his inner self and intermediate but
also his outer self and his actual body. As a result, he is the only one who
has ever risen into heaven with a body as well. The Gospel writers make
this abundantly clear when they talk about his resurrection. The words
of the Lord himself do too:

> "Why are thoughts rising in your hearts? Look at my hands and my
> feet, because I am he. Feel me and see, because a spirit does not have
> flesh and bones as you see I have." And when he had said this, he
> showed them his hands and feet. (Luke 24:38, 39, 40)

Genesis 14:19. *And he blessed him and said, "A blessing on Abram from*   **1730**
God the Highest, possessor of the heavens and the earth."

He blessed him means enjoying heavenly and spiritual benefits. *And
said, "A blessing on Abram from God the Highest,"* means that the Lord's
intermediate self enjoyed benefits from his inner self. *"Possessor of the
heavens and the earth"* symbolizes the bonding of his inner self (Jehovah)
with his intermediate and outer selves.

He blessed him means enjoying heavenly and spiritual benefits. This   **1731**
can be seen from the symbolism of *blessing* as enjoying every possible
benefit, discussed in §§981, 1096. The people who enjoy every benefit are
those who enjoy heavenly and spiritual good, because this produces every
benefit of every description.

The ideas contained in the present verse announce and predict the
union of the Lord's human side with his divine side. True blessing
requires this union.

A blessing on Abram from God the Highest means that the Lord's inter-   **1732**
mediate self enjoyed benefits from his inner self. This too can be seen
from the symbolism of a *blessing* as, again, the enjoyment of benefits. It
can also be seen from the symbolism here of *Abram* as the intermediate
or rational self, discussed above at verse 13 [§1702], and can also be seen

from the symbolism of *God the Highest* as the Lord's inner dimension, also discussed earlier [§§1311:3, 1729].

Abram, as noted, symbolizes the Lord's intermediate or rational self, which was to become one with his inner self (Jehovah), by means of spiritual battles and victories.

The case with the intermediate self is this: The intermediate self, as noted, is midway between the inner and outer selves and makes it possible for the inner self to exert an influence on the outer self [§1702]. Without it there is no communication. Heavenly and spiritual properties are what are communicated. When something heavenly comes through, the intermediate self is called Melchizedek, but when something spiritual does, it is called Abram the Hebrew.

1733   *Possessor of the heavens and the earth* symbolizes the bonding of his inner self (Jehovah) with his intermediate and outer selves, as the symbolism of *heaven* and *earth* shows. Anything comparatively deep inside us is called heaven, and anything on the surface is called the earth. The reason *heaven* symbolizes what lies relatively deep inside us is that our deeper levels are an image of heaven and therefore are a kind of miniature heaven. The Lord's intermediate self is quintessentially heaven because he is the all-in-all of heaven and therefore is heaven itself. The fact that our outer self is called the *earth* follows naturally. The new heavens and the new earth mentioned in the prophets and Revelation, then, actually mean the Lord's kingdom and everyone who typifies the Lord's kingdom, or who has the Lord's kingdom inside. To see that heaven and earth have these meanings, look at what is said about heaven in §§82, 911, and about the earth in §§82, 620, 636, 913.

[2] The symbolism here of *God the Highest, possessor of the heavens and the earth,* as the bonding of the inner self with the intermediate and outer selves in the Lord can be seen from this: In regard to his inner self, the Lord was Jehovah himself. Because his inner self or Jehovah guided and taught his outer self, as a parent does a child, his outer self is called Child of God [divine offspring] in relation to Jehovah, but Child of Humankind [human offspring] in relation to his mother. The Lord's inner being, Jehovah himself, is what is being called *God the Highest.* As full union (or oneness) has not yet occurred, it is also called *possessor of the heavens and the earth*—that is, possessor of everything in the intermediate and outer selves meant here by the heavens and the earth (as noted).

Genesis 14:20. *"And a blessing on God the Highest, who has delivered* **1734**
your enemies into your hand." And [Abram] gave him a tenth of everything.

A blessing on God the Highest symbolizes the Lord's inner self. *Who
has delivered your enemies into your hand* symbolizes victory. *And [Abram]
gave him a tenth of everything* symbolizes the remnant gained through
victory.

The symbolism of *a blessing on God the Highest* as the Lord's inner **1735**
self can be seen from the remarks about his inner self just above.

Jehovah was called *God the Highest* in the ancient church because
height represented and therefore symbolized inner depth, so that the
Highest meant the deepest within. That is why the ancient church
worshiped on heights, mountains, and hills. The relationship of the
deepest level within to the shallower and shallowest levels is exactly like
that of the highest to the lower and lowest. The highest level, or the
deepest level within, is heavenly love, or love itself; Jehovah (the Lord's
inner level) was the most heavenly love, or love itself. There is no ade-
quate way to describe him except in terms of pure love and so in terms
of pure mercy toward the whole human race. That mercy is his desire
to save everyone, to make everyone happy forever, and to give us everything he has. Anyone who is willing to follow is someone he wishes to
draw toward heaven, or in other words, toward himself, out of pure
mercy, by the powerful force of love.

[2] This "love itself" is Jehovah. No other entity but love can be
described as being the I Am, or as having independent existence. The
essential reality of all life—life itself, in other words—comes from this
love because it is innate in love, is integral to love itself. Because Jehovah
alone is the essential reality of life (is life itself), since he alone is love,
absolutely everything has its reality and its life from him. Not a single
person has the capacity for independent existence or life but Jehovah
alone, that is, the Lord alone. And since no one has independent existence or life but the Lord alone, the fact that we seem to ourselves to live
independently is an illusion of the senses. Angels perceive clearly that life
is generated not by themselves but by the Lord, because living as they do
in the Lord's love, they live in the essential reality of his life. Even so, the
appearance of independent life is granted to them more than to anyone
else, along with happiness beyond words.

This, then, is to live in the Lord, which we cannot do in the least if
we do not live in his love—that is, in charity for our neighbor.

1736   The Word makes it quite clear that the Lord is Jehovah, who is called
God the Highest here. In Isaiah:

> *Jehovah Sabaoth is his name;* and your *Redeemer,* the Holy One of
> Israel, is called *God of the whole earth.* (Isaiah 54:5)

This states explicitly that the Redeemer, the Holy One of Israel—who is
the Lord alone—is Jehovah Sabaoth and God of the whole earth. In the
same author:

> This is what *Jehovah* your *Redeemer,* the Holy One of Israel, has said:
> "*I am Jehovah* your *God.*" (Isaiah 48:17)

In the same author:

> "I myself am helping you," says Jehovah, "your *Redeemer,* the Holy
> One of Israel." (Isaiah 41:14)

The names "Holy One of Israel" and "God of Israel" are used many
times. It is obvious that they refer to the Lord.

> They saw *the God of Israel.* Under his feet was a seeming work of sap-
> phire stone, and it seemed like the substance of the sky for purity.
> (Exodus 24:10)

[2] The Jewish religion also did not acknowledge or name anyone else
[than the Lord to come] as Jehovah, because it worshiped Jehovah as the
one God. That religion focused all the more on the Lord because all its
rites represented him and the whole of the Word symbolized him on an
inner level, although most of the people were unaware of this. In Isaiah:

> He will swallow death up evermore, and the *Lord Jehovih* will wipe
> away the tear from all faces. And they will say on that day, "Look! *This
> is our God!* We have awaited him, and he will save us. *This is Jehovah,*
> whom we have awaited; we will rejoice and be glad in his salvation."
> (Isaiah 25:8, 9)

This is about the Lord's Coming. [3] In the same author:

> Watch! The *Lord Jehovih* will come in might, and his arm is ruling
> for him. He will pasture his flock like a shepherd; he will gather them
> into his arm; he will carry little lambs on his chest; he will lead the
> unweaned. (Isaiah 40:10, 11)

This is plainly about the Lord, who is being called the Lord Jehovih. "He will come in might, and his arm is ruling for him" stands for the fact that he would conquer the hells by his own power. Pasturing his flock, gathering it into his arm, carrying little lambs on his breast, and leading the unweaned refers to his love, or mercy. [4] In the same author:

> This is what *Jehovah* has said; *he is God,* creating the heavens, forming the earth and making it; he is firming it; he has not created it an emptiness, he has formed it to be inhabited: "*I am Jehovah, and there is no other.* Is it not so, that *I am Jehovah and except for me there is no other God?* I am a just *God,* and there is no Savior except me. Turn to face me and be saved, all you ends of the earth! For *I am God, and there is no other.*" (Isaiah 45:18, 21, 22)

This clearly says that the Lord is the one Jehovah and God. Creating the heavens and forming the earth is regenerating us, so the creator of heaven and earth is the Regenerator; see §§16, 88, 472, and other places. As a result, the Lord in many places is called the Creator, Fashioner, and Maker. [5] In the same author:

> You are *our Father,* because Abraham does not know us and Israel does not acknowledge us. You are *Jehovah, our Father,* our Redeemer; *your name* is age-old. (Isaiah 63:16)

This is obviously about the Lord, who is the only Redeemer. In Moses:

> Be careful before him and listen to his voice, so as not to vex him, because he will not put up with your transgressing, since *my name is in the middle of him.* (Exodus 23:21)

The name of something is its essential character (see §§144, 145), and what is "in the middle" is the deepest core (§1074). [6] In Isaiah:

> A child has been born for us, a son has been given to us, and sovereignty will be on his shoulder; *his name* will be called Miraculous, Counselor, God, Hero, *Eternal Father,* Prince of Peace. (Isaiah 9:6, 7)

Clearly this is the Lord. In Jeremiah:

> Look! The days are coming when I will raise up for David a just offshoot, and he will reign as monarch, and he will act with understanding and exercise judgment and justice in the land. In his days Judah

will be saved and Israel will live securely. And this is *his name that they will call him: Jehovah our justice.* (Jeremiah 23:5, 6)

Clearly this is the Lord. In Zechariah:

Jehovah will become *monarch* over the whole earth. *On that day Jehovah will be one, and his name one.* (Zechariah 14:9)

Clearly this is about the Lord. His name stands for his essential nature.

1737   The fact that *who has delivered your enemies into your hand* symbolizes victory can be seen without explanation.

The Lord achieved and created the union of his human and divine qualities through the constant conflicts and victories of his spiritual trials, and he did so by his own power. Anyone who thinks this union and oneness occurred in any other way is very much mistaken. As a result, the Lord became the embodiment of uprightness. What he eventually united or identified with was heavenly love, that is, love itself, which is Jehovah, as noted above [§1735].

Our own close connection with the Lord also comes about through times of trial, and through the grafting of faith onto love. Unless faith is implanted in love, or in other words, unless the tenets of faith lead us to live a life of faith—which is charity—the bond will never develop. This alone is *following him,* or forming as close a bond with the Lord as the Lord's human part formed with Jehovah. A life of faith is also what causes all who live it to be called God's children (after the Lord, who is the only child of God) and to become images of him.

1738   *And [Abram] gave him a tenth of everything* symbolizes the remnant gained through victory. This can be seen from the symbolism of *tenths,* or tithes, as a remnant, which was discussed previously (§576). For the definition of a remnant, see §§468, 530, 560, 561, 661, 1050. To be specific, a remnant is all the phases of love and charity—and therefore all the phases of innocence and peace—with which we are gifted. These states are given to us from infancy on, although they dwindle as we continue on into adulthood, until we start to regenerate. Then in addition to the earlier remnant, we also receive a new remnant, and with it, new life. It is our remnant that makes us human. When we lack an outlook of love and charity and an outlook of innocence that permeate all the other moods of our life, we are not human but worse than any wild animal.

The remnant acquired during spiritual battle is what is meant here. This remnant is what the tithes that Abram gave Melchizedek symbolize. It is all the heavenly qualities of love that the Lord amassed through his unceasing struggles and victories, by which he was constantly integrating his divine nature, until finally his human side likewise became love, or in other words, the vital essence of life—that is, Jehovah.

Genesis 14:21. *And the king of Sodom said to Abram, "Give me the souls, and the property take for yourself."*

1739

The king of Sodom said symbolizes the evil and falsity that was conquered. *To Abram* symbolizes the Lord's rational mind. *Give me the souls, and the property take for yourself,* means to give [evil spirits] their lives and they would ignore the rest.

The king of Sodom said symbolizes the evil and falsity that was conquered. This is established by the symbolism of *Sodom* as evil and falsity, which was demonstrated earlier in the chapter [§1663]. Verse 17 above [§1721] says that the king of Sodom went out to meet Abram, meaning that evil and falsity surrendered. This verse now continues by depicting him as pleading.

1740

[2] The reason we overcome evil and falsity through the battles involved in a spiritual crisis, and become imbued with goodness and truth in the process, is that these battles dissolve evil and falsity, and when they are dissolved, goodness and truth replace them. Then the goodness and truth are reinforced more and more and in this way are solidified. There are evil spirits who stir up what is evil and false, you see. If they did not, we could barely recognize those things as evil and false; but when they are stirred up they are exposed. The longer the struggle lasts, the more obvious they grow until finally we gain a horror for them.

[3] All the while evil and falsity are disappearing, goodness and truth are taking their place. The more horror we acquire for evil and falsity, the more the Lord instills in us a love for what is good and true. Again, the more horror we acquire for evil and falsity, the less any evil spirits dare to draw near, because they cannot tolerate an aversion and horror for the evil and falsity in which their lives consist. Sometimes they feel the grip of terror with their first step toward us. The more we love what is good and true, the more the angels—and with the angels, heaven—love to be with us, because when they immerse themselves in the good impulses of love and the true ideas of faith, they are really alive.

The symbolism of *to Abram* as the Lord's rational mind is established by the representation of *Abram*. In the last two chapters, Abram represented the Lord's state during youth. Here in the present chapter, Abram represents the Lord's rational mind, and in those circumstances he is called Abram the Hebrew, as the remarks and proofs above at verse 13 show [§§1702–1703]. He represents the same thing here because no other Abram is meant in this chapter than Abram the Hebrew.

1741

The Lord's spiritual dimension (when connected to his inner self) is Abram the Hebrew, but his heavenly dimension (when connected to his inner self) is represented and symbolized by Melchizedek, as noted [§§1725, 1732].

1742   *Give me the souls, and the property take for yourself,* means to give [evil spirits] their lives and they would ignore the rest. This can be seen from the symbolism of a *soul* as life, as discussed earlier, in §§1000, 1005, 1040; and from the symbolism of *property* as the rest, which is not strictly speaking alive (or not as much so), discussed just below.

[2] The life that evil spirits have and desperately love is a life consisting in the urges of self-love and materialism. So it is a life of hatred, revenge, and cruelty. No other kind of life offers any joy, they believe. They resemble humans, since they once were human; and from their former life as humans they retain this belief that all life consists in the joy of such wicked urges. They remain wholly convinced that such a life is the only life, and that if they lose it they will be obliterated. The nature of the life these people love can be seen from their existence in the other world, where it turns into something that resembles reeking excrement. Amazingly, they perceive the stench to be an extremely pleasant fragrance, as shown by the personal experiences related in §§820, 954.

[3] They act like the demons that the Lord was casting out of a madman, who in terror for their lives begged him to send them into some pigs (Mark 5:7–13). These demons had been sordid misers during bodily life, as can be seen from the fact that in the other life they seem to themselves to spend their lives among pigs. The life of a pig corresponds to greed, which makes such a life pleasing to them, as indicated by the experience related in §939.

1743   Genesis 14:22. *And Abram said to the king of Sodom, "I have lifted my hand to Jehovah, God the Highest, possessor of the heavens and the earth."*

Abram said to the king of Sodom means an answer. *I have lifted my hand to Jehovah* symbolizes the mind the Lord had. *Possessor of the heavens and the earth* symbolizes union.

1744   The fact that *Abram said to the king of Sodom* means an answer can be seen without explanation.

1745   *I have lifted my hand to Jehovah* symbolizes the mind the Lord had, as can be seen from the symbolism of *lifting one's hands.* Lifting one's hand to Jehovah is a physical gesture corresponding to a state of mind, as everyone knows. The literal meaning is expressing intermediate characteristics (that is, characteristics of the mind) through external images that correspond to them, but it is inner things that are meant in the inner sense. The lifting of Abram's hand, then, is a mindset or state of mind.

[2] As long as the Lord was being tested, he talked to Jehovah as a separate person, but so far as his human quality became one with his divine quality, he talked to Jehovah as identical with himself. Many passages in the Gospels and many passages in the prophets and David offer evidence for this. The reason for it stands out clearly from previous remarks about the Lord's heredity from his mother [§§1414, 1444:1–2, 1573]. To the extent that any of that heredity remained, he felt absent from Jehovah; but to the extent that it was rooted out, he was present with and was himself Jehovah.

[3] This can be illustrated by the bond between the Lord and the angels. Sometimes angels speak not for themselves but for the Lord. When they do, they have no idea they are not the Lord; but their superficial traits are being suppressed. It is different when their outward traits are active. Their inner self is the Lord's possession, and so far as anything of their own does not get in the way in such a situation, their inner self belongs to the Lord and in fact is the Lord.

The Lord, however, achieved full union or eternal oneness with Jehovah, so that his human nature itself is also Jehovah.

Possessor of the heavens and the earth symbolizes union, as is established by the discussion above at verse 19 [§1733], where the words are the same and the symbolism is the same.

1746

Genesis 14:23. From the string of a shoe even to its strap, if I should take anything that is yours, . . . ! To prevent you from saying, "I have made Abram rich."

1747

From the string of a shoe even to its strap symbolizes everything that was unclean on the earthly and bodily levels. *If I should take anything that is yours* means that there was nothing of the kind in his heavenly love. *To prevent you from saying, "I have made Abram rich,"* means that the Lord never received strength from anything unclean.

The fact that *from the string of a shoe even to its strap* symbolizes everything that was unclean on the earthly and bodily levels can be seen from the symbolism of a *shoestrap.*

1748

In the Word, the foot and heel symbolize the periphery of the earthly level, as shown before, in §259. A *shoe* is what covers the foot and heel, so it symbolizes an even more peripheral part of the earthly level, which is to say the actual level of the body. A shoe's symbolism depends on the topic at hand. When mentioned in connection with something good, it is taken in a positive sense; when mentioned in connection with something bad, it is taken in a negative sense. The latter is how it is taken here, where the subject is the property of Sodom's king, symbolizing evil and falsity. So the *shoestrap* symbolizes what is unclean on the earthly and bodily levels. A *shoestring* symbolizes falsity, and a *shoestrap,* evil. Because it is so small, it symbolizes what is lowliest of all.

[2] This symbolism of a shoe can also be seen from other places in the Word. When Jehovah appeared to Moses in the middle of the bramble, for instance, he said to Moses:

> You are not to come near here; *strip* your *shoes* off your feet, because the place on which you are standing is holy land. (Exodus 3:5)

The leader of Jehovah's army said the same thing to Joshua:

> *Strip* your *shoe* off your foot, because the place on which you are standing is holiness. (Joshua 5:15)

Anyone can see here that a shoe would not detract from the holiness in any way, provided the individual were intrinsically holy. The order is given because the shoe was representing the earthly, bodily periphery, which needs to be shed.

[3] The fact that earthly and bodily things are unclean can be seen in David:

> Moab is my washbasin. On Edom I will set my *shoe.* (Psalms 60:8)

Something similar is involved in the command to the disciples:

> If anyone does not welcome you or listen to your words, coming out of that house or city shake off the *dust of your feet.* (Matthew 10:14; Mark 6:11; Luke 9:5)

The dust of the feet symbolizes the same thing as a shoe—namely, something made unclean by evil and falsity—because the bottom of the foot means the outer limit of the earthly level. In those days people were engrossed in representation and believed that representation alone, rather than the naked truth, held secrets of heaven within it. That is why they were commanded to shake the dust off.

[4] Since a shoe symbolized the periphery of the earthly level, having a shoe taken off meant being stripped of the outermost dimensions of the earthly plane. As an example, take a man who refused to perform the levirate, spoken of in Moses:

> If a man does not wish to perform the levirate, his sister-in-law shall come up to him in the eyes of the elders and *draw* his *shoe* off his foot

and spit in his face. And she shall answer and say, "This is what shall be
done to the man who does not build up the house of his brother." And
his name in Israel will be called the house of one *stripped of his shoe.*
(Deuteronomy 25:5–10)

This stands for a complete lack of earthly charity.

[5] A shoe symbolizes the outer limit of the earthly level in a good
sense too, as can also be seen in the Word. Moses, for instance, says of
Asher:

> A blessing on Asher because of his sons! Let him be acceptable to his
> brothers and dip his foot in oil; iron and bronze is his *shoe.* (Deuter-
> onomy 33:24, 25)

The shoe stands for the periphery of the earthly level. A shoe of iron
stands for earthly truth; a shoe of bronze, for earthly good. This is indicated by the symbolism of iron and bronze (§§425, 426). Because a
shoe symbolized the earthly, bodily periphery, it gave rise to this figure
of speech ["from the string of a shoe even to its strap"] that meant the
least important, lowliest things of all. The outermost part of our earthly,
bodily dimension is the lowliest of everything we have in us, which is
what John the Baptist meant when he said,

> One mightier than I is coming, and I am not worthy to undo the *strap*
> of his *shoes.* (Luke 3:16; Mark 1:7; John 1:27)

If I should take anything that is yours means that there was nothing of
the kind in his heavenly love, as can be seen from Abram's refusal to take
anything from Sodom's king. *Abram* represented the Lord in his new
role as victor, and consequently he represented the qualities of heavenly
love that the Lord had acquired through his victories. The *king of Sodom*
represented evil and falsity, of which nothing was present in the Lord as
victor—that is, in heavenly love.

[2] The inner meaning of these words is not clear unless you know
how matters stand in the other life. Among evil and hellish spirits, self-
love and materialism reign supreme, so these spirits view themselves as
gods of the universe and as having great power. Once conquered, they do
perceive that they have absolutely no power, but the illusion of authority and dominion remains, and they believe they can add greatly to the
Lord's authority and dominion. For this reason, in order to procure a
share of power, they offer good spirits their services. However, evil and
falsity are the only resources they think they can use in accomplishing

1749

anything, whereas the Lord—or heavenly love—can use nothing but goodness and truth. As a result, Sodom's king (who represents such spirits) here receives the answer that there is nothing of the kind in the Lord; in other words, that evil and falsity lend the Lord no power.

[3] The power exerted by evil and falsity is entirely contrary to the power exerted by goodness and truth. The power exerted by evil and falsity is the desire to enslave everyone; the power exerted by goodness and truth is the desire to free everyone. The power exerted by evil and falsity is the desire to destroy everyone, but the power exerted by goodness and truth is the desire to save everyone. This shows that the power of evil and falsity is the Devil's, while the power of goodness and truth is the Lord's. The diametrically opposite nature of the two kinds of power can be seen from the Lord's words in Matthew 12:24–30; and the idea that no one can serve two masters, in Matthew 6:24; Luke 16:13.

1750   *To prevent you from saying, "I have made Abram rich,"* means that the Lord never received strength from anything unclean. This can be seen from the symbolism of *being enriched* as acquiring power and strength. The situation with this can be seen from the discussion just above.

1751   Genesis 14:24. *Excepting only what the young men have eaten, and the share of the men who went with me—Aner, Eshcol, and Mamre; these shall take their share.*

Excepting only what the young men have eaten symbolizes good spirits. *And the share of the men who went with me* symbolizes angels. *Aner, Eshcol, and Mamre,* symbolize characteristics of [the angels]. *These shall take their share* means that they were given power over [the evil spirits].

1752   The symbolism of *excepting only what the young men have eaten* as good spirits can be seen from what comes before and after. As for what comes before, Mamre, Eshcol, and Aner are mentioned above at verse 13 as sworn allies of Abram's. They symbolized the state of the Lord's rational self, or at least its outward part, and what its goodness and truth were like [§1705]. Consequently they symbolized the angels who were with the Lord when he was fighting, as is evident from the explanation there.

The same thing can be seen from what follows, as will soon become clear.

Here the ones who went with Abram are called young men; what they actually mean are good spirits; fully adult men, discussed just below, mean angels.

The Word reveals that angels were present with the Lord when he fought the hells. The same thing can be deduced from the fact that angels simply had to be present during his struggles, to whom the Lord (by his own power) gave strength and the apparent ability to fight alongside him. Angels receive *all* their power from the Lord.

[2] The fact that angels fight evil spirits can be seen from many earlier remarks about the angels present with us, guarding us and turning aside the harm that hellish spirits attempt, as discussed above at §§50, 227, 228, 697, 968. All their power is from the Lord, though.

It is true that good spirits are angels too, but they are a lower kind, because they inhabit the first heaven. Angelic spirits inhabit the second, and those who are properly called angels inhabit the third, as mentioned in §§459, 684. The form of government in the other world is such that good spirits are subordinate to angelic spirits, and angelic spirits are subordinate to actual angels. As a result, they form a single angelic community.

Good spirits and angelic spirits are the ones called young men here, but actual angels are the ones called men.

The symbolism of *and the share of the men who went with me* as angels can be seen from the remarks directly above and in addition from the fact that when angels appear to people in the Word they are called men.

1753

Aner, Eshcol, and Mamre, symbolize characteristics of [the angels], as can be seen from remarks concerning these men above at verse 13 of the current chapter [§1705]. To be specific, their names symbolize good impulses and true ideas used in the struggle, and not so much the angels themselves, because it is the young men and adult men who symbolize angels, as noted. Angels never have any name but are differentiated by the quality of their goodness and truth. Consequently, a name in the Word symbolizes nothing else than a person's vital essence and its character, as already shown (§§144, 145, 340). The same thing can also be seen in Isaiah, where he says of the Lord:

1754

> *His name will be called* Miraculous, Counselor, God, Hero, Eternal Father, Prince of Peace. (Isaiah 9:6)

[2] His name means what he is like—miraculous, a counselor, God, hero, eternal father, and prince of peace. In Jeremiah, where he too speaks of the Lord:

> *This is his name that they will call him:* Jehovah our justice. (Jeremiah 23:5, 6)

This says explicitly that his name is his justice. In Moses, too, where he
also speaks of the Lord:

> He will not put up with your transgressing, since *my name* is in the
> middle of him. (Exodus 23:21)

Here too his name stands for the divinity of his essential nature. In addition it can be seen from many verses in the Word that say, "*they called on
Jehovah's name*"; that they were "not to take up *Jehovah's name* unwor-
thily" [Exodus 20:7]; and in the Lord's Prayer, "*may your name be held
sacred*" [Matthew 6:9; Luke 11:2]. It is the same with angels' names, and
here with the names of Eshcol, Aner, and Mamre, who represent angels:
they symbolize the characteristics of angels.

1755   *These shall take their share* means that they were given power over [the
evil spirits], as can be seen from what was said above at verses 21, 22, 23:
that the Lord wanted nothing from [the evil spirits], since they had no
strength to offer him.

As regards the power over them given to the angels: A great deal of
experience has made clear to me that angels are the ones who rule over
evil and hellish spirits, but the Lord sees and foresees absolutely everything, and provides for and arranges absolutely everything. Sometimes he
does so with bare tolerance, sometimes with reluctant permission, sometimes with acceptance, sometimes with pleasure, and sometimes with a
will. The *desire* to control others is a strictly human trait, at odds with
traits angels receive from the Lord, but when desire is absent, all control
comes of love and mercy.

This idea is fairly arcane, though, so it cannot be explained intelligibly in a few words. It is enough to know that evil and hellish spirits are
put under the angels' power and that the Lord governs absolutely everything, even the most minute details. I will say more about this below,
with the Lord's divine mercy, where providence and permission are discussed [§2447].

1756   This is the message of the inner meaning, in its general outlines; but
when every last word is explained according to its symbolism, the actual
train of thought and its beauty cannot be seen as well as it would be
if the whole were captured in a single mental image. When all of it is
grasped in a single idea, then scattered particulars are seen to cohere and
connect in a beautiful way.

The situation resembles that in which we hear someone talking and
focus on the words. We do not pick up on the idea of the speaker as well

as we would if we ignored the words and their definitions. Scripture's inner meaning (compared to its outer letter) is almost the same as speech whose words we only barely hear, much less pay attention to, when our mind is entirely absorbed by the ideas embodied in the speaker's words.

[2] The ancient method of writing used words and human figures to represent ideas in an entirely allegorical way. Secular writers of the day composed their histories in this way, and also [their works on] issues of public and private life. As a matter of fact, not a single written word was what it literally seemed to be; each represented another meaning. Ancient authors even presented the full range of passions as gods and goddesses, whom pagan peoples later began to worship as divine. Any literate person can see that this is so, since ancient books of the kind are still in existence.

This method of writing they inherited from the very earliest people, who lived before the Flood. The earliest people were in the habit of representing heavenly concepts and divine ones to themselves in the form of things visible in nature and in their culture. Because of this, it filled their minds and souls with pleasure and delight to observe the objects of the universe, especially those that displayed beauty of form or design. So all the books in the church of that time were written this way. Job is one such book. Solomon's Song of Songs is one that imitated them. The two books Moses mentioned in Numbers 21:14, 27 were of the same kind. And there were many more that did not survive.

[3] This writing mode was later admired for its antiquity by both Jacob's descendants and the surrounding nations—so much so that they revered nothing as divine that was not written in that mode. People inspired by the prophetic spirit spoke in a similar way: Jacob (Genesis 49:3–27); Moses (Exodus 15:1–21; Deuteronomy 33:2–end); Balaam, a "child of the east" from Syria, where the ancient church remained in existence (Numbers 23:7–10, 19–24; 24:5–9, 17–24); Deborah and Barak (Judges 5:2–end); Hannah (1 Samuel 2:2–10); and many others. They spoke this way for many hidden reasons. People did not understand their words, and only a very small number realized that the words symbolized the heavenly affairs of the Lord's kingdom and church. Even so, touched and filled with wondering awe, they sensed that something divinely sacred was present in those words.

[4] The histories of the Word are like this as well; in them too the individual names and the individual words represent and symbolize the heavenly and spiritual qualities of the Lord's kingdom. This has not yet

been recognized by the scholarly world, though, which knows only that the Word was inspired down to its smallest jot and that as a whole and in every word it contains secrets of heaven.

The Way Spirits Talk (Continued) and How It Varies

1757 SPIRITS talk to people in words, as noted earlier [§§1637, 1638]. They talk to each other in thoughts, however, which are the source of words and which combine to form whole concepts. The individual thoughts are not as dim and vague as they are in people still living in their bodies but are as sharp and clear as [the words] of speech.

Our thinking becomes more distinct and clearer after the body is discarded, and each thought then separates out to serve as a discrete unit of speech. Darkness dissolves with the body, freeing the mind of the fetters that bind it and so of the fog that envelops it. Our thinking becomes more spontaneous, and as a result we more readily see, grasp, and vocalize specific ideas.

1758 Spirits talk in different ways. Each community or clan of spirits can be identified by its speech, and in fact each spirit can too, much as is the case on earth. They are identified not only by the emotions that give life to their speech (and that fill and convey the words) and by their accent but also by the sound and by other characteristics less easily put into words.

1759 The language of heavenly spirits does not flow easily into the articulated sounds or words we use, because it cannot adapt to any word containing a harsh sound or hard, double consonants or a merely factual thought. As a result, heavenly spirits rarely flow into [our] speech except through emotion, which softens the words into something like a stream of water or breath of air.

Spirits who are midway between heavenly and spiritual have a sweet kind of language that flows along like the gentlest of breezes, caressing the listening ear and softening the actual words. It is also swift and sure. The reason for the fluidity and charm of their speech is that the heavenly goodness present in their thoughts has the same qualities, and that there is no discrepancy between their words and their thoughts. All sweet-sounding harmony in the other life comes from goodness and charity.

The language of those who are spiritual is also fluid but not as soft and gentle. They speak more than the others.

Evil demons are also capable of speaking smoothly, but only to the outer ear. On a deeper level their speech grates, because they are simulating goodness rather than responding to it emotionally.   **1760**

Their speech can also lack smoothness, and then the discrepancy with their thoughts is perceived in their speech as an undercurrent.

There are spirits who act on us not in such a streamlike way but by vibrating back and forth in a kind of straight line, more sharply or less. They bring with them not only a message but also an answer to it. They are people who reject the inner dimensions of the Word for many reasons, despise humans as mere tools for their use, and are completely self-absorbed.   **1761**

There are spirits who are mute but have shaped my face to reflect their own opinions, presenting their ideas in such a vivid way that their overall thinking lay open to view in visible form. This they achieved by changes in the area around my lips spreading into my face, and also around my eyes. When they were communicating their more profound thoughts, they worked in the area of my left eye if they were dealing with truth and the desire for truth, and around my right eye if they were dealing with goodness and the desire for goodness.   **1762**

I also heard a large group of spirits speaking all together. Their speech rose and fell like a wave, flowing into various destinations in my brain.   **1763**

Again, I listened to certain spirits using speech that had a fourfold ending, duplicating the pitch and sound of threshers. These spirits are separate from others, since they cause the kind of headache that suction through a syringe would cause.

I heard some who seemed to be talking to themselves but in an audible voice, so that their words reached my ears.

[2] Still others talked by belching the words up out of their stomach. They are the kind who have no interest in the meaning of a thing but are enlisted by others to speak.

I have heard spirits who spoke hoarsely, their voices cracking. They attach themselves to my left side under my elbow and also to my left ear.

Then there were those who had lost their voice, like a person with a cold. Some of them are the type that draw out others' secrets in order to hurt them by injecting [something contradictory] into their pleasure.

[3] There are small spirits who are few in number but still talk as if they were a huge crowd. They seem to thunder. I heard them above my head and assumed they were a large throng, but then one individual

approached me on my left side below my arm and spoke in similarly thunderous tones. He did the same thing again from farther away. Where they come from will be told elsewhere, the Lord in his divine mercy willing.

These types of speech are relatively unusual, however.

For one whose inner ear is open, and for spirits, these sounds and types of speech are as loud and clear as those of a person on earth, surprising to say. For one whose inner ear is not open, they are inaudible.

1764
Once some spirits also talked to me in pure visual representations. They presented images of flames in various colors, lights, rising and falling clouds, different kinds of cottages and platforms, utensils, people dressed in various ways, and many other things. All the images had symbolic meaning, and from them alone I could tell what the spirits meant.

Genesis 15

Sacred Scripture, or the Word, Which Conceals a Divine Message That Lies Open to the View of Good Spirits and Angels

SOME people love the Lord's Word and live a kind and charitable life. Others believe what it says in a simple-hearted way, without making assumptions that undermine the religious truth of its inner meaning. When the Word is read by either kind of person, it is displayed by the Lord before angels' eyes with tremendous beauty and charm, accompanied by visual representations and adapted with inexpressible variety to every phase they are then passing through. The beauty and charm are so great that every single facet is perceived as alive. This vital energy is the life that lies within the Word and that gave birth to the Word when it was sent down from heaven. For this reason, the Lord's Word by its very nature conceals spiritual and heavenly messages within, no matter how unpolished it seems in the letter. These inner messages lie open to the view of good spirits and of angels when people on earth read the Word.

1767

Since I have been given the opportunity to hear and see that the Lord's Word is presented in this way before good spirits and angels, let me report my experiences.

1768

A spirit came to me not long after he had left his body. (This I could tell from the fact that he did not yet realize he was in the other life but believed he was still living in the world.) I sensed that he had devoted his time to intellectual pursuits, which I discussed with him, but then to my amazement he suddenly soared into the air. I decided he was the type of person whose ambitions had been lofty (since people like this usually rise into the air) or that he thought heaven was at the top of the sky. (This kind of person too is usually raised aloft, in order to learn that heaven is not up high but deep within.) [2] I soon perceived, though, that he had been lifted up to a group of angelic spirits positioned a little

1769

out in front and to the right, on the first threshold of heaven. He then
spoke to me from there, saying that he was seeing sights grander than
the human mind could ever conceive. While this was happening, I was
reading in the first chapter of Deuteronomy about the Jewish people,
specifically the ones sent to scout out the land of Canaan and all that it
held. As I was reading it, he said that he caught none of the contents of
the literal meaning but only those of the spiritual meaning, which were
too astounding to describe.

This occurred on the very threshold of the angelic spirits' heaven.
What would it be like in their heaven proper, or in the heaven of true
angels?

[3] Then certain spirits present with me, who had previously doubted
that the Lord's Word was like this, began to regret their disbelief. In their
present state, they said they believed, because they had heard from the
spirit that he heard, saw, and perceived it to be so.

[4] Other spirits, however, stood by their disbelief and kept saying it
was not true, it was all imagination. So they too were suddenly swept up
high. They talked to me from there and confessed that it was anything
but imagination, because they really perceived that it was true. In fact
they perceived it more keenly than would ever be possible with any of
the senses available during physical life.

[5] Soon others too were raised into the same heaven, including
someone known to me in bodily life. He gave the same testimony, saying
among other things that he was too dumbfounded to describe the glory
of the Word in its inner sense. Speaking with a kind of pity, he expressed
astonishment that humans were completely unaware of such things.

What is more, he said that from there he could peer deeply into my
thoughts and feelings. In them he saw more than he could tell—what
caused them, how they interacted, where they came from, who inspired
them, how the mental images mingled with earthly sediment, the need
to separate the two completely, and so on.

1770   On two later occasions I saw yet others raised into the second heaven
to be with angelic spirits, and they talked to me from there while I read
Deuteronomy 3 from start to finish. They said they focused only on the
deeper sense of the Word and stated positively that not one tip of a letter
in it failed to contain a spiritual meaning that harmonized in the most
beautiful way with all the other parts. They added that the names symbolize something deeper. This proved to them as well that each and every

particular in the Word had been inspired by the Lord, which they had not believed earlier. They also wanted to swear to the truth of this in the presence of others but were not allowed.

Still another group of spirits had difficulty believing that the Lord's **1771** Word conceals these kinds of depths within, at its heart. (In the other life spirits keep the skepticism they had when they lived in their bodies; it is not broken down except through means provided by the Lord and through personal experience.) Accordingly, the inner eye of their mind was opened while I was reading some of David's psalms, although these spirits were not lifted up to join angelic spirits. They perceived the inner dimensions of the Word in the psalms I was reading and, stunned by them, confessed that they had never believed in such things.

[2] Many other spirits then listened to the same part of the Word, but they all perceived it in different ways. It filled the thoughts of some with many sweet, pleasant images and so with a kind of life, according to the capacity of each. It also had the strength to pierce through to their deepest core. With some its power was so great that they seemed to themselves to be lifted up toward the more inward parts of heaven. The more they were affected by its truth—and by the goodness interwoven with the truth—the closer they came to the Lord.

[3] At the same time the Word was read to some who grasped none of its inner meaning but only its outer or literal meaning. In their eyes, the letter was lifeless.

This showed what the Word is like when the Lord brings it to life and when he does not. When he does, it has the power to penetrate to our inmost core; when he does not, it is mere words, with hardly any life in it.

The Lord in his divine mercy has also granted me the opportunity **1772** to see his Word in all the beauty of its inner sense. This he has done many, many times. I am not talking about the way it appears when the inner meaning of each individual word is explained but about the way it appears when the whole and all the parts form a single chain of thought. This can be described as seeing heaven's paradise from earth's.

Spirits who loved and enjoyed the Lord's Word during their physical **1773** life feel a certain pleasant, heavenly warmth in the next life, and this too I was allowed to experience.

The spirits who had enjoyed the Word somewhat shared their warmth with me, and it resembled the balmy temperatures of spring. The warmth started in the area of my lips and spread through my cheeks and from there to my ears. It also reached up to my eyes and down toward the middle of my chest.

[2] Other spirits felt even more pleasure in the Lord's Word and in the deeper lessons that the Lord himself had taught. The warmth they shared with me was deeper and started in my chest, spreading up toward my chin and down toward my lower abdomen.

The warmth of those who felt still more pleasure was still more deeply gratifying and more springlike. It reached from my lower abdomen up to my chest and from there through my left arm to my hand.

I was taught by angels that this was the case, and they said that when such spirits come close, they trigger these waves of heat. The spirits themselves do not feel it, however, because they are inside it. The same is common with children, adolescents, and young adults; mostly they are not aware of the fire they have—although they have more than mature adults and old people do—because they are inside it.

[3] In addition, I sensed the warmth of those who did enjoy the Word but did not concern themselves with understanding it. The heat was restricted to my right arm.

As far as heat goes, evil spirits can also conjure up a type that mimics the pleasurable kind, and they can share it with others, but it is strictly superficial; it has no inner source. This is the kind of heat that turns into something putrid and dunglike—the heat that adulterers and hedonists have.

1774 There are spirits who are reluctant to hear about the Word's deeper layers. In fact they refuse to understand the subject, although they are capable of doing so. Mainly they are people who had believed that good works deserve credit and had therefore done good out of love for themselves and worldly reward. In other words, their goal had been to gain high position or wealth and the reputation that goes with it, not to benefit the Lord's kingdom. In the next world they are more insistent than any others on getting into heaven, but they stay outside, because they do not want to learn the truth and therefore be affected by goodness. They interpret the letter of the Word to suit their delusions, bringing forward any passage that smiles favorably on their selfish urges.

They were represented by a little old lady whose face was ugly and yet snowy white, her appearance marred by distorted features.

Those who welcome and love the deeper layers of the Word, on the other hand, were represented by a girl just grown up, in the bloom of early womanhood, dressed in beautiful clothes, wearing wreaths and other splendid finery.

With one group of spirits I discussed the Word and the need for some kind of revelation to have been given, in the Lord's divine providence. After all, revelation—the Word—is a broad container, holding within it both spiritual and heavenly elements and consequently uniting heaven and earth. Without it, heaven and earth would have lacked connection and the human race would have perished.

In addition, it was necessary that heavenly truth be available somewhere for people to learn, because we were born for heavenly purposes and should come among heavenly beings when bodily life ends. Religious truth forms the laws of order in the realm where we will be spending eternity.

It may seem perplexing—although it is absolutely true—that angels understand the Word's inner meaning better and more fully when young girls and boys read it than when adults who lack a faith born of neighborly love do. The reason I was given is that young boys and girls are at a stage of innocence and mutual love. So the vessels [of their minds] are very tender, almost heavenly, completely open to outside influences, and therefore capable of being molded by the Lord. (They are unaware of his molding, however, except perhaps through a kind of delight perfectly suited to their tastes.)

The Lord's Word, the angels said, is dead verbiage, but he brings it alive in the person who reads it. He gives it as much life as each of us is capable of receiving, and the more charity we express in our lives and the more innocent we are, the more living the Word becomes. This happens in countless different ways.

More on this subject will be found at the end of the present chapter [§§1869–1879].

Genesis 15

1. After these words, the word of Jehovah came to Abram in a vision, saying, "Do not be afraid, Abram; I am a shield to you, your very ample reward."

2. And Abram said, "Lord Jehovih, what will you give me? For I am walking childless, and my 'child,' the steward of my household, is the Damascene Eliezer."

3. And Abram said, "Here, you have not given me seed, and indeed the 'child' of my household is my heir."

4. And see, now: the word of Jehovah to him, saying, "This one will not be your heir; but one who will issue from your belly will be your heir."

5. And leading him outside he said, "Look, please, toward the sky and count the stars, if you can count them." And he said to him, "This is how your seed will be."

6. And he believed in Jehovah, and [Jehovah] credited it to him as uprightness.

7. And [Jehovah] said to him, "I am Jehovah, who brought you out of Ur of the Chaldeans, to give you this land to inherit."

8. And [Abram] said, "Lord Jehovih, how will I know that I will inherit it?"

9. And [Jehovah] said to him, "Take yourself a three-year-old heifer, and a three-year-old she-goat, and a three-year-old ram, and a turtledove, and a chick."

10. And he took himself all these things and split them in half and set each of the parts across from its other [half]; but the fowl he did not split.

11. And winged creatures swooped down onto the bodies, and Abram drove them away.

12. And the sun was about to set, and slumber fell on Abram, and look—terror of immense shadows was falling on him!

13. And [Jehovah] said to Abram, "You must know beyond doubt that your seed will be immigrants in a land not theirs; and they will serve [the people of that land], and these will afflict them four hundred years.

14. And also the nation they serve I will judge. And after this happens, they will depart with a great deal of property.

15. And you will come to your ancestors in peace; you will be buried at a good old age.

16. And in the fourth generation they will come back here, because the wickedness of the Amorites will not be complete until that time."

17. And it happened that the sun set, and darkness occurred, and see? A furnace of smoke and a torch of fire that passed between those pieces!

18. On that day Jehovah struck a pact with Abram, saying, "To your seed will I give this land, from the river of Egypt all the way to the great river, the river Phrath:

19. the Kenite, and the Kenizzite, and the Kadmonite;

20. and the Hittite, and the Perizzite, and the Rephaim;

21. and the Amorite, and the Canaanite, and the Girgashite, and the Jebusite."

Summary

THE inner sense here continues to speak of the Lord, in the period **1778**
after he endured the battles and spiritual trials of his youth. These
battles were severe assaults on the love he cherished for the whole human
race and in particular for the church. Therefore, since he was anxious
about what was in store, he received a promise. At the same time he
was shown what the condition of the church would be toward the end,
when it would begin to die. Still, a new church would be revived to take
the place of the former one, and the heavenly kingdom would increase
beyond measure.

Consolation of the Lord after the inward struggles portrayed in the **1779**
last chapter (verse 1).

The Lord's complaint that the religious culture was merely superficial **1780**
(verses 2, 3). The promise of a deeper kind (verse 4). Its fertility (verse 5).
The Lord embodied uprightness (verse 6). He alone had kingship in the
heavens and on earth (verse 7).

Because he wanted reassurance that the human race would be saved **1781**
(verse 8), he was shown what the church was like generally, specifically,
and in minute detail (verses 9–17).

The heifer, she-goat, and ram represent the church's heavenly aspects, **1782**
while the turtledove and chick represent its spiritual aspects (verse 9).
The church is on one side and the Lord on the other (verse 10). The Lord
routed evil and falsity (verse 11), but falsity still plagued the church (verses
12, 13). The church was delivered from falsity (verse 14), so the Lord was
comforted (verse 15). Evil would seize control, however (verse 16), and in
the end, false ideas and evil cravings would be in complete control (verse
17). Then the Lord's kingdom and a new religion would arrive, whose
extent is described (verse 18). The false thoughts and evil urges to be
driven out are meant by the nations mentioned (verses 19, 20, 21).

Inner Meaning

THE contents here, as I have said before, are true history. Jehovah **1783**
did talk this way with Abram, and promised him he would inherit
the land of Canaan. Jehovah did command Abram to arrange the heifer,

she-goat, ram, turtledove, and chick as he did. The winged creatures
did swoop down onto the bodies. Slumber did fall on Abram, and in
his sleep, terror of shadows. When the sun had set, he did see a furnace of smoke along with a torch of flame between the parts. And so on.
These details are historically true, and yet each and every one of them
down to the smallest action represents something, while the words of
the story themselves down to the smallest jot have a symbolism. In other
words, every last feature has an inner meaning. Everything in the Word
is inspired, and since it is inspired, it cannot come from any source but
a heavenly one. It cannot hide any message but a heavenly and spiritual
one in its inner recesses. Otherwise it would never be the Lord's Word.
[2] This is the message contained in the inner sense. When the inner
sense lies open, the literal sense is obliterated, as if it did not exist. Conversely when attention is paid only to the historical or literal meaning,
the inner meaning is obliterated, as if it did not exist.

    The relationship is like that of heavenly light to the world's light, and
that in turn of the world's light to heavenly light. When heavenly light
appears, the world's light seems dark, as I have learned from experience.
On the other hand, when anyone sees by the world's light, heavenly light
would seem dark if it appeared at all. It is the same with the human mind.
Anyone who relies exclusively on human wisdom, or in other words, on
book learning, sees heavenly wisdom as a dark hole. Anyone who enjoys
heavenly wisdom, though, finds human wisdom simplistic and vague—a
form of darkness, if it is unlit by heavenly rays.

1784   Genesis 15:1. *After these words, the word of Jehovah came to Abram in
a vision, saying, "Do not be afraid, Abram; I am a shield to you, your very
ample reward."*

    After these words, the word of Jehovah came to Abram in a vision, means
that after the struggles of his youth, he had a revelation; a *vision* is a profound revelation received through perception. *Do not be afraid, Abram;
I am a shield to you,* symbolizes protection from evil and falsity, and trust
in that protection. *Your great reward* symbolizes the goal of his victories.

1785   *After these words, the word of Jehovah came to Abram in a vision,* means
that after the struggles of his youth, he had a revelation. This can be seen
from the symbolism of *words,* of *the word of Jehovah to Abram,* and of a
vision. In Hebrew, *words* mean things, and here they mean accomplished
events, namely, the Lord's inward struggles treated of in the last chapter.

    The word of Jehovah to Abram is simply the Lord's word inside
himself. In his youth, though, and during his struggles, before his two

essential natures had united as one, Jehovah's word necessarily appeared to him as revelation. This is the only way the things inside manifest themselves when they reach the surface, during the phases and moments in which the surface is distant from the core. These phases are referred to as times when the Lord was humbled.

The fact that a *vision* is a profound revelation received through perception can be seen from visions, which vary with the visionary's state of mind. A vision is completely different for those whose deeper levels are shut off than for those whose deeper levels are open. When the Lord appeared to the whole congregation on Mount Sinai, for example, his appearance was a vision. The people saw it differently than Aaron, and Aaron differently than Moses. The prophets' visions, furthermore, were different from Moses'. There are many different kinds of visions, which will be discussed later [§§1882–1885, 1966–1975], the Lord in his divine mercy willing.

The deeper a vision is, the fuller it is. The Lord's visionary ability was the most perfect of all, because he then had a perception of everything in the world of spirits and the heavens, and he also had direct communication with Jehovah. This communication is represented and on a deeper level is symbolized by Jehovah's appearing to Abram in a vision.

Do not be afraid, Abram; I am a shield to you, symbolizes protection from evil and falsity, and trust in that protection, as can be seen from the symbolism of a *shield,* discussed just below.

These words—that Jehovah is a shield and very much a reward—are words of comfort after trial. All trial carries with it some kind of despair; otherwise it is not a trial. So consolation follows. Anyone who is being tested becomes anxious, and the anxiety causes a state of despair over the outcome. The actual struggle is nothing else.

Those who are sure of victory feel no anxiety, so they face no test.

[2] Because the Lord endured the most dreadful, fiercest trials of all, he too was inevitably driven to despair, a despair he was to overcome and dispel by his own power. This is quite clear from his crisis in Gethsemane, described this way in Luke:

> When Jesus was in the place, he said to his disciples, "Pray not to undergo trial." And he withdrew from them about a stone's throw, and dropping to his knees he prayed, saying, "Father, if you want this cup to pass by me . . . Still, let your will be done, not mine." An angel

1786

1787

> appeared to him from heaven, though, comforting him. And when he
> was in agony, he prayed more intensely. And his sweat became as drops
> of blood falling on the ground. (Luke 22:40–45)

In Matthew:

> He began to be grieved and distressed. Then he said to his disciples,
> "My soul is completely grief-stricken, even to death." And going on a
> little he fell on his face praying, saying, "My Father, if it is possible, let
> this cup pass by me. Yet not as I wish but as you do." Again a second
> time he went away and prayed, saying, "My Father, if this cup cannot
> pass by me unless I drink it, let your will be done." And he prayed a
> third time, saying the same words. (Matthew 26:36–44)

In Mark:

> He began to be terrified and greatly distressed. He said to his disciples,
> "My soul is wrapped in grief, even to death." Going on a little, he fell
> on the ground and prayed that, if it was possible, the hour pass by him.
> He said, "Abba, Father, all things are possible for you. Make this cup
> pass by me. Not as I wish, though, but as you do." He did this a second
> time and a third time. (Mark 14:33–41)

[3] These passages show what the Lord's crises were like: they were
the fiercest of all; he had very deep-seated anguish, to the point of sweat-
ing blood; he was then in a state of despair about the goal and the outcome; and he received comfort. The present words—"I Jehovah am your
shield and very much your reward"—also entail comfort after the spiritual battles described in the last chapter.

1788　　The fact that a *shield* is protection from evil and falsity, which inspires
trust, can be seen without explanation; frequent use of the saying "Jehovah
is a shield and buckler" has made it a familiar one.

The specific symbolism of a shield, though, can be seen from the
Word. In relation to the Lord it symbolizes protection. In relation to
human beings it symbolizes trust in his protection. Just as war symbolizes times of trial (as shown in §1664), every weapon of war symbolizes
a particular aspect of trial or of defense against evil and falsity. (Defense
against evil and falsity is defense against the Devil's horde, the source and
agent of our trials.) So a shield symbolizes one thing, a buckler another,
an aegis another, a helmet another, a spear or a javelin another, a sword
another, a bow and arrows another, and a corselet another. Each will be
discussed later, with the Lord's divine mercy.

[2] The reason a shield symbolizes protection from evil and falsity on the Lord's part, and trust in him on our part, is that it was a way of protecting the chest, and the chest symbolizes goodness and truth. (The chest symbolizes goodness because it contains the heart, and truth because it contains the lungs.) This symbolism of a shield can be seen in David:

> A blessing on Jehovah, my towering rock (teaching my hands *battle;* my fingers, war), my mercy and my fortress, my fortified citadel and my own rescuer, *my shield and he in whom I trust.* (Psalms 144:1, 2)

The battle and war are those of spiritual trial and, in an inner sense here, of the Lord's trials. The shield obviously means Jehovah's protection and humankind's trust in it. [3] In the same author:

> Israel, *trust in Jehovah;* he is their help and their *shield.* House of Aaron, *trust in Jehovah;* he is their help and their *shield.* All you who fear Jehovah, *trust in Jehovah;* he is their help and their *shield.* (Psalms 115:9, 10, 11)

The meaning is similar. In the same author:

> Jehovah my fortress, my God in whom I will *trust,* will cover you with his wing, and under his wings you will *feel confidence.* His truth is a *buckler* and *aegis.* (Psalms 91:2, 4)

The buckler and aegis stand for protection from falsity. [4] In the same author:

> Jehovah is my rock and my fortress and my rescuer, My God, my towering rock *in which I trust, my shield,* and the horn of my salvation. *Jehovah is a shield to all who trust in him.* (Psalms 18:2, 30)

The meaning is similar. In the same author:

> You, who examine hearts and kidneys, are a just God. My *shield* [rests] on God, who saves the upright at heart. (Psalms 7:9, 10)

The shield stands for trust. In the same author:

> You have given me the *shield* of your salvation, and your right hand will hold me up. (Psalms 18:35)

The shield stands for trust. In the same author:

> To God belong the *shields of the earth;* he has been greatly exalted. (Psalms 47:9)

[5] The shields stand for trust. In the same author:

> A sun and *shield* is *Jehovah God;* favor and glory Jehovah will grant. Good
> will not be withheld from those who walk in integrity. (Psalms 84:11)

The shield stands for protection. In Moses:

> Blessings are yours, Israel. Who is like you, a people finding salvation
> in Jehovah, the *shield* of your help and one who is the *sword* of your
> excellence? And your foes will be deceived concerning you. (Deuter-
> onomy 33:29)

The shield stands for protection.

[6] Just as people fighting their inward battles are said to have these
weapons of war, so are the enemies that attack and challenge them. In
that case, the symbolism of the weapons is the direct opposite. A shield,
for instance, is then the evil and falsity that they wield in battle, defend
themselves with, and trust in. For example, in Jeremiah:

> Arrange *shield* and *buckler,* and approach for *battle.* Harness the horses,
> and mount, riders, and present yourselves in your *helmets;* polish your
> *javelins;* don your corselets. (Jeremiah 46:3, 4)

There are many other passages as well.

1789 *Your great reward* symbolizes the goal of his victories. This can be seen
from the symbolism of a *reward* as the prize that follows one's inward
struggles. Here it symbolizes the goal of the Lord's victories, because he
never sought any victory prize for himself. The reward of his victories was
the salvation of the whole human race, and he fought out of love for the
whole human race. No one who fights from this love demands any self-
benefiting reward, because such a love by its very nature wants to give
everything it has to others for their own and to keep nothing for itself. The
salvation of the entire human race, then, is symbolized here by the reward.

1790 Genesis 15:2. *And Abram said, "Lord Jehovih, what will you give me?
For I am walking childless, and my 'child,' the steward of my household, is
the Damascene Eliezer."*

Abram said, "Lord Jehovih," symbolizes the Lord's perception. *Abram*
is his intermediate self; the *Lord Jehovih* is his inner self in relation to
his intermediate. *"What will you give me? For I am walking childless,"*
means that there was no inward religion. *"And my 'child,' the steward of
my household,"* symbolizes outward religion. *"Is the Damascene Eliezer"*
means outward religion.

Abram said, "Lord Jehovih," symbolizes the Lord's perception, as can **1791** be seen from the fact that the Lord had the deepest, fullest perception of all. His perception, again, was a sensation and perceptive awareness of everything that was happening in heaven [§1786]. It was also unbroken communication and internal conversation with Jehovah, which the Lord alone possessed. This communication is meant in an inner sense by "Abram said to Jehovah." In other words, it was represented by Abram when he talked with Jehovah. The meaning is the same wherever "Abram said to Jehovah" comes up below.

It has already been asserted that *Abram* is the intermediate self. In other **1792** words, Abram represented the Lord's intermediate or rational self. The last chapter told what the Lord's intermediate self was [§§1701–1702, 1707].

The fact that the *Lord Jehovih* is his inner self in relation to his inter- **1793** mediate can be seen from previous statements about the Lord's inner self: His inner self was Jehovah himself, from whom he was conceived and whose one child he was; and his human side eventually became one with this inner self, after he purified his maternal part (everything he inherited from his mother) by means of his struggles and trials [§§1414, 1444, 1573, 1602–1603, 1607, 1707:5, 1725:2, 1733:2].

The name *Lord Jehovih* comes up fairly often in the Word. In fact every time Jehovah is called the Lord, the name used is not the Lord Jehovah but the Lord Jehovih, especially in passages dealing with his trials. [2] In Isaiah, for instance:

> Watch! The *Lord Jehovih* comes in might, and his arm is ruling for him.
> Look! His *reward* is with him and his work before him. He will pasture
> his flock like a shepherd; he will gather the lambs into his arm and carry
> them on his chest; he will lead the unweaned. (Isaiah 40:10, 11)

"The Lord Jehovih comes in might" is about victory in his spiritual battles. "His arm will rule for him" stands for the fact that he used his own power. This passage tells what the "reward" of the last verse is: the salvation of the whole human race—that is, pasturing his flock like a shepherd, gathering the lambs into his arm, carrying them on his chest, and leading the unweaned. All these are acts of the deepest love, or divine love. [3] In the same author:

> The *Lord Jehovih* has opened my ear for me, and I have not rebelled;
> I have not drawn back. My body I have given to those striking it, and
> my jaws to those plucking them. My face I have not hidden from their

insults and spit, and the *Lord Jehovih* will help me. Watch: the *Lord Jehovih* will help me. (Isaiah 50:5, 6, 7, 9)

This is obviously about his trials. There are other passages too.

1794   *What will you give me? For I am walking childless,* means that there was no inward religion, as can be seen from the symbolism of *walking childless. Walking* in an inner sense is living, as shown earlier, in §519. Being *childless,* however, or having no seed, no descendants of one's own, is dealt with in verses 3, 4, 5 below, where you will find an explanation of childlessness, or lack of seed [§§1798, 1799, 1802, 1803, 1804, 1810].

1795   *And my "child," the steward of my household,* symbolizes outward religion, as can be seen from what the *steward of a household* symbolizes on an inner level, or in regard to religion. Outward religion is called the steward of a household when real, internal religion is the household itself and when the head of the house is the Lord. This is exactly the role of the outward church. All management belongs to the external aspect of religion. This includes administration of the rites and of other activities associated with the church building and with religion itself—that is, with the house of Jehovah, or the Lord's house.

[2] The externals of religion without the internals are nothing. The internals make the externals something and give them their quality. The situation resembles that of a human being. Our facade, or our person, is not much by itself, unless there is something inside to animate it and bring it to life. So what is inside determines how good the outside is. In other words, the nature of our thoughts and instincts determines the value of everything expressed through our outward, physical part. What the heart holds makes us who we are, not words or gestures. The same with the inward aspects of religion. Still, the externals of religion are like our own externals; they carry out all management and administration. To say the same thing another way, our outward, physical self can likewise be called the steward or manager of a household when the household is that of our inward parts.

This shows what childlessness is; it is a time when there is no inward aspect to religion, only an outward aspect, as was true in the period the Lord was deploring.

1796   *Is the Damascene Eliezer* means outward religion, which follows now from the above. It also follows from the symbolism of a *Damascene.* Damascus was Syria's most important city. In it were remnants of the ancient church's worship, and from it came Eber, or the Hebrew nation, which had only the outward shell of a religion, as noted before (§§1238, 1241). So that nation merely managed the household.

These details contain something of the Lord's despair and so of his trials, as is clear from the words and also from the message of comfort concerning inward religion that follows.

Genesis 15:3. And Abram said, "Here, you have not given me seed, and indeed the 'child' of my household is my heir."   **1797**

Abram said, "Here, you have not given me seed," means that the church had no inner dimension, which is love and faith. "*Indeed the 'child' of my household is my heir*" means that only the outer dimension would exist in the Lord's kingdom.

Abram said, "Here, you have not given me seed," means that the church had no inner dimension, which is love and faith. This is established by the symbolism of *seed* as love and faith, discussed earlier, in §§255, 256, 1025. It can also be seen from the symbolism of an heir, discussed below.   **1798**

It has been stated and shown several times before that love and the faith it inspires is the inner core of the church. In describing faith as the inner core of the church, I mean no other faith than the faith of love or charity, that is, the faith that comes of love or charity.

[2] In a broad sense, faith is everything the church teaches. A teaching devoid of love or charity, however, makes no part of the church's core. A doctrine is merely a piece of knowledge, and knowledge is memorization. The worst people—even those in hell—can memorize. When a doctrine develops out of charity, though, or is imbued with charity, it does go to make up the inner core, because it is part of life. Life itself is the inner core of all worship, so whenever a doctrinal teaching rises out of a life of thoughtfulness, it is the kind of teaching that belongs to the faith meant here.

The idea that this faith is the kind that forms the inner core of religion can be seen from a single fact: anyone who lives a life of love for others knows everything there is to know about faith. If you wish, simply look at various doctrines to see what they teach and where they tend. Do they not all lead to love for our neighbor? So do they not all belong to the faith that comes from neighborly love? [3] Take just the Ten Commandments. The first is to worship the Lord our God. Those who live a life of love or kindness worship the Lord God, because a life of love or kindness is his life. The second is to keep the Sabbath. Those who live a life of love, or live in charity, keep the Sabbath reverently, because nothing is sweeter to them than worshiping the Lord and glorifying him every day. The commandment against murder is all about charity. Those who love their neighbor as themselves would be aghast at doing anything to hurt others, let alone killing them. The ban on theft is the same. Those who live a life of kindness give what they have to their neighbor rather than take anything away. The ban on adultery likewise. Those who take up a life of kindness would rather protect their neighbor's wife, to prevent anyone from inflicting that kind of harm on her. They also look on adultery as a crime against conscience—one that destroys both the love between married partners and the duties they owe each other. Coveting what belongs to their neighbor also offends those who live a life of charity, because charity involves wanting others to benefit from us and our possessions. So people like this never covet what belongs to someone else.

[4] These are the commandments of the Decalogue, which are among the more accessible religious teachings. People who have charity and live thoughtful lives do not know these commandments by rote but hold them in their heart and have them written on their soul, because the Commandments are an integral part of charity and therefore of a charitable life.

The church does have other official doctrines, and people who love their neighbor know these simply as a result of their love too, because they live by what they know is right. If they cannot fully understand or figure out a given claim of rightness or truth, they still believe it in simplicity, or with a simple heart. They think, "This is so, because the Lord has said it." No one who has this kind of belief is doing anything wrong, even if the belief is not true in and of itself but only appears to be true.

[5] Take for example the idea that the Lord feels angry at us, punishes us, tests us, and so on. Take also the idea that the bread and wine of the Holy Supper is symbolic; or else that Christ's flesh and blood are actually present in some way that "they" explain. None of this matters, whether the authorities say one thing or the other. (Few even think about it, though. Those who do just need to make sure their thoughts come from an innocent heart.) None of it matters to people who love their neighbor because that is simply how they have been taught, and they live lives of kindness anyway. When they hear that bread and wine on an inner level symbolize the Lord's love for the whole human race—and everything entailed in this love, as well as the love we return to the Lord and our neighbor—they immediately believe and rejoice in it.

Not so those who devote themselves to doctrine rather than to a life of love. They quibble about everything and condemn anyone who does not speak (they use the word *believe*) as they do.

From this anyone can see that love for the Lord and charity for our neighbor is the inner core of religion.

Indeed the "child" of my household is my heir means that only the outer dimension would exist in the Lord's kingdom, as can be seen from the inner-level symbolism of an *heir* and of inheriting. *Becoming an heir,* or inheriting, symbolizes eternal life in the Lord's kingdom. All people in the Lord's kingdom are his heirs, because their life comes from the Lord's life, which is a life of mutual love. That is why they are called his children. The Lord's children, or heirs, are all those who share in his life (because their life is from him) and have been born from him (that is, regenerated). Those who are born to a person are that person's heirs, so all who are reborn from the Lord are his heirs, since they then receive the Lord's life.

[2] The Lord's kingdom has people of little depth, moderate depth, and great depth in it. Good spirits, who inhabit the first heaven, have little depth. Angelic spirits, who inhabit the second heaven, have moderate depth. Angels, who inhabit the third heaven, have great depth. Those with little depth are not as close to the Lord as those with moderate depth, who in their turn are not as close as those with great depth. In his divine love and mercy, the Lord wants to have everyone near him. He does not want us to stay outside in the first heaven but to enter the third. If it were possible, he would like to have us not just beside him but in him. That is the nature of divine love—the Lord's love.

Because religion at that time was purely superficial, he complained here, saying, "Indeed the 'child' of my household is my heir," meaning that as a result, only the outer dimension would exist in his kingdom. But a message of comfort follows in the next verses, as does the promise of deeper dimensions [§§1800–1810].

[3] The outer dimension of religion has already been defined (§§1083, 1098, 1100, 1151, 1153). Doctrine in itself does not make the outer shell; still less does it make the inner core, as noted above. The Lord does not differentiate religious movements by their doctrine, either, but by the way their members live what is taught. All doctrine—if it is true doctrine—looks to a life of love as its fundamental principle. What is the point of doctrine but to teach us how to be human?

[4] In the Christian world, it is doctrine that differentiates churches. Doctrine is the basis on which people call themselves Roman Catholic, Lutheran (or Evangelical), Calvinist (or Reformed), and other names as well. These names grow out of doctrine alone, which would never happen if we considered love for the Lord and charity for our neighbor the chief concern of faith. If we did, those distinctions would simply be differences of opinion on the mysteries of faith. True Christians would leave such issues up to the individual and the individual's conscience. In their hearts they would say, "A person who lives as a Christian—who lives as the Lord teaches—is a real Christian." One church would come out of all the different churches, and all disagreement due to doctrine alone would vanish. Even the hatred of one denomination for another would melt away in a moment, and the Lord's kingdom would come on earth.

[5] Right after the Flood the ancient church was like this, even though it was scattered through many countries. These countries differed greatly when it came to doctrine, but they still made neighborly love the main focus, and they regarded worship not from the viewpoint of doctrine (a matter of belief) but of charity (a matter of life). That is what is meant by the statement in Genesis 11:1 that they all had one language and the same words (concerning which, see §1285).

1800   Genesis 15:4. *And see, now: the word of Jehovah to him, saying, "This one will not be your heir; but one who will issue from your belly will be your heir."*

See, now: the word of Jehovah to him, symbolizes an answer. *Saying, "This one will not be your heir"* means that the outward part would not inherit his kingdom. *"But one who will issue from your belly"* symbolizes those who have love for him and love for their neighbor. *"Will be your heir"* means that they would become the heirs.

1801   *See, now: the word of Jehovah to him,* symbolizes an answer—the answer that it would not be the outward part of the church but the inward part, as can be seen from what follows. The *word of Jehovah*—the answer— is a message of comfort.

1802   *Saying, "This one will not be your heir,"* means that the outward part would not inherit his kingdom, as is established by the symbolism of becoming an heir, or inheriting, discussed just above. The heir of the Lord's kingdom is not the outward part but the inward part. The outward part does inherit it too, but only through the inward part, because they then act as one.

To see how the case stands, you need to keep in mind that everyone in the heavens is an heir of the Lord's kingdom. This includes those in the first heaven, those in the second, and those in the third, or in other words, those with little depth and moderate depth just as much as those with great depth, because they all make one heaven. The relation of inner planes to outer in the Lord's heavens is the same as it is in a human being. Angels of the first heaven are under the angels of the second, who are under the angels of the third, but their hierarchy has nothing to do with dominance. Instead, the inner reaches act on the outer ones as they do in an individual human. The Lord's life flows through the third heaven into the second and through this into the first, in prescribed order, as well as flowing directly into each heaven. The lower angels do not realize that the situation is like this unless the Lord inspires them to reflect on it. The hierarchy has nothing to do with dominance, then.

[2] The more depth an angel of the third heaven has, the more that angel is heir to the Lord's kingdom. The more depth an angel of the second heaven has, the more that angel is an heir. And the more depth an angel of the first heaven has, the more that angel too is an heir. Their depth is what makes them heirs. Deeper angels have more depth than shallower angels, so they are closer to the Lord and are more his heirs.

Depth consists in love for the Lord and charity for one's neighbor, so the more love and charity angels have, the more they are the Lord's children, or heirs, because the more they have of his life.

[3] No one can ever be taken from the first, outermost heaven into the second, deeper heaven without first being taught about the good impulses of love and the true ideas of faith. The more such spirits learn, the more they can be lifted up among angelic spirits. Angelic spirits need similar training before they can be lifted up among angels of the third heaven. Instruction shapes our intermediate levels and so our inmost levels. It prepares them to receive the good impulses of love and the true ideas of faith and therefore to receive a perception of goodness and truth. People cannot possibly perceive something they neither know of nor believe in. Consequently they cannot receive the gift of perceiving love's goodness and faith's truth except through the kind of knowledge that allows them to recognize and evaluate goodness and truth. Everyone is like this, even little children (and in the Lord's kingdom, every child receives instruction), but children learn easily, because false principles do not permeate their minds.

They are taught only general truth, however. When they have learned it, the perceptions they receive are countless. [4] They resemble people who become convinced of some overarching principle. Such people seize quickly, almost intuitively, on the specifics that support the general ideas, and on the individual details that support the specifics. The overarching truth resonates with them, and therefore the specifics and the smaller details supporting that truth do too. The particulars enter into the overall effect, adding pleasure and charm, so they are always perfecting it. These are the inner depths that allow people to be called heirs, or to inherit the Lord's kingdom. They do not become heirs or inherit that kingdom, however, until they devote themselves to what is good—that is, until they enter into the mutual love that angels share. Knowledge of and desire for goodness and truth introduce them into this emotion, and so far as they want what is good, or share in universal love, they are heirs, or inherit the kingdom. Mutual love is the most truly living quality there is, and they receive it from the very being of the Lord, their father. What follows just below in verse 5 also bears this out [§§1805–1810].

1803 *But one who will issue from your belly* symbolizes those who have love for him and love for their neighbor. This can be seen from the meaning of a *belly* and *issuing from one's belly* as being born. Here it refers to those who are born from the Lord.

People who are born from the Lord, that is, who are reborn, receive the Lord's life. As I have said, the Lord's life is divine love, or love for the whole human race, and the desire to save the entire race and all its members forever, if possible. Those who do not possess the Lord's love, that is, who do not love their neighbor as themselves, never possess the Lord's life, so they have never been born from him. They have not "issued from his belly." As a result, they cannot be heirs of his kingdom.

[2] This leads to the conclusion that in an inner sense, issuing from his belly here describes people who love him and love their neighbor. In Isaiah, for example:

> This is what Jehovah your Redeemer, the Holy One of Israel, has said: "I am Jehovah your God, teaching you to profit, making you go on the path you should walk. If only you had listened to my commandments! And like a river your peace would have been, and your justice like the waves of the sea; and like the sand your seed would have been, and those *issuing from your belly* like the grains of it." (Isaiah 48:17, 18, 19)

"Seed like the sand" stands for what is good; "those issuing from their belly like grains of it," for what is true. So it stands for those who love, because [those who are reborn] are the only ones who love what is good and true.

[3] In addition, inner organs mentioned in the Word symbolize the love that is mercy. This is because the reproductive organs—particularly a mother's uterus—represent and therefore symbolize the chaste love of marriage, so they stand for love of children. In Isaiah, for instance:

> The stirring of *your gut* and of your *compassions* toward me have kept on. (Isaiah 63:15)

In Jeremiah:

> Is Ephraim not a child precious to me? Was he not the offspring of my pleasures? Therefore *my gut* has churned for him; I will *take utter pity* on him. (Jeremiah 31:20)

[4] This shows that love itself—or mercy itself—and the Lord's compassion on the human race are what the belly and the act of coming forth from it symbolize on a deeper level. Those who have "issued from the belly," then, symbolize people who love.

To see that the Lord's kingdom is mutual love, see §§548, 549, 684, 693, 694 above.

Will be your heir means that they would become the heirs, as is established by the symbolism of an *heir,* already discussed.   **1804**

Genesis 15:5. And leading him outside he said, "Look, please, toward the sky and count the stars, if you can count them." And he said to him, "This is how your seed will be."   **1805**

Leading him outside symbolizes the eyesight of the intermediate self, which views the inner reaches from the outer. *He said, "Look, please, toward the sky,"* symbolizes a representation of the Lord's kingdom when one is gazing at the universe. "*And count the stars*" symbolizes a representation of goodness and truth when one is gazing at the constellations. "*If you can count them*" symbolizes the fertility of love and the prolificness of faith. *And he said to him, "This is how your seed will be,"* symbolizes the heirs of the Lord's kingdom.

Leading him outside symbolizes the eyesight of the intermediate self, which views the inner reaches from the outer. This can be seen from the symbolism of *leading someone outside* and also from what follows. Our inner depths are led outside when we contemplate the starry sky with our physical eyes and allow it to direct our thoughts to the Lord's kingdom. Our inner sight—the sight of our spirit or soul—is led outside whenever we view something with our eyes and it essentially disappears as it leads us to "see" or think about aspects of religion or aspects of heaven. The   **1806** eye itself is really just the sight of the spirit itself led outdoors. In fact its main purpose is for us to see inner realities from outward objects. In other words, the aim, as we look at objects in the world around us, is for us to reflect constantly on everything that exists in the other life, since that life is the goal of our life in the world. That is how the earliest church looked at things; that is how the angels with us look at things; and that is how the Lord looked at things.

1807   *He said, "Look, please, toward the sky,"* symbolizes a representation of the Lord's kingdom when one is gazing at the universe, as can be seen from the symbolism of the *sky*. In the Word, on an inner level, the sky means not the heaven that we see with our eyes but the Lord's kingdom as a whole and in each part. When people who see deeper meaning in external objects look at the sky, they do not think about the starry heaven at all but about the angels' heaven. When they see the sun, they do not think about the sun but about the Lord as heaven's sun. Likewise when they see the moon and also the stars. In fact when they see how vast the sky is, they do not think about its immense size but about the Lord's vast, infinite power. The same holds true for all other sights, because each one of them represents something.

[2] The same is true for sights on the earth. When such people see the sun rise, for example, they do not think about the dawn but about the way everything rises out of the Lord, and the way wisdom advances day to day. Again, when they look at gardens, orchards, and flower beds, their eye does not cling to any tree, or to its blossom, leaf, or fruit, but to the heavenly attributes these represent. Their attention is absorbed not by the loveliness or charm of any flower but by what it represents in the other life. Nothing beautiful or enjoyable can possibly exist in the heavens or on earth that does not in some measure represent the Lord's kingdom. (On this subject, see what was said at §1632.) That is what is meant by looking toward the sky, symbolizing a representation of the Lord's kingdom when one is gazing at the universe. [3] The reason each and every thing in the sky and on earth represents something is that a stream of influence from the Lord through heaven brought it into existence, and continues to do so, in order to keep it in existence.

The situation is like that with the human body. It is through our soul that our body comes into existence and remains in existence, so our whole body and everything in it represents something about our soul. The soul concerns itself with purposes and goals; the body, with executing them.

All effects of whatever kind likewise represent the purposes that caused them, and the purposes represent the ultimate goals that form their origins.

[4] People who think divine thoughts never restrict themselves to the objects of outward sight but are always seeing inner depths in those objects and from those objects. The very innermost depths have to do with the Lord's kingdom, so these people concern themselves with the very ultimate goal.

It is the same with the Lord's Word. People who care about divine concerns never view the Lord's Word in terms of the letter but view the letter and the literal meaning as representing and symbolizing the heavenly and spiritual attributes of the church and the Lord's kingdom. In their eyes, the literal sense merely serves as a vehicle for thinking about those subjects.

That is how the Lord looked at things.

And count the stars symbolizes a representation of goodness and truth when one is gazing at the constellations. This can be seen from the discussion just above and also from the representation and symbolism of *stars* as goodness and truth. The Word mentions stars quite often, and every time it does they symbolize goodness and truth or, in the negative sense, evil and falsity. To put the same thing another way, they symbolize angels or communities of angels and, in a negative sense, evil spirits and their assemblages. Stars that stand for angels and their communities are fixed, but those that stand for evil spirits and their assemblages wander. Wandering stars appear very often [in the other world].

1808

[2] A plain sign that everything in the heavens and on earth represents heavenly and spiritual traits was visible to me in this: that the same celestial and terrestrial sights appearing before our eyes also present themselves to view in the world of spirits. Such sights are as clear as day there, where they are nothing but representations. For example, when the stars come out and they are standing still, it is instantly recognized that they symbolize what is good and true. When wandering stars appear, it is instantly recognized that they symbolize what is evil and false. The very gleam and twinkle of the stars indicates the quality. Not to mention countless other phenomena. Anyone who is willing to think wisely can see from this where it is that everything on earth comes from—namely, the Lord. The reason things manifest themselves physically rather than metaphysically on earth is that all heavenly and spiritual entities from the Lord are alive and real. (These are called "substantial.")

So they also manifest themselves physically in the outermost, natural world. See §1632.

[3] The following passages in the Word show that stars represent and symbolize goodness and truth. In Isaiah:

> The *stars* of the heavens and their *constellations* do not shed their light; the *sun* has been shadowed over in its emergence, and the *moon* does not radiate its light. And I will punish the world for its evil and the ungodly for their wickedness. (Isaiah 13:10, 11)

This is about a day of punishment. Anyone can see that the stars and constellations mean not stars and constellations but true ideas and good impulses; that the sun means love, and the moon, faith. After all, it is talking about false ideas and evil impulses that cast a shadow. [4] In Ezekiel:

> When I blot you out I will cover *the heavens;* I will black out their *stars;* the *sun* I will cover with a cloud, and the *moon* will not make its light shine. All the *lamps of light* I will black out above you, and I will bring shadow over your land. (Ezekiel 32:7, 8)

The meaning is similar. In Joel:

> Before him the earth shook, the *heavens* trembled, the *sun* and *moon* turned black, and the *stars* withdrew their rays. (Joel 2:10; 3:15)

The meaning is similar. In David:

> Praise Jehovah, *sun* and *moon!* Praise him, all you *shining stars!* Praise him, heavens of heavens! (Psalms 148:3, 4)

The meaning is similar.

[5] John says explicitly that "stars" do not mean stars; they mean what is good and true or, to put it another way, people committed to what is good and true, such as angels:

> I saw the Son of Humankind, having in his right hand *seven stars.* "The mysteries of the *seven stars* that you saw atop my right hand, and the seven lampstands: *The seven stars are angels of the seven churches.* But the seven lampstands that you saw are seven churches." (Revelation 1:16, 20)

[6] In the same author:

> The fourth angel trumpeted, so that a third of the *sun* was struck and a third of the *moon* and a third of the *stars,* so that a third of them would

be shadowed over and the day would not shine for a third of it and the night likewise. (Revelation 8:12)

It is quite plain here that goodness and truth are what were shadowed over. In Daniel:

One small horn went out and grew mostly toward the south and toward the sunrise and toward the ornament [of Israel], and it grew right to the *army of the heavens* and threw down to the ground some of the *army* and some of the *stars* and trampled them. (Daniel 8:9, 10)

Clearly the army of the heavens and the stars are goodness and truth, and these are what were trampled.

[7] From this can be seen what the Lord meant by these words in Matthew:

At the close of the age, immediately after the affliction of those days, the *sun* will go dark, and the *moon* will not shed its light, and *the stars will fall down from the sky,* and the powers of the heavens will be shaken. (Matthew 24:[3], 29)

And in Luke:

Then there will be signs in *sun* and *moon* and *stars;* and on earth, the distress of nations in despair, as sea and surf make noise. (Luke 21:25)

Not in the least does the sun here mean the sun; or the moon, the moon; the stars, the stars; the sea, the sea; they each mean whatever they represent. The sun symbolizes heavenly aspects of love; the moon, spiritual aspects; the stars, goodness and truth, or knowledge of goodness and truth. Around the close of the age, when there is no faith, which is to say no charity, they will be darkened in this way.

If you can count them symbolizes the fertility of love and the prolificness of faith or, to put it another way, the fertility of goodness and the prolificness of truth. This is self-evident, considering that they cannot be counted.

1809

This is how your seed will be symbolizes the heirs of the Lord's kingdom, which can be seen from the symbolism of *seed* as love and the faith that comes of it or, to put it another way, people who have love and faith, whether they are angels or people on earth. This symbolism of seed has often been mentioned and proved before [§§255, 256, 1025, 1447, 1610, 1798:1].

1810

This verse as a whole is saying that the Lord's kingdom is so vast and populous that no one could ever believe it. The only word for it is immeasurable. Its boundless reach will be discussed elsewhere, with the Lord's divine mercy, and is symbolized here by the words of the current verse: "'Look, please, toward the sky and count the stars, if you can count them.' And he said to him, 'This is how your seed will be.'"

The same words also symbolize the countless points of goodness and truth that go into each angel's wisdom and understanding, which yield such happiness.

1811 Genesis 15:6. *And he believed in Jehovah, and [Jehovah] credited it to him as uprightness.*

He believed in Jehovah symbolizes the Lord's faith at that stage. *And [Jehovah] credited it to him as uprightness* means that at that juncture the Lord first came to embody uprightness.

1812 *He believed in Jehovah* symbolizes the Lord's faith at that stage, as can be seen from the words themselves. It can also be seen from the inner-sense train of thought, which is this: While the Lord was living in the world, he never stopped fighting and winning his inward battles. He did so with the constant, deepest trust and faith that he would inevitably win because he was fighting for the salvation of the entire human race, motivated by pure love. That is what *believing in Jehovah* is here.

The love from which a person fights reveals what faith that person has. People who fight from some other love than love for their neighbor and for the Lord's kingdom do not fight from faith. That is, they do not believe in Jehovah but in whatever they do love. The love they fight for is itself their faith. Take for example a person who fights out of a desire to become greatest in heaven. People like this do not believe in Jehovah but rather in themselves. Wanting to be greatest is wanting total control over others, so people like this are fighting for dominance. The same is true with all other kinds of love. So the actual love from which a person fights allows you to identify that person's faith.

[2] In all the struggles the Lord faced while he was being tested, though, he never fought out of self-love, or for his own sake, but for everyone in the universe. He did not want to become greatest in heaven, because this is contrary to divine love. He hardly even wanted to become least. All he wanted was for all people to make something of themselves and be saved. He says so, too, in Mark:

> The two sons of Zebedee said, "Grant us to sit one on your right and the other on your left in your glory." Jesus said, "Anyone who wants to be great among you must be your attendant. And whichever of you wants to be first must be everyone's slave, since even the Son of

Humankind did not come to be served but to serve others, and to give his soul as the ransom price for many." (Mark 10:37, 43, 44, 45)

This love, or faith, is what the Lord fought from, and it is what is meant here by believing in Jehovah.

And [Jehovah] credited it to him as uprightness means that at that junc- **1813** ture the Lord first came to embody uprightness, as can also be seen from the inner-sense train of thought, which has to do with the Lord.

The Lord alone became the epitome of uprightness, on behalf of the whole human race. The evidence for this is that he alone fought out of divine love, which is love for the whole human race, whose salvation was the one thing he sought (and sought ardently) in his battles.

In respect to his human side, the Lord was not born a model of uprightness, or justice, but became one by fighting his battles and winning them, and doing so under his own power. Every time he fought and won, he was *given credit for being upright.* That is, it contributed bit by bit to his transformation into a model of justice, until finally he became pure justice.

[2] When those of us born to human parents—of a human father's seed—fight on our own, we are incapable of fighting from any other love than self-love and love of the material world. So we do not then fight from heavenly but hellish love. This is the nature of the self-centeredness we inherit from our parents, as well as that which we develop on our own by the way we live. So if we think we can fight the Devil on our own, we are grossly mistaken.

The same goes for people who try to become virtuous on the strength of their own abilities. These are people who imagine that they generate their own charitable efforts and think up their own religious truth and who therefore see these efforts and this truth as earning them heaven. Such people violate religious goodness and truth in deed and thought, because what religion truly teaches—the truth itself—is that the Lord does the fighting. Because they violate religious truth in deed and thought, they deny the Lord his role and take it for themselves; or to put it another way, they install themselves and their own hellish tendencies in the Lord's place. That is why they want to become great in heaven, or even the greatest there. That is also why they falsely believe the Lord fought the hells to become the greatest. Our self-absorbed point of view carries with it these delusions that seem so true but are exactly the opposite.

[3] The prophets foretold that the Lord would come into the world to become the epitome of uprightness—a role that is his alone—so this could have been known before his Coming. The prophets also revealed

that he could not become the epitome of uprightness, or justice, without being tested by all evil and all the hells and winning victories over them. In Jeremiah, for example:

> In his days Judah will be saved and Israel will live securely, and this is *his name that they will call him: Jehovah our justice.* (Jeremiah 23:6)

In the same author:

> In those days and at that time, I will make an *offshoot of justice* sprout for David, and he will perform judgment and *justice* in the land. In those days, Judah will be saved and Jerusalem will live securely. *And this is what they will call him: Jehovah our justice.* (Jeremiah 33:15, 16)

In Isaiah:

> He looked, and there was no man, and he was astounded that no one was interceding; and his arm achieved salvation for him, and *his justice* sustained him. And he put *justice* on like a coat of armor, and a helmet of salvation on his head. (Isaiah 59:16, 17; see especially Isaiah 63:3, 5)

His arm stands for his own power.

As the Lord alone embodied justice, he is also called the *dwelling place of justice* (Jeremiah 31:23; 50:7).

1814   Genesis 15:7. *And [Jehovah] said to him, "I am Jehovah, who brought you out of Ur of the Chaldeans, to give you this land to inherit."*

He said to him, "I am Jehovah," symbolizes the Lord's inner self, which was Jehovah, the source of his perception. *"Who brought you out of Ur of the Chaldeans"* symbolizes the first state of his outer self. *"To give you this land to inherit"* symbolizes the Lord's kingdom, of which he is sole possessor.

1815   *He said to him, "I am Jehovah,"* symbolizes the Lord's inner self, which was Jehovah, the source of his perception. This can be seen from many earlier statements that the Lord's inner part (everything he received from the Father) was Jehovah in him, because he was conceived by Jehovah [§§1414, 1573:3, 1602, 1607:2, 1707:5, 1725:2, 1733:2].

We receive one thing from our father and another from our mother. From our father we receive everything inside us. Our soul itself—our life—is from him. From our mother we receive everything on the surface. In short, our inner self (our spirit itself) comes from our father, while our outer self (our actual body) comes from our mother. Anyone can grasp this simply by considering the fact that the soul itself is implanted by the father and sets about clothing itself in the tiny shape of a body in the ovum. Whatever is added after that, in either the ovum or the uterus, is the mother's, because the soul has no other supply of material to draw on.

[2] This shows that the Lord was Jehovah in respect to his inner dimensions. The outer dimension that he received from his mother, however, needed to become one with his divine aspect, or Jehovah, which was accomplished through times of trial and victories, as noted [§§1659:2, 1707:5, 1708, 1737]. As a result, at those stages, it could not help seeming to him as though he was talking to another person when he talked with Jehovah, despite the fact that he was talking to himself, at least insofar as the two were united.

The exquisite power of perception that the Lord had, more than anyone who has ever been born, came from his inner depths, that is, from Jehovah himself, as symbolized here on an inner level by "Jehovah said to him."

Who brought you out of Ur of the Chaldeans symbolizes the first state **1816** of his outer self, as can be seen from the symbolism of *Ur of the Chaldeans.* What the Lord received from his mother at birth (his maternal heredity) is what Ur of the Chaldeans symbolizes here. Its nature has already been described [§§1414, 1444, 1573].

This maternal heredity is what the Lord was led out of whenever he overcame evil and falsity, or in other words, hell.

To give you this land to inherit symbolizes the Lord's kingdom, of **1817** which he is sole possessor. This is established by the symbolism of *land*—in this case the Holy Land, or the land of Canaan, which is the heavenly kingdom—and by that of *inheriting,* both of which were dealt with in various places above.

It is the Lord's human side that is said here to inherit the land, meaning that it possessed the heavenly kingdom. After all, his divine side possessed the universe—and therefore the heavenly kingdom—from eternity.

Genesis 15:8. And [Abram] said, "Lord Jehovih, how will I know that I **1818** *will inherit it?"*

He said, "Lord Jehovih," symbolizes a kind of conversation between his intermediate and inner selves. *"How will I know that I will inherit it?"* symbolizes a test of the love felt by the Lord, who wanted reassurance.

He said, "Lord Jehovih," symbolizes a kind of conversation between **1819** his intermediate and inner selves, as can be seen from remarks on the words *Jehovah said to him* in the last verse. It can also be seen from the discussion of the *Lord Jehovih* at verse two in this chapter [§§1791–1793] as being conversation between his intermediate self and his inner self (or Jehovah), especially when he was being tested.

1820   The symbolism of *"How will I know that I will inherit it?"* as a test of the love felt by the Lord, who wanted reassurance, can be seen from the doubt that the words themselves express. Anyone who is being tested is unsure of the end. The end is love, and love is what evil spirits and evil demons attack, throwing the end into doubt. The more love the victim has, the more doubt they cast. If the cherished end did not become doubt-ful, even to the point of despair, there would be no struggle. Certainty about the outcome comes just before victory and is a part of victory.

[2] Few people know much about these challenges, so let me explain briefly here. Evil spirits never fight against anything but what we love. The more passionately we love something, the more bitterly they fight it. Evil demons combat anything good that touches our hearts; evil spirits combat anything true that touches our hearts. As soon as they become aware of something we love, no matter how small, or smell out anything dear and pleasing to us, they immediately attack and try to destroy it. In the process, they are trying to destroy the whole person, because our life consists in what we love. Nothing could possibly give them more pleasure than to destroy us. Nor do they ever stop trying (even if it takes forever) unless the Lord drives them away.

The malicious, deceitful ones worm their way into our central loves, stroking them and so awaking us to them. Once they have done so, they immediately set out to destroy what we love and consequently to kill us, by a thousand bewildering means.

[3] They do not fight by arguing against what is good and true. (That kind of fight is useless, because if they were beaten a thousand times they would continue to stand firm, since there is no end to the supply of arguments undercutting goodness and truth.) Instead, they pervert what is good and true, setting it aflame with the fire of appetite and delusion, so that for all we know we share their appetites and delusions. They also seize on some unrelated pleasure in us and feed the flames with it. In this way they very deviously infect and molest us. So skillfully do they work, as they spread their contagion, that if the Lord did not help us we would inevitably believe them.

[4] They level the same attack on the devotion to truth that forms our conscience. As soon as they detect a trace of conscience, no matter how imperfect, they take our misconceptions and weaknesses and shape them into a fog of emotion, which they use to block and distort the light of truth; or else they torture us with anxiety. Another device they use is to train our thoughts on a single issue, with no letup. They fill it up with crazy notions and at the same time secretly tie our cravings into the insanity. They have

countless other underhanded methods as well, which could never be described intelligibly. Little of this reaches our conscious awareness, and only in its most general outlines; and it is our conscious awareness of right and wrong (our conscience) more than anything else that these evil spirits take the greatest delight in destroying.

[5] These few details—very few—give some idea of what it is like to be tested; in general, the nature of our trials matches the nature of our love.

This in turn indicates what the Lord's trials were like: the very fiercest of all. A trial is as fierce as the love is large. The Lord's love was to save the whole human race—a love that burned intensely. So his love comprised every desire for everything good and every desire for everything true, in the highest degree. This is what the hells all fought against, employing the most malevolent tricks and the most poisonous venom; but the Lord still conquered them all decisively, by his own power. Victory carries with it the consequence that malicious demons and spirits no longer dare to do anything. Their whole life depends on being able to destroy things, but when they sense that their victim has what it takes to stand up to them, they retreat as soon as they attack. The same thing happens when they near the first threshold of heaven; fear and horror immediately seize them and they rush away as fast as they can go.

Genesis 15:9. And [Jehovah] said to him, "Take yourself a three-year-old   **1821**
*heifer, and a three-year-old she-goat, and a three-year-old ram, and a turtle-
dove, and a chick."*

[Jehovah] said to him symbolizes perception. *Take a three-year-old
heifer, and a three-year-old she-goat, and a three-year-old ram,* means items that serve to represent the heavenly aspects of religion—a *heifer,* the more superficial ones; a *she-goat,* the deeper ones; and a *ram,* the heavenly-spiritual aspects. They were to be *three years old* because they would cover all eras and conditions of religion. *And a turtledove and a chick* mean items that serve to represent the spiritual aspects of religion, a *turtledove* being the more superficial aspects, and a *chick,* the deeper ones.

The symbolism of *[Jehovah] said to him* as perception can be seen   **1822**
from the discussion above at verses 2 and 7 [§§1791, 1815]. Perception is just a kind of inward speech, which comes out in such a way that what is said is perceived. This is exactly what every inner dictate, including conscience, is as well. Perception is a higher or deeper form.

Take a three-year-old heifer, and a three-year-old she-goat, and a three-   **1823**
year-old ram, means items that serve to represent the heavenly aspects of religion. This can be seen from the animals' symbolism in sacrifices.

No sound-thinking person can believe that the different species of animals sacrificed had significance only as sacrifices—that an adult ox and young ox (or calf) symbolized the same thing as a sheep, kid, or she-goat; that these had the same meaning as a lamb; or that a turtledove and pigeon chicks meant the same. The truth is that each animal had its own particular symbolism. As evidence, consider the fact that one kind was never offered in place of another. It was specified which were to be used in burnt offerings, daily sacrifices, and Sabbath and festival sacrifices; in freewill offerings, vows, and thanksgiving; in atonement for guilt and sin; and in purification. This would never have been done if something particular had not been represented and symbolized by each animal. [2] It would take too long, though, to detail here what each kind symbolizes. It is enough to know here that heavenly traits are what animals symbolize, spiritual traits are what birds symbolize, and each species symbolizes some specific heavenly or spiritual trait. Religion itself, and everything involved in the Jewish religion, served to represent the kinds of things that exist in the Lord's kingdom, which contains only what is heavenly and spiritual. In other words, it contains only what relates to love and faith. This is also fairly clear from the symbolism of clean, useful animals, which are discussed in §§45, 46, 142, 143, 246, 714, 715, 776. In the earliest churches they symbolized heavenly goodness, so later, when the church came to view and acknowledge worship as nothing more than a superficial act (and a representative one at that), they were turned into representations.

[3] Because the subject of the current verse is the state of religion, including a prediction of its future character, this was presented to Abram's view by use of the same kinds of representations. It took place exactly as described here, and yet it symbolizes these things on an inner level. Anyone can see and consider the truth of this. What use would there be in taking a three-year-old heifer, a three-year-old she-goat, a three-year-old ram, a turtledove, and a chick, dividing them into two pieces, and positioning them just so, if each and every aspect of it were not significant? What that significance is can be seen in the following sections.

1824   A *heifer* means items that serve to represent the more superficial heavenly aspects; a *she-goat,* those that represent the deeper ones; and a *ram,* those that represent the heavenly-spiritual aspects. This can be seen from the sacrifices, which will be discussed later where they are the focus, the Lord in his divine mercy willing [§§2180:2, 2830, 3519, 9391, 10042].

There are heavenly qualities that are relatively superficial and ones that are relatively deep; there are also heavenly qualities that are spiritual.

The more superficial heavenly qualities are those that belong to the outer self; the deeper ones are those that belong to the inner self; and the spiritual ones are offshoots. Heavenliness itself is love for the Lord and for our neighbor. This heavenly influence flows from the Lord through the inner self into the outer. In the inner self, it is called the heavenly core; in the outer self, it is called the heavenly surface. The heavenly surface is formed of every desire for what is good; in fact it includes every form of sensual pleasure produced by that desire. So far as both of these—desire for what is good, and the resulting pleasures—contain a loving, charitable goodness, they contain what is heavenly and happy.

The spiritual side of heavenliness, however, is every desire for truth that contains within it the desire for what is good. In other words, it is a desire for truth generated by a desire for what is good. So it is faith that contains charity, or faith generated by charity.

The fact that *three years old* covers all eras and conditions of religion can be seen from the symbolism of *three* in the Word. Three symbolizes an entire religious era from beginning to end, so it symbolizes every state along the way. Consequently the end of a religious era is symbolized by a third day, week, month, year, or age, which all mean the same thing.

1825

Just as the number three symbolizes the condition of religion, it also symbolizes conditions in a religious person and in fact the condition of any feature of religion. This can be seen from the meaning of that number in the scriptural passages quoted in §§720, 901.

[2] This symbolism of a three-year-old heifer as an era or state of religion all the way to its end (when it has been devastated or stripped bare inwardly) can also be seen in Isaiah:

> My heart cries out over Moab; those who flee it as far as Zoar are a *three-year-old heifer.* For they will ascend in tears on the ascent to Luhith, since on the way to Horonaim they will raise a cry for the wreckage. (Isaiah 15:5)

And in Jeremiah:

> Gladness and exultation have disappeared from Carmel and from the land of Moab; and wine from the winepresses I will put an end to. No one will tread the hedad; the hedad will not be a hedad. From the cry of Heshbon all the way to Elealeh, all the way to Jahaz, they have uttered their voice, from Zoar all the way to Horonaim—a *three-year-old heifer;* because the waters of Nimrim will also become wastelands. (Jeremiah 48:33, 34)

No one could ever tell what these words mean without knowing what is symbolized by Moab, Zoar, the ascent to Luhith, the cry of Heshbon to

Elealeh, Jahaz, Horonaim, the waters of Nimrim, and the three-year-old heifer; although it *is* clear that they depict final devastation.

1826   *He took a turtledove and a chick* means items that [serve to represent] the spiritual aspects of religion, as is shown by the symbolism of birds in general and of turtledoves and pigeons in particular. The symbolism of birds as spiritual entities (which have to do with faith, or with truth), and so as intellectual and rational properties, has been demonstrated before, at §§40, 745, 776, 991. The symbolism of pigeons as faith's goodness and truth was demonstrated at §870. In addition, what they symbolized in the sacrifices will be told later, by the Lord's divine mercy, where sacrifices form the subject [§§10129:5, 10132:9, 10210].

In the Word—especially in the prophets—when the text speaks of heavenly subjects it also speaks of spiritual ones and in this way unites them. The one develops out of the other, so that the one belongs to the other, as noted before in §§639, 680, 683, 707, 793, 801.

1827   A *turtledove* means items that serve to represent the more superficial spiritual aspects, and a *chick,* the deeper ones. This can be seen from what was said about heavenly qualities: the superficial ones are symbolized by a heifer, the deeper ones by a she-goat, and the ones in between by a ram.

1828   Genesis 15:10. *And he took himself all these things and split them in half and set each of the parts across from its other [half]; but the fowl he did not split.*

He took himself all these things means it was done. *And split them in half* symbolizes the church and the Lord. *And set each of the parts across from its other [half]* symbolizes parallelism and correspondence regarding heavenly things. *But the fowl he did not split* means that spiritual things lack this symmetry and correspondence.

1829   *He took himself all these things* means it was done, as is self-evident.

1830   *And split them in half* symbolizes the church and the Lord, as can be seen from what follows. There were heavenly things, symbolized by the heifer, goat, and ram; and spiritual things, symbolized by the turtledove and chick. Since these were *split* and placed opposite each other, they can mean nothing else.

1831   *And set each of the parts across from its other [half]* symbolizes parallelism and correspondence regarding heavenly things. The evidence for this is that the pieces on one side symbolize the church, while those on the other side symbolize the Lord, and when they are placed opposite each other there is nothing but symmetry and correspondence. It was the heifer, goat, and ram that were split and set like this, and they symbolize heavenly attributes, as noted just above at verse 9, so it is clear that there is symmetry and correspondence in respect to heavenly attributes.

The case is different with spiritual attributes, however, and they will be discussed just below.

As I have frequently mentioned, heavenly attributes are all those that have to do with love for the Lord and love for our neighbor. The Lord is the one who bestows love and a sense of charity; the church is the one that accepts them. What unites the two is conscience, the soil in which love and charity are planted. So the space between the pieces symbolizes the capacity in us that is called perception, an inner voice, or conscience. Anything higher than perception, the inner voice, and conscience is the Lord's; anything below them is part of us. Since each side looks to the other, then, they are described as parallel; and since they answer or respond to one another as active and passive do, they are said to correspond.

But the fowl he did not split means that spiritual things lack this symmetry and correspondence. This can be seen from the symbolism of *fowl* as something spiritual, as dealt with at verse 9 just above [§§1826–1827]. It can also be seen from the fact that Abram did not divide the fowl in half, so that there is no symmetry or correspondence of this kind.

As noted many times before, "spiritual" means everything that has to do with faith. Consequently it means all doctrine, since doctrine is called the teachings of faith, even though these teachings are not a part of faith until they are united with charity, or love for others. There is no parallelism or correspondence between these spiritual entities and the Lord, because they are not the kinds of things that enter us by way of an inner voice or conscience, as attributes of love and charity do. Instead they enter us by way of instruction, and so by hearing. In other words, they enter not from inside but from outside and therefore create their own vessels or containers in us. [2] For the most part they seem to be true and yet are not, such as literal statements in the Word that either represent true ideas or symbolize true ideas and therefore are not true in themselves. Some are even false and yet are capable of serving as vessels and containers. In the Lord, though, they are pure truth, truth in its essence. So there is no parallelism or correspondence between the two. However, spiritual elements can still be molded to serve as vessels for heavenly contents, which are matters of love and charity. Spiritual things make up the cloud in our intellectual half that the Lord injects with charity in order to create conscience, as discussed earlier [§1043].

[3] Some people, for instance, restrict themselves to the literal level of the Word and believe that the Lord is the one who leads us into crisis and at the same time tortures our conscience. Because he permits evil, they consider him the cause of evil. They think he sends sinners to hell, and so on. To them these ideas seem true, but they are not, and because

1832

they are not strictly true, there is no symmetry or correspondence. Yet the Lord leaves them intact in such a person and adapts them in a miraculous way, by means of charity, to serve as vessels for heavenly impulses.

It is the same with the worship, doctrines, and moral code—even the idols—of honest non-Christians. These the Lord leaves equally intact, at the same time adapting them too, by means of charity, to serve as vessels.

It was the same with very many rituals in the ancient church and later in the Jewish religion. Of themselves these rituals were completely devoid of truth, but they were tolerated and allowed, and even ordered, because ancestors of the people in these religions had held them sacred. As a result, they had been grafted and etched onto these people's minds from infancy as being full of truth.

[4] These and other things like them are what are symbolized by the fact that the fowl were not split. Once an idea has been planted in our mind and we come to view it as holy, the Lord leaves it intact, as long as it does not violate divine order. Although it may not be parallel or correspond, he still adapts it.

These things are also what were symbolized in the Jewish religion by the practice of not splitting birds in sacrifice. Dividing something is putting the parts opposite each other so that like corresponds to like. Because the kinds of things being discussed here have no like to correspond to, in the other world they are erased from consciousness in people who allow themselves to be taught, and genuine truth is transplanted into their positive emotions.

It can be seen in Moses that birds were not divided in the Jewish religion, because of this representation and symbolism:

> If their offering to Jehovah is the burnt offering of a *bird,* they shall bring some *turtledoves* or some *offspring of a pigeon* and shall cleave it with its wings, not *divide* it. (Leviticus 1:14, 17)

Likewise in sacrifices for a sin offering (Leviticus 5:7, 8).

1833   Genesis 15:11. *And winged creatures swooped down onto the bodies, and Abram drove them away.*

Winged creatures swooped down onto the bodies symbolizes evil and the falsity it spawns, which would try to destroy [what was heavenly and spiritual]. *And Abram drove them away* means that the Lord put them to flight.

1834   *Winged creatures swooped down onto the bodies* symbolizes evil and the falsity it spawns, which would try to destroy [what was heavenly and spiritual]. This can be seen from the symbolism of a *winged creature* as falsity. In the Word, a flying creature symbolizes truth (as shown above [§§776–777,

986, 988, 1826]), and in a negative sense, falsity. Almost everything of this
type in the Word has both kinds of meaning. The fact that a flying creature also symbolizes falsity was demonstrated earlier, in §§778, 866, 988.

Anyone can see that this detail has a hidden meaning; otherwise
it would not have been worth mentioning. That hidden meaning has
been given, and it is also evident from the series of ideas in the inner
sense, which has to do with conditions in the church. [2] When the
Lord revives a church, it is innocent at first. Each person loves the next
as sister or brother, as we know from the early [Christian] church, the
church just after the Lord's Coming. In those days, all the sons and
daughters of the church lived together as siblings, and they also called
each other sister and brother and loved each other. As time passed,
though, love for their neighbors shrank and disappeared, and when it
did, evil took its place. Falsity also inserted itself, along with evil, giving
rise to schisms and heresies, which never would have come up if neighborly love had reigned supreme and thrived. They would not even have
referred to a schism as a schism, or a heresy as a heresy, but as doctrine
tailored to personal belief. They would have left that doctrine up to each
person's conscience, as long as it did not deny the fundamentals of the
Lord, eternal life, and the Word, or violate divine order, that is, the Ten
Commandments.

[3] The evil and resulting falsity that took over in the church once
neighborly love had vanished are what are meant here by the winged
creatures that Abram drove away, or in other words, that the Lord (represented here by Abram) put to flight. Abram merely drove off birds
rather than any amount of evil and falsity. Heaven does not acknowledge
Abraham except as a human like any other, entirely powerless on his own.
It is the Lord alone that heaven acknowledges, as Isaiah also says:

> You are our Father, because Abraham does not know us and Israel does
> not acknowledge us. You are Jehovah, our Father, our Redeemer; your
> name is age-old. (Isaiah 63:16)

And Abram drove them away means that the Lord put them to flight, **1835**
as can be seen from the remarks above.

It is the same with the church, too. When it begins to fall away from
love for others, evil and the falsity that comes from it can be chased off
fairly easily. Up to that point, conditions in the church are not very far
removed from neighborly love, so the mindset of the people in it is quite
flexible. Over time, though, evil and its falsity grow, and as they grow
they strengthen and stiffen, as will be told below.

[2] The Lord constantly drives as much evil and falsity away as he can, but he does so through conscience. When the bonds of our conscience loosen, the Lord has no means of influencing us, because he acts on us by flowing through charity into our conscience. A new means does develop to take its place, but it is an external one: fear of the law and fear for our life, status, money, and consequent prestige. These are not matters of conscience but only superficial restraints. They make it possible for us to live in the same community with others and to seem friendly, no matter what we are like inside.

[3] These means, or restraints, have no effect at all in the other world. Outward appearances are stripped away there and inner character remains. There are large numbers of people who have lived an upright life in private and public, avoided hurting anyone, acted in a polite and friendly way, and even done good to many others, but only for selfish reasons—for the sake of position, money, and so on. They end up among the inhabitants of hell in the other life, because inside them they harbor no goodness or truth but only evil and falsity. In fact hatred, vengefulness, cruelty, and adultery lurk inside them, remaining hidden from others; and they remain hidden to the extent that those fears or external restraints are in charge.

1836 Genesis 15:12. *And the sun was about to set, and slumber fell on Abram, and look—terror of immense shadows was falling on him!*

The sun was about to set symbolizes the period preceding the end, and conditions then. *And slumber fell on Abram* means that the church was then in shadow. *And look—terror of immense shadows was falling on him* means that the shadows were frightening; *shadows* are falsities.

1837 The symbolism of *the sun was about to set* as the period preceding the end, and conditions then, can be seen from the symbolism of the *sun*. On an inner level the sun symbolizes the Lord and therefore the heavenly qualities of love and charity, so it symbolizes love and charity itself, as discussed before at §§30–38, 1053. This shows that sunset is the church's final era, which is called the consummation, or end, when charity dies out.

The Lord's church is compared to times of day, because of resemblances between the two. Its early period is compared to sunrise, or dawn, and to morning. Its final period is compared to sunset, or evening, and to the shadows then. The church is also compared to the yearly seasons. Its early days are compared to spring, when everything blooms. As it nears its end it is compared to fall, when things start to fade. The church is even compared to metals. Its early days are called golden, its last days, iron and clay, as in Daniel 2:31, 32, 33. This clarifies what *the sun was about to set* symbolizes; it symbolizes the period preceding the end and conditions then, since it had not yet set. Later sections deal with conditions in the church after sunset, when darkness fell and the smoke of a furnace and a torch of fire passed between the pieces [§§1858–1862].

Slumber fell on Abram means that the church was then in shadow, as **1838** can be seen from the symbolism of *slumber.* Slumber is a shadowy state, compared to wakefulness, and this verse ascribes it to the Lord, who is being represented by Abram. Not that the shadowy state of slumber ever comes over him, but over the church. The situation resembles that in the next life, where the Lord is always the sun—the light itself—but appears to the evil as a shadow. He appears to each of us according to our mood. So the present verse is talking about the church when it is in a dark state.

[2] By way of example, let us also consider acts of devastation, punishment, and condemnation, which the Word often attributes to the Lord, when in reality they are committed by people in the church who devastate, punish, and condemn themselves. It seems to us as though the Lord would devastate, punish, and condemn, and because it seems this way, the Word speaks in the same terms, to suit appearances. If we were not taught in accord with appearances, we would refuse to be taught at all. Anything that contradicts appearances we disbelieve. We fail to comprehend it, until later when we learn to judge well and receive the gift of a faith rooted in love for others.

[3] The case is the same with the church. When shadows settle on it, the Lord becomes obscure in people's eyes. He grows so dim that they do not see him, or in other words, acknowledge him. Yet the Lord never grows dim. It is we who do so, although the Lord longs to be in us and with us; but the darkness is still ascribed to the Lord. Likewise the slumber here, which symbolizes shadowy conditions in the church.

Look—terror of immense shadows was falling on him means that the **1839** shadows were frightening; and *shadows* are falsities. This can be seen from the symbolism of shadows as falsities (discussed just below).

Conditions in the church before the end but when the sun was about to set are portrayed as *terror of immense shadows,* but conditions after sunset are portrayed as darkness and more in verse 17 below. [2] The Lord describes it this way in Matthew:

> The sun will go dark, and the moon will not shed its light, and the stars will fall down from the sky, and the powers of the heavens will be shaken. (Matthew 24:29)

It is not the world's sun that will go dark, but the heavenly radiance of love and charity. It is not the moon that will, but the spiritual luster of faith. It is not the stars that will fall down from heaven, but knowledge of goodness and truth in religious people, this knowledge being the powers of the heavens. And it is not in heaven that these things will happen, since heaven is never dark, but on earth.

[3] The terror of immense shadows that was falling on him is his shrinking in horror from such enormous devastation. The more devoted a person is to the heavenly qualities of love, the more horror that person feels on seeing the end approach—the Lord most of all, since he was moved by divine and heavenly love itself.

[4] The symbolism of *shadows* as falsities can be seen from quite a few passages in the Word. In Isaiah, for instance:

> Doom to those who put *shadow* for light and light for *shadow!* (Isaiah 5:20)

The shadow stands for falsity and the light for truth. In the same author:

> One will gaze on the land, and look—*shadow,* distress; and the light has been *shadowed over.* (Isaiah 5:30)

The shadow stands for falsity. The shadowing of the light stands for the disappearance of truth. [5] In the same author:

> Look—*shadows* cover the earth, and *darkness,* the peoples. (Isaiah 60:2)

In Amos:

> The day of Jehovah is one of *shadow* and lack of light. Is the day of Jehovah not *shadow* and lack of light? And is there not *darkness* and lack of radiance on it? (Amos 5:18, 20)

In Zephaniah:

> The great day of Jehovah is near. A day of wrath is that day, a day of anguish and distress, a day of devastation and ruin, a day of *shadow* and *darkness,* a day of *cloud* and *gloom.* (Zephaniah 1:14, 15)

The day of Jehovah stands for the last days and the final stage of the church. The shadow and darkness stand for falsity and evil.

[6] The Lord himself also refers to falsity as shadow, in Matthew:

> If your eye is bad, your whole body is dark, so if the light that is in you is *shadow,* how immense the *shadow!* (Matthew 6:23)

The shadow stands for the type of falsity that overcomes people who possess religious knowledge. [How immense the shadow] means how much more benighted they are than nations who lack that knowledge. [7] Again in the same author:

The children of the kingdom will be cast out into outer *shadow*. (Matthew 8:12; 22:13)

Outer shadow stands for the more heinous misconceptions of people in the church, because these people block the light and introduce false thinking that opposes truth, which people outside the church are incapable of doing. In John:

In him was life, and the life was the light of humankind; the light, however, appears in the *shadows,* but the *shadows* have not comprehended it. (John 1:4, 5)

The shadows stand for falsity within the church. [8] Falsity outside the church is also called shadow, but shadow in which light can shine. This shadow is mentioned in Matthew:

The people sitting in *shadow* have seen a great light; and on those sitting in the vicinity and gloom of death, light has risen. (Matthew 4:16)

The shadow stands for the false ideas that result when knowledge is lacking—the kind of shadow that people outside the church experience. [9] In John:

This is the judgment: that the light came into the world but people loved *shadow* more than light, since their deeds were evil. (John 3:19)

The light stands for truth and the shadow for falsity. The light also stands for the Lord because all truth is from him, and the shadow stands for the hells because all falsity is from them. In the same author:

Jesus said, "I am the light of the world; whoever follows me will not walk in *shadow.*" (John 8:12)

[10] In the same author:

Walk, as long as you have light, to prevent the *shadows* from overtaking you, because whoever walks in the *shadow* does not know where to head. I have come into the world as the light, so that no one who believes in me should stay in *shadow.* (John 12:35, 46)

The light stands for the Lord, the source of everything good and true. The shadow stands for falsity that the Lord alone dispels.

[11] The lies being spread during the [church's] final days, called shadows here, or at least referred to in the phrase "terror of immense shadows," were represented and symbolized by the *shadows* that fell on the whole earth from the sixth hour to the ninth [during the Crucifixion], and by the fact that the *sun was shadowed over* at the same time, which represented and symbolized the dying out then of love and faith (Matthew 27:45; Mark 15:33; Luke 23:44, 45).

1840 Genesis 15:13. *And he said to Abram, "You must know positively that your seed will be immigrants in a land not theirs; and they will serve [the people of that land], and these will afflict them four hundred years."*

He said to Abram symbolizes a perception. *You must know positively* means that it was certain. *Your seed will be immigrants* means that charity and faith would be rare. *In a land that is not theirs* symbolizes places where it would not seem as if the church belonged to those who had charity and faith. *And they will serve [the people of that land]* symbolizes oppression. *And these will afflict them* means that their trials would be heavy. *Four hundred years* means however long they would last and what conditions would be like then.

1841 The symbolism of *he said to Abram* as a perception is established by remarks above at verse 9 and other places, where the symbolism of these words is the same.

1842 *You must know positively* means that it was certain, as is self-evident.

1843 *Your seed will be immigrants* means that charity and faith would be rare, as can be seen from the symbolism of *immigrants* and of *seed*. *Immigrants* mean what is not native and so what is not acknowledged as belonging to the local area and therefore what is regarded as foreign. *Seed*, though, symbolizes charity and the faith that goes with it, as shown before, in §§255, 1025, and above at verse 3 [§1798:1]. The seed is described as immigrants, which are viewed as foreign, and what is foreign is what does not belong to the area, or come from it, so it follows that it is something rare. It also follows, then, that charity and the faith that comes of charity would be rare, since that is what the seed is. When it says that Abram's seed would be immigrants—that is, that charity and faith would be rare—it is speaking about a time before the end, when the shadows (falsity) would be immense.

[2] In Matthew 24:4–end, Mark 13:3–end, and Luke 21:7–end, which describe the close of the age, the Lord predicts that faith will be rare in the last days. Everything said there carries the idea that charity and faith

will be scant in those days, until finally they disappear. John predicts the same thing in the Book of Revelation, as the prophets also do many times, not to mention the narrative parts of the Word. [3] But by the faith that will perish in the final days nothing is meant but neighborly love. No other faith can possibly exist than the faith that grows out of love for others. People who do not love their neighbor cannot have the least faith. Love for others, or charity, is the actual base on which faith is planted. Charity is its heart, the source of its existence and life. As a result, the ancients compared love and charity to a heart, and faith to lungs, both of which reside in the chest. Charity and faith actually resemble the heart and lungs, too, because to imagine a life of faith without charity is like imagining we can live by our lungs alone, without our hearts. Anyone can see it is impossible. So the ancients called every impulse of charity a gesture of the heart, and every word of faith lacking in charity they called lip service, or a product of the lungs (by way of the breath that flows into speech). That is how they developed the habit of talking about goodness and truth as something that ought to "come from the heart."

In a land that is not theirs symbolizes places where it would not seem as if the church belonged to those who had charity and faith. This can be seen from the symbolism of the *earth* as the church, as discussed in §§566, 662, 1066, 1068.

Today people describe the church solely in terms of religious teachings, which they use as a means of distinguishing among the Lord's churches. They do not care how adherents of those churches live— whether they nurse hatred for each other, rip each other apart like wild animals, rob each other, strip each other of reputation and status and wealth, or privately deny all that is holy. Yet the church can never exist in such people. It exists instead in people who love the Lord, love their neighbor as themselves, have a conscience, and oppose the kinds of hatred mentioned. These people, though, are like foreigners among the others, who skewer and harass them as often as they can, or else look on them as sorry, contemptible simpletons. This, then, is what it means to say, "Your seed will be immigrants in the land."

And they will serve [the people of that land] symbolizes oppression, as can be seen from the discussion just above.

And these will afflict them means that their trials would be heavy. This can be seen from the symbolism of *afflicting* or affliction as persecution

1844

1845

1846

and so as putting a person to the test. Affliction means nothing else in the Lord's Word, as in Isaiah:

> I will purge you, and not with silver; I will choose you in the crucible of *affliction.* (Isaiah 48:10)

Affliction stands for a time of trial. In Moses:

> You shall remember all the path by which Jehovah your God has led you these forty years in the wilderness, in order to *afflict* you and to *test* you. Jehovah has been the one feeding you manna in the wilderness—which your ancestors did not recognize—in order to *afflict* you and in order to *test* you, to do good to you in the end. (Deuteronomy 8:2, 16)

Afflicting explicitly stands for testing. [2] In the same author:

> . . . when the Egyptians did evil to us and *afflicted* us and laid hard *slavery* on us, and we cried out to Jehovah, God of our ancestors, and Jehovah listened to our voice and saw our *affliction* and our labor and our oppression. (Deuteronomy 26:6, 7)

This passage contains the same themes as the present verse—the enslavement and affliction of Abram's descendants, which likewise symbolized the trials of the faithful, as did those descendants' hardships in the wilderness. These troubles also represented the Lord's trials, [3] as in Isaiah:

> He was despised, a man in pain, and we therefore hid our faces from him, so to speak; he was despised, and we did not value him. Nevertheless our sicknesses he bore and our pain he shouldered, but we counted him beaten, struck by God, and *afflicted.* (Isaiah 53:3, 4)

These things symbolize the Lord's trials. The idea that he bore our sicknesses and shouldered our pain does not mean that the faithful would never face terrible challenges, or that he bore our sins by deflecting them onto himself. What it means is that he overcame the hells through the struggles and victories of his trials and that as a result he alone, in his human capacity, would bear the weight of the trials that religious people undergo.

[4] The Lord himself calls times of trial *afflictions.* In Mark:

> Those who are sown on stony places, when they hear the message, do not have any root in themselves but are fickle. Later, when *affliction* and persecution arise because of the message, they immediately stumble. (Mark 4:16, 17)

Affliction stands explicitly for trials here. Not having any root in themselves is not having charity, since faith is rooted in charity. People who
have no such root succumb in times of trial. In John:

> In the world you will have *affliction,* but rest assured; I have overcome
> the world. (John 16:33)

The affliction stands for trials. [5] In Matthew:

> Nation will be roused against nation, and kingdom against kingdom.
> All these things will be the beginning of woes; then they will hand you
> over to *affliction.* Then there will be great *affliction* such as there has
> not been from the beginning of the world. Immediately after the *afflic-*
> *tion* of those days, the sun will go dark. (Matthew 24:7, 8, 9, 21, 29)

This concerns the close of the age, or the final days of the church. The
affliction stands for external and internal trials. External trials are persecution by the world; internal trials are persecution by the Devil. Nation
against nation and kingdom against kingdom symbolize absence of charity, as does the fact that the sun (the Lord; love and charity) will go dark.

Four hundred years means however long the trials would last and **1847**
what conditions would be like then. This can be seen from the symbolism of *four hundred,* which symbolizes the same thing as forty: how long
trials last and what conditions are like then, as discussed at §§730, 862.
The number forty in the Word depicts fairly short or fairly long spans of
tribulation.

On a literal level these words have to do with the length of time the
children of Jacob spent in Egypt. It was 430 years, as can be seen in Exodus 12:40 (although this period began not with Jacob's arrival in Egypt
but with Abram's stay there, as noted earlier). The time is referred to as
430 years because this number implies times of trial, which is what their
enslavement in Egypt represented, as did their later afflictions for forty
years in the wilderness.

Genesis 15:14. *"And also the nation they serve I will judge. And after this* **1848**
happens, they will depart with a great deal of property."

Also the nation they serve symbolizes the evil who oppress them. *I will*
judge symbolizes visitation and judgment. *And after this happens, they will*
depart with a great deal of property, symbolizes deliverance, and acquisition of heavenly and spiritual benefits.

The symbolism of *also the nation they serve* as the evil who oppress **1849**
them can be seen from the symbolism of a *nation* and *serving.* In a

positive sense, a *nation* symbolizes goodness or, to put it another way, good people. Although I mention goodness in the abstract, it exists in a being who feels it—a person on earth, a spirit, or an angel. In a negative sense, though, a nation symbolizes evil or, to put it another way, evil beings, as discussed at §§1159, 1258, 1259, 1260.

Serving, however, or enslavement, symbolizes oppression, as in the last verse [§§1840, 1844–1845, 1846:2].

1850   The symbolism of *I will judge* as visitation and judgment is self-evident.

Judging, or a judgment, does not mean any Last Judgment, as common thought holds. People picture the destruction of earth and sky, the creation of a new sky and a new earth (as the prophets and the Book of Revelation predict [Isaiah 65:17; 66:22; Revelation 21:1]), and therefore the passing away of everything that exists. This view has become so widespread that it has laid hold of the imagination in even the best-informed, and laid hold so strongly that people do not believe the dead will rise again until that time. Such a time was indeed predicted, yet people see that although many centuries have passed since the prediction it has not happened and does not seem imminent. These circumstances combine to strengthen the confident in their confidence that nothing of the kind *can* happen and therefore that they will not rise again.

It is important to know, however, that the Last Judgment and the obliteration of earth and sky does not mean anything of the kind. Such a picture does agree with the literal meaning but not with the inner meaning at all. According to the inner meaning, the Last Judgment means the church's final days. The sky and earth that will be destroyed mean the church, so far as its inward and outward worship goes, which becomes no church at all when charity fails.

[2] The last judgment of the very earliest church took place when all charity and faith died out and when perception ended. This happened just before the Flood. The same flood described earlier was the last judgment of that church [Genesis 6–8]. In it the sky and the earth—the church—were destroyed and a new sky and earth were created. In other words, a new church, called the ancient church, was created, and this church has also been discussed. It too had a final period, specifically when all charity froze and all faith went dark, around the time of Eber. This period was the last judgment of that church, which was the sky and earth that were destroyed. [3] The new sky and earth were the Hebrew church, which again had its final period, or last judgment, when

it became idolatrous. So a new church was raised up, this time among Jacob's descendants. It was called the Jewish religion and was nothing more than a church that *represented* charity and faith. In that religion, among Jacob's descendants, there was no charity or faith, so there was also no church, but only a representation of a church. The reason was that direct communication of the Lord's kingdom in the heavens with any true church on earth was impossible, so indirect communication was set up through representations. The final period or last judgment of this "church" occurred when the Lord came into the world, because representative acts—specifically, sacrifices and other rituals like them—came to an end at that point. The disappearance of these rituals was brought about by the expulsion of Jacob's descendants from the land of Canaan.

[4] Afterward, a new sky and earth were created. That is, a new church was created, which has to be called the nascent [Christian] church. It was started by the Lord and afterward grew gradually stronger, and in its early days it possessed charity and faith. The Lord predicts the death of this church in the Gospels, as does John in the Book of Revelation, and its death is what people call the Last Judgment. Not that heaven and earth will now be obliterated, but that a new church will be raised up in some region of the globe, leaving the current church to remain in its superficial worship, as Jews remain in theirs. The worship of these people is devoid of charity and faith, or in other words, of religion, as is fairly well known. Such is the Last Judgment in general.

[5] In particular, we each have an individual last judgment right after we die. We pass into the other world, where we come into the way of life we adopted in the body and receive a verdict of either death or life.

We have an even more particular last judgment if we receive a verdict of death. Absolutely everything in us then condemns us, since there is no detail of our thought or intent so small that it does not reflect our final judgment and drag us to our death. If we receive a verdict of life, it is the same: absolutely every detail of our thought and intent contains an image of our final judgment and carries us toward life. Our overall character is the same character we display in each of our thoughts and feelings.

This is what is meant by the Last Judgment.

And after this happens, they will depart with a great deal of property, symbolizes deliverance, and acquisition of heavenly and spiritual benefits. This can be seen from the symbolism of *departing* as being freed and from that of *property* as heavenly and spiritual good. This is the property acquired by people who suffer persecution and undergo trials,

1851

oppression, and affliction (slavery), as described in this verse and the last. Benefits of the same kind are also represented and symbolized by the property Jacob's descendants had when they left Egypt (Exodus 11:2; 12:36). The same is true of the property Jacob's descendants acquired in the land of Canaan, once they had driven off the indigenous nations [Joshua 11:16–12:6; 22:8], and it is true in passages throughout the prophets about taking plunder from one's enemies and growing rich on it.

1852   Genesis 15:15. *"And you will come to your ancestors in peace; you will be buried at a good old age."*

You will come to your ancestors in peace means that nothing good or true will be hurt. *You will be buried at a good old age* means the enjoyment of everything good by people who belong to the Lord.

1853   *You will come to your ancestors in peace* means that nothing good or true will be hurt. This can be seen from the symbolism of *ancestors,* of *coming to one's ancestors,* and of *peace.*

Ancestors in this instance symbolize the same thing on an inner level as female and male descendants taken together. The symbolism of daughters as goodness and of sons as truth has been shown earlier, in §§489, 490, 491, 533, 1147. So ancestors symbolize what belongs to daughters and sons together.

Coming to one's ancestors is passing from the life of the body to the life of the spirit, or from this world to the other. *In peace* means that nothing will be missing and therefore that nothing will be hurt. When we pass into the other life, we lose none of what makes us human. We keep possession of absolutely everything except our body, which has blocked the deeper exercise of our abilities.

What follows just below will show that it is not death, or passing over to our ancestors through death, that is symbolized here.

1854   *You will be buried at a good old age* means the enjoyment of everything good by people who belong to the Lord. This can be seen from the fact that people who die and are buried do not die but pass from a life that is dark and dim into one that is sharp and clear. Bodily death is merely a continuation and also a perfection of life. It is the point at which people who belong to the Lord first come into the enjoyment of everything good. This enjoyment is what a *good old age* symbolizes.

The Word very often mentions that people have died, been buried, and been gathered to their ancestors, but on an inner level these words do not have the same meaning they do on a literal level. The inner sense contains descriptions of life after death and of eternal things; but the literal sense contains descriptions of life in the world and of ephemeral things. [2] When this topic comes up, then, people who focus on the inner meaning (angels, for instance) never linger over thoughts of death and burial but thoughts of continued life. They view death as nothing more than a riddance of the crudest physical elements and of time, and as nothing but a continuation of life itself. In fact they do not know what death is, because they do not think about it.

The case is the same with the different ages of our life; when it says "at a good old age" here, angels form no picture of old age. In fact they do not know what old age is, because they are always heading toward life as lived in mid- and early adulthood. This kind of life—and consequently the heavenly and spiritual blessings connected with it—is what is meant when mention of a good old age and other stages of life comes up in the Word.

Genesis 15:16. *"And in the fourth generation they will come back here, because the wickedness of the Amorites will not be complete until that time."* **1855**

In the fourth generation they will come back here symbolizes a time and state of renewal. *Because the wickedness of the Amorites will not be complete until that time* symbolizes the final days, when there is no longer any good.

In the fourth generation they will come back here symbolizes a time and state of renewal, as can be seen from the symbolism of a *fourth generation*. A fourth generation symbolizes the same thing as forty and four hundred: how long trials last and what conditions are like then, as mentioned above at verse 13 [§1847]. It is a kind of reduction of the number. Whether a number is large or small, as long as it belongs to the same family it involves the same idea, as noted several times before [§§395:1, 433, 482, 575, 737:1]. **1856**

The fourth generation does not mean a generation descended from Abram, Isaac, or Jacob, as can be seen from the scriptural narrative. After all, when they returned, many generations had passed, and these generations were very different from their ancestors. The phrase *fourth generation* is used in other places too [Exodus 20:5; 34:7; Numbers 14:18; Deuteronomy 5:9; 2 Kings 10:30; 15:12], but in the inner sense it never means a generation. Here it means a time and state of renewal, because it means the end of the hardships symbolized by the number forty, or four hundred; see §§862, 1847.

Because the wickedness of the Amorites will not be complete until that time symbolizes the final days, when there is no longer any good, as can be seen from the symbolism of an *Amorite* and that of *completion*. **1857**

An *Amorite* in the Word symbolizes evil in general, because Canaan is called the land of the Amorites, as indicated in Ezekiel 16:3, 4 and Amos 2:9, 10. So in this verse the Amorites mean all the nations in the land of Canaan, which symbolized individual types of evil and falsity, as noted before [§§1205, 1444:4]. The Amorites, then, symbolize all evil in general.

Completion symbolizes the final days, when there is no longer any good.

[2] What it means in an inner sense to say that the wickedness of the Amorites will not be complete until that time, though, is a secret. The situation of the evil in the other life is that they are not punished before their evil reaches a climax, both generally and specifically. Things in the other world are in such perfect balance that evil actually punishes itself. In other words, the evil bring on themselves the penalty for their evil, but only when it has reached its peak. Every evil has its limit—a different limit for each individual—and no one is allowed to break that limit. When evil people go beyond the limit, they trigger their own punishment. This is true in every specific case, [3] and it is similar overall. (The evil do not push their way into hell abruptly but gradually.)

This situation traces its origin to a universal law of the pattern established by the Lord: The Lord never sends anyone to hell. Evilness itself (or the evil themselves) forces its way in, step by step, until it is finally complete and nothing good appears any longer. As long as we have a trace of goodness, we rise out of hell; but when sheer evil remains, we are thrust down into hell. Goodness and evil have to be separated first, since they are opposites. Straddling the fence is not permitted. These things are what are symbolized by the fact that the Amorites' wickedness needed to be complete.

It is different for good people, however. The Lord constantly lifts them toward heaven and gradually washes away their evil.

[4] The situation is the same with conditions in a church. Its divine visitation does not come until its evil is complete—that is, until it no longer has any charitable goodness or religious truth. The prophets very often speak of this climax. In Isaiah, for instance:

> I have heard from the Lord Jehovih Sabaoth of a *full end* and *final decision* on all the earth. (Isaiah 28:22)

In Jeremiah:

> You, Babylon, who live on many waters, great in treasures—your end has come, the *full measure* of your *dirty profits*. (Jeremiah 51:13)

In Daniel,

> Seventy weeks have been decreed upon your people and upon your holy city, to *bring an end to transgression,* and to *seal up their sins,* and to *atone for wickedness,* and to introduce everlasting justice, and to seal up vision and prophet, and to anoint the holy of holies. (Daniel 9:24)

> Then at last upon the abominable bird will come ruination; and all the way to a *full end* and *final decision,* [ruination] will pour itself out upon the wasteland. (Daniel 9:27)

[5] The Lord himself also predicts the end, in these words in Luke:

> They will fall by the mouth of the sword and be taken captive among all the nations. And in the end Jerusalem will be trampled by the nations, until *the times of the nations are fulfilled.* (Luke 21:24)

Falling by the mouth of the sword symbolizes being cut down by falsity, because in the Word a sword is the punishment of falsity. Jerusalem stands for the Lord's kingdom and the church (§402). The nations stand for evil (§1260). So the verse says that the end comes when evil and falsity take hold of the church, which consequently self-destructs.

Genesis 15:17. *And it happened that the sun set, and darkness occurred, and see? A furnace of smoke and a torch of fire that passed between those pieces!*   **1858**

And it happened that the sun set symbolizes the last days, when the end comes. *And darkness occurred* means when hatred displaces charity. *And see? A furnace of smoke,* symbolizes the thickest falsity. *And a torch of fire* symbolizes feverish cravings. *That passed between those pieces* means that this fever separated people in the church from the Lord.

The symbolism of *and it happened that the sun set* as the last days, when the end comes, is established by remarks above at verse 12 concerning *sunset* and its symbolism as the last days of the church [§1837].   **1859**

And darkness occurred means when hatred displaces charity, as can be seen from the meaning of *darkness.* In the Word, shadow symbolizes falsity, but darkness symbolizes evil, as discussed just below. Shadow occurs when falsity displaces truth, and darkness occurs when evil displaces goodness or (what is exactly the same) when hatred displaces charity. When hatred displaces charity, the darkness is so deep that we lose any awareness at all of the presence of evil. Still less do we see that the evil is bad enough to send us to hell in the next life. When people hate, they sense a certain pleasure and a certain energy in their hatred, and the   **1860** pleasure and energy themselves make it nearly impossible for those people to see hatred as anything but good. Whatever caters to their sensual desire or cravings seems good to them, because it caters to what they love. In fact if anyone tells them it is hellish, they can hardly believe it. They find it even harder to believe if told that in the other world this pleasure and energy turn into the stench of excrement or of a dead body. Still less can they believe that they themselves will become devils in the appalling image of hell. Hell consists of nothing but hatred and devilish figures like this.

[2] The ones who retain any ability to think are capable of seeing this. If they themselves were to describe hatred, or represent it, or draw some kind of picture of it (if they have the talent), they would invariably use devilish figures of the kind that they themselves turn into after death. Amazing to say, these people can still claim they will go to heaven in the next life—some relying simply on the fact that they say they believe— when in reality heaven contains nothing but models of charity. (See a description from experience of those models of charity in §553.) They need to contemplate, then, how those two figures of hate and love could live together in harmony in the same space.

[3] The fact that *shadow* symbolizes falsity, and *darkness,* evil, can be seen from these passages in the Word. In Isaiah:

> Look—*shadows* cover the earth, and *darkness,* the peoples. (Isaiah 60:2)

In Joel:

> Let all the inhabitants of the earth shudder, because the day of Jehovah has come: a day of *shadow* and *darkness.* (Joel 2:1, 2)

In Zephaniah:

> A day of wrath is that day, a day of devastation and ruin, a day of *shadow* and *darkness.* (Zephaniah 1:15)

In Amos:

> Is the day of Jehovah not *shadow* and lack of light? And is there not *darkness* and lack of radiance on it? (Amos 5:20)

The day of Jehovah stands for the final days of the church, which is the topic of the present verse. The shadow stands for falsity, the darkness for evil, which is why both are mentioned. Otherwise the text would be repeating itself, or piling up words for no purpose. On the other hand, the word for darkness in the present verse as it appears in the original language involves both falsity and evil, or dense falsity that gives rise to evil, and also dense evil that gives rise to falsity.

And see? A furnace of smoke, symbolizes the thickest falsity. *And a torch of fire* symbolizes feverish cravings. This can be seen from the symbolism of a *furnace of smoke* as thick falsity and from that of a *torch of fire* as feverish cravings.

1861

This verse speaks of a *furnace of smoke* because some people look exactly like a smoky furnace. They are those (especially in the church) who know truth and yet do not acknowledge it but deny it at heart and live a life opposed to truth. They themselves look like the furnace, while the distortions billowing out of their hatred look like the smoke; and the hateful urges that create the distortions look exactly like *torches of fire* from such a furnace. This can be seen from representative scenes in the other world, described from experience in §§814, 1528. It is the urges of hatred, vengefulness, cruelty, and adultery (particularly when deceit is mixed in with all of these) that look like and actually turn into such torches.

[2] The following passages show that *furnaces, smoke,* and *fire* have this symbolism in the Word. In Isaiah:

> Everyone is a hypocrite and an evildoer, and every mouth is speaking stupidity, because *wickedness blazes* like *fire;* bramble patch and brier patch it consumes, and it *ignites* the thickets of the forest, and they float up with the *rising of smoke.* In the wrath of Jehovah Sabaoth, the earth has gone dark and the people have become like *food for the fire;* a man does not spare his brother. (Isaiah 9:17, 18, 19)

The fire stands for hatred; the rising of the smoke from it, for hateful distortions. Hatred is depicted in the words "a man does not spare his brother." When angels examine people like this, they look exactly as they are portrayed here. [3] In Joel:

> I will give portents in the heavens and on earth: blood and *fire* and pillars of *smoke.* The sun will turn to shadow, and the moon, to blood, before the day of Jehovah comes, great and fearsome. (Joel 2:30, 31)

The fire stands for hatred; the pillars of smoke, for falsity; the sun, for neighborly love; the moon, for faith. [4] In Isaiah:

> The land will become *burning pitch.* By night and day it will not be quenched; forever its *smoke* will go up. (Isaiah 34:9, 10)

The burning pitch stands for dreadful urges, the smoke, for falsity. [5] In Malachi:

> Look: the day is coming, *blazing* like a *furnace!* And all the proud and everyone doing evil will be stubble, and the coming day will *light* them *on fire*. It will not leave them root or branch. (Malachi 4:1)

The blazing furnace stands for the same kinds of things. The root stands for neighborly love and the branch for truth, of which none will be left. [6] In Hosea:

> Ephraim acquired guilt through Baal; he will be like chaff [that] is storm-driven off the threshing floor, and like *smoke* from a *smoke hole*. (Hosea 13:1, 3)

Ephraim stands for a person with understanding who becomes like this. [7] In Isaiah:

> The strong will become tow, and their work will become an ember, and they will both *kindle* equally, and no one to quench them. (Isaiah 1:31)

This stands for the fact that people who love themselves, or what is the same, hate their neighbor, are kindled by their cravings in this way.

In John:

> Babylon has become a dwelling place for demons. Those seeing the *smoke* of its *conflagration* were shouting. The *smoke* goes up forever and ever. (Revelation 18:2, 18; 19:3)

[8] In the same author:

> He opened the pit of the abyss, so *smoke* went up from the pit, like the *smoke* of a large *furnace*. And the sun and the air went dark with the *smoke* of the pit. (Revelation 9:2)

In the same author:

> From the mouth of the horses went out *fire* and *smoke* and *sulfur*. By these a third of all human beings were killed—by the *fire* and by the *smoke* and by the *sulfur* that went out from their mouth. (Revelation 9:17, 18)

In the same author:

> Whoever worships the beast will drink of the wine of God's anger, mixed with pure wine in the goblet of his anger, and will be tortured with *fire* and *sulfur*. (Revelation 14:9, 10)

In the same author:

> The fourth angel poured out his bowl onto the sun, and it was granted
> to him to *scorch* humanity with *fire.* Therefore humans *burned* with
> great *heat* and blasphemed the name of God. (Revelation 16:8, 9)

In the same vein, Revelation 19:20; 20:14, 15; and 21:8 say that various
beings were thrown into the *lake of fire,* a lake *burning* with *sulfur.* [9] In
these passages, fire stands for cravings, or urges. The smoke stands for distorted thinking, which will reign supreme in the final days. What happens
with cravings and distortions in the other life is what John saw when his
inner eyes had opened. Spirits see the same things, as do souls after death.

This indicates what hellfire is: pure hatred, revenge, and cruelty (self-
love, in other words), which turns into scenes like these. When our nature
is like this, then as long as we live in our bodies, angels who inspect us
closely see us in exactly this way, no matter how different we look on the
surface. That is to say, our hatreds look like fiery torches and the false
thoughts they inspire look like smoky furnaces.

[10] Here is what the Lord said about such fire in Matthew:

> Every tree not making good fruit is cut down and thrown into the *fire.*
> (Matthew 3:10; Luke 3:9)

The good fruit means love for others. If we divest ourselves of this love,
we cut ourselves down and throw ourselves into this kind of fire. In the
same author:

> The Son of Humankind will send his angels, who will gather together
> out of his kingdom all the stumbling blocks, and those who do wicked-
> ness. And they will send them into a *fiery forge.* (Matthew 13:41, 42, 50)

Likewise. In the same author:

> The king says to those who are on his left, "Go away from me, you
> cursed ones, into *eternal fire* prepared for the Devil and the Devil's
> angels." (Matthew 25:41)

Likewise. [11] The fact that they would be sent into *eternal fire* or *fiery
Gehenna* and that their worm does not die and their *fire* is not put out
(Matthew 18:8, 9; Mark 9:43–49) stands for something similar. In Luke:

> Send Lazarus to dip the tip of his finger into the water and cool my
> tongue, because I am tormented in *this flame.* (Luke 16:24)

Likewise.

[12] People who do not know the secrets of the Lord's kingdom imagine that the Lord is the one who sends the ungodly down into hell, or into the kind of fire with which hatred blazes, as noted; but the true case is radically different. It is we ourselves and devilish spirits themselves who hurl themselves there. Since it seems as though the Lord sends them, however, it was phrased that way in the Word, in keeping with appearances and even with sensory illusions—especially in the eyes of Jews. They had no interest at all in understanding anything but what agreed with their senses, no matter how mistaken those senses were. As a result, the literal meaning is full of such appearances, especially in the prophetic parts. [13] In Jeremiah, for example:

> This is what Jehovah has said: "Render judgment in the morning and snatch spoil from the hand of the oppressor, so that my *fury* does not go forth like *fire* and *burn* (and no one to quench it) because of the wickedness of their deeds." (Jeremiah 21:12)

Rendering judgment is saying what is true. Snatching spoil from the hand of the oppressor is doing good deeds that embody love for others. The fire stands for the hellish punishment experienced by people who do not act that way—that is, who live by the lies that hatred spawns. In the literal meaning, this kind of fiery fury is attributed to Jehovah, but in the inner sense it is exactly the opposite. [14] Likewise in Joel:

> The day of Jehovah: before it, *fire* consumes all, and after it, a *flame blazes.* (Joel 2:1, 3)

In David:

> *Smoke* went up from his nose, and *fire* from his mouth consumed all. *Embers sent flames* from him, and darkness was under his feet. (Psalms 18:8, 9)

In Moses:

> A *fire* has kindled in my anger, and *it will burn all the way to the lowest hell,* and it will consume the earth and its produce and *torch* the foundations of the mountains. (Deuteronomy 32:22)

The fire stands for hatred, and the smoke, for falsity, which exist inside us. They are attributed to Jehovah, or the Lord, for the reasons given. It also appears to the hells as though he does these things, but the case is exactly the opposite; they are the ones who do it to themselves, because fiery hatred burns inside them. This shows how easy it is for us to succumb to delusions when we do not know about the Word's inner meaning.

[15] It was the same with the *smoke* and *fire* that the people saw on Mount Sinai when the law was issued. Jehovah, or the Lord, appears to each of us as we are. To heavenly angels he looks like the sun; to spiritual angels he looks like the moon; to all good people he appears as the light, in various pleasing, delightful ways; but to the evil he appears as smoke and a devouring fire. Jews had no neighborly love at the time the law was issued but were ruled by self-love and materialism; evil and falsity held complete sway in them. Jehovah, or the Lord, therefore appeared to them as *smoke* and *fire,* while at the same instant he appeared to angels as the light and sun of heaven. [16] Moses makes it clear that he looked this way to Jews because of their character:

> The glory of Jehovah resided on Mount Sinai. And the appearance of Jehovah's glory was like a *consuming fire* on the head of the mountain, before the eyes of the children of Israel. (Exodus 24:16, 17)

In the same author:

> Mount Sinai was smoking—all of it—because Jehovah came down on it in *fire,* and the *smoke* of it went up like the *smoke of a furnace,* and the whole mountain trembled violently. (Exodus 19:18)

And in another place:

> You came near and stood below the mountain when the mountain was *burning with fire* all the way to the heart of the sky; *shadow* and *cloud* and *darkness.* And Jehovah spoke to you from the *middle of the fire.* (Deuteronomy 4:11, 12; 5:22)

Again:

> It happened when you heard the voice from the middle of the *shadow* and the mountain was *burning with fire* that you came near to me and said, "*Why should we die? For this big fire will consume us.* If we continue to hear the voice of Jehovah our God anymore, *we will die.*" (Deuteronomy 5:23, 24, 25)

[17] It would be the same if anyone else living a life of hatred and the garbage it generates were to see the Lord; such a person could not help seeing him in terms of hatred and its loathsome by-products, which absorb

the goodness and truth he radiates and turn them into malevolent fire, smoke, and darkness.

The same passages also reveal what the smoke of a furnace and a fiery torch are—the thick falsity and foul evil that took over the church in its final days.

1862   *That passed between those pieces* means that this fever separated people in the church from the Lord. This can be seen from the discussion above at verse 10 about splitting the animals in half, which symbolized parallelism and correspondence regarding heavenly things [§§1830–1831]. Placing one part across from its other [half] symbolized the church and the Lord. The middle or intervening space symbolized what connects the Lord and the church (or the Lord and an individual in the church), and what connects them is conscience, the soil in which goodness and truth are planted by means of charity.

When hatred replaces charity, and when evil and falsity replace goodness and truth, we have no conscientious awareness of goodness or truth. Instead, this middle, intervening space seems to be filled with a smoky furnace and fiery torches. That is, it seems to be filled with persuasive lies and with hatred, which are the entities that completely sever the Lord from the church. [2] This is the symbolism of *it passed between those pieces*—mainly the torch of fire, or in other words, self-love, or in other words, the vice of hatred. This symbolism can also be seen in Jeremiah, where almost the same words appear:

> The men transgressing my pact, who have not established the words of the pact that they struck before me—[witness] *the calf that they cut in two and passed between the parts of:* the chieftains of Judah and the chieftains of Jerusalem, the eunuchs and the priests and all the people of the land, *passing between the parts of the calf*—yes, I will give them into the hand of their enemies and into the hand of those seeking their souls. And their corpse will serve for food for the bird of the heavens and the beast of the earth. (Jeremiah 34:14, 18, 19, 20)

1863   Genesis 15:18. *On that day Jehovah struck a pact with Abram, saying, "To your seed will I give this land, from the river of Egypt all the way to the great river, the river Phrath."*

On that day Jehovah struck a pact with Abram symbolizes the union of the Lord's intermediate self with his inner self, or Jehovah. *Saying, "To your seed will I give this land,"* symbolizes the consolation, after all these trials and horrors, that the people who possessed charity and faith in him would become his heirs. *"From the river of Egypt to the great river, the river Phrath,"* symbolizes the extent of spiritual and heavenly qualities; *to the river of Egypt* is the extent of spiritual qualities; *to the river Phrath* is the extent of heavenly qualities.

On that day Jehovah struck a pact with Abram symbolizes the union   **1864**
of the Lord's intermediate self with his inner self. This is established by the symbolism of a *pact* as union, which was discussed earlier, at §§665, 666, 1023, 1038. As the subject here in an inner sense is the Lord, the pact symbolizes a deeper union. The Lord went further and further in being joined and united to Jehovah his Father until they finally became one. In other words, his human side also became Jehovah, who was the Lord's actual inner self. These things were represented by the pact that Jehovah struck with Abram.

Anyone can see that Jehovah never strikes a deal with us. That would go against his divine nature. What are we but some contemptible bit of filth that cannot think or do anything but evil on its own? All the good we do comes from Jehovah. The conclusion follows, then, that this pact (like other pacts with Abram's descendants) was just a representation illustrating God's nature and the heavenly features of God's kingdom. Here it represented the union of the Lord's human side with his divine side, or Jehovah.

Earlier discussions indicate that what this pact represented was the bonding of the Lord's intermediate self with his inner self, or Jehovah. The earlier discussions showed that the Lord was joined and united to his inner self more and more closely, through the struggles and victories of his trials [§§1659:2, 1661:5, 1707:5, 1708, 1729:2, 1732, 1737, 1738, 1793:1, 1815].

His intermediate self has already been defined as the self midway between his inner and outer selves [§§1701–1702, 1707].

Saying, "To your seed will I give this land," symbolizes the consolation,   **1865**
after all these trials and horrors, that the people who possessed charity and faith in him would become his heirs, as is established by the symbolism of *seed* and that of the *land*. *Abram's seed* symbolizes love and the faith that comes of it, as shown before, in §§255, 256, 1025. So it symbolizes everyone who has charity and faith in the Lord. The *land of Canaan* symbolizes the Lord's kingdom. *Giving your seed the land,* then, means that the heavenly kingdom would be given as an inheritance to people who have a faith in the Lord that comes from charity.

[2] No explanation is needed to show that these things served to console the Lord after his trials and horrors. After all, he put evil and falsity

to flight (symbolized by Abram's driving away of the winged creatures that swooped down onto the bodies, as told in verse 11). Yet thick falsity was going to pour in, and this horrified him (symbolized by the terror of immense shadows that fell on Abram in his sleep, as told in verse 12). Furthermore, undiluted falsity and evil would take over the human race in the end (symbolized by the smoky furnace and fiery torch that passed between the pieces, as told in the last verse, verse 17). After foreseeing these distressing outcomes, he could not help feeling anguish and grief. A message of comfort now follows, therefore, like the one in verses 4 and 5 above saying that his seed would inherit the land—that is, people who have charity and faith in him would become heirs of his kingdom. The salvation of the human race was his only comfort, because he possessed divine, heavenly love and became divine, heavenly love itself even in regard to his human nature. Only this love aims to love everyone and finds heartfelt satisfaction in doing so.

[3] The fact that divine love is like this can be illustrated by the love parents have for their children, which grows with each generation. In other words, parents have more love for their later descendants than for their own direct offspring. Nothing ever exists without a cause and source, so neither does this constantly increasing love the human race has for ensuing generations. The cause and source have to lie with the Lord, from whom flows all love between married partners and all the love parents have for their children. The reason lies in the nature of the Lord's love. He loves us all as a father loves his children, wants to make us all his heirs, and provides an inheritance for those who have yet to be born, just as he does for those already born.

1866   *From the river of Egypt to the great river, the river Phrath,* symbolizes the extent of spiritual and heavenly qualities; *to the river of Egypt* is the extent of spiritual qualities; *to the river Phrath* is the extent of heavenly qualities. This can be seen from the symbolism of the *river of Egypt* and that of the *great river,* or the *river Euphrates.*

The symbolism of these rivers as the extent of spiritual and heavenly qualities can be seen from the symbolism of the land of Canaan as the Lord's kingdom in the heavens and on earth. That kingdom contains nothing but the spiritual qualities of faith and the heavenly qualities of mutual love. As a consequence, the boundaries of Canaan can only mean the extent of these qualities. The inhabitants of heaven have no notion at all of what the land of Canaan is, what the river of Egypt is, what the great river Euphrates is, or in fact what the boundaries of any land are. They do know how far spiritual and heavenly qualities reach, and they know in what direction spiritual and heavenly states lie and where they end. These are the subjects they have their minds on when people on earth read about such things. In this way the letter of the Word and its narrative content vanish, once they have served as a focal point for the heavenly thoughts of heaven's inhabitants.

[2] The reason the *river of Egypt* symbolizes the extent of spiritual qualities is that Egypt symbolizes facts. Facts, together with people's rational processes and moments of deep understanding, are spiritual entities, as noted before in §1443 and many other places. The symbolism of Egypt on an inner level as facts is mentioned in §§1164, 1165, 1186, 1462.

The symbolism of the *river Euphrates* as the extent of heavenly qualities can be seen from the lands which that river borders and which it separates from Canaan. These lands too symbolize facts and the knowledge of heavenly matters, in various passages. Here, though, since it is being called a river, and a great river at that, it symbolizes only heavenly matters and the knowledge of them, because a great river and size in general have to do with heavenly things.

Genesis 15:19, 20, 21. *The Kenite, and the Kenizzite, and the Kadmonite; and the Hittite, and the Perizzite, and the Rephaim; and the Amorite, and the Canaanite, and the Girgashite, and the Jebusite.*   **1867**

The Kenite, and the Kenizzite, and the Kadmonite, symbolize falsities that need to be banished from the Lord's kingdom. *The Hittite, the Perizzite, and the Rephaim,* symbolize persuasive lies. *The Amorite and the Canaanite* symbolize evil. *The Girgashite and the Jebusite* symbolize falsity rising out of evil.

It would take too long to prove from the Word at this point that   **1868** these nations symbolize such things, and there is no need to do it here, since the nations are merely named. Some of them have been discussed before. It was noted at §§567, 581, 1673, for instance, that the *Rephaim* symbolize persuasive lies; at §1680 that an *Amorite* symbolizes evil; above at verse 16 that a *Canaanite* symbolizes evil [§1857:1]; and at §1574 that a *Perizzite* symbolizes falsity. The specific symbolism of the other nations will be described later, by the Lord's divine mercy, where they come up.

[2] In regard to the "nations" that need to be banished from the Lord's kingdom, the case is this: In the other world, evil, diabolical spirits crave nothing more than to go up into the world of spirits and plague good spirits. But every time they do, they are thrown out. It is the same as in people who are regenerating: the falsity and evil that have taken

possession of them are subdued and scattered and are replaced with the truth and goodness that belong to the Lord's kingdom. These evil influences were represented by the nations that the children of Jacob expelled from the land of Canaan, and likewise by the Jews themselves, who were driven out later. [3] The same thing happened at one time to many other nations that represented similar influences. These included the Horites, driven from Mount Seir by Esau's descendants (as told in Deuteronomy 2:12, 22); the Avvim, driven off by the Caphtorim (as told in Deuteronomy 2:23); the Emim or Rephaim, driven off by the Moabites (as told in Deuteronomy 2:9, 10, 11); the Zamzummim, by the Ammonites (as told in Deuteronomy 2:19, 20, 21); and many others mentioned in the prophets.

Sacred Scripture, or the Word (Continued)

1869   HOW much a single word of Scripture contains has been shown to me by a revelation of people's individual ideas. Surprising to say, ideas can be revealed so vividly in the other world that they actually become visible and take on a shape, as if they were images in a painting.

One individual whose ideas were revealed in this way was a person who had lived a life of charity, or mutual love, and had taken pleasure in the Word during his time in the world. When his thoughts were revealed, countless beautiful objects appeared, bringing with them a delight and pleasure that touched the heart. I learned that these visible manifestations have further inward layers that can be revealed, and when they are revealed, sights still more beautiful and delightful present themselves, bringing happiness itself with them. All angelic ideas are like this, because the Lord himself lays them open.

[2] Physical vision was used to illustrate this principle for a group of spirits who were amazed that a person's individual thoughts can be revealed this way in the other world. The sight of the eye is so weak and dim that it sees the smaller objects of the physical world simply as spots, dark and shapeless, although they hold within them too many parts to count. When the same objects are observed through a microscope, however, the inward parts come into focus, connected in a beautiful series and flowing from each other in an elegant pattern. These parts likewise

could be laid open by an even stronger microscope. This showed what the case is with the inner eye, whose lines of sight are nothing but ideas: in themselves these ideas are about as hazy as anything can be in that realm—although human beings think otherwise. I will have more to say about people's ideas below, however, with the Lord's divine mercy [§§1971, 1980, 1981].

It is the same with the Lord's Word. The individual words in it create **1870** mental images of themselves, because a word is just a mental image given verbal form so that its meaning can be perceived. These images contain within them so very many elements incapable of coming to human consciousness (only to the consciousness of angels) that it is completely beyond belief. When the Lord lays them open, the forms inside them are presented in two ways: they are presented to the perception by sensations of pleasure and happiness, and they are presented to the eye by objects of paradise that hold a representative meaning. The former come from the heavenly and spiritual forces of the Lord's love, or mercy; the latter come from the light that his love and mercy radiate.

[2] I have been shown through amazing experiences that Sacred Scripture was inspired not only in its individual words but also in every tiny letter of each word. So it was literally inspired down to the smallest jot (as the idiom goes). Each jot contains a measure of emotion and vital energy, which affects the whole word it appears in and which therefore permeates the most minor details in a correspondential way. But in the absence of other background knowledge, these things cannot be explained at all intelligibly.

I cannot describe how the Lord's Word appears before angels, but it **1871** can be grasped to some extent by people who have seen optical cylinders in museums. These cylinders reflect beautiful images from distorted drawings projected in a circle around them. Although the surrounding drawing appears to have no shape, organization, or pattern but to be simply a confused projection, it presents a lovely picture when focused onto the cylinder. That is how the Lord's Word is, especially the prophetic part of the Old Testament. Hardly anything can be seen in the literal meaning besides a disorganized jumble; but when it is read by a person on earth (particularly a little boy or girl), it gradually rises up, turning more beautiful and more pleasing as it goes. In the end it presents itself to the Lord as a human figure representing the whole of heaven—not as heaven actually is but as the Lord wishes it to be; in other words, as his likeness.

A beautiful, bright-faced girl appeared to me, moving quickly to the **1872** right, darting slightly upward as she went. She seemed to be in the first bloom of her years, since she was neither a child nor a full adult. Her clothing was black, shiny, and attractive. She skipped happily from one patch of light to another this way. I was told that this is what the inner levels of the Word are like as they begin to rise. The black clothes were the Word in its letter.

Later a young woman flew to my right cheek, but I could see her only with my inner eye. I was told that these are the things in the Word's inner sense that do not reach our consciousness.

1873　Some spirits were talking about the Word's inner sense. In order to present its nature intelligibly, they illustrated it by asking what the fruit of faith is, for example, and said that good deeds are the fruit of faith in an outward or literal sense. Good deeds, though, are lifeless if they are not the product of charity, so that the fruit of faith in its next deeper meaning is charity. Since charity (or love for one's neighbor) ought to come from love for the Lord, however, this is the fruit of faith in an even deeper sense. And since all love comes from the Lord, the fruit of faith is the Lord himself. Accordingly, good deeds hold charity, which holds love for the Lord, which holds the Lord himself.

1874　In conversation with some good spirits I said that many statements in the Word (more than anyone could believe) are phrased to suit appearances and the illusions of the senses. For instance, the Word says that Jehovah feels anger, wrath, and fury against the ungodly, that he enjoys destroying and annihilating them, and even that he kills them. But these things are said in order to avoid shattering people's self-delusions and cravings, so as to bend them instead. To fail to speak in terms people grasp—in terms of appearances, fallacies, delusions—would be to sow seed on the water; it would be to say something that would immediately be rejected.

Still, those statements can serve as general containers for spiritual and heavenly ideas, because it is possible to inject certain notions into them. The first is that everything comes from the Lord; the next, that he allows things to happen but all evil comes from devilish spirits; then that the Lord provides and arranges for evil to be turned into good; and finally that nothing but good comes from the Lord. So the literal meaning disappears as it rises and turns spiritual and then heavenly and at last divine.

1875　I was given the opportunity to perceive angels' ideas on the following words in the Lord's Prayer: "Do not lead us into crisis but free us from evil" [Matthew 6:13; Luke 11:4]. The good spirits nearest me discarded *crisis* and *evil* by a certain way of thinking perceptible to me.

They rejected those ideas so thoroughly that what remained was purely angelic; specifically, what was left was goodness, without a hint of crisis or evil. In this way, the literal meaning died away completely. The first step of the process was to form countless ideas of this goodness—how something beneficial comes of our affliction, and yet the affliction rises out of us and our evil, which contains its own penalty. Attached to these ideas was a kind of indignation that anyone should think that crises and their evils come from anywhere else, and that anyone should think about evil when thinking about the Lord. These ideas were purified as they rose higher and higher. Their journey upward was represented by the discarding of certain elements, as also described in §1393. These elements were discarded in a manner and with a speed that are impossible to express, until the ideas finally passed into an area of thought that was shadowy to me. Then they were in heaven, where the angels think only of the Lord's goodness, in thoughts that are ineffable.

Like the words of human language, the names of people, countries, **1876** and cities in the Word vanish at the very first threshold of their upward path. Names are some of those earthly, bodily, material things that the soul gradually sheds as it enters the next life, and sheds completely if it goes to heaven. Angels do not hold on to the slightest mental image of people in the Word, so they do not retain the least idea of their names. What Abram is, what Isaac, and Jacob are, they no longer know. It is the qualities represented and symbolized by figures in the Word that form an angel's picture. Names and words are like chaff or scales that drop off when [the ideas] enter heaven.

This shows that names in the Word have no meaning besides a symbolic one. I have spoken about this many times with angels, and they have taught me the truth very fully.

When spirits talk to each other, they use not words but thoughts, of the kind we have when we are thinking wordlessly. Their speech, then, is common to all languages. When spirits talk to a person on earth, their speech falls into the words of the person's language, as noted in §§1635, 1637, 1639. [2] When I talked with the spirits about this, I was inspired to say that as long as they were conversing among themselves, they could not pronounce even a single word of human language, still less a name. Astonished to hear this, some of them went away and tried it. They came back admitting they could not, because human words were too coarse, too tied to the material world to rise into their sphere of existence. Such words are formed from the sound of air, articulated by physical organs;

or else they are formed by an inflow into the same organs traveling an internal pathway to the organs of hearing.

This also made it clear that not a syllable of Scripture could cross over to spirits, still less to angelic spirits, whose speech is even more universal (§1642). Least of all could it reach angels (§1643), with whom it retains none of the initial thoughts entertained by spirits. Among angels, such thoughts are replaced with spiritual truth and heavenly goodness that vary in indescribable ways in their very smallest forms. These forms are linked and connected in a harmonious series with the source elements from which representations are created. The happiness of mutual love renders the representations extremely sweet and beautiful, and sweetness and beauty render them happy, because their sources are animated by life from the Lord.

1877　　At first, people who are souls or spirits in the world of spirits (especially the bad ones) hold on to what they had during their physical life: earthly, bodily, and worldly concerns, and along with them, any principles they had adopted. Such people include those who are unwilling to hear anything about the Word's inner sense but only about the literal meaning. They even believe that the twelve apostles will sit on twelve thrones and judge the twelve tribes of Israel. Again, they believe that the only people who can go to heaven are those who are poor, unhappy, and persecuted. The truth is that both the rich and the powerful go there, if they have lived a life of charity and faith in the Lord.

Since people like this demand heaven as their just reward, they run around making fun of the message of the Word's inner meaning wherever they go, because it opposes their delusions and cravings. I saw them do so. What they want is to earn heaven and to be promoted above everybody else, but they resemble diseases and poisons that enter the bloodstream, spread through the veins and arteries, and pollute the whole supply of blood.

1878　　There are also people who despised the Word during physical life. There are others who misused phrases of Scripture by turning them into mocking jokes. Some considered the Word useless except for its ability to serve as a restraint on the masses. Others blasphemed the Word, and yet others profaned it. The fate of all these people in the next world is wretched, each according to the nature and degree of her or his contempt, derision, blasphemy, or profanation. As noted, the inhabitants of the heavens hold the Word so sacred that it is like heaven to them.

Therefore, because all thoughts are shared generally there, [the two kinds of people] cannot possibly coexist but are separated.

Once when I was lying in bed I was told that evil spirits were plotting against me, intending to suffocate me. The Lord was keeping me safe and sound, though, so I scoffed at the threat and went to sleep. Waking up in the middle of the night, however, I sensed that I was breathing not under my own power but heaven's. I had no respiration of my own, as I could plainly tell. Then I was told that the conspirators were nearby, and that they were the type that hate the deeper content of the Word, or in other words, genuine religious truth (since this is the deeper content of the Word). The reason they hate it is that it attacks their illusions, delusions, and desires, which the literal sense could be made to defend.

1879

[2] Later, when their efforts had failed, the ringleaders tried to invade the inner organs of my body and penetrate right to my heart, where they were even let in. I sensed quite plainly what was happening the whole time, since anyone whose inner levels (those of the spirit) are opened receives also the ability to sense these kinds of things. I was then brought into a certain heavenly frame of mind, in which I did not attempt to rid myself of these guests, let alone avenge the wrong they had done. This calmed them down, they said at the time, but directly afterward they seemed to go berserk. Seeking revenge, they tried to finish off their efforts, but in vain. Eventually they scattered on their own.

*   *   *   *   *   *

Furthermore, to speak generally of spirits and angels, who are all human souls living on after the death of their body, they have much sharper senses than people do: sight, hearing, smell, and touch, but not taste.

1880

However, it is impossible for spirits (much less angels) to see anything in this world by their power of sight, or in other words, by the eyes of their spirit. To them the light of the world, or of the sun, is like thick darkness. By the same token, it is impossible for us to see anything in the other world by our power of sight, or in other words, with the eyes of our body. To us the light of heaven, or of heaven's Lord, is like thick darkness.

[2] Still, when it pleases the Lord, spirits and angels can see objects in the world through the eyes of a person on earth. This is an experience

the Lord does not grant except to a person whom he allows to speak with spirits and angels and to associate with them. Through my eyes they were allowed to see objects in the world, and to see them as clearly as I did. They were also allowed to hear people talking with me. More than once a few of them saw friends they had had during bodily life. Looking through my eyes, they saw these people just as close at hand as before, and it stupefied them. They also saw their spouses and little children and wanted me to tell their loved ones they were present and could see them, and to relay how matters stood for them in the other world. But I was forbidden to talk to these people and reveal that they were being watched in this way. Besides, they would have called me crazy or believed me to be hallucinating, because I knew that although they would pay lip service to the idea that spirits exist and the dead have risen again, they would not believe it in their hearts.

[3] When my inner sight first opened, and they saw the world and all that is in it through my eyes, spirits and angels were so dumbfounded that they called it the miracle of miracles. They were moved by a new kind of joy at the thought that earth would have this kind of contact with heaven, and heaven with earth. This pleasure lasted several months, but now that the experience has grown familiar, they no longer marvel at all.

I was taught that the spirits and angels present with other people do not see anything in the world at all but only pick up on the thoughts and feelings of those they are with.

[4] These experiences established the idea that we were created to live in heaven among the angels at the same time as we are living on the earth among people, and vice versa. If that happened, heaven and earth would come together and form a single whole. We would know what was going on in heaven, and angels would know what was going on in the world. When we died, we would then be crossing over from the Lord's kingdom on earth to the Lord's kingdom in the heavens. It would not be as though we were passing into a different kingdom but into the same one we inhabited while we were living in our body. Instead we have become so body-oriented that we have shut heaven off from ourselves.

1881 Spirits become very upset and in fact outraged when you tell them that people do not believe spirits can see, hear, or touch anything. They told me that people ought to know that life does not exist without sensation, and the sharper the senses, the more vibrant the life. The objects of their senses, the spirits said, are as superior as their ability to sense them.

The representative things that the Lord gives them are real, because they are the source of everything that exists in the world of nature (§1632). *Their senses are much better and more impressive than ours!* This is how their indignation expressed itself.

There are two kinds of visions (both of them uncommon) that I was introduced to for the sole purpose of learning what they are like and what it means in the Word when it says that people were (1) taken out of the body or (2) led by the spirit to another place.

The case with the first—being taken out of the body—is this: The person is brought into a certain condition midway between sleep and wakefulness. In this condition, the person is fully convinced that he or she is completely conscious. The person's senses are all as wide awake as they are when the body is fully alert—sight, hearing, and (amazingly) the sense of touch, which is keener now than it could ever be during physical wakefulness. During this state, I have also seen spirits and angels literally as big as life, and I have heard and even touched them, surprising to say. Hardly anything physical was involved.

This is the condition in which people are said to be *taken out of the body* and to have no idea whether they are *in the body or out of the body* [2 Corinthians 12:2, 3].

Only three or four times have I come into this state, and then only to learn what it was like, and to see that spirits and angels enjoy sensation of every kind, even touch—a far better and far keener sense of touch than in the body.

As for the second kind of vision—being led by the spirit into another place—what it is and what it involves has been shown to me by living experience. But this has happened only two or three times. Let me cite a single instance.

Strolling city streets and country meadows while at the same time talking with spirits, I had no idea I was not as fully awake and aware as I am at any other time. I walked along like this without losing my way, and all the while I was having a vision, seeing woods, rivers, mansions, homes, people, and so on. After I had walked around this way for several hours, I suddenly found myself seeing with my physical eyes and realized I was somewhere else, which utterly astounded me. I perceived that I was experiencing the state of those who are said to have been *led by the spirit to another place.* While it is happening, you do not stop to think about the route, no matter how many miles long. You also fail to

1882

1883

1884

think about the time, no matter how many hours or days. Neither do you notice feeling at all tired. You are being led by paths you do not know until you reach the destination.

This happened so that I would also be able to see that we can be led by the Lord without knowing why or where.

1885   These two types of visions are unusual, however. They were demonstrated to me simply for the purpose of teaching me what they are like. All the sights you find reported, by the Lord's divine mercy, at the beginning or end of each chapter in these first two volumes are ordinary ones. They are not visions but sights that I have seen for many years now in full physical consciousness.

[Continued in Volume 3]

Biographical Note

EMANUEL SWEDENBORG (1688–1772) was born Emanuel Swedberg (or Svedberg) in Stockholm, Sweden, on January 29, 1688 (Julian calendar). He was the third of the nine children of Jesper Swedberg (1653–1735) and Sara Behm (1666–1696). At the age of eight he lost his mother. After the death of his only older brother ten days later, he became the oldest living son. In 1697 his father married Sara Bergia (1666–1720), who developed great affection for Emanuel and left him a significant inheritance. His father, a Lutheran clergyman, later became a celebrated and controversial bishop, whose diocese included the Swedish churches in Pennsylvania and in London, England.

After studying at the University of Uppsala (1699–1709), Emanuel journeyed to England, the Netherlands, France, and Germany (1710–1715) to study and work with leading scientists in western Europe. Upon his return he apprenticed as an engineer under the brilliant Swedish inventor Christopher Polhem (1661–1751). He gained favor with Sweden's King Charles XII (1682–1718), who gave him a salaried position as an overseer of Sweden's mining industry (1716–1747). Although Emanuel was engaged, he never married.

After the death of Charles XII, Emanuel was ennobled by Queen Ulrika Eleonora (1688–1741), and his last name was changed to Swedenborg (or Svedenborg). This change in status gave him a seat in the Swedish House of Nobles, where he remained an active participant in the Swedish government throughout his life.

A member of the Royal Swedish Academy of Sciences, he devoted himself to studies that culminated in a number of publications, most notably a comprehensive three-volume work on natural philosophy and metallurgy (1734) that brought him recognition across Europe as a scientist. After 1734 he redirected his research and publishing to a study of anatomy in search of the interface between the soul and body, making several significant discoveries in physiology.

From 1743 to 1745 he entered a transitional phase that resulted in a shift of his main focus from science to theology. Throughout the rest of his life he maintained that this shift was brought about by Jesus Christ, who appeared to him, called him to a new mission, and opened his perception to a permanent dual consciousness of this life and the life after death.

He devoted the last decades of his life to studying Scripture and publishing eighteen theological titles that draw on the Bible, reasoning, and his own spiritual experiences. These works present a Christian theology with unique perspectives on the nature of God, the spiritual world, the Bible, the human mind, and the path to salvation.

Swedenborg died in London on March 29, 1772 (Gregorian calendar), at the age of eighty-four.